GENESIS REVISITED

THE GENESIS STORY

BY:

ALAN HEWITT

First published by Willow Farm Press Godalming in 2006 (P & C) 2006

Published by:

Willow Farm Press
c/o "Waverley"
Oakdene Road
Godalming
Surrey
GU7 1QF

ENGLAND

Text copyright (P & C) 2006   Alan Hewitt

Alan Hewitt
95 Muirhead Avenue
Liverpool
L13 9BH

ENGLAND

A CIP catalogue record for this book is available from the British Library.

ISBN = 978-0-9554866-0-9 (pbk)   ISBN = 978-0-9554866-1-6 (hbk)

Printed in England by the Alden Group

Alden Group Ltd
De Havilland Way
Witney
OX29 0YG

www.alden.co.uk

Contents

ACKNOWLEDGEMENTS

This is always like writing your Christmas card list; you simply KNOW that you are going to forget somebody so I will apologise for that inevitable omission here and now - SORRY!

Before we go any further; some of you may be wondering what exactly makes this book any different to its predecessor: "Opening The Musical Box - A Genesis Chronicle" apart from the change of title and more importantly why I am asking you to shell out your hard earned £'s, $'s or Euros on it all over again? Well, rather a LOT actually. One of the main (and deserved) criticisms of the earlier book was the lack of illustrations. Sadly, that was a decision taken by the publishers rather than myself and one which hopefully, has been successfully resolved here. A book such as this is more than a mere collection of pretty pictures, however, and in this new edition I have endeavoured to bring the band's story up to date, correcting any factual mistakes or omissions from the previous work (yes folks, contrary to popular rumour the author **IS** human!) and hopefully what you now have in your hands now is the kind of work which Genesis fans have been asking for ever since Armando Gallo's superb meisterwerk back in the 1980's!

Let's get one thing straight here and now. This is NOT a work of biography. If you like, what you have here is more a "One Thousand Things You Didn't Know About Genesis And Didn't Know Where To Look" kind of a book - maybe that should have been the title, I don't know? What I do know is that, putting this material together has been the pre-occupation of more of my life than I care to think about! It has been put together with love and admiration for the musicians who collectively are known as "Genesis" and its various amazing off-shoots and also for the followers of those musicians - the greatest FANS in the world!

My grateful thanks therefore first of all to the musicians for the music and their active co-operation with this project and its predecessor so take a bow... Tony Banks, Phil Collins, Peter Gabriel (even if I never got an interview out of you!); Steve Hackett; John Mayhew; Anthony Phillips; Mike Rutherford; John Silver; Chris Stewart; Daryl Stuermer; Chester Thompson; Ray Wilson and Nir Z without whom none of this would have been possible - or necessary! Grateful thanks also to the other musicians whom have assisted in the wider picture over the years for helping our heroes bring home the musical bacon in so many ways!

My thanks to the people known collectively under the awesome title of "The Management" without whom this would not have been possible and in particular to Carol Willis and Jo Ann Greenwood at TSPM; Annie Callingham at Philip Collins Ltd; Billy Budis at Camino and not forgetting the able assistance of Ann Marie and Teresa at Voiceprint; Mary Lane at Real World and Caroline Turner at Hyperactive and Jake Locke; John Wood and Andy Lodge at the good ship Camino for all their help and encouragement over the years.

The Waiting Room is now streamlined and online and for that I have the work of Martin Dean, Tony Burton and of late Stuart Barnes to thank for their efforts, patience and perseverance. Thanks as always; to all the past Waiting Room and Pavilion "inhabitants" too of course - this would not have been thinkable much less possible without your efforts! That goes for Mario Giammetti at "Dusk"; the irrepressible Simon Funnell and David Dunnington whose magazines and sites have provided so much information to the fan base and to Manuela Thiele for her efforts on behalf of Tony Banks fans and to Mic Smith whose stewardship of the Kontakt magazine for so many years has kept Peter Gabriel fans up to date with the activities of their hero - good luck with the book, Mic!

The fans... for whom this was written, are too many to name individually but some "Mentions In Despatches" must be made. First of all the irrepressible Peter Gozzard for his continued faith in the cause. Mike Jackson for those box loads of audio tapes! To Richard and Andew Nagy, David Beaven for assistance above and beyond the call of duty. To Jana Shepherd, Mike Carzo and Frank Musilammi for persistence and patience. To Alan Perry, James Hendry; Albert Gouder and everyone else who contributed material and memories. To Kevin and Shirley Powell (and Rachel) for unending hospitality and encouragement and indeed to all the other unsuspecting fans who have had the "pleasure" or should that be "pressure" of hosting yours truly on my travels both here and overseas; I hope it wasn't too much of a chore and hey; let's do it again sometime?!

Thanks also to the various members of the growing Genesis "Tribute band" scene both here and abroad for keeping the music alive and for continuing to entertain us so wonderfully whatever "era" or "incarnation" they represent!

Finally a **BIG** thank you to Mark Kenyon and Anthony Hobkinson without whom this would definitely NOT have been possible!!

Some comments on the first book…..

"I have to say that I enjoy reading The Waiting Room and enjoy finding out what everyone else is doing. I looked through the book and it is interesting to look at all that stuff …the gigs and so on back to back…" **(Phil Collins - TWR interview Manchester MEN Arena June 2004).**

"I took his book on holiday and it is so detailed, you're reading things about your life you've forgotten. I think he knows more about us than we know…" **(Mike Rutherford - Record Collector Magazine December 2000).**

"When it comes to collecting information on a band there's nothing better than having an enthusiastic fan take on the job. It needs that type of dedication to see the thing through. The problem is that that when a band has as long a history as Genesis, it gets difficult to correlate all the facts so they are easy to interpret. Fortunately for Genesis fans, the information could not be in better hands, for Alan Hewitt is an enthusiastic and experienced writer who also produces the excellent Genesis fanzine The Waiting Room…. Everything you could want to know about the band is well presented here… Better still it's a darn good read and that is a welcome change for something this informative…" **(Roger Newell - Guitarist Magazine September 2000)**

"Congratulations on the book… excellent job!" **(Steve Hackett - 2001)**

"Many, many thanks for the book, I can see it becoming my new 'Bible' on the band and Phil! I have only had a quick glance through but I can see that a lot of hard work has gone into it…" **(Annie Callingham Personal Assistant to Phil Collins - June 2000).**

FOREWARD.

IN 1997, Alan Hewitt was asked to compile the questions for a Mastermind Contestant's chosen Special Subject : Genesis!

In thus being acknowledged as the leading expert in this field, it naturally followed that his expertise should have been committed to paper for the benefit of Genesis fans all over the world.

Alan has taken a wide, eclectic view of all aspects of the band's history and the cornucopia of disparate projects that have emanated from both past and present members. Thus the book can rightly claim to be the definitive reference bible for All fans.

The second edition brings us up to date with the recent activities of the inmates - and the outmates! - as well as providing arguably the most complete gig guide ever published. Exhaustive discographies and a wealth of illustrations are a huge added bonus and will prove invaluable for the man on the Clapham Omnibus who wishes to seek out the under-water reggae mix of some obscure, early 'B' side!

Alan's labour of love continues as the individual protagonists show no sign of letting up (despite the band itself "resting") and there is every reason to think that he will soon be hard at work both discovering nuggets of the band's history and chronicling the current creative output for the next edition !

Anthony Philips. London.

January 2005.

INTRODUCTION: "PROJECT GENESIS - REVISITED"

Any of you who purchased the original edition of this book back in 1999 (was it really THAT long ago?) will probably be scratching your heads wondering why you are being asked to shell out your hard-earned $s or £s or Euros or whatever currency to buy this tome again? Well, for a start since 1999 there have been so many developments within the Genesis camp and also in the various solo careers of the individual members, that it was obvious that it would need to be updated at some point to bring their stories back up to date.

That has been an ongoing task similar to painting the Forth Bridge really; just when I would think it was safe to take a break, someone would launch a new album or tour and off I would go again. Work on this project has been a regular and continuous part of my life ever since I sent the original manuscript off to the publishers back in 1998. Several things were brought home to me after the original edition was issued. First; there was still considerable work to be done on the massive and involved Gig Guide sections both for the band and the individual artists as I had very forcibly (but gently) demonstrated to me by a recent meeting with Phil Collins! Thanks to the kindness of Phil, his PA Annie Callingham; other band members and many fans of the individual members; the revised and updated Gig Guides are now as accurate as they reasonably can be with much new information contained in them which I am sure will prove useful.

Another bugbear, for me as well as the fans themselves was the comparative lack of illustrations. There is a LOT of text to wade through in this book and it really needs a suitable visual accompaniment. Thankfully, this time that will be provided. The archives of TWR and several fans and band members have been raided and suitable images have been found with which to accompany the text and hopefully give the project that extra element which was missing last time. I admit that much of the text will remain the same apart from obvious corrections although additional commentary and updates have been made within the confines of available space. I had several ideas for brand new sections for this edition but reality intervened and sadly they will have to wait for the deluxe coffee table edition!

Hopefully there will be sufficient new information contained in this book to be enjoyed by the fans who bought the first edition as well as to any first timers who are buying this one - so where were you, guys?!! The aim of the exercise remains the same however: to bring as much information about the band and its component parts together under one roof. I have worked long and hard on this project and I am still amazed by the enthusiasm of the fans who have been extremely kind to my mistakes and thanks to them hopefully they are at a minimum in this edition - enjoy it, it's for you!

Alan Hewitt
Liverpool November 2006.

CHAPTER ONE   ANON: THE BAND THAT TIME FORGOT

Britain in the 1960's can only be likened to the England of the Tudor period which saw the blossoming of the "English Renaissance" that gave us Shakespeare, Donne, Byrd, and so may other talents. The England of the second Elizabeth was likewise in the throes of a cultural upheaval the likes of which had never been seen before or since (sadly) as the nation gradually threw off the shackles of austerity which were the after effects of six years of war and began to breathe again.   Into this atmosphere of burgeoning creativity a group of Public schoolboys began a love affair with music which has now spanned four decades.

History has already related how the formative line-up of Genesis emerged out of the ashes of two school groups at Charterhouse; Anon fronted by Mike Rutherford and Anthony Phillips and The Garden Wall which included Tony Banks and Peter Gabriel. In the cloistered atmosphere of Charterhouse the individual members of the band were drawn to music as an escape from the repressive regime that permeated school life.Their earliest efforts at musical creativity were divided between the various school bands which sprang up in the wake of the musical revolution going on outside the walls of Charterhouse.

The history of Anon can be traced back to the now "semi-legendary" group formed by Anthony Phillips at St Edmunds Preparatory School in Hindhead; it was in "The Spiders" that Ant first teamed up with Rivers Job an older boy at the school and, in fact, his first experience of performing in front of an audience pre-dates the formation of "The Spiders" and was as lead singer. It was a memorable occasion but for all the wrong reasons as Ant recalls…

"Someone had heard My Old Man's A Dustman and so we went and rehearsed it and I forgot the words and was sacked as the singer..!"

As a result, Ant became more interested in playing the guitar and it was around this time that he met Rivers and the two of them discovered a common interest in pop music.

The formation of "The Spiders" soon followed and Ant and Rivers joined forces with Richard Francis who was known as "Sid" and "Bonehead" Goldsmith whom Ant describes as *"the legendary drummer"* who was thrown out of school for a variety of nefarious activities. Ant also remembers that "Bonehead" was *"years ahead of his time as he didn't worry about a regular rhythm!"* It was obvious that "The Spiders" were not destined for greatness but a longstanding friendship was forged between Ant and Rivers which survived his departure to Charterhouse and the disbanding of "The Spiders".

Rivers' arrival at Charterhouse was opportune and he soon teamed up with another pupil; Richard MacPhail who had similar interests, and it was during the Easter holidays of 1965 that Rivers took Richard to Anthony's house in Putney for a rehearsal where it soon became patently obvious that Richard was not cut out as a drummer, however, he did know the words to The Rolling Stones' songs which were the fledgling band's repertoire and he therefore became their singer as Richard himself confirms… *"That's basically how I became the singer in the band..."* At the same time, another Charterhouse pupil; Rob Tyrrell found himself equally drawn to music and especially drumming, and by the time that Ant, Rivers and Richard were looking for a drummer, he had become more than competent.

Another budding drummer at the school called Chris Stewart could only marvel at Rob's natural ability to play the drums and remembers… *" Rob was absolutely superb! He was a natural.. I was terribly jealous of him.."* Ant clearly recalls the first time that he, Rivers and Rob played together; the three of them got together in an empty classroom but Rob didn't have his drums with him at school at that stage and so Ant asked an older boy in his House if he would lend Rob his kit. As Ant recalls…

"This chap was quite kind to lend us his drums although he was almost a brooding presence as it were, quite understandably, as he didn't want his drums to be broken up! Of course, it was Peter Gabriel!"

Ant also remembers the material which comprised the band's set… *"The early stuff was just Stones numbers and it really had that kind of raw quality to it..."*

Mick Colman also has some fond memories of those days…

"Ant and I started to collaborate on songs. I wrote one called She's Got Those Lopin' Shoulders the first and by far the worst song I ever wrote... The first memory I have of actually playing with Anon is of what was probably my first rehearsal with the band, which I think took place in the room under the stage (Green Room) of the main hall one afternoon. I used to get a little bit frustrated by having to play little

more than 'ker-chunk, chunk, chunk, chunk, chunk, chunk, chunk, chunk, ker-chunk, chunk, chunk'
etcetera and even then being allowed the use of only the bottom two strings of the guitar in time-honoured
twelve bar fashion .

For relief I sometimes got to play 'did-dee, did-dee, did-dee, did-dee, did-dee, did-dee, did-dee' on the
same two strings, typical of the early Stones sound and I found it very difficult not to embellish or
overplay here and there sometimes. And then I would be rounded upon with cries of: "For Christ's sake,
Mick, can't you just play 'did-dee, did-dee, did-dee, did-dee, did-dee, did-dee, did-dee...?" Ah, those were
the days..."

Suitably inspired, the band were now on the lookout for both a name and a rhythm guitarist although Ant
remembers new guy Mike Rutherford being slightly more sociable than others…

"I don't know what happened to Mike (Rutherford). I think he was basically in the pub! He was a bit of a
lad in those days. He was unlike the others; he was with the "in" crowd..."

Mike's first band had been "The Chesters" which had been formed while he was at Preparatory School and
prior to that, his first public appearance had been memorable but once again for all the wrong reasons, as
Mike remembers…

"I couldn't really tune my guitar but there was a master who could tune it. At that show, between his
tuning in the early evening and me playing it, it went out of tune, so it sounded pretty horrible. I was
singing Travelling Light with an out of tune guitar but I was fairly uninhibited in those days and I wasn't
shy about performing.."

What does a new band need once it has its line-up? An audience, and soon Anon set about gaining that
and the band made their debut performance at a concert held at Charterhouse on 16th December 1965. The
show itself comprised a mixture of comedy sketches; music and a film made by the pupils . Anon were
due to perform three songs and even at this debut the spectre of the technical problems which were to later
dog Genesis, raised its head. Mike's guitar lead failed and the replacement was too short for Mike to play
in his proper place. Panic over; Anon started their first number; We've Got A Good Thing Going
followed after initial nerves had subsided by Talkin' About You and Mercy Mercy all of which were well
received by the pupils but not apparently, by the school's headmaster; Mr Van Oss who spent the entire set
with his fingers in his ears!

Other performances followed usually at friends' parties including a now legendary performance at Rob
Tyrrell's parents' house which was also a fancy dress party with guests invited to turn up as pub signs.
Mike couldn't resist joining in and he arrived dressed as a highway man complete with Tricorn hat and
mask! Other gigs are more difficult to catalogue and other difficulties overtook the band. Richard
MacPhail's parents were increasingly worried about their son's involvement with the band to the point
where he was forced to leave which meant that Anon now needed a new lead singer and Mike suddenly
found himself in the spotlight…

"It was a nightmare... I couldn't really reach the notes. I remember one particular moment when we were
doing a Stones song like Mercy, Mercy and I sang so high that my Adam's Apple kind of came out of
place!"

Mike's stint as singer was short lived as his House master; Mr Chare, then banned him from playing the
guitar. With Mike out of the group, the search was now on for someone who could fill his role as rhythm
guitarist and fortunately, Richard MacPhail was able to rejoin and he was present when they were
introduced to a music scholar from Mike's House called Mick Colman. Richard remembers…

"Mick had his own guitar and amp which was quite something. He played the introduction to The House
Of The Rising Sun which we all thought was very impressive..."

Eventually the group decided to try and record some of these gems with the help of fellow Charterhouse
pupil; Brian Roberts who had set up a home recording facility in two rooms over a pair of garages next
door to his father's surgery in Wellesley Road Chiswick. Brian recalls the set up…

"If you were sitting in the rooms above the garage you could hear all the traffic from the road as clear as
day. Air tight didn't come into it, it was more a case of wind open!"

A set of rehearsals took place before the group took themselves down to Chiswick where they recorded a set of demos during a couple of days in April 1966. Among the titles they put down were a version of The Stones' Lady Jane and at least three Anon originals. This was where they recorded Anthony's first song of any worth (his words, not mine) Patricia which eventually became In Hiding on Genesis' first album, along with two other Anon originals; Pennsylvania Flickhouse and Don't Want You Back. Anthony Phillips also remembers some of the antics which went on at this very primitive recording studio...

"Brian had this garage.. he was the guy with the German mother who used to call them both; the husband and the son, by their surname (laughter) Roberts you get ze tea. .She was wild actually. I remember a policeman came in once to see what we were doing because we were sort of sitting on this balcony and I've never seen a guy sent packing so quickly.. he was just gone!"

With Richard's encouragement, the idea of an end of term concert featuring the various Charterhouse bands took shape. To gain a wider acceptance amongst the sceptical authorities at the school; it was agreed that all the bands would be playing for charity, and, having got this far; Richard now set about finding other bands suitable to share the bill. Two others were found: The Climax (which were the band that Mike had joined during his brief exile from Anon); and another called The Garden wall which included both Peter Gabriel and Tony Banks who were joined by Chris Stewart who by this time had had drum lessons from Peter Gabriel!

They were lacking a bassist and lead guitarist and so, Ant and Rivers agreed to fill in. The Climax opened the show before The Garden Wall took the stage. The piano in the hall proved too difficult to move and so Tony Banks played it off-stage with the result that no one knew he was there until the fourth song; When A Man Loves A Woman which he started..

Anon, having already tasted the excitement of recording their own material, decided to have another go, and by pooling their resources, had managed to raise the grand sum of twenty Guineas with which to record two of their songs at a local studio: Tony Pike Sound in Putney. Having resolved problems in the band's line-up by re-enlisting Mike to replace Mick Colman who was unable to attend the session, the band decided to record Pennsylvania Flickhouse and Don't Want You Back two of the songs they had previously recorded with Brian Roberts and which featured frequently in their set. Upon arriving at the studio in Drybergh Road, the group soon found that their previous methods of obtaining a sound they were happy with were not suitable on this occasion as Ant recalls...

"We were used to playing our amps quite full so we got a lot more power from the overloading..."

The noise that the band were making was too much for Tony Pike to bear and he issued his now famous injunction: *"You mind my compressors!"*

Having completed the session, the band now had a master tape with their two songs on it and the question now arose of what to do with it and the suggestion arose that an acetate should be cut from the tape so that the band would in effect, have their own record as a souvenir of their first experience in a proper recording studio. No one can recall clearly why the eventual acetate was a one-sided affair with only Pennsylvania Flickhouse on it, but six copies were duly cut from the master tape, plus one for Brian Roberts, two of which still survive today in the hands of Mike Rutherford and Richard MacPhail. This recording was recently considered (and eventually shelved) for release as part of the second "Archive Collection" album by Anthony Phillips. The track certainly shows the influence of The Rolling Stones on the members of the band with Ant and Mike trying to emulate Mr Richards' greatest licks and Richard puts in a performance as Mick Jagger that would not endear him to the listening public on "Stars In Their Eyes"! (*)

(*) A UK talent show (allegedly!)

By the autumn of 1966, Anon seemed to have run their course, although whether by accident or design, they managed to get themselves a slot at the Charterhouse end of term concert in December which was to prove to be their final gig. With Richard, Rivers and Mick Colman out of the picture, Mike was free to rejoin after the dissolution of The Climax, taking up bass duties and a fair proportion of the vocals again, and there, effectively the story of Anon ends. In fact, it was during a later recording session at Brian Roberts' garage studio that fate played its part in bringing the fledgling Genesis together as Anthony himself remembers...

11

" Mike and I went to record our songs and since then I'd got to know this guy (Peter Gabriel) who could sing a bit and he was kind of a wild guy who used to stand on tables and so on... I got Tony Banks to come and play some keyboards on it and he was going to bring Peter his vocalist, who I hadn't really heard sing, to do one song. The deal was that Banks would come along and play keyboards if we recorded one song of theirs and, of course, their song was far better than any of our stuff and we eventually got the publishing deal on the basis of their song which was called; She Is Beautiful which became The Serpent and it was really good. Mike and I were writing dreadful songs.. I mean we wrote one called Listen On Five which was ghastly!"

CHAPTER TWO IN THE HALL OF THE STUDIO KING

Ghastly or not, the group had managed through the auspices of a friend of theirs at Charterhouse to gain the ear of Jonathan King, a Charterhouse old boy who had already gained a degree of chart success by writing and producing the hit Everyone's Gone To The Moon and following it up by writing and producing another hit for Hedgehoppers Anonymous; It's Good News Week. Hardly the most impressive credentials for a progressive band like Genesis but hey, everyone has to start somewhere and King had two points in his favour: first of all he was enthusiastic about the music the band were producing (so enthusiastic that he tried to sign the group to a five year contract in September 1967 before parental objections reduced this to one year), and second; he was able to give them recording time through his connections with Decca Records. Anthony remembers the compromises that the young composers had to make….

" We went progressive and I really liked a lot of that and then when the other boys did Silent Sun I thought it was a terrible sell-out and I really hated it to start with. I thought it was a real sort of Jonathan King... he loved the seven chord trick, basically that was all he knew (laughter). I wasn't with that stuff, I thought it was ok ..."

Interestingly enough; their contract with King covered four songs three of which ironically finally saw the light of day as part of the fourth disc on the band's recent Genesis Archive collection; these being; Image Blown Out and She Is Beautiful. And the third; a cover of the Soul standard Try A Little Sadness Looking back on it now, the fee they were paid (£40) seems pitiful but to a group of schoolboys in the late 1960's.

It represented a considerable investment! King's management company: Jonjo was also appointed as their management by the four band members; Mike, Tony, Ant and Peter, on 30th August 1967.

Under Kings' auspices, the band now comprising Anthony Phillips, Tony Banks, Mike Rutherford, Peter Gabriel and John Silver (Chris Stewart having checked out before the album came to be recorded) began to write much more intricate and complex music and as Anthony recalls…

"Peter's lyrics went very cosmic and there were songs like Barnaby's Adventure and The Mystery Of The Flannan Isle Lighthouse . "

Even in those early days the band had very strong ideas of what they wanted their music to sound like and there was some division of opinion when the band finally got to record their first album in 1968 as both Anthony and Tony Banks recall…

(Ant) *"We were dead naïve and some of the playing on that album was pretty rough but it seemed to sound pretty good to most of us and we had this idea that putting strings on meant a lovely sort of string "wash"... and I thought we were getting it with our twelve string sound; chords, rich and the worst thing about it was because of the way it was recorded was that they stuck all the backing tracks having been the full picture, it all suddenly went left in the stereo and the strings were suddenly on their own with the vocals I think dominating the whole thing..."*

(Tony) *"We did the album in a day and a half, we worked on it and then came back the following day to finish it. Then later we did a mono mix of it which sounded good but then these arrangements were added. We were involved in writing some of the parts, the awful thin string lines as opposed to the big banks of strings which we'd hoped for. It all sounded cheesy in the end...."*

The band's first single coupled The Silent Sun with That's Me and was released to an indifferent public reaction by Decca on 2nd February 1968 The reviews of the first single showed promise, one paper referring to it in the following glowing terms…

"Certainly a thought provoking song that holds the attention throughout. Competently handled by Genesis with a beautiful flowing arrangement of violins and cellos. A disc of many facets and great depth but it might be a bit too complex for the average fan…"

Percipient comments indeed, given the band's later history! Another reviewer went even further in their enthusiasm… *"great piano intro, Peter Frampton-ish poetic lyrics, soaring strings, tasteful production. By all that's happy , a great hit".* Sadly, the enthusiasm of this reviewer was not matched by single sales.

The album itself was recorded on 9th September 1968 at Regent Sound Studios and it was at this time that the unnamed band began looking for gigs to bring their brand of music to an audience beginning with an inauspicious gig at a local Sunday School teacher's home which Ant still has vivid memories of…

"Peter singing that song Babies in the corner and we couldn't hear him! He has this style.. which has obviously become a very endearing style but in those days it wasn't very confident which was where he appears to pick at the piano and that's fine if it's obvious for the rest of us to know what tempo he's in an, of course, that relies on HEARING him and he tended to drift and he was over in the corner and a lot of people were talking over on our side and he just drifted out of the frame really… he was still going but I don't think anybody else was listening to him!"

Looking back on that first album now; it is amazing to see that all of the classic Genesis trademarks were there even at this early stage; Tony's pop sensibilities and fondness of the odd jazz chord are there, Peter's soul man vocals shine through on several tracks. The irony of Am I Very Wrong? Would, I am sure come back to haunt Peter several years later when he finally left his friends and "the curse of the happiness machine" for pastures new. With The Conqueror, the blueprint for a much later Genesis classic can be clearly seen; the larger than life character that eventually fades away would eventually reappear on Duchess when that song would become an extended metaphor for the situation of the band itself. Musically, From Genesis To Revelation is an endearingly naïve effort although the fact that a band of schoolboys were allowed the luxury of recording an ALBUM at all back in those days was quite unusual.

Even in those formative days, the band's creative muse was taking them in different directions from most of their contemporaries as can be seen from the wealth of previously unreleased material from this period which eventually formed part of the band's first Genesis Archive box set in 1998. Tracks such as Hey!, The Magic Of Time and Build Me A Mountain certainly demonstrate the influence of Psychedelia or perhaps Magic Mushrooms (?) on the budding band of musicians. One track from this period; Going Out To Get You even survived as an occasional item in the live set until 1972. Others such as The Mystery Of The Flannan Isle Lighthouse display the band's penchant for extended fantasy storytelling which was to become one of their trademarks although probably few of these compositions ever saw the light of day in terms of live performance.

Life on the road soon beckoned to the band and the decision to go "professional" was one which the band agonised over. Their friend and one time co-band member in Anon; Richard MacPhail secured a place for them to rehearse and it was there that the formative Genesis really began to take shape as Tony Banks recalls…

"It was a slow process as both Peter and I were a bit unsure about going professional. We borrowed from each of our parents £150, most of which went into buying a Hammond organ and then we rehearsed. We wrote some material and then tried to get people to act as our agent or manager. We took some of the songs from the From Genesis to Revelation period such as Visions Of Angels as well as some of the things we'd written more recently and just slowly embellished them. We had this song which became The Knife which was originally written on the piano and which was then transferred to the organ and through that we found it sounded great…"

It is amazing to think now that even at this stage in their development, the band had distinct ideas about what would and would not work, often resulting in heated "artistic" discussions. The initial creative urge can produce much that is not necessarily representative of an artists' true talents but it is frightening to realise that even then material which was thought to be excellent could be discarded as was the case with a song; Everywhere Is Here which Anthony Phillips remembers well…

"There was another song from that same period called Everywhere Is Here. It was one of the Jonathan King ones (from the second batch of recordings the band provided King with AH) *that went walkies.*

That was done at the same time as Visions Of Angels and some people felt it was better! I have got a particular axe to grind though because basically both of them were my songs and after a period where I couldn't write anything decent , so Peter Gabriel and Tony Banks were writing the majority of the material and then I suddenly had a good phase!

I don't know why we didn't do Everywhere Is Here, it was a bit more commercial funnily enough than Visions Of Angels. It was almost a more conventional Pop song with a rousing chorus and people almost preferred that but that was one of the demos they couldn't find. It never emerged from the Jonathan King archive..."

This was one of a whole raft of songs created in that formative period which remain unheard and in many cases permanently lost to posterity, although there is still the tantalising possibility that some gems are still in the band's own archives including such intriguing titles as Barnaby's Adventure and Fourteen Years Too Long (both of which still reside in the Banks tape archive apparently) some of which Tony Banks still recalls…

"If we could find things like From The Bottom Of A Well it would be great to have that as well. We went and did a version of the song Going Out To Get You as a single as well which was quite good. - Peter was really screaming and squeaking his way through that one! Then there was another one which Mike remembered the other day which we also recorded as a single. It was called Wooden Horse, it was quite good but I don't know what has happened to that..."

Ever the perfectionists, the young group honed their craft with scant regard to the effect their single-mindedness was having on the personal relationships within the band and soon this was to have grave consequences. The strain soon began to tell as Anthony recalls…

"It was definitely a formative period and the group had to go through it and I look back at it and think that we made an awful lot of mistakes in terms of how we handled it which meant that personality difficulties were going to be inevitable, in the sense that we never stopped... we never left the place and you have to get away from it and from the people in order to keep the freshness and to stop things going sour. The music got better obviously but the personalities started to fray and to move apart. It's certainly NOT true to say that when I left I was the dissenting voice and everyone else was hunky dory - very much not so at all. I had grown very much apart from Mike and Tony Banks I would say, and I don't think he would mind me saying, had grown even further apart from Peter."

John Silver also recalls this period being one of intense work…

"We were all doing it quite seriously. The nexus of the band really was comprised of Mike; Peter; and Ant and I had become friendly with Peter in London and I'd said that I had been a drummer in a band; in a series of bands and so he said: 'well, come and meet the other guys' and we met at various flats and apartments in London and eventually I did some playing with them and we all hit it off and we all knew that it was quite possible that we would be successful and we all wanted the success a great deal but we weren't willing to compromise on the publicity and commercial side for that success..."

During this period, Decca released a second single from the as yet unreleased album and took the unusual step for the time of coupling two non album tracks. The single A Winter's Tale/One-Eyed Hound appeared on 10th May 1968 once again to public indifference, but the occasional excellent review, such as the following …

"An absorbing disc which opens quietly with the soloist singing intimately to just piano accompaniment - then it explodes into a pulsating crescendo, with sighing organ, crashing cymbals and intricate counter-harmonies. The soul-searching lyric is impressive and gripping - and while the melody could have done with a little more substance, it's a platter I can thoroughly recommend..."

Decca finally released the album in March 1969 and the release was not without its problems beginning with the fact that Jonathan King, having given the group the concept of the creation of the world to work around, then decided to call them band "Genesis" although several others were suggested including "Gabriel's Angels" and "The Champagne Meadow".

Decca pointed out that there was already a band by the name of Genesis in the USA and insisted that he change their name which he refused to do. Hence upon its release, the album carried the title From Genesis To Revelation which condemned it to being relegated to the "Religious" sections of most record stores and it sold a measly 649 copies. A final single was issued on 27th June 1969 coupling a further two album tracks; Where The Sour Turns To Sweet/In Hiding but to no avail, not that the band really noticed being far too busy sharpening their craft with their first "proper" gigs to a paying audience and further embellishing their repertoire of songs beginning with a gig at London's Brunel University in Acton on 4th November 1969.

By this time, John Silver had departed for the States as he recalls…

"The reason I left was because I had been offered an assisted place at a university in the States and this was at the time of The Graduate which had just come out and by the summer of 1969 we had already had an album out and some singles. I'd already heard myself on the radio and had the pleasure of 'phoning my pals and relatives up and saying to them; 'Listen; we're on the BBC Radio Light programme or it may have even been Radio One by this stage and we'd met lots of famous people and I thought that what was ahead was a pretty hard slog and so I decided to go to university a bit later rather than stick with it and the success that eventually accrued; accrued long after I had left and was a result of many years of traipsing up and down the M1 in the back of a transit van…"

Having no experience of playing to an audience led to several highly amusing incidents as the various band members recall…

(Ant) *"well I think you remember the terrible ones and the good ones. I remember the one that summer in the East End where there was only one guy in the audience and Peter said; "Any requests?" I mean, that was a legendary one! The one at Blaises which was this awful sort of night club and in those days Mike used to play the cello (*) and it was a teeny small stage and he bowed up a woman's skirt and that's obviously one that you couldn't forget! A terrible gig was at The Marquee where we had a showcase and my amp went wrong. The twelve string used to feed back and we'd got to the quiet bit in Stagnation and it was just a complete funnel of sound going on and so they whipped the lead out of the amp and I was playing the lead guitar and I wasn't sure what had happened and so I turned up rather than down , so when they plugged the lead back in there was a terrible roar so I remember that!"*

(* Ironically, this very cello is still extant and currently resides at Anthony Phillips' home minus several strings!)

Even at this early stage of their development the band were creating their own brand of music and one which was perplexing to their early audiences who wanted something they could dance to and the music that they were writing wasn't always to their putative audience's tastes and the band themselves weren't always sure about some of the tracks themselves as both Ant and Tony recall…

(Ant) *"Mike and I came into our own in 1969 and when we first went on the road Tony Banks found the organ a tricky proposition and he didn't naturally adapt to it straight away, so Mike and I suddenly found ourselves with the lions share of the cake for a while but we were also responsible for some of the more average stuff because our electric stuff was still forming the basis of some of our louder stuff, it wasn't the best stuff and I think Going out to get you was probably a hotch potch of some of our slightly Blues riffs and I don't really remember much more about it …*

We had loads of nice acoustic songs all of which were basically butchered not deliberately but by tech louts, the equivalent of lager louts in fact… We had a good second set at one time I remember playing at Brunel University with Fairport Convention and effectively blowing them off stage with a second set which had; Visions Of Angels, Twilight Alehouse; Pacidy and probably Stagnation and The Knife and it was a good set Pacidy lost out in the end because it was too slow and ponderous. The pressure came to accelerate everything because they weren't proper concert audiences and you had to get a move on…."

(Tony) *"I used to play guitar in the middle of Let Us Now Make Love and I think that song went through its best phase in the early version of it when Ant used to play it on the piano to us and it sounded great. It was a very good song, it sounded great live…"*

John Mayhew had been recruited by the band in late 1969 to replace the departing John Silver, in time for their first forays on the road. John had already had experience in several semi-professional outfits including Milton's Fingers, a four-part harmony group that he still recalls with some affection. He also remembers his first contact with Genesis…

"I put my telephone number around and Mike Rutherford called me some time in the afternoon and when I got home from work my wife told me that a guy called Mike Rutherford had called and was going to call back at six o'clock. I remember it was six o'clock and I was half way down the stairs when the 'phone rang and I picked it up and he spent about twenty minutes trying to convince me to join Genesis. He didn't know me, he didn't particularly want me because I was hot news or anything like that but because he felt he had to be convincing and argue a rock solid case for me leaving my precious life and joining Genesis..."

Even the manner of John's first meeting with the band took on the surreal appearance that surrounds so much of the early Genesis "experience"…

"I remember it was a beautiful summer's day here. I remember it was just the same on the day that I arrived at this little country railway station. I arrived there and I had all my drums and everything in these hard fibre case, and they were black and I was dressed in black. There was a London taxi that arrived and that was black. I got in and stashed all the drums in the storage space; got in and there was Peter Gabriel writing notes on little scraps of paper..."

By the beginning of 1970 the band had parted company with Jonathan King and were on the look out for a new record deal and new management. Their enforced exile at the MacPhail cottage (which is not to be confused with Ant's parents' then home : Send Barns as happened in a recently published book on the band) led to the creation of a plethora of pieces many of which are now sadly lost although a handful have recently been issued as part of the band's retrospective "Genesis Archive 1967 - 1975" four disc set . Many others have eluded fans and Tony Banks recalls some of them…

"For some reason Let Us Now Make Love wasn't recorded for Trespass . I think we'd seen it as a possible single and so we left it behind. It wasn't left off because we didn't think it was good; the idea was that we would do it as a single. Everyone seemed to want us to record Twilight Alehouse but we didn't particularly want to as we didn't think it was as good as some of the other ones… Pacidy sounded good live as well but part of the problem was that we had too much material.

Some of these early songs would be things you would never have heard of; things like Jamaica Longboat, Digby Of The Rambling Lake. There was also a song called The Light which later became Lilywhite Lilith, there was also an instrumental piece called Moss we used to call it The Epilogue. The Light was a popular live song as was the long version of Going Out To Get You and The Knife and it was a toss up between those two as to which would make it on to the album…Going Out To Get You started out with a riff of Ant's but we made it a much bigger thing and it went on for about twenty minutes..."

It was the band's extended version of The Knife which convinced record engineer John Anthony to take his boss at the newly formed Charisma Records; Tony Stratton-Smith, to see a gig and the band were signed to his label within a matter of weeks. Another witness to this formative period in the band's story was the artist responsible for the covers to their first three Charisma albums; Paul Whitehead….

"I met them through John Anthony and at the time I was Art Director for a magazine called 'Time Out' and John said; 'I'm producing this band and you're a natural: a perfect fit'. And the first time I met them I went to the Charisma office and it was like; you've got to understand; with the English class structure; English Public School boys are twits (laughter) and they were very naïve. The only guy that was real was Mike and basically I had an interview with them and I had no idea what they did….It was kind of weird I remember them going on the road with a picnic hamper and they were just not Rock & Roll you know. They didn't trust the food in the transport cafes….I spent time with them and listened while they wrote songs and gave them my feedback and brought books for them to look at and to me it was like they had the musical language and I had the visual language..."

The band's performances at this time are hard to document although apparently their show at London's Roundhouse on 11th March 1970 was filmed and the film still exists somewhere - a daunting prospect! Although Tony Banks does not rate the band's performance that day very highly…

"I can't remember much about that one. We were on for about half an hour. That's the one we did with David Bowie. I remember it being an awful gig from our point of view. It wasn't our sort of place and they didn't like us and we didn't fit in (laughs)"

The band also managed to secure a spot on the BBC's prestigious "Night Ride" programme in February 1970 the first of a series of sessions for the BBC that lasted until 1972 and captured the band at several important points on their rise to fame and this is a session which Mike Rutherford still remembers…

"The first one with Alec Reid sticks in my mind the most. We were just writing and writing then, with very little to work towards, and suddenly that first session appeared and we had a goal to work towards. I remember being very impressed with the way everyone was worried about the levels not peaking whereas normally you don't worry as long as it sounded good...."

Another vintage BBC recording from that era has recently re-surfaced too. In January 1970, the band were commissioned to record music for a BBC documentary about the work of Mike Jackson. This was a largely forgotten item in the band's catalogue until a copy master of the "Genesis Plays Jackson" tape surfaced for auction. Apparently, the second producer on the programme had given his copy master to his son and it was this copy which had surfaced, generating much excitement among fans of this era of the band.

The recording contained four pieces or "Movements" and these were titled: "Provocation", "Frustration"; "Manipulation" and "Resignation". The first of these was eventually reprised by the band as part of Looking For Someone and the second appeared as Anyway and an instrumental version of part of The Musical Box in the third. The final track "Peace" however has remained tantalisingly hidden and the tape itself disappeared from view again shortly after this announcement was made. However, hope of a release of this material was recently given to fans by Tony Banks in an interview with The Waiting Room...

"Talking about Musical Box, the thing that has emerged which has emerged quite recently is this thing we did with Paul Samwell-Smith...the 'Jackson tape' which the guy has finally tracked down and I have got it actually... I have got a copy of it and we are going to get hold of the original. To be honest the copy is probably as good as the original because it is just mono. I don't think it is a stereo mix. The thing is not bad; its just a copy. Paul Samwell-Smith was the producer and the other guy was the TV producer and the guy who has the tape is his son. And having got this thing; because it has got early versions of things that we used in things like Fountain Of Salmacis; Anyway ... most of Anyway is in there and Musical Box and stuff...it comes and goes a bit (laughs) and the first three pieces we pillaged extensively... lots of bits of Looking For Someone and stuff like that but the fourth piece we didn't really pillage at all and it is really rather nice .

It is a much softer piece and it has a loud bit in it. I found it out of all the retrospective stuff I found it one of the most interesting things actually because it was before Trespass but it was something, whereas the other stuff we have got prior to Trespass was really pretty basic stuff; which was the stuff that ended up on Archive 1;this was actually the first time that we sounded like the group we became and it is quite interesting really..."

Tony is the master of understatement there, as usual! Although, with the band's profile currently being higher than it has for a long time with the recent releases and the ongoing re-mastering of the back catalogue as well as a genuine interest in the archival material emerging from the band themselves, it is quite possible that this and other gems might still see the light of day.

With so much material to choose from the band's problems were exacerbated by their continuing attention to detail and there were several arguments during the recording of the new album as Anthony recalls...

"I remember having an argument with the engineer about the twelve string sound. I remember him telling me "that doesn't sound like a twelve string " and I'd been playing this thing on the road for nine months and I had my own sound which wasn't everybody's idea. I didn't go for this kind of washboard; percussive all plectrum kind of stuff, I was trying to aim toward the more orchestral thing..."

Gradually, the band began to gain an audience with their non stop round of playing any and every university and college hall they could play and the band's musicianship improved enormously as John Mayhew recalls...

"We progressed very quickly from an acoustic, reflective band. I think it would have spoiled the album if there had been too much of a contrast between The Knife which is about as sharp as it gets (laughs). I think if there had been a song like Pacidy on the album it would have been too much of a contrast on one album because there were quieter songs and shorter ones too and I think they would have been better on an album of their own. They weren't actually writing songs to record although they were song writers; they kept on churning out songs..."

Not all of these songs were well received by the band's prospective audience however, as John recalls...

"There was the night in Ronnie Scott's Club and there was this guy who was heckling and it got to Tony, he was the first and he stood up from the organ and said: 'Sir, we are no ORDINARY rock band!'..."

Mike Rutherford has related the difficulty of trying to tune 12 string guitars up in toilets and other surreal surroundings, and John Mayhew also recalls something similar at one gig…

"They would go to the extent of driving the van outside a gig to tune up. I remember there was one gig we played and I think it was either a football field or a cricket pitch next to the gig and they were trying to tune up the guitars because the quiet sets would have really shown up an out of tune guitar and they drove the van out to the middle of the pitch to get away from the noise of the gig so they could tune up!"

However, a serious problem loomed on the horizon; Anthony Phillips, the mainstay of the band was beginning to have doubts about the direction in which the band was going and about his own position within the group. Also playing live was proving difficult for him and he began to suffer from severe stage fright which was eventually to lead to his decision to leave the band in July 1970, before their first proper album with Charisma was finished. The news came as a shock as Mike Rutherford recalls…

"I remember him telling me in the back of our transit van which Richard MacPhail was driving and being very shocked actually...." Mike agrees to a certain point with Anthony's assessment that the band were trying too hard… *" I think the trouble was in those days, you were so committed to the road, and it took so much out of you; get to the gig; rehearse; move the gear; all that routine. You were like a train that couldn't slow down...."*

Another casualty of this drive to perfection was to be John Mayhew, already aware that he was not able to match the musicianship of the others, he was particularly aware of Anthony's dissatisfaction with the way the band was going and to some extent blamed himself for that - needlessly as it has turned out. Communication was never really a strong point of the guys at this stage and no-one ever actually said how they felt which is a shame really because a lot of unnecessary guilt could have been avoided all round perhaps by a good old fashioned barney. Nonetheless, he was not surprised when he was informed by Peter Gabriel that the band would be looking for another drummer…

"We met in a coffee shop, Mike and Peter were there, and I think it was Peter that said to me; 'How would you feel about leaving?' and I said; 'Sure'. I remember I had tears in my eyes because I had built up an affection for the band in that year but because I couldn't play as well as they could, I was holding them back and that was why I felt responsible for Anthony's dissatisfaction. It was a bit like somebody under sentence. Eventually you are going to get sentenced and I would like to think that I knew it more and more. I say boldly that I was pushed out or that they asked me to leave, yes all that happened, but I knew it was coming. There was no pretence. I didn't speak to anyone about it, but I could see that they were going to places where I probably wasn't destined to go. So, c'est la vie!..."

Anthony and John's last gig with the band was in Hayward's Heath on 18th July 1970 and although the band admit that it was the closest that they ever came to breaking up nonetheless that indomitable spirit which has characterised Genesis' career was there even at this early stage as Mike recalls...

"Ant's last gig was at Hayward's Heath because I remember thinking that this was going to last forever, we were breaking ground with Genesis, and I drove back with Pete... Pete and I were in the car together and we started to have a conversation and..."hang on a minute: maybe we should carry on?" That's how it seemed..."

It is ironic that both Anthony and John were carrying guilt about the way that they perceived each had treated the other. Anthony in particular always felt that he had treated John quite badly in his quest for musical perfection, and John had always felt that he was holding the band back and that that was the reason for Anthony's growing sense of frustration. The truth, as usual, is somewhere in between these two positions and fortunately at a recent meeting which the author was accidentally instrumental in setting up, the two of them finally set the record straight.

CHAPTER THREE LOOKING FOR SOMEONE

Genesis spent the summer months of 1970 playing a variety of gigs "traipsing up and down the M1" as John had put it, as a four piece as well as completing work on their delayed album for Charisma although the difficulties still remained of who (if anyone) was going to be Anthony's full time replacement in the band as well as their decision to find a replacement for John Mayhew who had departed the band at the same time as Anthony. There was also considerable discussion about the material which was to be selected for inclusion on the new album as Tony Banks recalls...

"It was probably a group decision which ones went on. The songs that could have gone on included Twilight Alehouse which we didn't want on the album - I can't remember why... Some songs were always going to be on the album such as Dusk , Looking For Someone was always a high point for us although Stagnation was the most significant track on the album..."

The album was defined by the unique sound generated by Mike and Anthony's combined twelve string sound which as Mike himself admits was the dominant force on several tracks....

"Having recently heard the re-mastered version of that album I listened to Stagnation and I couldn't hear where Pete came in at all, and it was Ant and I with the twelve string over everything else...".

Continuing their two song writing groups worked well and the two units fed creatively off each other as Tony Banks remembers…

"There was very much the two sides to the sound; one of which came from Ant and Mike in the form of the acoustic guitar sound. That was demonstrated best on tracks like White Mountain and the early part of Stagnation. Then there was the heavier sound which I like to think came from Peter and myself which was shown on things like Looking For Someone and The Knife . It's funny as things were not really played to be that way but that's how it happened; they were more guitar based and we were more keyboard based, then there were moments where we met like on Stagnation that's why it's a successful song as it was a combination of everyone's best parts..."

As a musical unit the band were firing on all cylinders during this period although live performances were continually dogged by technical difficulties which Anthony Phillips recalls quite vividly...

"In those days we did these big kind of multi big changes where everybody would suddenly end up by playing different instruments and nothing would ever work (laughter) and there would be long gaps between numbers where things would be tried out and passed across (laughter). There was a thing which used to be know as the "Strat procession" which was my guitar which Tony Banks would sometimes play through his Leslie and it would often go round two or three times to see if it would work in different sockets. I think this is probably where Gabriel's stories started because there was such a long time that had to be filled in because various bits of gear didn't work..."

Trespass was recorded in June - July 1970 and finally released by Charisma in October of that year by which time both Anthony Phillips and John Mayhew had departed for pastures new. The album brought together all of the classic elements that Genesis fans have grown to love and was the first real indication of the inspirations and ideals which motivated the band. The orchestral effect created by Ant and Mike on their twelve strings was, at the time, unique and no doubt more than compensated for the disappointment of the last album.

The variety and depth of the music drew welcome praise from both the fans and critics. Each track displayed the various elements that were the essential Genesis and they all finally gelled within Stagnation which is seen by fans and several band members alike as the key track from the album. The musical development of the band from their hesitant steps on their debut album are astonishing. Peter's vocals alternate between choral delicacy and screaming rocker which once again demonstrated the lessons which had been learned by the band's lengthy stint on the road where they had to grab an audience's attention - who could ignore The Knife?! The deceptive initial delicacy of White Mountain also gave way to a harder edged middle section before returning to a tranquil ending clearly showing that the band had learned how to work an audience both on record and in the live context. Tony Banks has also finally got to grips with the "new" technology of the organ to deliver some delightful phrasings hinting at the gems which were to come later.

Several of the tracks from this album had already been written before the recording sessions and two at least; Stagnation and Visions Of Angels had been considered for release as part of From Genesis To

Revelation but those versions had been shelved. This may be seen as a surprise decision; but with the benefit of hindsight it is obvious that these tracks would not have fitted into the format of that album. Stagnation in particular was to develop beyond the initial versions into a classic slice of Genesis, even being considered as a potential single release, and indeed promotional copies were pressed up. This abortive release even garnered a review by another band (sadly unknown) who had recently done a gig with the band...

"As soon as the voice comes in its Genesis and I like it. We know them, we did a gig with them not long ago. The lyrics are too much, and the singer is very interesting. He's surprisingly inconspicuous offstage but on it he is really good, He comes to life as soon as he walks on. He's like an actor - when hr gets onstage he can really do things. Listen to that combination of images in just one verse - the changes on the lyrics and the music. It seems to flow beautifully..."

The development of the tracks both in the studio and live was to stand the group in good stead... Genesis fans always have been discerning and demanding, haven't we?!

Trespass was also the first clear statement of the band's intent to push the musical envelope beyond the realms of the three minute single. For a band with no recognisable focus or established fan base, this was a brave step indeed. The composers' "art" was still very much focussed on the singles market and few bands had managed to grab the album market and create their own identity there with any great success. It was to be Genesis' good fortune that the label to which they eventually signed in 1970 was to stand them in good stead.

Charisma Records, the creation of raconteur and all round bon-viveur, Tony Stratton-Smith had been established in 1969. With an eye for the out of the ordinary, Stratton-Smith, populated Charisma with the most eclectic mix of artists that you could imagine. Here Art Rock acts such as Genesis and Van Der Graaf Generator rubbed shoulders with the archetypal anarchists; Monty Python's Flying Circus; and Folk Rockers Lindisfarne. No other record company then or since could boast such a varied roster of performers on its books! This was exactly the kind of creative atmosphere that a band of Genesis' nature needed to flourish and grow and over the coming years that growth was encouraged and stimulated.

Mick Barnard's contribution to the Trespass album has been hard to document but Mick has recently commented on his brief stint with the band to the Italian Genesis Magazine: "Dusk...

"I found the album (Trespass) quite weak I mean, I like The Knife but the other sort of more melodic and slow stuff I was not really into. I think one of the things that put me off a little bit was the fact that they threw the album at me and said: 'learn it'. I would rather have put my own contribution to parts..."

Mick's reminiscences about the famous Disco Two performance are also somewhat at odds to the rest of the band...

"It was quite a job. We actually had to take some equipment which was silly as we weren't playing it. Yes they did a nice backdrop which from our point of view was blue and they superimposed war scenes on it. When it was broadcast we were playing in Watford Town Hall supporting Johnny Winter, and I rushed back because that was not too far from my house and I just managed to get in and see us performing on Disco Two..."

This certainly does not tally with Mike's comments on this elusive performance... *"Disco Two was very much like TV AM these days; it was live TV and it wasn't very good and I believe it has been lost and I am not too disappointed about that, actually!"* This performance was broadcast on 14th November 1970 and featured the band performing The Knife. Sadly, like so much of the BBC's early music archive, this performance and most of the rest of the Disco Two series itself, has been erased from the archives.

There is also the vexed issue of the contribution made to the album by Kim Shaheen; an American guitarist. Kim apparently answered the band's advertisement for a guitarist following Anthony Phillips' departure which was prior to the release of the album. With their usual vagueness at this time even this important decision appears to have been overlooked in the various biographies to date (including the previous edition of this book!) although this might also be attributed to the fact that the band members themselves seem to have no recollection of Kim's involvement with the band, but here are Kim's memories of the situation...

"I rang up Peter and I met the three... it was Peter, Tony and Mike and they had an apartment in London they just had a desk and three chairs and it was kind of like a school exam ....They made me sit down and

Peter had this tape recorder. He had me play a couple of songs and he recorded them... We arranged to meet a few more times and I went out to the house in Chobham ...and we went back there and played ... I played some things - stuff where they kind of needed a beat. I'm not sure what got used and what didn't ..."

The attitude that was to get the band labelled as "snotty nosed bastards" was somewhat in evidence. The innate sense of "superiority" bred into Public School boys was on display to the interloper who dared to take Anthony Phillips' place, as Mick Barnard remembers…

"They were all excellent musicians. They were brilliant, all of them. Peter I found easy to talk to. He was a very straight person. He had quite a stutter but he didn't seem to have that on stage. Phil was very much more the type of person I was - the same upbringing. The others were very privileged in their upbringing. Mike Rutherford was very friendly and very good. He would help me out with some guitar parts... I wouldn't say that I really ever had a fall-out with Tony Banks but I always felt that he felt somewhat superior and that maybe was just his general attitude. I have often said that we didn't get on but it wasn't as if we ever came to blows. It was just a personal thing. I just felt that he kept me at a distance. That was it; there was no way he was ever going to get close, even on tours and things... With the others we had a great time on tours especially with Peter because he had a brand new Hillman Imp car at the time and we used to go off and tour the Lake District, while the roadies took the equipment to Scotland in the van, so we had a nice time touring around..."

The year ended with the band playing the last of their gigs with Mick Barnard at a free concert at London's Lyceum ballroom at which the final piece in the band's musical jigsaw saw them playing and liked what he saw as he recalls…

"I met them in 1970 and it was decided that I was going to join them at the earliest opportunity. They fulfilled contractual requirements at that moment with the existing guitarist who I think was a chap called Mick Barnard.. they did a further two gigs I think with him and then I was 'in' as it were..."

The band had seen Steve Hackett's advertisement in the back pages of the then illustrious "Melody Maker" asking for musicians "determined to strive beyond existing stagnant musical forms" and a meeting was arranged where Steve had the chance to shine and prove that he wasn't just into techno flash but could also lay down moods and layers of music; a quality which definitely appealed to Genesis!

CHAPTER FOUR OPENING THE MUSICAL BOX

By the time Steve joined, Genesis had begun rehearsals for their follow up album to Trespass at Farnham Maltings in late 1970. Trespass in the meantime had received favourable coverage in the press and audience reaction had bordered on the ecstatic but this had not been translated into sales as Tony Banks recalls...

"With Trespass the group weren't doing a lot and the album sold something like 6000 copies. I think we felt it was ok. Obviously we wanted it to do well but we didn't expect any fantastic sales figures. At that time the group were getting a live following but nothing astounding..."

However, the group's work ethic meant that they continued to gig up and down the country "They would play anywhere" recalls promoter Tony Chapman...

"I never had any hassles from them. They would pick up the details and be on the road even if they had to play a hundred capacity club miles away up North..."

Another promoter; Andrew Kilderry remembers them for different reasons...

"I remember once they were the only band who forgot to ask for their money. I had them in for £75 and they did the show, and they were too scared and nervous to ask anything and off they went!! The agent called me up a few days later and went mad because they hadn't been paid!"

Steve Hackett, the band's new guitarist remembers his first gig with the band vividly...

"It was University College in the City or City of London University in Moorgate. It was a very shaky concert...not a pleasant experience.. there were lots of mistakes and I had a fuzz box that I'd been rehearsing with all week and suddenly they gave me a different one on the night and this fuzz box started to feed back and I played bum notes all night long and I thought; that's it the game's up I haven't got the gig... then we did the Lyceum in London and there wasn't a bigger London gig at the time and we did the concert and it was well received and when it was finished I was still sitting there on my stool afterwards and Richard MacPhail came onstage, took my arm and said; "it's finished now, Steve" (laughter) I was that nervous after it!"

Fortunately for Steve, his view was not shared by the band as Mike Rutherford commented in an interview with Sounds in March 1972...

"Fortunately Steve fitted in really well and it's much stronger now than it ever was. People have criticised us for not improvising but I've never known people improvise to a standard I am happy to play at. When this happens people find that they often have to refer to their memory book of riffs and phrases, so what we do instead is keep going over bits during the composition stage until it's right. In fact most of our work goes into the composition and that's also why we sometimes get blamed for lack of communication with the audience. You see, it's what we have written rather than what we play that matters most to us..."

The writing and rehearsing for the band's new album took place at manager Tony Stratton-Smith's house in Crowborough and it was not an easy period for the band who were still coming to terms with the loss of Anthony Phillips the majority of the material which was to feature on the album had already been written before Steve joined the band and they now were in the process of embellishing these pieces as Steve recalls...

"Most of the album had been written out of rehearsals before I joined although there was still a lot of room to make improvements; no one was making the sound of a musical box for a start; so I felt well here's me for a start..."

Nursery Cryme, is by comparison to Trespass, a frustrating album to listen to. One can sense the direction in which the band were heading but the album still seems rooted in 1970 to a certain extent. The key track; The Musical Box was, as Tony pointed out, a hangover from Ant's time but the recent arrival of Phil Collins and Steve Hackett certainly ensured that it had a drive and edge that would probably have been lacking otherwise. The band's humour was evidenced, albeit very darkly, on Harold The Barrel and no doubt there was a small twinge of nostalgia on For Absent Friends? Harlequin and Seven Stones are mediocre by comparison to the "epic" Musical Box and Fountain Of Salmacis and even the bizarre story of a decorative garden plant getting its revenge in The Return Of The Giant Hogweed once again displayed the band's growing confident musicianship and Peter's skill with lyrics which are by turns humorous and wryly sarcastic.

Even Peter admitted how much the band had changed since the departure of Ant and the arrival of Phil and Steve and also the driving force for their continued existence...

"Yes, our style has changed a lot - evolved in the last year. It changed when Phil came along and Steve joined on guitar. Originally we tried to do Folk type numbers and it's all worked up to a crescendo. Now we've got an act we have started to take control of audiences. In the past we bodged our way through things. A lot of it is based on fantasies without them taking over from the music. There is a lot of freedom in the music. Nobody has to compromise too much. In our writing we are trying to do something that hasn't been done before and that is to write a combination of sections that match..."

The album still suffered from poor production, something which was to dog the band for some time to come and it is only recently with the re-mastering programme carried out by Virgin that fans have managed to hear this album in all its glory. However, once you do hear the re-mastered version; the contributions which new members, Phil and Steve made to the album are plain to see. Phil's powerhouse percussion gives the album an edge lacking previously and Steve's aural inventiveness, especially on The Musical Box and Fountain Of Salmacis takes these mini operettas to a new dimension.

In an effort to increase interest in their growing stable of acts, Charisma decided to package three of the best together and send them out on tour throughout the UK in January and February 1971 taking in some of the larger theatres on the gig circuit. Genesis, as the junior partners in the package opened the show for Van Der Graaf Generator and Lindisfarne who, by this time were a happening band with their massive hit "Fog on the Tyne". However, Genesis, with nothing to lose and everything to gain, went on and in many cases stole the other groups' thunder which was confirmed by a review by Michael Watts of Melody Maker...

"It would be insidious to single out any one of the bands for future success, but at Sunday's concert, the beginning of Charisma's package tour, Genesis emerged with the greatest honours and audience acclaim. They are harder and more incisive than the delicacy of their album would suggest, and their vocalist, Peter Gabriel, frantic in his tambourine shaking, his voice hoarse and urgent is a focus for all the band's energy..."

Another witness to those memorable early gigs is the band's long-time biographer; Armando Gallo who recalls the first time he saw Genesis....

The first time I saw them was in January 1971; 24th January at the Lyceum which was my birthday. I went to see Van der Graaf Generator there with a bunch of friends because they were my favourite band, and opening for Van der Graaf was Genesis and Tony Stratton-Smith was at the back at the bar with his usual drink (laughter) and he said; 'have a pint Armando' so I had the pint and then he said; you should check out this band, they're very good'.. and so I went forward and by the time they came out and did The Knife there must have been about fifty people in front who went crazy but all the others just didn't care..."

Despite the plaudits of the critics and the fans, sales of *Trespass* did not significantly increase and Charisma focussed their promotional activities around Lindisfarne. However, the band were to make gains in some unexpected places and gained a new audience after their first overseas gigs which were in Belgium in March 1971 where the band played a couple of college halls and also recorded sets for "Pop Shop" a Belgian equivalent of Top of the Pops. Sadly; like its visual predecessor this visual document of the band appears to have been wiped. An audio recording of one of these early overseas shows has, however, recently surfaced and, despite its rough quality it nevertheless serves as a record of the energy and invention of the band at this formative stage of their development with a set comprising an early version of Happy The Man, Stagnation, The Light, Twilight Alehouse, The Musical Box, The Knife and Going Out To Get You.

The band's live following increased and they continued to perform concerts up and down the country whilst continuing to work on the follow-up album to Trespass although it was not plain sailing as Tony recalls...

"It wasn't a particularly easy period as I remember, we were struggling a bit with some of the songs. At that point Musical Box was a live success. We wrote The Return Of The Giant Hogweed and that took over from The Knife as being the song to close the live set and it worked pretty well. The Fountain of Salmacis worked well; it was something of a departure from the norm..."

Indeed this was the facet of Genesis' music that not only appealed to their audience but to the players themselves as Steve maintains...

"Things like The Fountain Of Salmacis were often more of an odyssey than a song. I call them odysseys because you didn't really know where you were going to end up. The structure doesn't vary that much and this was very important; each song was an adventure - it was a journey..."

Charisma finally released the album; titled Nursery Cryme in November 1971 sadly with less promotion behind it than its predecessor, and having strangely decided to finally release The Knife as a single split into two parts and coming with the band's first picture sleeve which even more strangely omitted Ant! Another Charisma Package Tour was organised in the autumn with Genesis and Lindisfarne again and the year saw them consolidating their position as one of Britain's most popular live acts. In the meantime, something was stirring in Continental Europe.....

CHAPTER FIVE A BRAVE NEW WORLD

Finally coming to terms with the fact that Nursery Cryme was, in commercial terms, no improvement on Trespass as Tony recalls...

"I think we were considerably more depressed by the sales of Nursery Cryme as that only sold again about 6000 copies and by the time that that album came out the group was obviously a lot bigger. We were doing well in foreign countries at that point - Belgium and Italy - but not as well in England..."

In fact the New Year brought good news for Genesis - in late January the news broke that the Trespass album was Number One on the Belgian charts! And by the time that the band crossed the English Channel to play some more overseas gigs their new album had reached Number Four in the Italian charts which astonished the band as Phil himself recalls...

"When we heard it we were amazed, it was strange that it should come from anywhere abroad, considering the amount of work that we had put in, in England..."

However, the band were not without their supporters in the UK and a third radio session was recorded by the BBC on 9th January 1972 as part of the "Sounds of the Seventies" series followed shortly afterwards by a series of gigs in Belgium again including the recording of what is now their earliest surviving appearance on television as part of the "Rock of the Seventies" series where the band performed live in a studio. Looking at this film now, the band do look extremely self conscious but even so their music shines through and the choice of tracks was inspired including as it did highlights of their current live set; Musical Box, The Return Of The Giant Hogweed, Twilight Alehouse and Fountain of Salmacis. It was particularly significant to see Twilight Alehouse appear on this performance because it was over a year before it was finally committed to vinyl as the b-side of the band's fist minor "hit" single.

The band's touring schedule took them to Italy in April where they played a string of sell-out gigs to ecstatic audiences and it was during this tour that Watcher Of The Skies took shape with Tony and Mike writing the lyrics in Naples although other contributions were of equal significance as Steve Hackett recalls...

"For instance on Watcher Of The Skies I remember being the one who said; "we've got to get a Mellotron; we've got to get a light show...I remember being against doing Supper's Ready live before we had all these things because I felt it wouldn't work and I remember it was me and Peter saying; "we shouldn't do it unless we've got all the sound effects of the train doors slamming and Uncle Tom Cobley and all...because we had performed a number of these type of things live and people just wandered off to the bar and we wondered why? So we had to get the whole production together before things started clicking with Genesis in those days..."

The band's following despite the relatively disappointing sales for Nursery Cryme had increased to the point where they were given a spot on the bill for the prestigious Reading Festival in August 1971 and subsequently at the next two Festivals. Even then Genesis made an impression and the 1972 Reading Festival is vividly recalled by longstanding fan Andy Wilkinson...

"Still relatively unknown outside the club and college circuit of London and the Home Counties, this gig was to be an interesting test of their appeal in front of a very mixed bunch of festival goers, many present to see other, more prominent headlining bands. ...With forty odd minutes to play, it was going to be an interesting short set... They opted to go Hell for leather from the start and kicked off with a frenetic The Knife. They sure as hell grabbed a lot of people's attention as darkness fell and Peter was, as usual, the focus of everything up there on stage. Next Twilight Alehouse seemed to please the crowds with the slurred organ finale, then straight into Watcher Of The Skies by now it was getting pretty dark and the majestic choral opening really did capture the atmosphere of the evening and the crowd were definitely warming to the band who sounded totally and radically different to anything that appeared before. The Musical Box followed and was to be the conclusion to their set with a short but ear and eye catching Return Of The Giant Hogweed as an encore. They had stolen Friday evening musically and created a wonderful hour of festival atmosphere on a warm August evening..."

The band's touring schedule took them the length and breadth of the UK during 1971 and into 1972 culminating with an auspicious slot at the Great Western Music Festival in Lincoln on 28th May and it was there that the longstanding bogie of Genesis and open air concerts struck and the show was a disaster by their standards although the audience and critics were blown away especially by Peter's appearance dressed as an "an ageless Egyptian prince". Armando Gallo also remembers that particular show...

"The Lincoln festival was very good as well because it was a four day festival; it was raining and it was cold and they came out and thought they'd done a horrible show but that's when I got converted to Genesis at that show because the atmosphere was so against them; it was two o'clock in the afternoon - it was cold everybody was still covered in straw because it was raining so much they gave out hundreds of bales of straw and people were sleeping under it and people were waking up and I wrote in my first book that that was where I stood in the mud with my wellies entrenched in the mud and there were twelve Italian journalists there and I was taking care of them and we were all just raving about it..."

Other memorable shows at this time included the band's show at the Olympia Theatre in Paris where they were supported by Peter Hammill. They then began the process of rehearsing and recording their new material initially at a rehearsal room in Blackheath although the band were not too happy with Charisma's choice of producer as Tony remembers...

"Charisma wanted us to have a hit so they thought they'd bring in Bob Potter who had worked with Bob Johnson in America and people like Simon and Garfunkel and Bob Dylan and Charisma thought that he could tighten things up a bit and stop things getting too arty for their own good. He came in and we just didn't see eye to eye at all. I did the introduction to Watcher.. and he said it was awful, he felt it sounded just like 2001. Charisma scrambled about trying to find somebody else and they came up with Dave Hitchcock ... we changed engineer during the course of the album as well as we weren't happy with the sound the guy was getting.

We realised that when we got John Burns in as the engineer that we could communicate with him, we were after the same sort of thing...With Supper's Ready the whole thing came about by accident there were little parts on there like the Apocalypse section where the organ solo on that started off as a very tongue in cheek sort of thing, I thought I'd play like Keith Emmerson to see what it sounds like..."

Supper's Ready was to be the backbone of the new album Foxtrot upon its release in October 1972 and the press and fan reaction was universally favourable and Supper's Ready made an instant impression as Andy Wilkinson, remembers …

"Peter was as ever, in complete control. Slim; dressed all in black with the now familiar partly shaven head and totally unique stage demeanour. He teased and taunted and provided lengthy pithy surreal stories mixed with references from Monty Python and vague references to sexual innuendo and to the characters the songs portrayed... but what was different was Supper's Ready although only released a month before, the audience seemed to be very familiar with this piece and just sat and witnessed it in awe. The song was played pretty much as it sounded on Foxtrot . Peter and the rest of the band were in top form and gave a performance of unnerving power, subtlety and precision. There were NO costume changes, NO props, and NO zany theatrics; it was played honestly with a minimum of fuss but very intense..."

The band weren't necessarily as convinced about the track themselves, as Phil Collins pointed out in an interview for NME's Tony Tyler…

"The second side - Supper's Ready was left till last really. Peter was rushing through the lyrics while we were putting down the backing tracks. Perhaps more time would have made it better..." although, in the same interview he also praised part of the latter day epic... *"Apocalypse in 9/8 it's the best thing we've done. It started off as a jam. Steve and Peter were away for some reason and Mike started playing this movement on bass pedals - totally abstract with no time signature at all. Then we tied it down and we worked it out to a two bar riff. I just knocked a beat out and it became a bar of nine. That's the way things are often done in the band and that's the sort of thing I'd like to work more to because I - personally - like playing in time signatures..."*

The band also took an unusual step in releasing a non album track as a single; Happy The Man which had been around since the very earliest days of the band was chosen backed by Seven Stones from the band's previous album. It was not a success although Tony Banks remembers the song quite fondly...

"I didn't have that much to do with it really, I was sort of there if you know what I mean! (laughter)...Once again Mike had another tuning on the guitar where everything was tuned to a chord and he played a riff on that and that sounded good. I played guitar along with him and we built it up from there...I suppose it came as a result of being on the road just too long with Lindisfarne (laughter) we had to have one song like that!"

The band's new show drew heavily upon the new album and their audience was such that now they were capable of playing the largest theatres in the UK as a headline act in their own right although technical problems still reared their head and Tony Banks recalls the appalling P A systems which were used in those days...

"With the PA's in those days you could never hear the voice so we actually performed one song on stage with no lyrics, Peter was just making noises (laughter). He Introduced Get 'Em Out By Friday as a song called I've Been Travelling All Night Long and no one noticed the difference!"

Foxtrot was to be one of those defining moments in the band's story. Here, at last; the band melded musicality with imagination and adventure all in the space of one album. Steve's insistence that they utilise special effects to translate their stories came to the fore here. From the grandiose opening chords of Watcher Of The Skies, where Tony's Mellotron actually sounds like a spacecraft about to land; to Peter's paranoid vocalisations on Get 'Em Out By Friday which, I suppose, could almost these days be seen as a reference to "Ethnic Cleansing" with perhaps Ratko Mladic being today's ruthless version of "The Winkler"?

Nostalgia continues to be a regular theme with Time Table being a delightfully poetic lament for times gone by. Can-Utility & The Coastliners although ostensibly about the legend of King Canute's attempts to control the tide, is just as much about the stupidity of listening to the advice of hangers-on and as such shows that even during this period; Genesis were capable of writing observant lyrics about every day subjects. Steve's acoustic masterpiece; Horizons was the lull before the storm that broke with Supper's Ready, the band's symphonic opus which managed to embrace everything the band had been striving for and their apocalyptic depiction of the struggle between the forces of good and evil still takes the breath away even now!

Another tour with Lindisfarne took place in October to coincide with the release of the new album although this time the honours were shared. Europe had already taken the band to their hearts, now it was time for the band to focus their attentions upon the USA where the band were very much an unknown quantity. Buddah Records who were in charge of promotion of the Charisma catalogue in the USA had found the band's previous album a hard one to promote in the States, but with *Foxtrot* they finally felt that they had something they could work with. A showcase gig was arranged for the band at New York's prestigious Philharmonic Hall in aid of the United Cerebral Palsy Fund. A warm-up gig was arranged a couple of days before at Brandeis University in the Boston area which went off without fuss to a small audience. The Philharmonic gig itself however, was a different matter with problems piling on problems; Leonard Bernstein showed scant regard for fellow professionals by insisting on rehearsing the orchestra on the day of the gig and there were several problems again with the PA system as Tony recalls...

"The whole gig was a complete nightmare. We had this incredible hum all the way through Supper's Ready. Something was really wrong with Mike's gear and I couldn't get full volume out of the gear, no textures, no colours..."

However despondent the band felt however, the audience loved the show and fans started writing in to their local radio stations requesting that they play Genesis's records and the stage looked set for Genesis to take the States by storm. However, as they were to discover, a lot more work had to be put in before that goal was achieved....

CHAPTER SIX CONQUERING THE NEW WORLD

Having been bitten albeit briefly by the America bug the band returned there in March of 1973 not before they continued their upward rise at home consolidating their position with a series of sell-out shows across the UK in January and February which culminated with a show at London's Rainbow Theatre which was then the biggest gig a band could get in London. It was here that the band experimented with their new stage set up having finally perfected the musical side of things with Foxtrot their strongest offering to date. Rather than clutter the stage with as much gear as they could cram on it, Genesis opted for the other extreme and managed to find a way to make it appear as if there was no equipment on stage at all by the clever use of a gauze curtain (the "Sails") and ultraviolet light which also served to heighten the appearance of Peter's Day Glo makeup. This was also, as mentioned previously, Gabriel's first appearance with all the costumes; bat wings, cape etc.

His previous dalliance with costume at Dublin's National Stadium the previous September where he had emerged during The Musical Box wearing a fox head and red dress had been met with stunned silence by the audience. Surviving footage of Peter's appearance at the Bataclan Club in Paris the following February where he appears in this costume gives a small sample of exactly what this theatrical element was like although sadly it is unlikely if it will ever be released officially! The band were also filmed during their appearance at the Frankfurt Festival in January, a further indication of how far they had progressed both musically and visually and public and press interest in this "happening" band continued to grow apace although there was no avalanche of press plaudits in the UK, Chris Welch being the sole voice in the wilderness and his review of the Rainbow gig sums up Genesis's predicament at the time...

"Did not the youths and maidens dance as if possessed? And you can't blame it on rock and roll because Genesis don't play any".

The art of presentation was indeed a lesson which Peter Gabriel had taken to heart as the band learned to their surprise when he opted to bring in a set of costumes for the band's showcase gig at London's Rainbow Theatre on 9th February 1973 as Steve recalls...

"He sprang that on us the night we were doing the Rainbow and I was very happy he did that. He just brought them along and they were just sitting there backstage before the show. He didn't rehearse with them, and he just put them all on during the numbers and I thought it was... there was a school of thought within the band that might have said; "I'm not too sure about that gold lame number (laughter). So I think he had the right sort of steamrollering approach; if he wanted to do it he just went ahead and did it and I felt the same musically, it was sometimes better to steamroller things than to try and do them by committee..."

This was indeed the band's problem; once again the spirit of the early audiences who had wanted "something to dance to" had come back to haunt Genesis. The music press, ever ones for an easy option, lazily and inaccurately categorised them in the same pigeonhole as ELP, Yes and Jethro Tull without realising that Genesis were an entity all of their own and Peter's appearance was perfectly in keeping with the surreal nature of the show as emphasised by the introductions Peter used for the Rainbow show...

"Michael Mellotron playing the part of Tony Banks, David Drums and Sally Cymbals as Philip Collins, myself, Peter Gabriel played by Patrick Moore, Michael Rutherford by Richard Rickenbacker, and Steve Hackett by Gary Gibson himself...".

Holding to the tenets of the old storytelling traditions, Genesis took you far beyond the mere artifice of Rock & Roll into their own world ,as a front man, Gabriel was transformed and Genesis gigs were never quite the same afterwards and neither were their audiences who packed out show after show in the UK and subsequently in Europe and as their long term friend and chronicler of their career; Armando Gallo was to say several years later - *"Welcome to the world of Genesis"*

After their brief initial foray to the USA, and the reaction to the Philharmonic Hall show, the band naturally thought that America would fall before the all conquering heroes as the UK and Europe had already done. Upon their return to the States in March however, their illusions were to be cruelly shattered.. With a massive stage production in tow there were to be very few shows where they could (even if they were willing to do so) compress their show into a thirty or forty minute show as support to some other artist and no self respecting artist would want a support act that could effectively blow them offstage with a presentation like Genesis's. Steve Hackett and Tony Banks both outlined the difficulties they experienced with American audiences on their first proper tour of the US in an interview with Barbara Charone…

(Steve) : *"Attitudes of American audiences were a bit like - 'well, come on show us what you can do'. It's like they have seen it all. One night someone screamed out; 'You better be fucking good!' which doesn't exactly make one play better. What saved us in the end was the visuals…"*

(Tony): *"Its quite a problem when you come face to face with an audience that doesn't like you, a crowd that wants you to play loud and play rock. In those situations it's easy to get the feeling that you are trying to educate the people which is obviously all wrong. I can understand now why so many English bands break up after American tours. You're in England secure and doing well and then once you get to the States it feels like you are getting nowhere. That situation can be quite a bring-down; smashed egos and all. But our American tour wasn't particularly straining. We didn't do that many concerts in a row because Peter's voice tends to go after two or three nights which was good for the band anyway. So many bands seem to kill themselves just making it big…."*

Consequently, apart from a few shows supporting Lou Reed and Richie Havens, the band were effectively on their own ironically even using Dale Newman; a member of what is now the longest serving road crew in rock as a support act at some shows and Mike's guitar roadie and now long-time minder of their studio; The Farm recalls how he first became involved with the band….

"I got the 'phone call from Craig Schertz and agreed to do two weeks as guitar technician. My guitar skills were just enough to do what he required at the time, which was just a few acoustic guitars and keeping them in tune… the two weeks went well and Mike asked me if I wanted to g to Europe so I said; "Here's my passport" and we were off! (laughter)"

This is another facet of Genesis which marks them out from other bands; their road crew have remained with them for many years and maintain the high standards which the band set themselves.

The band's shows at the Free Trade Hall Manchester on 24th February and the De Montfort Hall in Leicester on 25th February 1973 were recorded for an American radio show; "The King Biscuit Flower Hour" and it was at this point that the band's manager; Tony Stratton-Smith managed to obtain the unmixed tapes from the radio station with the aim of releasing a live album which the band themselves were not too keen on. Although, as Stratton-Smith quite correctly pointed out; such a release would enable the band to take a step off the album - tour- album treadmill which they had been on since their career began and give them some breathing space with which to reassess their position and to begin writing for a new album. Initially the album was pressed up as a double although eventually a truncated version was eventually released into the shops on 20th July 1973 and certainly it showcased some of the band's finest moments although sadly omitting Supper's Ready. The album was rightfully dedicated to the band's long time friend and sound engineer; Richard MacPhail whose devotion to the band's cause is well remembered by Phil…

"The sound in those early gigs around the Foxtrot time, in the small town halls, was probably amazing because Richard knew exactly everybody's head inside out and he was so in sympathy with what the band should sound like…"

Test pressings of the album on the Dutch Philips label do exist although fortunately for most fans' wallets, the recent Genesis Archive collection has finally brought the remaining concert highlights of this period to us at a much more acceptable price!

Once again, however, Genesis Live suffers from several flaws perhaps the most irritating is the omission of the between-song stories told by Peter Gabriel which had by now become semi legendary among fans. Once again, the production values are less than they should be and given that Richard MacPhail did give the band an incredible sound at these gigs; this is not reflected by the patchwork quality of sound on the album even after the recent re-mastering work it is still a sadly disappointing effort. Many fans have expressed the opinion that it would have been better to have released it as originally planned as a double album; although as outlined above, the band themselves do not seem to agree with that assessment, and also a double live album by anyone other than the MAJOR league artists of the day back then would certainly have been an expensive item which in itself would probably have mitigated against the very fans whom it was aimed at.

The band wound down live work during the summer months to work on their forthcoming new album. That didn't stop them pulling out all the stops for a breathtaking performance at the Reading Festival, which saw the band grab the audience by the scruff of the neck and shake them until they begged for more. Peter's entrance on top of a white hydraulic pyramid being just the latest in a line of visual gimmicks which would eventually culminate in The Lamb Lies Down On Broadway some twelve months later. Typically enough; the band were far from satisfied with that performance as they explained to Chris Welch…

(Peter) *"I don't think the music was very good. The reaction was very pleasing to us from that point of view. We have never had that sort of reaction at a festival before. We are always very sceptical about working in the open air. We work very much on atmosphere and that is easier to create inside. We had a bit of power trouble as well which caused the long delay. It wasn't intentional."*

(Steve) *"Your write-up was very complimentary compared to the actual performance, I think it showed we had been off the road for some weeks…"*

After the success of Foxtrot both at home and abroad, anticipation for the band's new work was high. Perhaps in fact, unlike previous efforts, they almost allowed themselves TOO much time to write and record and the end result in some aspects fell between two stools. Undoubtedly the music had improved and the over all technique was immeasurably better but there were still problems as Tony recalls…

"We had a few arguments about this at the time actually because really there was too much material to go on the album. I wanted to kick off After The Ordeal which I actually think is our worst song we've ever recorded, I really didn't like that. I don't like the whole sort of pseudo classical thing at all…We could have got it off the album without any trouble as we shouted about it quite loudly at the time! But Pete also said that he wanted to get rid of the instrumental bit at the end of Cinema Show and I said; 'We can't have that; it's great and it's got all the best bits!" So we ended up with a compromise which was to keep the whole bloody lot on and as a result the album sides were far too long; about twenty eight minutes as I recall. That was far too long for a vinyl album so it sounds pretty rough…"

Peter also pointed out a facet of the band's recording which might come as something of a surprise to fans who assumed that Genesis were always about extended soloing and lengthy compositions during the Gabriel period, only learning the art of self-editing after he left….

"I am never very objective about albums just after we have finished them. This one (Selling England) has more flow. We've fully explored the roots of the band on the past ones, when we've had contrast after contrast. The solos are longer on this one and we've played our things to their natural length. In the past we rather nervously tended to cut things short. The new album has longer solos - at the risk of being boring. We hope that the fans will stay with us at any rate…"

Steve's difficulties with the album were much more of a personal nature. By nature a quiet and rather shy individual, Steve had difficulty coming to terms with the sometimes heated and, it must be said, at times petty attitude which was evidenced by the core members who had grown up with each other as Steve maintained it was sometimes as trivial as...

"well you broke my ruler in 1963! To which the reply was ah, yes, but you pinched my sweets in 1964!.."

The other members were used to each others 'foibles and it was difficult for the new boys to sometimes find a position in which they were comfortable. Steve eventually overcame these doubts as he remembers…

"I had this with Genesis before Foxtrot I didn't think I'd contributed sufficiently to the songs on that album. I always felt they were strong enough without me and I felt…'You know I think I ought to leave, you guys are strong enough without me..' and they said…Tony and Mike said…'Oh, no Steve, we really like your guitar playing and we really want you to stay with the band..'"

And so, freed from that nagging doubt Steve threw himself into the writing and recording of Selling England by the Pound and without doubt it is his work which shines through the album which is one he remembers particularly fondly…

"Well, having been involved with a bunch of guys who were a song writer's collective as they originally presented themselves; at that point I felt I hadn't really come up with any songs for the band and at that time I felt that it was time to express myself spontaneously as a player and I felt this is never going to wash with the band but I said; 'I've got a few bits that go like this..(hums out tune that became Dancing With The Moonlit Knight) and I said 'what I'm really all about is this but I really don't think that you guys are in this ball park, are you?' and Phil said; 'Hold on, I think we've got something..''

That something turned out to be the one thing that had so far eluded them: a minor hit single. I Know What I Like which evolved out of a band jam session was to prove to be the unlikely "hit" of 1973 and it all originated out of a guitar riff of Steve's as Tony explains...

"It was a riff of Steve's that it was based on. We used to jam on it for hours and then I had the idea of playing it on fuzz piano and organ at the same time and because the piano was very out of tune with the organ, the whole thing had a nice quality about it, even when I was just playing these very simple chords. We knew we'd written something that had single potential although we were a bit embarrassed about it as we weren't supposed to be a singles band. Anyway Charisma put it out and we refused to go on Top of the Pops! (laughter). We thought that was enough of a stand..."

Selling England By The Pound took all the elements that made its predecessor a success and honed them to even greater perfection. This is without doubt their most musical album to date and although it was something of a struggle in artistic terms, the results were astonishing. It is certainly to my ears, the first Genesis album that is aurally satisfying although even now the production values were incredibly poor. The tale of poor old Britannia that opened the album demonstrated fine line in irony; "Can you tell me where my country lies…" can be interpreted in a variety of ways. In view of the creeping Americanisation of the UK at this time it is a singularly telling line. Peter expressed his own thoughts on that subject in an interview with Chris Welch prior to the album's release…

"Well, Christ, it's society's doom innit? Flogging England by the pound. We've always been keen on telling stories which we know nothing about. We get off on fantasy, you know. I hate patriotism but we try to be English if you know what I mean. A lot of bands try to go 'American' after their first tour there. I like America; I think New York has got a great feel about it and it's a very exciting city but as a visiting rock and roll band I think your experiences are limited and you don't get much artistic insight into the nature of the city…"

Intriguing comments, given the later developments within the band's story!

Once again, the band demonstrated their sense of humour with their lurid tabloid press-styled report on the sexual antics of a pair of star-crossed lovers at The Cinema Show and they even managed to predict the growth of Rap music with their take on the various UK supermarket chains in Aisle Of Plenty.

This is the album where Steve Hackett became a major force within the band and his soloing on Firth of Fifth became an indelible trademark of the band's sound. However, it does not work on every level. The Battle Of Epping Forest was one of those tracks where music and lyrics did not make ideal bedfellows.   It did however, unlike so many of Genesis's other opuses, have its feet firmly grounded in the real world as Peter Gabriel explained at the time….

"About two or three years ago I read a newspaper item about a gang battle that took place in Epping Forest. I like to collect cuttings from newspapers about any odd happenings. In this case I kept the cutting for ages, but could not find out any more about the battle. I even put an ad in The Times and checked the newspaper libraries but the story had disappeared off the face of the earth. Even my original cutting seems to have disappeared..."

A case of maybe the evidence being buried with the bodies, perhaps?   The resulting track is perhaps one of the most unsatisfying efforts that Genesis have committed to record. Throwing the kitchen sink in meant for a track that had simply too much going on in it for it to succeed; perhaps an early indication that editing can sometimes be a good policy?

Most tellingly of all, however was the little ditty; More Fool Me which featured Phil's first lead vocal for the band after performing so many harmonies. Again, the lyrics can be viewed in so many ways even perhaps in the case of the lines…

And there you are
Quite sure that you were right
Knowing full well
That I'd be the first one
To go down

Which could be seen as a reference to Peter's position within the band which was now being perceived as being of almost God like proportions by the fans.

The single eventually reached the number nineteen slot in the UK charts and the album itself the highest position to date in the charts reaching number three. At last Genesis had made the breakthrough to mainstream success and the ensuing tour was extremely successful and enjoyable as Steve remembering the band's famous gigs at Los Angeles' Roxy Theatre that December recalls...

"..Then we did these three nights at the Roxy; two shows a night and they sold out and they were hanging from the rafters and they loved everything we did and they were to my mind some of the greatest gigs the band ever did because it was a small room, it was very powerful and I felt very much at home and I knew what I was playing and I knew who I was and I was wearing a terrible jacket with strawberries all over it! (laughter). I was going through my phase of looking like the guy from Spinal Tap who had the moustache! (laughter).

*Nonetheless they loved us and I felt we were right; this was the greatest stuff this band is ever going to do, this is **IT**! And there were things happening on stage; Pete and Phil were so loose and they would start going into comedy routines (laughter) at one point they would start doing this thing where I think it was Pete, would start doing an impression of Alan Whicker (laughter) and then Phil started doing the same thing, and of course, the audience didn't know what they were doing but the band were falling about; we were in tears of laughter and we were so relaxed. Then we did a Christmas Eve show where; in those days in order to sound like Mickey Mouse you couldn't get your voice up that high and so Pete took helium and he took so much that he hiccups for a day afterwards but he went for it and he was dressed up as Father Christmas and it was just great..."*

The band even found time to record a concert film at Shepperton Studios outside London. Titled "Tony Stratton-Smith Presents Genesis in Concert" it was filmed in front of an invited audience on 30th and 31st October 1973 and featured the current highlights from the band's new set: Watcher Of The Skies, Dancing With The Moonlit Knight, Musical Box, I Know What I Like and Supper's Ready and managed to capture something of the spirit of the band at this crucial stage in their development. In fact, the live sequence from this film was to have been the promotional video for the I Know What I Like single but the band rejected this at the last minute. Sadly the plans for this film to be given a cinematic release also fell through and it remains unseen to this day although tantalising glimpses have been given on various television programmes and more recently in the band's own documentary histories although frustratingly enough, it is also known that earlier shows were also captured for posterity on film although these too, are sadly languishing in vaults somewhere.

Also at this time, during a brief lull in the band's touring schedule, Mike Rutherford was briefly reunited with his old friend Anthony Phillips for the recording of a song which dated back to the halcyon days of 1969. Silver Song had been written by Phillips as a tribute to the Genesis drummer; John Silver and having enlisted Mike to record it, they also involved Phil as singer which, along with his solo spot on More Fool Me during the band's new show, was perhaps an early indication of what was to happen later? Anthony recalls how this elusive recording came about...

"That summer ('73) Genesis had a bit of a lull, writing Selling England By The Pound. Mike and I were talking about possible solo things. We heard about the Charisma album of modern hymns (Beyond An Empty Dream) and Silver Song came to light at the same time. Phil came down and sang on the demo of the hymn (Take This Heart) with a few friends. Then the Silver Song idea came up - I can't remember how we played it to him, but he loved the idea.

The demo is great because it has a lovely country feel to it but the sound is so wild. The drums do sound seriously 'cardboard box-ey' on that. The finished version sounded a little clinical - with the twelve strings; we didn't get the feel of it. Phil sang it well but he didn't sing it in the really loose way he did on the demo. He sang it correctly and brilliantly at the end with the improvised part, but it lacked the loose sort of summer afternoon feel the demo had.. We had to do it in a day, both songs (another song; Only Your Love was also recorded at the time).."

Either way, the recording including the prospective B-side; Only Your Love was recorded and proposed as a Phil Collins solo single although this idea was subsequently shelved and the recording still lingers somewhere in the Charisma archives. The hymn which Ant and Mike recorded; Take This Heart finally appeared on the Charisma album Beyond An Empty Dream in 1975 and is now one of the most collectable items for fans of both Ant and Mike's work.

Such breaks were to prove a rare luxury for the band as they continued their gruelling concert schedule into the following year beginning with five sell-out shows at London's prestigious Drury Lane Theatre the first of which is vividly recalled by Andy Wilkinson...

"Mid way through a so far stunning and unbelievable evening, time to play Firth Of Fifth. Tony began unaccompanied with the breezy piano intro leading into the song. Suddenly things began to go seriously wrong: one or two blindingly obvious bum notes were played, the tempo began to skew; more wrong notes. Tony had totally lost the plot!! He bravely continued, struggling heroically to get his piano back on course. Too late, the beautiful piano introduction was reduced to an unqualified disaster. Tony had no option but to stop dead...Phil rescued the situation somewhat, when he swiftly called 'two, three, four' and the band continued in unison with the rest of the song. Thankfully Tony had not lost his composure over this faux pas, and the song and the rest of the set was completed in fine style...

Although this technical hiccup did have long term effects and the song has NEVER been played with its introduction since! Another memorable moment from these shows occurred when Peter decided to avail himself of another theatrical prop common in these old English theatres: a "Peter Pan Rope" with which he was hauled up to "fly" across the stage during Supper's Ready giving an already dramatic song even more style. It almost ended in tragedy however, when Peter was almost strangled by the guide rope and on the repeat of this "flying" incident at a gig in New York, Peter came very close to becoming a castrato if the photographs of the incident are to be believed, at any rate! The band rounded off their most successful tour to date with a string of US shows which ended with a two night stint at New York's Academy of Music in early May 1974. The stage was now set for them to embark on work for another new album; one which was to take their fans and critics by surprise….

CHAPTER SEVEN TAKING THE LAMB TO MARKET

1973 and 1974 were difficult years in the UK; the oil embargo placed on the West by the Oil Producing States in the Middle East, hit industry hard and especially the record industry. The "three day week" was one misery but added to that restrictions on products made from petroleum (including of course; records) was another. Perhaps these difficulties influenced the direction the band was taking; their previous album's title: Selling England By The Pound was ostensibly a reference to the Labour Party manifesto of the time and perhaps the general frustration rubbed off on the band, who knows? What isn't in doubt is that by the summer of 1974 things in the Genesis camp were far from ideal.

Phil, sensed the restrictions that the structured approach to composition which was very much the Genesis approach most keenly and began to look for other outlets for his music outside of the band including his own "scratch band": Zox and the Radar Boys which included such alumni as Bill Bruford and Peter Banks and this freedom of expression is something which Phil enjoyed as he explained during a Radio One interview at the time…

"just keep it very loose and just have a good time... because I'm at home with the arranged things that we do but sometimes I get a yearning to get on stage and not know what is going to happen. Occasionally we've had improvised things when equipment has broken down with various members like me and Steve or me and Mike and Steve and they can turn out to be quite fun... The stuff on the new album... a lot of it is heading that way, towards having a very loose theme to work with and keeping a lot more of whatever happens on the night...the freer you can keep it, the better really..."

Ironically, given the turn of events which was to follow, it was Phil's unrest with the band which led him initially to consider leaving the band as Armando Gallo recalls…

"I moved to England and I was going back to the USA and maybe on the Wednesday or Thursday of the week before I was due to leave it was the presentation of the gold disc for Selling England by the Pound and they were finishing the tour of The Lamb... and Phil came up to me and said; 'You're leaving for Los Angeles and so I better tell you before somebody else tells you; I'm leaving the band' and I said 'really?' and he was getting this band together which became Brand X and so I left and went back to California and then in the August there was the news that Peter had left the band and I said; 'what do you mean, Peter's left? Phil was supposed to be leaving..?"

As mentioned, previously, Mike also took up work outside of the band being reunited with his friend Anthony Phillips for what eventually, some three years later was to appear as his first solo album; The Geese & The Ghost. Peter Gabriel also was tempted by working in the area of film which is something which has always fascinated him. In particular an extremely tempting offer was made by William Friedkin who had gained a certain notoriety by directing the classic horror film; The Exorcist. In particular he was taken by the story on the back of the Genesis Live album and thought that Peter might be able to work in the field of screen writing. Naturally , Peter was tempted and briefly left the band to try his hand. Steve also started writing various bits and pieces during the initial break between albums and tours, maybe as therapy for the growing problems in his first marriage.

The "team ethic" which had guided Genesis thus far was thrown into turmoil by Peter's decision and Tony in particular was adamant that any individual project shouldn't be put before the interests of the group. Added to these difficulties, Peter's wife was expecting their first child and there were complications which placed an even greater strain on him and Steve Hackett was in a similar position with the impending breakdown of his first marriage. The band themselves, perhaps in an attempt to return to the early days, opted to record the album out in the country and retreated to Hedley Grange a rambling pile which had previously been the home of notorious occultist Aleister Crowley and also home to the arch hedonists of the rock world; Led Zeppelin.

At an early stage it was decided to make the album into a concept which in itself was a brave step given that the rock world was by now beginning to tire of such things as Yes discovered when they took their"opus" Tales From Topographic Oceans out on the road and were soon forced to reduce the amount of new material in their set and reintroduce several old "favourites". The backlash against rock and roll excess which was some two years later to unleash the so-called "New Wave" was beginning to gather momentum and so Genesis's decision to create a concept album at this point in their career may be seen in that context as perhaps a strange decision? However, Genesis are nothing if unpredictable and the album that they were to create was the one which took everyone, fans and critics alike totally by surprise and which remains to this day, their most talked about and indeed, argued about, recording.

There were two main ideas for the story up for grabs and here it was Peter who was perhaps slightly more worldly wise who insisted upon the story of Rael, the Puerto Rican street kid who was the central figure in the new work and perhaps here Peter also saw the chance to indulge both his desire to create a musical story of his own and to experiment with a putative film script into the bargain, for the album that emerged; The Lamb Lies Down On Broadway is Genesis's most visual album . Having decided to write the story himself, the rest of the band threw themselves in to the task of creating the soundtrack to go with it as both Tony Banks and Steve Hackett remember...

(Tony) ..*" it was a chance to do all sorts of things like improvisations. During the writing of the album we brought in all these little bits that we had and worked on them and for me that was such fun to do. We just set ourselves an idea and improvised on it. Some of them became more solid pieces than others...we had this sort of Chinese jam which ended up somewhere in The Colony Of Slippermen I think, we had one called Victory At Sea which became Silent Sorrow In Empty Boats. Then there was obviously The Waiting Room which was called Evil Jam we just sat there and tried to frighten ourselves! (laughter)..*"

Steve also recalls some of these moments...

"The same thing happened with the bit on The Lamb that we used to call Pharaohs which became Fly On A Windshield the bit that has no melody but is full of portent and has the idea of almost the "Ben Hur" rhythm; the guys in the galley (laughter) and I thought; 'oh that's good' and so the guitar became this sort of screaming voice over it and I went for Egyptian phrases as we made the same modulation from E to F sharp that roughly parallels the modulation on Ravel's Bolero at the end.."

Collaborative efforts aside, however, the album was to bring its own problems. Peter's decision to wrote the story line and lyrics did create some friction. Fans were already beginning to set Peter up on the dreaded pedestal from which it was inevitable he would either fall or be pushed. His decision to leave the band was not something entered into lightly but the problem of who did what was one which did exacerbate the problem as Tony points out...

"As Peter decided it was his story he was going to write all the lyrics. It was a reasonable decision as it was his story but I don't think it would have suffered if other people had been involved as well. A different lyric writing style has been very much a feature of Genesis over the years although perhaps people assumed Peter wrote all the lyrics which, of course, he didn't...

This is particularly true even of this album where Peter's tardiness with lyrics meant that eventually Mike and Tony wrote some of the lyrics for the final side of the album. The frustration with that assumption and the attention that was being paid to Peter at the expense of the rest of the band and indeed, the music they created collectively was expressed by Phil in an interview which the band gave to Barbara Charone of Sounds in October 1974...

"People that are seeing us for the first time really aren't ready for the music. They are prepared to see a visual show and a few weird costumes. But they are surprised to see that we can PLAY aside from Peter's thing. Sure, all of Peter's press bothers us because we're an equally spread band. And it brings us down that people often can't see beyond the superficial thing of Peter wearing funny masks. Fantasy is what we're aiming for and the visuals are there to help the music. Peter wouldn't be wearing a flower mask if it wasn't required in Willow Farm and he doesn't wear a nylon on his head for sexual fantasies; it's because he is imitating a rogue.

People assume that the costumes were just an attempt to get front pages of the music papers but it's really all related to the music. Peter gets more press than the rest of us and he's running out of things to say. People always ask him the same questions about why he had his hair cut the same way they ask me questions about what drummers I like or Tony what keyboards he uses. People seem to forget about the fact that all of us write music and all of us write lyrics. What annoys us intensely is when people come backstage after a gig; ignore everybody and go up to Peter and say; 'amazing show man, really dug it, your music's fantastic'..."

Mike Rutherford confirmed that view in the same interview...

"The thing that hassles the band most though is people who assume that Peter automatically writes all the songs because he is the front man visually. I'm not so proud as a player, but as a writer I don't take criticism well..."

Steve also had reservations about the way the album was going. In fact, there is very little of Steve to actually be HEARD on the album apart from the glorious Fly On A Windshield where his guitar soars over the rest of the band. As he revealed in an interview which he gave to Circus Magazine in June 1978, he received short shrift from Peter when he voiced his objections... *"I was very pissed off at the way The Lamb Lies Down On Broadway was going. I told Pete so and he said; 'I don't give a fuck'..."* Steve was also annoyed with Peter's comments about his accident and the postponement of the tour and the blame for it which appeared to be aimed in his direction by Peter... *"Peter did an interview in which he said, in so many words; 'We've had to cancel the tour - Steve goes out and gets a little drunk, and look what happens!' He was prepared to make me a scapegoat. My credibility was on the line so I went to America and played the tour - with my arm in a sling..."*

Without doubt, the resulting album; The Lamb Lies Down On Broadway is the most talked about and indeed, argued about, album in the entire Genesis canon, and with good cause. However, the album itself does not thrill this listener in the way it does so many other fans, nor has the haze of nostalgia clouded over the many inconsistencies within the work itself. The modern day "fairy tale" of Rael is all well and good, after all it is based on a character whom most people can identify with, if not relate to and therein lies my major problem with this album. I do find it difficult to relate to the story of an American street kid, as narrated by a bunch of English ex-public school boys (Steve and Phil excepted). Indeed, the idea of a story such as this being written by English musicians is very hard to credit Even Peter himself seems to have anticipated some of the furore the new album would generate if his comments in an interview carried in the November 2nd edition of New Musical Express were anything to go by...

"Yes we expect a good slagging this time. I suppose it's an album and ticket sales... to be er, WORTHY of slagging.... The new album is a lot more direct than some of the things we have done in the past and all the songs are seen from the point of view of Rael who is a very earthy sort of character, so there aren't any wishy-washy... pseudo cosmic areas for people to get lost in. Or at least not as many. We know that concept albums are very passe and boring for most people but for those people who can get into what we

are trying to do - which is fantasies and everything - this album is a logical development and a good thing for us to try..."

The lazy comparisons of the band to the likes of ELP and Yes were also beginning to rankle as Tony commented .....

"I suppose people think we're more airy-fairy than Yes or ELP, more fey because we don't sweat as much, but I've never thought we've been at all like those bands and I think this new album will end those comparisons forever. The most important thing to us is the song, then the playing and only then the presentation. We're not as concerned with flaunting musicianship; Yes and ELP are more dependent on solos. I'm not a soloist as such. I think of myself more as an accompanist who colours the sound..."

Musically it contains some of the band's finest work of that there is no doubt, however, the work is in places too obscure for its own good and frankly I find it to be at least as pretentious, if not more so than some of its predecessors which was the whole point in the first place to get away from what was becoming perceived as the "arty, farty nonsense" that Progressive Rock was becoming. Also, and here the band were in good company; Yes and Jethro Tull having succumbed to the same failing by trying to take themselves far too seriously; the work contains some seriously irritating "noodling" of the kind that mid period King Crimson did to so much better effect. It is strange that both Yes's opus Tales From Topographic Oceans, and Genesis's would have fared far better had they omitted the third side of their respective albums.

A case of synchronicity perhaps? Over indulgence? Certainly! Obviously, I am speaking from a minority viewpoint here... Genesis fans in general have continued to revere this album and no doubt will continue to do so. Peter Gabriel, in the same interview which has been quoted from previously, seemed to share some of those viewpoints...

"We wanted him (Rael) to be this earthy and aggressive sort of person, but instead of making him a British earth person whom almost the entire staff of the NME would knock us for writing about because we know nothing about British earthy people, or so it goes... We've chosen an American earthy person who clearly we can't even pretend to know anything about. We can only observe as casually as any other British export will observe American life . And it seems acceptable for any artist to write about the American way of life. Also it is set in New York because New York is more aggressive and speedy than any other city, which is a useful feel to start this particular story from. So there is that separation, partly resulting from our being subjected to the rights and wrongs of the class struggle..."

The album after many delays, eventually appeared in late November 1974 by which time the band were on tour in the USA a tour which had been postponed due to an injury which Steve sustained to the tendon in his thumb which delayed things even more although Tony reckons that may have been a blessing in disguise...

"Well, Steve's hand was a very useful excuse! (laughter) He genuinely cut his hand and couldn't play but we were nowhere near finishing the record and we needed the time desperately so it gave us a bit of a breathing space. A lot of people thought that we had made it up, but it was true..."

Not everyone was as sympathetic to Steve's situation however, as Peter's comments in an interview for New Musical Express on 2nd November 1974 reveal....

"It seems ridiculous that such a vast operation has had to be cancelled due to Steve indulging in a tentative piece of raving and it's a complete drag for us as well as the fans because not only did we want to do the tour but it looks like we stand to lose quite a bit of money in the way of compensation..."

A further result of the injury was that Steve had time while recovering to work on some ideas of his own which were to bear fruition a year later. The upshot for the band was that the tour began before the album had been released which was certainly not an ideal situation for the band as Tony recalls...

"I love the idea of playing it live and I wish it had worked better. The people that came to see us wanted to hear Musical Box and Supper's Ready - the things they knew. When we started, we were playing in America to an audience that hadn't even heard it as the record wasn't even out at this stage. So it was completely new music that they were hearing and it was difficult. We had so many special effects going which in the rehearsal room looked marvellous but on stage they never all worked at the same time, we always had something going wrong. I hate it when something goes wrong on stage!"

Someone who recalls just how often things went "wrong" on stage is David Lawrence who worked as head of lighting on the band's US and European tours…

"…This (The New York show) was going to be a good two nights; all the music press were there; and all the music people. Nothing could go wrong. In the past the New York shows had had lots of problems. The year before someone had hijacked all the guitars and held them for ransom; so we were more careful about this show than most. In the middle of the jam section (The Waiting Room) there is a long crescendo of sound getting louder and louder; the lights get brighter and brighter and then suddenly all the stage sound equipment went off; no keyboards; guitars; just Phil on drums. Backstage there is panic.

The band; all except Phil came offstage leaving him to do a quick solo. We were all running round back stage looking for the power supply board to see if a fuse or circuit breaker had blown. This took about two minutes as everything had been painted matt black; including the two big fuse boxes; which we just could not find in the dark. When power came back and the band went back onstage to start playing again as if nothing had happened I think the audience thought it was part of the show and we got on with it. Unfortunately; the same thing happened at the same place during the next night but we were ready for it; this fuse blowing never happened again - ever. New York was fighting back!"

Another person who has vivid memories of the band's gigs in New York during The Lamb… tour is Steve's wife, Kim Poor. Her then fiance was a fan of the band and it was he who played his part in getting Steve and Kim together by asking her if she wanted to see the band's show in New York. Kim remembers the show as being given a very mixed reception; it was not received with quite the adulation that legend would have you believe; Kim remembers a distinctly tense atmosphere at the gig, with sections of the audience booing the new show and others cheering, she maintains that it was likely that a fight might have broken out at any moment - New York was fighting back, indeed!

Her first encounter with a member of the band was with Peter, whom she recalls was incredibly shy. She and Steve hit it off immediately however, and the pair were soon an item much to the despair of Kim's parents apparently!

Nowhere were these mechanical gremlins that dogged the tour demonstrated more fully than on the first night of the band's re-scheduled European tour at the Falkoner Theatrit in Copenhagen where at one point in the show there was supposed to be a flash but the guy mixing the flash powder got the ratio wrong and there was an enormous bang and the band stopped playing and the guy poked his head round the curtain and said; *"sorry!"* to which Phil's humorous riposte was: *"You're fired!"* It was also at this gig that "audience participation" took on a whole new meaning as Dave Lawrence recalls…

"In Oslo the night before the first show of the European tour; one of the trucks broke down; just ten miles outside the town. Nick; the head of the road crew woke everybody up at around 2am and dragged them out of the hotel. The truck that had broken down was stuck at the top of a big hill in the snow with its brakes locked on and its engine dead. The only option was to unload all the equipment into another truck and then take it to the concert hall. Sounds OK when you say it like that; but the only truck we had was full of lighting equipment; so we managed to wake up the concert hall caretaker who let us in and unload all ten tons of gear quickly into the hall and then drive this, now empty, truck out to the broken down one. But we had no transport for the crew.

Luckily for us; some fans of the band were waiting outside in the cold hoping for a glimpse of the band. We persuaded several of them that if they gave the crew lifts in their cars to the broken down truck; they may get some tickets for the show. We all jumped in their cars and sped off and were given a demonstration of hand brake turns in the snow at the same time. Those fans saved the day for us and helped us unload tons of gear… "

One can only imagine now the sheer sense of adventure that pervaded the shows supporting the album from Peter's introduction.. *"We've written a great big lump of music and story and we'd like to play it for you, this is the story of Rael…"*

Almost immediately, fans were taken aback by Peter's appearance - gone were the flower masks and other paraphernalia of yore and instead he was clad in a leather jacket, jeans, T shirt and sneakers with his face heavily made up to reflect the swarthy complexion of street kid; Rael. However, anyone mourning the loss of these costumes must surely have been compensated by the bizarre "Slipperman" costume which was to be the creative apogee of this period in the band's theatrical development and the impact that the new-look Genesis show made on the audience is recalled by Andy Wilkinson…

"The now familiar solo piano opening and out bounces our hero in a guise totally foreign - was this REALLY Peter Gabriel? Short cropped hair, harsh and threatening face make-up; open leather jacket denim and trainers... A total transformation and we were being taken to the urban streets of NY and the world of Rael...One of those rare moments when sound and visuals melt succinctly together in perfect harmony. The screens portrayed a beating crimson heart gently being shaved by a scalpel-like instrument.. the band moved into a musical area never before touched or attempted by them; like it or detest it; The Waiting Room proved a fascinating insight to the band experimenting with the art of improvisation. A real cacophony of every imaginable sound from birds calling to howling synth; frantic twenty second guitar licks and even a brief vibes solo somewhere in the middle of this..."

Musically challenging, as it was Andy also recalls the moment when Peter unleashed his most surreal costume to the unsuspecting audience...

"What happened next, no one was quite ready for. The strange quirky opening phrase of The Arrival reveals a long transparent plastic tunnel worming its way across the stage. Something was crawling along it. Gasps of sheer astonishment then laughter as the strangest; ugliest; lumpiest thing you could ever imagine emerges out of a cocoon. The beast (or Slipperman) proceeds to inflate a pair of giant testicles - SURREAL! Not content with this, the figure dances remarkably well, bellowing out: 'You're in the Colony of Slippermen'..."

The tour was to be the band's largest to date, initially 102 shows were planned although several were cancelled due either to poor ticket sales (difficult to believe now, I know) or due to other circumstances beyond the group's control, bit none more so than the antics before and after the shows in Cascais Portugal, remembered in vivid detail again, by David Lawrence....

"The concert hall was a bit small, only seating around 2,500 people and there was no power when we arrived. The dressing rooms were quite primitive and the feel of the hall was not good. After unloading the trucks and putting up the equipment; the local electrician came in who could not speak English, and we could not speak Portuguese. He gave us three power cables and we needed five. A few minutes of head scratching told us that we only had half the power we needed and there was no earth. The electrician then took us outside to a pole in the street; he climbed it and clipped on our three cables to the top of the pole; power was now on and live but we didn't want to touch it!

Using lots of gloves and towels to wrap around his hands; Peter managed to connect us to our power box without killing himself; and we found an earth for the system via the trusty water pipe. Things were a bit basic in Portugal and soon we heard the sound of tanks outside the hall. It would seem that we had walked into a small revolution which was about to start. Troops were walking around with guns in one hand and a can of beer in the other. A few shots were fired over people's heads and the place went mad. Nick was running backstage telling everyone to arm themselves with anything heavy- the microphone stand now had more than one use! At one point; half the crew were under the sound mixer; with Craig (Schertz) shouting... 'Just like 'Nam!'

Teargas was now being fired everywhere as fans were trying to get inside the small hall; the army trying to keep them out. The fans outside with no tickets were standing on top of tanks as they were driving around. It was all very nasty; the band went on and did the shows and during this time Craig had two guards at his side by the sound mixer; I had one by me complete with automatic rifle and beer! This was not a good time to be in show business. When the show ended; all the army disappeared with the fans; leaving us to pack up and go. We think it was just a show of force but it was a very nasty time.

Around 2am everything was in the trucks apart from our big mains cable which was still connected to the outside power pole. The electrician had gone home and it needed someone to climb up the pole and disconnect the cable while it was live. Nobody was going to do this; so Peter picked up two pairs of working gloves and a hacksaw and shouted to me....

'You hold the cable; I'll cut it!'

Peter cut through a 300 amp cable live and much sparking and we all ran to the bus. The drivers needed no directions on the way to go - OUT! A few hours after we had left Portugal; they closed the borders and had a small revolution, we were lucky to get out of that one...

Genesis have never gone down in history as abusers of hotel rooms, that isn't to say that some amusing incidents haven't happened and one of these is also recalled by David Lawrence...

"Back to the tour... we played in Denmark; France; Germany; Switzerland; Spain; all without too many problems but then we go to Portugal. The trouble started with the hotel; one of those very nice; flash hotels that road crews do not normally get let loose on. For some reason; a few of the sound crew got drunk- VERY drunk; and on returning to their hotel room late at night decided to wreck it. I only found out the next morning at breakfast; when all the contents of the hotel room were bobbing up and down in the swimming pool, and I mean ALL! Everything including the bed and all the light fittings and the shower were in the pool- the room was empty. This did not go down too well with the hotel who started a stock check on all rooms counting everything. Nick; the head roadie took the costs for the damage out of the wages of about five crew members. Jim, one of the sound men shouted - 'On the Deep Purple tour; they let us do it!' This was the only bit of hotel wrecking I ever saw during the tour; shame really..."

Critical reaction to the new live show was mixed but generally favourable and the fans loved the show. Genesis had managed against the odds to turn a concept album into a triumph. During the tour however, Peter's unease at the growing adulation heaped on him at the expense of the rest of the band became too much and at a dinner with the rest of the band he announced his decision to formally quit the band at the end of the tour. This decision was kept from the public until the band could decide upon their options. Peter's decision cast a shadow over the tour to some degree and as Phil remembers everyone had prepared themselves psychologically for the last show which......

"Was in Besancon, it was supposed to be in Toulouse, but due to poor ticket sales it was cancelled and we had all prepared ourselves for this last show and suddenly it was; 'oh tonight's the last gig' which was a bit of an anti climax and Pete played the "Last Post" on the oboe which was strange really..."

The tour finished in Europe in late May 1975 and the band took a well earned rest before reconvening to consider their options without Peter. The news of his departure was finally broken to the public by his now famous press release in August by which time Steve Hackett had almost completed work on what was to be his first solo album; Voyage of the Acolyte a very apt title for the album given the circumstances surrounding it at the time and this album on which both Mike and Phil played, served to indicate that interest in the band was still high when it achieved silver disc status upon its release later that year which was extremely gratifying for Steve but the band's problem remained: who was going to replace Peter?

The announcement of Peter's departure from the band was finally made in the music press on 18th August 1975 and took fans totally by surprise, including as we have mentioned before, several of the band's own inner circle. The press took to writing obituaries and eulogies for the band almost immediately which was to prove to be as futile an exercise as it was to prove to be again in 1996 but before we run ahead of our story, back to 1976…

CHAPTER EIGHT. Out of the fire and into the fight...

The summer and autumn of 1975 were taken up by writing and rehearsals for the new album which the band were soon preoccupied with, so much so, in fact that it could almost be said that they blocked out the fact of Peter's departure to concentrate on the matter in hand: the new Genesis album. Steve Hackett was already hard at work on his solo project which gave him much needed confidence in his abilities as he recalls...

"The difference was that everyone had become a slightly different person. I had had some solo success in terms of being able to produce a whole album for myself whereas if I'd just come up with a bunch of out-takes. So I was writing more material and I was at the point where everybody had gone off and done separate things, apart from Tony who was very disappointed that everybody hadn't been saving material particularly for Genesis and he said; 'I'm the only one who has been writing material for this band...' and he was very disappointed about that but as far as everyone else was concerned, no one was even sure if the band had a future..."

Steve's solo album; "Voyage Of The Acolyte" appeared in the autumn of 1975 and was received well by fans and critics alike eventually going silver in the UK and in doing so proved that interest in the band's material was still high. The band continued to work on the new album although they still had no idea who was to take over from Peter. Numerous musicians were auditioned from the hundreds that sent in audition tapes but none of these lucky hopefuls were deemed to be quite right for the band although to some outside observers, the answer was patently obvious as Steve remembers...

"Well, funnily enough one of the first people to suggest that Phil should be the singer was Jon Anderson who came to Phil's wedding at the time and I said ' I've just done a solo album and Phil sang wonderfully on it' and Phil had sung the first song I'd ever written for Genesis; For absent friends and I said 'Phil's got a wonderful range' and he said 'why don't you get in an extra instrumentalist and make the band stronger? Phil's got a nice voice you seem to be aware of that already..."

Phil's decision to take on the singer's job was motivated as much by his dissatisfaction with the quality of the people the band were auditioning as anything else as Steve vividly remembers...

"So eventually we did take somebody in to the studio and record and he sang a version of Squonk and he had considerable trouble with the melody lines because it was written by instrumentalists where the melody was up and down weaving all over the place and he found it very difficult to respond to it and Phil deliberately stayed away on the day when we had the guy come in and we'd been through a series of auditions by now and he was the best of the bunch but he had enormous problems with the melody ... the guy had a perfectly good voice he just wasn't right for the part and so, I remember Mike and Tony saying to Phil: ' what do you think, Phil?' and he said: 'I'll tell you what I think ; I think it sounds fucking average! Let me have a go...' "

The rest, as they say is history and Phil took on the role for the rest of the rehearsals and without knowing it, the band had solved their vocalist problem. The only one who didn't seem to be at all surprised by the choice was the band's record company manager Tony Stratton-Smith whose reaction was typically understated...

"God, he sounds just like Pete. Looks like you've found your vocalist, chaps!"

The resulting album; "A Trick Of The Tail" was everything that its predecessor wasn't; melodic, lush, and above all immensely accessible. The album also laid to rest any doubts that the band were not capable of writing without Peter which had been one of the most irritating assumptions which fans and the press had made about the band. Each track was credited to the people who wrote it and revealed the collective talent that makes Genesis so special. This decision was something that the band felt strongly about as Tony Banks explains...

"I'd said it before really as we'd got slightly fed up because obviously in the very early days there was a tendency through the whole period with Peter to suggest that he was obviously the dominant writer and who tended to write most of the lyrics. You got this impression that he was doing all of this while the rest of us were just sitting round watching him do his creative thing. Of course, Genesis was never like that; everybody was writing and some songs were written by individuals..."

Phil too was quick to stress that the band were all pulling together and were perhaps finding it easier to be creative and told BBC disc jockey John Peel very much the same in an interview broadcast at the time of the album's release..

"It has changed in the studio because we found it very easy working with the four of us in the studio. Everything was a lot quicker just because there were four mouths instead of five..."

The first Gabriel-less album, A Trick Of The Tail was certainly a revelation to many fans (myself included). Without Peter, the very accessibility that they had striven for with The Lamb.. fell into place, giving the band their most successful album to date and yet, quality had not been sacrificed in any way. The band even dusted off their trust ol' twelve strings on several songs.

The album's opener could even have been a veiled reference to the perils of nonconformity within the music biz and if fans had been feeling a little deprived of melody then they could only have been completely satisfied by this effort, and as for comedy? Well... Robbery, Assault & Battery's Vaudevillian style and hilarious accompanying video must have brought a smile to most fans' faces! Entangled with its acoustic driven middle section certainly harks back to the early days of the band and the album's title track : A Trick Of The Tail an extended metaphor for the desire of youth to escape from the pressures to conform; certainly shows that far from being isolated from events; Genesis were well aware of them but unlike the exponents of the "New Wave", the band were prepared to make their observations in their own "special" way, and after all, had they not demonstrated their own unwillingness to conform by daring to continue as a band without Peter?

What is perhaps the most amazing thing about this album however; is exactly that, it is MELODIC. Given that by the end of 1976 the emphasis in the UK music scene had switched from melody to discord, and from craftsmanship to amateurism of the worst kind, and yet this album was a massive seller and brought in even more fans than the band's previous efforts -why? Well that; my friends is anyone's guess but my own take on the reasons is simply that after the strife and austerity of the 1973/74 period, the public at large were ready for a reminder perhaps of a perceived "Golden Age" and this album with its emphasis on traditional musicianship and craft was the tonic that 1976's somewhat jaded senses needed!

With the album's release and subsequent chart success both at home and abroad the band were about to set off on their first tour without Peter with one problem still remaining: who was going to fill the drummer's set while Phil was up front "wiggling his bum" and singing? At the time, there was no doubt in Phil's mind, the only drummer who was, in his opinion capable of the task was his long time hero Bill Bruford who was taken on board as the guest drummer for the tour. The choice was an inspired one because of Bruford's credibility with the progressive rock fans who were Genesis' audience particularly in the USA where his influence was enormous and both Tony and Steve remember his time with the band fondly...

(Tony) *"Well, Bill was an easy person to get along with; he's still a friend of mine in fact, and obviously he's a very versatile drummer... When we got on stage there'd be calls for 'Bruford' and I think that helped us through what was obviously quite difficult period trying to establish ourselves without Peter as a singer..."*

(Steve) *"So Phil became the singer and Bill Bruford came into the band and gave us a big up because he was someone who Phil admired and we'd all admired in Yes and King Crimson and when he arrived he was immediately cracking jokes and that and he dispelled any feelings of... and he jammed along with us and said; 'yeah, that sounds great and this will be fine...' and it wasn't any kind of angst-ridden is this going to work out right? So he immediately put everyone at ease with his humour which was great..."*

Bruford himself was not the likeliest of choices. He explained how he came to get the job in an interview which appeared in the April 10th edition of "Sounds"....

"I'd been cavorting around with Phil for quite some time in Brand X and we were rehearsing in this little place in Shepherds Bush. He kept on talking about needing a drummer for Genesis on stage because he had decided he could handle the vocals out front and I said; 'why don't you ask me, you prick?' and he said; 'yes'... I had never seen them or heard their albums before I had to learn them to go on tour.... I respected Phil and knew he wouldn't be involved in any rubbish... Obviously they need to get out on the road and reassert themselves. I think there's quite a refreshing change in their music now that Gabriel has left. They may have got bogged down in his theatrics I suspect..."

The tour started at the end of March 1976 at the Civic Auditorium in London Ontario ostensibly at a low key gig originally planned for about four hundred people but in the end over two thousand fans gave Phil a hero's welcome in spite of the odd fan or two who appeared dressed as one of Peter's more esoteric creations! Their new show drew upon all the strengths of both the older material and the new album and managed to leave the fans happy in fact, Genesis' reviews flew in the face of established rock lore at the time, the "New Wave" had broken over the UK and was soon to sweep over the rest of Europe and the United States leaving many established bands and artists as casualties in its wake.

To their credit, Genesis continued to plough their furrow and the fans and critics alike were more than happy with the "new" singer who had filled Peter's shoes so capably. It is difficult to credit now though, but Phil Collins **DID** have some reservations about performing certain tracks from the back catalogue and for the first three shows of the tour the set was deprived of its glorious centrepiece: Supper's Ready which Phil was uncertain about performing. He need not have worried… Supper's Ready carried all before it and by the time the tour reached London's prestigious Hammersmith Odeon in June 1976 there could no longer be any doubt that Genesis were here to stay and they were already planning their next album when another crisis loomed…

CHAPTER NINE "Unquiet slumbers for the sleepers.."

The success of 1976's album and tour must have been sweet for the band, surrounded by the hysteria which attended the so-called "New Wave" which swept through the UK music scene in 1976 and continued to dominate into the following year. Ironically 1977 was also to see the re-emergence of two key personnel in the Genesis story with Peter Gabriel releasing his first solo album to critical acclaim from press and fans alike, and another founder member's first solo effort in the shape of the classic "The Geese & The Ghost" album by Anthony Phillips which was also well received. For a member of that most vilified of groups a "Progressive" rock group, Genesis and Co certainly were putting up a spirited resistance to the running dogs of Punk!

The music press were caught up in the hype as well and bands which they had steadfastly championed up to this point were soon the recipients of the critical backlash which had, in some cases, been long overdue. Genesis too were to be on the receiving end of some stringent criticism when they released their new album at the beginning of the year with such headlines as; *"Pretentious old superstars refuse to lie down"* and more tellingly still in the headline of Chris Welch's review of the band's first gig of their tour… *"Cold Genesis"* .

The album itself *"Wind & Wuthering"* is in many fans' opinions the last classic Genesis album; dramatic and full of character and yet also possessed of the deprecating humour which is also one of Genesis' most undervalued elements.   The band recorded the album at Relight Studios in Holland during the autumn of 1976 which was mainly to benefit from the cheaper recording costs which were afforded to artists in Holland at the time although Tony Banks also recalls that it was …

"Quite good too in a way; getting away from all the distractions and that helped give the album quite a strong identity.."

Certainly the album was a fine one from the dramatic opener; Eleventh Earl Of Mar perhaps even another nod to the fans still mourning Peter's departure especially in the exhortation to *"bury your memories, bury your friends; leave it alone for a year or two, till the stories go hazy and the legends come true"* Anyone thinking that the band were devoid of humour should certainly listen to the almost Tom and Jerry-like storyline of All In A Mouse's Night there was something here for Genesis fans of every shade of musical persuasion. Upon its release on 23rd December 1976, the album also gave the band their first UK number one album although this is disputed among fans and chart pollsters alike.

The drama that was unfolding itself within the UK music scene during 1976 and 1977 was not lost on Genesis, and Wind & Wuthering is a much more dark and dramatic album than its predecessor. The key track; One For The Vine tells of the adulation that can be heaped undeservedly on an individual and the cost both mental and physical that that can have both for the "leader" and the "followers" and once again, can be seen as a metaphor for what was happening in the UK. Fans and critics who had previously adored Genesis and others of their ilk now hurled invective at them.

Certainly, the brickbats aimed at many in the established world of Rock 'N' Roll for excess might have had an easy target with Genesis's new stage production which took their shows to new heights. A few of the statistics for the band's shows at Earls Court in late June 1977 still make impressive reading: Four onstage roadies, two laser beam operators; six Rainbow lighting operators; two ShowCo lighting operators; four ShowCo sound men plus one ShowCo rigger along with five truck drivers to drive the four articulated lorries, oh and one spare electrical generator! The costs for the lighting system and PA also beggared belief; £300,000 for the PA and £100,000 for the lighting rig - a far cry from starving yourself if a set of guitar strings needed replacing! All of this equipment was, however, necessary and the band's manager; Tony Smith explained the reasoning behind it in a feature on the band in a July edition of New Musical Express…

"We spend most of the money on the lighting because it emphasises the music. With a band like Genesis who don't have a Jagger or a Mercury or a Rotten you need to make it visually as well as aurally entertaining….I am anti the ELO, ELP 25 trucks on the road syndrome. I think people become bored with all that very quickly. I think that Genesis could go and play some club dates which we are thinking of doing and be just as exciting. But when you are playing a 15,000 seater hall, you have to have something extra…"

Many musicians and groups had come to believe their press reports. Not so, Genesis who were still challenging themselves and their musical identity and their audience with each new album. Eleventh Earl of Mar can also be seen as a sly dig at the New Wave; a populist rising which was doomed to failure just like the Jacobite rising from which the song draws its story; as its arch proponents eventually became that which they professed most to despise: Rock stars!

Your Own Special way also demonstrated that the band could write simple and effective love songs too …Mike's composition has stood the test of time and was a fine choice of single; even being re-worked by Steve Hackett on 1996's Genesis Revisited album, where it still shone as brightly as ever! Blood On The Rooftops; a brilliantly observed examination of suburban life on which Steve's guitar work really shines through. The contrast between the two instrumentals on the album couldn't be more marked. Wot Gorilla? Is Genesis' passing nod to Jazz Fusion which to my ears does not sit well within the somewhat darker context of this album. Unquiet Slumbers For The Sleepers/In That Quiet Earth however, takes the listener on an aural trip to the dark and lonely world of the Yorkshire Moors with whistling wind and cold comfort farm a wonderfully orchestrated piece in which all of the players shine. That leaves… Afterglow… my all time favourite Genesis track. An emotional look at the aftermath of a disaster in which the character has lost everything. One of Tony's finest compositions but also one which encapsulates (maybe unwittingly) some of the feelings of other band members especially the line…

And walk upon stranger roads than this one

Which exemplifies Steve Hackett's position perfectly. Steve had trodden the path of solo work and (unbeknownst to most fans) would do so again soon. Nonetheless, an amazingly dramatic and emotional end to the band's most dramatic album.

Having faced the problem of too little material available for the last album, this time round the band were faced with the direct opposite of having too much material as Tony recalls…

"The main weakness was that we couldn't include the tracks that ended up on the EP later: Match of the day and Pigeons so none of the lighter tracks got on…"

It was also at this time that the crisis which had been brewing for a couple of years finally surfaced. Steve Hackett's solo success with "Voyage Of The Acolyte" back in 1975 had proven to him that he was capable of both writing and more importantly to Steve; producing his own music. The confidence which this gave him was apparent on both "A Trick Of The Tail" and "Wind & Wuthering" which Tony Banks recalls as being the moment when Steve's writing really gelled with the band for the first time…

" There were also things like Blood On The Rooftops which I didn't have that much to do with in terms of writing but quite a lot to do with in terms of arranging. This was the first time that Steve's writing had really fitted in to the band and it was Phil's chorus with Steve's verse and that's a really strong, great track. Eleventh Earl of Mar as well which quite a lot of the chorus parts were Steve's as well…"

However, Steve was to experience the same difficulty that Peter Gabriel had during the writing of "The Lamb Lies Down On Broadway" and failed to get some of his best music past the "Committee Stage" of the band and this was a frustrating time for him as he remembers…

"The track that became Please Don't Touch was something that Genesis rehearsed up originally and we didn't include it on the album and we did not develop it and I felt that was a gem and I felt: 'hang on; here's one of my best ideas and we're not using it why are we including that one and not this one?' So I became aware that the intensity of playing that was important to me was not quite so high a priority to the others and they were starting to relax a little bit more..."

The band's tour was to be their biggest yet commencing with a sell out run of shows in the UK's most prestigious theatres, beginning with three shows at London's famous Rainbow Theatre which Genesis were asked to re-open after its extensive refurbishment. For this tour, the band had to find another drummer. Bill Bruford's position with them had always been of a temporary nature and he was currently occupied with the formation of AOR super group in the making; UK with Eddie Jobson and John Wetton. Eventually the band opted for their first American member in the shape of respected session player Chester Thompson whose previous credits included stints with Alphonso Johnson and Frank Zappa. Ironically, Chris Welch's review of their opening night singled Thompson out for venomous treatment as the following extract from his review shows...

"...But for me the missing ingredient was in the percussion department. New drummer Chester Thompson has worked with Frank Zappa and is skilled and accurate,. He coped with a difficult score but failed to inject personality into his playing and this became all the more marked when Phil Collins finally ceased singing and returned to his drum kit. As soon as Phil got down to work, the band took off...."

His review ended with what for many was an extremely fatuous exhortation...

"Bring back Bill Bruford - at least he can be relied on to help cast out demons!"

The band's personal demons were still to be exorcised and Steve's decision to leave the band became definite during the tour which was an enormous success with the band also playing their first gigs in South America with a series of record breaking shows in Brazil during May 1977. An indication in the huge increase in popularity that the band had undergone both at home and elsewhere was given when the band returned to the UK in June for a series of three shows at London's cavernous Earls Court Arena supported by Woodstock veteran and long time hero of the band; Richie Havens.

Not only that but a successful single awaited the band when they released their first EP in May 1977. Comprising the remaining tracks from the album sessions it reached the number 18 slot in the UK charts, aided no doubt by a humorous video which included Phil in QPR top at a football match! The humour of the band which to many fans was lacking on the album was much in evidence here. Phil's comic complaints about the vagaries of football and in particular football referees in Match Of The Day and the absurd ballad to those creatures who:

Who puts fifty tons of shit on the Foreign Office roof?

Whatever possessed Genesis to write a song such as Pigeons is anyone's guess but nevertheless, it is a brilliantly observed song. Inside & Out is definitely the one song which should have been included on the album. A superbly crafted song about the injustices of the legal system it was perfectly in keeping with the darker edge to the album and one on which the humour of the band was further displayed during Phil's introduction to the song which formed a part of their later tour when he referred to it as...

"This next song is all about a poor unfortunate man who goes to a party where he meets a man with.... sorry meets a lady with very large knockers... and err, it depends who you know really. And unfortunately she seduces him and claims that he raped her it's all very eternal triangle. It's off our Spot The Pigeon EP which is currently racing up the Indonesian charts and it's called Inside & out..."

There was a further treat in store for fans if treat is the right word for the band's first attempt at a concert film which was given a gala premiere in July 1977 in the presence of Princess Anne although the Princess' thoughts about the move have not been recorded. Tony Maylam's cinematic record of the band's hugely successful 1976 tour shared the billing with Rick Wakeman's "White Rock" . The film "Genesis In Concert" was certainly not as indulgent as Led Zeppelin's effort a couple of years later but it has to be admitted it came pretty CLOSE! Even Tony recalls that it is not the best visual record of a Genesis concert...

"I remember doing the film. We actually did it primarily as a film for whatever it was and Tony Maylam used to go round saying 'wonderful footage' and so on and then used dancing girls on a beach or something during Entangled (laughter). It was ok ... a couple of things on it are quite nice and I suppose

it's quite nice to have a record of Bill's time with the group... I think things like Cinema Show were probably at their best when Bill was playing with us..."

Sadly this visual record of the band has never been officially released in this country or anywhere else for that matter.

The band's last show of the tour was at Munich's enormous Olympiahalle on 3rd July 1977 and during the remaining summer months they attended to the task of whittling down the enormous amount of material for a long overdue live album. Having recorded just about every show from both the 1976 and 1977 tours, it was a difficult decision and it was during the selection process that Steve eventually decided to leave the group. The story of how he told the band has already been well documented but his reasons have been the subject of debate by fans ever since and with the benefit of hindsight Steve's decision was a vital if painful one both for him personally as a musician and the group as a whole and he explained his decision to "The Waiting Room" in a recent interview ...

"I feel that it is only now that I feel that I can truly express myself in music. I think at the time I was anxious to do a string of solo albums and that was something that worried both Tony and Mike. Phil wasn't in the least bit worried; he'd been operating with Brand X for quite a while but I think it was regarded as less of a threat because at least he wasn't pushing albums out under his own name...perhaps if I'd come up with another group title or something it would have been less of a political hot potato but it did seem to create waves.

Nonetheless I felt that I was coming up with far too many ideas for the band to fully exploit... explore is perhaps a better word, and in order to develop I felt I had to work with other people... I already WAS working with great people in Genesis . I realised at this point that they were a GREAT band and they were great at doing what they did and they'd done great things but I felt to prove, or to attempt that level of greatness for myself, I had to do that outside the band..."

Steve was much more forthright about his reasons for leaving in an interview he gave with Circus Magazine in June 1978...

"The real telling point for me came with Wind & Wuthering when I had a full album's-worth written but eventually got credited on only four tracks. So when the next Genesis album came round, I had the choice of having most of my work discarded or making a separate album. What was the point of working in such a situation? The only reason I stuck with Genesis as long as I did was to prove to myself that, in fact without Peter Gabriel, Genesis could still make it..." Nor did he stint in laying the blame for his departure, and Peter's before him at the door of the person he held responsible... *" I know that Peter left the band because of Tony, and I would say that I did too. Genesis will probably end up as only Tony Banks..."* The bitterness of the split was to result in a rift between Steve and the remaining members which has only recently begun to heal properly.

Steve's wife; Kim Poor remembers that at the time, the band were not happy with Steve's intentions to pursue a solo career parallel with Genesis and said so in no uncertain terms; "no more solo albums" was the ultimatum delivered to him. In addition to this, the band were also unhappy that Tony Smith was continuing to manage the now re-emergent Peter Gabriel whose first solo album had been a great success at exactly the same time as Genesis were promoting Wind & Wuthering. A conflict of interests was certainly something that the band could do without as far as management issues were concerned, but to demand of Steve that he cease his own work when he was patently never going to be allowed to upstage Tony Banks in particular in the band's writing department, was simply unreasonable. Steve is one of those people who takes a lot to get angry but once he is backed into a corner he will fight for whatever he believes is right. With the prospect of not being allowed to continue his own work and no sign of any negotiated agreement with the rest of the band in sight; he opted for the harder option of pursuing his own musical career instead of settling back in the comfort of the Genesis "machinery" and quit the band during the mixing sessions for their new live album.

The band eventually released the live album in October 1977 and once again, displayed their own fine sense of ironic humour by titling it "Second's Out" and upon its release it achieved a number two slot in the UK charts, a position somewhat overshadowed by the announcement in the music press of Steve's departure. As a record of both Steve's time in the band, and indeed, Peter's this album is hard to beat containing most of their classic tracks from that era as well as much of the material that was in the band's current live set. A line had very firmly been drawn under that period of the band's history what remained now was to consolidate on their success and to search for the one thing that had so far eluded them - a hit single!

CHAPTER TEN. "And then there were three…."

Genesis reconvened quickly in the wake of Steve's departure and rapidly regained the momentum which had been created during the last two years working again in the Relight Studios in Holland. By this time the band were facing the harsh realities of Mid Seventies England. Gone were the certainties which had ensured that a new album by the group would automatically be well received. In fact, the New Wave backlash had had a healthy tonic effect upon most of the members of the Establishment of the musical world and Genesis were well aware that something different was the order of the day this time round.

Steve's departure had given the band a chance to re-evaluate themselves as musicians and to draw more deeply and freely upon the collective talents of the remaining members as Mike was quick to point out…

"Because there's a different atmosphere with less people. People have to work harder in certain areas"

Nowhere was this more in evidence than with Mike's role in the band itself, he now had to fill the vacuum left by Steve and not only that but the entire band also realised that they had to change in musical terms too. The lengthy instrumental passages so revered by the fans were a millstone which had to be ditched if the band was to have any future as Mike explained…

"It was definitely a conscious effort to make songs shorter. On Wind & Wuthering we were definitely disappointed that we couldn't get the EP on, time-wise, because it would have made a better balance. So, we consciously cut down quite a few tracks which could have been anything from five to eight minutes long. We kept them down to about five as we felt that the strength of the track came across and there was much more variety on the album; eleven tracks for us is quite a lot. It's easy for us to elongate things and we enjoy doing that; going off an coming back to themes at the end of a song. It was quite hard for us to keep some of the songs a bit shorter…"

Certainly there was a greater sense of freedom about the album and the variety of songs took the fans by surprise and the sound had certainly changed reflected by the band's change in work methods as Phil explained…

"We used to go in for rehearsals for much longer and spend a shorter time in the studio whereas now it's nearly the other way round - we leave more to chance in the studio rather than playing a song to death… I think we spent six or seven weeks really with the tracks we had written ; we rehearsed a couple of times so that we knew the chorus and knew the changes and the rest of the time we tried to put together several group tracks; putting someone's verse with someone else' s chorus with someone else's introduction which we probably didn't do as much on Wind & Wuthering . We've tried to get back to group tracks a bit…"

The first fruits of Genesis' new album appeared in March 1978 in the shape of the first single which heralded in the new look Genesis in a BIG way. Follow You Follow Me was that rarity in the Genesis canon - an instantly catchy song one which propelled the band into the top ten of the UK charts and ushered in their first appearance on Top of the Pops perhaps to the horror of their longstanding fans who felt perhaps in the same way as members of an exclusive gentlemen's club felt when it was opened up to women (shock horror!). Here at last, was a song which the girlfriends of the band's fans could relate to and enjoy.

And Then there Were Three manages to bring an element of social realism to the band in ways which The Lamb… didn't. The album opener; Down And Out about a businessman's desperation to keep his place in the hierarchy is, once again a brilliant observation of the struggles the band had had to renew itself…

"I don't want to beat about the bush
but none of us are getting any younger.
There's people out there who could take your place.
A more commercial view! A fresher face!"

Telling words indeed, and ones which the band were very much at pains to ensure didn't happen to them. Gone were the extended epics of yesteryear and the shorter format worked extremely well.   Mike Rutherford explained how this track caused problems for Chester Thompson during the rehearsals…..

"the three of us wrote that while we were rehearsing for the album. When Chester Thompson came over to start rehearsing for the American tour he just couldn't get that right at first. When we wrote it Tony Banks and I thought of the riff in a different way to Phil. We were looking at the same structure from different directions and Phil couldn't explain the riff to Chester which added to the confusion. Its funny because once you get used to a strange time signature it sounds very natural and you forget that other people will take time to get used to it..."

Nothing was lost in terms of quality; the lyricism and musicality that the fans cherished were all still there but trimmed back and given a new coat of paint and the new realism was reflected in the subject matter of several of the songs, none more tellingly than on Say It's Alright, Joe which became one of the highpoints of the band's set. Not only is this a great example of social commentary; Joe is one of life's casualties who sees life from the bottom of a whiskey glass; but also a prime example of the storytelling that makes Genesis different from the rest. What was different this time? The character is someone whom we can all easily identify with and whose troubles we have all shared at some point or other and his story a succinctly told within the bounds of a five minute song rather than twenty three minutes and without reference to a Thesaurus or Dictionary of Phrase and Fable! Genesis were just as observant as always, only more concise!

There were other, equally well executed tracks including another beautiful love song from Tony: Undertow but one with a harder edge to it as the characters reflects that while they are snug and warm, that could all change… once again maybe a reflection on the situation the band were in? In danger of becoming too comfortable with their superstar status in a love affair with the public that could not last forever. Burning Rope reflects upon similar sensibilities. This track also acted as the showcase for Mike's guitar playing talents, long submerged under those of Steve Hackett. Mike pronounced himself pleased with the result… *"I'm very pleased with the way it has come out. I think it's the best solo on the album. This is also the longest track on the album. It goes through more moods than any of the others. The basic track was drums, piano and bass which didn't really excite anyone. Tony did a lot of building up on the keyboards later on..."*

Ironically, given Phil's marriage problems which were to surface later in the year; Tony's track Many Too Many is a perceptive observation of a relationship which has run its course; a simple song or an extended metaphor for the realisation that the band had to change to survive? You decide, folks.

Once again, a mammoth world tour was undertaken by the group with no less than three separate US tours in an attempt to break up the length of time spent away from home and their families. Once again the group broke all the rule and record books with a stage show that incorporated all the latest available technologies: lasers; computerised mirrors, you name it Genesis had it. Fans were also surprised to see another new face on stage as the band had taken another American into the fold for live work. Mike quickly realised that it was not going to be possible to play both lead guitar and bass during live performances and so he began to look at likely candidates. Like Chester Thompson, Daryl Stuermer's background was impeccable including a time spent with Jean Luc Ponty and it was on Alphonso Johnson's recommendation after he himself realised that he wasn't suited to Genesis' style of music, that he got the gig with Genesis and Daryl still recalls his audition for the band…

"I met Mike and we played along to Squonk and Down and Out and we just did those two songs and Mike said; 'I think that will be enough' and I thought to myself 'Is he saying that because he doesn't like my playing, or is he saying that because he knows how good I can play?'

Mike was more than satisfied and Daryl's playing on the subsequent tour was a revelation as this writer can recall when I saw Genesis for the first time at their only UK show of the year at the enormous Knebworth Park Festival on 24th June. Having been grounded in the music of Gabriel, Hackett and Co to finally see the band with this new guitarist was an experience never to be forgotten. Ironically enough, the band experienced some real slating's from the music press that had adored them only the year before with a particularly damning critique of the band's only UK show appearing in Melody Maker which provoked Phil to respond during a subsequent interview with Chris Welch for that august periodical… *"I wrote several draft letters to the MM and tore them up. I still think Knebworth was good despite what Allan Jones said. I decided in the end it was better to turn the other cheek but I have never been so livid with anybody than I was with him. I was glad that there was a whole bunch of letters from Genesis fans to the MM a week later. That made me feel a little bit better. I know that kind of criticism is done all the time now and you have to put it in perspective..."*

Phil shouldn't have worried; the new album was riding high in the charts; the band had scored their first Top Of The Pops appearance for the BBC and, even more shocking for the critics; screened a sixty minute documentary about the tour on the BBC "Nationwide" programme which was duly screened on 21st August 1978. The latter gave some small insight into just how much hard work and preparation goes into presenting a tour of such magnitude.

"And Then There Were Three" also became the band's first album to reach the number one slot OFFICIALLY in the UK and also achieved a healthy position in the US Billboard charts helped no doubt by the enormous efforts that the band made during the year to break the USA in a big way. Just about every major venue in the country had the pleasure of hosting the band during their tours. Once again, the band had written far too much material for the album and released an EP of which alongside an album track also contained a further two non album cuts; "The Day The Light Went Out " and "Vancouver" . The latter was to prove to be strangely prophetic as it turned out. To fans, everything in the Genesis camp appeared rosy - a top ten album and successful singles and above all a massively successful and entertaining live show which was drawing praise from everyone who saw it what more could they ask?

The answer to the above question was easy to answer if you were Phil Collins' wife: a husband who spends slightly more time at home. During the year preceding the making of the And Then There Were Three album, Phil's wife Andrea had become increasingly disenchanted with her husband's peripatetic lifestyle and during the recording of the album matters came to a head. Phil was torn between breaking the band in the USA which would, if successful, give everyone not only the time but the financial freedom they had been striving toward for so long.

To gain that freedom however, one final push in the USA was needed and this was to prove the undoing of Phil's marriage. Andrea moved to stay with her parents in : Vancouver, and Phil continued the tour with the band. The year ended with a series of shows in Japan, the band's first in that territory and ones which Phil desperately wanted to avoid although as the surviving footage from these gigs shows, he was the consummate showman on stage. At the end of the tour, Phil made a valiant attempt to rescue his marriage and moved to Vancouver in a last ditch effort to patch things up but to no avail even the offer of his moving to Vancouver was not sufficient and his ultimatum to the band, born out of his desperation was not one which lent itself to any confidence in the group's future... *"if we can record in Vancouver then, I'm still in the band, if not..."*

Fortunately, the success of the band's album (And Then There Were Three was the ONLY UK album to achieve platinum status in 1978- the discs were awarded in late November 1978 while the band were on tour in Japan) and tour meant that the much needed break from the incessant round of recording and touring could now be taken. The band were even given a gift from Charisma boss Tony Stratton-Smith in the form of a race horse: "Trick Of The Tail" in tribute of this success and the fact that the album whose name it bore was also approaching platinum status itself! Mike and Tony wisely decided that the time was now ripe for them to have a go at solo albums of their own. This would give Phil time to try and resolve his personal problems and would also give both Mike and Tony a chance to extend their own creative muscles.

The resulting albums; "Smallcreep's Day" and "A Curious Feeling" respectively were released during the following year and gave the label (along with Steve Hackett's third solo album: Spectral Mornings) a welcome boost in a financially lean year. It is interesting to read Stratton-Smith's prophetic comments given to an edition of Music Week in September 1979...

"We haven't yet seen the full potential of Peter Gabriel and I believe he will go right to the top. We have great hopes of his new association with producer Steve Lillywhite... Again I feel we have only seen half the potential of Steve Hackett and his last album (Spectral Mornings) was the first album that had a 'band' feel. His next album in April (Defector) will be very important to the company as it will be the first on the Charisma label in the States. Just before they broke many people thought we were too heavily invested in Genesis but I reckon the best thing I ever did was say; 'If Genesis go, I go' I remember using the phrase: 'Genesis are the flagship of Charisma'...."

Mike and Tony's solo efforts were warmly if not ecstatically received by the fans and critics. It is interesting however to look at that same article in Music Week and reflect on what night have been. That same article as quoted above also mentioned plans for the newly-formed "Charisma Films" to release a "Big budget film treatment of The Lamb Lies Down On Broadway featuring Peter Gabriel is planned for the end of 1980 and a one hour TV special inspired by the music of Tony Banks of Genesis is also being made.." Sadly, neither has seen the light of day as yet!

However, many once again misinterpreted the situation and saw in the appearance of solo projects from what to most Genesis fans at the time were the two key players, a split in the band signalling its demise and many wondered what the new decade would bring……

CHAPTER ELEVEN. Enter the Duke…..

Genesis reconvened in the autumn of 1979 to begin work on their new album. The end of the decade brought new challenges for the band and the music scene in the UK had irreversibly changed with the New Wave and Disco fever taking the place of what had gone before. Challenging times indeed, and the band were to prove themselves equal to the challenge.

The solo successes by Mike and Tony meant that the remaining members returned to the collective fold with fresh confidence that the fan base was prepared to listen to their efforts outside of the band.   They also had plenty of ideas as well as a greater appreciation of each other's roles within the band. Phil too had had plenty of time in which to write and compose material of his own once it became obvious that his attempted reconciliation with his wife was not going to work and it was the material which he brought to the new album which was perhaps the first indicator of the direction which the band was to pursue increasingly throughout the coming decade. In fact, the new album: "Duke" was to be very much a transitional work for the band as Mike himself admitted…

"1980 was the year we should have changed. We started to on Duke to me some of the songs on Duke were the end of an era and some were the start of another era…"

The old era was most definitively represented by the album's closing cut: a rambling instrumental overture titled "Duke's Travels/Duke's End" and at one point the "Duke Suite" as it became known was considered as a full blown concept tying all the tracks together as Tony remembers…

"At one point we were going to join together all the group compositions on the album - they were all going to be one long song. But we decided, for a variety of reasons to keep them separate. One felt that the album wouldn't be so well balanced if you had all the individual tracks on one side. The other thing was we didn't want to repeat ourselves; you know, having done something like Supper's Ready a long time ago…there would be comparisons and we didn't really want that…"

Mike, however recalls that there is some common thread between several of the songs…

"There isn't really any definite concept behind the album, although there are a couple of numbers with compatible themes. The cover concept; using Koechlin's children's book character to tie things together was rather an after-thought. I suppose he just represents the little Everyman character who is a bit confused by life in the Eighties; some of the songs reflect that worry, though there is no consistent line throughout the album…"

The album certainly managed to depict the confusion felt by many as the new decade began and many of the songs were certainly of a darker shade than those on the album's predecessor. In particular the deceptively simple Heathaze which contained the line…

Time to stop this dreaming, must rejoin the real world

The band had come face to face with the reality that substantial changes had to be made in order to avoid becoming the cliché'd dinosaur which they were viewed as by many in the music business at the time. Punk had shaken the tree and the casualties had been many; Genesis were determined not to suffer the same fate and Duke was to be the transitional album that straddled both the Progressive and the Pop sides of Genesis as fans saw at the other end of the spectrum where Phil's pop sensibilities came to the fore with Misunderstanding which was to become the band's biggest hit single to date in the USA and might have done as well in the UK had it been released as the opening single but the honours went to Turn It On Again a song destined to become Genesis' anthem throughout the Eighties.

Phil underlined the determination of the band to continue to grow and experiment in an interview for Sounds in May 1980…

JMLS/SMK   1st September, 1967.

Dear Mr. Gabriel,

I have sent revised Agreements to Jonjo Music Company Limited and send you herewith a copy of each: I have also sent copies to the other fathers.

I hope to hear from Jonjo Music Company Limited that they agree the alterations and as soon as I do so, I shall get in touch with you.

Yours sincerely,

J.M.L. Stone

R.P. Gabriel, Esq.,
Central Rediffusion Services Ltd.,
Carlton House,
Lower Regent Street,
London S.W.1.

Encs.

12.5
Night Ride
Jon Curle with swinging sounds on and off the record featuring tonight
GENESIS
Produced by ALEC REID

10.45 *Colour*
Disco 2
Introduced by Mike Harding featuring **Duncan Brown**, singer-songwriter; **Dream Police**, a Scottish group known around the Northern clubs for their progressive music; **Genesis**, whose name implies 'The Beginning' but who intend to become 'The End'; and **Zoo**, France's number one group, appearing for the first time on British television.

Designer JAMES HATCHARD
Producer director STEVE TURNER
Executive producer MICHAEL APPLETON
(This Week's Sounds: page 15)

14th November 1970

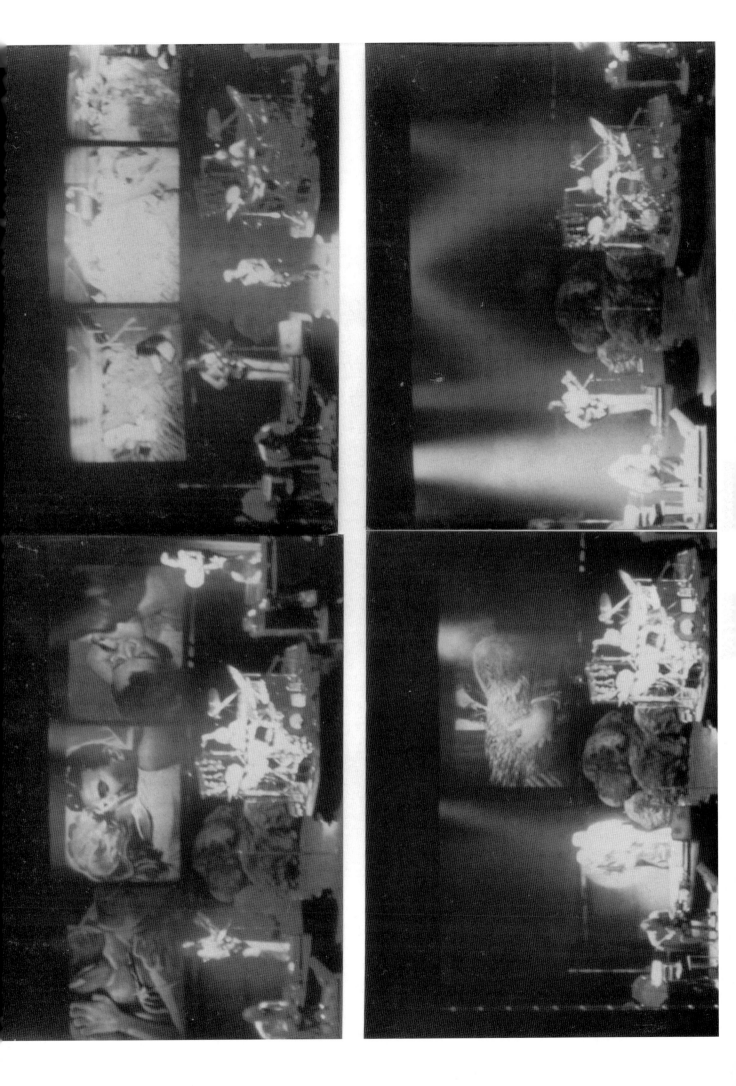

GENESIS, BACK WITH A FLICK OF THEIR TALES...

HAMMERSMITH ODEON HAMMERSMITH

GENESIS
New Single
'Your Own
Special Way'
Co-produced by Genesis and David Hentschel
Previously unreleased track on 'B'side
'It's Yourself'
CB 300

GENESIS

THE NEW ALBUM

**WIND
&
WUTHERING**

CHARISMA

CDS 4005

EMPIRE THEATRE, Liverpool

Jo Chester and Tony Smith
for Hit and Run Music present—

GENESIS

SATURDAY, 3rd MAY 1980
Evening 7-30

FRONT CIRCLE

£4.00

ROW

F   **69**

THIS PORTION TO BE RETAINED

BIRMINGHAM INTERNATIONAL
ARENA
NATIONAL EXHIBITION CENTRE

JO CHESTER AND TONY
SMITH FOR HIT AND
RUN MUSIC PRESENT

BLOCK
ARENA A

GENESIS

ROW
B

COMMENCING 8:00PM
DOORS OPEN 6:00PM

£6.50

SEAT

14

MONDAY
21ST DEC
1981
8:00PM

ARENA A

(including VAT)

(plans & conditions
see reverse)

TO BE RETAINED

BIRMINGHAM INTERNATIONAL
ARENA
NATIONAL EXHIBITION CENTRE

ANDREW MILLER
PROMOTIONS LTD
BY ARRANGEMENT WITH
TONY SMITH
PRESENTS
*** GENESIS ***
IN CONCERT
DOORS OPEN 6.00 PM

BLOCK
02

ROW
V

SEAT
29

£ 8.50

(Including VAT)

SATURDAY
25TH FEB
1984
8:00PM

EAST
STAND

TO BE RETAINED

(plans & conditions
see reverse)

Ref. 41999

Good News von **Blick**

Invisible Touch Tour

GENESIS

Special Guest: **PAUL YOUNG**

Samstag, 13. Juni 1987, 19.00 Uhr

Kassa- und Türöffnung: 17.00 Uhr

Fussballstadion St. Jakob
Basel

EINE GOOD NEWS PRODUKTION

Fr. 35.—
Billettsteuer
inbegriffen

No. 6 0 9 7

Keine Haftung für Sach- und Körperschäden. In keinem Falle
Rückerstattungsanspruch auf den Kaufpreis. Vor Missbrauch
wird gewarnt.
Das Mitnehmen von Tonbandgeräten, Filmkameras, Foto-

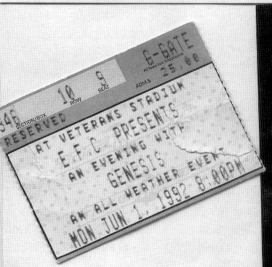

A1108 RIGHT   2 7 A   35.00 EBA1108
00CCTX ORCHESTRA
4.00 ISU ENTERTAINMENT COMM.   CN 61406
RIGHT   ***   RIGHT
OH 1X   PRESENTS   ADULT
2 7   G E N E S I S   2
271123   BRADEN AUD/NORMAL.IL   MC 35.00
13OCT7   SAT NOV 8 1997 8:00 PM   7

TM
NO REFUND NO EXCHANGE
ONLINE INFORMATION:
http://www.ticketmaster.com
ADMIT ONE
SUBJECT TO CONDITIONS
ON BACK

MasterCard

Capital productions présente, en accord avec Tony Smith pour HIT & RUN®

GENESIS
...CALLING ALL STATIONS...
...CALLING ALL STATIONS...
CALLING ALL STATIONS...
CALLING ALL STATION

GENESIS
Calling All Stations
Europe 1998

N
W   E
20/2 FANCLUB
After Show
S

Europe 2
100.3

EN CONCERT
Vendredi 20 Février 98 - 20 h 30
HALLE TONY GARNIER - LYON

Locations : Points habituels   Collectivités : Eldo

GENESIS
NEC ARENA BIRMINGHAM
THURSDAY 26TH FEBRUARY '98
SHOWTIME 8.00PM
DOORS OPEN 6.30PM
BLOCK B C 15

...CALLING ALL STATIONS...
...CALLING ALL STATIONS...
...CALLING ALL STATIONS...

TOURNÉE EUROPE 2

GENESIS
en concert

...MS AND CONDITIONS PRINTED OVERLEAF

Europe 2
LE MEILLEUR DE LA MUSIQUE

"My commitment to Genesis is much greater than it ever was before. I would fight for it more now than I would have done before because its more me. That's what it comes down to. There's more of me in it. I've come a long way since And Then There Were Three, I really have...."

Phil also gave a curious insight into the creation of what fans now refer to as the "Duke Suite"... *"The way we perform Duke on stage is the way we originally intended to do it on record. I wanted to do a long song with some substance. So, basically we put a lot of things together between us. Turn It On Again is a mixture of Tony's bit; Mike's bit and me saying; 'I want it to sound like Earth Wind And Fire'. Duchess was basically a drum machine pattern with Tony's Guide Vocal at the end. And Duke's Travels and Duke's End were riffs that we wrote as we went along. We intended it all to be one twenty five minute piece but when we came down to the practicalities of the album, the solo songs on the second side wouldn't have run so well so we had to split it up..."*

The true heart of the album however, belongs to the second track; "Duchess" which was not as lyrically straightforward as it might seem as Tony explains...

"Duchess is one of my favourite tracks it's so simple and yet it seems to capture so much atmosphere. It was at that time that girl singers were becoming popular and that's where the idea came from. Also, seen from that perspective it would take it away from the group a bit because if it had been written about a man, people would have thought it was talking about the group but talking about it that way gave it another dimension..."

Maybe another reflection on the need for the band to change or die can be seen *in* Cul-De-Sac. Ostensibly a song about the demise of the dinosaur; perhaps but with a closer look the realisation that changes had to be made can be seen. The direction in which those changes were to take the band were soon to be dramatically demonstrated.

Duke was released in March 1980 and the band scored a number one in the UK the first of a string of number one albums that were to span the 1980's, so much for the doubts about their popularity expressed in the music press!

The album achieved gold status a full TWO weeks before its actual release giving the lie to the nay sayers who were writing Genesis as off as "boring old farts". The award of the gold discs took place at a surprise party organised after the band's gig at the Gaumont Theatre Ipswich on 1st April 1980.

The announcement of the band's tour itinerary for the year took many by surprise: a full UK tour of the provincial theatres which hadn't been graced by a band of Genesis' stature since 1977 and an accompanying tour of larger venues in the USA with a few smaller dates mixed in. Taking the band back to their roots was a wise decision giving them a chance to feed off their audience and also to "dust off their twelve string guitars" and play several older pieces in the set.

The 80,000 tickets for the band's UK shows were soon snapped up with over half a million ticket applications being received and if anyone doubted the band's popularity in the UK, their appearance on Top of the Pops for the single "Turn It On Again" was followed by not only an ITV documentary on the band's shows in Liverpool but also the unheard of for Genesis fans - a live TV broadcast of part of their show from London's Lyceum Ballrooms. The band's last show of the tour was at the Performing Arts Centre in Saratoga Springs on 30th June after which the band took a well-earned rest Except for Phil who having whetted his creative appetite on Duke, wanted to expand his talents. Working in his own home studio he carefully created an album which was to make Genesis fans and the rest of the music world sit up and take notice upon its release in February 1981.

The success of "Face Value" with it's stripped down sound and strident opening single led many to believe that the demise of the group was imminent. Once again the eulogies proved to be premature and the creative impetus which the band's new found solo outlets had released gave the group a new lease of life and a new direction which many fans were to find hard to take when the groups next album appeared in September 1981....

CHAPTER TWELVE. Like it or not

Returning to studio work in their own purpose-built studio: The Farm, which had finally been completed, the band opted to re-invent themselves even further as Tony explained…

"We'd made changes consciously in order to get away from the compulsory keyboard solo; the tambourine on the chorus and all that sort of 'wet' sound if you like and just go for a different approach with this sort of very dry kind of thing: very streamlined and we were very pleased with the result and so this album, the cover and everything was crucial and I know that many people didn't like it but for us it was crucial. I don't think the band could have carried on, we couldn't have done… if we'd done another album like 'Duke' ,another album in the old tradition…"

This is also a point that Phil was keen to emphasise. Having survived the "slings and arrows of outrageous press reviews" to paraphrase a certain well-known playwright the band were equally as keen to keep on changing ….

"A group is a compromise and I suggested the horns on Abacab purely because I thought that 'wouldn't it be interesting to see what people would think?' You know, 'Genesis and earth Wind and Fire - Christ! Gotta check this out..' I tried to shake people up a bit and take them off automatic pilot. A lot of people have blamed me for the change in Genesis and it's not anything that's set a precedent. If it happens on the next album, it'll be because it works for the next album.. It's good for us to change…"

Certainly the album's opening single and title track; "Abacab" was different - a hard rocking track with a sharper edge to it and sporting an abstract cover which was repeated on the album itself which also sported the first picture of the band themselves on the inner cover - this was a million miles away from the pastoral Genesis which their fans had loved and which the critics had grown to despise. Once again the album charted at the number one position aided no doubt, by Phil's solo success earlier in the year. Abacab showed Genesis at their best and worst in fans opinions. Tracks such as the title track and "Me And Sarah Jane" easily fitted in to the fans' conception of the traditional Genesis song. Fans were mortified however, by the inclusion of horns on No Reply At All and they cringed at what most have agreed since is one of Genesis' worst musical moments: "Whodunnit?" which perversely, is one of Tony's favourites from the album…

"I listened to that album recently and one of my favourite tracks was the one that everybody hates: 'Who-dunnit' I thought that's a great track, why don't we do more like that? I remember playing that and trying to get this sort of computer noise and Mike and Phil were listening and they thought: 'you've got something there' so we put it down on tape with this drum music that Phil was playing and we improvised on it for thirty minutes…"

Abacab managed to divide fans in ways which no album since The Lamb… had managed. Reaction amongst old fans was openly hostile to the new stripped down sound and the more radical approach to the music nowhere more forcefully evinced than on Who Dunnit and No Reply At All The former still ranks as the worst ever Genesis track to my ears, and if it was intended as a joke then it almost certainly backfired. As shocking as that track was, the presence of the Phoenix Horns on the latter was a surprise. Their presence opened up new musical horizons and certainly challenged any preconceived ideas that outside observers might have had about this most venerable of rock "dinosaurs". Genesis also finally played some good old fashioned Rock and Roll in the shape of Abacab itself and the intriguing Dodo/Lurker which soon became high points of the new live set, perversely enough another highlight of the new set was WhoDunnit, replete with fantastic lighting effects!

The transition which had begun with Duke continued as the band evolved even further, a point that both Mike and Tony pointed out in an interview for Sounds in September 1981…

(Mike) *Duke set the scene in many ways. It was the end of one era and the beginning of another I think. There were old songs and new songs and there are more new songs on this album. There are more changes. Our writing has changed a lot, even since Duke. It's been two years since we wrote that…"*

(Tony) *"I find the lyrics have changed a lot too. We're doing Firth Of Fifth again on this tour and musically it stands up very well but lyrically I feel it's a bit dated. It's a sort of period piece. On this album the lyrics are much less up front. We're not even putting them on the album. They are meant as more of an abstract thing; more a part of the sound. We've tried to take some of the emphasis away from them. Not everywhere, but I think some of them have been overemphasised in the past".*

This was the key element that Genesis needed to keep the group alive: a spontaneity to recording and writing, gone was the shyness and self-doubt which had coloured the early band as Mike commented at the time...

" *The art of recording is to be adaptable, I would go away and work on a part; spend a couple of hours with a tape recorder working on a part I played on bass, developing some ideas. I'll get in the studio with a whole part worked out... and it's just not happening. So a musician reaches a certain maturity where he says; 'to hell with it' and starts again. You'll do it until it feels right. That's the sort of thing we would do in the past - no one would compromise. You have to be adaptable in the studio you can't MAKE ideas work...*"

The apparent simplicity of the music was deceptive however, unlike previous efforts where every musician was trying to have their voice heard over everyone else's this time there was space for everyone as Phil explained...

"The music that we write together is much different from the music that everybody writes individually because when you write on your own you fill in the gaps but on this one you get lots of gaps but it's a very corporate unit - the gaps are there because you're listening to somebody else playing..."

Having their own studio; the recently purchased Farm on the outskirts of the village of Chiddingfold, certainly gave the band the room to explore areas which they might not have done previously, more from the need to keep an eye on the studio clock and the resulting bill, than any musical uncertainty as Phil explained...

"There was a big difference between working in our own studio and going away to do it - which is what we used to do - and feeling that you had to keep to a schedule. We spent fourteen weeks doing the album. If something wasn't happening we'd just stop and do something else. Before we have felt obliged to keep on trying to get it right. There are a couple of songs on the album that would have died under the old method. But we were able to stop and come back to them..."

The album certainly created a furore among Genesis fans with many bemoaning the lack of exactly the characteristics which Tony has described above, while others felt that this band was now a much more acceptable proposition. The music was infinitely more acceptable to those people who were not necessarily cerebral about their music although the fans who mourned the old Genesis were missing the point as Tony explains...

"There was this reaction against songs like Who-Dunnit and Man On The Corner because it was simple and yet that has always been a part of Genesis and there's this illusion that it has taken over and I don't think it has taken over at all; there's just a little more emphasis and we do it better than we used to and therefore it gets a much higher profile because the singles are actually HITS. It has always been there and it used to be things like For absent friends..."

Once again, the band undertook a lengthy tour to promote the new album beginning in Europe in late September where their reception was mixed including two shows at the Groenoordhal in Leiden Holland where the band were booed which Tony remembers...

"We used to get booed when we played Who-Dunnit.. we played Leiden in Holland and we got booed and so we went back and played there again..."

Fans bemoaning the new album certainly took heart from the live set which drew on just about every album in the band's repertoire aided by their new look light show incorporating the world's first Vari-Lites which Genesis themselves had a hand in creating. This new computerised system of lights which could change colour and shape was to revolutionise rock shows and has since become a standard requirement at rock gigs and strangely enough, one of the high points of the 1981 shows in this fans' opinion at least, was during "Who-Dunnit" when these lights really came into their own! The band also felt confident enough to return to the field of live films with a handful of their shows including the last night of the tour at the NEC in Birmingham in December 1981 being filmed and released the following year under the title of "Three Sides Live" which with its accompanying double live album was to continue Genesis' success into the following year.

If Duke had been the beginning of the band's studio transition, then Abacab saw that transition translated into the live show as well, as the set for the tour was revamped to reflect the band's internal growth, as Tony Banks reflected....

"We're not trying to change the old songs. Its nice in some ways to recreate the era because you are playing in a way that you don't play now but did play then. It also means that the songs stand up for themselves; the old and the new. Some songs do sound dated and we just can't do them. We tried doing Dancing With The Moonlit Knight on the last tour and we just couldn't bring ourselves to play the end convincingly but other bits worked very well... once you start pandering to an audience it becomes transparent that you are doing that..."

Another indication of the creativity of this period was demonstrated when the band released the "3 x 3" E .P. in May 1982 combining the remaining tracks from the "Abacab" sessions niftily housed in a sleeve which harked back to the halcyon days of the 1960's and was a send-up of The Beatles' "Twist and Shout" cover the humour of which was totally lost on the reviewers of the single! The single charted well in the UK ensuring yet another appearance on Top of the Pops which Genesis fans were now fast becoming used to. The band also undertook a two month tour in August and September in support of the live album and at one show in Europe they were supported by their heroes: King Crimson. Essentially the same show as the year before, there was however, one fundamental difference in the inclusion of the entire Supper's Ready which Phil teased the audience about during his introduction...

"This next song is ten years old, so we thought we would dust off our twelve string guitars. This song has got lots of LOUD bits , and lots of quiet bits...this then is Supper's Ready..."

The highlight of the year for Genesis fans was without doubt, however, their unexpected reunion at a wet and windy Milton Keynes Concert Bowl on Saturday 2nd October with Peter Gabriel and Steve Hackett. The gig billed as "Six Of The Best" was the band's way of helping their old comrade out of the financial quagmire that had resulted from the first WOMAD festival which Peter had helped to organise earlier in the year. and for the fans who were there it was an actual quagmire as torrential rain hit the event although it was an emotional evening both for fans and band members as Phil recalls...

"When we did the benefit, we all laughed about it because it all came flooding back, falling over things, pulling microphone leads out of sockets, it was chaos but it was also great fun to do..."

For the show the band rehearsed a special set of "oldies" which sent every one of the sixty thousand or so soaked fans (myself included) away happy and left them wondering "what next?" The show was sound recorded and also filmed despite the band's denials - sorry guys, from where I was standing on the night I could clearly SEE the two guys on stage with film cameras! The likelihood of the film ever being released is minimal but there has been some discussion recently about the possibility of issuing the audio recording of the show as part of a proposed series of "Official Bootlegs".

CHAPTER THIRTEEN Just a job to do?

Phil's first solo tour in support of his "Hello, I Must Be Going" album took him away from the Genesis camp for what remained of 1982 and early 1983 with a highly successful album and tour emphasising his growing stature as a writer and performer. The remainder of the year also saw the release of Tony and Mike's second solo projects which were released to mixed reactions from the critics and fans alike. The summer saw the band return to collective endeavours for their first album to be entirely produced at their now completed studios: The Farm. The remainder of the 1980's were to be the creative apogee of Genesis' career both as a band and individuals with each and every member past and present giving their fans a selection of music which was, and still is, unparalleled in both the sheer amount and diversity of styles which were encompassed.

However, the band's follow-up to 1981's highly successful "Abacab" album was to be something of a struggle if the fact that there were no non album b-sides to any of the singles released from it, apart from the live version of 1980's classic; "Turn It On Again" is any indication. Perhaps the growing number of solo projects by the various members took its toll on the group and to many fans the eponymously titled album: "Genesis" was to many fans something of a disappointment although it did include the band's most successful single to date, the surprise hit of autumn 1983; *"Mama"* which once again re-wrote the rule books. For a start it was a song ostensibly about a man's obsession with a prostitute (!) and was another song which weighed in at over six minutes in length - not ideal chart fodder in the pop-orientated 1980's.

"Mama" was however, made of sterner stuff and gained the band their highest position in the UK's singles charts to date with the single peaking at number four helped no doubt by a Top of the Pops showing of the almost complete and very dramatic video for the song. Once again, the track was the kind of thing which emerged from collective endeavours in the studio as Tony explains…

"Mama was the other thing and because we had the studio we were able.. we had this little germ of an idea and Mike was playing through a fuzzbox or something like that and we thought: 'don't worry about that' it sounded so good on its own and the drumbox sounded so good and I put a drone on it somewhere and we had the skeletal idea and we put it down and we could do that in the studio which we really couldn't have done without a studio of our own…"

Mike Rutherford was emphatic about his delight in the success of the single…

"Its fantastic but what's even better - and this is by far the most important thing - is that we've done it with a song which is very much what we do, if you see what I mean. Our problem in the past has been that very often the best stuff we've done on an album hasn't stood a chance as a single because it has been so wrong in that context. So, we've put out songs that I've liked and have worked well as singles but have simply not been the best songs we've had at the time. But Mama is, I think one of the best songs on the new album and it is at the same time very much what Genesis is all about. To have a hit with a song which is six minutes long is also very exciting. We wanted it to be the single but I expected to play it to our manager Tony Smith and the bods at the record company and be told; 'You're crazy' but full marks to them; they agreed we should go with something that was a bit different…"

Following albums as radically different as the last two Genesis albums had been, would have been a tough task for any band and it is obvious listening to this album that the band were struggling. Maybe this album was that typically "difficult" twelfth record? When the ideas work as they do on the stunning opener; Mama, they work well. Even the dreaded Country & Western of That's All manages to bring a light hearted moment to the proceedings. However, tracks such as Taking it All Too Hard and It's Gonna Get Better hardly rate as the band's finest moments indeed, the title of one of the other tracks may just indicate the position the band found themselves in: Just A Job To Do. Maybe they simply needed to take a break or explore avenues outside of the band which was precisely what they did at the end of the extensive 1983/84 tour.

The album also contained another Genesis long-form classic in the shape of "Home By The Sea" which with its extended instrumental passages could almost have been at home on several of the band's earlier albums and which went on to become one of the favourites in the band's live shows. Fans might be surprised to hear how the song evolved as Tony recalls…

"Well, it was a traditional thing but with a different approach and if you're talking about the second half rather than the first half; we were out there improvising and Phil was just playing in three and Mike and I were playing over the top of that and all of the little moments coalesced and it sounded fantastic… and so we came in here and we had two thirty minute tapes of it and Mike and I just sat down and marked all the best bits; the things we thought were good… learned exactly what we played and then we just stuck it all together.."

Fans have never really seen Genesis as an improvising band but with their own studio and a growing willingness to take musical risks their individual identities gradually emerged more so on this album than perhaps on any of their previous efforts. However, perhaps the band tried too hard to avoid the pitfalls of recycling old themes and the irresistible pressure which all the band felt as Mike remembers…

"I've always felt that we've been tied down by our history, it's often felt like a weight around our neck having to keep recording albums in a similar vein and that's something we've tried to break away from. Each year there is a big question mark and each year it is getting bigger and bigger. This year (1983) when we started I was thinking - and I am sure the other two were too - 'am I just going through the motions?' Certainly the first couple of days were a bit slow, but then we wrote two or three things on the third day and I knew we were all hooked for an album and tour…"

To avoid simply re-jigging existing Genesis trademarks, the band even attempted a Country and Western style number in the shape of "That's All" which Phil hilariously introduced during the band's subsequent live shows as…

"A little country and western number where all of you boys can hitch up your pants and all of you girls can take off your dresses.." This

single was also the subject of a humorous reunion with original producer Jonathan King when he "ambushed" the band after their performance of the song on Noel Edmonds' "Late, Late Breakfast Show" and censured them for promoting "Koala Bars". In fact this album certainly saw the band's visual profile increase in the UK with numerous television interviews and the unheard of for Genesis: full screening of ALL THREE promotional videos from the album!

The success of both the single and the album which went straight to the number one slot both at home and abroad, stung the critics into even more vehement attacks on the band which Tony was at pains to refute and it is impossible to deny the logic of his response…

"We're in the world of commercial music. Let's face it; so if a record sells it must be relevant; that's all there is to it. It doesn't matter whether it's 'The Birdies Song' or The Sex Pistols, if it's top five music then it's relevant in some kind of way or another…All you're trying to conjure up is enjoyment for the moment, escapism through listening to a certain piece of music - that's all we're going for…It's a different world - and I think Mama too plays with your emotions to a far greater degree than your average pop song…"

Certainly the band courted a certain degree of controversy not only with the subject matter of the albums' debut single but also with a subsequent single: "Illegal Alien" which took a slightly tongue in cheek look at America's immigrant problems and which featured a hilarious video. The song was not well received either in the US where a dim view was taken of the band's apparent criticism of the illegal immigrant situation in the US; or indeed here where the single was deemed to be in similarly poor taste. That said, the song still managed to convey some of the problems and pressures associated with the glittering façade presented by the USA to people from an impoverished background and indeed the bureaucracy attached to the whole process of immigration….

"Down at the office had to fill out the forms,
a pink one, a red one, the colours you choose,
Up to the counter to see what they think
They said 'It doesn't count man, it ain't written in ink' "

However, the single was not appreciated by certain authorities in the US which completely missed the point and Tony Banks was at pains to deflect any accusations of latent racism within the Genesis ranks….

"It IS a tongue-in-cheek thing. In fact, it's meant to be sympathetic towards illegal aliens. It isn't about any particular race though in America you hear about Mexicans coming across the border on the TV all the time. Mike Rutherford just wrote some lyrics about it and we did the promotional video as well with us all dressed up for the part. You can see a picture from it on the LP sleeve, with us in false moustaches. Some said that Phil looked like Lech Walesa (leader of the Solidarnosc Trade union movement in Poland at the time). It goes into a reggae feel in the middle so it's not… its not just about Mexicans…"

However controversial some of the band's subject material might have been any doubts which the fans may have had about the quality of the band's new album were more that blown away when they embarked upon another lengthy tour in November a tour which, apart from the last five shows at Birmingham's cavernous National Exhibition Centre, was an entirely US/Canadian affair much to the disappointment of European fans. However, the band's position in the USA was such that this tour was to be their defining moment with shows taking in all the largest venues with a dramatically improved light show which took full advantage of the new Vari Lite system which the band had been instrumental in creating a few years earlier. The massive sound and light system certainly gave added impetus to several of the older pieces in the set and who can forget the sight of the lighting gantry threatening to take off during the latter part of Home By The Sea and a set which still included classic "oldies" like In The Cage and Carpet Crawlers alongside newer material including the hilarious routine for Illegal Alien and the extended homage to the Sixties that ended Turn it on again.

The tour finished, as mentioned above with five sell-out shows at the NEC in late February 1984 each one being for a different charity and with the final one being attended by both the Prince and Princess of Wales although what the Royal couple thought of Genesis' hi-tech rock show has never been recorded. These shows were also the subject of the band's second attempt at a live video which was subsequently released later in 1984 under the title: "Genesis: The Mama Tour" .

With another hugely successful album and tour under their belts, the band went their separate ways after the completion of the tour, and as was mentioned before, the intervening period between this album and the next one saw a proliferation of solo projects which increasingly called the band's rationale for existence into question as far as the fans were concerned; Phil's solo success continued with his third album and a mammoth world tour. Mike finally found his solo niche with the establishment of his "part-time" band; The Mechanics and Tony devoted his time to soundtrack work. The gaps between albums began to lengthen and it was to be almost two years before fans saw the fruits of the groups' collective work - an album that was a surprise to many and a shock to some: "Invisible Touch".

CHAPTER FOURTEEN. "Feeding the fire"

Another lengthy lay off from group activity including Phil's now legendary "Live Aid" performances, sparked concern once again among the fans that perhaps the end was nigh for the band. The relative dearth of material on the previous album although more than compensated for by the inventiveness of the live show had nonetheless cast doubts about the band's longevity. Fortunately, the summer of 1986 saw those doubts swept away beginning with the re-emergence of the band on television for a rare appearance on BBC's famous "Whistle Test" programme with a behind the scenes look at the band rehearsing for the forthcoming album. What was apparent even from that appearance was that the band were relaxed and still creatively coming up with the goods as a collective unit.

For a band as supposedly uptight as Genesis, their work ethic certainly revolved a lot more around humour than anyone might suspect and that innate sense of trust in your colleagues as Tony Banks explained…

"Oh, you have days when nothing comes but normally if you are stuck you can draw upon something that you've had in mind for years - sometimes TEN years and work on that. But if you are having an off day, something that one of the others comes up with will spark you off. That spark between you is very important in a band like ours and we bring things out of each other that we would never do on our own. For example; Phil is more rhythmically imaginative than me, so he will bring that side out in me… We're not conscious of each other and I think that helps. You know you can play a whole day of bum notes and no one is going to take any notice, whereas if you are working with other people you feel as if you should be trying to sound good - you know; 'Hey, here I am and I've got a reputation to protect!' …"

The improvisational nature of the band's work and the fact that at long last the effects of the claustrophobic atmosphere of Public School had finally worn off, led eventually to the band's most instantly accessible album: "Invisible Touch" which was to re-define the band as a musical unit and move them firmly into the pop mainstream. The single was an instant hit when it was released on 15th May 1986 charting at the number 15 position in the UK with higher positions in Europe and the USA. The single signalled Genesis' emergence as a true pop band to rival the likes of U2 whom they easily outsold on their subsequent tour in support of the album.

What made this album so special? There is no doubt about it, the sheer scale of the material is astounding with everything from the pure power pop of the title track, to love ballads such as In Too Deep and for the longstanding fans still reeling from their band's surrender to the pop infection; there were traditional Genesis pieces such as Tonight, Tonight, Tonight and Domino. The album brought in a whole new Genesis audience which easily replaced the older fans who no doubt found the new-look Genesis a very hard pill to swallow although even this new look band were still the victim of the venom of the music press who could not reconcile the band's success with the image they had in their minds of the band and who took to savaging the band on the most personal of levels as their manager Tony Smith commented

"Criticism is fine, but you don't get that. Quite often in a review they don't even mention the bloody music. They go on a diatribe about the band or what Phil looks like, and that infuriates me. It's non-journalism and it hurts when they spend a lot of time making records they are very sincere about, only to have it dismissed as ' another commercial record by those millionaires'. We've never done things just for the money and we never will. OK, we earn good money. But that is a by-product. In the past we have always spent more on our shows than we've earned. Genesis have always kept their feet on the ground and stayed normal. Maybe that's what bugs some critics…"

Invisible Touch made Genesis' claim to the pop crown of the late Eighties indisputable. The title track was everything that the band had been striving for since they started; quirky, catchy and irresistible and above all - FUN! In Too Deep was another fine example of how the band's ear for a good tune had developed into a killer instinct. However, the old Genesis was not ignored either and among these lighter moments, there were still some genuine moments of fire and drama too; especially in the post nuclear holocaust drama of Domino and Tonight, Tonight, Tonight which could easily be about drug addiction, alcohol abuse or obsession, you choose for yourself! This album silenced the critics as it took the pop world by storm on its release bringing in millions of new fans into the bargain.

The album was released in June 1986 and achieved number one positions both at home and in the USA and the statistics concerning the album were remarkable as reported in the somewhat bemused music press…

"Genesis remain at the top of the album chart for the second week with Invisible Touch. On it's first week in the shops 100,000 copies, of which a remarkable 10.27% were on compact disc. No other CD has sold 100,000 copies in Britain in a single week…"

In fact the album was another Genesis "First" being the first rock album to have a simultaneous release on both vinyl, cassette AND the new compact disc format. The album also ensured that the Genesis camp were well represented throughout the summer of 1986 and in fact, the band were knocked off the number one spot in the USA by former band member Peter Gabriel's new album; *"So"* and Steve Hackett's new band GTR also scored a chart success in the USA that summer with their debut album; GTR and single; "When The Heart Rules The Mind". It certainly did Genesis fans a power of good to hear people who had only recently derided the band suddenly raving about how good they were!

The success continued with the release of the second single in August 1986. "In Too Deep" almost repeated the chart success of its predecessor reaching the number 19 position. An indication of just how fruitful the recording sessions had been was indicated by the presence on that single and the subsequent three singles by a host of non album tracks several of which were certainly candidates for the album itself. Between the UK and USA the album spawned an unheard of FIVE hit singles in all between its release and the end of the summer of 1987. The third single; "Land Of Confusion" was also another first with an award for best video well deserved because the highly amusing video, designed by "Spitting Image" animators Fluck & Law certainly laid to rest any thoughts that the band had no sense of humour! The band also treated their fans to a video collection of the assembled tracks from the new album called "Visible Touch" which included videos which had not been available previously all of which added nicely to the fans' growing collections of visual memorabilia of this period in the group's history.

All that remained for the band now was the ubiquitous tour in support of the album which kicked off in Detroit on 18th September 1986 and was destined to become the band's largest scale tour since "The Lamb.." almost twelve years before with over 112 dates being performed to over one and a half million fans. Once again, the band utilised state-of-the-art technology including the new MKIII Vari Lites which once again gave an added emphasis to the stage show and enabled the band to play successfully in the large open air arenas and stadiums in Europe and the USA. The band also took in several shows in Japan, only their second visit to that country and finally got round to playing their first ever shows in New Zealand and Australia just prior to Christmas 1986 which were made even more special by the band's use of a four piece string section to comply with local Musician's Union rules which gave the band a chance to play a couple of numbers in a slightly different setting and to revive Mike's 1977 classic: "Your Own Special Way" which undoubtedly benefited from the addition of a string section. Without doubt the band were 1986/87's "Hottest ticket" with a string of sell-out shows at every venue they played culminating with a record breaking four consecutive nights at London's enormous Wembley Stadium in July 1987 which were filmed for the now obligatory live video of the tour which was eventually released some two years later under the title of "Invisible Touch Tour" with the initial 5000 copies coming with a bonus one-track live CD single. This video also set standards for video presentations being the first to be filmed using experimental Sony Hi Definition film to give an almost cinematic appearance to the film.

Fans were also treated to a further two videos by the band in 1988 during the increasing hiatus between this album and the group's next effort with the long overdue release of the Genesis Videos Volume One and Two which comprised most (but not all) of the band's promotional videos since 1976 certainly an indispensable item for fans and one which was well received and helped to keep interest in the band at a high level. The remainder of the 1980's saw both Phil and Mike's solo careers take off with a vengeance.

Mike's second album with the Mechanics; 1988's "The Living Years" spawned one of that years' biggest hit singles and Mike was finally able to tour in the UK and Europe throughout the early part of 1989 to public acclaim. Phil's fourth solo album, released in November 1989 was the one which catapulted him from star to Superstar status: "But Seriously" re-wrote the record books upon its release and the attendant demands on Phil's time inevitably delayed the commencement on the band's follow up to "Invisible Touch" giving Mike a chance to consolidate his solo career with the Mechanics' third album; "Word Of Mouth" which was released in the spring of 1991.

The band did put in two brief but memorable appearances during this extended hiatus however, first of all both Genesis and Phil Collins took part in the birthday celebrations for the 40th anniversary of Atlantic Records which was held at New York's Madison Square Garden on 15th May 1988 and for which the band performed a medley incorporating solo material by both Tony and Mike with Phil singing - the only time that this is likely to happen and Phil showed his true showmanship by carrying on through even when he forgot the words! The band also put in an appearance at the "Silver Clef" concert at Knebworth Park on 30th June 1990 where once again, they shared the billing with Pink Floyd as well as Elton John, Paul McCartney and a host of others on what was once again another extremely wet day. Genesis' performance that day was certainly lacklustre and a predictable choice of songs which I am sure led many fans to wonder about the future of the band and 1991 was to prove a pivotal year in more ways than one…..

CHAPTER FIFTEEN "Watching the fading lights"

Having waited such a long time for an album from the band, fans were not to be disappointed by the next offering from Genesis. Taking full advantage of the extra playing time on the now commonly available compact disc format, the band released only their second double studio album in their history. Preceded by the first single; "No Son Of Mine" which was released on 21st October 1991 and which signalled a new realism in the band's material. The song, accompanied by a dramatic monochrome video broached the taboo subject of child abuse - a million miles away from Genesis' usual lyrical fare. The single peaked at the number six position in the UK announcing once again that Genesis were very much alive and kicking and with plenty of musical ideas to play with . Collectively the band were as strong as ever with all the tracks being written in the studio with no material "imported" from outside projects as Mike Rutherford commented in the album's press release…

"It makes the first week a bit nerve-wracking, because you've got no songs to fall back on. We were a bit rusty, but it didn't take long to get going really. You just start jamming around, and out of chaos hopefully comes a strong moment. It's a good way for us to go, because we do a lot of work outside the band. It keeps Genesis for what it's all about; which is the chemistry of the three of us playing together…"

In all, the album contained some thirteen songs and once again, the band displayed a fine line in self-deprecating humour with the album title - "We Can't Dance*"* which upon its release gave the band their fourth consecutive number one album in the UK and in many other territories it achieved the same position in particular in Germany where it was top of their charts for over sixteen weeks! Certainly the album was a wholly different proposition than its pop orientated predecessor and was an entirely more satisfying prospect for the older fans whilst retaining enough of the band's growing pop sensibilities to not only keep but increase their fan base both at home and abroad.

Phil's writing for the band certainly included his best work to date and was a reassuring return to extended format pieces as well as the shorter pieces which had dominated the last couple of albums although Mike had a slightly different perception of events to those expressed in increasingly vehement tones by the more die- hard element of the fans…

"A lot of people thought we'd 'Gone American' with the last album but the fact is that in America a hit single and video can be so high profile that they can dwarf an album and people tend to forget everything that has gone before and it can overshadow an album. I certainly felt it was time for a change…"

And change it was with songs dealing with subjects as diverse as dietary fads (Living Forever), the building of the English railways *(*Driving The Last Spike*)* as well as a wry dig at the obsession with fashion models (I Can't Dance*)*. The album covered a lot of ground and gave fans something to digest and enthuse about and even the older fans couldn't have too much to complain about as the band had striven hard to make the album a more traditional one in some aspects as Tony explained…
"

Invisible touch was perhaps the most direct album we've ever done. This one has a bit more mystery in it. We tried very hard to get each track so that it has an individual quality about it, but at the same time there's an atmosphere which runs through all the songs…"

Change was in the air too as long-time Genesis producer Hugh Padgham was replaced by Nick Davis at the controls although this was not due to any falling out with Padgham as both Tony and Mike were keen to emphasise in their December 1991 interview in "Vox" magazine…

(Mike): *"We were very happy with Hugh, we all like his work but it was time to do something different".* Tony Banks was more keen on Nick's pushing of Tony into areas he might not have considered otherwise... *"Nick has definite opinions about certain things which is great. Perhaps over the years I have been over-liberal with the string sounds, but Nick would make me search for something else and I think that's good because there are easy options - you can get used to doing things a certain way..."*

The band even courted controversy in the USA again with a scathing attack on the television Evangelists so popular there in the song "Jesus He Knows Me" which was banned in certain parts of the USA and even the poor old BEEB got in the act here in the UK by banning the video when the song was released as one of the clutch of singles from the highly successful album.

Unusually for the band as well, a television crew were given access to the recording studio during the album sessions, an act unprecedented in the history of the group and the resulting documentary: "No Admittance" showed the band at work and at play and looking extremely relaxed apart from one moment when the frustration of trying to get the lyrics right got the better of Phil. The documentary also served to emphasise what the band had always maintained about their way of working which Mike outlined in an interview with The Waiting Room...

"The obvious one is I Can't Dance which was my guitar riff and Tony's keyboard part and that to me was a great little song because it just happened and we wrote it by deciding we'll try it out for the album and it will be great; or if it doesn't work: we'll throw it away, and Phil had the lyrics and it just happened in the morning and that's what I like..."

With the album a massive success world wide, the band were soon to prepare for the obligatory tour in support of it which this time round was to be a shorter affair than previous efforts. However, no expense was to be spared in the presentation of the band's latest show. Having decided that the tour was to be predominantly of larger venues and in particular the massive outdoor stadia in both the USA and Europe the band invested heavily in the latest technology to enable them to bring an accessible show to the massed hordes waiting to see them in concert. This technology included the world's first three Sony "Jumbotron" video screens which were deployed either singly or joined together to give extra emphasis on the visual effects which have always figured so largely in Genesis' show. Certainly it was to be the most complex show the band had ever staged as Mike admitted...

"This is the most elaborate show we've ever done and the first just in stadiums...in the past we did arenas as well which meant our hands were tied a bit. Now we've designed the show for stadiums which gives us more freedom..."

Technical problems were not to be the main worry on this tour however, but personal and logistical ones were to dog the tour from its opening night when Phil's vocals were affected by a severe cold resulting in the band leaving the stage after a mere three songs almost provoking a riot from disgruntled fans! Other problems were to occur when the band's tour finally reached Europe with a trucker's strike affecting several gigs and the band also had personal tragedy to deal with when a member of their road crew died. Even the band's British shows were not unaffected, with an initial announcement of three UK shows the first at Roundhay Park near Leeds the scene of their triumph in 1987 which was to be followed by a record breaking two night stint at the massive Knebworth Park in Stevenage which the band hadn't played since 1978. Many fans were therefore both surprised and somewhat disappointed when the band cancelled the first of these shows on 1ˢᵗ August 1992 citing logistical difficulties for the cancellation although an unkind and somewhat sceptical press remarked that the band were victim to poor ticket sales.

The shows themselves were a technical triumph incorporating the visual and musical excitement expected of the band with a growing sense of fun as evidenced by Phil's introduction to the medley of older tracks... *"This goes back to the dim and slightly damp Seventies when we wore bell bottom trousers and some of us had more hair!"* The new material fitted in easily with the established components of the Genesis set and they managed to take the audience by surprise with a new slant on tracks such as "Home By The Sea" and "Domino" which benefited enormously from the improved visuals. The tour statistics also made impressive reading with Genesis playing to an average audience of 56,000 per show over the sixty or so shows on the tour and even the one show at Knebworth achieving an audience of over 100,000 not bad for a band consistently branded unpopular by the press?

Knebworth was the culmination of the band's summer tour and fans were naturally expecting the band to return to the usual round of solo projects. The band, however, had other plans as Tony Banks explained...

"The last time we played in England, we only played at Leeds and Wembley. This time it seemed as if maybe we would only play Leeds and Knebworth, but we didn't want to short-change any of our fans. So we decided on the Earls Court dates - and from the point of view of the look of the show - it will probably look much better at Earls Court. It's more controlled indoors, it's a different kind of show.."

The shows in question were a series of six concerts at London's prestigious Earls Court Arena which took place in early November 1992. What was surprising for the fans was the announcement prior to this of a series of shows at several theatre venues in the Provinces beginning with a show at Southampton's Mayflower Theatre on 23rd October and a series of similar venues which the band hadn't played since the halcyon days of 1980 and which the band were looking forward to playing for a variety of reasons as Mike commented…

"I think half the time what we're looking for in our careers is variety and change. It's going to be refreshing to go back and play in some of the venues that we used to play in to smaller, more intimate audiences and with no production, just some lights. That'll be very fresh for us, we haven't done it for a long time. In a way I'm surprised more bands don't do the same…and I feel we know the venues very well. In my mind I can picture Newcastle City Hall very clearly, the way the balcony goes, the way it curves at the back. Newcastle always reminds me of Lindisfarne because when we first played there Lindisfarne were like The Beatles. You felt that you wanted to tell the audience that you were friends of theirs in order to get in…"

The new live set was fundamentally the same for these shows as it had been for the outdoor summer tour although as Tony remarked above, with the benefit of being indoors, the lighting effects certainly worked much better although the real treat was the stripped down and more intimate atmosphere of the theatre shows which were one of the hottest tickets of the year with tickets for the show in Edinburgh for example, changing hands for over £400 for a £17.00 ticket!

The last show of the tour took place at Wolverhampton's Civic Hall on 17th November the night after the band played a prestigious gig at London's Royal Albert Hall which was broadcast on the radio and the band must have taken great satisfaction in the success of both the album and tour but also the fact that they were still giving the "young guns" of pop a run for their money with a string of hit singles any band would be proud of as well as an increasing round of television appearances including a behind the scenes look at the band's gig in Nottingham by Blue Peter of all things and another first for the band: an appearance on Top of the Pops in support of a live single version of *Invisible Touch* which had been released in time for the tour although the lyrics were once again judiciously edited by the BBC so as not to offend the kiddies!

To capitalise on the band's high profile, Virgin also released a two-part live album featuring the "Short" and the "Long" tracks from the current live set. This effort, the band's fourth live album certainly demonstrated both the traditional and commercial faces of Genesis but was the cause of some criticism from the fan base who maintained that it should have been a double album entire show and released as one package were Virgin beginning to milk the cash cow that was Genesis? The following year was a relatively quiet one for the band as the individual members concentrated on solo projects. They were briefly reunited however, for a charity gig at Cowdrey Ruins in aid of the King Edward VII hospice where they were joined by such rock alumni as Pink Floyd and the remaining members of Queen.

Intriguingly enough, the question of what would happen to the band if another member were to quit was posed again to the band during a further interview with "Vox" magazine in December 1992. The responses from Tony and Phil in particular, with the benefit of hindsight, make fascinating reading…

(Tony): *"I think the chances are that would be it. We wouldn't try another incarnation. But I don't know, it really would depend on the situation and how bloody minded you are. The fact is that we are all doing things outside of the band - to varying degrees I must admit, but we all do have alternatives…"*

(Phil): *"Any pressure that I would have felt or any desire, would have surfaced by now, so it's really a question of us getting into the studio next time, and if it doesn't work, fine. That would be the point when we would most likely knock it on the head…."*

1993 and 1994 were to be traumatic years for Phil as his marriage to Jill gradually came apart and the couple and their young family became victims of the tabloid press search for a story. Phil's 1993 album "Both Sides" certainly went to town on the critics and was his darkest and most angry album yet. Another massive solo tour occupied him throughout 1994 and into 1995 and with Mike also taking advantage of the lull in Genesis activity to bring the Mechanics back to life for the highly successful "Beggar On A Beach Of Gold" album and tour there were many doubts expressed as to whether a band with so many successful members could sustain itself as a working entity.

The situation was certainly not helped by the ever growing gap between Genesis projects although Virgin kept the band's profile high with a series of releases including the long overdue re-mastering of the band's back catalogue from "Trespass" to "Three Sides Live" which were released in two blocks at varying intervals in 1994 although these releases were not without some attendant problems not least being the sleeves which were in some cases completely botched, a problem which has still not been properly rectified. The band were also captured live again on another concert video filmed over the six nights at Earls Court and capturing just about an entire show in glorious sound and vision.

By the end of 1995, however, fans were beginning to worry - four years since the band's last studio album and still no sign of the long awaited return to the studio and, as events would prove there was still to be almost another two years before the band re-emerged by which time fans were to be faced with their biggest challenge in twenty years : a new singer!

CHAPTER SIXTEEN "Across the dividing line"

Rumours began circulating towards the end of 1995 that all was not well in the Genesis camp. Various sources maintained that Phil had quit the band. In the face of these rumours, the band's record company and management maintained a stoical silence which did nothing to allay the disquiet of the fans and it was strange to hear people begin to write the same obituaries of the band which had been trotted out in 1975 when Peter made his now famous announcement.

As usual, however, the speculation and rumour were to be proven groundless. True, Phil had announced his decision to leave the band as early as 1994 at a dinner organised by the band's manager Tony Smith. With such a lot of activity from the solo members of the Genesis camp it was both unnecessary and possibly harmful to the band's future prospects to make any announcement prematurely as Tony Banks explained…

"Well, we let it ride for a little bit because we felt that Phil was probably going to leave but rather than forcing the issue, we thought we'd leave it until it was 100% definite and there was an official announcement between ourselves in the summer of 1995. So, we had already decided by then that Mike and I thought we would like to try and carry on by certainly seeing what we got out of the writing stage and seeing what was produced…. I thought Mike might not be too keen because Mike & The Mechanics was going well, but he was definitely up for it…"

The official announcement of Phil's departure was made by the Virgin Press office on Monday 29th March 1996 and even at this time of uncertainty the band displayed a great sense of humour with the headline: **"Genesis end 20 year experiment, decide to replace Peter Gabriel as vocalist"**. The decision still took fans by surprise and many were disappointed that the band hadn't had the faith to make the announcement sooner although how they could have made the announcement prior to finding a replacement is beyond me. However, the suspense of waiting for the announcement of who (if anybody) was to replace Phil was to be even more nail biting with a further year of silence to be endured before the decision was made public on 6th June 1997 and I am sure the irony of the choice of day was not lost on the band (6th June for those of you who don't know your history, is the anniversary of the D Day Landings in Europe during the Second World War).

An apt choice because this certainly was to prove to be the D Day for the band. If anything the situation was even more precarious now than it had been upon Peter's departure back in 1975. The band's status then was that of a large cult band, now in the 1990's Genesis were perceived by a large section of their audience as Phil's backing band and, indeed, the music press were increasingly running advertisements for Genesis gigs in the late '80's and early '90's under the banner: **"Phil Collins _and_ Genesis"**. How was the change of singer going to impinge on the huge fan base dedicated to Phil's version of the band and just who was the new singer?

The band's choice of new front man was almost as surprising as Phil's departure itself. Instead of choosing a high roller to replace Phil, the band almost perversely in many people's opinion, went the other way and chose a comparatively unknown singer. Ray Wilson was a surprise choice for a variety of reasons; first of all his previous experience had been as singer of Grunge rock outfit and one-hit wonders Stiltskin, second he was a mere twenty eight years old and third, he was by Genesis standards, a good looking guy still possessed of a full head of hair! Initial reaction to the band's choice was mixed but generally favourable although with reservations which were quite natural given that as yet, the fans had no evidence to go on.

For some however, it was to be a step too far particularly in the USA where reaction was at best lukewarm and at worst, openly hostile. Fans wondered at the band's logic in their choice but it is quite simple as Tony explains…

"I think we always felt that we didn't want it to come out like a supergroup or something. We wanted very definitely the group to carry on having the kind of character it has, and if you can imagine any singer you care to name, whether they would or wouldn't do it is irrelevant but if you said Steve Winwood with Genesis or whatever you would say that it is something else entirely…So we didn't consider singers like that we wanted somebody like Ray… Ray was good because he'd had enough experience so you felt he'd done it in front of a big audience and he'd proved that he had something of that… I think we were initially going for the voice and he was the voice out of everything I'd heard that personally I liked best of all and so it was quite lucky that the rest of it fell into place…"

The band's new album their seventeenth studio recording was called "Calling All Stations" and was eventually released on 2nd September 1997 preceded by a single "Congo" which peaked at the number 28 slot in the UK charts. The album itself peaked at number two being kept off the top slot by the ubiquitous Oasis. The position in the USA however, was far more daunting with the album peaking at the number 54 slot in the Billboard chart hindered by an extremely lacklustre promotion campaign by Atlantic. Perhaps they too had some doubts about the band's new look? Ray himself admits that the band's position this time round was somewhat difficult…

"I think with this album we are caught somewhere between what the band has done more recently and what they've done in the past.." although he also displayed a healthy sense of realism about the position as well… _"I couldn't come in and replace Phil and expect to sell 11 million albums, it just doesn't make sense and my view always was of it; if people who really love Genesis.. if those people like the album then I've achieved it; it has been a success…"_

Mike also summed up the problem the band faced in America…

"We are going to battle on we've got to get a vibe going and at the moment things are a bit cold. The trouble is until they hear something; until they hear Ray, they can't get excited about it and it's all based on hearsay…"

It was not all doom and gloom however, in Germany the band received silver discs for sales of 300,000 copies of the album within three weeks of it being released.

"Calling All Stations" as an album was for most fans who actually LISTENED to it, a welcome return to the darker more melodramatic Genesis of old. The title track itself was a genuine piece of traditional Genesis with sterling work by both Mike and Tony, and with it's story line being loosely Based around events currently taking place on the Mir Space Station at the time, perhaps it was a case of "Watcher Of The Skies revisited"? Who knows, either way the album certainly restated Genesis' credentials as a ROCK band and with a lead singer who was prepared to get behind the idea of Genesis as rock rather than pop…

"The idea was to establish us as a rock act; and if we'd started with one of the more obvious ballads such as Shipwrecked or Not about us it would have given the wrong impression and made people think: 'more *fucking middle-of- the -road Genesis here we go..' and really the album isn't middle of the road, it's got a lot of stuff on it that's definitely not middle of the road although there are one or two songs that ARE but I think Calling All Stations, The Dividing Line and There Must Be Some Other Way; these aren't middle of the road songs; these are rock songs of a Genesis type for me and I thought it was right to start off saying 'this is a rock band' and 'this is a rock album'..."*

Certainly, the album took on the darker side of life... One Man's Fool being an examination of the motivations for terrorism and the justification (if there can ever be justification) for such activities. The Dividing Line could perhaps be seen as an apt description of the band's current situation. A "dividing line" had been definitely crossed in many fans' opinions by the continuation of the band with Ray in the vocal position expressed even more forthrightly in the lyrics to another track from the album: Small Talk...

Going round in circles hearing too many points of view
Just words to tire me out, small talk I could do without
I would be amazed if you returned to see things my way
Now that you've been disrespectful to my sense of pride...

Indeed, the band's ego took an almighty dent from reaction to the new album. The overall feel of the album is decidedly downbeat after the optimism of Invisible Touch and We Can't Dance. That being said; there was no shortage of material for this project however, with a further six songs being shelved with five of them eventually appearing as B Sides to the three singles which were released from the album between August 1997 and February 1998. The underlying sense of bitterness and disappointment can be clearly be heard in the lyrics to several of these tracks.

Ironically, given the public apathy to the album in the USA, and the band's disappointment with the fans' reaction there; the band chose to premiere their new look band and album with a performance at the Kennedy Space Centre on 26th August 1997 a week before the album's release. The album followed and the fans were treated to a full range of tour dates beginning in the USA in November and winding up in the UK and Europe the following spring. However, the situation in the USA led to a drastic realignment of the shows originally scheduled for the major arenas in the US and then downgraded to theatres with a capacity of between three and five thousand. The situation was certainly not one which the band relished and their reaction was characteristically feisty:

(Ray) *"The American thing is obviously, very disappointing but we will play them. If we have to play smaller shows; then fuck it; we'll play smaller shows but we WILL play them. All they give a fuck about is that the places we play are busy; they don't want to play a half empty arena, stadium or anything. The way we look at it is; if we have to do theatres in America let's do FULL theatres rather than do half empty arenas..."*

Unfortunately for Ray, his desire to play Madison Square Garden in New York was to remain unfulfilled as the US tour was eventually cancelled entirely down to the fact as the band's manager Tony Smith remarked to The Waiting Room...

"The vibe simply wasn't happening in America"

And the only chance the US fans had to see the band was at the pre album launch mentioned above. This naturally led to a lot of griping by US fans although it has to be pointed out that throughout the '80's and early '90's they did infinitely better out of the band with regard to tours than either the UK or Europe. Reaction to the cancellation of the US tour was hostile and worrying for fans in the UK and Europe who expected the same thing to happen to the proposed tour here. In fact, after some rescheduling of dates, the Calling all stations tour finally got under way with a warm-up gig at Bray film studios on 23rd January 1998 in front of an invited audience of fans followed by the first proper gig at the Sports Hall in Budapest on 28th January followed by a tour of most of the major arenas in both the UK and Europe finally winding up with a show at the massive brand new Hartwall Arena in Helsinki on 5th April.

For the new show, the band also took fans by surprise by not only having a new singer to show off but also a new guitarist replacing Daryl Stuermer whose commitments to Phil's touring schedule prevented him from taking part. His replacement was almost as much of a surprise as Ray and proved that Genesis were not prepared to sacrifice anything in the music department: Anthony Drennan proved to be an inspired choice although he may have upset purists by his interpretation of Steve's solos during the older material but he certainly gave them a new lease of life as well. Phil's replacement in the percussion department was, if anything the most surprising of all.

Nir Tzidkyahu, a thirty year old Israeli drummer based in New York took over the rhythm section to startling effect although he admits that rehearsing for the tour did cause some problems…

"The dividing line is a pain in the butt! It was just one of those experimental jam sessions in the studio and I have no idea what I played and before we started rehearsals I said 'ok, let's listen to it now..' and there are different spots for you as drummer during the set…"

Once again, the band utilised the "Jumbotron" screens from the last tour to a somewhat mixed effect this time round primarily because they were stationary and not able to link up as they had been able to do on the "We Can't Dance" tour. The reason for this was quite simple: money as the band's lighting engineer Dave Hill explained…

"Every time the screen move it costs about £10,000 and besides, even The Rolling Stones didn't have the screens moving…"

Musically however, there were no such disappointments as the band treated us to a show that lived up to the billing on the posters: ***"Genesis Through the Ages"*** a somewhat misleading advertising campaign which got the band into some small degree of trouble with the UK Advertising Standards Council with its depiction of the band including both Peter and Phil on the posters! However, fans who contacted the box offices at the venues in the UK were left in no doubt as to who was in the band and it was quite astonishing to be asked the following question when booking tickets: *"You do realise that Phil Collins is no longer in Genesis, don't you?"* The tour in Europe and the UK was a qualified success with the combination of a rejuvenated band and a set drawing on the strengths of the Genesis catalogue the band managed to convince their fans that there is still plenty of life in the old (or should that be not so old?) dog yet. The band even managed to headline two of the most prestigious German festivals in the summer of 1998 over such alumni as Bob Dylan and Page and Plant rounding off the touring obligations for the album in fine style.

The relative failure of the album, obviously upset the band somewhat although sales of over three million units world wide is nothing to be sneezed at and fans were shocked when it became apparent that the band were in the process of winding down. Tony Banks explained the position to the author in a recent interview for The Waiting Room Magazine…

"I wanted to do a second album; I wasn't keen to do the first one but I was quite keen once we had done the first one to do a second one. Mike persuaded me in many ways to do Calling All Stations Project and I thought.. why not; let's give it a go and then once we had done it I thought we should do another one because I thought we were learning a bit how to use Ray's voice and it certainly warranted another one but Mike wasn't keen. I think that he felt that there was a very big fall in sales if you like…"

Calling All Stations as an album, certainly deserved a better reception than it received at the time. The fans' reaction to the decision to continue with a new singer, especially a comparatively unknown one, was hard for many fans (myself included initially) and this bitter pill might have been made easier to swallow if the band had had the courage to make the announcement sooner. Responsibility for the debacle in the US lies with the appalling decision taken by Atlantic Records to pull the planned advertising budget for the new album and to re-allocate it elsewhere. Result: a new album emerging to a public generally unaware of its existence! Not a shrewd move in the publicity motivated Nineties!

With hindsight, the decision not to tour in the US was also ill-advised and was almost certainly a knee-jerk reaction to the poor sales of the album. The band had always toured in support of albums as the standard way of garnering extra publicity and sales for albums and Calling All Stations should have been no different. A US tour would certainly have boosted sales of the album as well as giving the fans a chance to make up their own minds about the new-look band Effectively, the decision not to do this, condemned the album and band to their poorest ever showing in the States and also to all intents and purposes closed the book on Genesis as a touring entity, although this was not obvious at the time as Ray explained….

"The plan was to meet again in September 1999 and to start writing again with a view to releasing another Genesis album in the spring of 2000; April time. That was the plan and when wen finished the very last concert that was what I thought was happening, and I think; to be honest; Mike and Tony both thought that was what was happening as well. I don't think anyone finished that last gig thinking 'well.. that's it we're not going to do anymore..' I think everybody thought; 'let's do another album' because we all enjoyed doing it and the tour was good fun….

What happened between that last concert and August 2000, I don't honestly know. I don't know why all of a sudden it changed. I just got a phone call to say that I was going to be singing on Carpet Crawlers. I was going to do a verse of the song; Peter Gabriel was going to do a verse and so was Phil Collins and then I wasn't singing on the song anymore. Then I was told that the band weren't going to continue anymore and I don't know why.."

Ray's evident disappointment and bitterness at the way in which he was treated have obviously moderated somewhat and he is currently touring with his own band performing music from the Genesis catalogue as well as material from his growing catalogue of solo albums. His recent comments on the subject of the band make interesting reading…

"I enjoyed my time with Genesis, original members Mike Rutherford and Tony Banks who were still in the band with me, are musical geniuses and the following the band has is tremendously fanatical, they know more about the group than its members in some cases. They also have very clear ideas about which tracks they like - the earlier ones seemed to be the most popular and fortunately they were ones I felt I could do justice to. At times it used to slightly annoy Mike and Tony - they wanted to do more new stuff…"

CHAPTER SEVENTEEN The Final Curtain?

For fans still shocked by the new line up and all the personnel changes attendant on it, still further surprises were in store when it was announced that Virgin Records were planning to release the first of a proposed series of boxed sets by the band. Covering the period from the band's inception in 1967 to the end of the Gabriel era in 1975, the first of these boxes titled "Genesis Archive 1967 -1975" was finally released to the eager fans on 22nd June 1998 and which ironically charted at the number 35 position in the UK charts. What took the fans completely by surprise however, wasn't so much the fact that the boxed set had finally seen the light of day after so many false starts but the accompanying publicity which saw an undreamed of "Reunion" between the original band members including both Anthony Phillips AND John Silver for a series of interviews and photo opportunities at London's Heathrow airport on 11th May an event which was captured for posterity by VH1 and subsequently broadcast as part of their "Genesis Day" special and ironically narrated by Genesis "New Boy" Ray Wilson!

The four CD set compiled quite nicely just about everything that fans of this period and newer ones still finding their feet in the band's enormous back catalogue, could wish for including classic live recordings from both the "Selling England By The Pound" and "The Lamb Lies Down On Broadway" tours as well as the elusive rare single b-sides and a whole disc of previously unheard material from the very beginnings of the band's story. The release of this set sparked off the usual round of speculation on a grand reunion by the classic band line-up for a tour and album. Whilst no one in the band's camp either confirmed or denied the prospect of such a reunion both Steve Hackett and Anthony Phillips maintained that it was a prospect which they wouldn't rule out or, to use Steve's words…

"I would be involved but only if I can play my harmonica!"

However there were howls of complaint from some die-hard fans when it became apparent that some of this material was not quite what it seemed. The excitement over the release of a live concert from the legendary Lamb… tour was mitigated somewhat when it was revealed that parts of the vocal had been completely re-recorded by Peter Gabriel and that certain guitar parts on the live material from the 1974 Selling England By The Pound show had also been re-recorded by Steve. To many this was tantamount to drawing a moustache on the Mona Lisa, but there were valid reasons for it, as the band's producer; Nick Davis explained…

"I think about thirty or forty per cent of it (The Lamb..) was re-sung. There were problems on tape…I don't know if it were costume changes or technical reasons and so there were no lead vocals and I know all these people say you can't repair a concert, its sacrilege but to me a concert without a lead vocal would annoy me and so you can either be a purist about it and have no lead vocal, or you can get it repaired and have a lead vocal. Anything that was useable was used and anything that was sung was sung because it didn't exist on tape. I think it was about thirty per cent on The Lamb… the band would never repair anything out of choice ,they would sooner not repair it and it was only when you were listening to a good version of a song without a lead vocal and it was a shame not to use it for the sake of re-singing a vocal. Steve came in and did a bit of guitar too, because it wasn't on tape".

The release, on 6th November 2000, of the second Genesis Box set; "Genesis Archive #2 1976-92" spawned a whole new round of press and fan speculation about the band. Critical reaction to this collection was mixed although speaking from a fan's perspective, it draws together most (but not all) of the remaining threads from the Collins era of the band. Phil has gone on record as saying that he would like to work with Mike and Tony again although not calling the project "Genesis". I don't think however, in all honesty, that it would matter what it was called. If the three of them were to record again the fans would only have one name for it: "Genesis".

There is, for me at least one remaining bugbear: the documentation of the band's career has signally failed to acknowledge the final incarnation of the band. OK, so Calling All Stations was one album and Ray's tenure with the band lasted approximately two years. However, the album sold over THREE MILLION copies compared to the SIX THOUSAND copies that Trespass initially sold. The lack of acknowledgement of that magnificent achievement, against all the odds; has to be redressed. In fact, original indications were that the series of Box Sets were to span the band's entire career over three sets which, to my mind at least would have made for a much more satisfying resume of their career. Ray's contribution to the band's story has, in my opinion; been understated and undervalued by both the band themselves and a large proportion of the fans. I obviously cannot speak for any of the band themselves and their comments on this subject have been suitably diplomatic and guarded. However, to a great many fans, it seems that Ray's tenure with the band is an area which the band (by which I mean Mike and Tony) would rather forget, which is a sad reflection on an excellent effort, and the only real black mark on their career.

The rehabilitation (if you can call it that) of the Genesis catalogue has continued to inspire speculation from the fans and recent comments from Tony Banks with regard to the vexed question of a potential reunion and the re-mixing of the back catalogue for the 5.1 Stereo versions have been very interesting to put it mildly…

" The album I enjoyed the most was the second Archive album because it had all those B sides on it because I thought some of those tracks were really good… On The Shoreline was excellent and should have been on We Can't Dance but I was shouted down by the other two (laughs) and I thought it sounded better than that awful Since I Lost You, and the other one which is good is Hearts On Fire and those two should really have been on that album…. I talk about them now to Mike and Phil and they say… yeah, we should have had them on ,and I go… bastards! (laughs)…"

The re-mixing of the back catalogue CDs has certainly meant that the band themselves have to revisit their catalogue and perhaps realise that there might be life in the old dog yet. The prospect of live archival recordings has enticed fans and is definitely being taken seriously as Tony recently comment …

"Yeah we did have a lot of tapes ; hundreds of the things from quite early days and also all the rehearsal tapes. We were quite surprised that the one thing that didn't get a particularly good response off the second Archive album was the version of Mama which we put on and which I thought was really good…that was we could find actually… we were looking for the Home By The Sea stuff because we have three reels of that with all the improvisation stuff which we selected bits out of at the end and we couldn't find it but we thought the Mama bit was quite fun because it showed how the middle bit wasn't developed and there were a couple of little extra bits which were quite nice…"
At present; the most recent comments about the much discussed "reunion" of the classic Genesis line-up has come from Tony Banks and Phil Collins….

" I would have no particular qualms about it but there are no particular plans at the moment. I have to say that it is not something I am particularly itching to do one way or the other (laughs) but Phil always seems quite keen to do something and I think that Mike and I would probably be happy enough to do it…If you wanted to go back and do stuff with Peter… nightmare! (laughs) the Milton Keynes thing was bad enough… I am also not sure that it is quite the right moment …

I just don't think the band at the moment is very hot you know; but it may well happen in five years' time. I think the problem is that now no one really knows how to judge us because you have the Phil Collins sort of period and people tend to equate it with Phil's career and obviously; particularly in this country his career is seen as a bit iffy and then there is the Peter era which is more "deep" and it is all a bit schizophrenic and form where I stand it is something completely different. I only see the Genesis stuff … I am not that acquainted with everybody else's stuff and so it is a totally different career for me …"

Phil's explanation of his current tour also sheds some light on the prospects of a reunion tour by Genesis…

"Here I am, playing the songs and saying 'Goodbye'. So it is a kind of turning a page. Every night it gets very emotional at the end and at this stage it is the last tour but it isn't the LAST performance..."

The above comment does not effectively close the door to any further musical endeavour by Phil with either Mike or Tony in the future but it is has made the likelihood of the much talked about reunion tour an extremely unlikely event and perhaps the most telling comment about the prospects for the future of Genesis has come from Tony's recent TWR interview...

"We didn't need the hassle (of recording a follow-up to Calling All Stations) ... we could do things on our own...Mike has The Mechanics and I have had a chance to do this Classical thing, and I think there just comes a time really and it is possible that we have worked out what Mike and I can do together and that might have run its course now really. If we are going to work in that way where we are both writing at the same time and if we want to play on each other's pieces like we did in the early days that is slightly different I think but it is a certain way of writing and I did feel while we were doing Calling All Stations that I had run out of ways of playing chords against a repeated riff or bass and there are only so many chords you can use and I have done this too many times and I can't do this again..."

Mike and Tony's most recent comments on this subject do hold out a glimmer of hope for those fans craving a reunion however...

(Banks) "We never rule it out but there is nothing planned! I think the concept of doing something and playing some of this stuff is... it must be a possibility but there really is nothing planned... I think in fairness reunions are very dangerous things really because nothing ever quite lives up to how it was and I also think that you have got to ... and I know what you will say to this and with The Beatles to reform EVERYBODY wanted them to reform and I don't think with Genesis it is quite the same... Yes there are a certain number of people out there who would love it but others would say : 'Oh no, not them again!' and I think that we haven't quite got to a stage where ... I don't want to go out there and be pilloried all the time.."

(Rutherford) "The only people who have any input is... its down to us.."

Having said that, the band still managed to take everyone by surprise with the announcement at a Pan-European press conference held at the May Fair Hotel in London on 7th November 2006. There the band stated their intention to "turn it on again" one more time with a twenty date "selection of shows" through most if the major European territories in the summer of 2007. Fans were delighted at the news although some sceptics were more critical accusing the band of cashing in on the popularity of nostalgia at the moment. Sadly, from the plans announced at the conference, the band have no plans to record together again under the name "Genesis" but their revitalised back catalogue which is to be re-issued on the new 5.1 Surround Sound format in time for the tour should certainly generate some new interest.

The band always admitted that the line up that finished with the We Can't Dance album in 1992 had unfinished business to attend to and here at last they are ready to do exactly that. I certainly never thought I would see the band on a concert stage again in any form and so this is certainly something that this particular fan is looking forward to seeing and so let's hope that the band go out with a bang rather than a whimper and that they leave us with even more great memories than the thirty or so years that I already have under my belt – see you on the road next year somewhere guys!

Genesis UK Discography 1968 - 2004

Part One: 7" Vinyl singles

A- side title	B- side title	Catalogue number	Release Date
The silent Sun	That's me	Decca F12735	2.2.68
A winter's tale	**One-eyed hound**	Decca F12775	?.3.69
Where the sour turns to sweet	In hiding	Decca F12949	27.6.69
The knife (Pt1)	The knife (Pt2)	Charisma CB152 (PS)	?.9.71
Happy the man	Seven Stones	Charisma CB181 (PS)	12.5.72
I know what I like	**Twilight Alehouse**	Charisma CB224	?.10.73

Twilight Alehouse
(one-sided flexi disc issued free with October 1973 issue of "Zig Zag" magazine and subsequently re-issued as free single to first 1000 members of the Genesis Information fan club in 1976)

Counting out time	Riding the scree	Charisma CB238	1.11.74
The Carpet Crawlers	**The Waiting Room (Evil jam live)**	Charisma CB251	18.4.75
A trick of the tail	Ripples	Charisma CB277	?.3.76
Your own special way	**It's yourself**	Charisma CB300	?.2.76
Match of the day	**Pigeons/Inside & Out**	Charisma GEN001 (PS)	?.5.77
Follow you follow me	Ballad of big	Charisma CB309 (PS)	?.3.78
Many too many	**The day the light went out/Vancouver**		
		Charisma CB315 (PS)	?.6.78
Turn it on again	Behind the lines (Pt2)	Charisma CB356	?.3.80
Duchess	**Open door**	Charisma CB363 (PS)	?.5.80
Misunderstanding	**Evidence of autumn**	Charisma CB369 (PS)	?.8.80
Abacab	Another record	Charisma CB388 (PS)	?.8.81
Keep it dark	**Naminanu**	Charisma CB391 (PS)	?.10.81
Man on the corner	**Submarine**	Charisma CB393 (PS)	?.3.82
Paperlate	**You might recall/Me & Virgil**	Charisma GEN1 (PS)	?.5.82

The lady lies (Live)
(One- sided flexi disc free with June 1982 issue of "Flexipop" magazine)   ?.5.83

Firth of fifth (live)
(One-sided flexidisc issued free to members of "Genesis Information" in May 1983 with limited edition numbered sleeve)   ?.8.82

Mama	It's gonna get better	Charisma/Virgin MAMA1 (PS)	?.9.83
That's all	Taking it all too hard	Charisma/Virgin TATA1 (PS)	?.11.83
That's all	Taking it all too hard	Charisma/Virgin TATA-Y1 (Picture disc)	?.11.83
Illegal Alien	**Turn it on again (live)**	Charisma/Virgin AL1 (PS)	23.1.84
Illegal Alien	**Turn it on again (live)**	Charisma/Virgin ALS1 (Picture disc)	23.1.84
Invisible touch	The last domino	Virgin GENS1 (PS)	19.5.86
Invisible touch	The last domino	Virgin GENSY1 (PS)	19.5.86

(White vinyl limited edition with fold -out sleeve)

In too deep	**Do the neurotic (Edit)**	Virgin GENS2 (PS)	?.8.86
Land of confusion	**Feeding the fire**	Virgin GENS3 (PS)	?.10.86
Tonight, tonight ,tonight	In the glow of the night	Virgin GENS4 (PS)	?.1.87
Throwing it all away	**I'd rather be you**	Virgin GENS5 (PS)	?.5.87
No son of mine	Living forever	Virgin GENS6 (PS)	21.10.91
I can't dance	**On the shoreline**	Virgin GENS7 (PS)	30.12.91
Hold on my heart	Way of the world	Virgin GENS8 (PS)	6.4.92
Jesus he knows me	**Hearts on fire**	Virgin GENS9 (PS)	13.7.92
Invisible touch (Live)	Abacab (Live)	Virgin GENS10 (PS)	9.11.92

(Initially issued as a limited edition with photo booklet and numbered sleeve)

Tell me why (Live)	Dreaming while you sleep (Live)	Virgin GENS11 (PS)	9.11.92

Part Two: 12" Vinyl Singles

A-Side	B-Side	Catalogue number	Release Date
Keep it dark	**Naminanu**/Abacab (album version)	Charisma CB391-12 (PS)	?.10.81
Mama	It's gonna get better	Charisma/Virgin MAMA1-12 (PS)	?.8.83
That's all	Taking it all too hard/**Firth of fifth (live)**	Charisma/Virgin TATA1-12 (PS)	?.10.83
Illegal Alien	**Turn it on again (Full live version)**	Charisma/Virgin AL1-12 (PS)	23.1.84
Invisible Touch (Extended)	Invisible touch/The last domino	Virgin GENS1-12 (PS)	19.5.86
In too deep	**Do the neurotic (Unedited)**	Virgin GENS2-12 (PS)	?.8.86
In too deep	**Do the neurotic (Unedited)**	Virgin GENSY 2-12 (Picture disc)	?.8.86
Land of confusion (remix)	Land of confusion/**Feeding the fire**	Virgin GENS3-12 (PS)	?.10.86
Tonight, tonight, tonight (Edit)/In the glow of the night	**Paperlate/Tonight, tonight , tonight (Remix)**	Virgin GENS4-12 (PS)	?.3.87
Tonight, tonight , tonight (Edit)/In the glow of the night	**Tonight, tonight, tonight (12" Remix)**	Virgin GENS412 (PS)	?.3.87

(Limited edition with gatefold sleeve and European tour map issued in time for UK tour dates)

Throwing it all away(Live)	**I'd rather be you/Invisible touch (Live)**	Virgin GENS5-12 (PS)	?.5.87
No son of mine	Living forever/**Invisible touch (live)**	Virgin GENS6-12 (PS)	21.10.91

(Limited edition with gatefold sleeve and watercolour print)

Part Three: Compact Disc singles.

Match of the day/Pigeons/Inside & Out	Virgin CDT40 (PS)	?.?.91
Mama (Long version)/It's gonna get better (Long version)	Virgin CDT5 (PS)	?.?.91
Land of confusion/**Land of confusion(extended version)/Feeding the Fire/Do the neurotic**	Virgin SNEG3-12 (PS)	?.10.86
Tonight, tonight, tonight (edit)/In the glow of the night/Paperlate/ **Tonight, tonight , tonight (12" remix)** Domino (live)	Virgin DRAW412 (PS)	?.3.87

(Limited edition with first 5000 copies of the "Invisible Touch Tour" live video) ?.5.87

No son of mine/Living forever/**Invisible touch (live)**	Virgin GENDG6 (PS)*	21.10.91
I can't dance/**On the shoreline/In too deep(Live)/That's all (Live)**	Virgin GENDG7 (PS)*	30.12.91

(Limited edition with pocket biography)

I can't dance/**On the shoreline/I can't dance (Sex mix)**	Virgin GENSD7 (PS)	6.1.92
Hold on my heart/Way of the world/**Your own special way (Live)**	Virgin GENDG8 (PS)*	6.4.92

(Limited edition with artwork postcard set)

Hold on my heart/Way of the world/**Home by the sea(live)/Second Home by the sea(live)**	Virgin GENSD8 (PS)*	13.4.92
Jesus he knows me (single mix)/Hearts on fire/Land of confusion (Rehearsal version)	Virgin GENDX9 (PS)*	13.7.92
Jesus he knows me(Single mix)/Hearts on fire/I can't dance (The Other Mix)	Virgin GENDG9 (PS)	20.7.92

(* these discs combined to form "The Invisible Series" which was housed in a slip case available with the final volume)

Invisible touch(live)/Abacab(live)/The Brazilian (live)	Virgin GENDX10 (PS)	9.11.92

(Issued as a limited edition numbered edition with box and photo booklet)

Tell me why/**Dreaming while you sleep(Live)/Turn it on again (1992 live)**	Virgin GENDG11 (PS)	8.2.93
Tell me why/**Dreaming while you sleep (Live)/Tonight, tonight, tonight (Full live version)**	Virgin GENDX11 (PS)	15.2.93
Congo (Edit)/Papa he said/Banjo man	Virgin GENSD12 (PS)	28.8.97
Congo (Edit)/Second home by the sea(edit)	Virgin GENSDX12 (PS)	28.8.97

(Limited edition with enhanced CD Rom footage and promotional video for "Congo")

Shipwrecked/**Phret(Instrumental)/7/8 (Instrumental)**	Virgin GENSD14 (PS)	1.12.97
Shipwrecked/**No son of mine + (live)/Lover's leap + (Live)/Turn it on again + (live)**	Virgin GENDX14 (PS)	8.12.97
Not about us (Edit)/Anything now/Sign your life away/Run out of time	Virgin GENSD15 (PS)	23.2.98

Not about us (Edit)/Dancing with the moonlit knight (Live)/Follow you follow me (Live)/Not about us (Extended version)

Virgin GENDX15 (PS) 23.2.98

The lamb lies down on Broadway (live)/It (live)/Counting out time (live)/Carpet crawlers (live)/Dancing with the moonlit knight (live)/I know what I like (live)/**Happy the man**/Watcher of the skies (Re-mixed edited version)/**In the wilderness (without strings)/Shepherd/Twilight Alehouse**/Supper's ready (live)

Virgin G Box 98   (PS)   ?.9.98

(Limited edition ten track promotional sampler from the "Genesis Archive 1967 -1975" four CD set)

Carpet Crawlers 99

Virgin CRAWL CDJ 8 (PS) ?.5.99

(1 track promotional single for Turn It On Again - The Hits album)

You Might Recall/Evidence Of Autumn/Inside & Out/I Can't Dance 12"/Illegal Alien (Live)/Deep In The Motherlode (Live)/Ripples (Live)/The Brazilian (Live)/Entangled (Live)/Vancouver/It's Yourself/**Mama (work in progress)**.

Virgin CDBOXDJ 7 (PS) ?.6.00

(Limited edition 12 track sampler from "Genesis Archive #2 1976 - 1992" three CD set)

Tracks in **bold** type are non album tracks.
PS denotes singles issued with a picture sleeve.
+ These tracks were recorded at the bands acoustic launch for **"Calling all Stations"** at Cape Canaveral **Space Centre 26.8.97.**
# These tracks were recorded at the RTL studios Paris 17.11.97.

Part Four: Vinyl and Compact Disc Albums.

Album Title	Catalogue Number	Release Date
From Genesis to Revelation	Decca SKL4990 (Stereo edition)	?.3.69
From Genesis to Revelation	Decca LK4990 (Mono edition)	
Rock Roots	Decca ROOTS 1	1976
From Genesis to Revelation	Music Club MCCD133 (CD)	
(This is only one of numerous re-issues on both vinyl and compact disc of this first album)		
Trespass	Charisma CAS1020	21.10.70
Trespass	Charisma/Virgin CASCD1020 (CD)	
Trespass	Virgin CASCD1020 (CD) (*)	
Trespass	Virgin CASCDX 1020 (Re-mastered CD edition)	
Nursery Cryme	Charisma CAS1052	20.11.71
Nursery Cryme	Charisma/Virgin CASCD1052 (CD)	
Nursery Cryme	Virgin CASCD1052 (CD) (*)	
Nursery Cryme	Virgin CASCDX1052 (Re-mastered CD edition)	
Foxtrot	Charisma CAS 1058	21.10.72
Foxtrot	Charisma/Virgin CASCD1058 (CD)	
Foxtrot	Virgin CASCD1058 (CD) (*)	
Foxtrot	Virgin CASCDX 1058 (Re-mastered CD edition)	
Genesis Live	Charisma CLASS 1	?.8.73
Genesis Live	Charisma/Virgin CLACD1 (CD)	
Genesis Live	Virgin CLACDX 1 (Re-mastered CD edition)	
Selling England By The Pound	Charisma CAS1074	?.9.73
Selling England By The Pound	Charisma/Virgin CASCD1074 (CD)	
Selling England By The Pound	Virgin CASCD1074 (CD) (*)	
Selling England By The Pound	Virgin CASCDX1074 (Re-mastered CD edition)	
The Lamb Lies Down On Broadway	Charisma CDS101	?.11..74
The Lamb Lies Down On Broadway	Charisma/Virgin CGSCD101 (CD)	
The Lamb Lies Down On Broadway	Virgin CGSCD101 (CD) (*)	
The Lamb Lies Down On Broadway	Virgin CGSCDX101 (Re-mastered CD edition)	

(*) Discs marked are part of either Volume One or Two of two picture disc edition sets released by Virgin in 1991 with the catalogue numbers TPAK1 and TPAK17 respectively.

A Trick Of The Tail	Charisma CDS4001	13.2.76
A Trick Of The Tail	Virgin CDSCD4001 (CD)	
A Trick Of The Tail	Virgin CDSCDX4001 (Re-mastered CD edition)	
Wind & Wuthering	Charisma CDS4005	23.12.76
Wind & Wuthering	Virgin CDSCD4005 (CD)	
Wind & Wuthering	Virgin CDSCDX 4005 (Re-mastered CD edition)	
Seconds Out	Charisma GE2001	2.10.77
Seconds Out	Virgin GECD2001 (CD)	
Seconds Out	VirginGECDX2001 (Re-mastered CD edition)	
And Then There Were Three	Charisma CDS4010	?.3.78
And Then There Were Three	Virgin CDSCD4010 (CD)	
And Then There Were Three	Virgin CDSCDX4010 (Re-mastered CD edition)	
Duke	CharismaCBR101	12.3.80
Duke	Virgin CBRCD101 (CD)	
Duke	Virgin CBRCDX101 (Re-mastered CD edition)	
Abacab	Charisma CBR102	15.9.81
Abacab	Virgin CBRCD102 (CD)	
Abacab	Virgin CBRCDX102 (Re-mastered CD edition)	
Three Sides Live	Virgin/Charisma GE2002	3.6.82
Three Sides Live	Virgin/Charisma GECD2002 (CD)	
Three Sides Live	Virgin GECDX2002 (Re-mastered CD edition)	
Genesis	Charisma/Virgin GENLP1	8.9.83
Genesis	Charisma/Virgin GENCD1 (CD)	
Invisible Touch	Virgin GENLP2	15.6.86
Invisible Touch	Virgin GENCD2 (CD)	
We Can't Dance	Virgin GENLP3	11.11.91
We Can't Dance	Virgin GENCD3 (CD)	
The Way We Walk Volume One:The Shorts	Virgin GENLP4	16.11.92
The Way We Walk Volume One:The Shorts	Virgin GENCD4 (CD)	
The Way We Walk Volume TwoThe Longs	Virgin GENLP5	9.1.93
The Way We Walk Volume Two:The Longs	Virgin GENCD5 (CD)	
Calling All Stations	Virgin GENLP6	2.9.97

(Released as limited edition with three sided record and a fourth vinyl side etched with a picture of the band)

Calling All Stations	Virgin GENCD6 (CD)	
Genesis Archive 1967-1975	Virgin GENBOX6 (CD)	15.6.98
Genesis BBC Recordings (2 CD set)	Virgin (No Catalogue number)	

(Promotional double CD set comprising all of the band's BBC live/studio sessions 1970 -72)

Trespass	VirginVJCP -68091 (CD) +	29.3.99
Nursery Cryme	Virgin VJCP-68092 (CD) +	29.3.99
Foxtrot	Virgin VJCP-68093 (CD) +	29.3.99
Genesis Live	Virgin VJCP-68094 (CD) +	29.3.99
Selling England By The Pound	Virgin VJCP-68095 (CD) +	29.3.99
The Lamb Lies Down On Broadway	Virgin VJCP-68096-97 (CD) +	29.3.99
A Trick Of The Tail	Virgin VJCP-68098 (CD) +	29.3.99
Wind & Wuthering	Virgin VJCP-68099 (CD) +	29.3.99
Seconds Out	Virgin VJCP-68100-01 (CD) +	29.3.99
And Then There Were Three	Virgin VJCP-68102 (CD) +	29.3.99
Duke	Virgin VJCP-68103 (CD) +	29.3.99
Abacab	Virgin VJCP-68104 (CD) +	29.3.99
Three Sides Live	Virgin VJCP-68105-06 (CD) +	29.3.99
Genesis	Virgin VJCP-68107 (CD) +	29.3.99
Invisible Touch	Virgin VJCP-68108 (CD) +	29.3.99
We Can't Dance	Virgin VJCP-68109 (CD) +	29.3.99
The Way We Walk Volume One: The Shorts	Virgin VJCP-68110 (CD) +	29.3.99
The Way We Walk Volume Two: The Longs	Virgin VJCP-68111 (CD) +	29.3.99
Calling All Stations	Virgin VJCP-68112 (CD) +	29.3.99

Turn It On Again - The Hits	Virgin GENCD7 (CD)	25.10.99
Genesis Archive #2 1976 -1992	Virgin GEN BOX 7 (CD)	6.11..00
Genesis - The Platinum Collection	EMI 72438 637302 1 (CD)	29.11.04

(+) These are the Japanese limited editions of the Genesis catalogue complete with fully restored artwork and centre labels as on the original vinyl albums.
All release dates listed here and for the following solo artists' discographies are the release dates for the original versions of albums etc, and not the subsequent re-issues unless these are known.

GENESIS: A CHRONOLOGY

The following is a somewhat brief guide to the key events in the history of Genesis and the band's various solo off-shoots over the last thirty or so years.

February 12th 1950:	Stephen Richard Hackett born.
February 13th 1950:	Peter Brian Gabriel born.
March 27th 1950:	Anthony George Banks born.
October 2nd 1950:	Michael John Cleote Crawford Rutherford born.
January 30th 1951:	Philip David Charles Collins born.
December 23rd 1951:	Anthony Edwin Phillips born.
September 1963:	Peter Gabriel and Tony Banks enter Charterhouse.
September 1964:	Mike Rutherford enters Charterhouse
April 1965:	Anthony Phillips enters Charterhouse.
December 16th 1965:	Anon perform their first gig at Charterhouse.
Summer 1966:	Anon record "Pennsylvania Flickhouse" at Tony Pike Sound.
1st August 1967:	Genesis (un-named) sign publishing contract with Jonjo Music.
30th August 1967:	Genesis appoint Jonjo Music as their management company.
2nd February 1968:	The Silent Sun single released by Decca Records.
15th May 1968:	A Winter's tale single released by Decca Records.
8th September 1968:	Ray Wilson born.
March 1969:	From Genesis to Revelation album released by Decca records.
27th June 1969:	Where the sour turns to sweet single released.
23rd September 1969:	Genesis' first gig at Mrs Balme's dance Chobham.

October 1969: Guide me Orion (Flaming Youth's first single) released on Fontana Records

November 1969: Ark Two album released by Flaming Youth (featuring Phil Collins) released on Fontana Records.

4th November 1969:	Genesis' first "Professional" gig at Brunel University.
22nd February 1970:	BBC "Night Ride" Session recorded.

February 1970: The Road album released by Quiet World (featuring Steve and John Hackett) released by Dawn Records.

March 1970:	Genesis sign to Charisma Records.
11th March 1970:	Genesis gig at the Roundhouse London filmed.
July 18th 1970:	Anthony Phillips' last gig with Genesis at Haywards Heath.
August 8th 1970:	Phil Collins joins Genesis.
21st October 1970:	Trespass album released on Charisma Records.
January 1971:	Steve Hackett joins Genesis.
February 1971:	First Charisma Package tour of UK.

March 7th 1971: Genesis' first gig overseas at "La Ferme" Woluwe St Lambert Belgium.

26th June 1971:	Genesis appear at the Reading Festival for the first time.
September 1971:	The Knife single released.
November 20th 1971:	Nursery Cryme album released.
April 1972:	Genesis' first overseas tour in Italy.
May 26th 1972:	Great Western Festival Lincoln.
October 21st 1972:	Foxtrot album released.
December 16th 1972:	Genesis' first US gig at Brandeis University Boston.
April/May 1973:	Genesis' first headlining tours of Europe.
June 1973:	Genesis Live album released.
17th June 1973:	Zox and the Radar Boys gig Aylesbury (featuring Phil)
October 1973:	Selling England by the Pound album released.
October 1973:	Silver Song single recorded at Island Studios.
30th &31st October 1973:	Genesis record the "In Concert" film at Shepperton Studios
December 1973:	Genesis' first US tour.
February 1974:	I know what I like released as single charts at no 19 in the UK.
January/May 1974:	Genesis' first headlining tours of the USA and Europe.
November 1974:	The lamb lies down on Broadway album released.
November 20th 1974:	First gig of The Lamb… tour in the USA.
February 19th 1975:	First European gig of The Lamb… tour.
May 25th 1975:	Last gig of The Lamb… tour.
August 18th 1975:	Peter Gabriel announces his departure from Genesis.
August 1975:	Steve Hackett's first solo album; Voyage of the Acolyte released.
September 1975:	Beyond an empty dream album released featuring the hymn "Take

This Heart" composed by Anthony Phillips/Mike Rutherford

December 1975:	Brand X first gig at London School of Economics
13th February 1976:	A trick of the tail album released.
March 30th 1976:	First gig of the "A trick of the tail" tour in London Ontario.
11th July 1976:	Last gig of the "A Trick…" tour at Bingley Hall Stafford England.
July 1976:	Unorthodox behaviour Brand X's first album released.
31st December 1976:	Dress rehearsal gig at the Rainbow Theatre London

January 1st 1977: Wind & Wuthering album released and band commence world tour with a series of sell-out shows at The Rainbow Theatre in London

February 1977:	Peter Gabriel releases self-titled first solo album.
March 1977:	Anthony Phillips's first solo album: "The Geese & The Ghost" released.
March 1977:	Solsbury Hill first solo single from Peter Gabriel reaches no 13 in the UK charts.
5th March 1977:	Peter Gabriel's first solo gig at Passaic New Jersey USA.
April 1977:	Moroccan Roll album released.
May 1977:	Genesis play their first gigs in South America.
3rd July 1977:	Last gig of Genesis' "Wind & Wuthering" world tour in Munich.
8th October 1977:	Steve Hackett announces his departure from Genesis.
15th October 1977:	Seconds Out live album released.
November 1977:	Livestock album released.

March 1978: Follow you follow me released becoming Genesis' biggest hit reaching number 7 in the UK chart.

30th March 1978:	Genesis begin their massive "And then there were three" world tour
April 1978:	And then there were three album released.
May 1978:	Steve Hackett's second solo album: Please don't touch released.
June 1978:	Peter Gabriel's second solo album released.
June 1978:	Anthony Phillips' second solo album: Wise after the event released.
24th June 1978:	Genesis headline the Knebworth Park Festival.
August 1978:	Peter Gabriel's second solo tour begins in UK.

24th December 1978: "Rob & Gab" Christmas show featuring Peter Gabriel and Tom Robinson at Hammersmith Odeon London

August 1979: Peter premieres material from his third solo album at the Reading and Glastonbury Festivals.

September 1979:	Brand X "Product" album released.
September 1979:	Tony Banks' first solo album: "A curious feeling" released.
September 1979:	Steve Hackett releases "Spectral Mornings" album.
September 1979:	Anthony Phillips releases "Sides" album.
February 1980:	Mike Rutherford's first solo album: "Smallcreeps day" released.
February 1980:	Games without frontiers single released (video banned by BBC).
21st February 1980:	Peter starts his tour in support of his third solo album in Oxford.
3rd March 1980:	Turn it on again single released.
17th March 1980:	"Duke" tour begins at the Festival Hall Paignton.
March 1980:	Steve Hackett releases the Defector album.
March 1980:	Defector tour starts in UK.
28th March 1980:	Duke album released.
June 1980:	Private Parts & Pieces II: Back to the Pavilion released.
December 1980:	In the air tonight single released reaching no 2 position in UK chart.
11th February 1981:	Face Value Phil Collins' first solo album released.
March 1981:	Anthony Phillips' 1984 album released.
August 1981:	Abacab single released.
September 1981:	Abacab album released.
25th September 1981:	Genesis commence Abacab tour in Barcelona Spain.
23rd December 1981:	Final show of Abacab tour at the NEC Birmingham.
3rd May 1982:	3 x 3 ep released.
16th -18th June 1982:	First WOMAD Festival Shepton Mallet.
July 1982:	Private Parts & Pieces III: Antiques released.
August 1982:	Mike Rutherford's second solo album: Acting very strange released.
2nd August 1982:	Genesis commence the Three Sides Live tour in Peoria USA.
August 1982:	Three Sides Live album released.
6th September 1982:	Shock the monkey single released.
September 1982:	Peter Gabriel's fourth solo album released.
September 1982:	Phil Collins' second solo album: Hello, I must be going" released.
2nd October 1982:	"Six of the best" reunion concert at Milton Keynes Concert Bowl.
28th October 1982:	Peter Gabriel commences tour in support of his fourth solo album
21st November 1982:	Phil's first solo gig at Den Haag Holland.
April 1983	Steve Hackett releases Highly Strung album.
15th April 1983:	Tony Banks releases "Wicked Lady" soundtrack.

19th April 1983:	Highly Strung tour commences in Worthing UK
June 1983:	Peter Gabriel "Plays Live" album released.
September 1983:	Anthony Phillips's musical "Alice" opens in Leeds.
September 1983:	Anthony Phillips' "Invisible Men" album released in USA.
24th September 1983:	Genesis release "Genesis" album.
26th October 1983:	Steve Hackett releases Bay of Kings album tour of UK universities
7th November 1983:	First gig of the "Mama Tour" at Normal Illinois USA.
29th February 1984:	Last gig of "Mama Tour" at the NEC Birmingham UK.
May 1984:	Anthony Phillips' "Invisible Men" album released in UK.
August 1984:	Anthony Phillips' Private Parts & Pieces IV released.
August 1984:	Steve Hackett's Till we have faces album released.
October 1984:	Anthony Phillips' Private Parts & Pieces V released.
12th February 1985:	No Jacket Required album released.
14th February 1985:	No Jacket Required tour starts in Nottingham UK.
March 1985:	Mike + The Mechanics debut album released.
May 1985:	Anthony Phillips' Harvest of the heart compilation album released.
May 1985:	Peter Gabriel releases the "Birdy" soundtrack.
13th June 1985:	Live Aid Wembley Stadium and JFK Stadium Philadelphia.
August 1985:	Anthony Phillips' Private Parts & Pieces V album released
3rd October 1985:	No Jacket Required tour ends in New York USA.
March 1986:	GTR debut album released.
May 1986:	Peter Gabriel releases "So" album.
May 1986:	Tony Banks releases "Soundtracks" album.
June 1986:	Invisible Touch single released.
June 1986:	Peter takes part in the "Conspiracy of Hope" tour of USA.
June 1986: Mike Rutherford's first solo tour with the Mechanics the "Miracle Tour" commences in the USA	
10th September 1986:	Invisible Touch album released.
17th September 1986:	Invisible Touch World Tour commences in Detroit USA.
17th September 1986:	Peter Gabriel plays concert at the U N Building in New York.
7th November 1986:	Peter Gabriel commences the "This way up" tour in Rochester N Y
November 23rd to December 17th 1986:	Genesis play first ever gigs in Australia and New Zealand.
20th and 21st December 1986:	Peter Gabriel plays benefit gigs in Tokio Japan.
July 4th 1987:	Genesis' "Invisible Touch" world tour ends at Wembley Stadium UK.
August 1987:	Anthony Phillips' Private Parts & Pieces VII released.
October 30th 1987:	Peter Gabriel's "This way up" tour ends in Athens Greece.
25th April 1988:	Steve Hackett commences tour in support of new "Momentum" album.
May 1988:	Steve Hackett releases the "Momentum" album.
August 1988:	Phil stars in "Buster" film with Julie Walters.
2nd September 1988:	Peter takes part in the "Human Rights Now!" Amnesty International tour
15th October 1988:	"Human Rights Now!" tour ends in Buenos Aires Argentina.
November 1988:	Mike + The Mechanics' second album "The Living years" released.
November 18th 1988:	Anthony Phillips releases the "Tarka" album.
22nd February 1989:	Mike + The Mechanics' first UK/European tour commences.
14th August 1989:	Tony Banks releases the "Bankstatement" album
September 1989 :	Peter Gabriel releases the "Passion" soundtrack to Martin Scorsese's "Last Temptation Of Christ film
21st November 1989:	Phil Collins releases the "But Seriously" album.
December 1989:	Anthony Phillips releases "Missing Links Volume 1" album
16th April 1990:	Phil Collins commences the "But Seriously" world tour in Brussels
November 1990:	Peter Gabriel releases the "Shaking the tree" compilation album.
25thMarch 1991:	Mike + The Mechanics' "Word of mouth" album released.
7th June 1991:	Tony Banks releases the "Still" album.
21st November 1991:	Genesis release the "We can't dance" album.
16th May 1992:	"We can't dance" tour begins.
2nd August 1992:	"We can't dance" tour ends.
10th August 1992:	Steve Hackett begins first tour of USA in almost four years.
24th August 1992:	Anthony Phillips releases Private Parts & Pieces VIII: "New England".
21st September 1992:	Peter Gabriel releases "Us" album.
23rd October 1992:	Genesis begin series of provincial UK theatre shows at Southampton Mayflower Theatre
2nd to 8th November 1992:	Genesis play six shows at Earls Court Arena London.
16th November 1992:	Genesis release "The way we walk Volume One: The Shorts" album.
17th November 1992:	Genesis' last theatre show at the Civic Hall Wolverhampton.

11th January 1993:	Genesis release "The Way we walk Volume Two: The Longs" album.
13th April 1993;	Peter Gabriel commences "Secret World" tour in Stockholm Sweden.
17th May 1993:	Steve Hackett releases "Guitar Noir" album.
21st May 1993:	Steve Hackett commences first UK tour in five years at Liverpool's
Neptune Theatre	
18th September 1993:	Phil's last gig with Genesis at Cowdrey Ruins.
2nd November 1993:	Phil Collins releases "Both Sides" album.
April 1st 1994:	Phil's "Both Sides" world tour commences in Utrecht Holland.
May 1994:	Anthony Phillips releases the "Sail the world" soundtrack.
June 1994:	Anthony Phillips releases "Missing Links Volume Two: The Sky Road" album.
14th August 1994;	Peter Gabriel's "Secret World" tour ends at Saugerties NY
15th August 1994:	Genesis re-issue "Trespass" to " The lamb lies down on Broadway"
re-mastered albums.	
19th September 1994:	Steve Hackett releases "Blues with a feeling" album.
4th October 1994:	Genesis re-issue "A trick of the tail" to "Three Sides Live" re-
mastered albums	
24th November 1994:	Steve Hackett commences Italian tour at Congeliano Veneto.
January 1995:	Anthony Phillips releases "Gypsy Suite" album.
February 1995:	Mike + The Mechanics release "Beggar on a beach of gold" album.
17th March 1995:	The second leg of Phil Collins' "Both Sides" world tour titled "The Far Side" tour commences in Johannesburg South Africa
May 15th 1995:	Phil Collins' "Far Side" tour end in Manila.
3rd June 1995:	Mike + The Mechanics commence their "Beggar on a beach of gold" tour in Durban South Africa
August 1995:	Anthony Phillips releases "Anthology" album.
August 1995:	Steve Hackett releases "There are many sides to the night" album.
11th September 1995:	Tony Banks releases "Strictly Inc" album.
16th October 1995:	Anthony Phillips releases "Echoes" album.
28thFebruary 1996;	Mike + The Mechanics commence their UK "Hits" tour in Belfast.
4thMarch 1996;	Mike + The Mechanics "Hits" album released.
29th March 1996:	Press announcement detailing Phil's departure from Genesis.
June 1996:	GTR release "King Biscuit Flower Hour" live album.
11th July 1996:	Phil Collins commences first Big Band Jazz tour at the Royal Albert Hall London
22nd August 1996:	Anthony Phillips releases Private Parts & Pieces IX album.
September 1996:	Anthony Phillips releases "The Meadows of Englewood" album.
October 1996:	Steve Hackett releases "Genesis Revisited" album
21st November 1996:	Phil Collins releases "Dance into the light" album.
December 16th to	
December 20th 1996:	Steve Hackett performs handful of shows in Japan
28th February 1997:	Phil Collins commences the "Dance into the light" tour at Tampa
Florida USA	
6th June 1997:	Genesis announce Ray Wilson as replacement for Phil also announcing
title of new album:	Calling All Stations and 1997/98 Tour plans
26th July 1997:	Anthony Phillips releases "Survival the music of nature" album.
15th August 1997:	Congo single released.
26th August 1997:	Genesis play acoustic promotional show in Berlin.
28th August 1997:	Genesis play acoustic promotional show in Florida.
August 1997:	Anthony Phillips releases "Live Radio Sessions" album.
2nd September 1997:	Genesis release "Calling all stations" album.
September 1997:	Steve Hackett releases "A Midsummer night's dream" album.
22nd September 1997:	Steve Hackett releases UK version of "Genesis revisited".
22nd October 1997:	Anthony Phillips releases "Missing Links Three album.
15th November 1997:	Genesis radio show Hotel Richmond Copenhagen Denmark.
13th December 1997:	Genesis radio show at RTL Studios Paris France.
23rd January 1998:	Genesis play first full gig with Ray Wilson at Bray Studios
28th January 1998:	First gig of "Calling all stations" tour in Prague
25th February 1998:	First UK gig of "Calling all stations" tour at NEC Birmingham.
5th April 1998:	Final gig of "Calling all stations" tour in Helsinki Finland.
11th May 1998:	Genesis "reunion" at Heathrow Airport London for promotion of "Genesis Archive 1967-75 box set
30th May 1998:	Genesis perform at the "Rock in Ring" Festival Germany.
31st May 1998:	Genesis perform at the "Rock in Park" Festival Germany.
12th June 1998:	Phil Collins commences his second Big Band Jazz tour in USA.

22nd June 1998:	Genesis "Archive 1967-75" 4cd set released.
24th July 1998:	Phil's last Big Band show at the Symphony Hall Birmingham UK.
6th September 1998:	"Strictly Banks" concert Orchard Theatre Dartford.
5th October 1998:	Phil Collins "Greatest Hits" album released.
November 1998:	Anthony Phillips' "Archive Collection Volume One" album released.
8th February 1999:	"Another Day" first single by Ray Wilson's band 'Cut' released.
8th March 1999:	"Millionairhead" first solo album by Ray Wilson's band 'Cut' released.
5th April 1999:	Virgin Japan re-issue their entire Genesis back catalogue as limited edition CDs.
27th April 1999:	Cut's first gig at Room at the Top night club Bathgate Scotland.
30th April 1999:	Cut's tour as "Special Guests" of The Scorpions begins at Deggendorf
Germany	
26th April 1999:	Steve Hackett releases his "Darktown" album.
10th May 1999:	Mike + The Mechanics showcase gig for new album
13th May 1999:	First date of Mike +The Mechanics' UK tour in York
17th May 1999:	"Now that you've gone" first single released.
24th May 1999:	"A Hot night in Paris" Phil Collins' Big Band Jazz live album released.
24th May 1999:	"A Joyful Noise" Chester Thompson's solo album re-released.
31st May 1999:	"M6" 5th studio album by Mike & The Mechanics released.
15th August 1999:	"Whenever I stop" second single from the "M6" album released in UK.
25th October 1999:	"Turn it on again - The Hits" Genesis greatest hits album released
1st November 1999:	"Private Parts & Pieces X: Soiree" album by Anthony Phillips released.
1st May 2000:	"Sketches Of Satie" album by Steve and John Hackett released.
12th June 2000:	Peter Gabriel's Ovo album released.
9th July 2000:	First gig of Steve Hackett's Italian tour at the Vivegano Festival.
15th July 2000:	Last gig of Steve Hackett's Italian tour at the Arena Stella Maris Pescara.
15th July 2000:	Death of Paul Young, singer with Mike & The Mechanics.
21st September 2000:	Genesis "reunion" with Phil Collins at awards dinner for Tony Smith.
9th October 2000:	Steve Hackett releases the Feedback '86 album.
6th November 2000:	Genesis Archive II Box set released.
28th June 2001:	Steve Hackett begins South American Tour in Venezuela.
May 2001:	Genesis Songbook Video/DVD released.
September 2001:	Peter Gabriel performs concert for WOMAD in Seattle.
22nd July 2001:	Steve Hackett concludes South American Tour in Mexico.
12th November 2001:	Steve Hackett Live Archive 4 CD Box set released.
26th November 2001:	Genesis release " The Way We Walk Live In Concert" double DVD.
December 2001:	Ray Wilson "Unplugged" live CD released.
January 2002:	Steve Hackett performs acoustic shows in Tokio and Budapest.
March 2002:	Steve Hackett Genesis Files CD released.
23rd-28th April 2002:	Steve Hackett Italian tour.
September 2002:	The Barry Williams Show PeterGabriel's first single in eight years released.
23rd September 2002:	Peter Gabriel releases UP , his first solo album in ten years.
20th October - 2nd November 2002:	Steve Hackett tour of Italy and Malta.
28th October 2002:	Phil Collins' Can't Stop Loving You, single released.
3rd November 2002:	Peter Gabriel commences US leg of the "Growing Up" tour in Mexico
4th November 2002:	Phil Collins - A Life Less Ordinary documentary broadcast by BBC.
11th November 2002:	Phil Collins' Testify album released.
9th December 2002:	Steve Hackett "Somewhere In South America" live video released.
9th December 2002:	Steve Hackett "Somewhere In South America" live double CD released.
18th December 2002:	Peter Gabriel concludes the US leg of the "Growing Up Tour in Vancouver
30th December 2002:	Peter Gabriel releases "More Than This" single.
23rd January 2003:	Mike Rutherford featured on BBC TV's "This Is Your Life"
17th February 2003:	Steve Hackett "Somewhere In South America" DVD/CD released
17th March 2003:	Phil Collins releases The Least You Can Do single
23rd April 2003:	Ray Wilson releases Change his first solo album
24th April 2003:	Peter Gabriel commences European tour in Stockholm Sweden.
April 2003:	Anthony Phillips issues Intergalactic Touring Band archive album.
22nd May 2003:	Peter Gabriel ends the European tour in London England.
7th June 2003:	Peter Gabriel commences second US "Growing Up"
9th June 2003:	Steve Hackett releases To Watch The Storms album
2nd July 2003:	Peter Gabriel ends his second US "Growing Up" tour
5th July 2003:	Steve Hackett performs acoustic show at the Guilfest Festival Guildford
July 2003:	Anthony Phillips re-issues "Intergalactic Touring Band" album.
July 2003:	Steve Hackett releases NEARfest 2002 double live CD

July 2003:	Anthony Phillips reissues "Radio Clyde Session" archival album.
July 2003:	Steve Hackett releases "Hungarian Horizons" CD/DVD live recording.
27th September 2003:	Steve Hackett tour starts in Tilburg Holland
October 2003:	Peter Gabriel "Hit" album and "Growing Up Live" DVD released.
14th November 2003:	Steve Hackett concludes his European tour in Krakow Poland.
17th November 2003:	Genesis "Live At Wembley" DVD released.
17th November 2003:	Phil Collins releases See Through My Eyes CD single.
21st November 2003:	Phil Collins announces initial details of his "First Final Farewell Tour" 2004/05
24th November 2003:	Peter Gabriel releases Burn You Up, Burn You Down CD single
December 2003:	Steve Hackett releases Japanese edition of To Watch The Storms.
January 28th 2004:	Steve Hackett releases Live Archive 03 album.
March 1st 2004:	John Hackett releases his first solo album: Velvet Afternoon.
4th March 2004:	Steve Hackett commences UK/European tour in Dartford England.
3rd April 2004:	Steve Hackett ends his European tour in Budapest Hungary.
May 2004:	Anthony Phillips releases "Archive Collection 2" album.
5th May 2004:	Peter Gabriel commences his "Still Growing Up" European tour in Dortmund.
7th June 2004:	Mike & The Mechanics release Rewired, their seventh studio album.
28th June 2004:	Steve Hackett releases Live Archive 04 album
July 2004:	Nick Magnus releases Hexameron album (featuring Steve Hackett, John Hackett)
26th July 2004:	Steve Hackett performs live gig in Rome
28th July 2004:	Steve Hackett performs live gig in Palermo
1st August 2004:	Steve Hackett performs live gig in Valetta Malta
7th September 2004:	Mike + The Mechanics only UK gig for "Rewired" album in London.
13th September 2004:	Mike + The Mechanics release "Perfect Child" the first single from "Rewired"
24th October 2004:	Peter Gabriel releases the "Play" Promotional video compilation DVD.
1st November:	Phil Collins releases "Love Songs - A Compilation Old And New" double CD and "Finally… The First Final Farewell Tour" DVD.
22nd November 2004:	Steve Hackett releases "Once Above A Time" Live DVD.
29th November 2004:	Genesis release The Platinum Collection triple CD collection and The Video Show DVD.
7th March 2005:	Mike & The Mechanics release live DVD from their London 2004 gig.
March 2005:	Gramy Records issue a limited 180grm vinyl edition of the Sketches Of Satie
13th March 2005:	Steve Hackett commences acoustic tour in Verviers Belgium.
28th March 2005:	Steve Hackett releases his Metamorpheus album.
29th April 2005:	The first leg of Steve Hackett's acoustic trio tour ends in Schio Italy.
20th May 2005:	ARD release the DVD of Steve Hackett's "Beat Club" TV performance from 1978.
6th June 2005:	Steve Hackett releases his Live Archive 05 album
13th June 2005:	Steve Hackett commences his German tour at the Staatstheater in Oldenburg.
19th June 2005:	Steve Hackett ends his German tour at the "Lorelei Festival"
19th September 2005:	Virgin Records release the remastered versions of Steve Hackett's first four solo albums.
28th September 2005:	Steve Hackett commences his first proper US/Canadian tour in twelve years in Quebec
10th October 2005:	Anthony Phillips releases his Field Day album.
30th October 2005:	Steve Hackett plays final gig of tour in Mexico City.
31st October 2005:	Peter Gabriel releases his "Still Growing Up Live & Unwrapped" DVD.
November 2005:	Phil Collins commences the second leg of the "First Final Farewell" tour.
20th February 2006:	Steve Hackett releases the Live Archive 83 album.
11th March 2006:	UK national press carries reports of Genesis "Reunion" with Phil and Peter. This report remains unconfirmed.
8th May 2006:	Tarzan musical opens on Broadway.
11th September 2006:	Steve Hackett releases the Wild Orchid album.
28th September 2006:	Steve Hackett commences short tour with the acoustic trio in Bodo Norway.
7th November 2006:	Genesis announce the reformation of the We Can't Dance album lineup for a series of gigs throughout mainland Europe and the UK next summer.
11th June 2007:	First date of the Genesis "Turn It On Again" tour at the Olympic Stadium Helsinki Finland
14th July 2007:	Last date of the Genesis "Turn It On Again" European tour at the Palatine Forum Rome.

COLLECTOR'S CORNER

Being a fan of Genesis, or any other band for that matter, is an expensive business, especially in the current commercially minded world of music. The revenue generated by the sales of a single or album by any established group or solo artist is frequently outstripped by sales of 'merchandise' at concerts and by other items which are released by record companies. The most frequently seen items which fall into this category are tour programmes, T-shirts and badges all of which have their own horde of fans dedicated to collecting them. In addition to these there are those dedicated souls who spend their time trying to collect video and audio material by their favourite artists.

As long as there has been recorded music their have been those willing to bootleg material by artists. To write anything on that particular subject would merit a book in its own right as Genesis and its various off-shoots have to be one of the most frequently bootlegged groups of musicians in the world and the amount of material is, quite frankly staggering. It is far easier to try and outline the material which is either commercially available to fans in the field of official merchandise and tv and video material which anyone can record for themselves and thus begin a collection of their own.

Hence in this chapter I will deal with two or three specific areas which include: Tour programmes, books, and fan magazines, official videos and tv appearances and performances and an outline of a selection of the bootlegs currently available to those interested in such things. My thanks to Mic Smith, Peter Vickers and Ted Sayers for the additional information on some of the tour programmes.

ONE: TOUR PROGRAMMES 1972 -

In these days when rock memorabilia is fast becoming an area considered to be a "worthwhile investment" anyone who possesses a collection of tour programmes, handbills and other material from concerts would do well to ensure that their collection is well taken care of. Genesis and the individual members of the band have generated a great deal of material in this field enough to satisfy even the most dedicated collector. Tour programmes have been in existence for over a hundred years and they have always been collected. For Genesis the story really starts in 1972 with the first of a batch of increasingly intricately designed programmes.

Prior to this period, Genesis were usually relegated to the role of support slot on a show by another artist and, as such, did not merit any special mention in the main artists' programme, if they had one. All of this was to change in 1972 beginning with the now legendary appearance by the band at the Lincoln Festival for which there was a programme which cost the princely sum of ten pence! This was a 44 page booklet designed by David Wills and, as the artists included on the bill included Roxy Music, The Faces, Rory Gallagher and Status Quo, this is a highly sought after item by collectors. Genesis are mentioned on page 18 with a brief text by Geoff Ward and a small black and white photo of Peter Gabriel.

The second programme of the year to feature Genesis in any depth was produced for the Melody Maker "Poll Concert" which featured the bands and artists who had won the varying categories in the annual reader's poll. The concert took place at the Kennington Oval London on 30th September 1972 and this time Genesis were in the company of such alumni as Focus, ELP and Wishbone Ash. The sixteen page booklet included articles on the main bands and Genesis's appearance is restricted to a photo on the last page. However, by now Genesis were beginning to draw attention as a major attraction themselves and to merit more space in a tour programme.

In early 1971 Genesis had been on the bill of the first of the Charisma package tours, later titled the "Six bob" tours because as a ploy to attract people to the shows, ticket prices were pegged at 6 shillings (about 50 pence in current money). In October 1972 Genesis were again touring with Charisma stable mates, Lindisfarne who were current flavour of the month with their hit album and single: "Fog on the Tyne". The Lindisfarne autumn tour featured a programme which was the first to include Genesis's name on the cover and the sixteen page booklet also included a two page spread on the band with two black and white photos and full page advertisement for both the new Lindisfarne album and Genesis's latest album "Foxtrot" with a text by Jerry Gilbert from the music paper "Sounds". Even at this time, it is obvious that Genesis were an act to look out for and all of these programmes are extremely difficult to find now and represent a sound investment to any collector lucky enough to have them in their collection.

December 13th 1972 saw the band play their first gigs in the USA and a special commemorative programme was issued for the gig at the Philharmonic Hall in New York featuring a colour picture of the

Hall and black and white photos of both Genesis and their support act for this occasion; String Driven Thing.

1973 began with Genesis's first headlining tour in the UK and the first programme dedicated entirely to the band. Frankly it is not much to look at, being a rather simple eight page booklet with a rather garish yellow cover incorporating a photo of the band outside the Bottom Line Club in New York. Inside, there is a brief biographical outline of the band and its members and details of their equipment and a list of the UK tour dates.

The early part of the year also saw the band perform a couple of Festivals in Italy for which a programme was issued, which took the form of almost a newspaper with basic text and photographs spread over eight pages.

A rather unusual item also appeared at this time; a four page booklet which announced "John and Tony Smith in conjunction with Charisma present: Genesis on tour.." The cover features a photograph of the band in Central Park New York. It also announces that the special guests on the tour are String Driven Thing, another well known Charisma act from the period. The booklet seems to have been give out at gigs on the February 1973 tour, mine is accompanied by a handbill for the band's show at Exeter University on 14th February. The interior of the booklet is given over to the full lyrics of "Supper's Ready" accompanied by a rather intriguing explanation of the lyrics to each section.

The band performed at New York's prestigious Philharmonic Hall again on 2nd April 1973 and once again a tour leaflet was prepared, fundamentally the same as the one for the previous year although this time; the support act was Sandy Denny.

Perhaps the most intriguing programme ever produced by the band is that which accompanied their UK tour in October 1973. The entire package was enclosed in an envelope which, once opened had the following contents; a "Genesis Compendium" including cut-out dice and revolver, a page of programme notes by Michael Wale and a poster and flexidisc copy of 'Twilight Alehouse' the b-side from the band's first 'hit' single: 'I know what I like'. A complete copy of this particular package will fetch a considerable amount of money these days.

1974 saw the band consolidate it's position both at home and Europe which began with a series of sell-out shows at the Theatre Royal Drury Lane accompanied by a twenty four page booklet issued by the Charisma Press Office complete with full biographical notes on the band and reproductions of several features from the music press. This appears to be the only programme from the UK for the year. Strangely enough, it also appears that the 1973 eight page programme mentioned above was also available at these gigs, the only difference being the colour of the cover which, this time, was bright red. Who said recycling doesn't pay, eh?

Before the end of 1974 the band had released what, to many fans, was to be their finest album; "The Lamb lies down on Broadway". As usual, a tour brochure was published and this one is one of the best about the band. The cover features a design supposed to look like a tree, with the knots in the wood making it appear to smile on the front cover and frown on the back. Inside there is a full colour series of photographs taken by Armando Gallo as well as a full text and reproduction of the story from the album cover. The US version of this programme consisted merely of a sheet containing the storyline text from the new album as an introduction to the album which, as yet, had not been issued in the US.

There was also a special programme produced for the band's two shows in Portugal on 6th and 7th March 1975 which featured text and colour illustrations substantially different to the standard European edition, making this one of the rarest Genesis programmes around.

Strangely enough for a band of their stature, Genesis did not issue a commemorative programme for the "A trick of the tail" tour in 1976. Instead, a brochure was issued to commemorate the release in early 1977 of the film; "Genesis in concert" which was available at the premiere of the film on 31st January 1977. This was also issued in other territories including a German version.

The New year opened with the band playing three sold out shows at London's Rainbow Theatre for which another special unofficial brochure was issued featuring a blue cover with a group shot of the band on it. This item is now very hard to find.

The year's tour for "Wind & Wuthering" saw a welcome return to form with the release of two brochures of which the first is undoubtedly the best Genesis programme ever issued. The "World Tour '77" programme has it all, excellent photography by Robert Ellis, an inspired text by journalist Barbara Charone even an advertisement for ex-member Anthony Phillips's first solo album; "The Geese & the Ghost". This programme is quite common and should be an essential purchase for collectors.

Later in the year another brochure was issued; "Genesis European Tour '77 Picture Book". This was exactly what it's title proclaimed it to be; a 24 page collection of pictures by Robert Ellis. I must admit that this is my least favourite programme mainly because the photography included is, compared to its predecessor, very poor.

1978 was the best year for Genesis tour programmes. No fewer than four were produced beginning with the US tour postergramme which accompanied the massive tour that the band undertook in that country in April 1978. This folds out into a full colour poster of the band while on the other side there is a mixture of information about the band and their stage equipment and brief extracts from the first book by Armando Gallo; "Genesis the evolution of a rock band" which was published in the UK that year.

The band only played one show in the UK during their mammoth trip around the world in 1978. This was a prestigious headlining appearance at the Knebworth Festival on Saturday 24th June and a special programme was produced for the event. Titled: "Knebworth A Midsummer Night's Dream" the cover was a delightful cartoon style image of a couple of characters one of whom looks suspiciously like Tony Banks! The text includes items on all of the major acts appearing at the show including Tom Petty, Jefferson Starship and Brand X as well as a list of the available food and refreshments at the show (30p for a pork pie, those were the days!).

The band continued on tour throughout the summer headlining numerous festivals in Germany for which a special programme was produced. This has to be one of the nicest programmes in the collection including a beautiful artwork front cover and great live shot of Genesis on the back. More interestingly, however, it is the only programme to be written in more than one language; the text on Genesis and the other artists on the bill is written in both English and German, a nice touch for fans whose first language isn't English.

The band also travelled to Japan for the first time at the end of November 1978 and a special programme was issued to commemorate the historic event. Text is, of course, in Japanese but the excellent photographs included make this a worthwhile addition if you can find a copy.

After the surfeit of programmes in 1978, the brochure produced for the band's 1980 UK/US tour was something of a disappointment. Sporting a black cover with "Genesis in concert 1980" on the front the interior 28 pages are a mix of advertisements and extracts from Armando Gallo's second book on the band; "Genesis: I know what I like" which had been published in the UK that year. Copies of this particular programme are amongst the easiest to find and should pose no problem to anyone trying to find a copy.

The worrying trend towards rather poor programmes continued with the 1981 "Abacab" programme. Maybe the band had just run out of things to say or didn't want to produce an elaborate, and therefore, more expensive brochure. Either way, the programme for the tour was particularly disappointing. The booklet bore a white "Abacab-style" cover with colour live shot and the interior pages were another mixture of live and backstage shots with no text apart from a letter reproduced from a fan who had applied for tickets for the shows without enclosing payment! The US version of this programme also bore an advertisement for the band's back catalogue on Atlantic Records on the inner back cover in place of the advertisement for the year's tour merchandise which appeared in the UK/European edition, other than this, the programme is exactly the same as its UK counterpart.

Fortunately, the trend did not last and the following year's effort for the "Three Sides Live" tour of Europe, the USA and the UK was a much better production. Again the brochure mixed live photos with an informative text written by Andy Mackrill who was Genesis's tour manager at the time. This was coupled with a full tour itinerary and advertisements for the tour merchandise.

1982 was also the year which witnessed the event Genesis fans had been dreaming of since 1975; a reunion between the band and former frontman; Peter Gabriel. A one-off concert was organised as a benefit to pay off the debts Peter had incurred as one of the organisers of the ill-fated WOMAD Festival earlier in the year. Titled; "Six of the Best: A Benefit for WOMAD" the programme had a black and white cover incorporating a live shot of Peter with the band rehearsing for the show in London's Hammersmith Odeon a few weeks before. Inside there was a mix of colour photos as well as a series of quotes by all the band about the event and brief biographies about the other acts on the bill; John Martyn,

Talk Talk and The Blues Band. This is a MUST for any collection.

The "Mama Tour" of the USA in 1983/84 with the five dates at the National Exhibition Centre in Birmingham England produced another rather lacklustre programme. Sporting a grey cover with the album logo on the cover the interior was taken up by a rather uninspired series of photos some of which were taken from the 'Illegal Alien' video shoot and tour rehearsals. The five UK shows saw some slight variation because each night was dedicated to a different charity and as such, each night's programmes bore a different cover.

The 1986/87 tour is Genesis's biggest to date, the tour took in Europe, the USA and Canada, Australia and New Zealand as well as a second visit to Japan with over 112 dates played. There are two variants on the tour programme for this series of concerts. The first is the US/Australian programme which bore a beige cover with a stylised 'Domino' on it. Inside again is the usual mix of live and studio photos. The Japanese programme is fundamentally the same as its European counterpart - text is in Japanese obviously! The European programme differs from the US variant in several aspects. Most noticeable is the black 'Domino' cover. Inside there is, in addition to the mix of photos and adverts there is a two page spread about support act on the European leg; Paul Young, and a page dedicated to Tony Stratton-Smith the founder of Charisma Records, Genesis's record label of so many years, who had died of cancer in March 1987, halfway through the tour.

Either version of these programmes can be easily found at record fairs and are very common. There are however, two noticeable variations on this programme; both sport text about the band's supporting act: Paul Young, however, one variant has a greater amount of text, almost an entire page, whilst the other has a much briefer synopsis of Paul's career. The following two pages which feature advertisements for the band's back catalogue and Pernod respectively are transposed with each other depending on which edition you happen to possess. The Japanese edition, like its predecessor back in 1978 is considerable harder to track down.

Genesis' tour for their "We Can't Dance" album in 1992 produced another two programmes. First was a large format edition with a white cover with the band in their now famous 'I can't dance' dance routine. Inside again is a mix of photos of the new stage show and biographical text. The second programme was produced solely for the UK shows in October and November and was, like the venues the band played, a smaller affair which apart from a different cover a-la; "The Way we walk Volume Two: The Longs" album cover, is exactly the same as its larger predecessor.

Genesis's latest tour programme appeared in 1998 with that produced for their "Calling all stations" European/UK tour and was a glossy affair once again; featuring the new album cover and inside was a brief text outlining some of the band's thoughts on the album and their past history as well as an interesting selection of photographs which were somewhat marred by the "sci Fi" artwork design and graphics. This programme will be of particular interest to US fans because of the cancellation of the band's US tour.

TWO: SOLO TOUR PROGRAMMES 1977-

Genesis have not been alone in releasing tour programmes. So far, all of the solo members who have toured in their own right have issued brochures too and it is these which I will now take a look at. The first out of the traps as a solo artist was Peter Gabriel whose first album; "Peter Gabriel" was released in March 1977. He toured the USA, Europe and UK with the album and his first tour brochure appeared to coincide with this outing. This booklet set the trend for all of Peter's subsequent programmes and is bizarre to put it mildly. Sporting a grey cover with a picture of Waterloo Bridge with one of the passers by circled in red and no titles to indicate what the booklet is. The interior twelve pages are just as unusual, featuring demographic details of Europe, a medical report on Peter and reprints of the album lyrics. It also came with a promotional poster for the 'Modern Love' single.

As far as I have been able to find out, Peter did not release a programme for his 1978 tour. A brochure was produced for the Knebworth Festival September 1978 appearance which is fundamentally a Frank Zappa programme with additional text about both Gabriel and The Tubes who were also on the bill.

Peter's next booklet proper was issued to coincide with the UK tour in 1980. Another unusual production this booklet was titled "Peter Gabriel Tour of China 1984" a sly dig at the fondness of artists at the time who were falling over themselves to be the first to play in China and the kudos that they sought to attract from doing so. Modelled on Chairman Mao's famous "Little Red Book" the booklet incorporated a series of advertisements culled from Chinese newspapers along with the UK tour dates. This is one of the more difficult items to find and is a worthwhile, if strange, item in any collection.

The UK tour in 1983 also saw another tour brochure. This one was a little bit more traditional with details about Peter's band and the WOMAD festivals but still incorporated unusual features including a centre page dedicated to a cut out and keep Peter Gabriel mask! There was also a special souvenir booklet published for the gig at Crystal Palace on 9th July 1983 although there is little information about Peter in it - the same can also be said for the WOMAD Festival programme from 1982 and both of these are now very difficult to find.

The "This way up" tour in 1987 produced what to many fans is the best of Peter's programmes, a 48 page brochure incorporating a mix of information about Peter and his band as well as details about Amnesty International and a three page spread about American poet Anne Sexton whose poetry had inspired Peter's song "Mercy Street". Peter had collaborated with Sting and U2 in the US-only "Conspiracy of Hope" tour in 1986 and this was followed by the more ambitious "Human Rights Now!" world tour in 1988 a celebration of the fortieth anniversary of the signing of the International Declaration of Human Rights by the United Nations. The tour featured Sting, Bruce Springsteen, Youssou N'Dour, Tracy Chapman and Peter Gabriel and the tour brochure incorporated details on each artist as well as the full text of the Declaration itself.

Peter's involvement with humanitarian causes continues to this day and an interesting brochure was released to commemorate his involvement in the three day "WOMADELAIDE" Festival held in Adelaide Australia in February 1993 as part of the United Nations' "International Year for the World's Indigenous Peoples". The fifty six page brochure gives full details of the festival and its participating artists who were drawn from all over the world including brief biographical notes and black and white photography.

Peter's "Secret World" tour was a truly global one lasting over a year and reaching almost every conceivable part of the world. The tour brochure, in stark contrast with his stage presentation, was extremely disappointing and also very expensive. The thirty eight page booklet is housed in a black and white cover with a padlock on the cover, and a suitcase on the back. The interior has photos of the band and some information on a couple of humanitarian projects which Peter is giving his support to but is otherwise extremely uninspired.

Peter also appeared in the programme issued for the concert in aid of "Amnesty International" which was held at Paris' cavernous Palais Omnisports de Bercy on 10th December. Peter was one of numerous guests at this gig and the programme itself is a rather lacklustre large format programme with accompanying text in French.

The tour programmes for Peter's "Growing Up" and "Still Growing Up" tour s unusually for Peter, were actually crammed full of information about the tours, the musicians and Peter's other activities. Both are large format programmes and represent the best value productions in this field that Peter has produced thus far.

Steve Hackett's touring career began in 1978 but his first proper tour programme didn't appear until 1981. The "Cured" tour brochure set the standard by which all of Steve's subsequent programmes can be judged. The cover incorporated a live shot and advertisement for the new album. Inside the text gave a brief and informative biography of Steve's career as well as details on the other members of his band and a full tour itinerary for the tour and equipment lists for each band member.

1983 produced two tour programmes from Steve. The first was the brochure accompanying the "Highly Strung" UK tour in April/May. Again the brochure contained a good mix of information on Steve's career and his band within its sixteen pages and it is a worthwhile addition to your collection if you can find a copy.

Steve was out on the road again in October 1983 promoting his new acoustic album "Bay of kings" with a tour of the university halls in the UK. For these shows, a small fold out brochure was made which featured a colour photo of Steve on the cover with the title; "Bay of Kings: An evening of solo acoustic guitar with Steve Hackett". the interior had basic information including the venues on the tour and colour photos of Steve's live show from earlier in the year and it folded out to a small colour poster of Steve on stage. This is certainly one of the hardest programmes to find and although small, is a lovely addition to a collection.

Steve's most lavish programme is that which was produced for the "Momentum" UK tour in 1988. This is a very stylish affair with full colour album artwork cover and sixteen pages of text and photographs.

Another collectable offering from Hackett to your tour programme collection came in the shape of the commemorative programme for the first shows that Steve performed in Malta on 28th and 29th October 2002. An A5 sized glossy programme was issued including brief biographical notes and a discography.

Steve's To Watch The Storms UK/European tour in 2003 and the subsequent Live Archive 04 tour were covered by the same tour programme. Similar in style to previous A4 efforts, and full of the usual mix of photos, an informative text and plenty of information about Camino Records and Steve's own web site.

Steve's most recent tour; the Acoustic Trio 05 tour also produced a tour programme. An A5 sized booklet similar in style to the Malta 02 programme. Contained within is an excellent interview with Steve by Paul Clark, a brief biography and details of the other musicians accompanying Steve: John Hackett and Roger King.

Phil's solo career began with a vengeance in 1981 and his first tour as a solo artist was in support of his "Hello, I must be going" album in 1982. As usual, a tour brochure was issued which featured the album artwork to the "Hello, I must be going" album on the cover and inside there was the usual mix of photos and text including amusing spoof school reports on Phil and the other band members. Phil's school report included the comment; "Tries hard and is quite short.." which, I suppose is still a fair reflection of Phil's career, he is still trying VERY hard!

Phil's next solo outing was in support of his "No jacket required" album in 1985, a truly global affair taking in Europe, the USA and Canada, Australia and Japan. The twenty four page brochure was the usual mix of photos and background information although no actual text was included which was quite surprising given Phil's rapidly growing status both at home and abroad.

By 1990, the trend toward photo booklets rather than tour programmes in the old manner had really taken hold. In the main these were frequently overpriced and only of interest to collectors. Phil's 1990 tour brochure fell into this category. The booklet itself was a large format design featuring a picture of Phil on the cover dressed as a circus ringmaster, in keeping with the stage design for the tour. Inside was a rather motley collection of photos of the band attired in the costumes of several circus acts. No text accompanied the photos and the entire packaging was rather disappointing.

Phil's tour programme for the 1994/95 "Both Sides" world tour is a far superior effort and probably the best of his programmes to date. Another large format design incorporating a picture of Phil's drum kit disguised as oil drums once again in keeping with the idea behind the stage design. Inside again there are photos of the various members of the ever-growing orchestra that Phil takes on the road with him and the text accompanying them is both informative AND amusing!

Phil's produced another lavish programme for his "Dance into the light" US and European tour of 1997 continued the above trend with a large format glossy brochure packed with (not altogether flattering) photos of his ever expanding band and a very tongue in cheek text no doubt written by Phil himself.

With no tour programmes in evidence for either the 1998 Big Band Tour and the handful of shows for 2002's Testify album, Phil's current First Final Farewell Tour has redressed the balance with an excellent brochure containing a good mix of archival and new photographs and an informed text housed in a nifty hard card slipcase; an excellent finale to Phil's touring career.

The most recent member of Genesis to venture out on to the road is Mike Rutherford who, with his other band; The Mechanics, has done four tours so far. The first in 1986 was a solely US affair and, as far as I am aware, provided no tour programme.

His second tour in 1989 in support of the highly successful "Living Years" album, brought forth a postergramme which apart from a tour itinerary provided little more than a series of live shots that included a large full group portrait. I suppose the band had still to fully establish a reputation hence the lack of supporting text within this effort.

Mike's tour in support of the equally successful "A Beggar On A Beach Of Gold" album surprisingly produced no tour programme at all much to the disappointment of collectors but the most recent "Greatest Hits" tour was provided with something in the tour programme department. The "Hits Tour Manual 1996" was a twenty page colour booklet with a selection of photos from the 1995 tour including some from the band's shows in South Africa, along with informative and amusing text. It was also unusual for including the addresses of the various fan clubs that have sprung up in recent years. To fans of the Mechanics outside of the UK this programme will be extremely collectible because the 1996 tour only took in the UK.

May of 1999 saw the Mechanics' most recent tour in support of the "M6" album which once again gave the fans another tour brochure which was a large format publication with a very basic text and some very lacklustre photographs but once again, this is destined to become a sought after items to collectors due to the fact that the band once again, only played a handful of shows outside of the UK.

The Mechanics' Rewired album released earlier in 2004 generated a handful of shows in support of Phil Collins in Europe and a solitary UK show in London but no tour programme to commemorate the event.

That concludes this examination of the available tour programmes by the band and its solo off-shoots.

Now it is the turn of the various publications about the band which have appeared over the years...For a band the size of Genesis, it is surprising to find that there have been less than a handful of books about the band. The same can be said of fanzines, official or otherwise which have appeared in droves about acts with less than half of Genesis's staying power! However, what has been lacking in quantity has more than been made up for in the quality as we shall see.

The first book of any note about the band that was worth its weight in gold to fans was "Genesis: The evolution of a rock band" by respected journalist Armando Gallo. This was first published in the UK by Sidgwick and Jackson in 1978. Gallo had followed the band since 1971 and he managed to blend his superb photographs with an informed, intelligent and at times, amusing text in a way which has set the trend for rock biographies since. Sadly, this edition is no longer in print however, it was updated two years later under the title "Genesis I know what I like" which brought the band's story up to the beginnings of work on the "Duke" album along with sections on each member as well as a useful discography. The book was also issued as a limited edition hardback in calfskin with embossed autographs by the band and with only 1000 copies made these are now much sought after. Gallo has in fact re-issued this book recently as a limited edition hardback with a new cover although surprisingly enough with no additional text

Genesis - The Evolution of a Rock Band Armando Gallo Sidgwick & Jackson ISBN 0 283 98439 2 (Cloth)/0 283 98440 6 (Paper) 1978.
Genesis - I know what I like Armando Gallo DIY Books Distributed by Sigwick & Jackson ISBN 0 283 98703 0 1980.

A French language book was published on the band in 1979. Titled "Genesis" it was written by Herve Picart and Jean-Yves Legras. This edition contained many unseen black and white photographs and an informed text.
Genesis Herve Picart & Jean-Yves Legras ISBN 73 1499 0 (Paper).

Published at about the same time as Armando's first book on the band, there also appeared an interesting artwork book on the band: "Genesis Lyrics". This was designed by Steve Hackett's wife; Kim Poor, a longstanding fan of the band (she must be, she married a band member, after all!). The book drew upon Kim's designs for lyrics to published Genesis songs, and makes an interesting contrast to the other biographical works available as well as showcasing some of Kim's fantastic artwork.
Genesis Illustrated Lyrics Kim Poor Sidgwick & Jackson ISBN 0283 985267 (Hard back), ISBN 0283 985265 (Paperback) 1979.

In 1981 an Italian language book appeared, written by Giampiero Vigorito. Titled once again, simply "Genesis" this one contained a biography and black and white photography spread throughout its 158 pages.
Genesis Giampiero Vigorito Gammalibri (Italian language edition no ISBN number) 1981.

There was a four year gap before anything else of note was published on the band, but 1983/84 saw a plethora of books on the subject of Genesis. Hugh Fielder, the stalwart follower of the band, and music correspondent for "Sounds" in the UK set the ball rolling with his book; "The book of Genesis" which took the form of an extended interview with the various members, accompanied by numerous photographs.

The Book of Genesis Hugh Fielder Sidgwick & Jackson ISBN 0283 99074 0 1984.

This was soon followed by another book by Armando Gallo. This one took a slightly different approach and drew exclusively upon his amazing photographic archive of the band, with supporting text kept to a minimum enabling the photographs to more or less tell the band's story for him. Titled; "Genesis: from one fan to another" this forms another highly recommended addition to the growing canon of books about the band.

Genesis - From one fan to another Armando Gallo Omnibus Press ISBN 0-7119-0515-0 (Paperback)/ 0-7119-0514-2 (Hardback)

Another example of the "Genesis Mania" which was sweeping the music press during 1983/84 appeared in the shape of Janis Schacht's book "Genesis" which was published by Proteus books in 1984. Textually, the book was certainly quite well-informed and was also blessed with several photographs which had not seen the light of day before making it another useful addition to the canon of books about the band.

Genesis Janis Schacht Proteus Books Limited ISBN 0 86276 257 X 1984.

The final book to appear in 1984 was another interesting peek into the world of the band by photo journalists Philip Kamin and Peter Goddard and titled; "Genesis: Peter Gabriel, Phil Collins and beyond" a somewhat prophetic title given recent developments within the Genesis camp. The writers took another different tack opening the book with a chapter about the now legendary reunion concert in 1982 before looking back fondly on the individual members and their careers with a great selection of photographs making this book a perfect foil to the others published at this time.

Genesis - Peter Gabriel, Phil Collins and beyond Philip Kamin & Peter Goddard Sidgwick & Jackson ISBN 0-283-99093-7 1984.

Initially released in 1981 and republished in 1984, Geoff Parkin's book; "Genesis: The Illustrated Discography" was a goldmine of information to collectors of Genesis records and gave full details of most of their world wide releases both as Genesis and as individual solo artists. The re-issue in 1984, titled: "Genesis: Turn it on again" brought even more detail to light and both editions were to remain indispensable to fans until very recently. After the deluge of printed word about the band in 1984, those fans left still wanting more were to be in for a long wait with the next book on the band appearing in 1987.

Alain Bayeulle and Laurence Berrouet's "Genesis" appeared as a French language edition in 1987. Once again featuring a biographical text and some excellent unseen black and white photographs.

Genesis by: Alain Bayeulle/Laurence Berrouet Rock & Folk Press ISBN: 2-226-02789-0 1987.

Also appearing in 1987 was the first, and so far, only Hungarian language book on the band written by Laszlo Gobolyos. This featured a 200 page biography and colour and black and white photographs of the band. No publisher details are available but a catalogue number is shown.

Genesis by: Laszlo Gobolyos 1987. ISBN: 963 02 49081.

This was done as a spin off from the "Genesis a history" video project which was released in 1991. The authors; Dave Bowler and Bryan Dray were supposedly consultants on the band's "Genesis a history" video project and their book: "Genesis an authorised biography" was released in 1991. The authors; Dave Bowler and Bryan Dray were rather studious in their approach to the band's lengthy history and incredibly patronising toward their prospective audience although in their favour, it has to be said that theirs was the first book to deal with the band's solo careers in any depth. This book has also been re-issued in paperback with a slightly updated text and some different photographs.

Genesis - A Biography Dave Bowler and Bryan Dray Sidgwick & Jackson ISBN 0 283 061324 1992.

1994 saw the issue of a book by long time fan and editor of the Italian Genesis fanzine; Dusk Mario Giammetti. As its title: "Genesis Discografia 1968 - 1993" suggests, this publication examined the recorded output of the band and its solo members and is little more than a list of their recordings (official and otherwise!) which will prove useful to collectors for the details it provides. This was in turn followed in 1995 by another book outlining Genesis' recorded output. This time the detail is outstanding, and Max Demont's book; "Genesis Counting Out Time the World Wide Singles Discography" certainly lives up to its name with a tremendous amount of detail on its subject and is indispensable for collectors.

Francois Ducray's "Genesis - De Peter Gabriel A Ray Wilson" (From Peter Gabriel To Ray Wilson) appeared in December 1997. A French language pocket sized book similar to the Chris Welch volume mentioned below although far superior in content! Featuring some previously unseen photos and an informed text, spread over 98 pages.

"Genesis - De Peter Gabriel A Ray Wilson" Rock Serie ISBN 2-912836-01-8

Fortunately for fans of the band's formative period, Armando Gallo was finally persuaded to re-issue his magnificent tome; *"Genesis I know what I like"* earlier this year. Fundamentally, this is the same book as the 1980 edition but in view of the fact that that edition and its predecessor; *"Genesis The Evolution of a Rock Band"* are now long out of print, this is an essential purchase for Genesis collectors. The book is published in hard back with a magnificent new cover designed by Paul Whitehead and with an introduction by that artist. As Mike Rutherford said in his original introduction to this book : " It would be easy if we could just say to people; here - read this…" and those words are still true today. This is without doubt the most indispensable biography of the band and the yardstick by which all others are still measured. The book is available direct from Armando at his address: Armando Gallo P O Box 198, 12405 Venice Boulevard, LOS ANGELES, California 90066 USA.

The next book to appear about the band to date is long time Rock critic Chris Welch's pocket sized volume "The Complete Guide to the Music of Genesis" which sadly does not live up to its title and is full of quite glaring mistakes which is disappointing given Welch's long time championing of the band's cause although there are some insights to be gained from the text. Welch has also more recently issued a book about Peter Gabriel similar to the above.
Genesis - The Complete Guide to the music of… Chris Welch Omnibus Press ISBN 0-7119-5428-3 1995.

Genesis X File Volume 1 (private printed edition) Yashima Tsukamoto.

The next book to appear in the Genesis field (apart from the one you are reading, obviously) is a recent, privately published Japanese book which outlines in graphic detail all the available bootlegs which have been released in Japan. As such, it is similar in style and scope to Max Demont's monumental tome on Genesis singles mentioned earlier and will prove very useful to anyone wishing to find such things, and has the added bonus of giving details in both Japanese and English. The author; Yashima Tsukamoto is to be praised for this brave effort and with a second edition promised some time soon, this may become a standard text on the subject of the band's bootlegs.

The next book on the band was published in 2002 by Canadian journalist, Robin Platts. A modest volume, Inside & Out combined the main elements in several other books (including the one you are reading, folks!) along with an informed text which draws upon interviews conducted by Platts himself including several interesting ones with people who had not given their comments on the band. Another worthwhile addition to the Genesis library.

Genesis: Inside & Out Robin Platts Collectors Guide Publishing Inc ISBN 1-896522-71-8.

One of the latest Genesis books to appear is by longstanding Genesis fan Mario Giammetti whose previous woks are mentioned elsewhere here. His latest book : Genesis Il Fiume Del Costante Cambiamento" was published in 2004 by Editori Riuniti. This is another Italian language edition illustrated with a wealth of photos many of which are previously unseen, accompanied by an informed and detailed text.

Genesis: Il Fiume Del Costante Cambiamento Mario Giammetti Editori Riuniti ISBN 88-359-5507-6 2004 (Italian language edition)

The long delayed book by Record Collector journalist Paul Russell finally emerged in 2004. Titled: Genesis - Play Me My Song A Live Guide 1969 To 1975, this is an anorak's bible for fans of Gabriel era live recordings. Paul had access to the band's live tape archive and assistance from several well-known traders in the Genesis fan community to produce an informative but somewhat repetitive guide to the better live recordings (both official and unofficial) from the band's formative years. Accompanied by a highly amusing interview with Tony, Mike and Anthony Phillips and a gig guide which looks suspiciously familiar to me(especially the mistakes!) this is another useful reference work.

Genesis - Play Me My Song A Live Guide 1969 To 1975 Paul Russell SAF Publishing ISBN 0 946719 58 6

More recent still, is Dave Thompson's *Turn It On Again - Peter Gabriel, Phil Collins & Genesis* which was published at the start of 2005. An informed although Gabriel -biased text includes much background information about several aspects of the band's career including the beginnings and development of Charisma Records and their eclectic leader: Tony Stratton-Smith although prone to some glaring errors and a distinct lack of proof-reading. Another welcome addition that sheds more light on this enthralling band.

Turn It On Again - Peter Gabriel, Phil Collins & Genesis. Dave Thompson Backbeat Books ISBN 0-87930-810-9

The most recent addition to the growing number of books about the band is Peter Vickers' "The Top 200 Worldwide Genesis Rarities". Privately published by its author, this is a mine of information for collectors of the rare and the unusual in the world of Genesis records. Published as a limited edition of 200 copies, this is likely to become a collectors' item itself! Peter has been a regular contributor to Record Collector on the subject and certainly knows his stuff.

Genesis The Top 200 Worldwide Rarities. Peter Vickers (Private Edition No ISBN Number)

Genesis's solo members have been singularly ignored in the biographical department with only Peter Gabriel and Phil Collins receiving anywhere near the attention that their careers deserve.

Phil was the first to receive a biographical treatment with Johnny Waller's book: "The Phil Collins Story" published by Zomba Books in 1985. This took Phil's career from the beginning up to and including the release of his third solo album; "No jacket required".
Johnny Waller The Phil Collins Story Zomba Books ISBN 0-946391-78-5 1985.

This was followed in 1997 by Ray Coleman's "Phil Collins - The Definitive Biography" published posthumously after the author's death and sadly this is another volume which does not live up to it's title and instead concentrates an inordinate amount of its time on Phil's marriage break up in 1993/94.
Phil Collins The definitive Biography Ray Coleman Simon & Schuster ISBN 0-684-81784-5 1997.

Most recently; at the beginning of January 2005, the irrepressible Mario Giammetti published his book on Phil's career. Titled "Phil Collins - The Singing Drummer" Mario covers Phil's career in depth focussing on the solo years and including an in-depth sessionography by Enrico Geretto. Spanning nearly 400 pages and including a wealth of photographs, this is another essential addition.

Phil Collins - The Singing Drummer By: Mario Giammetti Edizioni Segno ISBN 88-7782-836-8 2005 (Italian language edition)

Armando Gallo turned his attentions to Peter Gabriel's career with the release of another of his excellent photo books which covers Peter's career up to and including the release of his "So" album in 1986. As you would expect, the book is an excellent photographic chronicle of Peter's career to date and is an essential addition to any collection although Armando's introductory comments are likely to surprise many Genesis fans!

Peter Gabriel Armando Gallo Omnibus Press ISBN 0-7119-0783-8 1986.

Peter's next appearance in print was two years later in 1988 with the publication of Spencer Bright's worthy tome: "Peter Gabriel - An Authorised Biography" which dealt in graphic detail with Peter's career both in and out of Genesis up to the release of "So" and the subsequent tour and is an insightful look behind the artist who many Genesis fans still see as the artistic heart of the band. Bright update the book in 1990 upon its release in paperback and more recently still updated again this year to take account of recent developments within Peter's career.

Peter Gabriel An Authorised Biography Sidgwick & Jackson ISBN 0-283-99498-3 1988.

With the completion of the "Human Rights Now!" tour in 1988, Peter was a contributor to the book which chronicled this milestone in musical political awareness. The book chronicles the entire tour and gives a useful background to the United Nations' Declaration of Human Rights itself and the accompanying photographs are worth the price alone.

Human Rights Now! James Henke Bloomsbury Press ISBN 0-7475-0318-4 1988.

Chris Welch has rejoined the fray with another book titled "Peter Gabriel in his own words" which appeared in 1997 and which is little more than a collection of extracts from interviews which Peter has given over his career and is rather more of an insight into the mind of a rock journalist than into the artist himself.

Steve Hackett's story was finally transferred to book form with the latest in the line of books on the band by Italian fan and founder of the Italian Genesis fan magazine: Dusk; Mario Giammetti who has been indefatigable in his chronicling of the band's activities. His latest effort; the second in the "Genesis Files" series covers Steve's career under the title "The Defector". Lavishly illustrated with many previously unseen photos and with an informed Italian language text, this is the first book to outline Steve's career in any detail.

Steve Hackett - The Defector Mario Giammetti Edizioni Segno ISBN 88-7282-903-8 2005. (Italian language edition)

Surprisingly enough, given their solo successes, neither Mike Rutherford or Tony Banks have been the subjects of a biography yet and the final work of any note to date has that other Genesis Founding Father" Anthony Phillips as its subject. The author; Sara Cavalle is a colleague of Anthony's friend and fellow musician Guillermo Cazenave and the book "From Genesis to Revelation Biografia Official de Anthony Phillips Co-fundador de Genesis" was written in Spanish for the Spanish record company Astral who market several of Guillermo and Anthony's albums.

From Genesis to Revelation Biografia Oficial de Anthony Phillips: Co-fundador de Genesis Antropovision ISBN B-22.618/ 96.

At the time of writing, there are plans afoot for further books on several individual band members. Mic Smith, long time organiser of the Kontakt, Peter Gabriel magazine is planning a major biography of that enigmatic artist., and yours truly will be ensconced in work on the first authorised biography of Steve Hackett by the time you read this.

Bootleg Recordings

Bootleg or illegal recordings of music have been around for a very long time in fact, before the advent of recorded sound the bootleggers were still plying their trade in the shape of unauthorised transcripts of existing sheet music and orchestral scores. If that sounds like a rather obvious statement; then perhaps it is, but nonetheless, it is still worth reiterating for the benefit of those people who may be new to this particular area of collecting.

The argument still rages over the validity of bootleg recordings. The record companies quite correctly maintain that such recordings deprive them of revenues that may be spent on nurturing new talent and of course, depriving the artists themselves of royalties on their work. At least one member of Genesis when asked about the vexed issue of bootlegs answered that he wasn't concerned by them ..."because the fans who buy them buy all the official stuff anyway..." and indeed several members of the band are reputed to collect their own "bootlegs" so who is right and who is wrong?

To fans and collectors, and sad anoraks like me, however, the bootleg is sometimes seen as an essential part of any collection be it as a memento of a favourite gig which they attended or as historical documents detailing their live output or sometimes unusual or otherwise unheard studio material and live version of songs no longer in the band's live repertoire. Whatever the relative merits of either argument, Genesis and its solo members are without doubt, extremely well represented by bootlegs initially pressed up on vinyl many of these are ironically enough, now highly sought after collectors items in their own right and, more recently on compact disc where a veritable explosion of "new" titles has occurred over the last few years. What follows is by no means a comprehensive list of these items but will give fans a flavour of exactly what you can expect should you decide to embark on this particular avenue of the Genesis "Collection" although of course, I have no knowledge where such items can be obtained so, in the words of the song: "Please Don't Ask!"

My thanks in particular to Mario Giammetti , and Yashima Tsukamoto for all their help in compiling this updated version of this section and to all the other collectors who have sent in details which have been added to this part of the text, and to Eric Reitinger for the use of extracts from his concise FAQ on this subject

Bootlegs : Some of your Frequently Asked Questions answered by: Eric Reitinger.

What is a bootleg/ROIO?

The term "bootleg" originates in the smuggling world where smugglers would hide contraband inside the long boots they wore to escape detection by Customs men. It gradually came to be used to describe any item with dubious origins (implying some kind of criminal activity) and eventually ended up as a convenient name for unauthorised recordings which were sometimes pressed on to vinyl or CD and issued by obscure record labels without the consent of the recording artist or their record company. These would take the form of live concert recordings, demo versions of tracks; and sometimes even completely unreleased songs by popular artists (as in the case of the first important bootleg: Bob Dylan's "Great White Wonder").

Bootlegging should not be confused with piracy. Piracy is the act of making (and selling or trading) illegal copies of officially available material. Material contained in bootlegs is not available to buy in the shops and although in some cases, the record labels have noticed the demand and issued some of this rare material, the vast majority of it will only ever be available through these "unofficial" lines. Bootleg is a term which has some quite negative connotations and so traders sometimes prefer the term ROIO: "Recording Of Indeterminate Origin".

What is on these bootlegs and where do they come from?

Bootlegs, as explained above, contain any material from a particular artist, which has never been released by themselves or their record company. This can include:

Live performances, sound checks, and rehearsals.
Studio demos, different mixes or alternate takes of tracks.
Completely unreleased, totally new tracks.

As for where they come from; there are various sources for bootlegs. Most traders will have this information on their trade lists so that you can make an informed guess on how any particular bootleg is going to sound.

Audience Recordings (AUD): As the name suggests, these are recordings made at live concerts by a member of the audience, using a portable recording device and a microphone. Although the sound is not usually comparable to that of a sound board or radio recording, audience recordings have certainly come along way since the early '70's when an enterprising member of the audience in Belgium recorded the first Genesis concert outside of the UK with a very crude cassette recorder! Nowadays, thanks to DAT recorders, Minidisc recorders and even pocket PCs, an audience recording can actually be an enjoyable listen.

Sound board Recordings (SBD): This term is often used to describe any recording which is made using professional equipment but in fact should only be used properly to describe recordings which are made directly from the mixing desk at a concert. This term is usually used to describe any recording that was taped directly from the mixing desk so you hear what the audience hears. This means that the recording quality is usually excellent. However, sound board recordings often have a lack of bass, as bass is naturally loud at the venue and so is often turned down on the mixing desk. The other problem with sound board recordings is that they often lack much crowd noise. This can be a good thing but often sounds odd, when an excellent performance ends and it sounds like the audience are asleep!

Radio Recordings (FM): Fairly self explanatory; these are the shows which are broadcast on the radio and then recorded off-air by the fans. The sound quality of these will depend on the quality of the broadcast and the equipment used to record it at home, but is generally very good. Unlike sound board recordings, these have a proper mix with decent bass and the right level of crowd noise.

Pre-FM Recordings: The best of the best, these are recordings taken from the radio station's master LPs, CDs or DAT tapes which they used to broadcast the show. As they have not been transmitted over the air and recorded at home, the quality on these is usually the best, and they do not suffer from the compression, which can affect the FM recordings.

Studio Recordings: Anything which is not from a live concert is hard to pin down to an exact source; however demos, outtakes and unreleased songs are usually professionally recorded and then somehow leaked from the studio; either via promo or reference CDs or in some cases by theft from the studio itself.

Sounds great. So, how can I get hold of these bootlegs, then?

Bootlegs started out in the late 1960's as actual releases, pressed in factories onto official vinyl and later CDs and then sold (often for extortionate amounts of money) at record fairs; small record shops and other outlets . The practice of buying and selling bootlegs is still around today but has been made largely redundant by the advent of the Internet; the widespread availability of CD-R and the vast trading communities which have been built up between fans. It should be pointed out that buying and selling bootlegs is legally no different to trading them; however where there is so much material available for free if you look in the right places; then there is no need to be spending money on this stuff!

For further information on the technical side of these recordings, check the feature that Eric has written as part of the "Genesis FAQ" on the Official Genesis "Talking Shop" part of the band's official website.

Genesis Bootleg Recordings

"The Hiding Place" Comprises the now famous tracks from the BBC "Night Ride" Session of 1970 : Shepherd/Pacidy/Let Us Now Make Love/Stagnation along with Looking For Someone taken, strangely enough; from the "Trespass" album itself. GNV1000.

This particular combination of tracks is also duplicated on the appropriately titled **"The Shepherd"** compact disc (Flashback 09.90.0126.33) which ruins the recording however, by including dubbed in applause! This disc also contains Twilight Alehouse/Watcher Of The skies/Get 'Em Out By Friday and The Musical Box from various BBC sessions making it an interesting addition to a collection as many of the BBC sessions have yet to be released officially.

For live recordings the earliest of any known show appeared last year, titled **Beside the silent Mirror"** (ARC012) this recording is ostensibly from the band's first overseas gig in Belgium on 7th March 1971 and, as such is of historical interest alone for the formative set which is represented on it which comprises: Happy The Man/Stagnation/The Light/Twilight Alehouse/The Musical Box/The knife/Going Out To Get You. Sound quality is not of the best but that is more than compensated for by the unusual set including the as yet unofficially released The Light parts of which were later used in Lilywhite Lilith .

Nursery Cryme/Foxtrot Tours 1971-73.

Twilight Francehouse Compact Disc (Highland HL203) Same as above.

From 1972 onwards the band's live shows are increasingly well represented beginning with **The Musical Fox** (Wild Bird Records WBR 9016) from the Charleroi Festival 16th January 1972 comprising the following tracks: Happy the man /Stagnation/The Fountain Of Salmacis/Twilight Alehouse/The Musical Box/The Return Of The Giant Hogweed.

There was once a harvest in this land Is a useful addition to any collection, comprising, as it does; an excellent quality recording of the band's gig at Watford Technical College on 4th March 1972 including rare performances of several tracks. Track listing is as follows: Harlequin/Stagnation/Fountain of Salmacis/Twilight Alehouse/Musical Box/The Return Of The Giant Hogweed/The Knife.

Another interesting recording from this period is **Genesis Rome 18 Aprile 1972** (Tintagel TICD009) which documents the band's first Italian tour in good sound quality and comprising the band's set from that period: Happy The Man/ Stagnation/The Fountain Of Salmacis/Twilight Alehouse/Improvisation/The Musical Box/The Return Of The Giant Hogweed/The Knife/Going Out To Get You.

This set is complimented by **Old Man's Tale** (GNV004) which is taken from the band's shows at Naples (19.4.720 and Pavia (14.4.72) including an unusual version of Can-Utility & The Coastliners under the title of Bye, Bye, Johnny! As well as a rare version of Seven Stones. More recently still a recording of the band's show in Ravenna (15.4.72) has been released on Lizard records (LZCD010) comprising the same set as Rome '72.

Another recent addition to the Genesis catalogue appears in the shape of **The Almost Complete BBC Sessions** (MDF Recordings) Which as its title suggests, gathers up all of the recordings that Genesis made for the BBC between 1970 and 1972 omitting only those which have already appeared elsewhere details are as follows:
Disc One: "Night Ride" BBC 22/2/70: Shepherd/Pacidy/Let us Now Make Love/Stagnation/Looking For Someone. **"In Concert" BBC Paris Studios London 2/3/72:** Fountain Of Salmacis/Musical Box/The Return Of The Giant Hogweed.
Disc Two: "Sounds Of the Seventies" 10/5/71: Musical Box/**"Sounds Of The Seventies" 9/1/72:** Harlequin/Harold The Barrel/The Return Of The Giant Hogweed/**"John Peel Sessions" 25/9/72:** Twilight Alehouse/Watcher of The Skies/get 'Em Out By Friday.

Other recordings from this period include:
The Story So Far... (BRUSH 1) Charleroi Festival 16.1.72
Shades Of Dawning (Highland HL069) Watford Technical College 4.3.72
Euchre Show (Highland HL498) Watford Town Hall 28.6.72.
Come Ancient Children (ARC/GNV 015 Picture LP) Reading Festival 11.8.72.
Piper 2000 Club Viareggio 20.8.72.
Through the looking Glass (ARC/GNV017) Genoa Teatro Alcione 22.8.72.
Sharpened to the hilt (ARC/GNV016) Lugo 15.4.72 and Verona 9.4.72.
Genesis Live In Pavia (FU203) CD Palasport Pavia 14.4.72.
Lugo Di Ravenna (No catalogue number) CD Lugo Di Ravenna 15.4.72.
Seven Stones (No catalogue number) Teatro Alcione Genoa 22.9.72.
Dublin 1972 (No catalogue number) National Stadium Dublin 28.9.72.
Live at the Marquee Club In London (The Amazing Kornyfone Recording) LP Marquee Club 10.11.72.
Imperial College (Night Sun 001) Imperial College London 18.11.72.
Violent Dreams (Highland HL103) Imperial College London 18.11.72.
The Coastliners (Highland HL313/314 2 CD set) Viareggio Club 2000 (afternoon and evening shows) 20.7.72.
Philharmonic Hall NYC 16.12.72

The following year saw the band's popularity grow and with it the number of recordings representing the various tours with perhaps the best ones being from the band's later tours in support of the "Selling England by the Pound" album. Recordings from this period include....

Heidelberg '73. Stadthalle Heidelberg 15.1.73. Track Listing: Watcher Of The Skies/Twilight Alehouse/Drum Solo/Get 'Em Out By Friday/The Musical Box/The Return of The Giant Hogweed.

Best of British Frankfurt Festival/Pop Shop Belgian TV 17.1.73 & 20.3.72.
Moonswept Paradise (Clean Sound Records LP CS1004) Palasport Rome 22.1.73.

Live in Glasgow Greens Playhouse Glasgow 16.2.73. Track Listing: Watcher of The Skies/Drum Solo/Musical Box/Get 'Em Out By Friday/Supper's Ready/The Return of The Giant Hogweed.

Live in Sheffield Sheffield City Hall 17.2.73 (2 CD set).
Quebec City (Wombat Records CD WOMBAT73) Quebec City Grandstand 3.3.73.

Selling England By The Pound Tour 1973-74.

The band's popularity continued to grow with the release of their fifth studio album: Selling England By The Pound in October 1973. This period is well documented by a series of live and studio recordings.

Live from Toronto Massey Hall Toronto 8.11.73 (2 CD set). Track Listing; Watcher Of The Skies/Dancing With The Moonlit Knight/Cinema Show/I Know What I Like/Firth Of Fifth/Musical Box/More Fool Me/Supper's Ready.

Fantasia (Exposure EX002) which is a recording of the band's show at Los Angeles's Roxy Theatre 19.12.73 comprising the following: Watcher of the skies/Dancing with the moonlit knight/The cinema show/I know what I like/Firth of fifth/The Musical box/Horizons/Supper's ready.

Welcome to Epping Forest (Rus Foley RFCD8) Rainbow Theatre 20.10.73

Chloe in The Garden (Laughing Clown Records LC48043 LP) Rainbow Theatre 20.10.73.
Live In Newcastle (The Amazing Kornyfone Record Label TAKRL 24905 Double LP) Newcastle City Hall 26.10.73.
This Planet's Soil (NEWOX 73) Ostensibly a recording of the band's filmed performance at Shepperton Studios on 30th October 1973.
First we were five (Rock Calendar Records RC2113) Tufts university 7.11.73.
Romeo Show (Highland HL072/73 2 cd set) Felt Forum NYC 22.11.73
Live at The Felt Forum (Laughing Clown Records double LP LC3222) Felt Forum 22.11.73.
Skywatchers (Double LP TMQ 72115) Roxy Club NYC 19.12.73.

Selling England by the Session (Highland HL032/33 2 cd set). This set is extremely interesting because as its title suggests, it is comprised entirely of out-takes and demos from the "Selling England.." album. Track Listing: Studio Improvisations #1-2/The Battle Of Epping Forest (Intro Parts 1-5)/The Cinema Show(Instrumental Take Fast and Slow Instrumental Takes #1-4)/Dancing With The Moonlit Knight (Instrumental Takes Fast #1-3)/The Battle Of Epping Forest (Part 6)/The Last Time(*)/You Really Got Me(+)/ The Battle Of Epping Forest(Part 7)/The Battle Of Epping Forest (Parts 8-9 Takes #1-6 and #1-4)/I Know What I Like (No lyrics #1-2)/The Cinema Show (No lyrics)/Drum Solo (1/2)/Firth Of Fifth (Slow)/Firth Of Fifth (Fast)/The Cinema Show/After the Ordeal(Fast)/Dancing With The Moonlit Knight (Vocal & Piano#1-2)Dancing With The Moonlit Knight (Band Version #1-2)/The Battle Of Epping Forest 1/The Battle Of Epping Forest (Jam #1-3)/The Cinema Show (Rehearsal)/Dancing With The Moonlit Knight (Second Version #1-2)/More Fool me/After The Ordeal (Part 1 & Part 2)/I Know What I Like.

In the Beginning (Volumes 1-6) (Extremely Rare EXR005/006/013/014/018/022) This ever expanding series of discs chronicles the band's 1973/74 studio out-takes in great detail with more demos than you could shake a stick at!

Live at Drury Lane Theatre Royal Drury Lane London 20.1.74 (2 CD set). Track Listing: Watcher Of The Skies/Dancing With The Moonlit Knight/Cinema Show/I Know What I Like/Firth Of Fifth/Harold The Barrel/Musical Box/Horizons/More Fool Me/The Battle Of Epping Forest/Supper's Ready.

The Battle Of Dusseldorf Philipshalle Dusseldorf 30.1.74 (2 CD set).
More fool me (Highland HL029/30 2 CD set) Orpheum Theatre Boston 24.4.74.
Moonlit Queen (Highland HL101/02 2 CD set) Massey Hall Toronto 2.5.74.
Live in Montreal (The Swingin' Pig TSPCD-040-2) Perhaps one of the most famous (or should that be "Infamous"?) bootlegs of all time originally issued as a single lp vinyl release titled **L'Ange Gabriel** (and under several other guises as well) this one captures the band at their peak with an excellent radio broadcast of the Montreal University show and tracks from one of the later BBC sessions 20.4.74.
Voices In The Academy (Highland HL189/90 2 CD set) Academy of Music NYC 6.5.74.

The Lamb Lies Down On Broadway Tour 1974-75.

The band's "The Lamb lies down on Broadway" shows are also well documented on bootleg including the following…

The Lamb Demos Down On Broadway Demo studio recordings 2 CD set. Track Listing: The Lamb Lies Down On Broadway (different mixes #1-2)/Fly On A Windshield (Rehearsal take/Demo mix)/Cuckoo Cocoon (Different Mix demos #1-4)/In The Cage (Demo #1and Rehearsal instrumental tale)/The Grand Parade Of Lifeless Packaging (Different Mix #1/Incomplete Demo Mix #2/Demo Mix #3)/Back In NYC (Demo Mixes #1-4)/Counting Out Time (Incomplete Demo Mix)/The Carpet Crawlers (Demo Mixes #1-2)/Lilywhite Lilith (Demo Mix)/The Waiting Room (Sound effects only demo/Different Mix Demos)/Anyway (Different Mix demos)/Here Comes The Supernatural Anaesthetist (Vocal Demo/Rehearsal Instrumental Takes #1-4)/The Lamia (Demo Mixes #1-2)/The Colony Of Slippermen (Rehearsal Instrumentals Takes #1-4)/The Light Dies Down On Broadway (Vocal Rehearsal Take)/Riding The Scree (Different Mix Demo)/In The Rapids (Incomplete demos #1-2/Demo Mix #1-2/Rehearsal Take)/ It (Rehearsal Take #1-2).

Hedley Grange Spring 1974 Tape 17 (2 CD set) A famous "hidden" recording taken direct from a master reel of demos for The Lamb… album and comprising the following tracks: Here Comes The Supernatural Anaesthetist (Takes 1-2)/In The Cage (Instrumental solo takes 1-5)/Evil Jam 1/Evil Jam 2/Evil Jam (Long version)/Flute Solo/Flute & Guitar/A Visit To The Doktor/Here Cones The Supernatural Anaesthetist (Jam)/Here Comes … (Takes 3-5)/The Colony Of Slippermen (Flute instrumental)/In The Rapids/It/The Light Dies Down On Broadway/Here Comes The Supernatural Anaesthetist (Take 6).

The lamb descends on Waterbury (OXY 089-090 2 cd set) comprising the entire show from the Palace Theatre Waterbury 12.12.74 as well as a delightful series of studio demos and out-takes from the rehearsals.

Rael Imperial (Highland HL059/60 2 cd set) West Palm Beach 10.1.75 (plus studio demos)

Supper's ready with a little lost lamb (Coloseum records 97-C-025 2 cd set) Lakeland Arena 11.1.75/Rainbow Theatre London 20.10.73

Rael Live in Manhattan (Suite 2) Madison Square Gardens NYC 28.1.75.

Live in Italy Palasport Turin 29.3.75 (2 CD set).

Live from Frankfurt Frankfurt Festhalle 3.4.75 (2 CD set)

The lamb lies down on Dusseldorf Philipshalle Dusseldorf 6.4.75 (2 CD set).

The Lamb Tour Westfalenhalle Dortmund 7.4.75 (2 CD set).

Live in Manchester (No catalogue number) Manchester Opera House 27.4.75

Tales of ordinary madness (Dream Weaver Records DWR396078-2) Birmingham Hippodrome 2.5.75. (Another well known bootleg when originally released on vinyl as **Swelled and Spent**).

The Waiting Room (Flashback Records) Wembley Empire Pool 15.4.75.

Awed Man Out (ACL records ACL 008) Wembley Empire Pool 15.4.75.

Memories of Wembley (No catalogue number) complete audience recording of the Wembley 15.4.75 gig (2 CD set).

A Trick Of The Tail Tour 1976.

1976's "A Trick of the tail" tour has also been documented by an increasing number of excellent recordings of which, the following are a representative sample.

A Trick Of The Takes Trident Studios rehearsals. ?.11.75. Track Listing: It's Yourself/Ripples/Robbery, Assault & Battery/Los Endos/Mad Man Moon/A Trick Of The Tail/Entangled/Dance On A Volcano/Squonk.

Memorial Auditorium Kitchener 27.3.76 (2 CD set). The first show currently available documenting Phil's arrival as singer, this one and the next show listed are also interesting for the set list which ran as follows… Dance On A Volcano/The Lamb Lies Down On Broadway/Fly On A Windshield/Carpet Crawlers/Cinema Show/Robbery, Assault & Battery/White Mountain/Firth Of Fifth/Entangled/Squonk/I Know What I Like.

Century Theatre Buffalo 28.3.76 (2CD set)

Watcher Of Toronto Maple Leaf Garden Toronto 1.4.76 (2 CD set). This was the first show at which the "standard" 1976 set was performed and the complete track listing for this and all subsequent gigs on this tour was as follows.. Dance On A Volcano/The Lamb Lies Down On Broadway/Fly On A Windshield/The Carpet Crawlers/Cinema Show/ Robbery, Assault & Battery/White Mountain/Firth Of Fifth/Entangled/Squonk/Supper's Ready/I Know What I Like/Los Endos/It-Watcher of the Skies.

Boston '76 Orpheum Theatre Boston 10.4.76 (2 CD set).

Syria Mosque Pittsburgh PA 13.4.76 (2 CD set)

Music Hall Cleveland 15.4.76 (2 CD set)

Just A Pool Of Tears Ford Auditorium Detroit 20.4.76 (2 CD set).

Live at the Ambassador Ambassador Theatre St Louis 23.4.76 (2 CD set).

"Dance on a Berkeley" (Highland HL094/95) Berkeley Community Theatre 29.4.76.

"Best Of British" Hammersmith Odeon 11.6.76 (1 CD) FM Radio broadcast

Dusseldorf '76 Philipshalle Dusseldorf 2.7.76 (2 CD set).

Los Endos Bills (Highland HL396/397 2 C D Set) Lorelei Festival St Goarshausen Freiluftbuhne 3.7.76.

There were also several earlier vinyl editions of shows from this tour all of which are now long since deleted and would form the basis of a collection in themselves.

Wind & Wuthering Tour 1977.

1977 and 1978's tours are documented by a fine series of recordings mainly taken from either soundboard or radio recordings and the following are among the most easily located….

Wot Gorilla, Lilith? (Highland Records HL329/330 " CD set) Rainbow Theatre London 1.1.77. Track Listing: 11th Earl Of Mar/Carpet Crawl/Firth Of Fifth/Your Own Special Way/Robbery, Assault & Battery/In That Quiet Earth/Afterglow/Lilywhite Lilith/The Waiting Room/Wot Gorilla?/One For The Vine/Squonk/All In A Mouse's Night/ Supper's Ready/I Know What I Like/Dance On A Volcano/Inside & Out/The Lamb Lies Down On Broadway/Musical Box (Closing section)

Second Night At the Rainbow (Digital Bros SAB10) As its title suggests, this is from the following night at the Rainbow and is taken from Pre-FM tapes of the British Biscuit Radio broadcast. (1CD). Track Listing: Intro/Squonk/In That Quiet Earth/Afterglow/One For The Vine/All In A Mouse's Night/Eleventh Earl Of Mar/I Know What I Like/Outro.

Live In London (Progressive Rock Remastering Project) Rainbow Theatre London 3.1.77. Track Listing: Eleventh Earl Of Mar/The Carpet Crawlers/Robbery, Assault & Battery/Your Own Special Way/Squonk/One For The Vine/Firth Of Fifth/All In A Mouse's Night/Supper's Ready/I Know What I Like/Dance On A Volcano/Los Endos/The Lamb Lies Down On Broadway/The Musical Box (Closing Section). Sourced from a soundboard recording this is another excellent release.

Live In Liverpool Empire Theatre Liverpool 9.1.77 (2 CD set). Track Listing: Squonk/ One For The Vine/Robbery, Assault & Battery/Your Own Special Way/In That Quiet Earth/Afterglow/I Know What I Like/11th Earl Of Mar/Firth Of Fifth/Supper's Ready/ Dance On A Volcano/Los Endos/The Lamb Lies Down On Broadway/Musical Box (Closing section).

In A House Of Dreams Southampton Gaumont Theatre (i4Detail 04 2 CD set). Track Listing: Squonk/One For The Vine/Robbery, Assault & Battery/Your Own Special Way/Firth Of Fifth/In That Quiet Earth/Afterglow/I Know What I Like/11th Earl Of Mar/Carpet Crawlers/All In A Mouse's Night/Supper's Ready/Dance On A Volcano/Los Endos/The Lamb Lies Down On Broadway/Musical Box (Closing Section).

On the Air (LaXious 03-04 2 CD set). Track Listing: Squonk/One For The Vine/ Robbery, Assault & Battery/Your Own Special Way/Firth Of Fifth/In That Quiet Earth/Afterglow/I Know What I Like/11th Earl Of Mar/Supper's Ready/Dance On A Volcano/Los Endos.

Ibirapuera Stadium Sao Paolo 15.5.77. (2 CD set)

Before Riches (Silver Rarities SIRA124/125 2 CD set). Earls Court Arena London24.6.77. Track Listing: Squonk/One For The Vine/Robbery, Assault & Battery/Inside & Out/ Firth Of Fifth/Carpet Crawlers/In That Quiet Earth/Afterglow/I Know What I Like/11th Earl Of Mar/Supper's Ready/Dance On A Volcano/Los Endos/The Lamb Lies Down On Broadway/Musical Box/The Knife.

Zurich Hallenstadion 2.7.77 (2 CD set)
Live In Munchen Munich Olympiahalle 3.7.77 (2 CD set).

And Then There Were Three Tour 1978.

Genesis - Tour Rehearsal (Highland HL037/38 2 CD set) comprises a soundboard recording of the band's rehearsals for their massive 1978 tour and as such is interesting to listen to in order to see what tracks they finally omitted from their set.

Real Mustard Palais Des Sports Dijon 3.6.78 (2 CD set). Excellent soundboard recording of the entire concert including a rare performance of Ballad Of Big. Track Listing: 11th Earl Of Mar/In The Cage/ Burning Rope/ Ripples/Deep In The Motherlode/Fountain Of Salmacis/Ballad Of Big/One For The Vine/Squonk/Say It's Alright, Joe/The Lady Lies/Cinema Show/Afterglow/Follow You Follow Me/Dance On A Volcano/Drum Duet-Los Endos/I Know What I Like.

Once in a while (Highland HL106/07 2 CD set) Gothenburg Scandinavium 7.6.78.
Ballad of Oslo Ekeberghallen Oslo 8.6.78 (2 CD set)
Supper in Dortmund Dortmund Philipshalle 14.6.78 (2 CD set) comprises complete audience recording of show including rare performance of Down And Out and unique encore of Apocalypse in 9/8.
Knebworth Show (Highland HL078/79 2 CD set) Comprises almost the entire show from Knebworth Park 24.6.78. (A much superior 2 CD set taken from the Pre-FM tapes of the British Rock Hour presentation of this gig also exists).

A Scream From Below (Highland HL187) Summerfield Showgrounds Milwaukee 19.7.78.
Show It Again Peter (Highland HL321/322 2 CD set) Madison Square Garden NYC 29.9.78.
Follow you follow me (Great Dane GDRCD 8918 2 CD set) comprises the entire show from Chicago's Uptown Theatre 13.10.78 and has been released under various other titles including the famous vinyl album; **From the mouth of the monster.**
"Audacious Atlanta" (MDF Records 2 CD set) The Omni Centre Atlanta 4.10.78.
Coming Down From Houston Hofheinz Pavilion Houston 22.11.78 (Highland HL 168)
Arigato Tokyo Sun Plaza Hall Tokyo 2.12.78 (2 CD set).

The tours which spanned 1980 through to 1982 are also well represented by recordings including the following:

Duke Tour 1980

The First Duke (No Catalogue Number) 2CD set Festival Hall Paignton 17.3.80

The Keepers Of The Key Come Home (No record company details). 2 CD set comprising entire show from Friars Club Aylesbury 22.3.80. Track Listing: Back In NYC/Dancing With The Moonlit Knight/The Carpet Crawlers/The Lady Lies/One For The Vine/Behind The Lines/Duchess/Guide Vocal/Turn It On Again/Duke's Travels/Duke's End/Say Its Alright,Joe/In The Cage-Ravine-Afterglow/Follow You Follow Me/Dance On A Volcano/Los Endos/I Know What I Like/The Knife.
First Hammersmith Hammersmith Odeon London 27.3.80. 2 Cassettes.
Second Hammersmith Hammersmith Odeon London 28.3.80. 2 Cassettes.
Third Hammersmith Hammersmith Odeon London 29.3.80. 2 Cassettes.
"Duke Stops To see The Lights" ABC Theatre Blackpool 3.4.80 2 CD Set.
ABC Theatre Peterborough 6.4.80. 2 CD set.
Sophia Gardens Cardiff 9.4.80. 2 Cassettes.
Gaumont Theatre Southampton 11.4.80 2 Cassettes
Conference Centre Brighton 12.4.80 2 CD set.
Sheffield City Hall 17.4.80 2 CD set
Guildford Memories (No Catalogue Number) 2 CD set Civic Hall Guildford 20.4.80
Swinging Sporrans (No Catalogue Number) 2 CD set Edinburgh Playhouse 23.4.80
Glasgow Apollo Theatre (No Catalogue Number) 28.4.80 2 CD Set.
Duke Meets The Geordies (No Catalogue Number) 2CD set City Hall Newcastle 30.4.80
Genesis - Duke Side Live (Highland HL019/20 2 CD set) Lyceum Ballroom London 7.5.80. This is also available under the title: **Musica** (Stonehenge STCD 2110/11 2 CD set).
A Sleepy Night (No Catalogue number) Liverpool Empire Theatre 2.5.80 (2 CD set).
Another Sleepy Night (No catalogue number) Liverpool Empire Theatre 3.5.80 (2 CD set).
For Hecklers Only Theatre Royal Drury Lane London 5.5.80 (2 CD set). Yes, this IS a bona fide recording from this elusive gig and the title becomes quite obvious when you listen to it!
Live In Pompey (No Catalogue Number) 2 CD set Guildhall Portsmouth 9.5.80
Oakland Coliseum Los Angeles 23.5.80 2 Cassettes.
Long Beach Arena 24.5.80. 2 Cassettes.
Sports Arena San Diego 26.5.80. 2 Cassettes
Live In LA (No Catalogue Number) 2 CD set Los Angeles Forum 27.5.80
Civic Arena Milwaukee 9.6.80. 2 Cassettes.
Where's Daryl? Pine Knob Music Theatre Clarkeston 12.6.80 (2 CD set). This recording captures the only Genesis gig at which Daryl Stuermer has not played since he joined the band.
Montreal Forum 19.6.80 (2 CD set).

The Lamb Lies Down On Albert (No Catalogue Number) Capitol Theater Passaic NJ 28.6.80. Track Listing: Deep In The Motherlode/Dancing With The Moonlit Knight/ Squonk/One For The Vine/Behind The Lines/Duchess/Guide Vocal/Turn It On Again/Duke's Travels/Duke's End/The Lady Lies/Ripples/Misunderstanding/In The Cage-Afterglow/Dance On A Volcano/Los Endos/I Know What I Like.

Madison Square Garden New York 29.6.80. 2 Cassettes.

Abacab Tour 1981

Abacab Complete Studio sessions 1981 (1 Disc)Track Listing: Abacab/Jangly (You Might Recall)/Nationwide (No Reply At All)/German 1 & II(Dodo/Lurker)/Sub (Submarine)/ Vocal 3/4 (Naminanu)/Chunky (Me & Virgil)/Odd (Keep It Dark)/Spike (Me & Sarah Jane)/Westside (Another Record)/Wierdsynth (Whodunnit?)/Lonely Man (Man On The Corner)/Don (Like It Or Not)/Paperlate/Abacab (Single version).

Running The Bulls Plaza De Toros Monumental Barcelona 25.9.81. 2 Cassettes.
Me And Virgil (Highland HL337/338 2 CD set) Velodromo Anoeta San Sebastian 26.9.81/Frejus Amphitheatre 29.9.81.

Picture About (No record company details) Frejus Arena 29.9.81. (2 CD set) Track Listing: Behind The Lines/Duchess/The Lamb Lies Down On Broadway/ Dodo/ Lurker/Abacab/Misunderstanding/Firth Of Fifth/No Reply At All/Me And Sarah Jane/In The Cage-Cinema Show/Afterglow/Turn It On Again/Los Endos/Man On The Corner/Who-Dunnit?/I Know What I Like.

Live In Lyon Palais Des Sports Lyon 1.10.81. 2 CD Set.
Like it Or Not (No Catalogue Number) Groenoordhal Leiden 3.10.81 2 CD Set
Stadthalle Bremen 5.10.81. 2 Cassettes.
Grugahalle Essen 6. 10.81. 2 Cassettes.
Karl Diehm Halle Wuerzburg 10.10.81. 2 CD Set.
Eis Sporthalle Kassel 13.10.81. 2 Cassettes
Live In Hanover Eilenriedhalle Hanover 15.10.81.
Guten Abend Hamburg Congresshalle Hamburg 18.10.81 2 Cassettes.
Live In Paris L'Hippodrome Pantin Paris 19.10.81. 2 Cassettes.
Hallenstadion Zurich 24.10.81. 2 Cassettes.
Perpetual Soundwave (Oh Boy 1-9098) Savoy Theatre NYC 28/11/81, Nassau Coliseum NY 29/11/81 and Lyceum Ballroom London 7/5/80.

Me & Cincinatti Riverfront Coliseum Cincinatti 21.11.81 (2 CD set). Track Listing: Behind The Lines/Duchess/The Lamb Lies Down On Broadway/Dodo-Lurker/ Abacab/ Me & Sarah Jane/Misunderstanding/No Reply At All/Firth Of Fifth/Man On The Corner/Who-Dunnit?/In The Cage-Cinema Show/Afterglow/Turn It On Again/Dance On A Volcano/Los Endos/I Know What I like.

Abacab To The Savoy (No Catalogue Number 2 CD set) Savoy Theater NY 28.11.81
Perfect Three Sides Live (Highland HL081/82 2 CD set) Nassau Coliseum 29.11.81.

Three Sides Live Tour 1982.

Civic Center Peoria 1.8.82. 2 Cassettes
Poplar Creek Chicago 2.& 3.8.82. 2 Cassettes (each).
Los Angeles Forum 9& 10..8.82. 2 Cassettes (each).
Postgate Pavilion Merryweather 19.8.82. 2 Cassettes.
JFK Stadium Philadelphia 21.8.82. 2 Cassettes.

Follow Me To Forest Hills Forest Hills NY 22.8.82 (2 CD set) This one captures one of only a handful of shows at which the Phoenix horns performed on stage with the band. Track Listing; Dance On A Volcano/Behind The Lines/Follow You Follow Me/Dodo-Lurker/Abacab/No Reply At All (with Phoenix Horns)/Paperlate(with Phoenix Horns)/Supper's Ready/Misunderstanding/Man On The Corner/Who-Dunnit/In The Cage Medley/Afterglow/Turn It On Again/Los Endos/TheLamb Lies Down On Broadway/It-Watcher Of The Skies.

Summer Of Saratoga (No record company details) 2 CD set comprising entire show from Saratoga Springs Performing Arts Centre 26.8.82.
CNE Grandstand Toronto 28.8.82. 2 Cassettes.
Jarry Park Montreal 29.8.82. 2 Cassettes.
Tirrenia Film Studios Pisa 6.9.82. 2 Cassettes
Palasport Rome 7.9.82. 2 Cassettes.
Autumnal Movement (MDF Recordings 2 CD set) Wilhelm Koch Stadion Hamburg 10.9.82.
Johanesshovs Isstadion Stockholm 12.9.82. 2 Cassettes.
Broendbyhallen Copenhagen 13.9.82. 2 Cassettes.
Scandinavium Gothenburg 14.9.82. 2 Cassettes.
Doyens of Deesside MDF Recordings 2 CD set) Deesside Leisure Centre 22.9.82. Track Listing: Dance On A Volcano/Behind The Lines/Follow You FollowMe/Dodo-Lurker/Abacab/Supper's Ready/Misunderstanding/Man On The Corner/Who-Dunnit?/In The Cage medley/Afterglow/Turn It On Again/Los Endos/The Lamb Lies Down On Broadway/It-Watcher Of The Skies/I Know What I Like.

Small Club at Marquee (Highland HL104/05) Marquee Club London 27.9.82.
Apocalypse (Ghost Records Ghost 0101/0102 2 cd set) Palasport Rome 7.9.82.
Get It Right Next Time Hammersmith Odeon London 29.9.82 (2 CD set).
Six Of The Best (Highland HL388/389 2 CD set) Milton Keynes Bowl 2.10.82

Mama Tour 1983-84.

Normal Illinois (No Catalogue Number) Horton Fieldhouse Normal Illinois 7.11.03. First night of the US tour with a different set: Dodo/Lurker/Carpet Crawlers/That's All/Mama/IllegalAlien/11thEarl Of Mar-Ripples-Squonk-Firth Of FifthMedley/Man On The Corner/Who-Dunnit?/Home By The Sea/Second Home By The Sea/Keep It Dark/It's Gonna Get Better/Follow You Follow Me/In The Cage-Cinema Show-In That Quiet Earth-Colony Of Slippermen Medley/Afterglow/Abacab/Drum Duet/Los Endos/Misunderstanding/Turn It On Again.

Civic Arena Milwaukee 10.11.83. 2 Cassettes
Rosemont Horizon Chicago (No Catalogue Number) Rosemont Horizon Chicago 11.11.83.
Toronto National Exhibition Halls (No Catalogue Number) National Exhibition Halls Toronto 23.11.83
Three Nights In Philly (Buccaneer RecordsBUC 051/2) Philadelphia Spectrum 27.11.83 and Nassau Coliseum Long Island 29.11.81.
Carrier Dome Syracuse NY 2.12.83. 2 Cassettes
Municipal Auditorium Buffalo NY 3.12.83. 2 Cassettes.
Pittsburgh Civic Center (No Catalogue Number) Pittsburgh Civic Center 7.12.83
Genesis - Los Cage (Highland HL171) Los Angeles Forum 14.1.84.
Fugitives From Justice (American Concert Series ACS001) Philadelphia Spectrum 27/11/83.
Straight In My Eyes (American Concert Series ACS014) Philadelphia Spectrum 25/11/83
 and Los Angeles Forum 12,13.,or 14/1/84.
Live In Seattle Tacoma Dome Seattle 10.1.84 2 CD Set.
Lloyd Nobel Center Norman IL 19.1.84 (2 CD set) Unusual for the inclusion of "Behind The Lines" as part of the 11th Earl…. Medley.
The Night the light went out Kemper Arena Kansas City 29.1.84 (2 CD set). Track Listing: Dodo/Lurker/Abacab/That's All/Mama/11th Earl Of Mar-The Lamb Lies Down On Broadway-Firth Of Fifth-Musical Box Medley/Illegal Alien(interrupted by power failure)/ Misunderstanding/Home By The Sea/Second Home By The Sea/Keep It Dark/It's Gonna get Better/Follow You Follow Me/In The Cage-Medley/Afterglow/Los Endos/Turn It On Again Sixties Medley.
Market Square Arena Indianapolis 1.2.84. 2 Cassettes.
The Steam Of The Medley (Highland HL335/336) Civic Auditorium Arena Omaha 3.2.84. 2 CD Ser
Dane County Coliseum Madison WI 5.2.84 2 Cassettes.
NEC Birmingham (MDF Recordings 2 CD set) Birmingham NEC 25.2.84
Live In Birmingham NEC Birmingham 26.2.94 (2 CD set).
Two Down, Three Left NEC Birmingham 27.2.84 (2CD set).
Birmingham Beauties NEC Birmingham 28.2.84 (2CD set).
Royal Cinema Show NEC Birmingham 29.2.84 (2 CD set).

This dearth of material has been more than compensated for by the plethora of recordings from the band's last three tours with an increasingly varied range of recordings appearing on the market…..

Invisible Touch Tour 1986-87

Invisible Touch World Tour (Gen69191/2 2 LP set) Joe Louis Arena Detroit 19.9.86. Track Listing: mama/Abacab/Land Of Confusion/In Too Deep/Domino/Follow You Follow Me/That's All/Tonight, Tonight, Tonight/Throwing It All Away/In The Cage-In That Quiet Earth-Apocalypse In 9/8 Medley/Invisible Touch/Turn It On Again.

Land Of Confusion (That's Life TL930015) Los Angeles Forum 17/10/86.
Outvisible Side (Highland 2 CD set) Madison Square Garden NYC 30.9.86
Illegal Alien (Beech Martin Records CD005) Los Angeles Forum 1986.

Melbourne's Own Special Way (No Catalogue Number 2 CD set) National Tennis Centre Melbourne 10.12.86. Track Listing: Mama/Abacab/Domino/Your Own Special Way(*)/In Too Deep(*)/The Brazilian/That's All/Home By The Sea/Second Home By The Sea/Throwing It All Away/In The Cage-In That Quiet Earth/Afterglow/Invisible Touch/Drum Duet-Los Endos/Turn it On Again. (*)= Tracks performed with a four piece string section.

Follow me To Melbourne (No Catalogue Number 2 CD set) National Tennis Centre Melbourne 11.12.86
That's Osaka (Platinum & Gold PG-870319 2 CD set) Osaka Castle Hall 13.3.87
Triangle on domino (Highland HL108/09 2 cd set) Berlin Reichstagsgelande 8.6.87.
Touch to Supper's ready (Highland HL127/28 2 cd set) Los Angeles Forum 17.10.86.
The Invisibles In Paris (MDF Recordings 2 CD set) Palais Omnsiports De Bercy Paris 2.6.87.

Invisible Cage (Kiss The Stone KTS042/43 2 cd set) Mannheim Maimarktgelande 20/6/87.
Live In USA & Germany 1987/1988 (part one) (International PF INP004) Mannheim Maimarktgelande 20/6/87.
Live in the park (MDF Recordings 2 CD set) Roundhay Park Leeds 28.6.87
Three down… One left!" (MDF Recordings 2 CD set) Wembley Stadium 4.7.87.

The Domino Principle (I4Detail I4Detail02 2 CD set) Wembley Stadium 4.7.87 Track Listing: Mama/Abacab/Domino/That's All/The Brazilian/In The Cage-In That Quiet Earth/Afterglow/Land Of Confusion/Tonight, Tonight, Tonight/Throwing It All Away/Home By The Sea/Second Home By The Sea/Invisible Touch/Drum Duet-Los Endos/Turn It On Again.

We Can't Dance Tour 1992.

Living Rehearsals Texas Stadium Irving TX 6.5.92 (2 CD set)Track Listing: Hold on My Heart/Way Of the World/Domino/Throwing It All Away/Dance On A Volcano(Radio announcement)/I Can't Dance/Tonight, Tonight, Tonight/Turn It On Again/Follow You Follow Me(*) (*)= Acoustic performance from the Dorchester Hotel 2002.
Astrodome (Red Line - Postscript PSCD2198 2 cd set) Houston Astrodome 9.5.92.
Live at the Skydome (Flashback flash08.92.0180 2 cd set) Toronto Skydome 9.6.92.
Luxury (BB 692) Three Rivers Stadium Pittsburgh 26.5.92.
Live in the Big Apple (Red Phantom 2093/94 2 cd set) Giants Stadium East Rutherford New Jersey 3.6.92.
Vienna (Backstage BKCD003/04 2 cd set) Vienna Wiener Prater Stadion 16.7.92.
Legend (Men at Work - Vox Populi 5554 2/1 2 cd set) St Jakob Football Stadium Basle 25.7.92.
Dancin' (Best Beat BB592) Pittsburgh Three Rivers Stadium 26/5/92.
Live - L'Espace Grammont Montpellier (WN- EG3 PC12 1-2 2 cd set) L'Espace Grammont Montpellier 20.7.92.
Legend (Men At Work WORK5554.2/1 2 cd set) St Jakob Football Stadium 26/7/92.

Live in the park Roundhay Park Leeds 31.8.92 (2 CD set). Track Listing: Land Of Confusion/No Son Of Mine/Driving The Last Spike/Dance On A Volcano-The Lamb Lies Down On Broadway-Musical Box-Firth Of Fifth-I Know What I Like Medley/ Throwing It All Away/Fading Lights/Jesus he Knows Me/Home By The Sea/Second Home By The Sea/Hold On My Heart/Domino/I Can't Dance/Tonight, Tonight, Tonight/ Invisible Touch/Turn t On Again.

There are also a whole batch of discs representing the band's final show at Knebworth Park on 2nd August with the following being a representative selection…
Summer nights (Kiss the Stone KTS 106-107 2 cd set).
Sincerely yours (Why not records WOT 2006 2 cd set).
Hold on my heart (On stage ON2234 2 cd set).
World dance (HM Digital Recording OHM 4-A 2 cd set).
Never Forget Jesus (Highland HL 315/316 2 CD set) Royal Albert Hall London 16.11.92.
Rare Material (PIG002 2 cd set) B-sides and rare material 1977/92.
Gold Collection (Rus Foley RFCD3) More B-sides and unreleased material 1970/90.

Rare Tapes Volumes 1-5 (No Catalogue Number). As its title suggests, this is a collection of unusual performances by the band from 1970 onwards culled from a variety of sources with the one exception being the studio track: Nowhere Else To Turn from the Calling All Stations album sessions.

Disc One: Looking For Someone (BBC Night Ride Session 22.2.70)/The Light (Live 7.3.71)/Twilight Alehouse(Live 26.2.72)/Harlequin (Live 4.3.72)/Bye, Bye Johnny (Live 14.4.72)/Happy The Man (Live 18.4.72)/Going Out To Get You (Live18.4.72)./One Handed Drum Solo (Live 28.6.72)/Can-Utility & The Coastliners (Live 20.8.72)/Seven Stones (22.8.72).

Disc Two: Supper's Ready (Live 18.11.72)/Harold The Barrel (Live 20.1.74)/Horizons (Live 4.5.74)/Watcher Of The Skies (Live 24.1.75)/It (Live 24.1.75)/The Musical Box (Live 24.1.75)/The Waiting Room (2.5.75).

Disc Three: Lilywhite Lilith-The waiting Room-Wot Gorilla? (Live 1.1.77)/All In A Mouse's Night (Live 2.1.77)/Inside & Out (Live 24.6.77)/Down & Out (Live 7.6.78)/Apocalypse in 9/8 (Live 14.6.78)/Ballad Of Big (29.7.78)/I Know What I Like (Live 29.7.78)/Dancing With The Moonlit Knight-Musical Box (Live 13.10.78).

Disc Four: Back In NYC (Live 29.6.80)/Me And Virgil (Live 27.9.81)/Like It Or Not (Live 30.11.81)/The Knife (Live 23.12.81)/No Reply At All -Paperlate(Live 22.8.82)/11th Earl Of Mar-Squonk-Firth Of Fifth (Live11.11.83)/11th Earl Of Mar-Behind The Lines-Firth Of Fifth-Musical Box(Live 17.1.84).

Disc Five: In The Cage-In That Quiet Earth-Apocalypse In 9/8 (Live 15.10.86)/Mama (Live 9.5.92)/Carpet Crawlers (Live 23.10.92)/Nowhere Else To Turn (Unreleased B Side 1997)/Small Talk (Live 13.12.97)/That's All (Live 23.1.98)/Hold On My Heart (Live 29.1.98).

Genesis Archive 2.5 (No Catalogue Number) As its title suggests; this is 2 CD an extension of the second Genesis Archive box set containing a further selection of live and studio material filling in the gaps from the official compilation.

Disc One: 11thEarl Of Mar (live)/Fly On A Windshield (Live)/Guide Vocal (Live)/Inside & Out (Live)/Follow You Follow Me (US single remix)/White Mountain (Live)/Say It's Alright, Joe (Live)/Tonight, Tonight, Tonight (Live)/Your Own Special Way (US single edit)/I Can't Dance (Live)/Who Dunnit (Live)/Keep It Dark (Live)/Me & Virgil (3x3 EP)/Burning Rope (Live)/The Knife (Live).

Disc Two: Abacab (7" single edit)/Dancing With The Moonlit Knight (Live)/Match Of The Day (Spot The Pigeon EP)/All In A Mouse's Night (Live)/The Lamb Lies Down On Broadway-It-Watcher Of The Skies (Live)/Mama (12" Extended version)/I Can't Dance Sex Mix)/Turn It On Again + Sixties Medley (12" single B Side)/Your Own Special Way (Live)/Tonight, Tonight, Tonight (7" single edit)/It's Gonna Get Better (12" single extended version).
Phil's decision to leave the band, and the installation of Ray Wilson as the band's new singer took many fans by surprise. The resulting Calling All Stations album and tour has, ironically, probably been the best documented album and tour out of the band's thirty plus year career.

Calling All Stations Tour 1998.

Alternate Calling All Stations (Highland HL256) alternative mixes and demos, B sides etc from album sessions. Track Listing: Shipwrecked (different vocal mix and guitars)/Congo (Extended ending different mix)/Alien Afternoon (Different ending guitar solo)/Not About Us (Alternative Mix)/Small Talk(No effect long version)/Calling All Stations (Alternative long version)/If That's What You Need (Different Mix)/One Man's Fool (Alternative Vocal Version)/Sign Your Life Away (Alternative Demo Version)/Run Out Of Time (Alternative Demo Version)/Papa He said (Non Album Track)/Banjo Man (Non Album Track)/7/8 Instrumental (Non Album Track).

Calling Chiddingfold Station (No catalogue number 1 CD) Chiddingfold Working Mens' Club rehearsal session 23.9.97. Track Listing: Domino (#1-4)/Talking & Tuning/The Lamb Lies Down On Broadway/Talking & Tuning/No So Of Mine/Talking & Tuning/ Firth Of Fifth
.

Calling RTL (No recording details) A live studio performance at the RTL Studios Paris 1997. Track Listing: No Son Of Mine/Congo/Land Of Confusion/Small Talk/ Mama/ Not About Us/Dancing With The Moonlit Knight/Follow You Follow Me/Calling All Stations/Invisible Touch/Shipwrecked/Alien Afternoon/Turn It On Again.

Berlin Rehearsal 1997 Radio broadcast from the Telecom Tower Berlin 26.8.97 and also includes a US radio interview from 1998. Track Listing: Band Introductions/Not About Us/Interview/No Son Of Mine/Interview/Lover's Leap/Interview/Turn It On Again/US Radio Interview.

Nothing Left Now Studio performances at Copenhagen 15.11.97 and Berlin 26.8.97. Track Listing: No Son Of Mine/Congo/Land Of Confusion/Calling All Stations/Turn It On Again/Alien Afternoon/Invisible Touch/Shipwrecked/No Son Of Mine/Not About Us/Lover's Leap/Turn It On Again.

There must be some other way to Bray (MDF Recordings 2 CD set) Bray Film Studios 23.1.98. Audience recording includes the only UK performance of Hold On My heart and That's All. Track Listing: No Son Of Mine/Land Of Confusion/The Lamb Lies Down On Broadway/Calling All Stations/Hold On My Heart/That's All/There Must Be Some Other Way/Domino/Carpet Crawlers/Firth Of Fifth (Instrumental section)/ Congo/ Home By The Sea/Second Home by The Sea/Dancing With The Moonlit Knight-Follow You Follow Me-Lover's Leap Acoustic Set/Mama/The Dividing Line/Invisible Touch/ Turn It On Again/Throwing It All Away/I Can't Dance.

Nervous Restart Sportshall Budapest (2 CD set) 28.1.98 (final dress rehearsal gig). Track Listing; No Son Of Mine/Land Of Confusion/The Lamb Lies Down On Broadway/ Calling All Stations/Hold On My Heart/Alien Afternoon/There Must Be Some Other Way/Domino/Carpet Crawlers/Firth Of Fifth (Instrumental)/Congo/Home By The Sea/Second Home By The Sea/Dancing With The Moonlit-Knight-Follow You Follow Me-Lover's Leap Acoustic Set/Mama/The Dividing Line/Invisible Touch/Turn It On Again/Throwing It All Away/I Can't Dance.

Nervous Restart 2 Sportshall Budapest (2CD set) 29.1.98 (First gig of the Calling All Stations tour). Track Listing: No Son Of Mine/Land Of Confusion/The Lamb Lies Down On Broadway/Calling All Stations/Alien Afternoon/The Carpet Crawlers/There Must be Some Other Way/Domino/Shipwrecked/Firth Of Fifth (Instrumental)/ Congo/ Home By The Sea/Second Home By The Sea/Dancing With The Moonlit Knight-Follow You Follow Me-Lover's Leap Acoustic Set/Mama/The Dividing Line/Invisible Touch/Turn It On Again/Throwing It All Away/I Can't Dance.

The Lamb Lies Down in Katowice (E S Recordings 2 CD set). Spodek Arena Katowice Poland 31.1.98. Polish Radio/TV Broadcast. Track Listing: As for Budapest 29.1.98.
Not About Us? (No Catalogue Number 2 CD set) Sportovinhala Prague 2.2.98 Czech Radio/TV Broadcast. Track Listing: Mama/Calling All Stations/There Must be Some Other Way/The Lamb Lies Down On Broadway/Alien Afternoon/ Congo/ Domino/ Home By The Sea/Second Home By The Sea/Turn It On Again/No Son Of Mine/Land Of Confusion/Shipwrecked/Invisible Touch.

Live After Diving (Highland HL283/284 2 CD set) Sportovinhala Prague 2/2/98 and NEC Birmingham 25 & 26/2/98.
Mannheim Magic (2CD set) Maimarktgelande Mannheim 4.2.98.
Live In Dortmund (2 CD set) Westfalenhalle Dortmund 10.2.98.
Through The Ages (Highland HL136/37 2 cd set) Stuttgart Schleyerhalle 12/2/98.
Strictly Mechanic (RFCD 13A/B 2 cd set) Stuttgart Schleyerhalle 12.2.98 (also available under the title **Through the ages**)
Live In Zurich (No Catalogue Number 2 CD set) Hallenstadion Zurich 13.2.98
Bologna 98 (No Catalogue Number 2 CD set) Palasport Casalecchio Bologna 17.2.98
Live In Roma (No Catalogue Number 2 CD set) Palasport Rome 18.2.98.
Live In Milan (No Catalogue Number 2 CD set) Filaforum Milan 19.2.98.
Doris' Day Out (MDF Recordings 2 CD set) Halle Tony Garnier Lyon 20.2.98.
Radio Waves (MDF Recordings) Birmingham NEC 25.2.98.
A new Beginning (Gentle Three 001 CD) NEC Birmingham 25.2.98.
More Radio Waves(M D F Recordings) Birmingham NEC 26.2.98 (2 CD set).
Live At Earls Court (M DF Recordings) Earls Court Arena London 27.2.98 (2 CD set)

Back Home By The Clyde Glasgow SECC 28.2.98 (2 CD set). Track Listing. A now standard set comprising: No Son Of Mine/Land Of Confusion/The Lamb Lies Down On Broadway/Calling All Stations/Carpet Crawlers/There Must Be Some Other Way/Domino/Firth Of Fifth (Instrumental)/Congo/Home By The Sea/Second Home By The Sea/Dancing With The Moonlit Knight-Follow You Follow Me-Lover's Leap Acoustic Set/Mama/The Dividing Line/Invisible Touch/Turn It On Again/Throwing It All Away/I Can't Dance.

Back In Toon (M DF Recordings) Telewest Arena Newcastle 1.3.98 (2 CD set)
A Welcome In The Valleys (M D F Recordings) Cardiff Arena 4.3.98 (2 CD set)
Cariad Caerdydd (M D F Recordings) Cardiff Arena 5.3.98 (2 CD set)
Live At NYNEX (M DF Recordings) NYNEX Arena Manchester 6.3.98 (2 CD set).
Live in Dublin (No Record company 2 cd set) The Point Theatre Dublin 9.3.98. (Also available under the title of **A single lonely voice**).
Calling All Stations From The Ahoy Ahoy Hall Rotterdam 12.3.98 (2 CD set)
Live In Lille (No Catalogue Number 2 CD set) Le Zenith Lille 13.3.98
Bordeaux Brilliance (No Catalogue Number 2 CD set) Patinoire de Malley Bordeaux 16.3.98
Hola Madrid! (No Catalogue Number 2 CD set) Pabellon Dos Desportos Madrid 19.3.98
Viva Barcelona! (No Catalogue Number 2 CD set) Palau St Jordi Barcelona 21.3.98
Erfurt Excellence (No Catalogue Number 2 CD set) Messehalle Erfurt 28.3.98
Guten Abend Hamburg! (No Catalogue Number 2 CD set) Sporthalle Hamburg 30.3.98.
A Finnish Symphony (MDF Recordings 2 CD set) Hartwall Arena Helsinki 5.4.98.
Live at the Ring Rock Am Ring Festival 30.5.98 (2 CD set).

The Solo Artists

As you may expect, the varied solo outings by the band members have also been well documented and the following is a concise outline of some of the material which has appeared for collectors…

Phil Collins/Brand X

Nightmore Patrol (Highland HL158) Glass Union Rochester NY 28.9.77 and Stockholm 30.8.78.
Phil's Masques (Highland HL031) A Brand X show from Park West Chicago 25.9.79.

Hello, I Must Be Going Tour 1982-83

First Time Behind The Lines Congresgebouuow Den Haag 21.11.82.

Live In London Hammersmith Odeon 30.11.82/Royal Albert Hall London 22.2.85. 2 CD set with the following tracks: I Don't Care Anymore/Thunder & Lightning/I Cannot Believe It's True/This Must Be Love/Thru These Walls/I Missed Again/Behind The Lines/You Know What I Mean/The Roof Is Leaking/Don't Let Him Steal Your Heart Away/The West Side/If Leaving Me Is Easy/In The Air Tonight/Like China/You Can't Hurry Love/It Don't Matter To Me/Hand In Hand.

4th Night At Hammersmith Hammersmith Odeon London 1.12.82. 2 CD set . Track listing: As above plus: And So To F/Why Can't It Wait Till Morning/People Get Ready.

Philadelphia '82 Tower Theatre ?.12.82. Edited version of above set list.
Phil Collins - The Fabulous Jacuzzis and One Neat Guy (Oh Boy 2-9096) Perkins Palace Pasadena 23.1.83. (2 CD set). Track Listing: As for Hammersmith.

No Jacket Required Tour 1985.

"Who said I would?" (MDF recordings 2 CD set) Manchester Apollo Theatre 12.2.85.Track Listing: I Don't Care Anymore/Only You & I Know/I Cannot Believe Its True/This Must Be Love/Against All Odds/Inside Out/Who Said I Would/If Leaving me Is Easy/Sussudio/Behind The Lines/Don't Lose My Number/The West Side/One More Night/In The Air Tonight/House Muzak/Like China/You Can't Hurry Love/It Don't Matter To Me/Hand In Hand/Take Me Home/People Get Ready/It's Alright/And So To F…

National Exhibition Hall Sydney 4.4.85 (2 CD set). Track Listing; As above
.
"Live at Live Aid" (ES Recordings) Wembley Stadium/JFK Stadium Philadelphia 15.6.85. Track Listing (Wembley): Against All Odds/Message In A Bottle/In The Air Tonight/Long, Long way To Go/Every Breath You Take. (Philadelphia): Against All Odds/In The Air Tonight.

But Seriously Tour 1990.

National Exhibition Hall Sydney 15.3.90 (I4Detail PCCD01) 2 CD set. Track Listing: Intro Music/Hand In Hand/Hang In Long Enough/Behind The Lines/Against All Odds/Doesn't Anybody Stay Together Anymore?/All Of My Life/Don't Lose My Number/Do You Remember?/Something Happened On The Way To Heaven/Another Day In Paradise/Separate Lives/I Wish It Would Rain Down/Saturday Night And Sunday Morning/The West Side/That's Just The Way It Is/Heat On The Street/One More Night/Colours/In The Air Tonight/You Can't Hurry Love/Two Hearts/Find A Way To My Heart/Groovy Kind Of Love/Easy Lover/Always/Take Me Home.
National Tennis Centre Melbourne 23.3.90 2 Cassettes. Track Listing: As above
"Something happened on the way to Brum" (MDF Recordings 3 CD set) Birmingham NEC 10.7.90. Track Listing: As above.
Berlin's Big Night Waldebuehne Berlin 15.7.90 2 Cassettes. FM radio broadcast.
"With Or Without Genesis" (American Concert Series ACS 062) Madison Square Garden NYC ?.9.90 Track Listing: As above.

Both Sides Tour 1994-95.

Prins Van Oranje Hal Utrecht 1.4.94 (2 CD set) This was the first date of the Both Sides world tour and featured a different set to later shows. Track listing: We Wait & We Wonder/One More Night/I've Forgotten Everything/Both Sides/In The Air Tonight/ Hang In Long Enough/Find A Way To My Heart/Easy Lover/Something Happened On The Way To Heaven/Invisible Touch (Jazz band intros)/You

Can't Hurry Love/Two Hearts/Sussudio/Burn Down The Mission/Always/Against All Odds/Take Me Home.

Westfalenhalle Dortmund 15.4.94. (2 Cassettes). Track Listing: Intro/I Don't Care Anymore/Don't Lose My Number/Everyday/Survivors/Another Day In Paradise/I Can't Turn Back The Years/I Wish It Would Rain Down/One More Night/A Groovy Kind Of Love/We Wait & We Wonder/I've Forgotten Everything/Both Sides Of The Story/In The Air Tonight/Hang In Long Enough/Find Away To My Heart/It Don't Matter To me/I Missed Again/Behind The Lines/Easy Lover/Only You & I Know/Something Happened On The Way To Heaven/You Can't Hurry Love/Two Hearts/Sussudio/ Helpless heart/Against All Odds/Take Me Home.

"Both Sides Of The Spectrum" Philadelphia Spectrum 22.6.94. (2 Cassettes)
Niedersachsenhalle Hanover 3.9.94 (2 Cassettes).
"Both Sides In Bercy" Palais Omnisports De Bercy Paris 10.9.94. (2 Cassettes).
National Exhibition Centre Birmingham 3.10.94 (2 CDs).
National Exhibition Centre Birmigham 4.10.94 (2 CDs)
Hallam FM Arena Sheffield 23.11.94 (2 Cassettes/CDs).

Live at G-Mex G-Mex Arena Manchester 28.11.94 (2 CD set). Track Listing: Intro/I Don't Care Anymore/Don't Lose My Number/I Cannot Turn Back The Years/ Survivors/Another Day In Paradise/I Wish It Would Rain Down/One More Night/A Groovy Kind Of Love/We Wait & We Wonder/Separate Lives/Both Sides/In The Air Tonight/Hang In Long Enough/Find A Way To My Heart/It Don't Matter To Me/Easy Lover/I Missed Again/Behind The Lines/Something Happened On The Way To Heaven/Knockin' On Heaven's Door/Two Hearts/Sussudio/Get Ready/My Girl/Take Me Home.

Buster's Big Night G_Mex Arena Manchester 29.11.94 (2 CD set). Track Listing: As above.
National Exhibition Centre Birmingham 4.12.94 (2 CDs).
National Exhibition Centre Birmingham 5.12.94 (2 CDs).
Saying Grace At The Arena Wembley Arena 11.12.94 (2 CDs)
Both Sides Tour (Twilight Music TMCD 003/04 2 CD set) Wembley Arena 13.12.94. Track Listing: As above

Mr Nice Guy (Oxygen OXY021) Fukuoka The Dome 7.5.95. Track Listing: As above

Live in Santiago Estadio Mundialista Santiago Chile 1995 (2 CD set).Track Listing: Drum Duet/I Don't Care Anymore/Don't Lose My Number/Everyday/Survivors/Another Day In Paradise/One More Night/A Groovy Kind Of Love/We Wait & We Wonder/Separate Lives/Both Sides/In The Air Tonight/Hang In Long Enough/Find A Way To My Heart/It Don't Matter To Me/Easy Lover/Only You & I Know/Something Happened On The Way To Heaven/Two Hearts/Sussudio/Take Me Home.

"Unplugged And More" Shepperton Film Studios 30.8.94. 1 Disc. Track Listing: I Don't Care Anymore/Both Sides/You Can't Hurry Love/One More Night/This Must Be Love/Separate Lives/The West Side/In The Air Tonight/Lady Madonna-Sussudio-Medley/Its In Your Eyes/The Tines They Are A-Changin'/Something Happened On The Way To Heaven/Helpless Heart/Two Hearts-Groovy Kind Of Love Medley/Oprah Medley: In The Air Tonight-Against All Odds-One More Night-Another Day In Paradise-Sussudio.

Dance Into The Light Tour 1997.

Going Loco In Tampa Ice Palace Tampa FL 28.2.97. (2 Cassettes). Track Listing: Hand In Hand/Hang In Long Enough/Don't Lose My Number/River So Wide/Take Me Down/Find A Way To My Heart/Another Day In Paradise/Against All Odds/Just Another Story/Lorenzo/Separate Lives/The Times They Are A'Changin'/You Know What I Mean/One More Night/In The Air Tonight/Timbantiocha/Loco In Acapulco/ Dance Into The Light/Easy Lover/Wear My Hat/You Can't Hurry Love/Two Hearts/ Something Happened On The Way To Heaven/Sussudio/The Same Moon/Take Me Home.

"Dancing Into Orlando" Orlando Arena 1.3.97 (2 Cassettes) Track Listing: As above.

"Something Happened On The Way To The Forum" Filaforum Milan 9.10.97 (2 Cassettes). Track Listing: Hand In Hand/Hang In Long Enough/Don't Lose My Number/River So Wide/Take Me Down/Find A Way To My Heart/Another Day In Paradise/Just Another Story/Against All Odds/Lorenzo/Separate Lives/Both Sides Of The Story/Do You Remember?/Long, Long Way To Go/One

More Night/in the Air Tonight/Timbantiocha/Easy Lover/Dance Into The Light/Wear My Hat/You Can't Hurry Love/Two Hearts/Something Happened On The Way To Heaven/Sussudio/Take Me Home

"Dancing Into The NEC" National Exhibition Centre Birmingham 6.11.97. (2 CDs). Track Listing: As above.

"Another Day At The NYNEX" NYNEX Arena Manchester 19.11.97. (2 CDs). Track Listing: As above.

"Dancing Into Earls Court" Earls Court Arena London 13.12.97. (2 Cassettes FM Radio broadcast). Track Listing: As above.

La Pinede Abtibes 16.7.96 (2 CD) Set.
Big Band Big Noise Stravinsky Auditorium Montreux 17.7.96 (2 CD set) Track Listing: Tony Bennet set/Los Endos/Two Hearts/That's All/Another Day In Paradise/Invisible Touch/The West Side/Against All Odds/Take Me Home/Radio Interview/Always/Do Nothin' Till You Hear From Me/Sussudio.

On The Air That Night (PC9697) Radio City Music Hall NYC 26.10.96 and RTF1 French TV studios "Tataratata" programme 3.2.97.
Phil Collins - Man of the year (Optimum 05 CD) New York 28.10.96/ Paris 3.2.97 .
Don't you know? I'm mad (Gizmo Dick GDR 9801/02 2 CD set) Palais Omnisports de Bercy Paris 13.12.97.

Big Band Big Noise II Symphony Hall Birmingham 24.7.98. 1CD. Track Listing: Intro/That's All/Invisible Touch/Against All Odds/I Don't Care Anymore/ Interview/ I've Got A Right To Sing The Blues/Watch What Happens/Chips And Salsa/Jazz track/Sussudio

"Unplugged At The Garden" Madison Square Garden New York NY 1.11.99 (1CD) This was an awards ceremony performance which featured the following tracks: Against All Odds/You'll Be In My Heart/Separate Lives/Take Me Home/In The Air Tonight (solo piano version).

Grand Casino Geneva 19.2.02 (No catalogue number). (1 CD) Track Listing: Groovy Kind Of Love/In The Air Tonight/Against All Odds/Another Day In Paradise/One More Night/ Something Happened On The Way To Heaven/You'll Be In My Heart/Separate Lives/You Can't Hurry Love/Easy Lover/Lady Madonna/The Way You Look Tonight/I Can't Dance/Take Me Home. Source: Mixing Desk.

Testify Tour 2002/03

The Scala Club London 6.11.02 (I4Detail PCCD02) 1 CD. Track Listing: In The Air Tonight/Something Happened On The Way To Heaven/Another Day In Paradise/I Can't Stop Loving You/I Missed Again/Against All Odds/You Can't Hurry Love/Two Hearts/Easy Lover/Lady Madonna/Sussudio/Take Me Home.

Little Dreams Grand Casino Geneva Switzerland 12.8.03. (1CD) A fundraiser for the "Little Dreams Foundation" for which Phil performed the following tracks: Intro by Orianne Collins/You Can't Hurry Love/Easy Lover/Follow You Follow Me (with M Rutherford)/I Can't Dance (With M Rutherford)/Throwing It All Away (With M Rutherford).

First Final Farewell Tour 2004/05

"Arrivederci Milano" Fila Forum Milan 1.6.04 (2 CD set) Track Listing: Don't Lose My Number/Intros/You'll Be In My Heart/One More Night/On My Way/Cant Stop Loving You/Hang In Long Enough/True Colours/Come With Me/A Groovy Kind Of Love/I Missed Again/Another Day In Paradise/Drum Thing/No Way Out/Separate Lives/In The Air Tonight/Dance Into The Light/You Can't Hurry Love/Two Hearts/Wear My Hat/Easy Lover/Sussudio/Its Not Too Late/Drum Thing/Take me Home.

"Aurevoir Geneve" Geneva Arena 6.7.04 (2 CD set) Track Listing: Drum Trio/ Something Happened On The Way To Heaven/Against All Odds/Don't Lose my Number/Intros/You'll Be In My Heart/One More Night/Can't Stop Loving You/Hang In Long Enough/True Colours/Come With Me/A Groovy Kind Of Love/I Missed Again/Another day In Paradise/No Way Out/Separate Lives/In The Air Tonight/Dance Into The Light/You Can't Hurry Love/Two Hearts/Wear My Hat/Easy Lover/Sussudio/Its Not Too Late/Drum Thing/Take Me Home.

"Farewell Amsterdam" Amsterdam Arena 19.6.04 2 CD set. Track Listing: Drum Trio (Los Endos/Timbantiocha)/Something Happened On The Way To Heaven/Against All Odds/Don't Lose My Number/You'll Be In My Heart/One More Night/Can't Stop Loving You/Hang In Long Enough/True Colours/Come With Me/Groovy Kind Of Love/I Missed Again/Another Day In Paradise/No Way Out/Separate Lives/In The Air Tonight/Dance Into The Light/You Can't Hurry Love/Two Hearts/Wear My Hat/Easy Lover/Sussudio/It's Not Too Late/Take Me Home.

"Winding Down At Wembley" Wembley Arena 27.6.04 (2 CD set) Track Listing: Intro/Drum Trio/Something Happened On The Way To Heaven/Against All Odds Don't Lose My Number/You'll Be In My Heart/One More Night/Cant Stop Loving You/Hang In Long Enough/True Colours/Come With Me/A Groovy Kind Of Love/I Missed Again/Another Day In Paradise/Separate Lives/In The Air Tonight/Dance Into The Light/You Can't Hurry Love/Two Hearts/Wear My Hat/Easy Lover/Sussudio/ Always/ Not Too Late/Drum Thing/Take Me Home.

"Always Manchester" Manchester Evening News Arena 28.6.04 (2 CD set). Track Listing: As above.

"All Right Anaheim!" Arrowhead Pond Anaheim 26.8.04 (2 CD set). Track Listing: Intro/Drum Thing/Something Happened On The Way To Heaven/Against All Odds/ Don't Lose My Number/You'll Be In My Heart/One More Night/Can't Stop Loving You/Hang In Long Enough/True Colours/Come With Me/A Groovy Kind Of Love/I Missed Again/Another Day In Paradise/Misunderstanding/No Way Out/In The Air Tonight/Dance Into The Light/You Can't Hurry Love/Two Hearts/Wear My Hat/Easy Lover/Sussudio/It's Not Too Late/Drum Thing/Take Me Home.

"OK Oklahoma!" Ford Center Oklahoma City OK 26.8.03 (2 CD set). Track Listing: As above.

"Tearing It Down In Orlando" TD Waterhouse Center Orlando FL 3.9.04 (2 CD set) Track Listing: As above.

"Phil In Philly" Wachovia Center Philadelphia 22.9.04 (2 CD set) Track Listing: as above.

"Skating On Ice" New Ice Arena St Petersburg 18.10.05 (2 CD Set). Track Listing: As below.

Belgrade Arena 28.10.05. (2 CD Set) Track Listing: Drum Trio/Something Happened On The Way To Heaven/Against All Odds/Don't Lose My Number/You'll Be In My Heart/One More Night/Can't Stop Loving You/Hang In Long Enough/True Colours/ Come With Me/A Groovy Kind Of Love/Another Day In Paradise/We Wait And We Wonder/Separate Lives/In The Air Tonight/Dance Into The Light/You Can't Hurry Love/Two Hearts/Wear My Hat/Invisible Touch/Easy Lover/Sussudio/Its Not Too Late/Drum Trio/Take Me Home.

Peter Gabriel Live Recordings.

Peter Gabriel 1 Tour 1977.

Before The Flood 1975.   A recent appearance this one and very interesting it is too, comprising as it does, several demos from the first solo album and several other tracks which Peter had written with lyricist Martin Hall who also later worked with Anthony Phillips on his 'Sides' album. Track Listing: Howling At The Moon/Excuse Me/Funny Man/No More Mickey/Get The Guns/Here Comes The Flood/God Knows.

Ain't That peculiar?   (Q-9011 LP) Cleveland Music Hall 15/3/77. Track Listing: Here Comes The Flood/On The Air/Moribund The Burgermeister/Waiting For The Big One/A Song Without Words/Excuse Me/Solsbury Hill/Ain't That Peculiar/Why Don't We?/Humdrum/Slowburn/All Day And All Of The Night/Modern Love/Down The Dolce Vita/Back In NYC.

Broken Eyes And Contact Lenses (PRRP SAE02 CD) Cleveland Music Hall 15/3/77. Much improved and COMPLETE version of above. Track Listing: Here Comes The Flood/On The Air/Moribund The Burgermeister/Waiting For The Big One/A Song Without Words/Excuse Me/Solsbury Hill/Ain't That Peculiar/Why Don't We/ Humdrum/Slowburn/All Day And All Of The Night/Here Comes The Flood/Modern Love/Down The Dolce Vita/Back In NYC. Bonus Track: PG Interview Picadilly Radio Manchester 1977. 2 CD Set.

Gilded Sleeve (Flat 8234 LP) L A Roxy Club 9/4/77. Track Listing: As above.

Manchester Apollo 23.4.77 (MUPPET 09). An excellent complete 2CD audience recording of this early show .

Like A Possessed Twelve Year-old (3047 LP) New Vic Theatre 30/4/77. Track Listing: Here Comes The Flood/On The Air/Moribund The Burgermeister/Waiting For The Big One/Song Without Words (Indigo)/Excuse Me/Ain't That Peculiar/Solsbury Hill/ Slowburn/All Day And All Of The Night/Down The Dolce Vita/Back In NYC.

Palais Des Sports Courtrai 2.9.77 (2 CD set) Track Listing: White Shadow/On The Air/Down The Dolce Vita/Waiting For The Big One/Excuse Me/Solsbury Hill/Indigo/ Modern Love/DIY/Humdrum/Heard it Thru The Grapevine/Modern Love/Here Comes The Flood/Back in NYC.

Live In Liverpool Empire Theatre Liverpool 23.9.77. Track Listing: Here Comes The Flood/Slowburn/Moribund The Burgermeister/Modern Love/Indigo/Humdrum/White Shadow/Heard It Thru The Grapevine/Excuse Me 1/Excuse Me 2/Waiting For The Big One/Solsbury Hill/Down The Dolce Vita/On The Air/All Day And All Of The Night/Here Comes The Flood/Back In NYC/Animal Magic.

Free Trade Hall Manchester 29.9.77

The Egg Was A bird (How To Walk Silly Records HTWSR 101 LP) Tivoli Gardens Copenhagen 9/10/77.

Peter Gabriel 2 Tour 1978.

Knebworth Park Festival 9.9.78. Track Listing: Me & My Teddy Bear/On The Air/Moribund The Burgermeister/Perspective/Flotsam & Jetsam/White Shadow/Here Comes The Flood/Waiting For The Big One/A Whiter Shade Of Pale/Slowburn/Home Sweet Home/I Don't Remember/Solsbury Hill/Modern Love/The Lamb Lies Down On Broadway.

On The Air (Musichien MCH 9104 91 LP/ 0304 CD) Essen Grugahalle 15/9/78. Track Listing: On The Air/Moribund The Burgermeister/Perspective/Here Comes The Flood/ White Shadow/Waiting For The Big One/Humdrum/I Don't Remember/Solsbury Hill/Modern Love.
Battersea Park Battersea Park Festival 16.9.78.

A whiter shade of pale (Highland HL015/16 (2 CD set) Chateau Neuf Oslo 31.8.78/Bottom Line Club NYC 4.10.78.Track Listing: On The Air/Moribund The Burgermeister/Modern Love/Flotsam & Jetsam/White Shadow/Have A Wonderful Day (In A One Way World)/Humdrum/Waiting For The Big One/D.I.Y/Home Sweet Home/A Whiter Shade Of Pale/Here Comes The Flood/Slowburn/Mother Of Violence/I Don't Remember/Solsbury Hill/Animal Magic/Perspective/**On The Air(*)/D.I.Y(*)/Solsbury Hill(*)/The Lamb Lies Down On Broadway(*)/Ain't That Peculiar(+)/A Song Without Words(+)/Waiting For The Big One(+)/Excuse Me(+)/Slowburn(+)/All Day And All Of The Night(+).**
(*)= Bottom Line Club NY 78 (+)= Cleveland 77.

The King Of The Rhythm (Vols 1 & 2) (Clean Sounds CS 1010/Amazing Record Company ARC0081/82 LP) Montreal University Sports Centre 15/10/78.

Kent State University 21.10.78

Mr Mozo Risin' (ML 9621) Stoneybrook University 28.10.78. Track Listing: Me & My Teddy Bear/On The Air/Moribund The Burgermeister/Perspective/Humdrum/Song Without Words/White Shadow/DIY/Waiting For The Big One/Flotsam & Jetsam/ Exposure/ Slowburn/I Don't Remember/Solsbury Hill/Modern Love/The Lamb Lies Down On Broadway.

Live In Geneva (Ganescha Rec 91 LP) Geneva Palaias des Sports 17/12/78.

Meeting at the Reading (Ghost Records Ghost 0103) Reading Festival 26.8.79. Track Listing: Biko/On The Air/D.I.Y/Humdrum/No Self Control/White Shadow/Mother Of Violence/I Don't Remember/Moribund The Burgermeister/Perspective/Solsbury Hill/Here Comes The Flood/The Lamb Lies Down On Broadway.

Peter Gabriel 3 Tour 1980.

Odeon Theatre Taunton 21.2.80 2 CD set.
Sheffield City Hall 25.2.80 2 CD set.
City Hall Newcastle 3.3.80 2CD set.
Empire Theatre Liverpool 4.3.80 2 CD set
Apollo Theatre Manchester 5.3.80 2 CD set
Chromedome (Rock Solid Records RSR113 LP) Sophia Gardens Cardiff 7/3/80. Also available as the much improved MUPPET 07 version.
The Intruder Hammersmith Odeon London 11/3/80.
Front Tear Games (Edition Export LG 00181 2 Lp set) Hammersmith Odeon 12/3/80. Also available as a 2 CD set.
Live At The Greek Greek Theatre Los Angeles 19.6.80 (2 CD set)
I Lost My Teddy Bear On The 1980 Tour (Alternative Vinyl Productions AVP 107 LP) Cleveland Music Hall 27/6/80.
At The German Front (Rentner records RR003 LP) Hamburg Audimax 1/9/80.

Utrecht '80 Nieuemusikcentrum Utrecht 6.9.80 (2 CD set). Track Listing: Intruder/The Start/I Don't Remember/Solsbury Hill/Family Snapshot/Milgrams' 37/Modern Love/ Not One Of Us/Lead A Normal Life/Moribund The Burgermeister/Mother Of Violence/Humdrum/Bully For You/Games Without Frontiers/And Through The Wire/I Go Swimming/Biko/On The Air/DIY.

Vin de Bordeaux Patinoire de Malley Bordeaux (2 CD set) 24.9.80
On Stage (Ghost Records 0100 CD) Florence Parco Le Cascine 28/9/80.
Chinatour (Lizard records LZCD011/12 2 CD set) Palasport Genoa 29.9.80.

Peter Gabriel 4 Tour 1982/83.

Shock The Dog (Trans World Communications DOG 001/002/003 3 LP set) Shepton Mallet Showering Pavilion 16 & 18/7/82. (Also available as a 2 CD set MUPPET 04)
Family Snapshot (Inferno PG 0083 2 LP set) Werchter Festival 3/7/83.

Intruder at the Palace (E S Recordings 2 CD set) Crystal Palace Football Ground 9.7.83. Track Listing: Across The River/I Have The Touch/Not One Of Us/The Family & The Fishing Net/Shock The Monkey/Family Snapshot/Intruder/Humdrum/Games Without Frontiers/Lay Your Hands On Me/Solsbury Hill/I Don't Remember/San Jacinto/On The Air/Biko/Kiss Of Life.

Live In Seattle Paramount Theatre Seattle 10.8.83 (2 CD set) Track Listing: Across The River/I Have The Touch/Not One Of Us/The Family & The Fishing Net/Shock The Monkey/ Family Snapshot/Intruder/Humdrum/Games Without Frontiers/Lay Your hands On Me/Solsbury Hill (Take 1)/Solsbury Hill (Take 2)/I Don't Remember/San Jacinto

Intruder (TMQ 71120 LP) Hammersmith Odeon 8/9/83
Kiss Of Life In Glasgow Apollo Theatre Glasgow 12.9.83. (2 CD set) inlcudes extra encore performance of Kiss Of Life.
Newcastle City Hall 15.9.83 2 CD set..
"Wallflower" Congressgebouw Den Haag 27.9.83 (evening show) (2 CD set). Track Listing: The Rhythm Of The Heat/I Have The Touch/Not One Of Us/The Family & The Fishing Net/Shock The Monkey/Intuder/No Self Control/Wallflower/Lay Your Hands On Me/Solsbuy Hill/I Go Swimming/San Jacinto/On The Air/Biko/Here Comes The Flood.

Con-Tact (The Famous Charming Label 347 153-1 3 LP set) Falkoner Theatrit Copenhagen 1/10/83.

Wallflowers In Vienna Vienna Stadthalle 8.10.83 (2 CD set) Track Listing: Rhythm Of The Heat/I Have The Touch/Not One Of Us/The Family & The Fishing Net/Shock The Monkey/Family Snapshot/Intruder/No Self Control/Wallflower/Lay Your Hands On Me/Solsbury Hill/I Don't Remember/San Jacinto/On The Air/Biko/Here Comes The Flood/Across the River/Intruder/Humdrum/Milgram's 37

"Conspiracy Of Hope" and So Tours 1986/87.

.
So Alive (Manic Monster Music MMM 003) Giants Stadium New Jersey 15.6.86. Track Listing: Red Rain/Shock The Monkey/Family Snapshot/Sledgehammer/San Jacinto/Biko.

Live In Rochester Rochester NY War Memorial 7.11.86. (2 CD set). Track Listing: Floating Dogs/San Jacinto/Red Rain/Shock The Monkey/Family Snapshot/That Voice Again/No Self Control/Mercy Street/This Is The Picture/The Family & The Fishing Net/Don't Give Up/Big Time/Lay Your Hands On Me/Sledgehammer/Here Comes The Flood/In Your Eyes./Biko.

Civic Arena Syracuse NY 9.11.86 (2 CD set) Audience recording.

State Of Mind (Jester Productions JP 103-2 NOV 86 A/D 2 LP) Largo Capitol Centre 11/11/86.
Montreal Forum 25.11.86 2 CD Set
Live In Philly Philadelphia Spectrum 30.11.86 (2 CD set MUPPET 08)

Take The Sledgehammer (Dr Gig DGDC009 CD) Tokio Jingu Arena 20 & 21/12/86. Track Listing: Here Comes The Flood/Red Rain/Shock The Monkey/San Jacinto/ Sledgehammer/Biko/In Your Eyes.

In Your Eyes (Red Phantom RPCd2105/06 2 CD set) Palasport Bologna 12/6/87.
Live In Rome (RL-03 LP) Palasport Rome 13/6/87.
Mystery Meeting Kim Sue Records KS 088700; AB2 2 LP set) Sporthalle Cologne 19/6/87.
In Your Eyes (Spacematic Recs 198-70127; PG198-70626 2 LP set) Earls Court Arena London 26/6/87.
Intruder (MDF Recordings 2 CD set) NEC Birmingham 30.6.87. Track Listing: Floating Dogs/San Jacinto/Red Rain/Shock The Monkey/Family Snapshot/The Family & The Fishing Net/Games Without Frontiers/No Self Control/Mercy Street/This Is The Picture/Big Time/Don't Give Up/Solsbury Hill/Lay Your Hands On Me/Sledgehammer/ Here Comes The Flood/In Your Eyes/Biko.

No Self Control at the NEC (MDF Recordings 2 CD set) NEC Birmingham 1.7.87. Track Listing: Floating Dogs/San Jacinto/Red Rain/Games Without Frontiers/Family Snapshot/Intruder/Shock The Monkey/No Self Control/Mercy Street/This Is The Picture/Big Time/Don't Give Up/Solsbury Hill/La Your Hands On Me/Sledgehammer/ Here Comes The Flood/In Your Eyes/Biko.

Live in Philly (E S Recordings 2 CD set) Spectrum Philadelphia 21.7.87. Track Listing: As above.
Live Blossoms Blossom Music Centre Cleveland 27.7.87 (2 CD set).
No Self Control (Victory Records XAV41-46 3 LP set) Verona Piazza Bra' Amphitheatre 18/9/87.
Music Without Frontiers (Collectors Pleasure Recordings COP009). Various venues on the 1987 US tour.

"Human Rights Now!" Tour 1988.

Of These Hope (MDF Recordings) Wembley Stadium 2.9.88. Track Listing: Of These Hope/Games Without Frontiers/Family Snapshot/Shock The Monkey/Don't Give Up/Sledgehammer/In Your Eyes/Biko.

Palais Omnisports De Bercy Paris 4.9.88.
Palais Omnisports De Bercy Paris 5.9.88.

"US" Tour 1993-94.

Laguna Beach (German Records GR031) Grand Slam Club 3.4.93.

Union (No recording details 2 CD set) Le Galaxie Amneville 23.4.93 Track Listing: Come Talk To Me/Steam/Games Without Frontiers/Across The River/Blood Of Eden/San Jacinto/Love Town/Kiss That Frog/Washing Of The Water/Solsbury Hill/Digging In The Dirt/Sledgehammer/Secret World/In Your Eyes/Biko.

Live from a Secret World (Pluto records PLRCD 9318) Le Zenith Paris 24.4.93. Track Listing: Come Talk To Me/Steam/Games Without Frontiers/Across the River/Shakin' The Tree/Blood Of Eden/San Jacinto/Love Town/Kiss That Frog/Washing Of The Water/Solsbury Hill/Digging In The Dirt/Sledgehammer/Secret World/In Your Eyes/Biko.
Secret World (Front Row 27/28 2 CD set) Academy of Music NYC 8/4/93.
Live To Be Loved (RTCDPG 1-2 2 CD set) Stockholm Globe 13/4/93.
Live From A Secret World (Pluto Records PLR CD 9318/AB 2 CD set) Le Zenith Paris 24/4/93.
Digging In Europe (Fun Factory 003 CD) Rotterdam Ahoy Sportpaleis 27 & 28/4/93.

Nimes '93 Amphitheatre De Nimes 13.5.93. (2 CD set). Track Listing: Intro/Come Talk To Me/Steam/Games Without Frontiers/Across The River/Shaking The Tree/Blood Of Eden/Shock The

Monkey/Washing Of The Water/Solsbury Hill/Digging In The Dirt/ Sledgehammer/Secret World/In Your Eyes/Biko/Here Comes The Flood.

From Steeltown to Lovetown (E S Recordings 2 CD set) Sheffield Arena 24.5.93. Track Listing: Come Talk To Me/Quiet Steam/Games Without Frontiers/Across The River/ Slow Marimbas/Shaking The Tree/Blood Of Eden/San Jacinto/Lovetown/Shock The Monkey/Washing Of The Water/Solsbury Hill/Digging In The Dirt/ Sledgehammer/ Secret World/In Your Eyes/Biko/Here Comes The Flood.

I Left My Red Dress In The Stadium. Dublin Point Depot 29/5/93. 2 CD Set.

Games Without Frontiers (On Stage Records CD/ON 2301 2 CD set) Earls Court Arena London 31/5/93. Track Listing: Of These Hope/Come Talk To Me/Steam/Games Without Frontiers/Across The River/Shaking The Tree/Blood Of Eden/San Jacinto/ Shock The Monkey/Washing Of The Water/Solsbury Hill/Digging In The Dirt/ Sledgehammer/In Your Eyes/Biko.

Chicago 1993 Rosemont Horizon Chicago 10.7.93. (2 CD set MUPPET 05) Track Listing: Come Talk To Me/Steam./Games Without Frontiers/Across The River/Slow Marimbas/Shaking The Tree/Blood Of Eden/San Jacinto/Shock The Monkey/Washing Of The Water/Solsbury Hill/Digging In The Dirt/Sledgehammer/Secret World/In Your Eyes/Biko.

Los Angeles 1993 (Red Line PSCD2278 2 CD set) Los Angeles Great Western Forum 22/7/93. Track Listing: Come Talk To Me/Steam/Games Without Frontiers/Across The River/Slow Marimbas/Shaking The Tree/The Blood Of Eden/San Jacinto/Only Us/Shock The Monkey/Washing Of The Water/Solsbury Hill/Digging In The Dirt/ Sledgehammer/Secret World/In Your Eyes/Biko.

Arco Arena Sacramento 21.9.93. (2CD set). Track Listing: Come Talk To Me/Steam/ Games Without Frontiers/Across The River/Shaking The Tree/Blood Of Eden/San Jacinto/Family Snapshot/Kiss That Frog/Washing Of The Water/Solsbury Hill/Digging In The Dirt/Slesgehammer/Secret World/in Your Eyes/Biko.

Across The River (Flying Tigers FTCD 0055 CD) Modena Palasport 16/11/93 and Tatarata French Tv studio performance 19/6/93.
Secret Sacramento (E S Recordings 2 CD set) ARCO Arena Sacramento 21.9.93.
Alive & Bumpin' (Octopus records OCTO 016/017 2 CD set) Modena Palasport 16 7 17/11/93.

Live In Sydney Entertainment Centre Sydney 1.3.94. Track Listing: Come Talk To Me/Steam/Games Without Frontiers/Shock The Monkey/Across the River/Shaking The Tree/Blood Of Eden/San Jacinto/Family Snapshot/Kiss That Frog/Solsbury Hill/ Digging In The Dirt/Sledgehammer/In Your Eyes/Biko.

Secret World (PG-001/002 2 CD set) Tokio Nippon Budokan Hall 8.3.94.
Glastonbury Festival (Festival Music FMCD-001/002 2 cd set) Glastonbury Festival 26.6.94.

Woodstock (Wood 99410) Saugerties New York "Woodstock II Festival" 25.8.94.

A Friend of mine (T Rex Records TRCD123) Compilation of Peter's more recent tv appearances and the Paris Amnesty gig 10.12.98. Track Listing: Red Rain/Signal To Noise/In Your Eyes. Film Tracks: Party Man/I Have The Touch/I Grieve/We Do What We're Told (Milgram's Progress)/Seven Zero.

Signal To Seattle Marymoor Park Seattle 29.7.01. Track Listing: Here Comes The Flood/ Red Rain/Digging In The Dirt/Family Snapshot/Come Talk To Me/Mercy Street/ Solsbury Hill/Signal To Noise/In Your Eyes/Father, Son/When You're Falling.

"Growing Up Tour 2002-03.

Real World Studios (No catalogue number 1 CD) 13th September 2002. Track Listing: The Barry Williams Show (CD)/Introduction and interview/Darkness/Interview/More Than This/Interview/Mercy Street/Interview/My Head Sounds Like That/ Interview/ Sledgehammer/Interview/Growing Up/Interview/The Barry Williams Show/Massimo Cotto Introduces/Burn You Up Burn You Down(CD).

Growing Up in Milan (No catalogue number 2 CD set) Milan Alcataz 16.9.02 Track Listing: Darkness/Red Rain/Growing Up/No Way Out/Mercy Street/My Head Sounds Like That/The Barry

Williams Show/More Than This (Take 1)/More Than This (Take 2)/Digging In The Dirt/Animal Nation/Sledgehammer/In Your Eyes/Father Son.

Up In The Flood (No catalogue Number) Munich 21.9.02. Track Listing: Darkness/Red Rain/Growing Up/Solsbury Hill/Mercy Street/Barry Williams Show/More Than This/ Digging In The Dirt/Family Snapshot/Jetzt Kommt Die Flut.

Live From RTL RTL Studios Paris 24.10.02 (I4Detail PGCD01) 1 CD. Track Listing: Darkness/ Red Rain/Growing Up/Mercy Street/My Head Sounds Like That/The Barry Williams Show/More Than This/Sledgehammer/In Your Eyes.

Auditorio Nacional Mexico City 4.11.02. (2 CD set). Track Listing: Father, Son/ Darkness/Red Rain/The Barry Williams Show/My Head Sounds Like That/Technical Fuck-Up #1/Downside Up/More Than This/Technical Fuck-Up #2/Come Talk To Me/Mercy Street/Digging In The Dirt/Growing Up/Animal Nation/Solsbury Hill/Sledgehammer/In Your Eyes/Family Snapshot/The Tower That Ate People.

United Center Chicago IL 12.11.02 (2 CD set)

Continental Airlines Arena East Rutherford NJ 17.11.02 (2 CD set). Track Listing: Here Comes The Flood/Darkness/Red Rain/Secret World/Sky Blue/Downside Up/The Barry Williams Show/More Than This/Mercy Street/Digging In The Dirt/Growing Up/ Animal Nation/Solsbury Hill/Sledgehammer/Signal To Noise/In Your Eyes/Family Snapshot/Father, Son.

Spectrum Arena Philadelphia 18.11.02. (2 CD set). Track Listing: Here Comes The Flood/Darkness/Red Rain/Secret World/Sky Blue/Downside Up/The Barry Williams Show/My Head Sounds Like That/Mercy Street/Digging In The Dirt/Growing Up/ Animal Nation/Solsbury Hill/Sledgehammer/Signal To Noise/In Your Eyes/Be My Woman And I'll Be Your Man/Father, Son.

Madison Square Garden New York NY 21.11.02 (2 CD set). Track Listing: Here Comes the Flood/Darkness/Red Rain/Secret World/Sky Blue/Downside Up/The Barry Williams Show/My Head Sounds Like That/Mercy Street/Digging In The Dirt/Growing Up/Animal Nation/Solsbury Hill/Sledgehammer/I Grieve/In Your Eyes/Family Snapshot/Father, Son.

MCI Center Washington DC 24.11.02 (2 CD set). Track Listing: Here Comes The Flood/Darkness/Red Rain/Secret World/Sky Blue/Downside Up/The Barry Williams Show/My Head Sounds Like That/Mercy Street/Digging In The Dirt/ Growing Up/ Animal Nation/Solsbury Hill/Sledgehammer/I Grieve/In Your Eyes/Come Talk To Me/Father, Son.

"The Moon And The Menstrual Cycle" Mohegan Sun Arena Uncasville 26.11.02 (2 CD set). Track Listing: Here Comes The Flood/Darkness/Red Rain/Secret World/Sky Blue/Downside Up/The Barry Williams Show/My Head Sounds Like That/Mercy Street/Digging In The Dirt/Growing Up/Animal Nation/Solsbury Hill/Sledgehammer/I Grieve/In Your Eyes/Father, Son.

Air Canada Centre Toronto 2.12.02 (2 CD set). Track Listing: Here Comes The Flood/ Darkness/Red Rain/Secret World/Sky Blue/Downside Up/The Barry Williams Show/My Head Sounds Like That/Shock The Monkey/Mercy Street/Digging In The Dirt/Growing Up/Animal Nation/Solsbury Hill/Sledgehammer/I Grieve/In Your Eyes/Come Talk To Me/Father, Son.

Oakland Coliseum 14.12.02 (2 CD set MUPPET 03). Track Listing: Here Comes The Flood/ Darkness/Red Rain/Secret World/Sky Blue/Downside Up/The Barry Williams Show/ More Than This /Mercy Street/Digging In The Dirt/Growing Up/Animal Nation/ Solsbury Hill/I Grieve/In Your Eyes/Shock The Monkey/Father, Son.

Milan Filaforum 9.5.03 (No catalogue number 2 CD set). Track Listing: Here Comes The Flood/Darkness/Red Rain/Secret World/Sky Blue/Downside Up/The Barry Williams Show/More Than This/Mercy Street/Digging In The Dirt/Growing Up/Animal Nation/Solsbury Hill/Sledgehammer/I Grieve/In Your Eyes/No Way Out/Father, Son.

Palasport Florence 12.5.03 (No catalogue number 2 CD set). Track Listing: Here Comes The Flood/Darkness/Red Rain/Secret World/Sky Blue/Downside Up/The Barry Williams Show/More Than This/Mercy Street/Digging In The Dirt/Growing Up/ Animal Nation/Solsbury Hill/Sledgehammer/I Grieve/In Your Eyes/Come Talk To Me/Father, Son.

Live in Poznan Poznan Arena 30.5.03. (2 CD set) Track Listing: Here Comes The Flood/ Darkness/Red Rain/Secret World/Sky Blue/Downside Up/The Barry Williams Show/ More Than This/Mercy Street/Digging In The Dirt/Growing Up/Animal Nation/ Solsbury Hill/Sledgehammer/Signal To Noise/In Your Eyes/Biko.

Brighton Conference Centre 24.11.03. (2 CD set). Track Listing: Burn You Up, Burn You Down/Red Rain/More Than This/Secret World/Games Without Frontiers/ Downside Up/Mercy Street/Darkness/Digging In The Dirt/Signal To Noise/Growing Up/San Jacinto/Shock The Monkey/Solsbury Hill/Sledgehammer/Signal To Noise/In Your Eyes/Biko.

"Still Growing Up" Tour 2004.

All of Peter's European shows in 2004 have been issued officially as another batch of "Encore" series recordings.

Studio Compilations.

With Peter's current high profile it is interesting to see the proliferation of compilations of unreleased studio material, B sides and unusual live recordings. Here is a representative selection of what is currently available.

"Games Without Words" (Gaba Rec GABA 1-2) Studio recordings from the Ashcombe House Sessions for Peter's third album ?.11.79. Track Listing: I Don't Remember/Games Without Frontiers/Milgrams' 37/The Start/And Through The Wire/I Go Swimming/ Walk Through The Fire/Intruder/Biko.

"Book Of Memories" (Three Cool Cats TCC 033/034 2 CD set) A compilation of B Sides, unreleased material and live tracks. Track Listing: Another Day (Kate Bush TV Special 1979)/Why Don't We?/Ich Und Mein Teddy Bear/A Whiter Shade Of Pale (Live)/Mother Of Violence (Live)/Exposure/I Heard It Thru The Grapevine/Let It Be/Shosholosa/Soft Dog/Across The River/Intruder/Games Without Frontiers/Solsbury Hill/Red Rain/Mercy Street/Biko 1987.

Demos, Rehearsals & Out-Takes 1980-88. Track Listing: Intruder/Family Snapshot/ Bully For You/And Through The Wire/I Have The Touch (1)/I Have The Touch (2)/Games Without Frontiers (Soundcheck)/Solsbury Hill (Soundcheck)/I Have The Touch (Demo)/And through The Wire (Live)/The Family & The Fishing Net (Live).
(Tracks 1-4 are studio recordings from the Peter Gabriel 3 Sessions including different lyrics and Peter's vocal version of Bully For You subsequently recorded and released by Tom Robinson).

Peter Gabriel Rarities Volume 1-4. Four CD compilation of demos, B sides unreleased material; and live recordings.

Volume 1: Strawberry Fields Forever/Me & My Teddy Bear/Jetzt Kommt Die Flut/ Shosholosa/Across the River/Soft Dog/Walk Through the Fire/Out Out/No More Apartheid/Don't Break This Rhythm/Curtains/I Go Swimming (Instrumental)/ Steam (Demo)/Downside Up/Love Town.

Volume 2: Summer Time/Bashi Bazouk/Party Man/Suzanne/Untitled Instrumental/ May God's Love Be With You/Solsbury Hill (Live)/Not One Of Us (Live)/Humdrum (Live)/Ain't That Peculiar (Live)/Kiss Of Life (Live)/Biko (Live)/Games Without Frontiers (Live)/In Your Eyes (Special Mix).

Volume 3: Mercy Street (Live)/Across The River (Live)/Signal To Noise (Live)/Excellent Birds/This Empty Room/Fallen Angel/My Special Place/Time Gets Hard/Untitled/ Don't Let Them Go (Deep Forest Mix)/Coming Home/Where You Go In Peace.

Volume 4: Don't Give Up (Live with Paula Cole)/Carpet Crawlers 99/Light Of Love/ Signal To Noise(Live)/And The Fainter Beat Her Heart/I Grieve/Big Time (Big Mix)/ Don't Break This Rhythm/And The Fainter Beat Her Heart (Live)/Cuckoo/Signal To Noise (Live)/Red Rain (Live)/Get Up, Stand Up (Live)/Don't Give Up (Live with Sinead O'Connor).

Passion Out Takes 1988. Track Listing: The Feeling Begins (Extended)/Disturbed (Alternate)/Passion (Alternate)/Cor Anglais Theme/It Is Accomplished (Film Version)/ Bass Bowl/With This Love (Alternate)/Wall Of Breath (Extended)/Location Recording (Morocco)/Location Recording (Unknown)/It

Is Accomplished (Alternate)/Trills/Bread And Wine - Flute Version/The Feeling Begins (Drum Version)/Of These Hope (Alternate)/Lazarus Raised (Alternate).

Rarities Track Listing: That Voice Again (Demo)/The Tower That Ate People (Steve Osbourne Mix)/Father Son (Live)/Sledgehammer (Ben Liebrand Remix)/I Don't Remember (Alternate Version)/Mercy Street (Piano Version).

Ashcombe Works (Highland Records HL462) Track Listing: On The Air (Other Version)/Bully For You/Bully For You (Instrumental)/I Go Swimming (Ga Ga Demo)/I Go Swimming (Ga Ga + Vocal Demo)/Wallflower (Other Version)/Milgrams 37 (Instrumental)/That Voice Again (Demo)/Strawberry Fields Forever/Intruder (Instrumental)/Games Without Frontiers (Instrumental)/Start (Saxless Version)/I Don't Remember (Instrumental)/No Self Control (Instrumental)/Walk Through The Fire (Instrumental)/And Through The Wire (Instrumental).

Sound Fruit (PMS Records CID 2 49 97). Track Listing: Preface/Here Comes The Flood/Taboo/Shaking The Tree(Remix)/Qualquer Coisa A Haver Com O Paraiso/Another day/Fallen Angel/Fisherman's Song/Sledgehammer (Dance Mix)/In Your Eyes/Reach Out (I'll Be There)/I Know What I Like (Live)/Not One Of Us/Humdrum/me & My Teddy Bear/Postscript.

Peter Gabriel Mix (No catalogue number). Track Listing: I Grieve (Live 01)/Another Day (Kate Bush TV Special 1979)/Qualquer Coisa A Haver Com O Paraiso/Big Time (Big Mix)/While The Earth Sleeps/Zaar/Troubled/Sledgehammer (Dance Mix)/Strawberry Fields Forever/Bread And Wine/Soft Dog/Why Don't We?/My Secret Place/Of These Hope/Come Talk To Me(Live)/Don't Give Up (Live)/I Shall Be Released (Live with U2).

UP Alternate Album 2002. Pre-release version of album Track Listing: Darkness/ Growing Up/Sky Blue/No Way Out (A.K.A: Don't Leave)/I Grieve/Burn You Up, Burn You Down/The Drop/The Barry Williams Show/My Head Sounds Like That/More Than This/Signal To Noise.

Steve Hackett/GTR Live recordings

Please Don't Touch Tour 1978

Star of Sirius (Highland HL050/51 2 CD set) Stockholm Gota Lejon 5.10.78. Track Listing: Please Don't Touch/Racing In A/Star Of Sirius/Carry On Up The Vicarage/Ace Of Wands/Hands Of The Priestess/Icarus Ascending/Narnia/Acoustic Set/Kim/The Optigan/A Tower Struck Down/Spectral Mornings/The Lovers/Shadow Of The Hierophant/Clocks/I Know What ILike.

Hail The New Messiah (MDF Recordings) Cardiff University 23.10.78.
Manchester Magic Manchester Apollo Theatre 24.10.78. (2CD set)
Carry on up the Apollo Glasgow Apollo Theatre 26.10.78 (2 CD set)

Spectral Mornings Tours 1979

Live in Liverpool (M DF Recordings 2 CD set) Empire Theatre Liverpool 24.6.79. Track Listing: Please Don't Touch/Tigermoth/Every Day/Narnia/The Red Flower Of Taichi Blooms Everywhere/Ace Of Wands/Carry On Up The Vicarage/Acoustic Set/Kim/The Optigan/A Tower Struck Down/Spectral Mornings/Star Of Sirius/Shadow Of The Hierophant/Clocks/I Know What I Like/Racing In A/Ace Of Wands/Racing In A (Acoustic section reprise).

If You break It, It's Yours Reading Festival 25.8.79. 1 CD. Track Listing: If You Break It, It's Yours/Tigermoth/Every Day/The Optigan/A Tower Struck Down/Spectral Mornings/Clocks/I Know What I Like.

Live At Drury Lane (MDF Recordings) Drury Lane Theatre Royal 11.11.79
(Also available as Steve Hackett Remastering Project SHRP 02)

The Virgin & The Gypsy (MDF Recordings) Poole Arts Centre 12.11.79. 1 CD. Track Listing: Please Don't Touch/Tigermoth/Every Day/Ace Of Wands/The Virgin & The Gypsy/The Steppes/Narnia/Sentimental Institution/The Red Flower Of Taichi Blooms Everywhere/The Lovers/Shadow Of The Hierophant/Spectral Mornings/A Tower Struck Down/Clocks.

Defector Tour 1980

Hercules Unchained (M D F Recordings) Sheffield City Hall 17.6.80 (2 CD set)
Grand Casino Montreux 13.7.80 (Steve Hackett Remastering Project SHRP 09)

Spectral Horizon (Neo Digital NDAL 1003) Chicago 10.10.80 (Also available as Steve Hackett Remastering Project SHRP 01). Track Listing: Slogans/Everyday/The Red Flower Of Taichi Blooms Everywhere/Tigermoth/Time To Get Out/The Steppes/Blood On The Rooftops-Horizons/Kim/Narnia/Jacuzzi/Sentimental Institution/Spectral Mornings/A Tower Struck Down/Clocks.

Spectral Evenings Palais Des Sports Geneva 19.11.80 (2 CD set).
Palasport Turin 29.11.80 (Steve Hackett Remastering Project SHRP 03) 2 CDs.

Cured Tour 1981

Steve Hackett - In Concert (Evening Star Records ES-001) Reading Festivals 26.8.79/28.8.81. 81 set is as follows: The Air-Conditioned Nightmare/Every Day/Ace Of Wands/Funny Feeling/The Steppes/Overnight Sleeper/Slogans/A Tower Struck Down/ Spectral Mornings/The Show/Clocks.

Carre Hotel Amsterdam 31.8.81 (Steve Hackett RemasteringProject SHRP 06) ·
Hertogenbosch Postcard Casino Den Bosch Hertogenbosch 26.9.81

Kill or Cure (MDF Recordings 2 CD set) Liverpool Empire Theatre 3.10.81. Track Listing: The Air-Conditioned Nightmare/Jacuzzi/Funny Feeling/Ace Of Wands/Picture Postcard/The Steppes/Every Day/The Red Flower Of Taichi Blooms Everywhere/ Tigermoth/Horizons/Kim/Overnight Sleeper/Hope I Don't Wake/Slogans/A Tower Struck Down/Spectral Mornings/Please Don't Touch/The Show/Clocks.

Cleveland Music Hall 20.10.81 (Steve Hackett Remastering Project SHRP 08 2 CD set)

Highly Strung Tour 1983

Venue Club London 13.12.82. (No Catalogue Number). Track Listing: The Steppes/ Funny Feeling/Hackett To Pieces/A Tower Struck Down/Spectral Mornings/Acoustic Set - Horizons - Kim/Overnight Sleeper/Slogans/Tigermoth/Please Don't Touch/The Show/Clocks - The Angel Of Mons/The Air-Conditioned Nightmare/Hackett's Boogie.

I know what I like (Heart Breakers HB807-1 CD) Guildford Civic Centre 29.1.83. Track Listing: The Steppes/Funny Feeling/Jacuzzi/Hackett To Pieces/Every Day/A Tower Struck Down/Horizons/Kim/Narnia/Slogans/The Show/Clocks/Here Comes The Flood(*)/Solsbury Hill(*)/Reach Out (I'll Be There) (+)/I Know What I Like(+)
(*)= Track with Peter Gabriel. (+)= Track With Mike Rutherford.

Weightless at the Empire (MDF Recordings 2 CD set) Liverpool Empire Theatre 26.4.83. Track Listing: The Steppes/Camino Royale/Funny Feeling/Can't Let Go/Funny Feeling(Reprise)/Weightless/Always Somewhere Else/Hackett To Pieces/Slogans/Give It Away/Spectral Mornings/Acoustic Set/Kim/Overnight Sleeper/Cell 151/Please Don't Touch/Every Day/Walking Through Walls/The Show/Clocks/Hackett's Boogie.

Norwich UEA 9.5.83 (No Catalogue Number). Track Listing: As above. 2 CD Set.

Bay Of Kings Tour 1983

Jazz on a summer's night (MDF Recordings) Liverpool Mountford Hall LSU 26.10.83. 1CD . Track Listing: Horizons/Time-Lapse At Milton Keynes/Bay Of Kings/ Calmaria/ Hands Of The Priestess/Jacuzzi/Overnight Sleeper/The Barren Land/Blood On The Rooftops/Guitar Exercise/Tales From The Riverbank/Second Chance/Chinese Imrovisation/Petropolis/Kim/Silver/Untitled Track/The Journey/Ace Of Wands/Cradle Of Swans/New Track/Horizons (Reprise)

Warwick University 27.11.83
Keele University 2.11.83 + Signal Radio interview 2.11.83
Leeds University 3.11.83
Heriot Watt University Edinburgh 4.11.83 (Steve Hackett Remastering Project SHRP 10).
Tales from the Left Bank (MDF Recordings) Barbican Theatre London 7.11.83

Live In York (No catalogue number) York University 13.11.83

GTR Tour 1986

GTR-Nerotrend (Elements of Crime Elements-083) Demos and out-takes from the second GTR album.

Birmingham Odeon 10.9.86. (No Catalogue Number). 2 Cassettes. Track Listing: Howe acoustic set/Hackett acoustic set/Jekyll And Hyde/Here I Wait/Prizefighters/ Imagining/ Hackett To Bits/Spectral Mornings/I Know What I Like/Sketches In The Sun/Pennants/ Roundabout/The Hunter/You Can Still Get Through/Reach Out (Never Say No)/When The Heart Rules The Mind.

A Two Headed Steve Show (Highland HL386/387 2 C D Set) Hammersmith Odeon 14.9.86.

Momentum Tour 1988

The Carrot That Killed The Opera House (MDF Recordings) Manchester Opera House 1.5.88. 1 CD. Track Listing: The Journey/Horizons/Bay Of Kings/A Bed, A Chair And A Guitar/Time-Lapse At Milton Keynes/Tales From The Riverbank/Ace Of Wands/Hands Of The Priestess/Jacuzzi/Overnight Sleeper/Cavalcanti/Second Chance/Portrait Of A Brazilian Lady/Still Life/Jazz On A Summer's Night/Concert For Munich/Notre Dame Des Fleurs/Momentum/Guitar-Synth Improvisation/Silver/The Carrot That Killed My Sister.

Live At The Cliffs (MDF Recordings) Cliffs Pavilion Southend 2.5.88 1 CD.
Nottingham Horizons (MDF Recordings) Royal Centre Nottingham 14.5.88 1CD.
Teatro Colosseo Turin 19.5.88 1 CD.
Teatro Orfeo Milan 20.5.88 1 CD.
Teatro Verdi Genoa 21.5.88 1 CD.
Teatro Tenda A Strisce Rome 22.5.88 1 CD.
New Morning Paris 19.9.88 (Steve Hackett Remastering Project SHRP07) 2 CDs.
Tour Noir Tour 1992.

Bottom Line Club New York City NY 20.9.92
Max's On Broadway Baltimore MD 23.9.92.
23 East Cabaret Philadelphia PA 24.9.92

Guitar Noir Tour 1993

The Spectral King Returns (MDF Recordings 2 CD set) Neptune Theatre Liverpool 21.5.93. Track Listing: Medley/Camino Royale/A Vampyre With A Healthy Appetite/Sierra Quemada/Take These Pearls/In The Heart of The City/Walking Away From Rainbows/There Are Many Sides To The Night/Dark As The Grave/Depth Charge/In That Quiet Earth/Bass-Drum Duet/Always Somewhere Else/Lost In Your Eyes/Every Day/Blood On The Rooftops-Horizons/Cincma Paradiso/Spectral Mornings/Firth of Fifth/Clocks.

Live At the Hop & Grape Manchester University 25.5.93 (M D F Recordings 2 CD Set).
Wonderful Wolverhampton (MDF Recordings 2 CD set) Wulfrun Hall Wolverhampton 28.5.93
Bier Keller Bristol 7.6.93 (Steve Hackett Remastering Project SHRP 05) 2 CDs.
Brewery Nights (M DF Recordings 1 CD) Kendal Arts Centre 11.6.93
Woughton Centre Milton Keynes (MDF Recordings) 12.6.93. 2 CD Set.
Full moon and empty spaces (Alternative Record Company ARC009-10 2 CD set) Villa Torlonia Frascati 5.7.93 and several tracks from earlier shows from 1978 and 1980.
Jekyll & Hyde (Highland HL360) Hammersmith Odeon 14.9.86.

Acoustic Tour 1994

The Italian Job 1 Sonny Boy Club Treviso 24.11.94 1 CD. Track Listing: Kim/ Black Light/Second Chance/Oh How I Love You/Blood On The Rooftops-Horizons/The Journey/Bacchus/Walking Away From Rainbows/Cavalcanti/Andante In C/Concerto In D/A Blue Part Of Town/There Are Many Sides To The Night/Ace Of Wands/Cinema Paradiso/Cuckoo Coccoon/Chinese Improvisation/Jazz On A Summer's Night/End of Day.

The Italian Job 2 Olgiate Comasco 26.11.94 1 CD.

Italian Tour 2000

Vivegano Castello 9.7.00 (Cassette)

Castello Negro (Path Records Path 001 2 CD set) Castello Malatestiana Cesena 11.7.00. Track Listing: Mechanical Bride/Serpentine Song/Watcher Of The Skies/Hairless Heart/Firth Of Fifth/iding The Colossus/The Steppes/Walking Away From Rainbows/Sierra Quemada/A Vampyre With A Healthy Appetite/Gnossienne #3/A Tower Struck Down/Darktown/Camino Royale/In Memoriam/Los Endos.
Teatro Della Ciminiera Catania 13.7.00 (Cassette)
Piazza Duomo Vecchio Molfetta (Bari) 14.7.00 (Cassette)

"Somewhere In South America" Tour 2001

Argentine Pollution (El Bocha Records 2 CD set) Teatro Coliseo Argentina 1.7.01. Track Listing: Mechanical Bride/Hackett To Bits/Serpentine Song/Watcher of The Skies/ Hairless Heart/Firth Of Fifth/Riding The Colossus/Pollution B/The Steppes/Gnossienne #3/Walking Away From Rainbows/Sierra Quemada/A Vampyre With A Healthy Appetite/A Tower Struck Down/Lucridus/Darktown/Camino Royale/In Memoriam/ Acoustic Set: Black Light-Horizons/Los Endos/In That Quiet Earth.

Chilean Sierra (E S Recordings 2 CD set) Santa Rosa Los Condes Chile 3.7.01.

Italian, Japanese and US shows 2002

Rosignano (No catalogue number 2 CD set) 23.4.02. Track Listing: Horizons/Gnossienne #1/Bacchus/Firth Of Fifth/bay Of Kings/Syrinx/Imagining/Second Chance/ Jacuzzi/ Overnight Sleeper/The Barren Land/Kim/Time-Lapse At Milton Keynes/Blood On The Rooftops/Improvisation/Concerto In D/Hairless Heart/Cinema Paradiso/ Mustardseed/ Gymnopedie #1/Jazz On A Summer's Night/Cavalcanti/Walking Away From Rainbows/ Tales Of The Riverbank/Concert For Munich/The Journey/Skye Boat Song-By Paved Fountain/Hands Of The Priestess/Ace Of Wands/Idylle-Aubade-Meditation/Hairless Heart (Reprise).

Trento (No catalogue number 2 CD set) 29.4.02

An Acoustic Evening In Tokio 12.1.02 (No catalogue number 2 CD set) Odaiba Aqua City Tokyo Japan. Track Listing: Horizons/Gnossienne #1/Bacchus/Firth Of Fifth/ Syrinx/Imagining/Second Chance/Jacuzzi/Overnight Sleeper/The Barren Land/ Kim/ Time-Lapse At Milton Keynes/Chinese Improvisation/Concerto In D/Hairless Heart/ Cinema Paradiso/Mustardseed/Gymnopedie #1/Jazz On A Summer's Night/Little Cloud/Cavalcanti/Walking Away From Rainbows/Tales Of The Riverbank/The Journey/Skye Boat Song/By Paved Fountain/Blood On The Rooftops/Hands Of The Priestess/All Is Mended/Ace Of Wands/Idylle-Aubade-Meditation/Bacchus.

Another Acoustic Evening… 13.1.02 (No Catalogue Number 2 CD set) Odaiba Aqua City Tokyo Japan. Track Listing: Horizons/Gnossienne #1/Bacchus/Firth of Fifth/Bay of Kings/Syrinx/Imagining/Second Chance/Jacuzzi-Overnight Sleeper/The Barren land/Black Light/Kim/Time-Lapse At Milton Keynes/Chinese Improvisation/Concerto In D/Hairless Heart/Cinema Paradiso/Mustardseed/Gymnopedie #1/Jazz On A Summer's Night/Little Cloud/Cavalcanti/Walking away From Rainbows/Tales Of The Riverbank/Concert For Munich/The Journey/Skye Boat Song-By Paved Fountain-Carcassi/Blood On The Rooftops/Hands Of The Priestess/All Is mended/Ace Of Wands/Idylle-Aubade-Meditation/Jacuzzi (Reprise).

Yet Another Acoustic Evening… 14.1.02 (No Catalogue Number 2 CD set) Odaiba Aqua City Tokyo Japan. Track Listing: Horizons/Gnossienne #1/Bacchus/Bay Of Kings/ Syrinx/ Jacuzzi-Overnight Sleeper/The Barren Land/BlackLight/Kim/Time-Lapse At Milton Keynes/Chinese Improvisation/Concerto In D/Hairless Heart/Cinema Paradiso/ Mustardseed/Gymnopedie #1/Jazz On A Summer's Night/Little Cloud/Cavalcanti/ Walking Away From Rainbows/Tales Of The Riverbank/Concert For Munich/The Journey/Skye Boat Song/Overnight Sleeper-Blood On The Rooftops/Hands Of The Priestess/All Is Mended/Ace Of Wands/Idylle-Aubade-Meditation/Jazz On A Summer's Night (Reprise)

Birchmere VA (No Catalogue number) Birchmere VA 27.6.02. Track Listing: The Floating Seventh/Mechanical Bride/Medley/Serpentine Song/Watcher Of The Skies/Hairless Heart/Firth Of

Fifth/Riding The Colossus/Pollution B/The Steppes/Gnossienne #1/Walking Away From Rainbows/In Memoriam/A Vampyre With A Healthy Appetite/Spectral Mornings/Darktown/Camino Royale/Shadow Of The Hierophant/Los Endos.

Live At BB Kings BB Kings Club New York 28.6..02 (No catalogue number) 2CDs.
Club Forli Naima Italy (No Catalogue number 2 CD set) 1.11.02.

To Watch The Storms Tour 2003-04

Endobre Polska (No Catalogue Number) PR3 Studios Warsaw ?.6.03. (Acoustic performance)
Festival Hall London (No Catalogue Number) 21.7.03 (With Evelyn Glennie)
Cleveland (No Catalogue Number) 11.8.03 (Acoustic performance)

Tilburg Club Het Noorderlight(No catalogue number 2CD set) 27.9.03 Track Listing: Mechanical Bride/ Serpentine Song/Watcher Of The Skies/Hairless Heart/Darktown/Camino Royale/The Steppes/Acoustic Set/Walking Away From Rainbows/Slogans/Every Day/Please Don't Touch/Firth Of Fifth/A Vampyre With A Healthy Appetite/Clocks/Spectral Mornings/ Brand New/Los Endos/In That Quiet Earth.

Zoetermeer 13 (No catalogue number 2 CD set) 28.9.03
Milton Keynes The Stables (No catalogue number 2 CD set) 3-4.10.03
Wolverhampton Wukfrun Hall (No catalogue number 2 CD set) 5.10.03
Leeds City Varieties(No catalogue number 2 CD set) 6.10.03
Newark Palace Theatre (No catalogue number 2 CD set) 7.10.03
Worcester Huntingdon Hall (No catalogue number 2 CD set) 9.10.03
Cardiff Coal Exchange (No catalogue number 2 CD set) 10.10.03
Rotherham Oakwood Centre (No Catalogue number 2 CD set) 11.10.03 *
Glasgow Renfrew Ferry (No Catalogue number 2 CD set) 12.10.03
Liverpool Neptune Theatre (No catalogue number 2 CD set) 13.10.03
Newcastle Opera House(No catalogue number 2 CD set) 18.10.03
Manchester Academy 2 (No catalogue number 2 CD set) 19.10.03
Leicester De Montfort Hall (No catalogue number 2 CD set) 20.10.03 *
High Wycombe Town Hall (No catalogue number 2 CD set) 21.10.03
London Queen Elizabeth Hall (No catalogue number 2 CD set) 28.10.03
Croydon Fairfield Hall(No catalogue number 2 CD set) 29.10.03 **
Braunschweig Meier Music Hall (No catalogue number 2 CD set) 8.11.03
Stuttgart Villa Berg (No catalogue number 1 CD) 9.11.03 FM Radio broadcast includes: In Memoriam.
Mannheim Capitol (No catalogue number 2 CD set) 10.11.03 (also included In Memoriam as an additional encore)

* These shows featured a bonus track: Jacuzzi as an addition to the acoustic set and featuring Steve's brother John on flute.
** This show featured another bonus track: Kim in place of Jacuzzi with John Hackett on flute.

Dartford Mick Jagger Centre (No Catalogue Number 2 CD set) 4.3.04 Track Listing: Valley Of The Kings/Mechanical Bride/Circus Of Becoming/Frozen Statues/Slogans/Serpentine Song/Ace Of Wands/Hammer In The Sand/Acoustic Set (Inc: Skye Boat Song-Classical Gas-Horizons)/Blood On The Rooftops/Fly On A Windshield/Please Don't Touch/Firth Of Fifth/A Dark Night In Toytown/Darktown/Brand New/The Air - Conditioned Nightmare/Every Day/Clocks/Spectral Mornings/Los Endos

Northampton Derngate Arena (No Catalogue Number 2 CD set) 5.3.04 *
Birkenhead Pacific Road Arts Centre(No Catalogue Number 2 CD set) 6.3.04
Blackburn Windsor Rooms St George's Hall (No Catalogue Number 2 CD set) 7.3.04 *
Cambridge Corn Exchange (No Catalogue Number 2 CD set) 12.3.04
London Shepherd's Bush Empire Theatre(No Catalogue Number 2 CD set) 13.3.04 +
Bristol Colston Hall (No Catalogue Number 2 CD set) 14.3.04
Birmingham Alexandra Theatre (No Catalogue Number 2 CD set) 15.3.04
Nottingham Rock City (No Catalogue Number 2 CD set) 16.3.04
Middlesbrough Town Hall "The Crypt" (No Catalogue Number 2 CD set) 18.3.04
Oxford New Theatre (No Catalogue Number 2 CD Set) 19.3.04 *
Southampton Guildhall (No Catalogue Number 2 CD set) 20.3.04
Turin Kubo (No Catalogue Number 2 CD set) 25.3.04

Venice 041 Marghera (No Catalogue Number 2 CD set) 26.3.04
Rome Stazione Birra(No Catalogue Number 2 CD set) 27.3.04
Erfurt Gewerkschafthaus (No Catalogue Number 2 CD set) 31.3.04
Dortmund Dietrich-Keuning-Haus (No Catalogue Number 2 CD set) 1.4.04

*   **These shows featured performances by John Hackett.**

+   **This show featured a guest appearance by John Paul Jones.**

Acoustic Trio 05 Shows

The Platform Morecambe 1st April 2005. Track Listing: Medley/Tales Of The Riverbank/Segovia
Tribute/The Pool Of Memory , The Pool Of Forgetfulness/Bay Of Kings/Medley: Classical Gas-
Improvisation-Cuckoo Cocoon/New Piece/Brand New/Black Light/The Barren Land/The Skye Boat
Song/Horizons/Mustardseed/Jacuzzi-Overnight Sleeper/Bacchus-Firth Of Fifth/Whole Tone Jam-The Red
Flower Of Taichi Blooms Everywhere-Hands Of The Priestess/There Are Many Sides To The Night/After
The Ordeal/Hairless Heart/M3/Inagining-Second Chance/Jazz On A Summer's Night/Next Time
Around/Kim/Idylle-Aubade-Meditation/The Journey/Ace Of Wands/Walking Away From
Rainbows/Gnossienne #1. (No Catalogue Number 2 CD set)

Steve varied the set considerably during this tour and each performance constitutes and individual one.
Other shows recorded from this tour include…

Pacific Road Arts Centre Birkenhead 30.3.05 (No Catalogue Number 2 CD set)
Quays Theatre Lowry Centre Manchester 31.3.05 (No Catalogue Number 2 CD set)
Darwin Suite Assembly Rooms Derby 2.4.05 (No Catalogue Number 2 CD set)
The Rum Store Carnglaze Caverns Liskeard 8.4.05 (No Catalogue Number 2 CD set)
Wulfrun Hall Wolverhampton 10.4.05 (No Catalogue Number 2 CD set)
Maddermarket Theatre Norwich 11.4.05 (No Catalogue Number 2 CD set)
The Stables Milton Keynes 13.4.05 (No Catalogue Number 2 CD set)
The Stables Milton Keynes 14.4.05 (No Catalogue Number 2 CD set)
The Broadway Barking 16.4.05 (No Catalogue Number 2 CD set)
Ashcroft Theatre Fairfield Halls Croydon 17.4.05 (No Catalogue Number 2 CD set).
Saschall Florence 26.4.05 (No Catalogue Number 2 CD set)
Harmonie Bonn 16.6.05 (No Catalogue Number 2 CD set)
St Maximin Trier 17.6.05 (No Catalogue Number 2 CD set)
Waldbuhne Hardt Wupertal 18.6.05 (No Catalogue Number 1 CD)
Freilichtbuhne Loreley St Goarshausen 19.6.05 (No Catalogue Number 1 CD)

Steve also undertook his first extensive tour of the US and Canada in almost ten years and so far, the
following recordings from that tour have emerged…

Le Medley Montreal QC Canada 29.89.05. (No Catalogue Number 2 CD set). Track Listing:
Medley/Horizons/Japonica/Tales Of The Riverbank/Segovia/The Pool Of Memory, The Pool Of
Forgetfulness/Bay Of Kings/Classical Jazz/Mexico City/The Skye Boat Song/Jacuzzi/Bacchus/Whole
Tone Jam-The Red Flower Of Taichi Blooms Everywhere-Hands Of The Priestess/After The
Ordeal/Hairless Heart/M3/Imagining/ Second Chance/Jazz On A Summer's Night/Next Time
Around/Kim/Idylle-Aubade-Meditation.

Hamilton Place Theatre - The Studio Hamilton ON Canada 2.10.05. (No catalogue Number 2 CD
set). Track Listing: Medley/Horizons/Japonica/Segovia/Tales Of The Riverbank/The Pool Of Memory,
The Pool Of Forgetfulness/Mexico City/The Skye Boat Song/End Of Day/Classical
Jazz/Jacuzzi/Bacchus/Whole Tone Jam-The Red Flower Of Taichi Blooms Everywhere-Hands Of The
Priestess/M3/After The Ordeal/Hairless Heart/Imagining/Second Chance/Jazz On A Summer's Night/Next
Time Around/Kim/ Idylle-Aubade-Meditation/The Journey/Ace Of Wands/Walking Away From
Rainbows/ Gnossienne #1.

Somerville Theatre Boston MA 9.10.05. (No Catalogue Number 2 CD Set). Track Listing: Classical
Jazz/Japonica/Horizons/Andante In C/Tribute To Segovia/ Metamorpheus Medley/Bay Of Kings/Mexico
City/BlackLight/The Barren Land/The Skye Boat Somg/Jacuzzi/Bacchus/Whole-Tone Jam-The Red
Flower Of Taichi Blooms Everywhere-Hands Of The Priestess/After The Ordeal/Hairless
Heart/M3/Imagining/ Second Chance/Jazz On A Summer's Night/Next Time Around/Kim/Idylle-Aubade-
Meditation/The Journey/Ace Of Wands/Walking Away From Rainbows/Gnossienne #1.

Troy Music Hall Troy NY 10/10/05. (No Catalogue Number 2 CD Set). Track Listing: Classical Jazz/Japonica/Horizons/Tribute To Segovia/The Pool Of The Pool Of Forgetfulness/Bay Of Kings/Andante In C/Mexico City/The Skye Boat Song/Jacuzzi/ Bacchus/Whole-Tone Jam-The Red Flower Of Taichi Blooms Everywhere-Hands Of The Priestess/After The Ordeal/Hairless Heart/M3/Imagining/Second Chance/Jazz On A Summer's Night/Next Time Around/Kim/Idylle-Aubade-Meditation/The Journey/Ace Of Wands/Walking Away From Rainbows/Gnossienne #1.

XM Radio Station Washington DC 12.10.05. (No Catalogue Number 1 CD). Track Listing: Horizons/Classical Jazz/Jacuzzi/Bacchus/Segovia/jazz On A Summer's Night/Mexico City/Ace Of Wands/Hands Of The Priestess/The Journey/Interview. FM Radio Broadcast

Town Ballroom (The Sphere) Buffalo NY USA 14/10.05. (No Catalogue Number 2 CD set). Track Listing: Classical Jazz/Cuckoo Coccoon/Horizons/Japonica/Tribute To Segovia/Metamorpheus Medley/Bay Of Kings/Mexico City/Black Light/Skye Boat Song/All is Mended/Jacuzzi/Bacchus/Firth Of Fifth/Impovisation-The Red Flower Of Taichi Blooms Everywhere-Hands Of The Priestess/After The Ordeal/Hairless Heart/M3/Imagining/Second Chance/Jazz On A Summer's Night/Next Time Around/ Kim/The Journey/Ace Of Wands/Walking Away From Rainbows/Gnossienne #1.

The Swedish American Music Hall San Francisco CA USA 27.10. 05. (No Catalogue Number 2 CD Set). Track Listing: Classical Jazz/Cuckoo Cocoon/Horizons/Tribute To Segovia/Metamorpheus Medley/Bay Of Kings/Mexico City/Black Light/Skye Boat Song/All Is Mended/Jacuzzi/Whole-Tone Jam-The Red Flower Of Taichi Blooms Everywhere-Hands Of The Priestess/After The Ordeal/Hairless Heart/M3/Imagining/ Second Chance/Jazz On A Summer's Night/Kim/Idylle-Aubade-Meditation/the Journey/Ace Of Wands/Walking Away From Rainbows/Bacchus-Firth Of Fifth.

Studio Compilations

Similarly to Peter, Steve's studio work has been the subject of various unofficial releases documenting his studio output. So far no less than six unofficial compilations have been made available compiled from various sources by fans under the generic title: "Hackett Rarities".

Hackett Rarities Volume 1. Track Listing: Narnia (1978 7" single A Side with vocals by John Perry)/Clocks (1979 7" single A Side remix)/Acoustic Set (1979 live 7" & 12" single B Side)/Kim (1979 12" Single live B side)/Tigermoth (1979 live 12" single B Side)/Clocks (1979 live 12" single B Side)/Hercules Unchained (1980 7" single B Side)/Hope I Don't Wake (1981 7" single A Side edited version)/Tales Of The Riverbank (1981 7" single B Side)/Second Chance (1981 7" single B Side)/Funny Feeling (1981 single A Side edited version)/Walking Through Walls (Extended version only available on US version of 1983 Highly Strung album)/The Air Conditioned Nightmare (1983 live B side of 12" single)/ Cell 151 (1983 7" single A side edited version)/Time Lapse At Milton Keynes (1983 7" & 12" single B side)/Paint It Black (1983 Brazilian 7" single A side by Kim Poor produced by Steve)/Just For You And I (1983 Brazilian 7" single B side by Kim Poor produced by Steve)/Vao Do Coracao (1983 Brazilian album track by Ritchie produced by Steve).

Hackett Rarities Volume 2. Track Listing: A Doll That's Made In Japan (1984 7" single A side edited version)/A Doll That's Made in Japan Instrumental (1984 7" & 12" single B side)/Just The Bones (1984 12" single B side)/A Life in Movies (1984 Guitar Speak II album track)/A Night Of Mystery (1984 Nightwing track from "My Kingdom Come" album featuring Max Bacon)/Cell 151 (1984 Nightwing cover version from "My Kingdom Come" album featuring Max Bacon)/Cell 151 (1984 Nightwing live version from "A Night Of Mystery" album featuring Max Bacon)/Wind In The Willows (1985 Eddie Hardin & Friends Wind In The Willows album track featuring Steve)/The Hunter Special GTR Mix (1986 12" single A side)/Average/Trouble (Tracks from 1986 Box Of Frogs album featuring Steve)/I Know What I Like (1986 live version by Marillion at Hammersmith Odeon London featuring Steve)/Heart To Heart/Flamemco (1987 tracks from Mae McKenna album produced by Steve)/Wasteland (1987 track)/Sailing/Sailing Instrumental (1990 7" single A and B side).

Hackett Rarities Volume 3. Track Listing: Face In The Mirror/Alone Again/Between Different Worlds/Another Dream/Song Of The unicorn/Lady Of The Golden Forest/ End Of The Rainbow (1992 tracks from "Gallery Of Dreams" album by Gandalf featuring Steve)/Old Faces At Heaven's Gate/Faces From Old Photos Rediscovered/Prelude V (1992 tracks from "Back To Bach" album by Julian Colbeck featuring Steve)/ Cassandra (1993 US album version from "Guitar Noir" album)/Lost In Your Eyes/Dark As The Grave (1993 edited versions from "Guitar Noir" promotional radio CD single).

Hackett Rarities Volume 4. Track Listing: The Well At The World's End/Coming Home To The Blues (1999 bonus tracks on Japanese edition of Darktown album)/Twice Around The Sun (2000 cover version by Karda Estra on the "Constellations" album)/ Carpet Crawlers 99 (1999 edited radio promotional CD single version)/You Are Part Of Me/Straight Back To You (1999 tracks from Ian MacDonald "Drivers Eyes" album featuring Steve)/Nothing Happens For Nothing/All Grown Up(2000 tracks from "Arkangel" album by John Wetton featuring Steve)/Timeless Radio Mix/Timeless Downtown Mix/Timeless Late Night Mix (2001 CD single tracks by Sonic Obsession featuring Steve)/Real World (2003 track from "Sinister" album by John Wetton featuring Steve)/Janowska/Nightmare Years/Outwitting Hitler (Tracks from the soundtrack to the "Outwitting Hitler TV documentary).

Hackett Rarities Volume 5: Track Listing: Brand New (2003 edited version)/Pollution B/Fire Island/Marijuana (Assassin Of Youth)/If Only You Knew (2003 tracks from Special Edition of "To Watch The Storms")/Flame (2003 bonus track on Japanese edition of "To Watch The Storms")/Reflections Of Thierache (2003 Djabe "Sheaves Are Dancing" track featuring Steve)/Muttersprache/Some Brighter Thing/Singing Deep Mountain (2003 tracks from the Gordian Knot album "Emergent" featuring Steve)/Some Day In May/The Flying Scroll/Why Me (2003 tracks from the "Postmankind" album featuring Steve).

Hackett Rarities Volume 6: Track Listing: Singularity/Seven Hands Of Time/The Power Of Reason (2004 tracks from Nick Magnus "Hexameron" album featuring Steve)/ Late Trains/The Hallway & The Pram/Ego & Id/Headlights/More (2005 tracks from John Hackett "Checking Out Of London" album featuring Steve)

Mike & The Mechanics

"The Miracle Tour" 1986

"Live In St Louis" (MDF Recordings) Kiel Open House St Louis 11.6.86. 1 Disc. Track Listing: Hanging By A Thread/Half Way There/Silent Running/Taken In/I Don't Wanna Know/Maxine/Par Avion/A Call To Arms/Tempted/I Get The Feeling/Take The Reins/All I Need Is A Miracle/Gimme Some Lovin'.

"Allegiance to the Flag" (MDF Recordings) Six Flags Over Texas 27.6.86. Track Listing: As above.
Miracle Mania (Elements of Crime Elements-041) Tower Theatre Philadelphia 19.6.86.

"The Living Years" Tour 1989

Hearing Is Believing (MDF Recordings 2 CD set) Manchester Apollo Theatre 5.3.89. 2 CD set. Track Listing: Nobody's Perfect/Seeing Is Believing/Silent Running/ Don't/ Nobody Knows/Hanging By A Thread/Why Me?/Taken In/Beautiful Day/Black And Blue/Par Avion/A Call To Arms/The Living Years/I Get The Feeling/Take The Reins/All I Need Is A Miracle/Poor Boy Down.

Poor Boy Down" (MDF Recordings 2 CD set) Newcastle City Hall 18.3.89. Track Listing: As above.
Live In London Hammersmith Odeon London 19.3.89.
All I need is a Miracle (Viva CD7539) Tower Theatre Philadelphia 30.3.89.

"Beggar On A Beach Of Gold" Tour 1995

"They Can't Dance But They Sure Can Play!" Civic Hall Wolverhampton 21.6.95. (1Cassette). Track Listing: Beggar On A Beach Of Gold/Get Up/Silent Running/Plain And Simple/Over My Shoulder/Another Cup Of Coffee/Someone Always Hates Someone/You Really Got A Hold On Me/Web Of Lies/Every Day Hurts-How Long-We Can't Dance Medley/Living Years/All I Need Is A Miracle/I Believe (When I Fall In Love It Will Be Forever)/Word Of Mouth.

"Plain And Simple" Royal Centre Nottingham 25.6.95. (1 Cassette). Track Listing: As above.

Live At The Bush Shepherds Bush Empire Theatre London 18.7.95. 1 CD. Track Listing: Get Up/You Really Got A Hold On Me/Over My Shoulder/Silent Running/Plain & Simple/Another Cup Of Coffee/Someone Always Hates Someone/Web Of Lies/The Living Years/Word Of Mouth.

"Hits" Tour 1996

The Miracle Goes On" Apollo Theatre Manchester 9.3.96. 1Cassette. Track Listing: Silent Running/I Believe(When I Fall In Love It Will Be Forever)/Get Up/Beggar On A Beach Of Gold/Someone Always Hates Someone/Another Cup Of Coffee/Web Of Lies/Plain And Simple/Eyes Of Blue/Nobody's Perfect/Every Day Hurts-How Long-We Can't Dance Medley/Living Years/All I Need Is A Miracle/Word Of Mouth/Over My Shoulder.

"Still Believing" Civic Hall Wolverhampton 21.3.96. 1 Cassette. Track Listing: As above.
"Living By Word Of Mouth" Civic Hall Wolverhampton 22.3.96. 1 Cassette. Track Listing: As above.

Live In Liverpool (MDF Recordings) Liverpool Empire Theatre 14.5.96. 1 CD. Track Listing: Silent Running/Seeing Is Believing/Get Up/A Beggar On A Beach Of Gold/Someone Always Hates Someone/Another Cup Of Coffee/Plain & Simple/Eyes of Blue/Nobody's Perfect/Everyday Hurts/How Long?/I Can't Dance/The Living Years/All I Need Is A Miracle/Word Of Mouth/Over My Shoulder.

St David's Hall Cardiff 15.4.96. 1 Cassette. Track Listing: As above.

M6 Tour 1999

Whenever I Play (MDF Recordings) Hanover Grand London 10.5.99. 1 CD. Track Listing: Ordinary Girl/Now That You've Gone/Another Cup Of Coffee/Whenever I Stop/All The Light I Need/Every Day Hurts/How Long?/I Can't Dance/The Living Years/All I Need Is A Miracle/Over My Shoulder.

"Live In Manchester" (MDF Recordings 2 CD set) Manchester Apollo Theatre 14.5.99

"Live In Dreamland" (MDF Recordings 2 CD set) Oxford Apollo Theatre 31.5.99

RTL Studios Paris 1999. 1 CD. Track Listing: Get Up/Ordinary Girl/Now That You've Gone/Whenever I Stop/Silent Running/My Little Island/All The Light I Need/The Living Years/Every Day Hurts/How Long?/I Can't Dance/Over My Shoulder.

Rewired Tour 2004.

"Two Left Standing" Amsterdam Arena 19.6.04 1 CD. Track Listing: Falling/Now That You've Gone/Silent Running/If I Were You/One Left Standing/Living Years/Over My Shoulder/Word Of Mouth.

Cologne Rhein Energie Stadion 12.6.04 1 CD. Track Listing: As above

Munich Olympic Stadium 6.6.04 1 CD. Track Listing: As above

Daryl Stuermer

"Live At Summerfest" Milwaukee 6.7.01. 1CD. Track Listing: Icarus/Banjo/Morning Train/Urban Island/Copenhagen/Follow You Follow Me/Land Of Confusion/Wading In The Wind/Wherever You Are/Festival City/American Fields.

Ray Wilson/Cut Recordings

"Who's Sarah?" Radio Café SWR3 Club Germany 1999. (1 CD). Track Listing: Young Ones/Reason For Running/Dark/Another Day/Millionairhead/Not About Us/Inside/Sarah/Space Oddity/Ghost.

Complete Recordings & Unplugged. Studio compilation (1CD). Track Listing: Ghost/Reason For Running/Dark/Young Ones/Sarah/Another Day/Adolescent Breakdown/Space Oddity/Another Day/Millionairhead/Not About Us/Inside/ Gypsy/Knockin On Heaven's Door/Carpet Crawlers/7/8/Run Out Of Time.

"Live At The Lighthouse" Lighthouse Club Edinburgh 17ᵗʰ August 2004. (2 CD set). Track listing: These Are The Changes/In The Air Tonight/Carpet Crawlers/Love Ain't Enough/Follow You Follow Me/Change/Another Day/I Can't Dance/Inside/New Song/The Fool In Me/Ripples/Jigsaw/Biko/Swing Your Bag/Not About Us/ Shipwrecked/Knockin On Heaven's Door.

"Live in Spirit" Spirit Of 66 Verviers 24th October 2004. (2 CD set). Track Listing: Gypsy/The Actor/Alone/The Lamb Lies Down On Broadway/Jigsaw/Biko/ Shipwrecked/Not About Us/Swing Your Bag/Knockin On Heaven's Door/No Son Of Mine/Lover's Leap/The Airport Song/Rest In Peace/These Are The Changes/Goodbye Baby Blue/In The Air Tonight/Carpet Crawlers/Love Ain't Enough/Follow You Follow Me/Sarah/Change/Another Day/Ripples/Shoot The Moon/Inside/Electric Suicide/I Can't Dance.

This list is, by necessity only a sample of the material which is available to fans with the determination (and shelf space) to seek them out - good luck!

Private Video Recordings

Since the advent of hand held video recording equipment in the early 1980's, many fans have taken to recording shows visually and these recordings are an additional source of material for die-hard fans. Prior to this, hand held Super 8mm cameras recorded snippets of shows without benefit of a soundtrack. The following is a selection of material which is known to exist on the video format ….

Genesis

Atomic Sunrise Festival Roundhouse London (Excerpts)		1970.
Palasport Turin	(Excerpts)	1973.
Montreal University	(Excerpts)	1974.
Hamburg/Kiel	(Excerpts)	1975.
Grand Rapids	(Excerpts)	1975.
Sherbrooke University	(Excerpts)	1975.
Empire Theatre Liverpool	(Excerpts)	1975.
Berlin	(Excerpts)	1976.
Earls Court Arena	(Excerpts)	1977.
Castle Hall Osaka Japan	(Excerpts)	30.11.78.
Toronto CNE Grandstand	(Entire concert)	28.8.82.
Milton Keynes Concert Bowl	(Entire concert)	2.10.82.
Montreal Forum	(Entire concert)	21.11.84.
Oakland Coliseum	(Entire concert)	20.2.84.
Joe Louis Arena Detroit	(Entire concert)	17.9.86.
Madison Square gardens NYC	(Entire concert)	3.10.86.
Bernabeu stadium Barcelona	(Entire concert)	13.5.87.
L'Hippodrome de Vincennes Paris	(Excerpts)	3.6.87.
Wiener Prater Stadion Vienna	(Entire concert)	16.6.87.
Oakland Coliseum	(Entire concert)	20.6.92.
Parkstadion Gelsenkirchen	(Entire concert)	3.7.92.
Niedersachsenstadion Hanover	(Entire concert)	10.7.92.
Roundhay Park Leeds	(Entire concert)	31.7.92.
Chiddingfold Working Mens' Club	(Rehearsals CDV)	23.9.97.
Budapest Sporthall	(Entire rehearsal concert)	28.1.98.
Hallenstadion Zurich	(Entire concert)	13.2.98.
Bologna Palasport	(Excerpts)	17.2.98.
Palasport Rome	(Entire concert)	18.2.98.
Milan Filaforum	(Entire concert)	19.2.98.
Earls Court Arena London	(Entire concert)	27.2.98.
NYNEX Arena Manchester	(Entire concert)	6.3.98.

Peter Gabriel

Roxy Theatre Los Angeles	(Super 8mm silent footage)	1977.
Toronto CNE Grandstand	(Excerpts)	8.11.82.
Kemper Arena Kansas City	(Entire concert)	4.12.82.
Berkeley UOC	(Excerpts from two shows)	1982/83.
Empire Theatre Liverpool	(Entire concert)	18.9.83.
Falkoner Theatrit Copenhagen	(Entire concert)	1.10.83.
United Nations Building New York	(Entire concert)	16.9.86.
Rochester NY War Memorial	(Entire concert)	7.11.86.
Joe Louis Arena Detroit	(Entire concert)	17.11.86.

Houston Astrodome   (Entire concert) 7.12.86.
Cologne Muengersdorfer Sportstadion   (Entire concert) 19.6.87.
Palatrussardi Milan   (Entire concert) 10.7.87.
Philadelphia Spectrum   (Entire concert) 27.7.87.
Palau St Jordi Barcelona   (Entire concert) 30.9.87.
Offenbach Ruhrstadion   (Entire concert) 13.9.87.
Berlin Eisporthalle   (Entire concert) 11.11.87.
Wembley Stadium   (Entire concert) 2.9.88.
Palais Omnisports de Bercy Paris   (Entire concert) 4.9.88.
Nou Camp Stadium Barcelona   (Entire concert) 10.9.88.
Academy of Music NYC   (Entire concert) 6.4.93.
Frankfurt Festhalle   (Entire concert) 21.4.93.
Palagiacchio Marino Rome   (Entire concert) 18.5.93.
Stuttgart Schleyerhalle   (Entire concert) 20.5.93.
Munich Olympiahalle   (Entire concert) 21.5.93.
Sheffield Arena   (Entire concert) 24.5.93.
Montreal Forum   (Entire concert) 29.6.93.
Philadelphia Spectrum   (Entire concert) 6.7.93.
Philadelphia Spectrum   (Entire concert) 8.7.93.
Los Angeles Great Western Forum   (Entire concert) 22.7.93.
Glastonbury Festival   (Entire concert) 26.6.94.
Marienplatz Munich   (Complete concert on DVD) 31.8.02.
Alcataz Milan   (incomplete concert) 16.9.02.
United Center Chicago   (Complete concert on DVD) 14.11.02.
Madison Square Garden New York (Complete concert on DVD) 21.11.02.
Air Canada Centre Toronto   (Complete concert on DVD) 2.12.02.
Anaheim   (Complete concert on DVD) 12.10.02.
Poznan Poland   (Excerpts from concert on DVD) 30.5.03.
Jones Beach NY   (Entire concert on DVD) 24.6.03.

Steve Hackett

Reading Festival   (Entire concert) 26.8.79.
Teatro Orfeo Milan   (Entire concert) 20.5.88.
Het Noorderlight Tilburg   (Entire concert) 28.5.88.
Bochum Zeche   (Entire concert) 16.9.88.
Stadio Plebiscito Selvazzano Padua   (Entire concert) 6.7.93.
San Jose   (Entire concert) 12.11.93.
Palermo "Sonny Boy"   (Excerpts) 1.12.94.
Vivegano   (Excerpts) 9.7.00.
Cesena   (Excerpts) 11.7.00.
Theatre Of Living Arts Philadelphia (Complete performance) 1.7.02.
Borders Bookstore Columbus Ohio (Complete performance) 10.8.02.
Borders Bookstore Cleveland Heights (Complete performance) 11.8.02.
Borders Bookstore Bryn Mawr (Complete performance) 11.8.02.
Cologne Live Music Hall   (Complete) 11.10.03.
Pacific Arts Centre Birkenhead   (Excerpts) 6.3.04.
Leini "Kubo"   (Complete concert) 25.3.04.
Stazione Birra Rome   (Complete concert) 28.3.04.
Foro Italico Stadio del Tennis Rome (Incomplete concert) 26.7.04.
Palermo Stadio della Verdura   (Excerpts) 28.7.04.
Pacific Arts Centre Birkenhead   (Excerpts) 30.4.05.

Mike & The Mechanics

Philipshalle Dusseldorf   (Entire concert) 27.2.89.
Mainz Rheingoldhalle   (Entire concert on DVD) 10.3.89.
Hanover Grand London   (Entire concert) 10.5.99.

Phil Collins

Palau St Jordi Barcelona	(Approximately half of the concert)	17.5.90.
Frankfurt Festhalle	(Entire concert)	11.5.90.
Toronto Skydome	(Entire concert)	17.7.94.
Oslo Spektrum	(Entire concert)	4.4.94.
Frankfurt Festhalle	(Entire concert)	27.9.94.
Wembley Arena	(Entire concert)	7.12.94.
Toronto Skydome	(Entire concert)	20.3.97.
Philadelphia Spectrum	(Entire concert)	29.3.97.
Milan Palasport	(Entire concert DVD)	1.6.04.
Philadelphia Wachovia	(Entire concert DVD)	23.9.04.
New Ice Arena St Petersburg	(Entire concert DVD)	18.10.05.
Belgrade Arena Belgrade	(Entire concert DVD)	28.10.05.

Ray Wilson

Codevilla Pavia	(Excerpts from acoustic gig CDV)	20.1.02.
Limelight Club Crewe	(Excerpts from acoustic gig)	5.4.02.
Camberley	(Complete Recording)	22.6.06
Leamington Spa	(Complete Recording)	23.6.06
La attache Edinburgh	(Complete Recording)	10.8.06

As you would expect with a band of Genesis's stature there is no shortage of material on film by the band. Over the last few years in particular, TV appearances, interviews and so on have become increasingly common and form yet another area for fans to begin a collection. Here I have divided the available footage into two distinct sections; first the commercially released and recorded videos/films of the band, and second: television appearances. In both cases I have opted to include details of UK and foreign material for this revised edition, where details are available.

PART ONE: COMMERCIAL FILMS/VIDEOS

"Tony Stratton-Smith Presents: Genesis in Concert". As its title suggests, this is a live performance of the band's set from the time of the "Selling England by the Pound" tour. Unfortunately this film has never been domestically released although it was available recently on laser disc in Japan whether this was officially sanctioned however, is open to debate! The film was recorded at the Shepperton Film Studios on 30th and 31st October 1973 and features the following songs: Watcher of the skies/Dancing with the moonlit knight/I know what I like/Musical Box/Supper's Ready. The film is complete with all of Peter's costumes and between song stories and is sixty three minutes in length. This was the first Genesis film which Paul Flattery and Jim Yukich directed for the band.

"Genesis in concert" Another film sadly unavailable in this country. It was filmed at Glasgow and Stafford during the band's "A trick of the tail" tour and as such, is the only visual record of the band with Bill Bruford on drums. The film was shown in UK cinemas in 1977 and has gained several showings since although no domestic video release has been planned. The film features the following songs: I know what I like/Fly on a windshield/Carpet crawl/Cinema show(Pt2)/Entangled/Supper's Ready(pt2)/Los Endos. Filming was by Tony Maylam and the entire film lasts some forty minutes. Although this has not been released in the UK those of you with the latest technology (and money to burn) can obtain it on laser disc from Japan; NTSC VPLR70468, although this release was not officially sanctioned by the band at the time, it has also found its way onto VCD format.

The 1977 tour was also filmed although so far only a small segment of it has surfaced. This is from the shows at the Reunion Centre in Dallas although one of Phil's intro's has been mysteriously overdubbed (rather poorly in fact) in French and once again the project was organised by Yukich and Flattery. The tracks broadcast comprise a twenty five minute compilation including; Dance on a volcano/Los Endos/The lamb lies down on Broadway and Musical Box(closing section).There is rumoured to exist a complete film of one of the band's Paris shows from this tour although I have been unable to confirm this. The 30 minute video was released in the US as an official package by the Video Tape Network.

More recently, information has surfaced that the band's gigs in Sao Paolo in May 1977 were also filmed by the local TV company: Globo TV. So far, information is sketchy but the indications are that a substantial amount of footage from those gigs still resides in their archives.

Sadly no complete film from the 1978 tour has appeared in this country apart from the BBC's "Nationwide" documentary from the European tour which features some footage from Mannheim, Leiden and Knebworth including a complete performance of 'The Lady lies' which was originally broadcast on 21st July 1978. Japanese fans were luckier with a television screening of highlights the band's show at the Sun Plaza Hall in Tokio on 3rd December which comprised the following tracks; 11th Earl of Mar/Dance on a volcano/Los endos/I know what I like. There is also supposed to be a fuller version of this footage although it has not been shown since 1978.

The "Duke" tour in 1980 was featured in two different television programmes which were screened in the UK during the tour. First of these was the "Live in Liverpool" documentary filmed at the Empire Theatre on 2nd May and screened on Granada tv on 3rd. This was a film about the tour and featured live and interview footage lasting for fifty minutes.

The BBC made their contribution to the Genesis archive during this tour by filming the show at the Lyceum Ballrooms in London on May 7th which later featured as an edited special on their popular "Whistle Test" programme including the following tracks; Duchess/Guide vocal/In the cage-Cinema Show-Ravine-Raven/Afterglow/Dance on a volcano/Los Endos.

The test shot for this broadcast was made at the same venue on 6th May and has recently surfaced as an unofficial DVD release. The film lasts for 132 minutes and comprises the following songs:Deep in the motherlode/Dancing with the moonlit knight/Carpet crawl/Squonk/One for the vine/Behind the lines/Duchess/Guide vocal/Turn it on again/Duke's Travels/Duke's End/Ripples (instrumental end section only)/The lady lies/In the cage - medley/Afterglow/Follow you follow me/Dance on a volcano/Los Endos/I know what I like.

From 1981 onwards, Genesis fans have been fortunate enough to have a video release to commemorate each successive tour by the band begining with "Three Sides Live" which was recorded during the 'Abacab' US/UK tour in 1981. The video was released by Wienerworld Video in 1982 and featured the following tracks; Behind the lines/Duchess/Misunderstanding/Dodo-Lurker/Abacab/No reply at all/Who-dunit?/In the cage-Cinema Show-Colony of slippermen-Ravine medley/Afterglow/Me and Sarah Jane/Man on the corner/Turn it on again. The video also featured backstage and interview footage with Hugh Fielder and lasts for approximately ninety minutes. Wienerworld TVE 90 0982 2.

The "Mama" tour lasted several months and was recorded for posterity in the form of the "Mama Tour" video which comprised an almost complete recording of the shows at the National Exhibition Centre in Birmingham between 25th to 29th February 1984. The full set listing on the video was; Abacab/That's all/Mama/Illegal Alien/Home by the sea/Second home by the sea/Keep it dark/It's gonna get better/In the cage:Cinema Show-Raven medley/Afterglow/Turn it on again - Sixties medley. The running time of the video was 102 minutes and it sadly omitted what for many fans was the highlight of the show in the form of the first of the two medleys which incorporated 11th Earl of Mar/Firth of fifth/The lamb lies down on Broadway/Musical Box. However, the video does capture the essential drama of the show. This was also the first video by the group to be released by Virgin Video. VVD090.

To coincide with the European leg of the "Invisible Touch" tour the band released the "Visible Touch" video which compiled the promotional videos released for singles from that album. The tracks included were: Anything she does/Throwing it all away/Tonight tonight tonight/Land of confusion/In too deep/Invisible touch. There was also a small documentary on the tour and the entire video lasts 48 minutes. Virgin Video VVD 204.

The extended hiatus which occurred after the end of the 1986/87 tour gave the band time to compile and release two video collections which tied up the loose ends of the promotional videos released for singles by the band over the years. Titled "Genesis The Videos Volume One" and "Genesis The Videos Volume Two" these are an indispensible part of any Genesis collection. The tracks on volume one were: Mama/No reply at all/Land of confusion/That's all/Tonight tonight tonight/Duchess/Anything she does/Robbery assault and battery/In too deep/Abacab/Follow you follow me. This collection has a running time of 55 minutes.

Volume Two comprised the following tracks; Illegal alien/Throwing it all away/ Misunderstanding/ Ripples/Keep it dark/Trick of the tail/Home by the sea/Second home by the sea/Man on the corner/Turn it on again/Many too many/Invisible touch. This collection runs for 57 minutes. The confusing thing about these two collections is that the videos are not in chronological order and there are several ommissions; Turn it on again and Man on the corner are live films which is surprising because there were promotional videos made for these two tracks. It is also something of a surprise that the videos for both I know what I like and Match of the day are missing. The other complaint frequently voiced by fans is that they had already purchased the videos to 'Invisible Touch' on the 'Visible Touch' compilation. however, to new fans both videos serve as a great introduction to the band's career. Virgin Video VVD329/330.

As if the release of the two video compilations wasn't enough the band also released a visual record of their 'Invisible Touch' tour in the form of the 'Invisible Touch Tour' video filmed at the band's record breaking four night stint at Wembley Stadium in July 1987. The video captured the show in it's entirety with the exception of the 'In the cage medley' which was already available on previous videos, and the full track listing is as follows:Mama/Abacab/Domino/That's all/The Brazilian/Land of confusion/ Tonight tonight tonight/Throwing it all away/Home by the sea/ Second home by the sea/Invisible Touch/Drum duet/Los endos/Turn it on again - Sixties medley. This was the first music video to be filmed in high definition and marks the beginning of the group's association with Sony which was to culminate in the stage show for their next tour. The film also came with a limited edition cd of the live track 'Domino'. Virgin Video VVD358. This film has also been issued as a DVD including a photo gallery and interviews.

"Genesis - A History" appeared in 1991 and was a long overdue look at the band's career with interviews with all band members and also with brief interviews with ex members Anthony Phillips, Steve Hackett and Peter Gabriel. Another must for collectors featuring previously unseen live footage by the band. 90 minutes.The band's appearance at the 1990 Knebworth Festival was also recorded and released in 1991 as part of the two video package;"Knebworth - The Event" which also features appearances by all the other acts on the bill. The videos were released by Castle Music Pictures in May 1991. CMP 2058.

Genesis's "The way we walk in concert",captured their 1992 "We can't dance" tour and was filmed at their six night residence at London's Earl's Court Arena. The video managed to bring all of the visual excitment of the show to the small screen and features the following tracks; Land of confusion/No son of mine/Driving the last spike/Old medley (inc Dance on a volcano-The lamb lies down on Broadway-Musical Box-That's all-Follow you follow me)/ Fading lights/Jesus he knows me/Dreaming while you sleep/Home by the sea/Second home by the sea/Hold on my heart/Domino/I can't dance/Tonight tonight tonight/Invisible touch/Turn it on again. 135 minutes. 0864963.

There was also a video EP put together of the promotional videos from the We Can't Dance album which was, sadly, never released although the Laser disc edition of the live video had this attached at the end of it.

"The Way We Walk Live In Concert" was also subsequently issued as the band's first live DVD release on 26th November 2001 as a double DVD package including the full live show with video streaming which enables you to control your own camera angle as well as full commentary by the band, interviews and other items. This release brings Genesis' video releases into the 21st century and other projects are considered for further release in this format.
Gut Vision GUTDVD1.

"The Genesis Songbook" was initially a TV project for Channel 4 TV compiled by the company who brought you the "Classic Albums" series of documentaries. This one featured extensive interviews with band members past and present, as well as others associated with the band including journalists Chris Welch and Armando Gallo as well as an appearance by the editor of a certain Genesis magazine (!). It was subsequently issued as a commercial video and DVD late in 2000. The DVD contained an additional 40 minutes' worth of footage and interviews.
Eagle Vision ERE176 (Video), EREDV176 (DVD)

As far as is known at the moment, there is no plan to release any live visual record of the band's "Calling all stations" tour although at least two shows on the tour were recorded by local television crews these being the band's shows at the Spodek Arena Katowice Poland on 31st January 1998; the Sportovinhala in Prague on 2nd February 1998 and at the Stadthalle Vienna Austria on 15th February 1998. There are, of course, various extracts from other concerts which were broadcast on the relevant television networks in the respective territories.

Genesis The Video Show was released on 29th November 2004. Finally giving in to the demand from the fans for a repackaging of the various promotional videos for their massive catalogue of singles, including some that had seldom been screened on TV. The track listing is as follows: No Son Of Mine/I Can't Dance/Hold On My Heart/Jesus He Knows Me/Tell Me Why/Invisible Touch/Throwing It All Away/Land Of Confusion/Tonight, Tonight, Tonight/Anything She Does/In Too Deep/That's All/Mama/Illegal Alien/Home By The Sea/Second Home By The Sea/Paperlate/Abacab/Keep It Dark/No Reply At All/Man On The Corner/Turn It On Again/Duchess/Misunderstanding/Follow You Follow Me/Many Too Many/A Trick Of The Tail/Ripples/Robbery, Assault And Battery/Congo/Shipwrecked/Not About Us/The Carpet Crawlers 99.
Virgin/EMI 7243 5 442449 6 DVD.

GENESIS UK AND OVERSEAS TELEVISION APPEARANCES 1969 -

It is difficult to imagine nowadays with the coverage of the band on tv and film that this wasn't always the case. Film of any kind of the band in the period prior to 1976 is very hard to find and much sought after by fans of the band. The following represents as full a visual record of the band from this period and beyond as I have been able to piece together. Where no footage from the UK is known to exist I have included details of foreign footage for the sake of completeness.

BBC Training film 1968 (Unreleased) features a performance of 'In hiding' (The only known footage of original line-up). According to recent information this was done in a similar way to later "Top of the Pops" recordings with the singer 'live' and the band miming to a backing track of the song.
"Stagnation"; "Twilight Alehouse" and "The Knife" 8mm film shot at the band's gig supporting David Bowie at London's Roundhouse on 11th March 1970 as part of the "Atomic Sunrise Festival". As far as is known, this is the only live concert footage of the band from this period including both Anthony Phillips and John Mayhew in the line-up. Recent information has it that the entirety of this gig was filmed professionally and recorded on eight track sound recording equipment as well, although who actually owns this film is anyone's guess at present!

"Disco Two" BBC TV November 1970 performance of 'The Knife' with Mick Barnard (Anthony Phillips's replacement). The band's first appearance on television and the only recording featuring Anthony Phillips' replacement, now sadly believed lost.

"Rock of the Seventies" Belgian tv special broadcast in the UK and filmed in 1972. Includes studio performances of 'Musical Box/Fountain of Salmacis/Twilight Alehouse/The Return Of The Giant Hogweed. This footage has also recently been issued unofficially as a DVD. Sadly, earlier performances by the band for either this series or "Pop Deux" have been erased from the archives.

"Best Of British Festival" Frankfurt 17.1.73. An unusual one this, a German celebration of the best in British music! Genesis appeared at the festival which was televised and sound-recorded with two tracks; Watcher of The Skies and Musical Box performed. Sadly, the whereabouts of the film footage is, at present, unknown although the sound recording of these tracks has long since been made available on bootleg.

Bataclan Club Paris 10.2.73. A recent addition this film was shot by French tv and includes footage of Gabriel in his various costumes including the legendary "Fox's head" and also includes the only Gabriel period visual performance of "The Knife" currently available to fans although there are reports of a further two complete concerts from this period available in the television company archives. Recently additional footage from this concert has surfaced, suggesting that the entire show was possibly recorded.

Another item also re-issued as an unofficial DVD Midnight Special US TV broadcast 19.12.73 well documented TV appearance for which the band performed both Watcher Of The Skies and The Musical Box the latter being particularly interesting because it featured a different arrangement to that on the album.

"Melody" French TV studios Paris 12.2.74. Another recent addition to the archives. This was filmed during the band's European tour for Selling England By The Pound and features a complete studio performance of both Supper's Ready and I Know What I like with Mr Gabriel hamming it up in fine style at several points! This item has also founds its way onto an unofficial DVD.

Montreal University 20th April 1974. Filmed by the students at the University, this film captures the band at the height of their powers. A 45 minute extract compiled from both live and still photography is currently available although the entire concert is believed to exist possibly in the University's archives.
"Trefpunkte" A very highly sought after item this, being the only acknowledged OFFICIAL visual record of "The Lamb". Filmed at the Shrine Auditorium on 24th January 1975 it includes footage of "The Slipperman" as well as "In The Cage" and "Musical Box.

Match Of The Day (Promo) TOTP 2/6/77. Your Own Special Way Tyne Tees Tv 1977. Follow you follow me Top of the Pops BBC TV 23/3/78. Turn it on again Top of the Pops BBC tv 13/3/80. "Tiswas" ITV includes promo video for 'Misunderstanding' 1980. "Tiswas" ITV includes promo video for 'Abacab' 19.09.81. 'Abacab' Top of the pops BBC tv 27.08.81. 'Paperlate' Top of the Pops BBC tv 27.05.82. "Three sides Live in America" (Shortened version of official video) broadcast on ITV 1983. 'That's all' Late late breakfast show ITV 22.10.83. TV AM interview 17.11.83.Midlands News 26.2.84. TV AM interview 04.08.84 includes 'Illegal Alien' promo. "Freezeframe" ITV Documentary 1985. "Whistle Test" BBC tv 17.12.85."Whistle Test" BBC tv 10.6.86. "Whistle Test Extra" BBC tv 20.9.86 Montreux Festival BBC tv 1986 "Fast Copy" interview 1986. "Music Box" interview 1986. Montreux Festival BBC tv 1987. Look North News Roundhay Park Leeds 28.6.87."Coca Cola Live Report" Wembley Stadium 3.7.87."The Rock of Europe" Wembley Stadium 4.7.87."Throwing it all away" Wogan Show BBC tv 29.6.87. "Atlantic at Forty" Madison Square Gardens NYC 15.5.88. "The Story so far" BBC documentary 31.3.91.We can't dance (Electronic Press kit) 1991.'No son of mine' Top of the Pops BBC tv 31.10.91.'Hold on my heart' Top of the Pops BBC TV 9.4.92. Children's BBC 17.4.92.TV AM interview 21.7.92. TV AM interview 22.7.92.TV AM interview 23.7.92. "No admittance" Yorkshire TV documentary 24.7.92. 'Jesus he knows me' Countdown studios 29.7.92. Channel 4 daily news 31.7.92. Calendar Yorkshire tv news 1.8.92. Knebworth Park Concert 1.8.92. Anglia tv news ?.7.92. Granada Weekend Manchester Apollo 30.10.92. "The O-Zone" BBC tv 8.11.92. "Blue Peter" BBC tv 26.11.92. TVS interview 20.11.92. Calling all stations (Electronic Press kit) 1997 Congo (Promotional video) 1997. Berlin acoustic concert 22nd August 1997. Performed as part of the band's promotional duties for their new album "Calling all Stations" this includes performances of No son of mine, Lover's leap and Invisible touch. Cape Canaveral Launch 26/8/97 (Virgin Records Electronic Press Kit). Shipwrecked (Promotional video) 1997."Talking Music" VH1 interview at the Bray Studios tour rehearsals 23.1.98. Not about us (Promotional video) 1998. VH1 interview about first "Boxed Set" 13.5.98. VH1 "Genesis Archive" Special 6/7/98. "The Story so far…" Network (RTE Ireland) 6/7/98."Behind The Music" VH1 18.12.99.

French TV Appearances
Bataclan Club Paris 10.2.73 Canal Jimmy, "Melody" ORTF Studios 1974, "C Plus" Interview 1986. "M6 Story" 1986. In Too Deep ORTF Studios 1986. "Invisible Tour" 1987. "Top 50 C Plus" 7.12.91. "All Star Weekend" 1991. "La Saga Du Rock" 15.11.91. No Son Of Mine Sacre Soiree TV Show 4.12.91."Culture Rock" ?.11.91. "Star 90" TF1 ?.12.91. "Nouba" ?.2.93."Culture Rock" 1993. "Escale MCM Special" 1994. "Emission cadence" (?). Halle Tony Garnier 20.2.98.

Italian TV Appearances
"Superclassifica" 1981. "Live From Venice" (Studio performance)1981. Tirennia Film Studios Pisa 6.9.82. "Tandem" ?.9.81. "Disco Ring" 27.9.81. "Gondola D'Oro" 1981. Paperlate St Vicente Estate 1982. Mama "Bananas Show" 1983. Mama "Superflash" 1983. Mama/Home By The Sea "Premiatissima" 1983. Mama "Gian & Rick Follies" 1983. "Disco Ring" 1985. Fantastico Show 1986. Video Music 1986. Deejay TV 1987. "Estate Rock" ?.6.87. "Genesis Day In Milan" (TV Special) 15.5.87. "Live In Milan" 11.5.87. "Fantastico Show" 15.11.91. "Appuntamento a Roma" 15.12.91. Congo/Shipwrecked "Domenica Show" 15.2.98.

German TV Appearances
Abacab "Top Pop Show" 1981. "Countdown" ?.9.81. Paperlate "Na Sowas" 1982. "Na Siehste" 1982. "Music Szene" interview 1986. "Live Aus den Alabama" ?.6.87. "Showfenster" 1988. "Golden Europa Awards" 1988. "Peter's Pop Show" 7.12.91. "Wetten Das" 14.12.91. "Countdown" 1991. I Can't Dance/No Son Of Mine "Countdown" 1991. "Rudi Carrell Show" 1992. "POP" 19.7.92. Schleswig Holstein TV Magazine 1992. "Niedersachsen Report" 13.10.92.

"Hinter Den Kulissen Ein Rocklegende" 1992. "Das report" 9.10.92. "Halo Niedersachsen!" 13.10.92. "Mittagsmagazin" 6.7.92. Bravo 2.11.97. RSH Gold 7.2.98. Blitz 7.2.98. "Rock In Park" German TV 31.5.98. Via Jam Special 1999.VH1 Germany 1999.

Japanese TV Appearances
Rainbow Theatre 1.1.77. Firth Of Fifth 1.1.77(?). Sun Plaza Hall Tokio 3.12.78. "Hit" 16.11.91.
Norwegian, Danish, Swedish and Finnish TV Appearances.
Abacab 1981 (Finnish broadcast of TOTP performance). Ullevi Stadium Stockholm 8.6.92. No Son Of Mine (NRK 1) 1991. Folkcomedie (NRK1) 1991. I Can't Dance (NRK1) 1991. No Son Of Mine (NRK1) 1991. "Dagbrowski" (NRK1) 1991. NRK 1 interview 1991. "35 Minutter med.." (NRK1) 1991. MTV Broadcast (NRK1) 1992.
Polish TV Appearances Katowice Spodek Arena 31.1.98 (Complete concert).
Spanish TV Appearances "Toccata Special" 1987. "A Tope" interview 13.5.87. TVE interview 1991. TVE interview 16.11.91.
Belgian TV Appearances "Rock Of The Seventies" 1972, "Five Songs Live" 1984.
Dutch TV Appearances Abacab "Music Box" 1981. Feyernoord Stadium Rotterdam 11.6.87 (2 songs).
Australian TV Appearances "The Meldrum Tapes" 1986. "Today" interview 1986. Australian t v news report1986. "Sounds" 1986-87.
Austrian TV Appearances "Ohne Maulkorb" (Live from Vienna 20.8.78). "Ohne Maulkorb" 1986.
US and Canadian TV Appearances "Midnight Special" 1973. "Mike Douglas Show" 1977. "Atlanta Special" interviews and live footage 1984."Michelob presents…" 1985. Invisible Touch (Live from Richfield Coliseum Cleveland 27.1.87). "The New Music" 1991. "Spotlight" 1992.
Czech TV Appearances Sportovinhala Prague 2.2.98. Television broadcast of the band's Calling All Stations gig. Part of No Son Of Mine is missing and so is the acoustic medley but otherwise this is the entire concert.

Obviously, this is only a small selection of the material available, and any details of TV appearances which may have been missed from these listings; will be most welcome.

THE SOLO ARTISTS ON VIDEO

Fans of the various solo members of the band have been quite well served with video material either on tv or commercially available product, especially if you happen to be a fan of either Phil Collins or Peter Gabriel and the following is a break down of the material available in the UK and elsewhere, to collectors.

TONY BANKS ON VIDEO Tony has yet to release a compilation of the promotional videos to the singles he has released and many of these are highly sought after items

The Waters of Lethe (Promotional film1979
For A While (Promotional Film) 1979
Canadian TV 1982
This is love (Promotional video) 1983
Short cut to somewhere (Promotional video) 1986
"Formel Eins" (German TV) 7.10.89
Throwback (Promotional video) 1989
Raincloud (Promotional Film) 1989
'I'll be waiting' This morning show ITV 1.11.89
"Rock School" BBC tv 27.3.88
"Rock School" BBC tv 17.4.88
"Rock School" BBC tv 8.5.88
"Rock School" BBC tv 15.5.88
I wanna change the score (Promotional video) 1991
The Gift (Promotional video) 1991
Only Seventeen (Promotional video) 1995   Pebble
Mill BBC TV 'Walls of sound', 'Only seventeen' 1996

Tony's music also appears in the soundtracks to the following films all of which are available on commercial video.
The Shout (with Mike Rutherford) 1979.
The Wicked Lady 1983.
Lorca and the Outlaws 1985.
Quicksilver 1985.

PHIL COLLINS ON VIDEO

Phil's solo success has been amazing and he has appeared on just about every tv show in the UK that you could possible think of as well as several you couldn't! He has also released a series of highly successful commercial video collections all of which are part and parcel of any collection of his material.

PART ONE: COMMERCIAL VIDEOS

Phil's first video release was a video E.P. featuring the tracks released as singles from his highly successful first album: "Face Value" and its successor; "Hello, I must be going" The tracks included were; In the air tonight/I missed again/Thru these walls/You can't hurry love. Originally issued by PMI it was subsequently re-issued by Castle Music Video CMVG 5017.

Never one to keep his fans waiting Phil also released a live video from his 1983 US tour. Titled "Live at Perkins Palace" it featured sixty minutes of live concert footage from one of his US shows including the following tracks: I don't care anymore/I cannot believe its true/Thru these walls/I missed again/Behind the lines/The roof is leaking/The West Side/In the air tonight/You can't hurry love/It don't matter to me/People get ready.Picture Music International MC2059.

The E.P. format was repeated in 1985 with the release of the "No jacket required" e.p. combining the videos from the album again and comprising the following tracks; Sussudio/One more night/Who said I would/Don't lose my number/Take me home. Virgin VVC 095.

Another live video followed the completion of the tour and this release is an excellent example of how live videos should be made featuring as it does, almost an entire live show with little over all editing. The 89 minute video includes the following tracks;Only you and I know/Against all odds/Who said I would?/Sussudio/Behind the lines/The West Side/One more night/In the air tonight/Like China/You can't hurry love/It don't matter to me/Hand in hand/Take me home/It's alright. WEA Music Video 2 52411-3.

Phil's film career merited a video of its own and one was duly produced in 1989. "Phil Collins is 'Buster'" was the film of the making of the "Buster" movie. Released by Vestron video VA 17253. The film itself is also now available on commercial video.

"The Singles Collection" released in December 1989 re-issued the earlier promotional videos which had been deleted along with the two promotional videos from the "Buster"soundtrack. The full track listing is: Don't lose my number/I missed again/A groovy kind of love/Who said I would?/You can't hurry love/Thrue these walls/Sussudio/One more night/Two hearts/In the air tonight/Easy lover/Against all odds/Take me home. Virgin Video VVD 594.

The 1990 "But Seriously" tour produced another live video to add to Phil's growing collection. This one is a complete show recorded at the Berlin Waldebuehne in July and contains the following songs: Hand in hand/Hang in long enough/Against all odds/Don't lose my number/Inside out/Do you remember?/Who said I would?/Another day in Paradise/Separate lives/Saturday night Sunday morning/The West Side/That's just the way it is/Something happened on the way to Heaven/Doesn't anybody stay together anymore?/One more night/Colours/In the air tonight/You can't hurry love/Two hearts/Sussudio/A groovy kind of love/Easy lover/Always/Take me home. Virgin Video VVD783. This video was also issued in 2003 as an extended two disc DVD set which included bonus material and photo archives. Warner Music Vision 2564 60487-2.

Phil took the video E.P format to extremes with the 1992 "But Seriously - The Videos" collection which featured film of every track from the album including live footage to make a rather nice compilation including the following tracks; Hang in long enough/Another day in Paradise/Do you remember?/Colours/Something happened on the way to Heaven/All of my life/I wish it would rain down/Heat on the street/That's just the way it is/Saturday night Sunday morning/Father to son/Find a way to my heart. Virgin Video VVD1010 77 minutes.

Phil's only video from his concerts on the 1994/95 world tour was titled "A closer look" this video is a backstage look at the preparations for the tour and was sold at gigs to raise money for the homeless charities in each city on the tour. So far it has not gained a full commercial release although it was shown in the UK the day before Phil's shows at the Manchester G-mex!

Phil's 1997 Dance Into the Light tour spawned its own live video: "Live And Loose On Paris" was released on 20th July 1998 and featured edited highlights of Phil's show from Paris during the "Dance Into The Light" tour and captures the show brilliantly. It is strange however, that this show has been edited, after all; Phil's fans have always been treated to a full performance on video but nevertheless this is an essential addition to collections. Tracks are: Hand in hand/Hang in long enough/Don't lose my number/Another day in paradise/Against all odds/Lorenzo/Separate lives/Long long way to go/In the air tonight/Timbantiocha/Easy lover/Dance into the light/Wear my hat/Something happened on the way to heaven/Sussudio. Warner Music Vision 3984 23466-3

This video has also been issued as a DVD release featuring exactly the same footage as the above video. Warner Music Vision 3984 23466-2.

Phil's first solo album: Face Value was the subject of one of the "Classic Albums" series of TV documentaries and this too has been released on video. Eagle Rock Entertainment ILC0183

Phil's recent appearance as the subject of the BBC documentary "A Life Less Ordinary" has also been turned into a commercial DVD release including over thirty minutes of extra footage not shown on the original broadcast. Sanctuary Visual Entertainment SVE3031.

With Phil's announcement of his cessation of touring, his final tour; dubbed with a certain tongue-in-cheek humour as "The First Final Farewell Tour" has seen another live concert video "Finally... The First Farewell Tour" which was released on 1st November 2004. This one not only takes in the complete performance from Phil's gig at the Bercy Stadium in Paris on 14th June 2004 but there are enough DVD extras to shake a stick at! These include many of the promotional videos for the songs in the live set; footage from Phil's legendary performance at "Live Aid" and much more. The live track listing is as follows... Drums, Drums & More Drums/Something Happened On The Way To Heaven/Against All Odds/Don't Lose My Number/You'll Be In My Heart/One More Night/Can't Stop Loving You/Hang In Long Enough/True Colours/Come With Me/Groovy Kind Of Love/I Missed Again/Another Day In Paradise/No Way Out/Separate Lives/In The Air Tonight/Dance Into The Light/You Can't Hurry Love/Two Hearts/Wear My Hat/Easy Lover/Sussudio/It's Not Too Late/Take Me Home.
Warner Music Vision 2564 61982 -2 2 DVD set.

PART TWO: UK FILM AND TV APPEARANCES

From humble beginnings to the superstardom he now so rightly enjoys, Phil's rise to fame has been well documented by film and tv and the following charts that rise through the medium of film and video in the UK."Calamity the cow" Children's Film Foundation film 1967. "And so to F.." with Brand X Old Grey Whistle Test BBC tv 1979."Pop Quest" BBC tv 1979. "In the air tonight" Top of the Pops BBC tv 1981."I missed again" Top of the Pops BBC tv 18.3.81."In the air tonight" Prince's Trust Gala Concert 1981."In the air tonight" Secret policeman's Ball (Film) 1981."If leaving me is easy" Top of the Pops BBC tv ?.5.81."Wogan Show" BBC tv 1982."In the air tonight" Prince's Trust Gala Concert 1982."Freezeframe" ITV Documentary 1982.You can't hurry love" Wogan Show BBC tv 1982."Why can't it wait til morning"/"You don't know like I know" (Duet with Leo Sayer) Leo Sayer Show BBC tv 1982."I don't care anymore" Three of a kind show BBC tv 1982."The other side of the tracks" Channel 4 Documentary 1983."The making of 'There's something going on'" Documentary about Phil's involvement with Anni Frid's solo album ITV 1984."The Tube" Channel 4 tv interview 11.2.85."Sussudio" Top of the Pops BBC tv 1985."Take me home" Top of the Pops BBC tv 1985."Live Aid" Wembley Stadium/JFK Stadium Philadelphia ITV 13.6.85."We said hello goodbye" Joan Rivers Show BBC tv 1985."Against all odds" The Two Ronnies Show BBC tv 25.12.85."One more night" The Two Ronnies Show BBC tv 31.12.85."Sussudio"/"One more night" B P I Awards Ceremony ITV 20.2.86.Birmingham N E C (Eric Clapton concert featuring Phil drumming in Eric's band) ITV 1986."Earsay" Channel 4 interview 1986.Prince's Trust Rock Gala ITV 26.6.86."Film '87" interview BBC tv 1987.Prince's Trust Rock Gala ITV 1987.Prince's Trust Rock Gala ITV 15.5.88."Parkinson: One on One" interview BBC tv 16.7.88."A groovy kind of love" Top of the Pops BBC tv 8.9.88."Aspel & Company" interview ITV 10.9.88."A groovy kind of love" Top of the Pops BBC tv 15.9.88."The last resort" ITV 15.9.88."This is your life" ITV 16.10.88.BBC Variety Club Awards 1988."Wired" interview Channel 4 tv 23.10.88."Donahue" interview Channel 4 tv 1988."Two Hearts" Top of the Pops BBC tv 25.12.88.The "Brit" Awards Ceremony ITV 13.2.89."Entertainment USA" BBC tv 1989."Another day in paradise" Top of the Pops BBC tv 1989."Rapido" Channel 4 tv 1989."Tommy" Philadelphia 12.5.89 (Phil appearing as "Wicked Uncle Ernie") ITV .Jonathan Ross Show ITV 1989."Going live" BBC tv 1989."Big World Cafe" Channel 4 tv 1989."Off the wall" interview 1989."Big World Cafe" Channel 4 tv 30.10.89.Wogan Show BBC tv 13.1.90.
B P I Awards Ceremony ITV 20.2.90."Rock Steady" Channel 4 tv 30.4.90.I wish it would rain down Top of the Pops BBC tv 1990.TV AM interviews 1990.BSB Hit Studio 1990."What's that noise?" BBC tv 15.10.90.MTV Music Awards ITV 27.10.90.ITV Billboard Awards 1992."Symphony for the spire" BBC tv 15.8.92."Both sides of the story" Top of the Pops BBC tv 21.10.93."Both sides of the story" Top of the Pops BBC tv 28.10.93.Prince's Trust Gala Concert 25.12.94. "Balto" Disney Animated feature film for which Phil provided one of the voice-overs 1995 Prince's Trust Gala Concert Royal Albert Hall London 11.7.96.Dance into the light (Promotional video) 1996.Dance into the light TOTP BBC TV 1996.Dance into the light/It's in your eyes Des O'Connor Show ITV 1996.The Noise ITV 1996.Live & Kicking BBC TV 1996.It's in your eyes (Promotional video) 1996.It's in your eyes TOTP BBC TV 1996."The Phil Collins Big Band" Tour Documentary BBC tv 23/12/96.Granada tv interview 11.11.97.London Tonight tv interview 12.12.97.Wear my hat (Promotional video) 1997."Parkinson" BBC tv 06.02.98. "Live by request" LWT 1.10.98, National Lottery Live BBC TV 24.10.98. True Colours (Promotional video) 1998. Big Screen ITV 1999. You'll be in my heart (Promotional Video) 1999. Can't Stop Loving You (Promotional Video) 2002; TV AM 28 & 29.10.02, "A Life Less Ordinary" BBC TV 4.11.02. Des O'Connor Today ITV 7/11/02. Testify Electronic Press Kit (pt1) 2002,

Testify Electronic Press Kit (pt2) 2002. See Through My Eyes/Two Hearts (Children In Need BBC TV) 22/11/03, TV AM Interview 25/11/03, Two Hearts/See Through My Eyes (TOTP BBC TV) 28/11/03.

Australian TV Appearances "Rock Cinema" 1986. "Sixty Minutes" ?.6.94

Austrian/German TV Appearances "Beat Club" 1983. "RTL Star Mix" 1985."Bitte Umblattern Bericht" 7.10.89. "P.O.P." 3.1.90."Lokal TV" (Dortmund) 12.7.90. "Frankfurt Die 80-er" 28.1.90. ZDF Pop Show. "Dortmund Viva" ?.11.93. 31.12.93."Vestermen Sie Spas" 5.2.94."Die Goldener Kamera" 12.2.94. "Pop Gallerie" 8.12.96. "Wetten Das" 10.12.96. "Blitz" 26.3.97. "Blitz" 1.10.98.

US/Canadian TV Appearances
You Can't Hurry Love (Solid Gold Classics) 1985. MTV interview 1985. "Phil on Phil" 1989.MTV "Rockumentary" 1989. MTV Music Awards 27.10.90. "Larry King Live" 1993. "The New Music" 1994. "Conan O'Brien Show" 1996. "Jay Leno Show" 1996. "Entertainment '96" 2.1.97. "Mills 'N' Collins" 22.10.98. CNN interview 7-8.8.98.

French TV Appearances
ORTF Studios 1982. "Serious Tour" 1990."Tele Montecarlo" 28.11.93. "Taratata" 2.12.93. "La Plein Du Super Canal" 8.1.94. Everyday ORTF Studios 1994. "Star 90" 18.4.94. "Culture Rock M6" ?.4.94. "le Monde Est A Vous" 6.1.97. "Taratata" 14.2.97.

Italian TV Appearances Thru These Walls (Disco Ring) 1982. "Prisma" ?.2.85 "Ragazzi" 9.12.89. Everyday (San Remo Festival) ?.3.94. "Fantastico Show" 6.1.96.

Dutch TV Appearances Hilversum TV Studios 10.9.69 (Flaming Youth), "Countdown" 1982. "Countdown" 1983.

Norwegian, Danish, Swedish and Finnish TV Appearances
Swedish tv 1983. Swedish tv interview 1986. Swedish tv interview 1989. Another Day In Paradise (Swedish tv performance) 1989. Pori Jazz Festival 17.7.98 (Finnish tv).

Japanese TV Appearances The Dome Fukuoka 7.5.95 (Broadcast as a tribute to the victims of the Kobe earthquake disaster). South American TV Appearances. River Plate Stadium Buenos Aires 21.4.95. Estadio Mundalista Chile ?.5.95 South African TV Appearances. Ellis Park Johannesburg 17.3.95.

PETER GABRIEL ON VIDEO

Peter's record on the video front is not quite as prolific as Phil's but what material is available more than makes up for the gaps between releases.

PART ONE: COMMERCIAL VIDEOS

The first commercial release by Peter was 1987's "CV" a compilation of his promotional videos going back as far as 1982 and serves as a great compilation of these often hard to find items, several of which gained limited if any airing on tv. The track listing includes: Big time/Don't give up(2)/Shock the monkey/Mercy Street/Sledgehammer/I don't remember/Red rain/Don't give up(1). Virgin Music Video VVD241. 40 minutes.

Peter's second commercially released video "POV" appeared in 1988 and features footage shot at the last of Peter's shows on the "This Way Up" 1987 tour at the Lykabettus Hill Theatre in Athens.The video is an inventive mix of live footage interspersed with old super 8mm footage and even the odd snippet of Genesis although you have to be quick to spot them. The track listing is as follows: This is the picture/San Jacinto/Shock the monkey/Games without frontiers/No self control/Mercy Street/Sledgehammer/Solsbury Hill/Lay your hands on me/Don't give up/In your eyes/Biko. Virgin Video VVD626. 85 minutes

Peter's concerts for the University of Peace which took place at the Jingu Stadium in Tokio on 20th and 21st December 1986 were also released in 1987 under the title "Hurricane Irene" and the video included Peter's performance of the following songs at the concert: Red rain/Sledgehammer/No self control/Biko/Red Rain(Reprise). 30 Minutes.

"All about US" was issued in 1993 and included an interesting background to the making of the album as well as the complete promotional videos to; Digging in the dirt/Steam/Blood of Eden/Solsbury Hill/Zaar/Come talk to me/Kiss that frog.Sadly the version of Solsbury Hill was not the original 1977 version but that which was made for the 1991 "Shaking the tree" album. It is intriguing to speculate about the reasons why this video and those to 'Modern love' and 'Games without frontiers' were not included in this compilation?

"Secret World Live" continues Peter's live video documents and as its title suggests, it is a live concert video filmed at the Palasport Nuovo Modena Italy on 16th and 17th November 1993.The film manages to capture the drama and hi technology which made the shows on this tour so remarkable and contains the following live tracks; Come talk to me/Steam/Across the river/Slow marimbas/Shaking the tree/Blood of Eden/San Jacinto/Kiss that frog/Washing of the water/Solsbury Hill/Digging in the dirt/Sledgehammer/Secret world/Don't give up/In your eyes. Picture Music International PM898. 103 minutes

"Growing Up Live" is Peter's largest scale foray into live video with another concert from Italy on his recent "Growing Up" tour. Capturing the live "experience" of one of Peter's new shows in full visual and 5.1 stereo this is another must for Peter's fans. Tracks: Here Comes The Flood/Darkness/Red Rain/Secret World/Sky Blue/Downside Up/The Barry Williams Show/More Than This/Mercy Street/Digging In The Dirt/ Growing Up/Animal Nation/Solsbury Hill/Sledgehammer/Signal To Noise/In Your Eyes/Father To Son. Real World 5050466-8596-2-4

Peter has also finally given his fans the promotional video compilation which so many of then had craved with the DVD release on 24th October 2004 of "Play - The Videos" which brings together just about all of the promotional clips for Peter's singles as well as several new clips and enhanced versions. The track listing is as follows: Father, Son/Sledgehammer/Blood Of Eden/Games Without Frontiers/I Don't Remember/Big Time/Lovetown/Red Rain/In Your Eyes/Don't Give Up/The Barry Williams Show/ Washing Of The Water/Biko/Kiss That Frog/Mercy Street/Growing Up/Shaking The Tree/Shock The Monkey/Steam/The Drop/Zaar/Solsbury Hill/Digging In The Dirt. Warner Music Vision 50504675581 2-9

Continuing to document his live appearances with a visual record to match the expanding live audio releases, Still Growing Up Live & Unwrapped takes the process a stage further with footage from several of his recent European shows accompanied by interviews and TV footage making this an altogether more satisfying release than its predecessor. The track listing is as follows: Disc One: The Feeling Begins/Red Rain/Secret World/White Ashes/Games Without Frontiers/Burn You Up Burn You Down/The Tower That Ate People/San Jacinto/ Digging In The Dirt/Solsbury Hill/Sledgehammer/Come Talk To Me/Biko/In Your Eyes(*)/No Self Control (+)
(*) From the 2004 Still Growing Up Tour
(+) From the 1987 This Way Up Tour film "P O V" with 5.1 surround sound
Disc Two: Still Growing Up Unwrapped documentary/"Big Room" performances of Darkness/No Way Out and Growing Up/BBC TV performances of Downside Up and Father, Son for the "Later With Jools Holland" show. Warner Music Vision 50-51011-0458-2-0

PART TWO: UK FILM AND TELEVISION APPEARANCES

Peter's television and film appearances in the UK have increased steadily over the last few years. Always one to shy away from interviews he nonetheless has been the subject of an increasing number and they have frequently been insightful and on occasions; amusing.

Solsbury Hill (Promotional video) 1977.Modern love   (Promotional video)   1978."Kate Bush Special" ITV 28.12.79.No self control   Top of the Pops BBC tv 1980.Tour rehearsals and interview 1980.Games without frontiers (Promotional video) 1980."Whistle Test" interview BBC tv 9.10.82."The Southbank Show" documentary ITV 31.10.82.This is the picture (Promotional video) 1984."Whistle Test" BBC tv in studio 1986."Breakfast Time" interview ITV 18.07.86."Entertainment USA" BBC tv 08.01.87.B P I Awards Ceremony ITV 09.02.87.Here comes the flood "First Five Billion Show" ITV 1987."Whistle Test" BBC tv 1987."Wogan Show" interview BBC tv 29.11.87."Off the Wall" interview 12.03.88.Prince's Trust Gala Concert 23.06.88."Rapido" Channel 4 tv 15.04.89."Rapido" Channel 4 tv 21.06.89."Rhythms of the world" BBC tv 1989."Rock Profile" ITV 1989."One to one" interview 1989."Rock of Europe" Cable tv 31.10.89."Star Test" Channel 4 tv 30.11.89.Mandela Day Concert Wembley Stadium 16.04.90."Blue Night" Channel 4 tv 1990.Abrazo de Esperanza" Concert for Chile BBC tv 1990."Rapido" Channel 4 tv 19.03.91."What's that noise?" BBC tv 1992."Entertainment Express" 22.01.93.Be still (Promotional video) 1994.GMTV News 28.06.93.Saturday Night Live 1992.Late night with Letterman 1995. Later With Jools Holland BBC TV 28.5.00; TOTP 2 BBC TV ?.10.02, Later With Jools Holland BBCTV 1.11.02. Games Without Frontiers (Children In Need Merthyr Tydfil gig BBC TV) 22/11/03.

US/Canadian TV Appearances
"The New Music" (Canadian TV interview) 1980. US TV interview 1982. "Good Morning, America" 11.6.86. "Good Morning, America" 11.7.86. Giants Stadium New Jersey 15.6.86. "Entertainment Tonight" 18.6.86. US TV interview 1986. American Music Awards 1987. "Off The Wall" interview 12.3.88. MTV "News At Night" 2.9.88. MTV News At Night 7.9.88. "Rock Profile" 1989.US news 8.11.89. "The New Music" 1992. "Saturday Night Live" 1992. "Extreme Close Up" 24.12.92. "Extreme Close Up" 1993. "Charlie Rose Show" 1993. "The New Music" 28.6.94. Woodstock II Festival 25.8.94. "Children In Need" BBC TV performance of Games Without Frontiers from Merthyr Tydfil 21.11.03.

South American TV Appearances River Plate Stadium Buenos Aires 15.9.88. Velez Sarfeld Stadium Buenos Aires 2.10.93.

French TV Appearances "Casablanca" 11.10.82. "Platine" 1983. "Les Enfants Du Rock" 1987. "Escale MCM" 1992. "Culture Rock" 1992. "L'Oeil Du Cyclone" ?.6.92 "Ifo de 20 H" TF1 ?.6/92. "MCM Most Wanted" 29.9.92. "Le Top 50 C+" 29.12.92. "Nulle Parte D'Ailleurs" ?.12.92 "Nouba" 30.12.92. "Le Cercle Du Minuit" 24.2.93. "Soir" 25.4.93. "Giga" ?.4/93 "MCM Weekend Special" 19.6.93.ORTF Studios 1993. ORTF "Rockline Exclusive" 1993. "Le Plein Du Super Canal" 8.1.94. "MCM Magazine" ?.2.94. "Taratata" 1994.

German TV Appearances Essen Grugahalle (Rockpalast Show) 15.9.78. "Ohne Maulkorb" 1986. "Haus Vaterland" 1984. "Special LADR" 1987. "Illusions" 1988. "Wetten Das" 27.11.93. "Heute Journal" 1993. "ARD Morgen" 11.2.94. "Megamix - Arte" ?.3.94. "Das Portrait" 10.5.94. "Rock Am Ring festival" 1994.

Italian TV Appearances No Self Control (Disco Ring) 1980. Shock The Monkey/Lay Your Hands On Me (Popcorn) (latter is a re-mixed version of song) 1982. San Remo Festival (both nights)1983."Mixer" 1983. "Estate Bologna" 1983. "Vota La Voce" 1983. "Video Music" 1986. "DeeJay TV" 1986. "Superclassifica" 1986. "Be Bop A Lula" 1986. "Sera TV" 1986. "Estate Rock" ?.7.87. "Fantastico Show" 6.1.88. "Goggi Domani" 1988. Milan Tour Report 17.5.93. TG4 Report 1993. "Canal Grande" 2.6.93.

Japanese TV Appearances TV Interview 1982. Jingu Stadium Tokio 20 & 21.12.86.

Portuguese TV Appearances "Rock In Rio" Bela Vista Park Lisbon 29.5.04

Spanish TV Appearances "Documentos" 1987. "Telediario" 28.9.87. "Telenoticies" 30.9.87. "A Tope" 30.9.87.

STEVE HACKETT ON VIDEO

Steve has appeared on several commercial videos/ DVDs and has made numerous television appearances over the years.

"The Making of GTR" Appeared in 1987 to tie in with the recent tour by the group which featured Steve and Steve Howe. It is an interesting look at the making of the one and only GTR album and includes interviews with all the band members and rehearsal footage making it a worthwhile addition to any collection of material by Steve. RCA/Columbia Video 43396-60633. 1987 30 Minutes.

"Steve Hackett - Live" a long overdue live video from the guitar maestro appeared in 1991. Initially recorded for the Central tv "Bedrock" series and screened on UK tv this video was eventually issued on Castle Music Pictures in 1991. The video contained the following tracks; Camino Royale/Please don't touch/Everyday/In that quiet Earth/Depth charge/Wonderpatch/In the heart of the city/Black light/Horizons/Jacuzzi/Theatre of sleep/Jazz jam/Spectral mornings/Clocks. 60 minutes CMP6064. This was also subsequently re-issued as a DVD by Classic Rock Productions under the title "Horizons" in 2003. The track listing for this was as follows: Camino Royale/Please Don't Touch/Everyday/In That Quiet Earth/Depth Charge/In The Heart Of the City/Horizons/Theatre Of Sleep/Jazz Jam/Clocks. Classic Rock Productions CRL015.

"The Tokio Tapes" Steve's performances in Tokio for the "Genesis Revisited" album were captured on video and released by his own record company; Camino Records in 1997. The video captures the entire show as performed by Steve and his band of intrepid musos and contains the following tracks: Watcher of the skies/Riding the colossus/Firth of fifth/Battle lines/ Camino Royale/In the Court of the Crimson King/Horizons/Walking away from rainbows/Heat of the moment/In that quiet earth/A Vampyre with a healthy appetite/I talk to the wind/Shadow of the hierophant/Los Endos/Black Light/The Steppes/I know what I like. Camino Records CAMVT15.
This video was also subsequently re-issued in 2001 as a DVD package including additional footage of the rehearsals and interviews, making a nice addition to any Hackett fan's collection.
Camino Records CAMDV15

The next release from the Hackett camp was "Somewhere In South America" which captures Steve's latest live band in fine form on their South American tour in 2001 with a set list comprising the following tracks: The Floating Seventh/Mechanical Bride/Medley/Serpentine Song/Watcher of The Skies/Hairless Heart/Firth Of Fifth/Riding The Colossus/Pollution/The Steppes/Gnossienne No 1/Walking Away From Rainbows/Sierra Quemada/The Wall of Knives/A Vampyre With A Healthy Appetite/A Tower Struck Down/Lucridus/Darktown/Camino Royale/In Memoriam/Horizons/Los Endos. Camino Records CAMTV29

This was also issued subsequently as a three DVD/CD package including the complete audio soundtrack to the gig along with the full DVD footage of the concert accompanied by backstage and rehearsal footage from Steve's recent Italian tour. Camino Records CAMDV29

Steve has also issued a DVD only package of one of his acoustic shows in 2003. Titled "Hungarian Horizon" the DVD captures the entire show and also has bonus footage of rehearsals and interviews with Steve and the band. Tracks: Horizons/Gnossienne #1 / Bourree/ Bacchus/Firth Of Fifth/Bay Of Kings/Syrinx/Imagining/Second Chance/ Jacuzzi/Overnight Sleeper/The Barren Land/Black Light/Kim/Time Lapse At Milton Keynes/The Chinese Jam/Concerto In D/Hairless Heart/Cinema Paradiso/Mustard Seed/Gymnopedie #1/JazzOn A Summer's Night/Little Cloud/Cavalcanti/Walking Away From Rainbows/Andante In C/Concert For Munich/The Journey/The Skye Boat Song/By Paved Fountain/Etude In A Minor/Blood On The Rooftops/Hands Of The Priestess/C Minor Triplets/End Of Day/Ace Of Wands/Idylle/Aubade/Meditation. Camino Records CAMDV30

"Once Above A Time" released by Eagle Records on 22nd November 2004, captures an almost complete show from Steve's Live Archive 04 tour in 2004. Recorded at the Petofi Csarnok in Budapest on 3rd April2004 the video is an essential live document of Steve's most recent rock show. The DVD contains in addition to the concert itself; a behind the scenes documentary titled "Backstage In Budapest". The track listing is as follows: Valley Of The Kings/Mechanical Bride/Circus Of Becoming/Frozen Statues/ Slogans/Serpentine Song/Ace Of Wands/Hammer In The Sand/Blood On The Rooftops/Fly On A Windshield/Please Don't Touch/Firth Of Fifth/If You Can't Find Heaven/Darktown/Brand New/Air-Conditioned Nightmare/Every Day/Clocks/Spectral Mornings/Los Endos. Eagle Vision EREDV451.

"Spectral Mornings" Released by ARD in Germany on 20th May 2005 represents the first truly official re-issue of any part of Steve's visual archive. Comprising footage from the famous Musikladen/Beat Club performance in October 1978 this release captures Steve and his first touring band at an important stage in his career and is an essential addition to any Hackett Collection. The track listing includes several classic performances from Steve's first two albums as well as material from his as yet unreleased third solo album, Spectral Mornings, hence the title, folks!
Track listing: Please Don't Touch/Racing In A/Ace Of Wands/Narnia/A Tower Struck Down/Spectral Mornings/Kim/Acoustic Set/Shadow Of The Hierophant/Clocks - The Angel Of Mons/Carry On Up The Vicarage (*)/Band Intros (*)/Star Of Sirius (*)
(*) = DVD bonus tracks.
Radio Bremen ISBN 3-937308-57-1

STEVE HACKETT UK TELEVISION AND FILM APPEARANCES

How can I? (Promotional video) 1978. 1979.Everyday/Clocks (Promotional film by Polygram Records) one track was shown on the BBC "Old Grey Whistle Test" 1979.The show (promotional video) 1980.Nottingham Theatre Royal 27th August 1981. Shown as part of the "Videosounds" tv series in the UK. Strangely enough, this was also available for a limited time as a commercial video on the WOT Video label (catalogue number 81016). "Gas Tank" Channel 4 tv. Music and chat show hosted by Rick Wakeman on which Steve featured playing 'Camino Royale' and 'Hackett's bogie' 1983.Cell 151 (Promotional video) 1983.When the heart rules the mind (Promotional video) 1986."First Run" Steve & Steve Howe as resident vj's (!) Sky TV 1986.Sailing (Promotional video) 1990. All is mended/By a paved fountain "The Bridge" VH1 performance ?.04.97. Metamorpheus Promotional interview DVD 9.2.05.

US/Canadian TV Appearances Shadow Of The Hierophant "Circus TV" 1978.Triangle Theatre New York 31.10.81. "American Bandstand" (GTR) 1986.
Austrian/German TV Appearances "Beat Club" 17.10.78. A Doll That's Made in Japan (Studio performance) 1984. Munich Alabamahalle 22.9.86. "First Run" (Hackett/Howe as guest VJ's) 1986. "P.O.P." 24.4.90. "Face In The Mirror" (Promotional video for track from Gallery Of Dreams album by Austrian musician Gandalf) 1990.
French TV Appearances Elixii Festival Brest 15.7.82.
Hungarian TV Appearances Sketches Of Satie Hungarian TV interview with Steve and John Hackett about the Sketches Of Satie album. Recorded at Crown Studios London in 2000
Japanese TV Appearances
Montreux Jazz Festival 1980. Bottom Line Club NYC 18.8.92 (Pay per view channel broadcast).
Romanian TV Appearances Golden Stag TV Festival Brasov 7.9.94
Spanish TV Appearances TVE 3 Studios Madrid 21 4.05. Intro/Jam/Jacuzzi-Overnight Sleeper/Horizons/ Walking Away From Rainbows/Bacchus-Firth Of Fifth-Bacchus/The Pool Of Memory And The Pool Of Forgetfulness/Bay Of Kings/After The Ordeal/Hairless Heart/Ace Of Wands.

MIKE RUTHERFORD ON VIDEO

Mike has become increasingly well known as a solo artist since he instigated the Mechanics in 1985 and there are numerous tv shows on which he and the band have appeared. So far only two commercial videos have appeared, the first contains the promotional videos to the singles from the first two Mechanics albums along with amusing interviews with the band members.

"Mike and the Mechanics - A Closer look" was released in the UK in 1991 and contained the videos to the following tracks: Silent running/All I need is a miracle/Taken in/Nobody's perfect/Nobody knows/Seeing is believing/The living years. Warner Music Vision 9031 72543-3.

To tie in with the 1996 UK "Hits" tour, a further video compilation was released. In addition to the tracks contained on the above mentioned video which has long since been deleted, the new video also contained all the promotional videos from the band's third and fourth albums; Word of mouth and Beggar on a beach of gold along with the remixed version of their classic track; All I need is a miracle which had been released as a promotional device for the album. To collectors, this compilation is most useful because of the inclusion of the tracks from Word of mouth which gained little, if any, screening on terrestrial tv in the UK and so, this video represents the chance to complete video collections. The full track listing is as follows...All I need is a miracle (96 version)/Another cup of coffee/A beggar on a beach of gold/Over my shoulder/Word of mouth/The living years/A time and place/Everybody gets a second chance/Stop baby/Seeing is believing/Nobody knows/Nobody's perfect/Silent running/All I need is a miracle/Taken in. The video was issued by Warner Music Vision and had the following catalogue number: 0630-13851-3.

Mike & The Mechanics + Paul Carrack Live At Shepherds Bush released in late 2004 finally brought the fans a live concert from the band. Filmed at their only UK gig on the Rewired tour, this DVD only release captured the band performing an essentially "Greatest Hits" selection. Bonus features include interviews with Mike and Paul and a selection of promotional videos.   Track Listing: Falling/Now That You've Gone/Get Up/If I Were You/Another Cup Of Coffee/A Beggar On A Beach Of Gold/Perfect Child/Whenever I Stop/All The Light I Need/One Left Standing/Silent Running/Living Years/Over My Shoulder/Word Of Mouth. Bonus Material: Interview with Mike and Paul. Promotional videos for: Silent Running/Living Years/Word Of Mouth/Over My Shoulder/A Beggar On A Beach Of Gold/Another Cup Of Coffee/One Left Standing.
Eagle Vision EREDV453.

The Mechanics also featured as part of the line-up for the concert organised to celebrate the 50th anniversary of the creation of the Fender "Stratocaster" guitar which took place at Wembley Arena in the autumn of 2004. Featuring a star-studded line-up line-up, Mike and Paul Carrack performed a set which comprised How Long?/All Along The Watchtower/While My Guitar Gently Weeps/I Can't Dance. The concert was filmed and subsequently released by Eagle Vision under the title: "The Strat Pack - Live In Concert"
Eagle Vision EREDV464

UK AND OVERSEAS FILM AND TELEVISION APPEARANCES

Working in line (Promotional video) 1980.Half way there (Promotional video) 1982.Silent running Top of the Pops BBC tv 1985.Sky Channel interview 05.04.86.TV AM interview 08.11.88.Living years Wogan Show BBC tv 13.01.89.TV AM interview 15.01.89."Night Network" ITV 1989."Motormouth" ITV 1989.Prince's Trust Rock Gala ITV 26.08.89."In Profile" 07.04.89. Living Years Grammy Awards Ceremony 1990. "The making of word of mouth" (Official film) 1991.TV AM interview 13.03.91.Word of mouth (Promotional video) 1991.A time and place (Promotional video) 1991.Victory Club London (Album launch) 18.01.95Over my shoulder (Promotional video) 1995 Over my shoulder Des O'Connor Show 1995."The Bridge" VH-1 13.02.95.Over my shoulder GMTV 15.02.95.Over my shoulder David Letterman Show 07.03.95.Ellis Park South Africa (Rugby World Cup Programme ITV) 1995.Beggar on a beach of gold (Promotional video) Beggar on a beach of gold Top of the Pops BBC tv 22.06.95. Beggar on a beach of gold VH-1 1995. Another cup of coffee (Promotional video) 1995. VH1 interview and live performance 1996. All I need is a miracle '96 (Promotional video) 1996. All I need is a miracle Des O'Connor Show ITV 1996. Ordinary Girl (promotional video) 1999. "Unplugged" VH1 1999. Whenever I Stop (Promotional video) 1999. "This Is Your Life" BBC TV 23.1.03.

US/Canadian TV Appearances Silent Running 1985. House Of Blues 15.8.95
South African TV Appearances Sandton Towers Johannesburg 3.6.95 full concert broadcast.
French TV Appearances "Taratata" ?.3.95.
German TV Appearances "P.I.T" 1986. "Stars '95" ?.3.95. "Samstag Nacht" 23.9.95."Lowenverheilung" 29.10.95. "Harold Schmidt Show" 9.2.96. "Ohne Filter" 19.9.99.
Italian TV Appearances Half Way There (Disco Ring) 1983. Hideaway (Disco Ring) 1983. "Roxy Bar" 8.4.95. "Mio Capitano" 18.4.95. "Video Music Special" 1995.

ANTHONY PHILLIPS TV APPEARANCES

Strangely enough, the most prolific recording member of the group past or present has been conspicuously absent from television with only a handful of appearances I am aware of and not one of them from this country!

VH1 "New Visions" US tv 12.1.88 Anthony as guest vj on two hour programme promoting his new album "Slow waves soft stars" and playing two tracks from it; Elevenses and Sospirando.TV AM interview with Simon MacCorkindale about the "Tarka" album including footage of the famous whale rescue from the Alaskan pack ice including "The Anthem from Tarka" as its background music. ?.10.88.
"Hidrogen" A Spanish tv programme promoting "New Age " music on which Anthony and Guillermo Cazenave appeared in July 1997. Featured tracks are; Lucy an illusion, Sortilege, Peggy in the sky without diamonds.

"The Meadows of Englewood" and "From Genesis to Revelation" are the first attempts to bring Anthony's music to the visual arena. Both were produced and released by the Spanish company; Astral in early 1998 and are also distributed by his UK record company: Blueprint. Both videos contain footage of Anthony at work in his studio as well as tantalising snippets of him playing live and talking about his career to date and as such are essential additions to any collection of his work.
"The Meadows of Englewood" Astral GVA30 1997.
"From Genesis to Revelation" Astral GVA30 1997
"Ant Day 2000" Private film of fan club meeting with Anthony at his studio

Ray Wilson TV Appearances: Ray's tenure with Genesis may have been brief, but he has certainly put in some mileage since then with no less than four studio albums and two live albums to his credit. So far, he has eluded TV coverage here in the UK but there have been several live broadcasts of his performances elsewhere in Europe.

German TV Appearances Cologne "Underground" 29.9.03 (TV Broadcast for the WDR "Rockpalast" series).

Spanish TV Appearances TVE3 "Radio 3" Studio concert performance 2003.
Obviously, the above is only a representative selection of the enormous amount of television material which has been generated by the band and its various offshoots over the last thirty or so year.

FANS AND FAN CLUBS

Complementary to any band's activities it now seems increasingly necessary for the artist to be served by a fan club. In the thirty or so years of Genesis's career they have had several official and unofficial ones which have chronicled their careers with varying degrees of success and longevity. The first 'Official' fan club for the band was run by Amanda Gardner and called "The Hogweed Youth Movement" and consisted of regular newsletters on the band's activities. The club ran from 1971 to 1974 when Amanda was forced to give it up due to other commitments.

The gauntlet of running an information service on the band was taken up in October 1976 with the first issue of the 'Genesis Information' newsletter written and published by Geoff Parkin. Throughout the late Seventies and Eighties this was to be the mainspring of information on the band with quarterly newsletters and magazines. In all, from its inception to the bankruptcy of the club in 1992 fifty three magazines were published in addition to the two books which Geoff wrote and which are mentioned elsewhere in this text. Genesis Information also had a US branch run by Brad Lentz which was basically a US distributor for the magzine as written by Geoff. In addition to the Genesis magazine, Geoff also instigated "Phil Collins News" which was an A5 sized publication dedicated to Phil and his solo career. In all some three issues were published between 1983 and 1984.

The next magazine to appear was published in Australia and was to become Australia's Official fan club magazine. Titled "Ripples" the first issue appeared in early 1987 and was written and published by David Birtwell and Richard Harms. This was a well produced and designed magazine which set a standard for its successors. Unfortunately, due to a variety of problems, the magazine folded in 1991 having printed twenty one issues in all.

August 1987 saw the inaugural issue of "The Waiting Room" which is now the longest established Genesis magazine in the world. Originally written and produced by Ted Sayers, Peter Morton, Iain Buckle and Alan Hewitt, the magazine is now in its nineteenth year of existence although now published exclusively as an online edition on the Internet.

Two noteworthy foreign language magazines appeared within a few months of each other in 1991 beginning with "Dusk" the Italian Genesis magazine written and produced by Mario Giammetti and followed in December 1991 by the German magazine "Invisible Touch" (now called "IT") written and produced by Helmut Janisch, Bernd Zindler and Peter Schutz. Both of these magazines continue to write about the band and its solo members and have taken to issuing English language editions of their publications.

Peter Gabriel is now served by his own official fan club; "The Box" which apart from Peter's work also acts as an information service for the numerous "World Music" artists who are housed under Peter's "Real World" record label.

FAN CLUB ADDRESS'S

"Dusk"   C/O: Mario Giammetti Casella Postale 10
82100 BENEVENTO Italy

FAN CLUB WEBSITES

Dusk: www.dusk.it

It: www.genesis-fanclub.de

The Waiting Room Web Site: www.twronline.net

FAN WEBSITES

Genesis www.genesis-movement.org run by Simon Funnell

Genesis www.worldofgenesis.com run by Dave Negrin

Tony Banks www.tonybanks-online.com run by Manuela Thiel

OFFICIAL WEBSITES

Genesis Official Web Site: www.genesis-music.com

Phil Collins Official Web Site: www.philcollins.co.uk

Steve Hackett Official Web Site: www.stevehackett.com

Anthony Phillips Official Web Site: www.anthonyphillips.co.uk

Peter Gabriel Official Web Site: www.petergabriel.com

Ray Wilson Official Web Site: www.raywilson.co.uk

Daryl Stuermer Official Web Site: www.darylstuermer.com

Chester Thompson Official Web Site: www.chesterthompson.com

Bill Bruford Official Web Site: www.billbruford.co.uk

Dale Newman Official Web Site: www.dalenewman.net

Nick Davis Official Web Site: www.nickdavis.org.uk

David Hentschel Official Web Site www.thekeyboard.co.uk

Brand X Official Web Site : www.brandxmusic.org

Appendix A: "The fugitive from fame" Tony Banks' career as a solo artist.

If people only knew how much Tony brought to Genesis they would give his solo records a second chance..."

The words of Phil Collins in a recent interview accurately reflect the current position of the Genesis keyboards man. His solo albums have reflected the heart of the Genesis sound as well as a varied array of other musical styles and personas and yet the success which he has achieved with Genesis has, as yet eluded Tony as a solo artist. To those who know Genesis, Tony remains the true artistic centre of the band in terms of its sound and style and in his solo projects he has endeavoured to extend upon that but many may ask why, if he is so successful with the group, does he need a solo career at all? The answer to that question is quite simple; without an outlet for the material that they produce, the band would have long since ceased to exist. Tony, Mike, Phil and Peter, Anthony and Steve before them have all generated a massive catalogue of material, certainly too much for any band to cope with, hence the solo outings, which have not only served to keep the band fresh, but also giving each individual a chance to flex their creative muscles in ways which have certainly kept the band's fans both intrigued and inspired.

Tony's first solo album appeared in 1979 during the group's hiatus at the end of their mammoth 1978 world tour for the "And then there were three" album. Titled "A Curious Feeling" it was a very dark and dramatic album, reminiscent in many ways of 1977's "Wind & Wuthering" Genesis recording and to some extent Tony agrees with the assessments which compare the album to its predecessor...

"I also looked at it as an excuse to go a little further down the road like Wind & Wuthering. That was one of the most extreme Genesis albums - I think it was the most musical and the most grandiose album we ever did. With One for the vine I was confined to ten or so minutes and I wanted to try and expand that same sort of feeling over a whole album, which was what A Curious Feeling was. I wanted to be able to use all the little differences of quiet and loud and contrasting them within the same song with another but still to tell one story effectively throughout..."

The album came about due to Phil's marriage problems which had been exacerbated by the extended tour...

"When Phil was having problems with his marriage, in order to give him a bit of breathing space, Mike and I said; 'Well we want to do our solo albums, why don't we do them now?' and that would give us time and we could get back together after doing that..."

 Some of the material which ended up on the album originated from the "A Trick Of The Tail" period and was considered by Tony for a solo album then, especially after the success of Steve Hackett's first solo effort; "Voyage Of The Acolyte" although Tony did not consider the time to be right to release a solo project then and his patience was commendable and meant that the finished product benefits from being a more rounded whole effort. The album also expanded Tony's musical skills, he played lead guitar on it for the first time in many years.

Many people forget that Tony frequently played guitar in Genesis especially in the period after Anthony Phillips's departure and even on the epic 'Supper's Ready' and Tony recalled the problems he had as a budding guitarist during the album sessions...

"When I did A Curious Feeling I actually played the lead guitar and bass as well and I had to stick bits of foam under the strings to stop them vibrating. I could never work out how to stop the strings vibrating after you played them!"

With the trend in music at the time being still geared very much toward the New Wave element, Tony's decision to make the album a conceptual piece based around the idea of a man consciously losing his mind was an intriguing one..

"I liked the idea of the songs, the way in which they reflect the idea of this person going through this terrible sense of loss and knowing that he's going and to see what he's feeling at the time. In terms of a concept album, I always felt that Genesis were so out of tune with what was considered mainstream so I really didn't think twice about it..."

Originally inspired by the science fiction story *"Flowers For Algernon"* Tony even contacted the author and asked if it was ok for him to base the album around the premise in the story only to be told there was a musical coming out based around it! Another case of missed opportunities! Tony and Mike also became involved in the world of films and film soundtracks at this time when they were asked to contribute music to "The Shout" film although in the end, Mike and Tony's work was overlooked in the film..

"I liked the film, I thought it was quite good and we were involved with it quite closely but the day they decided to do the main credits which was where I thought the music would be the main thing, they did it without us, and we were really depressed by that..."

The track eventually surfaced as the opener on the album as 'From The Undertow' and, as its title suggests, it was originally written as an introduction to the Genesis track 'Undertow' and Tony thought it was too good not to use...

"I thought the piece of music was good and as it hadn't really been used in the film I thought why not use it as a starting point for the album, and it sets a certain kind of atmosphere I think because it has a slightly uneasy quality about it."

Tony even used a singer with a Genesis connection; Kim Beacon who was lead vocalist with the final incarnation of Charisma band String Driven Thing who had supported Genesis on their first headlining tour of the UK in 1973 and the Genesis connections were maintained in the production department as well with current Genesis producer; David Hentschel in control although due to his commitments with Mike's solo album at the same time it came down to a matter of preference, and Dave opted to work with Mike and Tony engaged the services of David Bascombe a tape operator at the time who has since gone on to produce many albums by established artists including Tears for fears. Tony's problem with the album was how to project the album ...

"Everyone seemed to be saying 'well; it's another singer; it's a solo album but it's not you singing' and it was a slight problem."

Ironically, "A Curious Feeling" was to give Tony his highest chart position and best sales and over all he still thinks fondly of the album...

"For me, 'A Curious Feeling' is out of all the music that I've ever done - including the stuff with Genesis - perhaps the most satisfying 45 minutes of music I've ever done."

For a first solo effort; A Curious Feeling was not only an excellent album but also a brave one. By the late 1970's New Wave and Disco had effectively replaced Rock as the main staple on the airwaves and here was Tony Banks; keyboard player with one of those most reviled of entities; a "Progressive" Rock band, releasing a concept album!

Musically, A Curious Feeling is a hark back to Wind & Wuthering in many respects. It is a dramatic and dark album redolent of that particular era of the band's story. However, even within the drama there are some wonderful moments. The delicious irony of A Curious Feeling itself; an exhortation to…

"Put back our bites from the apple of the Tree of Knowledge
Be like the beasts again"

Maybe rock had done exactly that with the advent of the New Wave? Certainly the "beasts" were having a field day in the charts. Undeterred, Tony had put together an album that although based around a specific concept had nonetheless enough power to break through the "concept album" mould. You, is a delightful love song written in the way that only Tony Banks can write them. From The Undertow and The Waters Of Lethe are classic Banks instrumentals which many would deem self-indulgent but hey, what is a solo album anyway? Either way, the album managed to garner respectable sales at a time when the band were questioning their own rationale for existence. Tony was also unconcerned by the need to pander to the conventions of the time. He had seen it all before with the critical and fan reaction to The Lamb… and was well aware of the potential pitfalls of such a project ..

"I thought that with The Lamb Lies Down On Broadway the one fault that it had was that the story was too complicated and therefore didn't allow the music to express the mood of the story because you didn't know what was happening next. It was too episodic so I wanted something that had a much simpler tale to tell which people could understand It had moments that I think anyone could relate to..."

The album also gave Tony that ability to explore the areas of music usually occupied by the other members of Genesis without any of the attendant hassles of fighting for space and give fuller rein to his own ideas; even exploring his love of the odd Jazz chord here and there….

"Well the thing about being in a group is that you always compromise to some extent via the opinion of the other people. With certain chord changes, they tend not to be as fond of as you might be. I have always liked to try unusual chord changes and all sorts of harmonies and weird things. You can wallow in it little and it is an excuse to be self indulgent..."

If Tony's first solo album was laden with the orchestral trappings of Genesis, his next effort, 1983's "The Fugitive" was to be a much more sparse affair. Overcoming the dilemma of who to have singing on the record, Tony opted to do the job himself and surprised both himself and his fans with an album of songs which should have improved his commercial position, even provoking one critic to remark…

"The Fugitive features some bright, catchy pop tunes which, would surprise a few of the cynics if only they'd bother to listen..."

The initial single *"This Is Love"* achieved a lot of airplay and yet still failed to make any dent on the more pop-orientated charts and Tony is very resigned to this state of affairs...

"As I'm sure you're aware, this business is so wrapped up in people's perceptions of what they think and what they want and it all tends to be based on image..."

If image was what was lacking, it was more than made up for by the music, which was an exciting mix of experimentation especially on the album's two instrumentals; *"Thirty Threes"* and *"Charm"* which showed a slightly more jazzy side to Tony's music although he admits to some doubts about the relevance of the latter track ...

"The other one; 'Charm' I don't know about that, I'm not so sure about that as I did it as a bit of a joke with the silly noises and things. It needed heavy drumming in the middle but the drummer I used on that; Andy Duncan, really wasn't up to it. At one point I thought I would play the drums myself on that as it was so simple even I could do that (laughter)".

The other significant difference from Tony's previous album was the predominance of the drum machine in the area of writing which had come to the fore with the last Genesis album; *"Abacab"* and which had been embraced wholeheartedly on this project...

"I guess at that point things like drum machines and so on were starting to come in more and more and the change in Genesis as a whole happened as well. Those machines do tend to tie you a little bit in certain ways. They give you a lot of freedom in a sense that there's so much you can do with them, but they do tend to lock you into a particular tempo; if it's in 4/4 then it's in 4/4 for ten minutes!.."

The Fugitive was an album which fans struggled with at the time. Its overall sound was far poppier than Genesis fans had been used to and the first time that fans had heard Tony's voice which, by his own admission is not the greatest, made this an album that challenged the fans' perceptions. Listened to now, it is a typically mid '80's album. The keyboard and drum sounds tie it firmly to the same era as Duran Duran and Spandau Ballet. Musically however, the album is a million miles away from those purveyors of ear candy. The songs are couched in Tony's usual style and several tracks demonstrate his ear for the quirky. Reviews were mixed and the album received less attention from fans than it deserved.

Sound wise however, The Fugitive has perhaps not fared so well as its predecessor. The use of drum machine and certain synthesiser sounds which were certainly perhaps the height of chic in the mid 1980's have not aged as well as others. However, the process of self-editing which had begun with the band's Abacab album in 1981 was continued here. Tony had certainly learned how to rein himself in from his indulgences and the results are tighter, leaner songs with a surprising Pop edge to them and even some room for improvisation on the instrumentals. If anything the only accusation of "indulgence" this time must be levelled at the director of the promotional video for the This Is Love single which for some inexplicable reason featured an iguana! Tony admits to having some doubts about the process...

"The director was really desperate to use an iguana in the video (laughter). Its kind of weird when you do things on your own. When I am with the group and it comes to videos I have as strong a role as anybody but when you are on your own; your self-confidence is a bit lower I think and so people do tend to get their ideas over on you. I just let them do more or less what they wanted to do. It was enough of a strength for me to be focal and central to the whole thing and I found that so much more difficult and it also made me realise that I could never front a band..."

Concurrent with the production of this album, Tony was also at work on his first proper film soundtrack for the Michael Winner re-make of the 1943 classic; *"The Wicked Lady"* which gained a certain degree of notoriety with the British Board of Film Censors who wanted to remove one scene in which the central protagonists try to whip each other to death with much displaying of cleavage into the bargain! Tony attributes that to Michael Winner's desire for publicity.

The album divides nicely into two halves with side one featuring the music as composed by Tony, and side two the orchestral variations which comprised the film's soundtrack. It was interesting for the fans to hear both sides and gave an insight into how such projects can change from initial idea to finished work although a lot of the work was done by an arranger. Musically the album was a pleasant affair, which worked well within the context of the film as well as standing up as an entity of its own. The piano "Variations" on the album were a nice insight into the development of the music....

"The guy from Atlantic Records over here: Phil Carson , was approached by Michael Winner. He had already done something with Jimmy Page and he said 'do you know anyone who might want to do this film thing?' and Phil Carson said... 'Well thus guy Tony Banks , he wants to do it'. So he came to me, and I must admit that I wasn't a hundred per cent sure about doing it but decided to do it anyway. I worked on that particularly as it was to be an orchestral soundtrack and I was doing The Fugitive at the same time , so I worked with an arranger on that. So, in a sense a lot of what you hear on that is him really in terms of what the orchestrations are. With a lot of the pieces I just played them on the piano and recorded them and then he orchestrated it, some of them very faithfully , and others he adapted perhaps more than he should have done but it was fun to do and all the main sequences sounded great with the orchestra... and in great contrast to The Shout, The Wicked lady had the music really up front and it sounded great and when I saw it in the cinema it sounded fantastic and it made me want to do more..."

The finished film convinced Tony to try for more work in this field and this search was to lead to the music that appeared on his next album. Surprisingly, this project also spawned a single in the shape of one side being themes played by Tony and the other giving the orchestral variations on those themes. The single was very low key and now forms one of the most collectable items in Tony's catalogue.

There was to be almost a three year wait before Tony re-appeared as a solo artist with 1986's "Soundtracks" album. As it's title suggests, the music on this project was drawn from two films which Tony had become involved with. Ironically, neither of the films involved were in the running when Tony had been approached to create the score for the follow up to the Science fiction extravaganza; "2001: A Space Odyssey". Tony had initially been approached by the producer who had liked his work on "The Shout" back in 1979...

"The guy chose me because he really loved the theme from 'The Shout', he could sing it!.."

Tony tried several pieces even writing one with the producer in attendance but to no avail and Tony reflects wryly on the whole experience...

"The whole thing wasted about six months and it really was a setback for me. There were quite a few film offers coming in. I was actually sent the script to 'Terminator' although I doubt that I'd ever end up doing the film but that was something that I was in the running for as much as anybody else. So, the whole '2010' thing meant that I had to turn down other offers, and the film writing side of things took a setback and it was obviously a big blow to my self confidence as well..."

Tony eventually was approached to write the soundtrack to a low budget Sci fi film; "Lorca and the Outlaws" which had a budget of £200, 000 and agreed to do the soundtrack for free just for the experience. The film was appalling and failed to gain a general release in the UK, even video copies are hard to find! However, the project wasn't entirely futile, because during the course of it Tony had the chance to work with Jim Diamond and Toyah Wilcox and two songs from the film featuring their vocals appeared on an e.p later in the year. Tony was particularly pleased to be able to work with a female singer after all his time with Genesis…

"The idea of a female voice on what is essentially a traditional Genesis song was an interesting idea, it just changed the whole character of it completely..."

Tony also worked with Marillion vocalist; Fish on the opening track of the album; "Short Cut To Somewhere" which was written for another low key film "Quicksilver". Ironically it was never used in the finished film...

"I wrote some demo pieces for them, which they liked and it went from there. It was a weird situation actually as I was writing for committees. I ended up being involved in conference calls with about six people in Los Angeles, and it was a complete nightmare. I survived that but the problem was that I had a song to write for the film, it was crucial. I wrote three pieces for one section - the first they liked but didn't feel that it was appropriate, and the second ended up as 'A House Needs A Roof' on 'Bankstatement' although it was just an instrumental at that point...."

Eventually the producers engaged Giorgio Moroder to compose a track with Roger Daltrey which achieved nothing upon its release as a single. The album perhaps serves best as an example of how NOT to do things although Tony was certainly badly served by those others involved on the two films, at least he did gain experience in this field including essential knowledge of the notorious vagaries of Hollywood!

The biggest problem really for Tony was communication. He was in the UK and the people he was working for were some four thousand miles away in Hollywood. As Anthony Phillips' experiences with TV work have proven if you cannot actually SEE the project you are working to, then it must be incredibly difficult to write music that is supposed to accompany and enhance the action that is going on, on the screen. It didn't stop him creating a whole plethora of musical tracks which fortunately did see the light of day on the Soundtracks album but it certainly left Tony with a very bitter taste in his mouth about film work

The contrast between this album and Genesis's next album: "Invisible Touch" could not have been greater. Upon its release in June 1986 (only a month after "Soundtracks") the album hit the number one spot both in the UK and USA and went on to spawn a massive five hit singles. It seems that Phil's remarks about not Genesis fans not realising Tony's contribution to Genesis and therefore giving his solo projects more of a listening was still true and that long sought after solo success was still as far away as ever. Compounding that sense of frustration, Tony's other compatriot in Genesis; Mike Rutherford had, after an initially shaky start with his first two solo albums, had finally struck pay dirt with his "other band" Mike and the Mechanics who scored a hit with "Silent running" from their self titled first album and who were to achieve even greater success in 1988. Tony must have been wondering what he had to do to get a hit!

Taking a leaf out of Mike's book; Tony's next effort was an attempt at a band persona; "Bankstatement" submerged Tony within a group ...

"The theory was that having tried all these different combinations, a group might be a better idea. Obviously Mike tried it with The Mechanics and it worked really well, so I thought I would try the group thing..."

The group was based around Tony with vocalists Janey Klimek (formerly of 'The Other Ones') and Alistair Gordon and production duties were taken on by Steve Hillage. The album contained a surprising mix of material from the straight pop of *Diamonds Aren't So Hard'* to lovely ballads such as *'I'll Be Waiting'* and *'That Night'* as well as the musically excellent *'The Border'*. *'I'll Be Waiting'* was actually to feature as Tony's first appearance on British TV as a solo artist when he appeared on the *"This Morning"* show on 1st November 1989. The album was not very well received by fans or critics. Many saw it as a diminution of Tony's talents although as Tony himself explained, the success or lack of success of a record is down to a great many features, most of which are not under the control of the artist...

"Now in the record business it's almost impossible to put out an album and expect it to do something without the hit single as well, the shops just won't take it, which is the problem...I don't think it's a very healthy situation at all.."

Tony's discomfort with the fashions and trends of the music business are perhaps best expressed in the lyrics to the album's opening track, Throwback…

"I Guess I don't fit the times
I'm just a throwback
I'm trapped but still I search for a clue"

The idea of an individual at odds with the society in which he/she lives is a common theme in Tony's work and is perhaps the closest indication of Tony's real persona that you ever get. This is also evident in Queen Of Darkness; a slightly cynical look at the false promises and hopes that are built up and more often than not, dashed in the entertainment industry where the "dream" so often becomes a "nightmare"

Once again, musically Tony was faced with being the public image for his music, a situation he was never comfortable with. He had tried the experiment of fronting an album with 1983' The Fugitive to mixed fortunes and on this album it didn't help that working with Steve Hillage as producer created additional unnecessary frictions…

"Virgin said that I should use a producer ,so I said 'fine'. I had a few conversations with people who I didn't really see eye-to-eye with. The n I met Steve Hillage and I thought.. 'well he's a musician and he is kind of weird' and I thought it would be quite fun to work with him.... Eventually though, I had to step in and take a few things back and one or two tracks for me suffered as a result of that..."

Tony's solo efforts were to continue with the release in 1991 of "Still" his sixth solo recording. Deciding to run through the whole gamut of possibilities, Tony engaged the services of no less than five singers on this album, a decision which has been discussed and argued over by his fans ever since. To many the album represents a great step forward in Tony's oeuvre, to others it represented a diminution of his own persona.

Certainly, the choice of Fish again as one of the singers raised more than a few eyebrows! Equally surprising to some was the use of pop supremo Nik Kershaw whose impressive writing credits include numerous hits in his own right as well as penning the hit song 'The One And Only' for Chesney Hawkes, among others. Tony's explanation for the plethora of singers is quite simple.

"Well, this was the chance to go through the whole catalogue of possibilities! The problem was that I'd decided it didn't matter what I did in terms of commercial success and so I decided to do an album and use whatever singer I want to use including those I knew and those who might be interested..."

The album contained over an hour's worth of music in a variety of styles and fully utilised the dynamics of the chosen singers and musicians. The first single: I Wanna Change The Score' should have been a massive hit, it's catchy hook and easy to listen to tune would have gained it a chart position if released by anybody else but again, the stigma attached to a solo release from the Genesis camp, ensured that this was not to be the case. However, additional complications hindered the song's chances...

"I think the thing we didn't realise was that there are two factors here...Nik Kershaw as a singer seems to have become very unfashionable. People seem to have put him down as an ex-weenybopper!...The other thing was that he himself didn't want to get back into the limelight, and he realised after he'd agreed to do the singing that it might also involve him in the video and promotional side of things and he didn't want to do that..."

Two further singles from the album; 'The Gift' and ' Still It Takes Me By Surprise' also failed to make any lasting impression on the charts. Tony himself, remains singularly unimpressed by the situation and still maintains that this album is one of his personal favourites..

"For me personally, where I stand and it's a totally undetached viewpoint I know, but of all my albums the two I am most satisfied with are 'A curious feeling' and 'Still' in terms of what I wanted to do..."

Certainly the choice of musicians helped give the album a more evenly rounded feel and sound to it including amongst others; Steve Gadd, Vinnie Colaiuta on drums, Daryl Stuermer on guitars and Martin Robertson on saxophone. Musically it contains several of Tony's finest moments including the hauntingly beautiful 'Water out of wine' with a soulful performance by Janey Klimek. The album also saw Tony moving from fantasy to realism with tracks such as Red Day On Blue Street brilliantly illustrating the lies that Politicians tell when seeking re-election and one of the album's most underrated tacks and the only one to showcase Tony's vocals: Hero For An Hour ; which brilliantly illustrates the dilemma of a witness to a crime and the possible repercussions. Tony's manic-tinged vocals give an element of drama to what is, on the surface, a deceptively simple song.

The continued theme of striving to be what others expect you to be is brought out again in both I Wanna Change The Score with the desire to change your life for the perceived "better" one just around the corner and the aspirations and hopes of youth which are so often cruelly shattered by the experiences of life in Water Out Of Wine.

Bitterness is tinged with wry resignation in the morality play that is Another Murder Of A Day with the victim of drug addiction being brilliantly portrayed not only in the cleverly written lyrics with so many references to various "substances" all given that additional twist by the potent vocal delivery by Fish whose own personal demons must have given him the insight to deliver one of his finest vocal performances.

The Final Curtain certainly could have been taken as Tony's swansong in much the same way that Fading Lights, the closing track from the next Genesis album : We Can't Dance which appeared a few months after Still, was viewed by Genesis fans. There is certainly a quiet resignation about this album which makes it one of Tony's most thought provoking efforts.

Tony's fans have had a long time to wait for another album. Indeed, after "Still" Tony went on record as saying that he would not release any further solo projects. Thankfully, this was not to be the case and Strictly Inc" was released in September 1995. Continuing the idea of a band, the album bears no mention of Tony on the cover instead bearing a computer animation from the video from the first single: 'Only Seventeen'. Even the video for the single does not feature either Tony or any musician, instead relying on a mixture of hand drawn and computer generated animation to tell the story of a young girl who becomes involved in a shady underworld far away from her comfortable up bringing. For this album, Tony has relied on one singer throughout the project; Jack Hues, former front man of '80's band Huang Chung. This has given the album something that has maybe been lacking on Tony's previous outings; consistency of vocals and Jack's voice is certainly impressive...

"His voice is actually a bit like mine only better and he can do all the things I want to be able to do.."

The album contains a vast array of music in its sixty three minutes and it manages to pull out several surprises including the beautiful 'A Piece Of You' and the bitterly ironic 'Strictly Incognito' where Jack Hues' slightly manic vocals give an added dimension to the track. There is also a degree of social comment on this album, be it the political sleaze detailed on *'Charity Balls'* to the temptations of money *in* 'The Serpent Said' there is something for all fans of Tony's music including the final track; a seventeen minute opus titled; 'An Island In The Darkness'...

"With all of the other tracks I kept myself pretty much well in check but with this one I just went for it really.. "

Tony has also experimented more with computers and programming on this album than ever before

"the great thing about a computer you can get various ideas and slot them together and see how they sound..."

Several of the tracks hark back to the most recent Genesis album although Tony also admits that he has dug a little further into his past for some pieces too, especially on the last track.

"It was a chance to introduce a bit of what I hadn't had on the last couple of albums; the big drama, the vocals are intense and it has a kind of moody feel to it and then going into the guitar solo which relates, if to any early songs to 'Firth of Fifth' because the theme is repeated; soft and loud. It's a definite Genesis kind of thing but a lot of the stuff in between is non repetitive and some of them were just piano improvisations which I just took as I played them, actually..."

Tony has continued his partnership with Nick Davis, who has produced Tony's last two albums as well as the last Genesis album and it certainly seems to be a fruitful collaboration although Tony admits that

"He occasionally steals a chord from me!" .

Whereas, its predecessor: Still had been a somewhat melancholy album, Strictly Inc has a distinctly playful feel to it. The opening single Only Seventeen although based on a serious subject nonetheless has its tongue firmly in its cheek. Charity Balls pokes acerbic fun at the sleazy world of politics and the delightful manic schizophrenia of Strictly Incognito tells a serious moral story without a highbrow approach to the listener.

In between these tracks there are other examples of Tony's art. Something To Live For, A Piece of You and Never Let Me Know are three of the best love songs that Tony has ever penned and ones which would not have appeared out of place on a Genesis album.

With An Island In The Darkness, Tony demonstrated that not only had his talent for musical extemporisation had not diminished but has been quietly waiting its chance to re-appear. Keeping to just one vocalist certainly gave the album a continuity which to some extent had been missing from the previous albums and in Jack Hues, Tony made an inspired choice. His vocal delivery managed to convey the right mix of wry humour and occasional mania that the occasion required resulting in an extremely satisfying album.

With work on the final Genesis album; Calling All Stations (1997) and the two Genesis Archive box sets (1998 and 2000 respectively) Tony had been far from idle but many fans were wondering what, if indeed, anything was in the pipeline with regard to a further solo album. Their curiosity was finally satisfied on 27th March 2004 with the release of *Seven*, his first full scale orchestral album since his dabbling with orchestral forces for The Wicked Lady film soundtrack.

Tony explained how the album came about during a recent interview for The Waiting Room Magazine…

"Well… I sort of … after Calling All Stations thing ended I was just writing the normal way I was, you know and I had this idea which was all done just on the string synthesiser and I thought rather than trying to do this as something I would do myself; why not do it with real strings and see how it sounds. Once I got that idea in my head I thought let's see what else I can do and I started writing some other pieces specifically thinking in those sort of terms and let it go where it will really rather than tying to tie it to verse/chorus…."

The album comprises seven pieces of extremely atmospheric music with echoes of both many of Tony's favourite composers as well as a couple of pieces with a slightly older pedigree as he explained…

"I had always had this piece which I wrote years ago and which I thought if I ever did anything with an orchestra would probably be good enough and I had kept it back as a possible film theme over the years and that had never come up (laughs) so why not use it on this and expand it and make it less systematic in a way and I had another shorter piece that I had done around the time of Strictly Inc and then put them all together.."

Getting the album to the fans was something of a hard struggle apparently. Despite being one of EMI's major artists; that record company were surprisingly not enthusiastic about the project ….

"I talked to EMI and asked them… how much did Steve's (Hackett: A Midsummer Night's Dream album released by EMI Classics in 1998) album sell? As a sort of yardstick. And they said; 15000 and I thought that is fantastic ;if I sell that many I will be really happy and they said… well… they were not really happy at putting something out that only sells that many; they want to sell 100,000 because they want to subsidise their slightly classier sort of Classical composers who sell 600 copies but who have a very strong reputation…"

The decision to offer the option to Naxos Records, one of the most popular Classical music distributors in the UK and world wide was a shrewd one. Their ethos is dedicated to the service of music and it certainly helps to see Tony's albums in practically any outlet so there is no excuse for not purchasing the album. Tony's future plans after this project are somewhat tenuous but his musical legacy , both as a member of Genesis and as a solo artist and composer is extraordinary.

Tony Banks UK Solo Discography.

7" and 12" Vinyl Singles

A-Side	B-Side	Catalogue Number		
For a while	From the undertow	CB344	(7")	20.10.79
For a while	A curious feeling	CB365	(7" PS)	?.7.80
This is love	Charm	BANKS1	(7" PS)	?.5.83
This is love (Extended version)**Charm** (Extended version)		BANKS12	(12" PS)	?.5.83
And the wheels keep turning	Man of spells	BANKS2	(7"PS)	?.8.83
The Wicked Lady(Banks)	The Wicked Lady (NPO)	A 9825	(7")	?.6.83
Short cut to somewhere	Smilin' Jack Casey	CB426	(7" PS)	?.9.86
You call this victory/Redwing	Lion of symmetry	CBEP415	(7" PS)	?.8.85
Shortcut to somewhere	Smilin' Jack Casey/**K2**	CB426-12	(12" PS)	?.6.86
Throwback	Thursday the Twelfth	VS1200	(7" PS)	?.7.89
Throwback	Thursday the Twelfth/This is love	VST1200	(12" PS)	?.7.89
I'll be waiting	Diamonds aren't so hard	VS1208	(7" PS)	?.10.89
I'll be waiting	Diamonds aren't so hard/And the Wheels keep turning	VST1208	(12" PS)	?.10.89
I wanna change the score	Hero for an hour	VS1347	(7" PS)	7.5.91
I wanna change the score	Hero for an hour/Big man	VST1347	(12" PS)	7.5.91
The Gift	Back to back	VS1362	(7" PS)	?.7.91
The Gift	Back to back/A house Needs A roof	VST1362	(12" PS)	?.7.91
Still it takes me by surprise (Edit) The final curtain		VS1402	(7" PS)	24.2.92

Compact Disc Singles

Throwback/Thursday The Twelfth/This is love	VSCD1200 (PS)		4.8.89
Throwback (Remix)/I'll be waiting/Queen of darkness/Big Man Bankscd1 (Promotional 4 track CD)			4.8.89
I'll be waiting/Diamonds aren't so hard/And the wheels keep turning	VSCD1208 (PS)		?.7.89
I wanna change the score/Hero for an hour/Big man/The Waters of Lethe	VSCDT1347 (PS)		7.5.91
The Gift/I wanna change the score/A house needs a roof/Redwing	VSCDT1362 (PS)		?.7.91
Still it takes me by surprise(Edit)/The final curtain/Still it takes me By surprise	VSCDT1406 (PS)		24.2.92
Only Seventeen/**Only seventeen(A Saabson/ Svenson remix)**/The Serpent said/**Only seventeen (House mix by Andy Falconer)**	VSCDG1553 (PS)		29.8.95
Only Seventeen (Radio edit)/Only Seventeen (Full length version)/The Serpent said/**Only seventeen (House mix by Andy Falconer)**	VSCDJ1553		29.8.95
Walls of sound (Remix)/Back to you/Only Seventeen (Instrumental)	VSCDT1575 (PS)		8.1.96

Tracks in **Bold** are non album tracks.
PS denotes a single issued in a picture sleeve.

Vinyl and Compact Disc albums

A curious feeling	Charisma Records	CAS1148/CASCD1148 (CD)	?.8.79
The Fugitive	Charisma Records	TB1/TBCD1 (CD)	?.4.83
The Wicked Lady	Atlantic Records	78-0073-1	?.5.83
Soundtracks	Charisma Records	CAS1173/CASCD1173 (CD)	?.5.86
Bankstatement	Virgin Records	V2600/CDV2600 (CD)	14.8.89
Still	Virgin Records	V2658/CDV2658 (CD)	?.6.91
Strictly Inc	Virgin Records	CDV2790 (CD)	11.9.95
Seven	Naxos Records	8.557466 (CD)	27.3.04

Appendix B: "No drum kit required" Phil Collins a brief solo biography.

Well, where do you begin to describe Phil Collins' solo career? Perhaps it might be as well to remind ourselves that Phil's solo career began under similar inauspicious circumstances to the band which he eventually contributed so much to: Genesis. His youth was spent at stage school and through a variety of guises including a stint in the hit musical "Oliver!" and a less auspicious appearance in the Children's Film Theatre production of "Calamity The Cow" but, despite his grounding in acting, Phil's first love was (and still is) drumming. His uncles were persuaded to organise his first drum kit when Phil was five years of age and, as the saying goes; he never looked back! Phil's dedication was decided at a very early age …

"From the age of five I never wanted to be anything else. That was why my uncles built me that drumkit. I never wanted to be a fireman or a truck driver I wanted to be a drummer and that's really what I have been all my life and I have gone out from that position and visited other places; like singing; like song writing and I still see it as that I live behind the drums and visit other places.."

Phil's earliest exposure to "performance" came when his mother; an agent for a West End Theatrical School, found him his first leading role as Humpty Dumpty when he was only six years old. From there it was a short step to the tortuous world of child modelling and by the his mid teens Phil had done it all . He also played extra parts in such famous films as The Beatles' "A hard days' night" and "Chitty Chitty Bang Bang". At the age of fourteen, Phil joined the Barbara Speake Stage School and was soon enrolled in the West End cast for the hit musical "Oliver!" which was to lead to some concerns by his school when the productions' needs over ran the needs of Phil's education.

Fortunately for all concerned, this problem soon resolved itself when Phil's voice broke. During 1967 Phil also appeared in the now famous (or should that be infamous?) Children's Film Foundation movie; "Calamity the cow" which gave Phil a brief and inauspicious introduction to the film industry; his precocious nature led to several disputes with the film's director which led eventually to his being almost completely written out of the script!

Shortly after this Phil joined another stage school where along with a friend he formed the first of a number of groups he was to appear in before the first "Big Break" - "The Real Thing" in addition to playing the drums Phil also sang with this band; an early indication of what was to come perhaps although one which didn't make itself obvious to Phil whose first love was still his drumkit.. Phil's first big break came in 1969 when, in the heat of the historic events taking place that year a young keyboard player named Brian Chatto had been approached by composers Ken Howard and Alan Blaikley with regard to putting together a band and since Chatto was friendly with the staff at London's Speakeasy club which was practically Phil's second home by this point, it was easy for him to recommend a drummer. After an initial rehearsal at the Marquee, Phil and his guitarist friend Ronnie Caryl, joined the band; Flaming Youth.

Howard and Blaikley had already made their names as the songwriters for Dave Dee, Dozy, Beaky, Mick and Titch and The Herd. Ever with an eye to the main chance, they also steered the band toward an event which had already captured the imagination of the world: the first moon landing and gave them their imaginative interpretation of what would happen if the human race had to abandon Mother Earth. To do so in a set of eight pop songs strikes us now as pretentious in the extreme but this was THE SIXTIES and people's perceptions were different then. The band moved into de Lane Lea Studios then one of the top recording studios in the capital and with a two week deadline to go on, the band set to work eventually taking the grand total of FORTY hours to record the album - an enormous amount of time fore the period.

The resulting album, titled "Ark Two" was issued by Fontana in October 1969and the album drew mainly favourable comments from the music press especially in the Melody maker which referred to it as *"pop album of the month"* even in the august company of new releases by Stevie Wonder, The Band and The Small Faces. The band got off to a good start with a showcase at London's Planetarium and at a party at Blaikley's home but sadly, neither the album nor its accompanying two singles was destined to make any headway in the charts. To be fair, however, 1969 was a heavyweight year for albums with albums by King Crimson, Led Zeppelin, Pink Floyd and of course, a fledgling release by a little known band called Genesis!

The band continued to play gigs throughout what remained of 1969 and into the early part of 1970 but by the time that it came to work on the follow-up album, it was plain to Phil and Ronnie Caryl that the writing was on the wall for the band. Howard and Blaikley's new material was esoteric to say the least and not at all to Phil's taste although by the end the band had evolved into a free-form jazz combo including Rod Mayall brother of famed Blues man John, on organ.

During the summer of 1970,Phil noticed an advertisement in the back pages of Melody Maker which caught his eye:

"Tony Stratton-Smith requires drummer sensitive to acoustic music and acoustic twelve-string guitarist…"

Phil decided to attend the auditions but not before he buttonholed Stratton-Smith at one of his usual haunts; London's Marquee Club. Having ascertained that the group were a worthwhile proposition, Phil and Ronnie Caryl attended the auditions at the lead singer's parents home. The group of course, were Genesis and Phil's part in their subsequent rise to superstardom is told elsewhere. However, Phil had other irons in the fire and apart from playing on several well known albums in the summer of 1970 he also considered joining Yes when Bill Bruford let it be known that he was leaving. However, the audition for Genesis was to be the making of a star and Peter Gabriel still recalls the initial impression that Phil made on the fledgling group....

I remember noticing him as he sat down on the stool. Before he even picked up the sticks, I thought: this guy can play. Because he had a confidence, a self-assurance I could feel. It was like watching a jockey getting into the saddle, and instinctively knowing, from body language that here is someone who knows what he's doing..."

Needless to say, it was several years before Phil finally climbed into the "saddle" so to speak with Genesis but Phil's restless nature meant that even during his tenure with the band his session work was capacious including work with several heavyweights of the music industry. His growing dissatisfaction with the formalised music in Genesis led in 1973 to the foundation of his own scratch band: Zox and the Radar Boys which gave Phil a chance to scratch the itch of improvisation which had been growing for a while as he recalled during an interview with Radio One prior to the "Lamb..." tour...

"Well, I mentioned it to Bill Bruford and he said he wouldn't mind having a bash, Steve (Hackett) has mentioned it to John Lord and he said he wouldn't mind having a bash so people are from different kinds of bands and it's a very loose thing and the idea behind it is to just go on stage and basically start from scratch and not knowing what you're going to play...it wasn't a formal band... we've stopped playing pubs and clubs and if I can get anybody that's in the same frame of mind to just keep it very loose and just have a good time...because I 'm at home with the arranged things that we do but sometimes I get a yearning to get on stage and not know what's going to happen... even the stuff on the new album a lot of it is heading that way towards having a very loose theme to work with an keeping a lot more for whatever happens on the night especially when you're touring night after night with very dense passages, nine weeks in America and playing every night, the freer you can keep it, the better really..."

Phil was also during this period involved in a small work with Mike Rutherford and Anthony Phillips who were at the time, working on what was to eventually become Anthony's first solo album; *"The Geese & The Ghost"* in 1977. Anthony had also unearthed a song he had written as a tribute to Genesis' first full-time drummer; John Silver and had decided to record it and asked Phil to sing on the recording; "Silver Song" which was duly recorded on a day off between gigs on the band's hectic UK tour for their "Selling England by the Pound" tour in October 1973.

During the hiatus caused by Peter Gabriel's departure from the band in the summer of 1975, Phil decided to become involved in another "scratch" band this one turned into a beast with a slightly longer pedigree however as the resultant band; Brand X became Phil's mainstay between Genesis projects throughout the late Seventies and early Eighties before demands on his time and talents led him into other fields of endeavour.

The first inkling of Phil's future solo career occurred during the hiatus which followed the end of Genesis' huge tour in support of their *"And then there were three"* album which was to be their most successful to date. Success with the band was paid for in Phil's case by the failure of his first marriage to Andrea Bertorelli his childhood sweetheart who was simply unable to cope with the enforced isolation which was part and parcel of life on the road with a successful rock band at this time. Initially, Phil tried to compromise by agreeing to move to Vancouver in Canada where Andrea's family lived. This was no solution for the situation the band found themselves in however, but fortunately both Tony and Mike were able to give Phil some much needed breathing space by recording their own debut solo albums; *"A Curious Feeling"* and *"Smallcreep's Day"* respectively which gave Genesis fans something to whet their appetites on while waiting for the next group project.

That album; *"Duke"* released in March 1980 was another success and featured the first songs which Phil had written for the band; *"Misunderstanding"* and *"Please don't ask"* both of which were part and parcel of Phil's personal exorcism of his problems. Having so much time on his hands while Tony and Mike worked on their solo projects meant that he was finally able to commit his ideas to record in his own mini studio at home and the first result of his own efforts appeared in December 1980 in the shape of the dramatic *"In The Air Tonight"* single which was an instant success reaching the number two position in the UK. Phil explained his decision to finally release a solo album during an interview with Johnny Waller...

My writing career started two years ago - with Genesis, although I've been in the band twelve years; I have only submitted bits of songs,. When I was married, my time was spent between being married and having a family, Genesis and Brand X - and so writing was something I did if I could. So, it wasn't until my marriage broke up that I actually found the time or HAD the time rather, and the emotional inclination to sit down at the piano and pour my heart out which is what I did with what then became Face Value - bit it was only at that point that I had finished songs that I could show the band.

Tony and Mike have been the most prolific writers in the band in recent years, and so I would just put little bits in. So when we came round to doing Duke, we all had little bits of music and I played Genesis In the Air Tonight, If Leaving Me Is Easy as well as Misunderstanding and Please Don't Ask, which were intended for Face Value and they liked..."

The fans were taken aback slightly by Phil's decision to release his first solo work on the Virgin Records label instead of Charisma which at that time housed every member of Genesis past AND present. His decision to use a label not associated with the band was to encourage people who would not normally look twice at a Genesis project and his decision was proven to be the right one when the album *"Face Value"* was released in February 1981 and achieved number one status both in the UK and in many other territories. He went to great lengths to explain the reasoning behind this in an interview he gave to Melody Maker in February 1981….

"I thought that anybody who would see an album by me out after I had been with Genesis for ten years and Brand X for five would think ; 'Oh, another Genesis album, thank you' whereas I think my album has great potential to appeal to more people than those who like Genesis. I thought for the casual buyer it would certainly help if it were on a different label. I had an awful lot of songs that were not really Genesis-ey and songs that if I brought into Genesis would not end up sounding like I wanted them to. Misunderstanding was one of my songs it was a song that everybody liked and we didn't change it…. I just think that I wrote things on the keyboards and I like to play keyboards on them. Tony bless his heart, is a classically trained pianist and if you ask him to play like 'that' or 'that' or play the wrong inversions or something, instinct will tell him not to do that. Instinct will tell him to play the 'right' inversions and sometimes the 'right' inversions don't sound right…"

The album was an angst-ridden exploration of the failure of Phil's marriage and his use of the first person in his lyrics gave the album an almost "Dear Diary" feel which appealed to a wider audience than Genesis' much more impersonal lyrics although Phil himself was still taken aback by the instant success of the record…

"it was just a complete shock - a solo album that was done under those circumstances, so lazily. I was very intense obviously when I was doing it, it wasn't 'OK I want to make a record' it was just suddenly there was a record and suddenly people liked it. …"

With a chart success in both the album and single charts, many fans were surprised that Phil didn't tour in support of the album however, his commitments to Genesis meant that the hard working Mr Collins was soon ensconced in Genesis' newly acquired studio; The Farm for work on the album that would finally bring Genesis and their fans kicking and screaming into the 1980's; *"Abacab"* an album which was to prove almost divisive amongst fans as *"The lamb lies down on Broadway"* had almost ten years previously. Phil's follow up to this record was recorded and ready to go by the end of 1982 and with a determination of character the first single from the album took everyone by surprise by its subject matter for the song was written about a "Peeping Tom" of all things although Phil was quick to emphasise the lightweight intent behind the song…

"I don't know why I always go for these seedy characters but it's all very lightweight. Thru these walls just came from a line I heard somewhere else…"

The album *"Hello, I Must Be Going"* was by comparison to its predecessor a somewhat lacklustre affair which fell between the two stools of continuing the examination of Phil's marriage break up with several songs being hangovers from the first album , and the more up tempo numbers which signalled Phil's emerging rehabilitation. Without doubt however, the track which was the album's saviour was Phil's homage to The Supremes' Motown sound which was one of Phil's biggest influences and his cover of their classic *"You Can't Hurry Love"* was to propel Phil to superstardom as it became his first UK number one single.

Phil finally toured in his own right for the first time in November and December 1982 and into the spring of 1983 with a show which drew on both his albums with a band which included Genesis stalwarts Chester Thompson and Daryl Stuermer as well as his cohort from Brand X Peter Robinson on keyboards. Success was compounded by success as Phil became a highly sought after producer including work with Anni Frid of Abba whose album *"There's Something Going On"* was to be one of his first production tasks. He also managed to get back behind his beloved drum kit again when Robert Plant asked him to guest on his tour for his *"Principle Of Moments"* album in 1983 which Phil had also played on. Phil returned to duties with Genesis for their self-titled album released in October 1983 and even during the subsequent enormous US tour, he managed to find time to contribute the title track to Taylor Hackford's film *"Against All Odds"* soundtrack which was another huge success.

Continuing the upward momentum, Phil was soon at work on that all important third solo album and with *"No Jacket Required"* he really hit the big time beginning with the catchy first single *"Sussudio"* released in January 1985.

The album was a huge hit around the world and the accompanying tour took Phil to every continent the amazing fact with this album was that some of the material was speedily constructed rather than thought about and pondered over…

"I wrote the songs very quickly this time, in about three weeks I had ten or eleven…"

As Phil pointed out in an interview in Genesis Information magazine at the time and maybe that spontaneity rubbed off on the fans who quickly sent the album to the top of the UK charts. The album was a fortunate mix of the classic pop which Phil's sensibilities had refined to a new height and several more introspective songs including the thought provoking *"Long, Long Way To Go"* . Phil had also worked as the producer on his friend and Earth Wind & Fire member, Philip Bailey's album *"Chinese Walls"* with yet another pop classic in the shape of *"Easy Lover"* which dominated the UK charts throughout March and April 1985 helped no doubt by an absolutely hilarious promotional video although both Phils experienced problems with the inherent racism still so rampant within the record industry with the black music department executive at Bailey's record company; Columbia who amazingly hadn't heard of Phil Collins, telling Bailey that if he made a pretty album, black radio might not play it. This in itself was a reiteration of Phil's own experience at the time of his first solo album when he suggested that they send a sampler to several black radio stations to which the retort was…

"They're gonna know you ain't black"

It also didn't help that the internal rivalry between the two record companies that the two protagonists belonged to almost stimied the record's release in the UK…

"Phil's (Collins) company, Virgin didn't want my company CBS to put out the record because Phil had a solo record out at the time and they didn't want sales of that damaged. I was very worried about the record being prevented from coming out here. It was already a number one in America and I reckoned it would do well here…"

`
Racism apart, Phil's entry to the "Big League" was confirmed however, by his appearance at June 1985's "Live Aid" concert organised by the then plain "Bob" Geldof in aid of famine relief in Ethiopia. The resultant global extravaganza saw two syncrhonous concerts in London and Philadelphia on Saturday 13th July televised live around the world. What made Phil's performance out of the ordinary however, was the fact that, courtesy of Concorde, he managed to play at BOTH events as well as squeezing in percussion duties for Eric Clapton and the reformed Led Zeppelin. Further soundtrack work also kept Phil busy including another hit with the single *"Separate Lives"* which formed part of the *"White Nights"* soundtrack in 1986. Phil also turned producer for his long time friend and guitar hero; Eric Clapton to produce his *"August"* and *"Behind The Sun"* albums as well as taking the time to sit in as drummer for several of Eric's shows in support of the albums a duty which he has sporadically fulfilled ever since.

Having seen Phil's rise to stardom many Genesis fans were beginning to predict his exit from the band although Phil himself was at great pains to explain his rationale for staying with the band…

"It's more important to me because it's me, but I never differentiate between what's more important to me. I enjoy playing with the band and we all enjoy writing with each other, and we do it all infrequently enough for it to be fun. We do an album every couple of years, that's what it boils down to. By the time I've done what I want to do and they've done what they want to do it always ends up being every couple of years… there's no legal or binding thing between us except that we actually enjoy doing it.."

This enjoyment was to shine through in 1986 and most of 1987 when the band were occupied with the writing, recording and performing of Genesis' hugely successful *"Invisible Touch"* album one of the decade's most successful "Pop" albums and one in which the new relaxed attitude of Genesis really came to the fore. Phil then returned to his own work with a stint at the acting game with a starring role alongside Julie Walters in the controversial life story of Great Train Robber "Buster" Edwards. Phil's acting talents, whilst not of the Lawrence Olivier school, were nonetheless sufficient to gain critical acclaim for his part although the self - styled moral majority took exception to the film's apparent "glorification" of crime, a charge which is easily refuted if you actually WATCH it!

Not content with merely acting in the film, Phil was also persuaded to contribute to its soundtrack and the resulting two singles; a cover of Wayne Fontana & The Mindbenders' classic *"A Groovy Kind Of Love"* and Phil's own *"Two Hearts"* achieved success and kept his profile high while he worked on what was in November 1989 to become his most successful album to date.

Always the workaholic, Phil's work rate was phenomenal and the quality of his work has not suffered by his constant work as was clearly demonstrated by his fourth album, titled *"But Seriously"* which was released in November 1989, preceded by its first single; *"Another Day In Paradise"* which clearly emphasised as if there was any doubt, that Phil was more than capable of writing songs which said more than your average pop fare. The single's story of a homeless person's plight was so effective that the US Senate Commission on homelessness used it as part of their campaign on the issue.....

"The day I cut the record I was leaving the cutting room in London, me and Hugh Padgham, and we crossed the street and we were walking towards my car and this lady was sitting on the side of the street with two kids...she said 'Lend us some money Guv...' and I froze... you know... I almost pretended I didn't hear it , the same as everyone else does. I mean I do a lot for charity and I'm not saying I look the other way.... Its just that in this particular instance I froze and I thought; 'God ...' and as I was carrying on walking I thought.. 'I'm carrying on walking and she's just asked..' She's obviously...she's got two kids and she hasn't got any money... maybe she hasn't got a home at all, who knows. She must have somewhere to live...she's got two kids. And here I am and I've just finished cutting the record so I've heard it a dozen times and... its frightening. People like me, and I think everybody's the same, have got to do something. But I am not talking about alcoholism or drug abuse. I'm talking about your man on the street who actually hasn't got a roof over his head and there's so much of that in Europe, in America, all over the world, its not just specific places that have always had the problem... its everywhere..."

The album in the meantime, became Phil's first to be issued with extra tracks on the by now ubiquitous compact disc format although the "extras" were released to vinyl collectors as single b-sides. Demand for Phil's shows reached fever pitch with the band undertaking an eight month tour in support of the album which had by now gone several shades of precious metal into the process and a subsequent live album; *"Serious Hits Live"* was released to acclaim in the autumn of 1990. Phil always had confidence in this album as he explained.....

"This I think is my most solid album that I've done since Face Value for me. I think it's an important album coming when it does five years after No Jacket Required. I think a lot of people who are out there who think of Buster, they think of Groovy Kind Of Love, Two Hearts think that in the last couple of years I've gone soft . Whereas in fact I really look at it as a project. You know I did Buster because I loved the story, I loved the script and I wanted to act. It was great vehicle for me but it was a '60's vehicle and therefore me and Lamont sat down and wrote Two Hearts you know, which is a '60's song and it wasn't what Phil Collins would do as a solo artist necessarily, although I am very proud of that song. But it's a project song, you know, like Groovy Kind Of Love was a project song. It's not what I would necessarily have fitted in on this album which is why I didn't really cover any songs on this album. But I feel that people don't see that, they just see another Phil Collins single.

So really I tried on this album to try and haul people in to back to where I actually am, which is a drummer/singer/songwriter if you like. That is capable of writing songs, I think very moving songs. My best songs for a while now are on this album..."

The years that followed the release of that album have seen many highs and lows for Phil. Success continued with Genesis releasing another hit album in 1991' s *"We Can't Dance"* and subsequent groundbreaking tour. Phil's work as producer, session musician and actor could fill a book all on their own. 1993 was however, to prove to be a pivotal year both in the fortunes of Genesis and Phil Collins. His second marriage to Jill Tavelman ran into problems at this time much to the obvious delight of the so-called Press who hounded the couple at every opportunity. Phil's growing disaffection with Genesis eventually led to him announcing his decision to leave to the band in 1994. His subsequent album: *"Both Sides"* released in late 1993 was by far his darkest and angriest and one in which Phil got all of his frustrations out in one rant against the press, his wife and social injustice all in one go....

"My albums have always been pretty autobiographical and in 1994 I was on tour with Both Sides and as it happened I was stuck in hotel rooms for a lot of that tour because of the tabloid frenzy basically I had gone against what people thought was "me" the perfect nice guy; family man and my marriage was breaking up and I had gone off with somebody else and I had faxed for divorce, which was a load of rubbish it was hairy... Orianne's father was dying of cancer and there were journalists in her backyard and they wanted an interview and she had just fallen in love with me and me with her and she didn't know this stuff existed and there were all these people intruding and asking questions into their lives and Jill and Lily in England they were besieging her school and camping out in the garden and it was just unpleasant for everybody and I felt that if this is where I have arrived after all this time then really I have had enough, I don't want to do this anymore.."

His decision to play all the instruments himself also took fans by surprise and led to some criticism that the tracks are a little "same-ey" although explained the reasoning behind it...

"One of the problems I had encountered on earlier albums was that I would always fill out the bass end of the demos because it would sound a bit tinny without... and Leland and Pino and all those guys who played bass would have to skirt around what I had already done because I was using the demos and that made life a bit difficult for them and so I thought at that time, because at that point I still thought I was going to bring these guys in to play and I hadn't really formed an idea about what I was doing yet.

150

So I started playing bass on the keyboard just to fill in and I started having a good time doing that and I started thinking; 'Hey, this is good' and I had never played bass before and the more I did the more I enjoyed it. And at the same time as feeling like that, these songs were starting to come out which were very personal and luck for me, the kind of songs they were helped the fact that I didn't want anybody else on it. Then I started to do the same thing on the guitar and I thought; 'If I can do this on the bass maybe it would be nice to make it sound a little bit different from a Phil Collins album with all the keyboards on'.

I had put in a little bit of guitar earlier on and I tried little lead lines and I have never played lead lines I am pretty much a chord man on the keyboards and I started playing the little lead lines that you can hear on Can't Turn Back The Years and Can't Find My Way and those were all the original parts that I did at home and I suddenly thought that these songs are far too personal for me to let anybody else loose on...."

Despite the flak that Phil endured during this period, the album charted at the number one position and his tour, nicely divided into two parts the "Both Sides" tour of Europe and the USA which ran from April to December 1994 and the "Far Side" tour in 1995 which took in more exotic locations including Phil's first solo shows in South America and South Africa among others was his most successful to date.

The decision to leave Genesis had been kept secret until the band managed to find someone to replace Phil and the news was eventually broken to fans on 29th March 1996. Many wondered what Genesis would do next and of course, what Phil's next project would be. His decision to go out with a Jazz combo and play at several of the most prestigious jazz festivals in Europe that summer was his answer and a documentary about the tour was screened by the BBC at Christmas 1996. By that time, Phil had already begun work on his fifth solo album which eventually appeared late in the year and once again contained a mix of upbeat and conscience songs. Titled *"Dance Into The Light"* it took Phil's pop sensibilities and merged them with his uncanny knack of writing lyrics which can talk at several levels making the album one of his most satisfying efforts although the public didn't think so and this album was Phil's first not to gain automatic entry to the number one spot here in the UK. The tour had no such problems, however, and the resulting spectacular received rave reviews and played to enthusiastic crowds both in the UK and the USA and Europe.

The jazz experiment of 1996 had whetted Phil's appetite and fans were not surprised when he returned to this format for his next outing in the summer of 1998 with a string of shows in Europe and the USA which gave Phil a much needed chance to stay behind his much beloved drum kit and perform a set drawn from his own material and that of Genesis along with many staples from the jazz repertoire all lovingly presented to an enthusiastic audience and which was subsequently captured on the live album; *A Hot Night In Paris* which, as usual for an offering from Phil, drew mixed reviews from critics always eager to say anything as long as it is not constructive. Phil had always been a fan of the Big Band Jazz sound and here was his chance to have a go at another facet of music....

"The Big Band is something I've wanted to do for about thirty years, ever since I heard Buddy Rich and his band in 1966 and I wanted to do it since then and as a drummer it's a wonderful opportunity to stretch yourself and believe me I had to stretch myself as far as I could go. I had a mountain to climb in terms of I've got a broken wrist here. I had to learn to play again ... its still broken but I can play.... I had to learn to read and I had to write my own charts out because I couldn't read proper music. I had to invent my own phonetic language - but it's the most exciting thing I've ever done. I mean it is something that I will pick up and put down over the next few years..."

Between the second Big Band tour and the eventual release of the latest album: Testify in 2002,Phil occupied himself increasingly with work on soundtracks especially the long awaited Tarzan animated feature by Disney. Many disparaged his involvement in this type of work but once again, it represents another different facet of Phil's work and a very demanding one as Phil himself recalled...

"With Tarzan I had to re-record everything every time they wanted a change and that got very time consuming and it would sometimes work the first time and sometimes, it wouldn't..."

One thing that this form of work did encourage Phil to do was to explore the advantages of the latest computer recording technology which was certainly to stand him in good stead for his next solo album: 2002's Testify certainly saw Phil in a happier frame of mind. One thing that would not be realised from that record was the fact that Phil had suffered a minor stroke in his ear and his hearing had been severely impaired he was effectively 80% deaf in one ear!

The lengthy break between 1997's Dance Into The Light and Testify took many by surprise although it wasn't as if Phil's profile was any the less. The Big Band tours and album and his success with the Tarzan soundtrack kept Phil pretty much in the limelight but as he himself explained...

"I started to see the positive side of it actually; that maybe its an opportunity for people to say; 'I wonder what he's doing now? I wonder if there's any change?' .."

Yes, certainly there was a change with this album. Gone was the anger and angst of Face Value and Both Sides and in its place came an altogether happier side of Phil's persona. Having gone through the wringer in a very public manner in 1993/94, and with all the attendant publicity that that had garnered to see a "happy" album from Mr Collins was perhaps the biggest surprise of all.

"There's just little touches here and there and if you skimmed the songs down to just me on a piano then maybe there aren't that many differences in style from before but with the way I was working; trying this; trying that and that's no different; but that's better then I think it's a new me..."

Simpler songs reflecting an altogether different Collins from the angry middle-aged man of 1993's Both Sides and very much a reflection of the current state of affairs in Phil's personal life. This has always been the manner in which Phil's albums have been projected; almost an open "diary" of his thoughts and feelings at any particular period. Unusually enough though, this album actually had a VERY long gestation period. Phil began compiling stuff that would eventually end up on Testify back in 1994 while he was out on the road promoting Both Sides...

"The album was written over a couple of years; a period of a couple of years and I was on tour with Both Sides and I took with me a keyboard; a sequencer and I started writing little bits; loads of little bits;16 bar bits; 32 bits and saved them on this keyboard and didn't know what to do with it. Then I did Tarzan and then Disney asked me to do another film and at that point I felt I had to get stuck into this computer world because the way film music is they will always ask you to do it shorter or longer; can we hear it faster; can we hear it without that verse.. so I thought now was the time to get my feet wet with the computer and with that I could finish these bits that I had written in 1994 and they became Testify; Wake Up Call "

Phil's work method for this album was exactly the same as it has been for all of his others as he himself explains...

"It's simple and the best way to understand the way I work I don't sit down and say 'I know what I am going to do; I'm going to write a love song for Orianne' I don't sit down and write it I have the music or what is gradually becoming a song and because I work on my own; I don't have anybody hanging around operating equipment and I push play and record and I sing and what you hear, lyrically is what I sing. Sometimes a whole verse, a whole chorus or a whole song comes out. In The Air Tonight was completely improvised....I have always written like that "

With his attendant hearing problems; Phil opted to perform only a handful of shows against his doctor's advice to promote the album and effectively, that seemed to be that. However, Phil certainly is not one to lie down and his workaholic attitude continued with his next film project for Disney: Brother Bear which was issued last year and that was followed with the surprise announcement of Phil's "retirement" from touring with a massive tour humorously titled... "The First Final Farewell Tour" which took in the UK, mainland Europe and the US and Canada between June and September of 2004 with a further leg covering other territories not usually graced by such a major rock show including shows in Dubai, Israel and Russia which ran from October to December 2005. There may yet be other shows for Japan, Australia and South America depending on Phil's other commitments.

As usual, there was a certain sense of self-deprecating humour in the choice of title for the tour, as Phil explained...

"The reason for that is really just English humour. I could easily have just called it The Farewell Tour but that is a little bit to the point and a little bit sentimental. So we thought; me and Smithy (Tony Smith) 'what can we call it?' and we came up with all these stark (laughter) titles and it is taken from Monty Python ...a sort of nod in their direction..."

Between the work on this tour and the up coming Tarzan musical ; Phil will also have to get used to family life again with the commencement of school for his son Nicholas and the recent birth of another child which should keep Mr Collins Senior occupied for the foreseeable future. Whatever path Phil decides to take next, his career to date leaves an amazing legacy of music to be appreciated and enjoyed.

For a more detailed look at Phil's solo career the following are recommended reading:

"The Phil Collins Story" Johnny Waller Zomba Books 1985.
"Phil Collins The Definitive Biography" Ray Coleman Simon & Schuster 1997.
"Phil Collins - The Singing Drummer" Mario Giammetti Edizioni Segno 2005.

Phil Collins Solo UK Discography

7" and 12" Vinyl Singles

A - Side	B - Side	Catalogue Number

With "Flaming Youth"...

A - Side	B - Side	Catalogue Number	
Guide me Orion	From now on (Immortal, Invisible)	Fontana TF1057. (7")	?.10.69
Man woman and child	**Drifting**	Fontana 6001 002 (7")	26.6.70
From now on (Immortal, Invisible)	Space Child	Fontana 6001 003. (7")	?.12.70

With "Brand X"....

A - Side	B - Side	Catalogue Number
Sun in the night/	Disco Suicide	Charisma Brand 1 (7")
Soho	Dance of the illegal aliens	Charisma CB340 (7")

(The B-Side to this single was in fact: "Noddy goes to Sweden")

Soho	Noddy goes to Sweden/Pool Room Blues	Charisma CB340-12 (12")
Modern; Noisy and Effective	Swan Song	CBS XPS155 (7")

As "Phil Collins"....

A - Side	B - Side	Catalogue Number	
In the air tonight	The roof is leaking	Virgin VS102 (7" PS)	?.1.81
In the air tonight	The roof is leaking	Virgin VSK102 (7"PS)	?.1.81

(This edition came with cartoon booklet created by Phil's brother: Clive)

I missed again	I'm not moving	Virgin VS402 (7" PS)	27.3.81
I missed again	I'm not moving	Virgin VS402-12 (12" PS)	27.3.81
If leaving me is easy	**Drawing board demos**	Virgin VS423 (7" PS)	10.5.81
If leaving me is easy	**Drawing board demos**	Virgin VS423 (7" Limited Poster sleeve)(The demos	

were: In the air tonight/I missed again/If leaving me is easy) 10.5.81

Thru these walls Do you know, do you care?		Virgin VS524 (PS)	?.10.82
Thru these walls Do you know, do you care?		Virgin VSY524(7"PD)	?10.82
You can't hurry love	I cannot believe its true	Virgin VS531 (7" PS)	?.11.82
You can't hurry love	I cannot believe its true	Virgin VSY531(7" PD)	?.11.82
You can't hurry love	I cannot believe its true/**Oddball**	Virgin VS531-12 (12" PS)	?.11.82
Don't let him steal your heart away Thunder & Lightning		Virgin VS572 (7" PS)	?.3.83
Don't let him steal your heart away	**And so to F... (Live)**	Virgin VS572-12 (12" PS)	?.3.83
Why can't it wait til morning?	Like China	Virgin VS603 (7" PS)	?.5.83
Against all odds	**Making a big mistake** (M Rutherford)	Virgin VS674 (7" PS)	1.3.84
Against all odds	**Making a big mistake** (M Rutherford)	Virgin VSY674 (7" PD)	1.3.84
Sussudio	**The man with the horn**	Virgin VS736 (7" PS)	?.1.85
Sussudio (Extended remix)	**The man with the horn**	Virgin VS736-12 (12" PS)	?.1.85
Sussudio (Extended remix)	**The man with the horn**	Virgin VSY736-12 (12" PD)	?.1.85
One more night **I like the way**		Virgin VS755 (7" PS)	7.3.85
One more night **I like the way**		Virgin VSS755 (7" PD)	7.3.85
One more night (Extended mix) I like the way		Virgin VS75512 (12" PS)	14.3.85
Take me home	**We said hello, goodbye**	Virgin VS777 (7" PS)	?.7.85
Take me home (Remix) Take me home/**We said, hello goodbye**			
		Virgin VS777-12 (12" PS)	?.7.85
Separate Lives Only you & I know		Virgin VS818 (7" PS)	?.11.85
Separate Lives Only you & I Know (Extended mix)		Virgin VS818-12 (12" PS)	?.11.85
Separate Lives Only you & I Know		Virgin VSY818 (7" Picture disc)	?.11.85
In the air tonight ('88 Remix) I missed again		Virgin VS102 (7" PS)	?.3.88
In the air tonight ('88 Remix) I missed again		Virgin VST102 (12" PS)	?.3.88
A Groovy kind of love Big Noise (Instrumental)		Virgin VS1117 (7" PS)	?.10.88
A groovy kind of love Big Noise (Instrumental)		Virgin VST1117 (12" PS)	?.10.88
A Groovy kind of love Big Noise (Instrumental)		Virgin VSTG1117 (12" PS)	?.10.88

(This edition appeared in a gatefold sleeve)

Two hearts	**The robbery (Excerpt) (Anne Dudley)**	Virgin VS1141 (7" PS)	?.12.88
Two hearts	**The robbery (Full length) (Anne Dudley)**	Virgin VST1141 (12" PS)	?.12.88

(This edition appeared with a limited edition set of four postcards)

Another day in paradise Heat on the street	Virgin VS1234 (7" PS)	20.10.89

Another day in paradise Saturday night, Sunday morning/Heat on
The street   Virgin VST1234 (12" PS) 20.10.89
I wish it would rain down **Homeless (Another day in paradise demo)**
Virgin VS1240 (7"PS)   15.1.90
I wish it would rain down **Homeless/You've been in love (That
Little bit too long)**   Virgin VST1240 (12" PS) 15.1.90
Something happened on the way to heaven
I wish it would rain down (Demo)   Virgin VS1251 (7" PS)   10.4.90
(Also issued as limited edition with photo booklet same tracks different catalogue number : VSP1251)
Something happened on the way to heaven (One world remix)
Something happened…(7" version)/**I wish It Would rain down (Demo)** Virgin VST1251 (12" PS)   10.4.90
That's just the way it is   **Broadway Chorus (Demo of Something
Happened on the way to heaven)**   Virgin VS1277 (7" PS)   6.7.90
That's just the way it is   **Broadway Chorus/In the air tonight
(Extended version)**   Virgin VST1277 (12" PS)   6.7.90
Hang in long enough **Around the world in 80 presets**   Virgin VS1300 (7" PS)   ?. 9.90
Hang in long enough (Pettibone 12" mix)
Hang in long enough/**Hang in long enough (Pettibone Dub Mix)**
Virgin VST1300 (12" PS)   ?.9.90
Do you remember? (Live)   Against all odds (Live)   Virgin VS1305 (7" PS)   16.11.90
Do you remember? (Live)   Against all odds (Live)/**Doesn't anybody
Stay together anymore? (Live)**   Virgin VST1305 (12" PS) 16.11.90
Both sides of the story   **Always (Live)**   Virgin VS1500 (7" PS)   18.10.93
Everyday   **Don't call me Ashley**   Virgin VS1505 (7" PS)   10.1.94
We wait & We wonder (Edit) Hero (Demo version)   Virgin VS1510 (7" PS)   25.4.94
Dance into the light   Take me down   Face Value EW066 (7")   21.10.97

Compact Disc Singles

You can't hurry love/I cannot believe its true/**Oddball**   Virgin CDT1 (PS)   ?.?.87
In the air tonight (Extended version)/In the air tonight ('88 remix)/I missed again
Virgin VSCD102 (PS) ?.10.88
A groovy kind of love/Big noise(Instrumental)/Will you still be waiting?
Virgin VSCD1117 (PS) ?.10.88
Two Hearts/The robbery (Full length version)   Virgin VSCD1141 (PS) ?.12.88
(Issued as a limited edition in heart-shaped box)
Another day in paradise/Saturday night, Sunday morning/Heat on the street
Virgin VSCD1234 (PS) 20.10.89
I wish it would rain down/**Homeless (Another day in paradise demo)/You've been
In love(That little bit too long)**   Virgin VSCD1240 (PS) ?. 2.90
Something happened on the way to heaven (7" version)/**Something happened on the way
To heaven(one world remix)/I wish it would rain down (Demo)**   Virgin VSCD1251 (PS) 13.4.90
That's just the way it is/**Broadway Chorus/In the air tonight (Extended version)**
Virgin VSCD1277 (PS) 6.7.90
That's just the way it is/**BroadwayChorus/In the air tonight (Extended version)**
Virgin   VSCDX 1277 (PS) 13.7.9 (Limited edition in shaped box)
Hang in long enough/**Around the world in 80 presets/Hang in long enough
(Pettibone 12" Mix)**   Virgin VCSDT1300 (PS)   ?.10.90
Hang in long enough/**That's how I feel/Hang in long enough (Pettibone Dub Mix)**
Virgin VSCDX1300 (PS)   ?.10.90
(Limited edition numbered disc)
Do you remember?(Live)/Against all odds (Live)/**Doesn't anybody stay together
Anymore (Live)/Inside Out (live)**   Virgin VSCDT1305 (PS)   16.11.90
**Do you remember? (Live)/Doesn't anybody stay together anymore? (Live)/
The roof is leaking (live)**   Virgin VSCDX1305 (PS)   23.11.90
(Limited edition in shaped "Carousel" style box)
Doesn't anybody stay together anymore? (Live)
(One -track single free with initial copies of Phil's video: "But Seriously: The Videos" in Woolworths stores only)
1990
Both sides of the story/**Always (Live)/Both sides of the demo** Virgin VSCDT 1500 (PS) 18.10.93

Both sides of the story/**Always (live)/Both sides of the demo/Rad Dudeski**

Virgin VSCDG1500 (PS) 18.10.93

Everyday/**Don't call me Ashley/Everyday (early demo)** Virgin VSCDT1505 (PS) 10.1.94

Everyday/**Don't call me Ashley/Everyday (early demo)/Doesn't anybody stay**

Together anymore? (Live) Virgin VSCDG 1505 (PS) 17.1.94

(Limited edition with 1994 "Phil Collins" Calendar)

We wait and we wonder (Edit)/Take me with you/Stevie's Blues(There's a Place For us demo)

Virgin VSCG 1510 (PS) 25.4.94

We wait and we wonder/**For a friend/Hero (Home demo)** Virgin VSCDX1510 (PS) 25.4.94

Dance in to the light/Take me down/**it's over (Home demo)** Face Value EWO66CD (PS) 21.7.97

It's in your eyes/**Always(live)/I don't want to go** Face Value EWO76CD (PS) 9.12.97

It's in your eyes/**Easy Lover (live)/Separate lives (Live)** Face Value EWO76CD (PS) 16.12.97

Wear my hat/ **Wear my hat (Edited hat dance mix)/Wear my hat (Hat dance mix)/**

Wear my hat (Wear my dub) Face Value 0630 19073-2 (PS) 30.5.98

True Colours/I missed again/In the air tonight Virgin/Face Value VSCDT1715 (PS) ?.?.01

True Colours/Don't lose my number/Take me home Virgin/Face Value VSCDG 1715 (PS) ?.?.01

Can't Stop Loving You Face Value EW254CD (PS) 23.10.02

Look Through My Eyes/**Look Through My Eyes(Instrumental)/Transformation** Disney Records 01/50 4669682 2
?.?.03

Tracks in **Bold** are non album tracks.
PS denotes an edition with a picture sleeve.

Phil Collins Vinyl and Compact Disc Albums.

As "Flaming Youth".....

Ark 2   Fontana STL5533   1969

As "Brand X"....

Unorthodox Behaviour   Charisma CAS1117
Moroccan Roll   Charisma CAS1126
Livestock   Charisma CLASS 5
Masques   Charisma CAS1138
Product   Charisma CAS1147
Do they hurt?   Charisma CAS1151
Is there anything about?   CBS 85967
X Communications   Ozone Records (USA) OZ-001
Xtrax (Compilation)   Passport Records PB6054 (USA)
The Plot thins - A history of Brand X   Virgin CDVM 9005
Live at the Roxy   Zok Records

As "Phil Collins".....

Face Value	Virgin V2185/CDV2185 (CD)	11.2.81
Hello, I must be going	Virgin V2252/CDV2252 (CD)	?.9.82
No jacket required	Virgin V2345/CDV2345 (CD)	?.1.85
But Seriously	Virgin V2620/CDV2620 (CD)	20.11.89
Serious Hits - Live!	Virgin PCLP1/PCCD1 (CD)	5.11.90

(Initial copies were issued as limited edition with slip case and photo booklet)

Both Sides	Virgin CDV2800 (CD)	8.11.93

(Australian import copies were accompanied by a live four-track single: "Live from the Board" featuring the following tracks: Sussudio/Easy Lover/Separate lives/My girl)

Dance into the light	Face Value 0630-1600-2 (CD)	22.10.96
Hits	Virgin CDV 2870	5.10.98
A Hot Night In Paris	WEA 3984 27221-2	24.5.99
Testify	Face Value Records	11.11.02
Love Songs - A Compilation...Old And New	EMI Records 724386680426	1.11.04

Soundtracks

Against All Odds	Virgin Records	1984
White Nights		1985
Buster		1988
Tarzan		1999
Brother Bear		2003

Promotional interview discs and samplers

Phil Collins…. Profiled!	Atlantic Records PR3092-2
Phil Collins…. The story - the interview disc	Atlantic Records PRCD5370-2
Phil Collins - Dance into the light interview disc	Warner Records PC008
You Ought To Know (Toyota cars promotional sampler)	Solo
The Phil Collins Big Band Big Hits Sampler	Greenwood Trust Company

Appendix C: "From the cocoon to the Secret World" A short biography of Peter Gabriel.

Peter Gabriel's decision to leave Genesis, announced officially in August 1975 took many of his fans by surprise. The question for those of us blessed with hindsight is: should we have been so surprised? The answer is perhaps as misleading as the question. Of course, any long-term observers of Peter's career would not have been surprised by his decision to leave the band - the two were no longer mutually inclusive; Peter's sense of a "Real World" did not equate with the slightly phantasmagorical world of Genesis circa 1976.

With no definite "Career" to follow, Peter's decision took on epic proportions but are these truly realistic? The answer is ,in my own opinion "No" Peter always knew that he could return to music for a living, what makes his decision to leave the band so much more of a shock than the previous departures from the band, was the element of realism which it injected into the band. Peter decided to put family first and as such, he was the first member of the band to do so. This was perhaps the element which neither the band or Peter himself were ready for - realism. Although "The Lamb Lies Down On Broadway" can perhaps be described as a "Modern Fairy Tale" perhaps the real world had not injected itself enough into the cosseted Genesis scene and so, Peter's departure was the best thing for everyone although, of course, not everyone thought so at the time and not everyone has agreed on this point ever since - and dare I say it; in the words of one of Clint Eastwood's famous characters: "Opinions are like ass-holes; everybody has got one!" The divisions which Peter's departure from the band have caused are not open to debate here; what follows is purely an examination of his career since he left the band....

Peter could not long resist the attraction of writing his own music and the summer of 1976 saw him begin work on what would appear in early 1977 as his first solo album. Intriguingly enough, he enlisted both Mike and Anthony Phillips to help with the initial demos for this project although none of that material was used on the finished product, it would nevertheless make for interesting listening if any of that material were to surface now. Interestingly enough, a Charisma demo cassette from these sessions was recently unearthed during a search through Anthony Phillips' tape archives which features some of the original material which Peter wrote with help from Phil, Mike and Anthony himself although it is highly unlikely if any of this material will be released. Peter was still unsure about the correctness of his decision to get back into the music business, even expressing such reservations during the limited handful of interviews he gave during the promotional work for his first album. He also took the opportunity of expressing himself further on the subject of his departure from Genesis....

"After I left Genesis, I wanted to spend a while completely away from the music business. I didn't want to rush ahead with a solo career, I needed time to look at things, to get into situations where I was something other than a focal point. So, I followed up various interests - made babies, worked in the garden. It was about a year ago when I decided to get back into things. I had kept on writing songs up until then but for along while I wasn't sure exactly how much I was willing to involve myself once again. You know, I'm still not REALLY sure. All I know is that my staying with the band was wrong. It's difficult to look back and fish out my reasons, but I suppose most of all I split because I didn't like what the band was becoming. Things were becoming too predictable, too stable and too stale - it was just like building a house and then renting it out...I'm sure in the light of day the decision has been good for me and good for them. When I was with the band the other members tended to hide behind me - so when I got out of their way they were put to the test and it kicked a lot of life into them...."

Peter's search for a new musical style was initially to take him into working with Bob Ezrin who had, up to then, produced every album by Alice Cooper as well as Lou Reed's "Berlin" and Kiss' "Destroyer" albums. The new album was recorded at Nimbus Studios in Toronto during the autumn of 1976. In many ways it can be seen as a transitional work, in which Peter was searching for his own musical voice and, as such, several of the tracks were a surprise including the delightful barbershop harmonies of "Excuse Me" and the melodrama of "Moribund The Burgermeister". The album was released in the UK in February of 1977 on Charisma Records to widespread critical acclaim. A twenty date tour of North America was set up to promote the album in March and April.

Perhaps the most surprising aspect of the tour was Peter's appearance: without any of the usual costumery associated with his time in Genesis. Instead, Peter relied on the music and a simple but effective light show to do the talking for him. He explained the rationale behind the drastic about-face during an interview with Barbara Charone for Sounds

"It's very reassuring when the audience recognises material from the album when you are up on stage. The first few gigs were a little shaky. I might do some Genesis material later but at this point it's important for me to endeavour something different from my days in Genesis.... I was thinking of doing Supper's Ready but at the moment I would rather be judged on new songs until I have gained a separate credibility..."

Even more surprising perhaps for fans, was the inclusion in the set of several Soul classics in the shape of "Ain't That Peculiar?" and "All day and all of the night" as well as the resurrection of Peter's alter - ego: "Rael" for "Back In NYC". The shows brought Peter an entirely new audience in the USA as well as the stalwart Genesis fans who welcomed their hero's return to the fray. This success was confirmed when the first single from the album;

"Solsbury Hill" was a hit on both sides of the Atlantic.

A further surprise in the shows came with the previously unheard of performance of unreleased material from the as yet unrecorded second album, still almost a year away. Peter's first UK shows took place in April 1977 and were a warm-up exercise for a full European tour which was to take place in September and October 1977. For these shows, Peter was joined by the same musicians as he had performing with him on the earlier US tour: Tony Levin (bass), Larry Fast (Synthesisers), Steve Hunter (guitars). Both Fast and Levin were to become long time members of Gabriel's band and Levin is still with him over twenty years on. The tour was another success with audiences although it wasn't quite as successful with the Swiss police during the final leg of the tour when the band were arrested on their way from Besancon to St Gallen for a gig. The police mistook them for members of the German terrorist group Baader-Meinhof. Even an a-capella version of "Excuse Me" wasn't enough to convince them that the guys weren't "fugitives from justice" and it was left to tour promoter; Richard MacPhail to convince them. As you can imagine , the music press had a field day with this story sparking off such headlines as New Musical Express' "Gabriel Gang Freed"

Throughout all of this, Peter retained one determined ideal which he has adhered to throughout his solo career since. To change, to be different and to challenge his own perceptions as well as those of his audience although he also admitted that he was still searching for that defining Peter Gabriel "sound"....

I wanted to make it sound varied and I wanted to make it sound different from Genesis. You see, Genesis had since reappeared, sounding much the same as before, and I had written off simply as a performer rather than as a musical figure. I think I'll approach the next album the same way, and maybe the one after that. I'll try to establish a definite Peter Gabriel 'sound' ..."

Despite a successful tour; album and single; Peter was still in debt to the tune of £200,000 at the end of 1977 and still not satisfied with his efforts so far. His decision to involve Robert Fripp whose work with King Crimson had so inspired the early Genesis, in the production of his second album took many fans by surprise. Fripp himself was very reluctant to produce the album and wanted to give Peter the freedom to express himself that was in some ways missing from his first record. This freedom of expression was not without its problems as long standing fans of Peter's will know; Peter's expression sometimes takes a LONG time to come to fruition and what in Peter's and Kate Bush's cases was later to be called the "Tortoise Syndrome" was already beginning to creep in.

For the new album, Peter enlisted the help of Bruce Springsteen's keyboard player; Roy Bittan along with Levin and Fast and extra help from respected session musos Sid McGinnis on guitar and Timmy Capello on saxophones. A single was released in advance of the album which contained two tracks from the forthcoming album: *DIY* and *Perspective* but the single was destined to make no impression on the charts. Later in the year it was re-issued with a re-mixed A-side and an unreleased track on the flip side but also to no avail. This was perhaps an indication that already, outside of the Genesis "brand name", Gabriel was still something of a difficult product for a record company to bring to market. A view that Gabriel himself expressed in an interview with Nick Kent for Sounds in June 1978...

"I am concerned that people think that there are no obvious singles on the album. I thought possibly that there were a couple of potential ones there... I don't know... I still believe in D I Y commercially..."

The album itself, also titled *Peter Gabriel* like its predecessor was released in June 1978 with far less critical comment than the first album and the lack of a high profile single release from it was to cause Peter problems later when his contract with Atlantic Records in the USA was up for re-negotiation. The first tour was also less of a success than expected although critically well-received, Peter often played to less than full houses, especially in the USA which remained unconvinced by his re-invented self.

The album itself was a darker affair than its predecessor especially in the lyric department with songs like *Home Sweet Home* really challenging the listener with its description of someone on the edge of a nervous breakdown which was certainly a million miles away from the allegorical world of mid Seventies Genesis! Once again, Peter undertook an extensive tour of the USA and Europe to promote the album and the shows continued to place the emphasis firmly upon the music and its performance with improvisation playing a large part of the show especially with the performance of further new pieces which were in many cases far from finished. This tour also saw Peter change his appearance once again; with a closely cropped head and what can almost be described as a bin liner for clothing he was rapidly putting clear blue water between his appearance now and his days as the "Caped Crusader" in Genesis. In particular, Peter's appearance at 1978's Battersea and Knebworth Park festivals where the "New Wave" in British music was enjoying its first flush of major league success was enough to cause several music critics serious doubts as one remarked of Peter's performance at Battersea.......

"Peter Gabriel was the first of the day to get the audience off its collective ass, but his recent surge to credibility is perplexing; to me he is as anonymous today as he ever was with Genesis. But the rest of the audience endorsed

Gabriel's oddly-arranged music and went quite wild over his Punk parody of A Whiter Shade of Pale which I found both unfunny and unspectacular..."

Not all of the critics found the new album such a daunting or confusing prospect and he drew several plaudits from the press and his fans continued to be as loyal as ever. Peter rounded off the year with a series of sell-out shows at the prestigious Hammersmith Odeon in London including an extra special event on 24th December which, thanks to an oversight on promoter Harvey Goldsmith's part led to a double booking of the venue by both Peter and Tom Robinson. The resulting show billed as "Rob & Gab Christmas '78" was one of the highlights of 1978's musical calendar with guest appearances by Elton John , Paul Jones, Phil Collins and Andy McKay for what turned into the Rock & Roll party of the year.

1979 saw Peter taking stock of his position and working on material for his third solo album although he did put in a couple of appearances at the Reading and Glastonbury festivals during August at which several new pieces were again given a pre-album airing and anyone who heard him perform *Biko* for the first time will, I am sure never forget it! The remainder of the year was taken up by studio duties in which Peter's mode of writing for an album was undergoing a fundamental change with the emphasis being placed more on rhythm over the more usual chords and melodies and trying to give a different slant to "ordinary" events as he explained in an interview with Smash Hits Magazine …

"My initial ideas come at any time and I write them down in a diary or a notebook, or on a cassette if it's a musical idea. The hard part is working through all those ideas, sifting out the good ideas from the rubbish and turning it into songs. I liked taking titles or phrases from ordinary situations and trying to put them up against a slightly different background that will give them a new slant. It's an area I am much more interested in than a totally fabricated artificial world. For Games Without Frontiers I was thinking about adults behaving like kids, countries behaving like kids in the way that modes of behaviour which were unacceptable in a normal society were perfectly acceptable on an international scale..."

To help him, Peter acquired the services of producer Steve Lilywhite whose previous credits included *Hong Kong Garden* for Siouxsie and the Banshees and *Making Plans For Nigel* for XTC. Peter was already striving to break out of the constraints binding the writing of rock music and anything that sounded like a standard "rock" sound was avoided. In addition to Lilywhite, Peter had also enlisted the help of Phil Collins on percussion and it was to be his sound; the now famous "Gated reverb" which was to become one of the features of Peter's new sound. Collins created the sound through a gate compressor unit, a device which both shut off sound and squashes it. *Intruder* was the first beneficiary and Collins later used it to great effect on his own first solo album; *Face Value.*

This new rhythmic approach gave Peter the opportunity to explore an idea that had been with him since 1977 when he first heard of the death of South African political activist; Stephen Biko . At the time he was writing the track which was destined to become *Biko,* Peter came across a soundtrack of the music used at Biko's funeral and he was intrigued by the rhythmic, uplifting quality of the music. Peter also used the marimbas; an African instrument similar to a xylophone on the album as well as the vocal talents of Kate Bush. It was this track that along with Games Without Frontiers which firmly brought the unacceptable side of behaviour; personal, national and international, into a sharper and much more disagreeable focus.

This new found artistic freedom was one thing but the adventurous (and some might say controversial) subject matter of some of Peter's new work was to prove too much for his American record company: Atlantic and their A & R man; John Kolodner in particular, who is reputed to have remarked upon hearing the new record that it was; *"Commercial Suicide"* . The meeting with the heads of the record company was far from successful; they objected to *Biko* on the grounds that no one in the US was aware of what was happening in South Africa (a crass indictment of the US music scene and their opinion of their own people). They also thought that *Family Snapshot* (a song based on the thoughts of an assassin as he stalked his prey) was too controversial. Atlantic's decision to drop Gabriel from their roster of artists was referred to in Gabriel's own words as…

"an example of the short-sighted, bigoted attitude commonly found in the hierarchy of the American record industry... It will be ironic if this album turns out to be more successful..."

Peter's prediction about the album was well founded. The first single from it; *Games Without Frontiers* reached the number four spot in the UK charts in April 1980. The video for the single was censored by the BBC because eof its use of children's dolls (?) in it, and the line: *"we piss on the goons in the jungle"* was also edited out (shame on you, BBC!). The album; once again bearing the moniker *"Peter Gabriel"* was eventually released in May 1980 by which time Peter had already had the satisfaction of an enormously satisfactory tour of the UK and upon its release the album became Peter's highest chart entry to date when it entered the UK charts at the number one position.

Peter also outlined some of the reasons behind the lengthy gaps between his albums in an interview with Ray Coleman for Melody Maker in February 1981.…

"Its true, three albums in five years is not much. I get pre-occupied with details and this slows down the whole thing. I enjoy the first part; finding the ideas, lyrically and musically. Inspiration can come at any time and that's a lot of fun but I can't just turn it on like a tap as some musicians and writers can. So I have to wait a bit. The next part is turning the ideas into songs and that's always hard work for, requiring great discipline and often takes me a disproportionate amount of time. I tend to get absorbed in subsidiary details…."

Once again, Peter had challenged convention by writing songs about what most people would consider taboo areas as mentioned above and also in the overt references to sexual intrusion implicit in the lyrics to *Intruder*. In all three singles were released from the album although none of them equalled the success of *Games Without Frontiers*. Without doubt, however, it was *Biko* which must have brought Peter most satisfaction as it went on to create a life of its own and became the anthem for all of those striving to bring an end to South Africa's repressive Apartheid system. More satisfying still for Peter must have been the frantic efforts of Atlantic records to re-sign him to their label with an attempt to by him back for an advance of $750,000 an enormous sum of money for 1980! Peter however, opted to join the newly established label of David Geffen whose promise of artistic freedom and record company support were much more important to Peter.

That freedom also extended into areas such as interaction with the audience. Peter's shows rapidly became known not only for musical excellence, but also for the increasing involvement of the audience and interplay between the entertainer and the "entertained"….

"part of the reason for walking through the audience at the start of our show is to get eyeball-to eyeball with everyone, a one to one thing. They know they can clock me on the head as I'm going through to the stage, if they want to. My relationship with the audience is absolutely vital to me. I like to go through a variety of emotional experiences and the positioning of Biko at the end of the set is important. Although the subject matter is negative, for me it is very positive and affirmative, and its rather like at a football match when the audience stand up and roar. On Biko it's a great feeling to be a part of the audience and when they get up and belt out the chant. Interaction between the stage and the audience will always be part of my aim…."

The success of the third album gave Peter a much needed respite to recharge his creative batteries and it is certain that he was now confident enough to branch out into the fields of exploration which has characterised his music ever since. The two year hiatus between third and fourth album was not, as some have supposed, an indication that Peter was out of ideas, far from it! Peter's influences and inspirations were taking him even further afield and it was during this period that he started gathering tapes of music from all over the world convinced that a new and powerful force was soon to be unleashed upon music…..

"I feel that an important influence on music over the next few years will be ethnic in origin and I can hear it being combined with electronics and more expressive, emotive use of synthesiser…"

Peter delayed his album still further by deciding to scrap a variety of pre-sets from his drum machine and investigate the potential of the new Fairlight CMI as he explained to Hugh Fielder of Sounds in October 1982…

"The process of recording was longer this time because I decided to wipe all of the pre-sets from my drum machine and start trying to find forty or fifty interesting rhythm patterns. That took a while - listening to non European bits, Tamla bits and invented rhythms. And also with this Fairlight CMI computerised musical instrument that I used. I went out searching for sounds to university engineering departments, scrap yards and other places getting all sorts of different sound sources. This gave me the possibility of having a library of fairly original sounds with which to try and build the pictures of the tracks…"

This fascination with rhythm was to lead him into a desire to produce and promote a festival which would bring this music to a wider audience and this would eventually lead him to stage the first World of Music Arts and Dance (WOMAD) festival in the summer of 1982. Altruism is one thing but the hard nosed realities of the early Eighties meant that what was originally planned for the summer of 1981 was delayed almost permanently due to a lack of a major backer for the proposed festival which in turn, led to delays on an already behind schedule album from Peter.

Peter's new record deal with Geffen gave him artistic freedom and a certain degree of financial security although there was some concern expressed by the lack of a title for Peter's new album. Having had three issues of what Peter saw as his periodic "Music Magazine" the new record company felt that a title was needed for this effort. The as yet untitled album was filled with the new sounds which Peter had been acquiring; Ethiopian pipes formed the harmonies around which *The Family & The Fishing Net* was written; but as usual with Peter nothing is quite as simple as it seems …. *"There are certain lyrics which fit into the ritualistic situations but what I was looking at was the undercurrent of that symbolism within a normal everyday Western wedding in a church. The territorial battles between fathers' daughters and mothers' sons , the ring all sorts of sexual undertones…"* While the surdo drum from Brazil was the rhythmic basis for *Kiss Of Life*.

The first single *Shock The Monkey* was an early indicator of the new direction that Peter was taking and it failed to make any impression on the charts and with the new album following hot on its heels in September 1982, it was all too much for one reviewer in the UK music paper; *"Sounds"*

"Forget Heavy Metal; Punk; The Rolling Stones; forget the most horrendous musical niche you can think of - because the most horrendous of the lot is this: the Comfortably Middle Aged Set at which Genesis and associates sit at the head of the (leather-bound) table..."

Not all of the reviews were quite as extreme as that and indeed, in many areas Peter was praised for breaking down further the barriers that segregate musical forms and he even received noteworthy reviews in several black music papers. As in 1979, Peter opted to premier the as yet unheard album at the event which he had spent so much time (and money) helping to organise; the WOMAD Festival which took place at the Showering Pavilion in Shepton Mallet over the weekend of 16th to 18th July 1982. Unfortunately one of the major problems facing Peter was the fact that the authorities had restricted the performances by Peter and other headliners: Echo & The Bunnymen to the four thousand seater Showering Pavilion which rather reduced the appeal of the festival to those who couldn't get tickets for what were, for them, the acts they wanted to see. Gabriel's performance that day was amazing as one fan recalls...

"Coming on stage dressed in the usual black uniform, he began singing over a backing tape, until the rest of the band joined in and the song built up to a crescendo. In fact this is how most of the songs from the first half of the set developed; beginning sparsely with just piano and drums.....Particularly effective were I have the touch, Lay your hands on me, and Shock the monkey ...However after Shock..a new dimension was added when Ekome the Bristol-based drummers from Ghana joined the stage....Rhythm of the heat which Gabriel described as being about a white man who finds himself surrounded by blacks and is consequently shit-scared. This was particularly apt since Gabriel and his band were outnumbered by Ekone. For this song, Gabriel seemed to get himself into a trance-like state and performed a strange kind of ritual dance. By the end of this intense song Peter seemed visibly exhausted...."

Peter's second set was even more challenging than the first where he was joined on stage by long time friend and hero Peter Hammill and Indian violin master; Shankar for an improvised set which drew warm applause from the crowd. Peter's new work had also been the subject of a documentary by ITV's *"Southbank Show"* which was finally broadcast on Sunday 31st October 1982 and which captured the artist at work in the studio and also some of the magical moments from the WOMAD Festival. During the interview which formed part of the programme, Peter was keen to reply to the detractors of his new work...

"One of the real satisfactions for me with this record is that I'm played on black stations in America and even though in the white press I had some fair slagging this time, I had some very good reviews in black magazines...there are definitely elements of this hybrid between electronic non-European influences. I think a lot more musicians are now working in this area and there will be a style of music to emerge in the Eighties which I think will be very important and influential..."

A second single from the album failed to make any impression on the charts even though it's B-side should have attracted interest being co-written as it was by Gabriel Shankar, David Rhodes and Stewart Copeland. The album, in the meantime and despite the critics' reservations reached the number ten spot in the UK charts and it was time for Peter to embark on his lengthiest tour to promote it. Beginning in Boston USA on 28th October 1982, the new tour lived up to everyone's expectations as Peter and his band played a set high on drama and comedy with Peter taking everyone by surprise again by appearing with his face adorned by make-up for the first time since his days with Genesis. The surreal element was taken to even greater heights (or should that be depths?) in 1983 when Peter was invited to appear at the San Remo festival in Italy for which a special performance was required in which Peter had to appear as an alien visitor to the festival asking questions of the presenter about the festival itself before finally appearing on stage with an appallingly under rehearsed studio band to perform *Shock the monkey* where on the second night he failed to amuse the highly reserved TV studio audience by swinging out over them on a rope half way through the song only to fall off!

Peter had taken to performing songs in the language of the country he was playing in and had previously issued his third album as a German language edition back in 1980, he did the same for his fourth album titling it originally enough *Deutsches Album* . It was particularly interesting for the alternative versions of several of the songs many of which were noticeably longer than their UK counterparts. By the end of 1983, Peter had also finally issued a long overdue live album; *Peter Gabriel Plays Live* which contained most of the highlights of his current live set. The success of the album and tour, were somewhat marred however, by a series of family problems which Peter turned his attention to as well as his increasing desire to branch out into other areas of endeavour which were to occupy an increasingly large amount of his time over the next few years.

After the completion of the 1982/83 tours, Peter spent an extensive amount of time pursuing a project which he had initially contemplated during the mid 1970's - the creation of an adventure theme park - "Real World" an idea which he is still struggling with now. He also submerged himself in his work and ideas for his fifth album which was still three years away. A lot of other events were to influence him before that however.

In 1984, during what must have been a particularly trying period for Peter, he and his wife Jill had a trial separation during which time Peter made two visits to Brazil and Senegal which were to expose him to even more of the rhythmic influences which were so evident on his fourth album. He began preparing rhythm tracks for the as yet untitled fifth album early in 1984 but made slow progress. The main reason for the delay came through his involvement in the soundtrack for the *"Gremlins"* film to which he contributed *"Out, Out"* hardly his best recording ever and another much better contribution to the *"Against All Odds"* soundtrack where he was in the company of tracks by both Phil Collins and Mike Rutherford. His contribution; *"Walk Through The Fire"* was an old track left over from Peter's third album which he re-recorded and added lyrics and which was eventually released as the second single from the soundtrack later in 1984.

Also that year, Peter became heavily involved with the soundtrack to Alan Parker's controversial film *"Birdy"* . This was an intriguing project which utilised both existing music and newly recorded pieces which succeeded in capturing the state of shock experienced by the film's central character upon his return to "society" at the end of the Vietnam War. Unlike many rock stars; Peter took the precaution of warning his fans that not all of the music on the soundtrack album was new, Peter put the equivalent of a Government health warning on the sleeve. The album sold fewer copies than his previous albums but the sales of 150,000 copies world-wide made a respectable total for a film soundtrack. Peter also enjoyed the experience of working in the film world, a hark back to his earlier aspirations and a change from the usual "day job" as he explained…

"Being part of the rock 'n' roll production circus of tour, album, tour, album is no longer interesting for me. I would rather just do things I know I will like, so I do other projects. Music is still my main activity and certainly the most time consuming. I was nurse-maided through the Birdy project by Alan Parker, and producer Alan Marshall. So I would write to picture and they would end up using it somewhere else. This is quite normal I understand. The film was a great experience because it was a good film and also it was good to work with a great director and explore looking at images in front of you and see how they change according to the sounds you put with them. It was a new science to me. The record I like - even without the film. If I am sending stuff to people who don't know my work, Birdy would be the first thing I would send to them because it represents part of what I am trying to do in instrumental terms - something that is neglected because I am a singer and songwriter…"

Another vital component to emerge from this period was Peter's involvement with another producer. In the past, Peter had not always been happy with the production on his records, but in Daniel Lanois, he had found the perfect foil to his own maverick creativity. Lanois' production credits included Martha & The Mufifns, and he had also co-produced U2's *"Unforgettable Fire"* album with Brian Eno another hero of Gabriel's who had worked with him on Genesis' *"The Lamb Lies Down On Broadway"* . As usual, Peter's slowly, slowly work ethic meant that the album was a very long time in the making, One deadline; 31st July 1985 passed and so did another on 14th December 1985. Lanois was so frustrated that he resorted to what was supposed to be a playful action: he locked Gabriel in a back room in the studio and said he wouldn't release him until some lyrics had been completed!

Finally, the finishing touches to Peter's fifth solo album were in place in January 1986 and on 8th February the executives arrived to hear the album. On Tuesday 11th the pressing of the album started and on 24th April 1986 the first single; *Sledgehammer* was released. It was certainly a departure for Gabriel; upbeat, up mood and rude! If the single was a surprise, then the accompanying video was even more so. Produced by Stephen Johnson; it involved a technique called "Pixellation" which was a method of shooting movement frame by frame to give the illusion of human animation. First used on the Talking Heads' video for their hit *"Road To Nowhere"* it was used to even greater effect on *"Sledgehammer"* . The final cost of the video which took over three weeks to make was to be £120,000 but it was money well spent for the single went into the UK charts at number four and number one in the USA in July, where it ironically knocked Genesis' *"Invisible Touch"* single from the top spot!

Not all of the material from the album was brand new; Milgrams' 37 was a hangover from the third solo album and had been performed as part of the live show even then. Peter even re-worked one track into two and he explained how the two developed on the new album in an interview he gave for Musician Magazine in July 1986….

"Milgrams' 37 has been around since early last year. it's what I should call a 'dark corner' and perhaps it's the only track that rests on texture and atmosphere as its key elements. Most of the others are songs that you could strum along with on a guitar.

I rewrote the verses in Mercy Street, the B Side of the single; Don't Break This Rhythm is the original version of that song. The other one was In Your Eyes which originally had different lyrics too. The current words belonged to another song which didn't make it on to the album. Mercy Street was one of those songs whose rhythms I had recorded in Rio with the Brazilian percussionist Djalma Correia. The rhythm incidentally is called 'forro' which I understand the Brazilians developed at parties which were held many years ago by British and Irish railway workers. They would invite the Brazilians to gatherings 'for all' an dthis became corrupted to 'forro' which came to mean party time at the British and Irish place. When I got back here I began to improvise with the triangle pattern and once the original song was written around it - which as I said was Don't Break This Rhythm - I became dissatisfied with it. I had an idea that I could use an English Folk melody that I had been developing and the new lyrics were based on the work of Anne Sexton, the writer. I had intended to use them for another song. Once I had got the folk melody locked in I then strapped the Mercy Street lyrics on to it..."

Another highlight of the album was the intense duet with Kate Bush on Don't Give Up; a deeply moving song which can be interpreted either on an individual or wider level as Peter explained in the same interview…

"I started off on that song singing both parts myself, but I thought it could work better with a man and a woman singing, so I changed the lyrics around. At one point I tried to work it up in a Gospel/Country style and there are still echoes of that approach in Richard Tee's piano playing.
It was a conscious decision. I was trying to put a personal slant against another backdrop. In Don't Give Up the lyrics were inspired by two things: one was a TV programme on how unemployment has affected family life and the other was a photograph taken by Dorothea Lange during the Dust Bowl Depression. The basic idea is that handling failure is one of the hardest things we have to learn to do..."

Peter also took time to refute some of the complaints about the growing length of time between his albums….

"It's strange - someone can write a book in seven days or seven years and no one grumbles. But when you are making records, people complain and ask what you were doing if you are not part of the album/tour circuit. This album was begun in February 1985 and we had the mixes done by the following Christmas, so it wasn't much more than twelve months until it was finished, although there was some writing done before that. It's slow compared with most people but it is all done here (Real World), so I am not paying vast sums for studio time. My advances from royalties go towards the studio equipment and it gives me the opportunity to experiment and make the record the way I choose. It also means that if I want to do other non-commercial projects, it's not prohibitively expensive...."

The album topped the charts on both sides of the Atlantic going straight to number one slot on its release in the UK on 19th May 1986. By the summer of 1987 it had sold over FIVE MILLION copies world-wide, going double platinum in the USA with sales of over two million and double platinum in the UK with sales of over 600, 000. The album was a re-affirmation of what Gabriel's fans had known for years - here was an artist who was able to lay bare the very soul of his subjects although not all his fans were pleased in fact many maintained that the album's title; *"So"* actually stood for *"Sell out"* they couldn't handle their hero actually having a (shock horror) commercial success on his hands! As usual, the critical reaction to the album was mixed dividing between the enthusiastic and openly hostile…. *"Brilliant"* said *The Guardian* *"Universal message that hope springs eternal"* ran *The Times* *"The music which Peter Gabriel makes is terrifically uninteresting. It says nothing, being merely an ordering of sounds mostly artificial.."* said John MCKenna of Eire's *Hot Press*.

Having contributed an anthem to the growing movement for human rights in the form of *Biko* it was only a matter of time before he became involved in that movement and so, to the probable despair of his record company he interrupted his promotional tour of Europe for the new album to take part in the *"A Conspiracy Of Hope"* tour of the USA in the summer of 1986 to help raise membership of Amnesty International. Peter was in good company as the Amnesty rock & roll circus also included such alumni as The Police, Lou Reed, Bryan Adams and U2. The shows were a huge success and led to an additional 100,000 new members for Amnesty in the USA. Peter was not the headline artist at these shows but there is no doubt that he stole the show with the existing footage from a couple of them showing Peter and his band turn in stunning performances of a mixture of both old and new material.

Peter's tour for the new album proper began in November but not before Peter had put in one more special performance outside the United Nations Building in New York on 16th September 1986 where he was joined by Shankar, Little Stephen and Youssou N'Dour whose plaintive vocals were such a high point on the new record. From the first show of the tour in Rochester NY on 7th November, the new look Gabriel took audiences on a trip filled with drama and humour with a new look stage show which was astonishing in its simplicity. Gabriel had ditched the facial makeup from the previous tour and instead a series of moveable lighting gantries were used which attacked Gabriel mantis-like at several points during the show. Peter interrupted his tour schedule again in December to fit in two gigs at Tokio's Jingu Stadium in aid of the University for Peace with appearances again by Little Stephen, Youssou N'Dour and Nona Hendryx who had previously been Peter's support act on his first solo tour back in 1977.

The tour continued well into 1987 with growing plaudits from fans and critics alike and to prove that the success of *Sledgehammer* had not been a mere fluke, the third single; *Big Time* released from the album in March 1987 proved to be made of equally stern stuff but was a totally different song quirky and with wryly humorous lyrics accompanied by another brilliant video where the lyrics were quite literally translated visually with Gabriel appearing in a loud evening jacket and tie with his big head being superimposed on a small body! The tour continued across Europe and the UK finally ending in Athens in October with the shows captured for a long overdue live video *"PoV"* which was released over a year later. Peter also contributed a live version of *Biko* to Richard Attenborough's film *"Cry Freedom"* which was the life story of Biko himself and which won several Oscar nominations.

The success of the tour and the financial security which it brought meant that Peter was finally able to invest in his own recording studio: Real World which has the dual purpose of enabling Peter to record in his own time but also to give other artists facilities which they might never otherwise have and which has since led to the creation of the Real World record label which has dealt with Peter's recorded output since 1989. During the hiatus after the end of the *"So"* tour Peter was able to return to writing for another soundtrack one which was to cause considerable controversy. Peter had been approached by Martin Scorsese to write music for his film *The Last Temptation Of Christ* which gave Peter a chance to explore a whole gamut of musical ideas and soundscapes and the resulting soundtrack titled *Passion* was to be his new record label's first release in 1989.

Peter did not long remain a stranger to the concert stage however, he became involved in the 1988 Prince's Trust Gala and performed two shows for them in June 1988 at which Peter performed *Sledgehammer* accompanied by Phil Collins amongst others. The second benefit concert was far more in keeping with Peter's ethnic involvements being the 70th birthday celebrations for the imprisoned South African; Nelson Mandela which was held at Wembley Stadium where Peter appeared with Sly and Robbie's posse to sing *Set them free* and then later to perform *Biko* in his own right backed by Simple Minds along with versions of *Sun City* and *Free Nelson Mandela*. This was Peter's first ever appearance at the stadium and many people were surprised to see him back there a mere three months later as part of the *"Human Rights Now!"* entourage. In order to prepare for this, Peter and his band had spent a week rehearsing and surprised everyone by appearing unannounced at the WOMAD festival (now an established part of the UK rock circuit) in August.

Peter's involvement with the *"Human Rights Now!"* tour was a concomitant effect of the success of the 1986 *"A Conspiracy of Hope"* tour of the USA and was a nineteen date tour taking in every continent apart from Australia. Accompanying Peter on the tour were Bruce Springsteen, Sting, Youssou N'Dour and Tracy Chapman along with other guests who appeared along the way at various concerts. Once again, Peter was not the headliner that honour being shared by Springsteen and Sting however, Peter's energy and genuine commitment to the cause of Human Rights gave his performances a special edge and it was wholly appropriate that he should be involved in this landmark tour commemorating as it did the 40th anniversary of the signing of the United Nations Declaration of Human Rights.

The tour ended in October in Buenos Aires and Peter's travels then took him in early 1989 to Moscow to promote the Greenpeace movement's *"Breakthrough"* album and the year also saw the release of the *Passion* soundtrack which is undoubtedly one of Peter's most dramatic and moving works. He also found time to help out fellow Real World artist and friend Youssou N'Dour with his album and to appear on the *Shaking the tree* single and video. Peter also joined in 1990 in the celebrations at Wembley Stadium following the release of Nelson Mandela from prison and also took part in a special concert from Chile *"Embrazo de Esperanza"* where he duetted with Sinead O'Connor. 1990 also saw the delayed release of the *"PoV"* video which gained good reviews as well as a compilation album of some of Peter's greatest "hits" not the most appropriate title but it did give fans some interesting alternative versions of some of his classic songs.

1991 was spent mainly in the studio trying to nail down ideas for the long overdue new studio album although Peter did manage to fit in a trip to Dakar to play a short set in honour of Nelson Mandela's visit there and also to appear at the *"Simple Truth"* concert being held in aid of Kurdish refugees. Peter also organised the first Real World recording week involving artists from all over the world ending with a gala concert at the studios and the event was captured for posterity by BBC TV cameras.

September 1992 saw the release of Peter's long awaited follow up to 1986's *"So"* and the album *"Us"* was in marked contrast to its predecessor's up beat mood, a rather introspective affair, influenced no doubt by Peter's marriage break up. It was nevertheless a powerful album and contained some of his strongest work courting controversy again with the video for the first single; *Digging in the dirt* which was banned by the BBC for its overtly violent nature. Exposing his own personal demons through the music; Us was Peter's most personal work to date...

"Digging In The Dirt is about digging up demons which are powerful when underground but lose their power when exposed to daylight. At one point I had planned to do an album project on Death Row, on capital punishment and I started reading about convicted murderers, what made them tick. I started thinking maybe I was interested in all this stuff because I had something murderous inside me.."

The album failed to reach the number one spot but did well enough both here and abroad and fans were soon to be regaled by Peter's lengthiest and most inventive tour when he embarked upon the mammoth *"Secret World"* tour in April 1993. Beginning with a series of warm up shows at the Grand Slam Club in the USA.

For the new tour Peter had enlisted the help of set designer Robert LePage and he designed the new look stage based round the "Male" and "Female" or "Yin" and "Yang" signs. Also featuring a telephone box and a tree, the stage set was without doubt one of the most visually stimulating and with Peter's band now including both Shankar and female singer Joy Askew the tour delighted fans world wide during the year or so of its duration including numerous WOMAD shows in the US and elsewhere and a guest appearance at the "Woodstock" anniversary in August 1994. Peter's involvement with technology also led to the release in late 1994 of his first interactive CD ROM called *"Xplora 1"* as well as a couple of additional music video compilations and a second live album and video from the *"Secret World"* tour .

Since the end of the tour Peter has submerged himself in a variety of projects many of which are still on going. His most recent appearance being for the release of the long overdue *"Genesis Archive 1967-1975"* four cd set which he helped to compile along with his cohorts from Genesis even appearing on a VH1 video special about the early years. December 1998 saw Peter's first live performance in almost four years as part of the Amnesty International celebrations for the fiftieth anniversary of the signing of the Declaration of Human Rights.

Peter's OVO project emerged out of the project he was commissioned to write for the Millennium Dome in London. What eventually emerged as a fifteen minute stage show at the Dome, was converted by Peter into a full-length album project which was released in June of 2000. Embracing a variety of ideas as it does, sadly this album falls between the twin stools of the requirements of being the backing track to the visuals of the stage show, and the expectations of the fans who have now been waiting some EIGHT years for a new studio album from Peter and who may well find this album a little too discursive for their expectations.

Peter's fascination with film work has continued and in recent years he has embraced modern technology creating his own music download site as we as contributing material to a plethora of film soundtracks including another full-scale soundtrack which was released in 2002. Another true story; Rabbit Proof Fence told of the treatment handed out to Aboriginal children in Australia. Using that country's vast open spaces and varied landcsapes, Peter once again created an aural landscape to match the physical one in an impressive work which accompanies but does not overpower its subject. The film eventually gained limited distribution here in the UK and was excellent viewing.

By now, Peter's fans (myself included), had grown a mite impatient for a proper album from Peter. It had been TEN years since US and expectations were high. Rumours had abounded that Peter had had the album ready for release on several occasions and had scrapped it and started again. Some of these tales must surely have been apocryphal but either way, the sense of expectation when eventually the release date of UP was finally announced. Preceded by a single: The Barry Williams Show which was a suitable successor to Sledgehammer in so much that it was up beat and rude… The accompanying video was crammed full of wry observations on the world of TV chat shows and their cynical manipulation of their guests and their audiences and was deemed unsuitable for screening on UK TV not the first time that Peter had fallen foul of our draconian viewing laws!

I admit that when UP finally appeared I did not get into it. This was an album with which I struggled enormously . I could not see why this record had taken so long to produce especially when two of the tracks; I Grieve and Signal To Noise had already appeared in film soundtracks. However, appreciation gradually took over from frustration and it has become apparent that on this record Peter has honed his art to an impossibly high degree. The reworking of those film tracks plus Sky Blue which evolved from the Ovo album contain along with the rest of the album tracks some of Peter's most thought provoking and evocative music. Signal To Noise is every bit as relevant a protest song about the current situation in the Middle East as ever Biko was about Apartheid; Growing Up evokes all the hopes and fears of childhood and each track examines a facet of life from cradle to grave in such an absorbing and detailed way that you cannot help but be drawn into the album and absorbed by it.

Even by Peter's standards, the tour which was to accompany the album was a lavish one. Working again with Robert LePage the stage design included such wonders as Zorb balls in which Peter roamed across the stage; motorised "Zimmer" frames for Games Without Frontiers and an upside down bicycle track round which Peter and Melanie chased each other during Downside Up. The showes were designed to be as visually challenging as the album had been musically. A lengthy US tour occupied the autumn of 2002 before continuing in 2003 accompanied by a lengthy trip around Europe which saw Peter cramming the available arenas with fans eager to see their hero again.

In the autumn of 2003,the HIT album was also released. An unusual compilation and not quite what the title would suggest. This two CD set comprised most of the singles which Peter had had success with in the charts ,along with a selection not only of those tracks which had in some cases, been released as singles but which had achieved little success, such as DIY along with a brand new track: Burn You Up , Burn You Down which was also released as the album's single. Another example of how frustrating Peter Gabriel can be… this track like Don't Break This Rhythm has been in 1986, was relegated to what was essentially a compilation album and yet to these ears it was one of the best tracks he had come up with in recent years! Typical Peter really.

Peter's touring activities continued into the summer of 2004 with a revamped set and further UK and European shows and there are already rumours of another album in the pipeline so once again Gabriel fans should "Expect The Unexpected".

Further information on Peter's career can be found in the following....

"Peter Gabriel - An Authorised Biography" Spencer Bright Sidgwick & Jackson 1988 (updated 1990)

Peter Gabriel UK Solo Discography

7" and 12" Vinyl Singles

A - Side	B - Side	Catalogue Number
Solsbury Hill	Moribund the Burgermeister	CB301 (7" PS) 10.3.77
Modern love	Slowburn	CB302 (7") ?.7.77
DIY	Perspective	CB311 (7" PS) ?.5.78
DIY	Mother of violence/**Teddy Bear**	CB319 (7") ?.9.78
Solsbury Hill (Live)		SFI 381 (7") 4.10.78

(This was a one-sided flexi disc given away to attendees at Peter's Christmas '78 shows in the UK)

A - Side	B - Side	Catalogue Number
Games without frontiers	**The start**/I don't remember	CB354 (7" PS) ?.2.80
No self control	Lead a normal life	CB360 (7" PS) ?.5.80
Biko	**Shosholosa/Jetzt kommt die flut**	CB370 (7" PS) ?.8.80
Biko	**Shosholosa/Jetzt kommt die flut**	CB370-12 (12" PS) ?.8.80
Shock the monkey	**Soft Dog**	Shock 1 (7" PS) 6.9.82
Shock the monkey	**Soft Dog**	Shock 122 (7" PD) 6.9.82
Shock the monkey	**Soft Dog**	Shock 12 (12" PS) 6.9.82
I have the touch	**Across the river**	CB405 (7" PS) ?.12.82
I don't remember (Live)	Solsbury Hill (Live)	GAB1 (7" PS) ?.6.83
I don't remember (Live)	Solsbury Hill (Live)/**Kiss of life (live)**	GAB12 (12" PS) ?.6.83

(This edition appeared with limited edition "white label" copy of Games without frontiers /**Schnapschuss: Family Snapshot**)

A - Side	B - Side	Catalogue Number
Walk through the fire The Race (Larry Carlton)		VS689 (7" PS) ?.5.84
Walk through the fire The Race (Larry Carlton)/I have the touch		VS689-12 (12" PS) ?.5.84
Sledgehammer	**Don't break this rhythm**	PGS1 (7" PS) ?.4.86
Sledgehammer	**Don't break this rhythm/I have the touch ('85 remix)**	PGS112 (12" PS) ?.4.86
Sledgehammer (Dance mix) Don't break this rhythm/Biko (12" Extended version)/I have the touch ('85 remix)		PGS113 (12" PS) ?.5.86

(Limited edition re-issue of single)

A - Side	B - Side	Catalogue Number
Don't give up	**In your eyes (Special mix)**	PGS2 (7" PS) ?.9.86

(Also issued as limited edition with video still poster sleeve)

A - Side	B - Side	Catalogue Number
Don't give up	**In your eyes (Special mix)**/This is the picture	PGS212 (12" PS) ?.9.86
Big time	**Curtains**	PGS3(7" PS) ?.3.87
Big time (Extended version)	Big time (7" version)/**Curtains**	PGS312 (12" PS) ?.3.87
Red rain	**Ga-Ga (I go swimming instrumental)**	PGS4 (7" PS) ?.6.87
Red rain	**Ga-Ga (I go swimming instrumental)**/**Walk through the fire**	PGS412 (12" PS) ?.6.87
Biko (Live)	**No more Apartheid**	PGS6 (7" PS) ?.9.87
Biko (Live)	**No more Apartheid**	PGS612 (12" PS) ?.9.87
Shakin'the tree Old Tucson		VS1167 (7" PS) 22.5.89
Shakin' the tree Old Tucson/Sweeping the leaves		VST1167 (12" PS) 22.5.89
Solsbury Hill	**Shakin' the tree**	VS1322 (7" PS) ?.12.90

Solsbury Hill	**Shakin' the tree/Games without frontiers**		
	(live version)	VST1322 (12" PS)	?.12.90
Digging in the dirt	**Quiet Steam**	PGS7 (7" PS)	7.9.92
Steam	**Games without frontiers (Massive DB Mix)**	PGS8 (7" PS)	4.1.93
Blood of Eden	Mercy Street	PGS9 (7" PS)	22.3.93
Kiss that frog (album edit) Kiss that frog (Mindblender mix edit)		PGS10 (7" PS)	13.9.93
Lovetown	Love to be loved	660480-7 (7" PS)	13.6.95

Titles in **Bold** are non album tracks.
PS denotes single issued in a picture sleeve.

Compact Disc Singles

Solsbury Hill/Moribund the Burgermeister/**Solsbury Hill (Live)**	CDT33 (PS)	?.?.95
Sledgehammer/**Don't break this rhythm/I have the touch ('85 remix)**	CDT4 (PS)	?.4.86
Big time (Extended)/Curtains/No self control/**Across the river/**Big time		
	GAILS3 12 (PS)	?.3.87
Biko(Live)/No more Apartheid/I have the touch ('85 remix)	CDPGS 612 (PS)	?.9.87
Shakin' the tree/Old Tucson/Sweeping the leaves	VSCD1167 (PS)	22.5.89
Solsbury Hill/**Shakin' the tree/Games without frontiers (live)**	VSCDT1322 (PS)	?.12.90
Digging in the dirt/**Digging in the dirt (Instrumental)/Quiet steam/Bashi-Bazouk**		
	PGSDX 7 (PS)	7.2.92

(This edition appeared in a limited edition box with fold out lyric sheet)
Digging in the dirt/**Digging in the dirt (Instrumental)/Quiet Steam/Bashi-Bazouk**

	PGD7 (PS)	14.2.92
Steam/**Games without frontiers (Massive DB Mix)/Steam (Oh, oh let off steam mix)/**		
Games without frontiers (live)	PGSDX8 (PS)	4.1.93

(Limited edition in shaped case the standard edition contained the same tracks with the catalogue number PGSDG8)

Blood of Eden/Mercy Street/**Blood of Eden (Special mix)**	PGSDG9 (PS)	22.3.93
Blood of Eden/Mercy Street/Sledgehammer	PGSDX9 (PS)	29.3.93
Kiss that frog (Edit)/Digging in the dirt (Rich E mix)/Kiss that frog (Mindblender Mix)		
	PGSDG10 (PS)	13.9.93
Kiss that frog (Edit)/Across the river/kiss that frog (Mindblender mix edit)/Shaking		
The tree (Bottrill remix)	PGSDX10 (PS)	20.9.93

(Limited edition with postcard set)

Red rain (Live)/San Jacinto (Live)/Mercy Street (Live)	PGSCD11 (PS)	15.8.94

(Limited edition numbered cd ep from "Secret World Live" album)

Lovetown/Love to be loved/A different drum	660480-2 (PS)	13.6.95
Father, Son/Downside-Up/The Tower that Ate People	PGDJ2000 (PS)	1999

(Promotional CD single for the OVO album)
The Barry Williams Show (Unadulterated radio edit)/The Barry Williams Show (Album version)/My Head Sounds Like That (Remix by Royskopp)/Cloudless (Radio edit)

	PGSCD13 (PS)	?.5.02
More Than This (Radio Edit)/More Than This (The Polyphonic Spree Mix)/More Than This (Elbow Mix)		
	PGSCD 14 (PS)	?.?.02

More Than This (Full album version)/Sky Blue (Martyn Bennett Remix)/The Barry Williams Show (Video)/Peter Gabriel Photo Gallery

	PGSDVD14 (PS)	?.?.03
Burn You Up Burn You Down(Radio Edit)/Darkness(Engelspost Remix)	GABRIEL 003 (PS)	?.9.03

Vinyl and Compact Disc albums

Peter Gabriel	Charisma CDS4006/PGCD1 (CD)	28.2.77
Peter Gabriel	Virgin PGCDR1 (Re-mastered CD	
Peter Gabriel	Charisma CDS4013/PGCD2 (CD)	3.6.78
Peter Gabriel	Virgin PGCDR2 (Re-mastered CD)	
Peter Gabriel	Charisma CDS4019/PGCD3 (CD)	10.5.80
Peter Gabriel	Virgin PGCDR3 (Re-mastered CD)	
Peter Gabriel	Charisma PG4/PGCD4(CD) 10.9.82	
Peter Gabriel	Virgin PGCDR4 (Re-mastered CD)	
Peter Gabriel Plays Live	Charisma PGDL1/ CDPGD100 (CD)	9.6.83
Peter Gabriel Plays Live Highlights	Virgin PDDLCDR1 (Re-mastered CD)	
Birdy (Film soundtrack)	Charisma CAS1167/CASCD1167 (CD)	18.3.85

Birdy (Film soundtrack)	Virgin CASCDR1167 (Re-mastered CD)	
So	Virgin PG5/PGCD5 (CD)	19.5.86
So	Virgin PGCDR5 (Re-mastered CD)	
Passion (Film soundtrack)	Real World RWLP1RWCD1 (CD)	5.6.89
Passion (Film soundtrack)	Real World RWCDR1 (Re-mastered CD)	
Shaking The tree (Twelve Golden Greats)	Virgin PGTV6 (Vinyl)	15.11.90
Shaking The tree (Sixteen Golden Greats)	Virgin PGTVD6 (Compact Disc)	15.11.90
Shaking The Tree (Sixteen Golden Greats)	Virgin PGTVDR6 (Re-mastered CD)	
Us	Virgin PG7/PG CD7 (CD)	28.9.92
Us	Virgin PGCDR7 (Re-mastered CD)	
Secret World Live	Virgin PG8/PGCD8 (CD)	2000
OVO The Millennium Show	Real World PGCD8 (CD)	?.6.00
OVO The Millennium Show	Real World RWPG01/02 (CD)	?.6.00

(Limited edition in slipcase with bonus CD Rom disc and booklet)

The Long Walk Home (Film soundtrack)	Real World PGCD10	2002
UP	Real World PGCD11	23.9.02
Hit	EMI 07243 595237 2 9	15.11.03
Encore Series Collectors Box	EMI ESD - PG03-CB	

(Miniature Collectors' box containing 19 concert recordings from the 2003 Growing Up US tour, miniature tour programme)

Encore Series Collectors' Deluxe Road Case   EMI ESD-PG03-RC
(Miniature Replica Flight Case containing 19 concert recordings from the 2003 Growing Up US tour, limited edition miniature replica flight case, tour programme and autographed postcard)

European Tour 2004 Box   EMI ESD-PG04-CB
(Miniature collectors' box containing 23 concert recordings from the 2004 Still Growing Up European tour, miniature programme)

European Tour 2004 Deluxe Road Case   EMI ESD-PG04-RC
(Miniature replica metal flight case containing 23 concert recordings from the 2004 Still Growing Up European tour, limited edition miniature programme and signed postcard).

There was also a strictly limited edition flight cased set of recordings from the European Festivals shows in 2004 which had the same format as above and contained all twenty of the open air shows which Peter played that year. This was only available to members of the road crew and band.

Soundtracks

Peter's fascination with the world of film and video work has been well known. As a frustrated director, Peter's contribution to film has mainly been restricted to contributing music to films. His soundtrack albums are documented elsewhere, but here is a listing of his contributions to films over the years - the track(s) he has contributed are in ( )

All This And Word War Three 1976 (Strawberry Fields Forever).
Against All Odds 1984 (Walk Through The Fire).
Gremlins 1984 (Out, Out)
Hard To Hold 1984 (I Go Swimming)
Lorca And The Outlaws (San Jacinto)
Project X 1987 (Shock The Monkey)
Say Anything 1989 (In Your Eyes)
The Desert And Her Daughters 1990 (Passion extracts)
Until The End Of The World 1991 (Blood Of Eden)
Philadelphia 1994 (Love Town)
Natural Born Killers 1994 (The Rhythm Of The Heat)
Virtuosity 1995 (Party Man)
Strange Days 1995 (While The Earth Sleeps)
Angel Baby 1995 (We Do What We're Told)
Phenomenon 1996 (I Have The Touch)
Jungle 2 Jungle 1997 (Shaking The Tree)
Phenomenon 1998 (I Have The Touch)
City Of Angels 1998 (I Grieve)
Babe - Pig In The City 1998 (That'll Do)
Tower Of Song 2001 (Seven Zero/Suzanne)

ODEON HAMMERSMITH Tel. 01-748-4081
Manager : Philip Leivers

Jo Chester for Tony Smith &
Hit and Run Music present
PHIL COLLINS
EVENING 5-0 p.m.
Sunday, Nov. 28th, 1982
STALLS
£7·50

BLOCK
22 | F36

NO TICKET EXCHANGED NOR MONEY REFUNDED
This portion to be retained   No re-admission

Phil Collins

VS PRESENTS
By Arrangement with Tony Smith
& Hit and Run Music Limited

the 'No Jacket Required' tour
Phil Collins
and his
Hot Tub Club
Dimanche
17 mars 1985 à 20 h.
Caisse et portes à 19 h.
HALLE DES FETES
BEAULIEU LAUSANNE
30 F.
Impôt compris

001292

Force 4
PANACHE

Canal
Productions
présente avec

La plus belle radio

Phil Collins
and the
Nine Senars Guys!

MERCREDI 18 AVRIL 90 / 20 h
PALAIS OMNISPORTS
DE PARIS-BERCY

160 F

N° 07910

wea

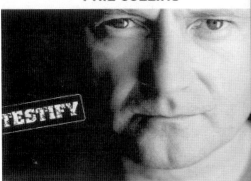

James Moir, Controller Radio 2 is delighted to invite you to a 'live and exclusive' performance by

PHIL COLLINS

GUESTS - STANDING

BBC RADIO **2** 88-91FM

To preview his forthcoming album **Testify**

Wednesday 6 November 2002
The Scala, Pentonville Road, Kings Cross, London N1 9NL
The nearest tube/BR station is Kings Cross

Doors from 7.00pm Show 8.00pm
Doors close at 8pm - admittance is prohibited after this time

Entrance subject to capacity
Please retain this portion of ticket
The BBC reserves the right to refuse admission

COMPLIMENTARY TICKET - NOT FOR SALE OR TRANSFERABLE
www.bbc.co.uk/radio2

FIRST FINAL FAREWELL TOUR EUROPE 2004
PC
Phil Collins
GUEST
668 MAN

EMPIRE LIVERPOOL

EVENING
FOR TIME SEE DAILY PRESS
£2·80
PETER
STALLS GABRIEL
2 3 SEP 1977
058
THIS PORTION TO BE RETAINED

EMPIRE THEATRE
Liverpool

Jo Chester for Gailforce Presents—

Peter Gabriel

Tuesday, 4th March 1980
Evening 7-30

STALLS
£3.50

16

ABC Printers, Manchester

THIS PORTION TO BE RETAINED

P000140
£8.30
(INCS. VAT & 30P BOOKING FEE)
NJF/MARQUEE AND JO CHESTER
PRESENT
IN AID OF THE LINCOLN TRUST

PETER GABRIEL

+ FULL SUPPORTING PROGRAMME
OPEN AIR CONCERT
SAT JULY 9TH 1983
SELHURST PARK
CRYSTAL PALACE F.C.
LONDON S.E.25
SUBJECT TO GLC APPROVAL
DOORS OPEN 2.30 PM
SHOW 4 PM - 10.30 PM
(USE HOLMESDALE ROAD ENTRANCES)

PETER GABRIEL

AREA C   P   51

TIERED SEAT

CHAS COLE FOR CMP & LCC
2004 LIVERPOOL SUMMER POPS
PETER GABRIEL
PLUS SUPPORT
KINGS DOCK - LIVERPOOL
WED 30-JUN-04 GATES 19:00

WAYAHEAD ALLOCATIONS
PRICE 32.50 S/C   TOTAL 32.50

ticketmaster.co.uk   08705 344 4444
W-WAYA 13-20615   TM2585   15-JUN-04 14:43

ticketmaster
ticketmaster.co.uk   08705 344 4444

PAUL KING for OUTLAW presents

STEVE HACKETT
IN CONCERT

21st June Edinburgh Odeon	27th June Hemel Hempstead Pavilion
22nd June Sheffield City Hall	28th June Wolverhampton Civic Hall
23rd June Leicester University	29th June Southampton Gaumont
24th June Liverpool Empire	30th June Hammersmith Odeon
25th June Brighton Dome	1st July Oxford New Theatre

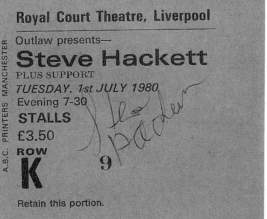

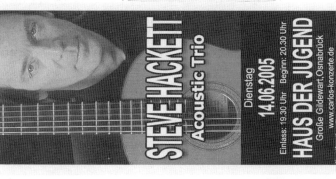

STEVE HACKETT
Acoustic Trio

Dienstag
14.06.2005
Einlass: 19.30 Uhr   Beginn: 20.30 Uhr

HAUS DER JUGEND

Große Gildewart, Osnabrück
www.carlos-konzerte.de

0444

Vvk: 22 € + Geb.
Ak: 26 €

ALICE

Book and lyrics	**Richard Scott**
Music	**Anthony Phillips**
Director	**Nicholas Hytner**
Designer	**Di Seymour**
Choreographer	**Heather Seymour**
Musical Director	**John Owen Edwards**
M D Performance	**Kevin Fitzsimmons**

with
Sally Ann Triplett
as Alice

The world premiere of **Alice**, an exciting new rock musical specially commissioned by Leeds Playhouse from Richard Scott and Anthony Phillips, a founder member of the famous group, *Genesis*.

It is set in a technological world of the future: a world where there is no place for spontaneity, passion or dreams. All human emotions are controlled by the Queen of Hearts, a vast computer.

On coming of age, Alice is computer matched with the mysterious 'Mathmagician' (He's a wizard with numbers). Through him, she encounters the 'forbidden' characters who have taken refuge within the memory banks of the Queen.

Visually stunning, tuneful, original and fun — this is Alice 2001!

Cast: **Sally Ann Triplett** (Alice); **Bruce Payne** (Magician); **Isabelle Lucas** (Duchess); **Peter Alex Newton** (Cat); **Andy Hampton** (Caterpillar); **Michael Skyers** (Robot); **David Easter** (Hacker); **Femi Taylor** (Queen); **Stanley Fleet** (Professor Turtle); **Jane Danielle**; **Lisa Dawn-Hart**; **Lisa Kent**; **Alan Forrester**; **Ray Lewis**; **Rory McDermott**.

Booking Information

Dates
Thursday 22 March - Saturday 14 April

Times
Mon/Tue 8.00pm
Wed - Sat 7.30pm
Matinee: Sat 14 April 3.00pm

Prices
Mon - Thu evenings and Sat matinee:
£3.80, £2.80
Fri and Sat evenings: £4.30, £3.30
Access, Visa, Diners Club, American Express cards welcome.

Concessions
£1.00 off: senior citizens, students, children, disabled and registered unemployed.
Suitable identification required.

Party Bookings
Groups of 10 - 39: 50p off each seat
Groups of 40 and over: £1.00 off each seat
Individual and group concessions not available on Saturday evenings.

LEEDS PLAYHOUSE

Calverley Street
Leeds LS2 3AJ

Box Office (0532) 442111
10.00am - 7.00pm Mon - Sat

Mike & The Mechanics

Hanover Grand
6 Hanover Street
London W1R 9HH

Monday 10th May 1999

Doors 7.30
Show 8.15

COMPETITION WINNER

88-91FM **BBC** RADIO 2

DOWNSTAIRS

ADMISSION: STRICTLY OVER 18s ONLY

SHOW SOUVENIR

THIS BOOK IS DESIGNED FOR YOUR FURTHER ENJOYMENT OF THE SHOW

GENESIS

Lindisfarne
GENESIS
TOUR-AUTUMN '72

OFFICIAL PROGRAMME

RECORD CORNER LTD.

genesis

Official Programme

 OFFICIAL PASS

HALL USHER.

CONCERT GENESIS

DATE 22ND APRIL 1975.

signed Mary Wade

position ASSISTANT TO HALLS MANAGER

genesis crew

74-75 tour

venue _____

date _____

signed _____

N°. 2931

TOEGANGSBEWIJS
voor koncert

GENESIS

DONDERDAGAVOND 10 APRIL 1975 20.00 UUR
MARTINIHAL-CENTRUM - GRONINGEN

PRESENTATIE: MAANDBLAD MUZIEK EXPRES

Produktie: Acket & Mojo

MEDEWERKER

GENESIS

6 e 7 de MARÇO
CASCAIS
pavilhão
dos desportos

DISCOS DISTRIBUIDOS POR phonogram

SATURDAY 2nd OCTOBER 1982

MILTON KEYNES BOWL

NJF MARQUEE on behalf of W.O.M.A.D. present
TONY BANKS : PHIL COLLINS : PETER GABRIEL
MIKE RUTHERFORD : DARYL STUERMER and
CHESTER THOMPSON IN CONCERT
plus SPECIAL GUESTS

BIRMINGHAM INTERNATIONAL ARENA
NATIONAL EXHIBITION CENTRE

JO CHESTER FOR
TONY SMITH AND
HIT & RUN MUSIC
PRESENT
*** G E N E S I S ****
DOORS OPENING 6:00PM
OFFICIAL MERCHANDISE
ON SALE INSIDE ARENA

BLOCK 02

ROW J

SEAT 37

£7.50

MONDAY
20TH SEP
1982
8:00PM
(Including VAT)

EAST
STAND

TO BE RETAINED   (plans & conditions
                          see reverse)

1982
Genesis
Live In Concert

★

V.I.P. GUEST

THE PAUL DAINTY CORPORATION
& EON-FM Presents

011966

MELBOURNE OLYMPIC PARK
No. 1 Ground
Saturday, 13th December, 8.00 p.m.
Please retain ticket.
(Subject to conditions on back of ticket)
WE PLAY RAIN OR SHINE
Please Note: Genesis will perform
the entire Concert.

GENESIS
INVISIBLE TOUCH
TOUR 1986

TONY BANKS ★ PHIL COLLINS ★ MIKE RUTHERFORD

GENESIS

DARYL STUERMER ★ CHESTER THOMPSON

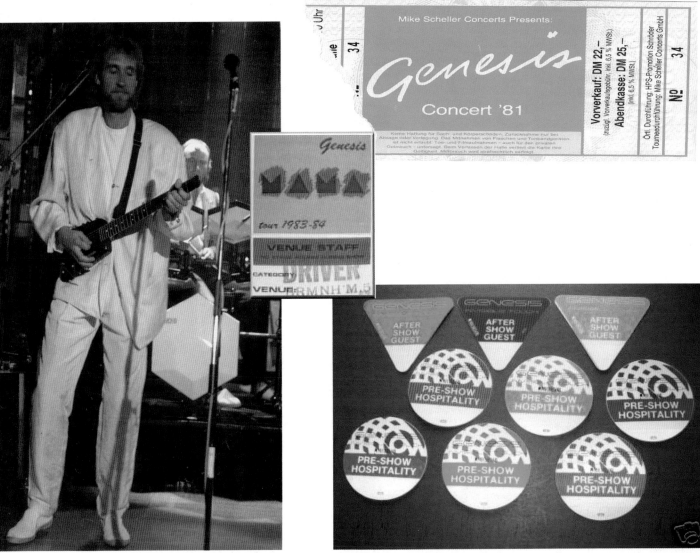

Mike Scheller Concerts Presents:

Genesis

Concert '81

Vorverkauf: DM 22,–
(zuzügl. Vorverkaufsgebühr inkl. 6,5 % MWSt.)
Abendkasse: DM 25,–
(inkl. 6,5 % MWSt.)

No. 34

Örtl. Durchführung: HPS-Promotion Schröder
Tourneedurchführung: Mike Scheller Concerts GmbH

Genesis

tour 1983-84

VENUE STAFF

CATEGORY DRIVER

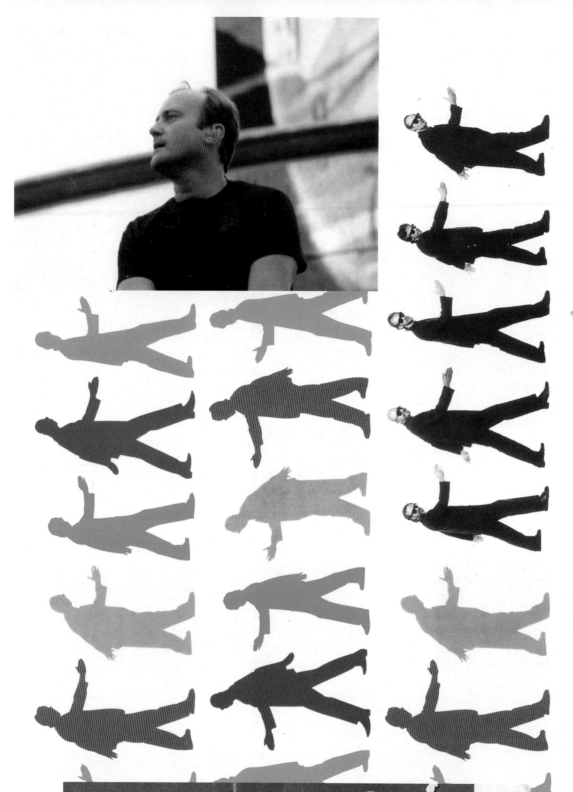

genesis

MANCHESTER EARLS COURT

UK TOUR 1992

SOUTHAMPTON NEWPORT WOLVERHAMPTON NEWCASTLE EDINBURGH

SOLO - ITG by arrangement with
TONY SMITH for HIT & RUN present

genesis

MANCHESTER APOLLO
Friday 30th October 1992
Tickets: £18   Show 8pm prompt - no support
STALLS   ROW E   SEAT 9

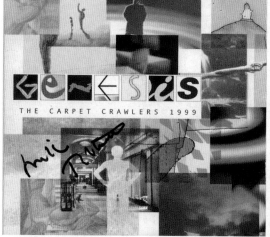

GE-E-IS

THE CARPET CRAWLERS 1999

A PRODUCTION BY ARRANGEMENT WITH TONY SMITH FOR HIT & RUN

GENESIS

...CALLING ALL STATIONS...
...CALLING ALL STATIONS...
...CALLING ALL STATIONS...

CALLING YOUR STATION

Das Beste aus fast 30 Jahren Genesis!
Denn Ihr bestimmt, was Genesis spielt!
Gewinnt ein Treffen mit Genesis

- MI. 04.2.'98 *MANNHEIM* MAIMARKTHALLE
- DO. 05.2.'98 *LEIPZIG* MESSEHALLE 7
- DI. 10.2.'98 *DORTMUND* WESTFALENHALLE 1
- DO. 12.2.'98 *STUTTGART* SCHLEYERHALLE
- FR. 27.3.'98 *MÜNCHEN* OLYMPIAHALLE
- SA. 28.3.'98 *ERFURT* MESSEHALLE
- MO.30.3.'98 *HAMBURG* SPORTHALLE

Kreuze hier die Stadt an, in der Du Genesis treffen möchtest.
Tickets an den bekannten VVK-Stellen. Bundesweiter Ticketservice: 0521-65070
Tickets im Internet: www.ticketworld.de

VH-1

Genesis Archive #2
1976-1992

ALAN HEWITT

Tony Banks   Phil Collins   Mike Rutherford

TURN IT ON AGAIN - the tour

PRESS CONFERENCE

TUESDAY 07/11/06
11:30am arrive / 12:00 conference

MAYFAIR HOTEL
Stratton Street
London, W1A 2AW
(entrance in Berkeley Street)

Appendix D: "The Acolyte's Voyage on the Transylvanian Express" Steve Hackett: A solo portrait.

Steve Hackett 's career as a solo artist has been an on-going love affair with the world of music. Over the last twenty five or so years, he has constantly managed to amaze both his fans and his critics with the breadth and depth of the music he has written.

Steve's career began before he joined Genesis with session stints in bands such as Canterbury Glass and Steel Pier and Sarabande to name but a few. His first foray into the world of recording came when he joined the band Quiet World in 1970. In a recent interview with The Waiting Room Magazine, Steve remembered the circumstances in which their album came to be recorded…

"It was three South African brothers: the Heathers who wrote the stuff, and their father was a medium and they had lived in England and then moved back to South Africa only to return to England later. Their father stayed behind in Africa and he used to send them tapes of various characters speaking through him and it was very strange as we used to sit down and listen to these tapes and one of theses characters was called: Koothume; who claimed to be the ' Spirit of Music' and funnily enough, he described music as… It depends on whether you like that album. I think of it more as a product of its time, rather than a great album but… he described the way in which music could be written and he described it in very visual terms. He said what was going to happen; there was going to be a kind of hybrid and modern music would include the sounds of the street. I still use that as an influence; some of the things he said…."

The album, titled: The Road was released in 1970 by Dawn records and has more recently still, been re-issued on compact disc by Tashiko records in Japan. It is certainly an interesting period piece although there is little indication of the musical direction which Steve was later to take to be found on it.

Steve's first proper solo effort actually appeared while he was still a member of Genesis and was released in 1975 whilst the band were still very much in the hiatus created by the recent departure of their charismatic front man: Peter Gabriel. The album was called Voyage Of The Acolyte and it was to give vital reassurance to the band that interest was still high in the band and their music when it achieved a silver disc in the album charts upon its release. Steve remembers the album fondly…

"Casting my mind back, I think it was during 1974 that there was a slight lull after touring… Anyway, at one point I had the Mellotron at home and I seemed to spend hours doodling on it. One or two ideas got put together because began to think without the restriction of the band and I wondered what I could come up with? I came up with one or two things that I was convinced that they would hate and that seemed to goad me even further on in that direction and try things that I felt they would avoid…"

The album would eventually feature both Mike Rutherford and Phil Collins and it was an extremely enjoyable outing for the fans, with an amazingly wide variety of music on it. Several tracks were destined to become favourites in Steve's live set including the maniacal; "A Tower Struck Down" and the lyrically gorgeous "Shadow of the Hierophant" Certainly there was much on this album that Genesis fans were used to; mysterious lyrics; lush instrumentation and it also gave Genesis fans the first real indications of what Phil's voice was capable of in the lead vocalists' role.

Musically however, the album was far more adventurous than might have been expected. Ace Of Wands and A Tower Struck Down demonstrated Steve's interest in and willingness to experiment with new sounds and instrumentation taking some of the experimentation from The Lamb…. project and putting his own stamp on the music. The album emerged out of the tremendous gaps in the amount of work Steve would be required to give within the Genesis framework as he explained…

"A lot of the time my services weren't really called for and I found that I had a lot of spare time. I started writing but not for any specific project just a few melody lines and for some reason managed to assimilate a lot of material and very quickly had a lot more than I could use.

Then I had six or seven months of solid touring and to keep myself sane in a very mechanical existence, I would write back at the hotel each night. And that way I progressed and kept sane because I get very nervous on stage. There was a time when I played a bum note on stage and I would think it was so bad that I'd committed such a heinous crime and sin that I couldn't really continue. I'd play a lot of muddy notes and it would be awful. Now I can divorce myself from everything and if I do play a wrong one, well the rest have got to be right.

After I had been writing various ideas it was time to get production ideas for an album and at the same time I was starting to get interested in Tarot cards ….."

Other tracks demonstrated the other, more melody dominated side of Steve. Hands Of The Priestess and The Hermit combined the well crafted lyrics with the talents of the musicians on the album to produce an almost orchestral end result which was to serve pretty much as the blueprint for the albums which Steve has released since. Steve's reasoning behind not putting out an album of guitar flash fretwork were also explained at the time….

"When I went in to do this album I wasn't trying to prove anything as a guitarist. I didn't want to and I don't think there is any amazing guitar work on it. I just feel better about having put something down that I would like to listen to rather than listen on one level - for technique. I have always thought in terms of other instruments you see, I'm very happy if the guitar can sound like something else in fact!"

Something that he is still proud of to this day!

Steve's commitments to Genesis' live and recording schedules meant however, that he was unable to tour with this album , and it was to be a further three years before the Steve Hackett road show would wend its way to a venue near you.

Steve's decision to leave Genesis after the conclusion of their highly successful "Wind & Wuthering" world tour in July 1977 was a very brave but necessary step if Steve was to be able to develop his own musical identity without the constraints of committee music writing which was very much Genesis' modus operandi. Although quoted with some venom at the time of the split; Steve is anxious to correct the misinterpretations that have been given to his position at this time…

"I did an interview in the States and I didn't realise that they were going to sell it to a British newspaper but I was particularly fiery that day and it came out sounding as if I hated their guts which is far from the truth. I had a lot of good times with the band and I consider that to be my formative period really…"

For the record, here are the offending comments from Circus Magazine …..

"I know that Pete left the band because of Tony, and I'd say that I did too. Genesis will probably end up as only Tony Banks. But Peter's just as bad. He's a little rat. I was very pissed off at the way The Lamb Lies Down On Broadway was going. I told Pete so and he said; 'I don't give a fuck' ".

Strong words indeed, but honest ones I think. Sadly, though, such comments were destined to sour relations with his former band mates for many years to come.

Steve was now free to concentrate on developing his own musical identity and the first fruits of this search for a musical "soul" if you like, came about with the album "Please Don't Touch" . This was a heavily guested project including appearances by Woodstock veteran: Richie Havens and the first appearance in the UK by Soul singer Randy Crawford who lent her delightful vocals to the track "Hoping Love Will Last" . A lot of the material for the album was written while Steve was still in Genesis…

"During that period I kept coming up with ideas and none of them, or less and less of them I should say, seemed to fit the band… I knew with a song like 'Hoping Love will last' there was no way that the band were in a position to do that. Obviously it was for a female singer, and with the greatest respect to Phil, I couldn't imagine him singing that…"

Once again, the album spawned several pieces that were to remain in the live set until very recently and it was amazing to hear the introduction to "Please Don't Touch" as a set opener as Steve finally commenced touring live for the first time with a set drawn from this album; its predecessor, and the as yet unrecorded third album. Steve's first solo gig was at the Chateau Neuf in Oslo Norway on 4th October 1978 and his first UK show took place at Cardiff University on 23rd October. Both the shows and the new album were favourably received by the fans and critics alike, and as Steve himself remembers…

"Yes, it was a marvellous thrill and Spectral Mornings was done off the back of that , so everyone was on a high really"

For touring purposes it was impossible to use the musicians who had appeared on the album itself and so Steve assembled his own band including several players who were to become firm favourites with the fans over the next few years including Pete Hicks on vocals; John Shearer on drums and, of course, Steve's brother John on flute and bass pedals. Together they formed an impressive array of talents on stage and the build up was now under way for what many fans still credit as being Steve's finest musical moment. After the success of the "Please Don't Touch" tour, Steve was soon back in the studio recording the tracks, some of which had already been aired live and arranged during that tour.

Musically, Please Don't Touch reinforced Steve's status as one of Britain's most adventurous musicians. Opening with the twin tributes to CS Lewis' Narnia stories and an irreverent and delightfully tongue-in-cheek acknowledgement of Agatha Christie's murder mysteries in Carry On Up The Vicarage here was a musician who was no interloper from outer space or some manic axe man determined to beat himself to death with the fastest riffs in history.

Hoping Love Will Last also displayed Steve's ear for Jazz and Soul and his choice of Randy Crawford was inspired and helped launch her career in the UK. Richie Havens a long time hero of the various members of Genesis also added his unique vocals to two tracks and Steve was not afraid to ladder his tights with a couple of rip-roaring instrumentals giving full vent to his talents.

Steve took the band to Hilversum Studios in Holland to record the follow-up album that became the yardstick by which all of his other efforts have since been measured, and that studio is still a place that Steve has fond memories of…

"Spectral was recorded at the beginning of '79. It was VERY , very cold: sixteen degrees below zero and very little sleep! I used to come in at 3 AM and the maids used to start making the rooms…I swear they used to start at four! It was a very big studio and the whole experience was absolutely wonderful.."

The album was a massive success both at home and across Europe where it was ecstatically received by the fans who packed out the theatres on Steve's first full length tour of the UK and Europe including a headline spot at one of the three days of the Reading Festival in August 1979.

The album had everything: lyrical ballads such as "The Virgin & The Gypsy" a delightful play on flower names which evokes so much more. Steve's masterful use and creation of aural moods and atmospheres was given free range on this album. The Red Flower Of Taichi Blooms Everywhere was another wonderfully evocative track and Clocks - The Angel Of Mons evoked that "Spectral" morning in 1916 when the famous apparition was seen by so many. There was even an anti drug song in the shape of "Everyday" … Cleopatra's "needle" being a clear reference to Heroin.

Steve also included another of those anarchic, left-of-centre pieces which had begun with "Carry On Up The Vicarage" on the previous album. This time it was found in the bizarre "Ballad Of The Decomposing Man" which many interpreted, quite wrongly as it happens, to be an anti Union song influenced by current event s in the UK. Steve, however, tells it quite differently…

"It was really a straight George Formby parody; probably a very bad impression of George Formby, but nonetheless it was meant to be humorous…"

That sense of humour was self evident during the stage show with the antics of the members of his band and the sheer talent of those players which certainly captivated this viewer at several shows on the tour. The set also included a couple of unreleased tracks in the shape of the dramatic "The Steppes" and the camp humour of "Hercules Unchained" the former went on to appear on Steve's next album and has retained its position as a highlight of Steve's live set while the latter was issued as a single b-side.

Once again, Steve's fans didn't have to wait too long for his next album. "Defector" was released a little under a year after "Spectral Mornings" and it seems that he was taking the words of the spirit Kitumbi from his Quiet World days quite literally; in trying to explain in music the idea that the defector from the Eastern Bloc who is the album's central character, arrives in the West and is amazed to find that everyone dreams in colour. The idea is a very striking one and Steve explained part of the rationale behind it…

Yes, in fact, we found that when we toured later and went to Estonia in what was then the Soviet Union , there was a limitation of colours. There were two colours that the buildings were painted, and the rest was concrete. I found that the insides of churches were the only places where there was any imagination and colour…"

The contrast between the Spartan existence of the Eastern Bloc and the decadence of the West was clearly defined in track such as The Steppes, an eerily windswept evocation of the landscape of Russia which jarred against the wry humour and luxuriant instrumentation of Jacuzzi. The Show could almost be read as an anthem for the youth of the East AND West united in their common language: music.

Musically the album was far heavier from Steve's previous efforts and Steve admitted the change in an interview with Hugh Fielder for "Sounds" in July 1980…

"I've felt more involved in every aspect of this tour than I've ever done... the music, the organisation and the audience. I want to get closer to them and to be more expansive. With Genesis it wasn't done to come offstage and cry 'Oh yeah' or anything like that. It was always more analytical. Perhaps it's that I'm reacting against now. I've moved to the centre of the stage now both mentally and physically..."

The change certainly showed in the stage presentation for which Steve dressed in anonymous black jeans and T-shirt finally discarded the gypsy player look which had become his trademark in Genesis. The album itself drew favourable reviews and contained the mix of music which always makes Steve's albums a pleasure to listen to including yet another masterpiece of eccentricity: "Sentimental Institution" for which Steve utilised a device which he had discovered in Holland during the "Spectral Mornings" sessions...

"I found this machine which was designed for lounge use in Holland at a place called Relight Studios which is where we did Wind & Wuthering. It was an amazing machine... on one side of the keyboard it would give you pre-recorded riffs with discs that you used in order to achieve them... I used it on Defector on Sentimental Institution doing the 'Big Band' sound which was produced to sound like an old 78 record. In fact it's one of my favourites because it is a send up of something traditional and you have to listen closely to it to realise that the lyrics are a total send up..."

The tour also saw Steve's first solo visit to the USA and his show drew upon all of his albums as well as a playful rendition of the operatic standard "Oh Sole Mio" which, apparently was not to well received in Turin where it was booed by several members of the audience!

Steve's next musical outing was to signal "All Change!" with a completely revamped band and musical style. The "Cured" album which appeared in 1981 has to be the one which has divided Steve's fans the most marking as it does Steve's first outright flirtation with the world of "Commercial" records a subject decidedly anathema to Steve's fans at this time most of whom had grown used to the more melodic side of his music and to his regular touring band, many of whom were almost regarded as members of the family by the fans and almost all of whom were conspicuous by their absence on this record. Steve stripped things down to basics and was accompanied on it solely by his brother and keyboard player Nick Magnus who also co-wrote a couple of tracks . The result was a more commercial sounding album although Steve is quick to explain his reasons behind such a career change...

"Well, at the time I was learning to sing and trying to develop a musical personality which at times ran contrary to my musical leanings.. it wasn't a conscious decision to start writing commercial songs...I think it was an album of finding my way..."

It was also a time to experiment with the latest technology and Steve was fortunate indeed to have the help of Nick Magnus, someone who was extremely "au fait" with this stuff and who was keen to try it out although it wasn't always easy as Steve explained....

"Well, with a real drummer you never do it all in one go. You may have to play a song several times with a drummer and say; 'This take is better than that one'. With the Linn drum computer, it's a case of spending the time to programme it and then let it run. The rhythm is very metronomic obviously, but people think that these drum machines are perfectly in time. They aren't. I had two separate units that I tried to hook up with each other at one point and I found that they didn't stay in time - they went out of sync. So, even drum machines play out of time. It's not just the drummer boys (laughs). Doing the album as a partnership with Nick, I found out that he was an extremely fine drummer - or at least an extremely fine writer of drum parts. He's very deft when it comes to playing the machine.

Very often we started with a drum track and then a keyboard track so that the song would have some sort of size. I found it very difficult to invent bass parts with just the drummer and nothing else because I had never really played bass before. So we put down keyboards or perhaps guitar - rather like an artist might do a sketch.... I'm nit sure that I would like to make every album like this in the future, but it's a way of working and it works very well. It's a very precise way of recording. It allows you to sidestep a lot of problems: the drummer's got to go home for dinner; or he's so tired that he just can't play the part anymore; or the first take was bit rough, but it's the one with the best feel, so we'll take it. It eliminates all that kind of stuff...."

Whatever the reasons, "Cured" was to be a turning point in Steve's career. The album surprised fans in many ways. The stripped down sound had its echo elsewhere. Genesis had taken their fans by surprise with Abacab and it could almost be seen as if there was a certain degree of synchronicity between Steve and his old band mates. Cured still contained the Progressive Rock element of Steve's music in numbers such as The Air-Conditioned Nightmare which is still a live favourite in Steve's set to this day. Picture Postcard and Hope I Don't Wake introduced a healthy dose of "Pop" into the proceedings although it took many fans (myself included) a while to get used to it! The biggest surprise really was Steve stepping centre stage and "wiggling his bum" as the singer! This took some getting used to. Steve's pipes were not the greatest at this time but the experiment worked in the live context as the tour in support of the album later that year showed.

The reasons for not employing the talents of his existing band were many, but sadly; the main one was financial although the band themselves also wanted a greater creative input in the music…

"On the second album I wrote the occasional track with the band and they wanted to have more and more of a creative input and they wanted to write songs. So there was a resistance to some of the ideas that they had on one level…On the other level it was impossible to maintain weekly wages…"

Steve again took to the road in order to promote the album with his largest European tour to date including several shows in the Eastern Bloc where, as Steve was quick to point out in an interview with Rick Wakeman on the *'Gastank'* series a year or so later; he was actually a bigger draw than his peers in Genesis. The tour also saw Steve incorporate into his live set up, two players who were later to feature heavily in other bands: Chas Cronk who played bass for Steve and later also played for Rick Wakeman before forming *Cry No More* and Ian Mosley who took over John Shearer's drum stool with Steve before going on to find more success with current stable mates: Marillion.

1982 was a relatively quiet year for Steve, apart from writing material for his next album; he also took time to become involved in a couple of charitable projects including the organisation of a special concert for the *"Poland Aid"* charity and another in aid of the Tadworth Children's hospital at which show he was joined on stage by his old cohorts from Genesis: Mike Rutherford and Peter Gabriel. Saturday 2nd October 1982 also saw the event that Genesis fans had dreamt of since Peter's departure in 1975 and of course, Steve's in 1977: a reunion of what most fans consider to be the band's Classic line-up for a benefit concert to help bail out Peter Gabriel's cash-starved WOMAD project. A nice gesture from the current band toward their ex-front man and one which was greatly appreciated by the sixty or so thousand wet and cold fans (yours truly included) who witnessed the event!

Early in 1983 the first indication of Steve's new direction was given by the appearance of a single from the as yet unreleased album. "Cell 151" was probably one of the most unlikely hits of the year and gave Steve his highest chart placing for a single in the UK. It was backed by a marvellous live version of "The Air- Conditioned Nightmare" . The irony of it all was that at this time, things were not going too well with Steve's record company. Charisma Records were at this time in the throes of a take-over by Virgin Records and Steve was one of the artists caught in the middle…

"A & R were starting to make comments that didn't fit the MD's ideas and so it left me in the middle trying to steer a sensible course…"

Sadly, the end result for Steve was an album: "Highly Strung" which, with the right amount of promotion, could have been extremely successful. However. disagreements were not just over A & R decisions, as Steve points out…

"There were two things that I also disagreed with Charisma at the time. Firstly; so many fans were asking for a live album and I wanted to deliver one but they were firmly against that. I felt it was the right move and I still think it would have been the best thing to do. The other was the idea of an all acoustic album which I started doing in my own spare time and with my own money as it were, which was the album that became Bay of Kings. I started recording that in 1980 but it wasn't released until much later…"

After Cured perhaps people could be forgiven for thinking that Steve was trying to tell them something through the titles of his albums. Was he unwell… mentally or physically? Far from it.. the title is simply another example of Steve's typically dry English humour as indeed perhaps was the hit single Cell151 which ostensibly took as its subject a prisoner's desire to escape from gaol…maybe also a guarded reference to Steve's "escape" from the confines of Genesis? Camino Royale was another tribute to one of Steve's heroes: James Bond.

Highly Strung took Steve still further down the road of self-discovery that he had embarked upon back in 1978 as he admitted in an interview in Sounds in May 1983…

"This is the right album for me at this time. It's more me than before and its more me than anybody else. The album was an all-out effort over a longer period of time. That's because I did each song separately, one at a time. It was a collection of songs rather than trying to do an album and nearly killing myself in the process. I tried to make the album more alive. I went for the jugular. Energy first, subtlety second…."

If further proof was needed that Steve's tongue was firmly in his cheek when he decided upon titles, try Group Therapy for size. Nothing dramatic or sinister… merely a chance for the new "group" to have a healthy instrumental work-out. India Rubber Man was perhaps the most directly biographical track possibly referring to Steve's then current problems with the record company and trying to "stretch" to be all things to all men fans and record company executives alike!

Having failed to resolve the problems with Charisma, and having tried to persuade them of the sense of releasing a live album, Steve sought an independent release for his new acoustic album: "Bay Of Kings" which was released in October 1983 on the Lamborghini Records label, itself a subsidiary of PRT. Yet another new album and another UK tour, this time taking in the smaller clubs and university halls which was very much a "back to basics" approach if you like, but one which definitely suited the more intimate nature of the music itself.

The shows themselves however, didn't pass off unremarked. A show at Ashton under Lyme had to be cancelled due to poor ticket sales and an appalling lack of publicity which led to a previous show being booed when the audience who had been led to believe it was to be an appearance by Steve AND his band were not too appreciative of a solely acoustic show! And what a show they missed! Steve drew not only upon the material on the acoustic album itself but also threw in some older favourites treating them to an acoustic setting.

That small hiccup aside, the tour was a great success and so was the album. It received its finest accolade from the virtuoso violinist Sir Yehudi Menuhin who used a track from it as part of the soundtrack to the television programme about his Music Foundation: *"From Kew To The Findhorn Foundation"* . Steve was also one of only two artists to sell out concerts at London's prestigious Barbican Centre so, obviously not everyone felt the same way as those who booed his show! Steve's own view of the album was simple and honest...

"I viewed it as music without props and that pre-dates New Age and Unplugged, so the derivations from the Classical and Flamenco and Folk and all of those kinds of areas are still there... There's also the influence of the nylon guitar, because with Genesis we had specialised in twelve string extravaganzas, so I felt that nylon was the area I was most interested in because it had the widest range of dynamics in all acoustic areas... I think it was a reaction against dependency... the pyrotechnics of rock; the smoke and lasers; and dancing girls in the wings!"

If Steve's view of "Bay Of Kings" was that it was a reaction against rock and roll excess, his next project took his fans off down a path which few musicians had explored successfully at that time: the area of "World Music". The new album; "Till We Have Faces" was a rhythmically charged exploration of the percussion and samba music of Brazil, where most of it was recorded. It came as a surprise to both Steve's fans and the critics who, in the main, loathed it, although Steve explains it in the following terms...

"I thought of it as a learning experience; being involved with that amount of rhythmic... percussion players who were...I would meet them in the street and they would demonstrate their skills and we would put them in the studio and the situation in Brazil was that I could only get recording studios that started at midnight and these things often conspire and so when I got home at eight in the morning they were doing renovations upstairs and so I did that album on very little sleep! Then I brought it back to England and mixed it and again.. it's an album that falls into two halves. I think of the cohesive song element and the more improvised; the more rhythmic..."

As Steve pointed out in the sleeve notes to the re-issue of the album; it was impossible to take a Samba School on the road and so the album remains the only Steve Hackett album which has never been played in a live context. Steve, however, still thinks he didn't go far enough with the project...

"I think, with hindsight, I would have gone even further with it and made it even more a World Music album, if that's the term; and abandon all Western civilisation whatsoever..."

Always one keen to try and push the envelope, Steve perhaps pushed a little too far with this album. Sure, there are still elements of the Steve Hackett his fans had come to know and love. The wonderfully camp humour of Matilda Smith-Williams Home For The Aged has its precursors in such tracks as Carry On Up The Vicarage and Sentimental Institution, for example. What's My Name is Steve's very own version of Genesis' Dodo/Lurker... a Gnomic Riddle of a track which has still eluded definition!

The album's single: A Doll That's Made In Japan is perhaps the most cohesive track on the album telling the tale of a Japanese prostitute through her own eyes. Myopia is a vivid description of the condition that has afflicted Steve since his childhood although as usual there is a self deprecating twist to the tale. Musically however, the album lacked that essential spark that made Steve's albums to this point special events.

Steve still has material from this period which was not released at the time although I suspect that several pieces may have appeared on projects since, and it is certain that had the project been released now, its reception would have been much better, and that is perhaps another example of how often Steve is ahead of the game as an innovative artist. Steve's outlook on producing work of this type is typical of the attitude which has shaped his entire career...

"I've usually found that the best thing to do is exactly what you wanted and then you've got a much better chance of pleasing the fans but then you've usually got a good chance of upsetting record companies, so it's very difficult to please both the business and the public..."

Steve made his first live appearance for two and a half years at a charity gig staged by Marillion at the Hammersmith Odeon in February 1986, where he joined in on a performance of the early Genesis classic: I Know What I Like . This was in between rumours that had started to abound that Steve had joined an AOR Supergroup with ex-Yes man; Steve Howe. Many fans were naturally sceptical especially after Steve's time in Genesis but; lo, and behold in March 1986 the debut single from the aptly titled GTR arrived in the shape of the track "When The Heart Rules The Mind" and Steve's fans had to sit up and take notice!

Steve's involvement in this project came about via a chance meeting with Brian Lane...

"Brian Lane who was manager of Yes had offices in the same area as where I was living at the time and we bumped into each other, funnily enough years earlier in Los Angeles when I'd done the Please Don't Touch album and he wanted to work with me not in a solo sense but in a group sense, and I didn't really want to work in a group, but we were talking one day and he said: 'Steve Howe's not doing anything at the moment; he's out of Asia' and he became very excited about forming a group with two guitarists, and over lunch one day he mentioned it and Kim was there and she said: 'why don't you do something with two guitarists?' I said I would meet Steve and this very quickly became the idea of forming a group, because we felt that if we just made an album and didn't tour it, we wouldn't give the album the best chance. And the group really grew up to facilitate the liaison between the two of us. Brian's association with Geffen Records was in the ascendant and they became very interested in the band which I had always seen as a project. They were on the boil and then they went off and Arista got involved. It was something that initially was going to take three months to record and ended up taking nine months to record in a top studio and became a big success in the States but was not as well received over here.... I don't think of it as the best record I've ever made and that's putting it diplomatically!"

The creative output between the two guitarists was evident on the first single which had been written on the very first day of recording. It went on to be a huge success in the USA and also achieved a respectable chart position here and in Europe during that remarkable summer of 1986 when Genesis & Co seemed to be sweeping all before them. A follow up single: "The Hunter" was issued in the USA and in several European territories as well but failed to make any impact on the charts. A lengthy tour was also undertaken to promote the album, culminating with sell-out shows at the Hammersmith Odeon.

The concerts themselves were divided into three sections with the two guitarists playing separate solo sets before being joined by the band for the main event, prompting one reviewer to remark: *"Three bands for the price of one"* . The other musicians in the band were well-known if not actually famous; Max Bacon the lead singer had formerly fronted Heavy Metal act: Bronz, Phil Spalding had played bass for Mike Oldfield amongst others and drummer Jonathan Mover had played numerous sessions, so it was a coherent band unit that the fans saw and in the main, the shows were well received.

The GTR line up was destined not to last as long as the production of a second album , however. Personality clashes and recording difficulties ensured that that band went their separate ways by mid 1987. Steve had already started work on a new rock album during the hiatus at the end of the GTR tour. For this album, he enlisted the help of some old friends; Nick Magnus and Ian Mosley who was by this time, firmly ensconced in the Marillion drum seat. Along with these familiar faces, Steve also managed to enlist the musical and vocal talents of Pete Trewavas, Brian May, Bonnie Tyler and Chris Thomson and you would think that with such a combination of talents that record companies would have been fighting each other to acquire the new album, wouldn't you? It is therefore, ironic that it was only in 2000, that this album finally appeared on Steve's own imprint: Camino Records. Some of the material from this album had been recycled elsewhere and some of the tracks have appeared on other re-issues from Steve's back catalogue but it is great to finally have one of the great "Lost" albums of the 1980's available to hear at last.

Almost two years were to elapse before Steve appeared with a new album . Once again he opted for the back to basics approach and released another acoustic album: "Momentum" a further demonstration of Steve's skills with the *"Small Orchestra"* as he calls the acoustic guitar, as well as showing his determination to...

"Just simply go out and play in front of people without any fuss and again to show that I could do it without the props, without the conglomerate; without the big budget all that... and so I started doing acoustic shows again, and again it was different pressures because what is simpler on paper is actually complex when you have to go out and play it yourself. In many ways there are much more pressures because you don't have a band..."

The tour in the UK was another extensive one taking in university halls and several theatres where the show would be well received. Steve also toured Europe and gained further acclaim from the audiences. The album also gained a respectable position in the New Age and Classical charts and also received generous plaudits from the normally hostile British Press.

Concurrent with this album; Steve was also at work on another rock album; in fact it was almost ready for release at the same time as "Momentum". It was to have been another heavily guested project featuring amongst others; Brian May; Chris Thompson; Bonnie Tyler and Marillion's Steve Rothery. However, die to various contractual problems, the project, under its working title of "Feedback" was never released although a few pieces from it have since sneaked out on other albums especially some of the re-issues of Steve's albums on compact disc. Steve himself admits to plundering from this as yet mysterious project…

"I'm plundering ideas from that album which I'm using on some things now… at the time it wasn't possible to release it… it wasn't contractually possible to release it… and although with the production we are capable of now, it doesn't feel contemporary enough and the production we have now on the Guitar Noir album is superior to that…"

The years between 1989 and 1992 were frustratingly quiet as far as the fans were concerned but far from quiet as far as Steve himself was concerned. During this time Steve was occupied with a variety of projects including the building of his own recording studio: Crown Studios as well as the setting up of his own record label : Camino Records, which now covers all of Steve's releases and is a highly respected independent record label in the UK. Once again Steve became involved in a charitable project when he heard about the forced repatriation of the Vietnamese "Boat People" from Hong Kong against their will…

"A lot of artists were involved in making yet another version of 'Sailing' … we were looking for an emblem for the cause, and it seemed perfect for it…"

The single was released as part of the "Rock Against Repatriation" project which was also accompanied by a charity auction of rock star memorabilia . 1992 itself saw the tying up of contractual "loose ends" with Virgin Records who were the inheritors of his catalogue when they took the ailing Charisma Records over in 1982 and the resulting compilation album: "The Unauthorised Biography" contained a selection of Steve's finest moments from his back catalogue as well as two new tracks one of which; "Don't Fall Away From Me" was another hangover from the "Feedback" project and although very much a stop gap measure it was nonetheless a chance to give newer fans a pocket introduction to Steve's work as he himself explained…

"It was a respite…I think that again, Billy (Budis) and I sat down and we decided that we would include tracks which hadn't received as much attention as others. So, instead of doing an album of stage favourites, we decided to include stuff like the Randy Crawford track: 'Hoping love will last'…"

That album was itself followed by the long overdue live album: "Timelapse" which was initially released by the Dutch Crisis record label and subsequently re-issued by Camino Records as part of their re-issue project in 1994. This album drew together two concerts with ten years separating them ; the first was performed in New York in 1981 and the second was a television broadcast in the UK in 1990. As such, it was a clever way of representing the way in which Steve's live sound and style had changed over the years. Live shows themselves became very much a part of Steve's life again later in that year when he embarked on a US tour for "Timelapse" but which also was used as a springboard for material from the new album which he was finishing off at the time. This new record: "Guitar Noir" was finally released in 1993 and was Steve's first rock album for almost ten years and his twelfth studio album to date.

"Guitar Noir" managed to capture Steve's early blues influences as well as combining both acoustic and electric elements in the same track more successfully than ever before…

"I tried to marry the acoustic influences, in other words, the acoustic guitar was incorporated into songs which I hadn't done before…it was either electric or acoustic… now I see all music as terribly similar…I see opposites as similar…"

Guitar Noir also saw Steve finally take that last step essential to his development as an artist. He had flown the nest from Genesis; developed his own musical style and continued to experiment. He had also taken on vocal duties, a brave step but a necessary one. So, what was missing? With Guitar Noir, Steve finally found his "voice" in terms of writing lyrics that not only really suited his voice which had undoubtedly improved over the years, but also in terms of being able; finally to actually express himself lyrically and emotionally.

Guitar Noir was indeed a "dark" album which threw light on the darker corners of life and the human condition from the observation of a prostitute's rationale for her work in There Are Many Sides To The Night to the searingly wonderful instrumental Sierra Quemada. Ever observant; Steve also took an acerbic look at the 9-5 routine in, In The Heart of The City and a wonderfully evocative examination of the commercialisation of Little America. Steve was certainly pulling no punches on this album!

However, it is not all doom and gloom. Steve's sense of humour still had time to shine through on the eccentric A Vampyre With A Healthy Appetite and the gorgeous tribute to Steve's wife Kim: Paint Your Picture as well as the awesome Like An Arrow which is really Steve's celebration of his release from the artistic strictures which had always seemed to bind his hands in some way or another previously... he was, perhaps becoming his own Hercules Unchained?

Steve's touring schedule took in his first comprehensive UK tour for over five years as well as visits to North America again and his first shows in South America as well as a handful of shows in Italy later in the summer into the bargain. The album received a less than complimentary press in some quarters, although the fans at the shows themselves, gave Steve and his new band a rapturous reception. The new stage show drew heavily upon the new material although Steve did have a few "oldies" which he pulled out later as a reward for the fans' patience.

Steve's tour itinerary took him back to Italy in the summer of 1994 for a series of acoustic shows with Julian Colbeck as well as a couple of shows as part of David Palmer's orchestral ensemble playing the orchestral variations on the music of Genesis; Yes; Pink Floyd; Queen and Jethro Tull. 1994 also saw Steve revisit his Blues roots in a BIG way with an album which mixed standards from the Blues repertoire and new tracks written in that vein. This came as a surprise to his fans although exactly why is a mystery because he has never made any secret of his love of the Blues and several of his earliest musical ventures were on the Blues Harmonica and he recalled auditioning for Genesis with parts of his Blues reprertoire...

"when I was auditioning for them I ran through a number of things I was able to do... one of which was the Blues harp... I'd wanted to do something in a Blues style as far back as the Sixties... and after years of doing very carefully crafted albums... meanwhile in my bedroom I would still be practising my blues vibratos, and thinking: 'when can I use this?'..."

"Blues With A Feeling" also included newly written tracks among the Blues standards he covered and Steve's reason for doing this was quite admirable...

"I noticed that Blues could be falling into the same trap as Classical music where a certain amount of writers perform wondrous works and we just repeat them endlessly... In the period of the Sixties Blues revival with bands like Fleetwood Mac doing originals, people didn't seem to mind as much. Maybe the word 'Purist' wasn't bandied about in the same way then, it can be very limiting..."

Certainly that is not an accusation that can be levelled at Steve's music, and the album was a wonderful romp and not at all politically correct!

While out on the 1994 Italian tour, or as he likes to put it: *"The Italian Job"* he got the inspiration for another live album but this one was certainly different. "There Are Many Sides To The Night" was a faithful rendering of the acoustic shows which he and Julian Colbeck in Italy in November and December of 1994. The idea behind the album was as ironic as the title...

"Well, every time I play Italy there's normally a bootleg album (laughter) there's at least one that gets made from the concerts and I don't think the quality of bootleg recordings is that great and so, if you like you can look at this as the 'Official Bootleg'..."

As an introduction to Steve's acoustic material and to give a different slant to several of the established rock tracks this album is hard to beat.

The remainder of 1995 and the early part of 1996 were spent working on a project that certainly surprised Genesis fans on its release. The very idea of Steve recording an album of Genesis "covers" would have seemed ridiculous to most fans at the time. Steve however, sees things quite differently...

"I'm always gonna be remembered for those Genesis albums above all, no matter what I do . There's still that but plainly I feel that certain things have changed over the years: my own experiences; my own techniques; ability to play; techniques have changed so much and I often wondered what those numbers would sound like if they were re-recorded with the technology of now...?"

Having taken that idea on board, Steve set about obtaining the services of a band of musicians many of whom had been associated with Genesis, including Bill Bruford; Chester Thompson; and Paul Carrack to name but three and throughout the project Steve has been very careful not to meddle with anything if it isn't broken...

"I took the philosophy that there was no point in changing everything just for the sake of it; if something was wonderful in the first place I wouldn't do that so to some extent some things have been extended..."

With Steve's previous involvement with David Palmer's orchestral treatment of the Genesis catalogue on the "We Know What We Like" album in the Mid Eighties, Steve certainly has treated the established Genesis repertoire with great respect; love and above all; humour, and this return visit to his heyday with the band is a delight. Steve also took to the road for a handful of shows in Japan where the album was initially released and subsequently issued in the UK on 22nd September 1997 with a different running order to its Japanese counterpart; Steve's own delightful re-working of "Los Endos" . The shows in Japan included both Julian Colbeck by now no stranger to Steve's fans, along with Chester Thompson and John Wetton. Steve himself thoroughly enjoyed himself on the tour, as he explained to "The Waiting Room" Magazine…

"It was a very interesting line-up; chock full of pals. We had ten days' rehearsals which was less than I would have liked…"

The shows from Tokyo on 16th and 17th December 1996 were recorded and subsequently issued as a double live album and initially the show was also broadcast on a "Pay Per View" channel in Japan. Nostalgia was the watchword when fans finally got to see the show and hear it as well when Camino released it under the title of "The Tokyo Tapes" in early 1998. As if that wasn't enough living in the past; the long-running US radio show: The King Biscuit Flower Hour, delved into its archives and treated Steve's fans to an archival disc of their recording of GTR's concert from the Wiltern Theatre Los Angeles in 1986 itself another welcome addition to the collectors' archives.

Late 1997 and early 1998 saw the re-issue of most of Steve's back catalogue on his own label: Camino Records which thankfully allowed fans to complete their collections and to avoid the difficulties which Steve had experienced with these releases on independent labels as his manager; Billy Budis explained…

"With the difficulties we've had with various independent companies we've decided to take control of them ourselves and use them as a launch base for our own record label…"

In the meantime, Steve had another project on the go in the form of an acoustic album accompanied by orchestra and based around Shakespeare's play: "A Midsummer Night's Dream" which was released by the Classics Division of EMI records on 2nd March 1997. This album was yet another surprise for Steve's fans and Steve explained how the album came about in an interview given to The Waiting Room Magazine in August 1997…

"The Midsummer Night's Dream thing came about as a result of a number of acoustic pieces which I'd recorded and had on the back burner thinking this will probably go out on some small independent label; probably our own, at some point. There won't be any interest from any major record labels. And I found out that, on the contrary, EMI were very interested in my musical activities…"

The album incorporated several older pieces within the weave of newer pieces written specifically for the project and the result was one of Steve's most satisfying albums to date and; shock horror; a successful one to boot the album actually reached the TOP of the Classical charts in the UK upon its release!

1999 saw Steve just as busy on a multitude of projects including his "Darktown" album released by Camino Records on 26th of April 1999. A startling album this one certainly challenges Steve's fans to look hard at themselves and the several taboo subject areas as well as serving as the closest thing to a biography in music yet from Steve it certainly lives up to the description given in the Press Release accompanying the album… *"A nightmare theme park of an album from a man truly possessed…"* (34). This one is certainly not for the fainthearted and gives added weight to the assertion by his fans that Steve is among the most challenging and talented of artists still to be working in the field of rock music in the UK.

In fact, Darktown could very easily be viewed as Steve's equivalent to Phil's Face Value album, although fortunately without the pain and aggravation of a divorce! It includes several tracks which exorcise several very personal ghosts from Steve's life. Guitar Noir had seen Steve step into the centre of his work and write in a way and about subjects which would have been unthinkable previously. None more so than Jane Austen's Door which describes in painful detail the circumstances surrounding the gradual decline of Steve's first girlfriend who succumbed to drug addiction. As an intensely private individual; the subject matter of this song does not sit easily when listened to but once again; it all fits into Steve's gradual rehabilitation of his past, as he explained…

"My first girlfriend lived on a housing estate called Churchill gardens in Pimlico and she lived in a house called Jane Austen House … so it was the story of my first girlfriend who, you know like all sort of puppy love if you like; you break up; you go your separate ways and in her case she became involved with drugs and became a schizophrenic and I always had the feeling that there was something more that I could have done to prevent that happening…It was a song that I had tried to write for many years because on one level it is a song about lost love nut on another level it was a song that I did because I had lost contact with her for many years and I wanted to contact her again and say: 'I've written a song about you and here it is..' and I did put it in her hand and it was a rather powerful moment for me…"

Certainly on this album Steve has stepped from behind the "mask" of writing in the third person and has begun to find his emotional and lyrical feet in ways which would have been inconceivable only a few years previously. The trend begin with Guitar Noir was continued here. Darktown itself examined the seedier side of school life and the effects of bullying on both the victims and the perpetrators…

It's all on camera it's all on film
On the couch in the shower
The stains are there still
Drink to the ones who dished
Out the marks
Rabid animals right from the start
It's happy hour shut the
Beasts away
Come along children it's time
To play…

In Darktown

Steve pulls no punches here, exhaling of a long suppressed anger ;this is a savage indictment of an educational system which in many cases has institutionalised bullying and which, thanks to a spate of recent well-publicised cases has finally begun to be addressed. The album covers a wide range of subjects and varies widely in styles as well with Steve reclaiming his title of "King Of Sustain" with another blistering guitar solo on Twice Around The Sun. In many ways, Darktown is an old-fashioned album... a final clearing of the decks and an exorcism of old ghosts to allow the artist to move on… emotionally and artistically.

Steve has branched out even further with a look back to one of his influences and an archival release with Sketches Of Satie and Feedback 86 released by Camino Records on 8th May 2000, and 9th October 2000 have taken his fans down yet more paths with an album of "covers" although, as you would expect from Steve; there is a difference. This album contains acoustic guitar and flute variations on pieces by the famous French Impressionist composer: Erik Satie which emerged from a desire to originally record some of the acoustic pieces which had formed a major part of Steve's shows in the past. In discussion with his brother and with his manager; Billy Budis, this idea was soon extended as Steve himself explained in an interview he gave to The Waiting Room magazine ….

"Well, John and I had talked about doing something for a long time… we hadn't worked together for quite some time and frankly I missed it and we talked about possible flute and guitar combinations and we were talking originally about an album that would have a mixture of things, a mixture of composers; a mixture of guitars… I remember talking to Billy (Budis) about one of John's suggestions which was all the stuff that we played on tour over the years; the acoustic tours we had done; the adaptations of electric things basically written for flute but still close to both our hearts. John was very keen on recording that stuff and I think he still is, in the long term but Billy said; 'Why don't you make it two separate projects? Why don't you do an album of Erik Satie stuff and do an album of the other stuff?' And that may be the way the cookie crumbles eventually…"

The fascinating thing about this project is exactly how many of the pieces you will instantly recognise upon hearing them. I was amazed at how much of this music I was actually familiar with without actually knowing it. It is certainly to be hoped that John and Steve will work together again in the future although when exactly that may take place is anyone's guess really because Steve still has a plethora of projects under his belt including a further rock album, another classical concerto and the album mentioned previously with Jim Diamond.

The Feedback 86 album has had, even by Steve's standards, an exceptionally long gestation period. The album was originally destined to appear as Steve's follow-up to the short-lived GTR project back in 1987 and featured a Who's Who of rock, including Chris Thompson, Bonnie Tyler and Brian May among others. However, getting the album finished and released was quite an involved process as Steve himself remembers…

"…I will be absolutely honest and say that I couldn't get a record deal with a single record company in Christendom (laughs) never mind Pagandom so, I think that my standing at this time, in the record industry was at an all time low and that was fifteen years ago… I felt; 'that's it' I must have reached thirty five and that's it; the doors are all closed to me now…"

Considering that Steve's experiences with GTR were not exactly of the best; this album nonetheless features another guitar maestro Brian May which was another surprising step for Steve's fans….

"Brian and I were talking about doing something when GTR was ending for me, and I felt again like working with guitarist which had proven to be an interesting combination and I felt that GTR was a little bit light on guitar if

anything and between Brian and myself... I had started this track (Slot Machine) off and then he said; 'Well, give me the tape and I will work on it' and he re-wrote one of the verses and put in loads of guitar work and it really rocked, and so you have got Chris Thompson doing vocals on that and you have got Brian singing away on it and you have got all three of us singing on some of the choruses. It had been around the houses a bit, as had the rest of the album..."

The album had several tracks on it which deserved greater recognition including the infectiously catchy Slot Machine which certainly deserved to be a single. Cassandra, was another excellent rock number. Social realism was also here in the shape of The Gulf... a somewhat prophetic look at the situation in the Middle East; a situation which had deteriorated greatly by the time the album finally saw the light of day. Stadiums Of The Damned may be seen as the successor to Genesis' 1977 track: Pigeons only a darker version exploring the seedier side of the so-called "beautiful game".

Another project which had been around the houses was the "Carpet Crawlers 99" track which eventually surfaced as part of the Genesis "Turn It On Again - The Hits" album. Fans had become extremely excited at the news of this putative reformation of the classic Genesis line-up. However, things were not so simple. Steve's original rationale for getting behind this project had been its proposed inclusion as part of the first Genesis Archive box set back in 1998. For one reason or another; and I will be extremely cynical and say that to many people's view (my own included) the decision to issue it as part of the "Hits" project was simply a marketing ploy to ensure that the older fans shelled out on this project too. Strangely, it was apparently not released as a single in any territories apart from Germany.

Steve's own views of this effort are mixed to say the least...

"I was roped into that on the understanding that it was going to be used with the box set, so it was going to make more sense as a retrospective that featured both me and Pete as well as the other three. They held on to it in order, I suspect to give the hit single making three man team some connection with, perhaps their roots... I felt very uncomfortable about it going on an album where it is a cameo appearance at best and most of that is on the cutting room floor.... The track was put together over about a period of three years or so I seem to recall. My contribution was an afternoon in my own studio. I don't think anyone really wanted to meet up and work together on that thing. It is really only worth doing if everyone is going to see eyeball to eyeball. The problem is; handing it off to another producer is a bit of a lottery, isn't it? I don't know if I am prepared to take those sort of chances..."

The rest of this album, is the usual mixture of electric and acoustic tracks which always makes Steve's albums so special and this one will certainly show Steve in yet another light. Always one to take musical chances; Steve's recent tour of Italy also saw him radically change his set with the omission of long time stage favourite; Horizons and introducing several new pieces into the set as well as a Genesis "oldie" in the shape of Hairless Heart...

"... I may release the new stuff as part of a live thing. It is an idea that I have mentioned to Billy (Budis, Steve's manager), and I am waiting for him to say; 'that's a great idea, Steve' or 'Don't be so bloody stupid!' (laughs)..... I was excited about doing some of the new stuff and we did it all live; the vocals were all live and that was the thing I was most concerned about... I did something off The Lamb... as well, which was Hairless Heart which hadn't been done by any band member for over twenty five years, and I figured that it was about time to see if it still made sense...."
Finally succumbing to the requests of his fans, Steve put together an archival live collection of what can be called "official bootlegs" in the shape of "Live Archive '70's, '80's, '90's" which drew upon live recordings from several of his shows throughout the period mentioned in the title. This was a long time in the making and Steve took a lot of time deciding on which shows to use as he recently explained to The Waiting Room Magazine....

"We started off with the best performances of the bunch in each case; each era; and I tried to do a minimum to them; tried to keep it as honest as possible. So, what you have are very honest live recordings. We listened to a lot of gigs; especially from the 1990's. It was wonderful listening back to the Hammersmith show and hearing the level of enthusiasm from the crowd - my favourite part of the show of course; is the applause - that's the bit I have nothing to do with!"

Once again, Steve has also been bitten by the touring bug and has undertaken tours of both Italy and South America within the last twelve or so months. His rationale in doing so is two fold. First of all; Steve has always been a performing as well as recording artist and he enjoys the live work very much. Secondly, this also gives him the opportunity to experiment in the live context in much the same way as he does in the studio....

"I find that the studio stuff informs the live stuff and the live stuff informs the studio stuff. I may even end up using part live and part studio recordings which would be the first time we have ever done that. Some of the newer stuff was pretty spontaneous...."

Steve continues to work on several projects and even found time recently to contribute material to the soundtrack of a television documentary called "Outwitting Hitler" which was yet another string to Steve's bow and the programme was well received when broadcast on US TV....

"Chris Ward who was the director, already knew my work and called up to pitch us his film which was a work in progress by that point. He gave us a tremendous amount of background so that is how I got involved. By the time the contract was signed they needed the soundtrack pretty fast and I could barely get hold of an engineer in time so the finished score includes some material that I had actually intended for my guitar and orchestra project. In some ways then, it is an insight into a future classical project. We plundered some of the future and we plundered some of the past. It was a case of numerous telephone calls across the Atlantic and playing him stuff on the 'phone as we were doing it. More of a quick skirmish rather than a major pitched battle (laughs). Luckily they were very happy with it..."

Work continues on Steve's new recording studio in which he has finished work on his new rock album and he also has material under consideration for a further orchestral/guitar project and another acoustic album.

"The new album is quite far down the line and I would like to complete that in my new studio. I am probably about half way through and still recording songs for it. There is some very lovely stuff there, and it is strange; I am doing all the things that people discouraged me from doing. I find myself writing quite a few love songs at the moment, and I am finding that I am singing a little bit softer but also enjoying the other things- the extravaganzas; the long things. I also sit there and strum a guitar and strum a guitar and sing, which has been something I have rarely had the opportunity to do these days...."

Since that last comment from Steve; the "new" rock album has emerged. To Watch The Storms is Steve's seventeenth studio album released in May 2003 and the first to be completed in his new studio . Once again, continuing the forward momentum Steve has explored his personal psyche and covered an increasingly wide range of subject material from a brilliant personal tribute to his artist father in Serpentine Song and an exotic instrumental romp through the world of the Silk Road a track which would not be out of place on one of Peter Gabriel's "Real World" artists' albums although in case we forget; Steve had produced an album of "World Music" years before Peter hi-jacked the term. 1984's underrated Till We Have Faces saw Steve experimenting with massed percussion and this track is perhaps a hark back to that era although influenced by subtler ideas, as Steve explains...

"I had done an album in Brazil where we had worked with massed drummers and armies of percussion and was it prior to Peter's involvement...? Yes it was before his involvement with what subsequently became known as 'World Music'. Pete has done some incredible stuff. That is why it is named after a specific trade route and the journey is everything, and lyrically it borrows from Oriental poetry where you get two line stanzas that accompany something like pen and wash and all the calligraphy that accompanies that stuff. So, that was how that one came about; the shortest lyrics for any song; two lines of poetry and the rest was...I was trying to write something that was in the spirit of Oriental poetry. I didn't borrow from any specific thing. I was after poetry with that thing..."

There was also another acerbic examination of the stupidity of mankind in Mechanical Bride with some amazingly observed lyrics...

Fox hunt, bullfight; animal's curse
Born again with the roles reversed

And the equally observant....

Electric Chair burned hair
Framed, fried you could be there
Wedded to remaining dumb
You just can't hide the Mechanical Bride.

This latter is a protest song on more than one level as Steve explains....

"I remember being at a charity dinner party and listening to these two people discussing how many grouse or whatever they had 'bagged' and I said... 'Wouldn't it be fun if the animals could fire back?' and they looked at me as if I had gone crazy and walked away.... At the end of the day it was all about innocent men dying in the electric chair and being tortured to death...state sanctioned torture and the idea that any civilised nation could do that rests very uneasily with me..."

No longer content to merely observe; Steve is now coming out of the shadows and expressing himself about things which he feels strongly in ways which, as he himself admits; he would not have done previously....

"I have explored things that concern me. I have found that as I get older I am writing from the inside out and expressing myself in terms of things which I maybe wouldn't have written about in the old days..."

There is humour too in the maniacal cover version of Thomas Dolby's The Devil Is An Englishman in which Steve delivers the vocals in a manner which has been described by one observer as akin to *"Lawrence Olivier on Speed"* and further examples of Steve's acoustic playing in the form of the delightful Wind Sand And Stars and If You Only Knew.

Vocally, Steve has definitely found his niche and this is admirably demonstrated on his homage to Daphne Du Maurier in Rebecca and also on Serpentine Song and Brand New. The strengths of the new material have been amply demonstrated during Steve's most recent tours which saw Steve and his new band road test the old and the new to the equal delight of Steve's fans.

The recent tours have also generated a further healthy dose of live recordings for the Live Archive series and also visual documents in a further series of live videos and DVDs which more than cater for his fans' desire for a souvenir of the shows they attended.

Steve's latest orchestral recording: Metamorpheus, was released on 28th March 2005. Once again, he has not taken the easy path. Metamorpheus is a guitar/orchestral project. To many this may not have come as a surprise after the highly successful A Midsummer Nights Dream; but this album is an entirely different one to its predecessor. Written very much conforming to the "Programme Music" which is the norm in Classical circles, the album attempts to re-tell the Orpheus story in that manner as Steve himself explains…

"I didn't want to do a myth re-told with motorbikes and black leather. I didn't want to do that; I wanted to stick with the spirit of the original and take you through someone's life; before their life; during their life and after their life. So you have got three stages in a way.. I have described the story in detail track by track so in a way it qualifies as a piece of Programme Music in Classical terms"

The album is an impressionistic telling of the various elements of the Orpheus story in which Steve expanded his compositional style aided and abetted by a member of the first band he recorded with : Quiet World…
"It was largely Dick Driver who put together the orchestra and he and I had not worked together since 1970, since the very first album: Quiet World and he was their bass player and he contacted me not that long ago and he said that he liked some of the stuff I had done and he told me he had been working with orchestras; he had worked with the Royal Philharmonic and mainly these days he was playing an upright bass."

The album has had another lengthy gestation with work beginning on it as far back as 1997 shortly after Steve's previous orchestral effort: A Midsummer Night's Dream was completed. The reasons for the delay in completion are nothing more than the sheer amount of projects which Steve has on the go at any one period and the simple operation of economics as he explains…

"It was a year to write but recording took longer because there were always other projects and orchestral projects are very expensive; they eat money; they eat time and resources and so you have always got to wait for the tight time and so I started it in 1997 and then had to wait while a number of other projects took precedence…. This is very hard to do live and I don't know if I will attempt any of it live because it is really designed for guitar and orchestra rather than guitar and trio.."

Certainly fans who heard the album have been surprised by the depth of the compositions; austere and complying to the demands of the classical "tradition" in places; the music demonstrates the fact that A Midsummer Night's Dream was no flash in the pan. Steve has taken a story of such essential magnitude that it deals with the twin questions of life and death and brought it shimmeringly to life. After such a magnificent effort; fans would surely be forgiven for thinking that the effervescent Hackett is due for a rest but far from it! He has continued to write and has recently completed writing a brand new song for his hero: Richie Havens; The Cedars Of Lebanon as well as brimming with ideas for several other projects.

Steve has continued to delve into his past. The original transfer of his Charisma albums from vinyl to CD format by Virgin Records in the late 1980's was, by anyone's standards a botched job. Fortunately, the various problems associated with these releases has recently been addressed with the re-mastering of his first four Charisma albums, a task which was supervised by Steve in conjunction with his engineer; Ben Fenner. The resulting re-issues were released to an expectant fan base on 19th September 2005 and were well received. More recently still; Steve has also issued another in the Live Archive series of albums, this time focussing on Steve's first acoustic tour back in 1983. Unusually for the series, this release was compiled from both desk and bootleg recordings because no complete desk recording from the Bay Of Kings tour survived!

The irrepressible Hackett has also completed work on Wild Orchid, a new rock album. Drawing his inspirations from an unbelievably wide variety of influences; Seventeenth Century poetry, Dickens; Stephen King; the 1940's Big Band era; Bach and many more, the new album is replete with a cast of characters some of whom will be familiar to Steve's fans and others who are making their first appearances on the Hackett "theatre of dreams" stage. One thing has remained constant; Steve's desire to knock down the prejudices within music.....

"I try not to be pigeonholed. People think they know what you can do but not even I know what I can do until I pick up a guitar. By the time I snuff it if I can look back at the time and there will come a day when the factory closes down .... There are so many different kinds of music around today... and I hope that in some ways they all meet up in me and my broad tastes... At one time I had a very tough time in the industry by trying to establish this two-pronged thing saying this is the nylon guitar and it is just as valid as the electric and the more I break down those prejudices within myself the more I find it is translated into an accepting crowd and so I have been very proud of that in a way and I have led people into areas which they might not have considered..."

Steve has always been fortunate to work in a genuinely creative environment; from his days in Genesis onwards, he has been surrounded by people willing to work towards a common goal: the creation of excellent music. His collaborations have often surprised his fans but what might surprise them even more is how far he is prepared to subsume his own persona in search of the music that fits what he is looking for. In this respect, his partnership with Roger King over the last few years has been particularly fruitful as the pair of them outlined recently...

(Roger): *"It's about half way. Steve writes the songs and my job is as a programmer and keyboard player and I guess recording engineer too. They are all Steve's songs but I am sure he won't mind me saying so; he isn't terribly technically literate; certainly not a computer operator!"*

(Steve): *"I'm a humble guitarist and I like to have conversations about what happens next and I think the danger is that, in the last .... How many years would it be? Twenty five years? More? Guys can make albums on their own but it is nice to sit down with a mate and say; 'what do you think? I'm not sure about that. Maybe we could try such and such?' which is a million miles away from the idea of the composer sitting down with the score sheet and it was set in stone and you can't change it and this is a very flexible way of working and I think it is wonderful..."*

Once again, Steve mixes it up on the new album. Several of the tracks have a darker edge; rather like musical "Tales Of The Unexpected" although laced with a degree of grim humour as Steve remarked...

"Yes, exactly he (the character in Down Street) is in his own Twilight Zone and he thinks he is going to be served and actually he is going to be served up, as it were. So, we are back to that ironic approach but all my spooks are not supposed to be taken seriously, they are more to do with the haunted house than they are with the... again its back to the fairground really..."

The fairground is indeed a neat analogy for the new album. All the fun of the fair is here; the thrills of the rollercoaster: On The Transylvanian Express or A Dark Night In Toytown; the ghost train: Down Street; the Waltzer and the Merry Go Round: A Girl Called Linda and To A Close.

In addition to that, Steve has also recorded a version of Bach's Chaconne; an incredibly difficult piece originally written by Bach as a memorial to his deceased first wife. It is acknowledged as a particularly demanding piece and Steve's interpretation is both a homage to Bach himself and also to Andres Segovia who was an early inspiration for Steve's work. Perhaps this might form part of another album in similar vein to 2000's Sketches Of Satie, either way, the rendition is a marvellous tribute to the composer and also to Steve as an interpreter and performer. With so many ideas still burgeoning within him, I am sure there will be many more musical voyages from this particular acolyte!

Steve Hackett UK Solo Discography

7" & 12" Vinyl Singles

A-Side	B-Side	Record Company	Catalogue Number
Children of the world	Love is walking	Dawn Records	DNS100 (7") 1970
How can I?	Kim	Charisma Records	CB312 (7") ?.5.78
Narnia (Remixed)	Please don't touch	Charisma Records	CB318 (7") ?.10.78
Everyday	Lost time in Cordoba	Charisma Records	CB334 (7") ?.6.79
Clocks -The Angel of Mons	**Acoustic set (live)**	Charisma Records	CB341 (7") ?.9.79
Clocks -The Angel of Mons	**Acoustic set(live)/** **Tigermoth (live)**	Charisma Records	CB341 12 (12")PS ?.9.79
The Show	**Hercules Unchained**	Charisma Records	CB357 (7") PS ?.3.80
Sentimental Institution	The Toast	Charisma Records	CB368 (7") PS ?.8.80
Hope I don't wake	**Tales of the riverbank**	Charisma Records	CB385 (7") PS ?.8.81
Picture Postcard	**Theme from "Second Chance**	Charisma Records	CB390 (7") PS ?.10.81
Cell 151	**Time-lapse at MiltonKeynes**	Charisma Records	CELL 1 (7")PS 16.4.83
Cell 151	**The air-conditioned Nightmare/** **Time Lapse At Milton Keynes**	Charisma Records	CELL 12 (12")PS 16.4.83

(This was also a limited edition with a bonus free "white label" copy of the "Clocks" 12" single).

A-Side	B-Side	Record Company	Catalogue Number
A Doll that's made in Japan	**A Doll that's made in Japan (instrumental)**	Lamborghini Records	LMG16 (7") PS ?.8.84
A Doll that's made in Japan	**Just the bones**	Lamborghini Records	12MHG16 (12")PS ?.8.84
When the heart rules the mind	Reach out (never say no)	Arista Records	GTR1 (7") PS 28.4.86

(This edition also appeared as a limited edition with poster "Family Tree" sleeve)

A-Side	B-Side	Record Company	Catalogue Number
When the heart rules the mind	Reach out (never say no)	Arista Records	GTRSD1 (7") PD 28.4.86
When the heart rules the mind Sketches in the sun/Hackett To bits	Reach out (never say no)/	Arista Records	GTR121 (12") PS 28.4.86
Sailing	Sailing (Instrumental)	Epic Records	EIRS 139 (7") PS ?.5.89

(This was the charity recording made for the "Rock Against Repatriation" project and includes Steve and a host of other celebrities)

Tracks in **Bold** type are non album tracks.
PS Denotes a picture sleeved edition.

Promotional Compact Disc Singles

Lost In Your Eyes/Dark As The Grave/There Are Many Sides To The Night
(Promotional album sampler)   Permanent Records   CDS Perm 11 1993

Your Own Special Way (one track single)   Snapper Music   SRECD100P (PS) 1997

Between The Cold Moon & The Earth (Excerpt)/By Paved Fountain (Excerpt)/Helena (Excerpt)/Starlight/Celebration.
(Promotional album sampler)   EMI Classics   HACK001   (PS) 1998

Days Of Long Ago (One track single)   Camino Records CAMCD17S (PS) 1999

Balfour Street (One track single)   (Promotional CD single featuring Steve and Annabel Lamb as a
Fundraiser for the Hope For Children charity).   INKYTHINGS LTD   (PS) 2006.

Vinyl and Compact Disc Albums

Voyage of the Acolyte	Charisma Records	CAS111	?.10.75
Voyage of the Acolyte	Virgin Records	CASCD111	?.8.91
Voyage of the Acolyte	Virgin Records	CASCDR111	19.9.05 +
Please don't Touch	Charisma Records	CDS4012	?.4.78
Please Don't Touch	Virgin Records	CDSCD4012	?.8.91
Please Don't Touch	Virgin Records	CDSCDR4012	19.9.05 +
Spectral Mornings	Charisma Records	CDS4017	?.5.79
Spectral Mornings	Virgin Records	CDSCD4017	?.9.89

(Initial copies of the compact disc of "Spectral…" had a bonus spoof track as a run out at the end of the disc).

Spectral Mornings	Virgin Records	CDSCDR4017	19.9.05 +
Defector	Charisma Records	CDS4018	13.6.80
Defector	Virgin Records	CDSCD4018	?.9.89
Defector	Virgin Records	CDSCDR4018	19.9.05 +
Cured	Charisma Records	CDS4021	21.8.81
Cured	Virgin Records	CDSCD4021	?.9.89
Highly Strung	Charisma Records	HACK1	23.4.83
Highly Strung	Virgin Records	HACKCD1	?.9.89
Bay of Kings	Lamborghini Records	LMGLP3000	7.11.83
Bay of Kings	START Records	SCD10	?.5.87
Bay of Kings	Permanent Records	PERMCDL20	?.5.94 (*)
Till we have faces	Lamborghini Records	LMGLP4000	?.9.84
Till we have faces	START Records	SCD11	?.5.87
Till we have faces	Permanent Records	PERMCDL19	?.5.94 (*)
GTR	Arista Records	GTR1	2.6.86
GTR	Arista Records	ARCD8400	2.6.86
Momentum	START Records	STLP15	28.3.88
Momentum	START Records	SCD15	28.3.88
Momentum	Permanent Records	PERMCDL21	?.5.94 (*)
Timelapse - Steve Hackett Live	Crisis Records	500 001-2	?.8.91
Timelapse - Steve Hackett Live	Camino Records	CAMCD11	?.10.97.
The Unauthorised Biography	Virgin Records	CDVM9014	?.10.92
Guitar Noir	Permanent Records	PERMCD13	21.3.93
Guitar Noir	Camino Records	CAMCD12	?.5.94 (*)
There are many sides to the night	Kudos Records	KUDOSCD2	?.10.94
Blues with a feeling	Permanent Records	PERMCD27	19.3.94
Genesis Revisited	Mercury Records	PHCR -1454	?.8.96
A Midsummer Night's Dream	EMI Records	5 56348 2	24.3.97
GTR Live	King Biscuit Flower Hour	70710-88021-2	?.7.98
Genesis Revisited	Reef Records	SRECD704	22.9.97
The Tokyo Tapes	Camino Records	CAMCD15	6.4.97
Darktown	Camino Records	CAMCD17	26.4.99
Sketches Of Satie	Camino Records	CAMCD20	1.5.00
Sketches Of Satie	Gramy/Camino Records	GR-055/CAMLP20	?.3.05

(This is a limited edition 180grm vinyl edition)

Feedback '86	Camino Records	CAMCD21	9.10.00
Steve Hackett Live Archive	Camino Records	CAMCD23	12.11.01

(This release is a four disc live set comprising recordings from Steve's 1979, 1981 and 1993 live sets - an official bootleg series, as it has been called by several fans)

Steve Hackett Live Archive

Newcastle City Hall 26.10.79	Camino Records	CAMCD23X	12.11.01

(This is the bonus disc from the archive set available only through Steve's record company)

Steve Hackett Live Recordings '70's, '80's

	Victor Records	VICP-61608~9	12.11.01

(The '70's disc in this case is the Newcastle '79 show, released as a bonus disc in other territories)

Steve Hackett Feedback 86 + Live '90's

	Victor Records	VICP-61610~11	12.11.01

(Both of the above are the Japanese editions of the Archive, released as two double CD sets. The latter contains the first release of Feedback 86 in Japan where it had previously been unavailable)

The Genesis Files (Double CD)	Snapper Music	SMDCD382	?.2.02
Somewhere In South America (Double CD)			
	Camino Records	CAMCD29	9 .12.02
To Watch The Storms	Camino Records	CAMCD31	26.5.03
To Watch The Storms	Camino Records	CAMCDSE 31	26.5.03 (+)

(+) Special edition contained four extra recordings.

NEARfest	Camino Records	CAMCD32	23.7.03
To Watch The Storms	Universal Records	UICE 1064	?.11.03 (^)
Live Archive 03	Camino Records	CAMCD33	8.1.04
Guitar Wars	Universal Records	UICE 1070	?.?.04
Live Archive 04	Camino Records	CAMCD34	28.6.04

Metamorpheus	Camino Records	CAMCD35	28.3.05
Live Archive 05	Camino Records	CAMCD36	6.6.05
Live Archive 83	Camino Records	CAMCD37	20.2.06
Wild Orchid	Camino Records	CAMCD38	11.9.06

(*) Albums marked thus were originally issued on the Lamborghini Records label and subsequent compact disc editions appeared on the START Records label and later on, on Steve's own labels: Permanent, Kudos and Camino. These albums have also subsequently had additional tracks added to them and have been re-mastered.

(^) This is the Japanese edition of the album which features a revised running order, one track unavailable on the previous releases and a different Kim poor artwork design on the sleeve.

+ These are the recently re-issued Virgin re-masters of Steve's first four solo albums each of which contains several bonus tracks .

Appendix E: "The Genesis of a mechanic" Mike Rutherford a solo biography.

He began his career hoping to be able to play London's Marquee club. Well, Mike Rutherford has certainly come a LONG way since that particular aspiration was fulfilled.

Mike's solo recording career began during the hiatus which followed the end of the band's massive "And Then There Were Three" world tour in 1978. With Phil Collins resident in Vancouver at the time, trying to resolve his marriage difficulties, both Tony and Mike opted to begin writing and recording material for their long-overdue solo albums. Previously such events had been very much frowned upon as Steve Hackett and Peter Gabriel can testify as perceived threats to the stability of the band. By this time, however, Genesis was a well established unit both at home and elsewhere and the opportunity to stretch their individual legs, so to speak, appealed to both musicians as Mike explained….

"I think the feeling was that it was about the right time to do it. Steve was a little bit unlucky, he left before the band reached this stage where the band was successful enough for us to take a year or so off and it just felt right to have a break from each other and do some solo stuff..."

Mike's solo effort was the first to be released in 1979. Titled Smallcreep's Day it took its title from a book by Peter Currell-Brown and was in part a concept album outlining the fascination of the character Smallcreep with what the end result of his day to day work in a factory might be. Half of the album was given over to this concept and the other half was dedicated to more straightforward songs although Mike was somewhat worried about the division as he recalls…

"I was thinking about writing some shorter songs as well and I was worried that a whole concept album might be too stodgy.. too heavy in a sense..."

Critically well received, the album also marked a brief reunion with Mike's long time friend and fellow Genesis founder; Anthony Phillips who contributed keyboard parts to the album which took many fans by surprise…

"I hadn't planned to use Ant actually but by then he was also a very good keyboard player and I thought this was something new; having Ant on keyboards and I was looking to try new and different things...."

There were two singles from the album although neither of these achieved chart success the B-side of one: Compression has a long history being one of Mike's famous "bits" from a much earlier Genesis recording session. Mike's credentials were now established although it was to be a further three years before his next solo effort.

With a break in recording duties with Genesis after the end of the Abacab album and tour, Mike returned to the studio to record his second solo album. Once again displaying a fine line in irony, Mike called it Acting Very Strange and took fans unawares by taking on the vocal duties himself which certainly gave the album a harder edge than its predecessor and this album gained grudging critical acclaim including these comments from Hugh Fielder of "Sounds"

If Mike Rutherford's first album dropped too easily into the 'solo- contribution-from-a-member-of-a-famous-band' category, the second makes no such mistake and contains virtually no references to his day job. Instead it contains more references and clues to Mike's own character and musical tastes than he's ever revealed on one piece of vinyl before....The self confidence this requires is there in abundance and suddenly he's not hiding behind the songs anymore..."

The album certainly displayed a heavier side to Mike's character as evidenced by such numbers as Maxine and Acting Very Strange as well as a great sense of humour in Couldn't Get Arrested. Unusually, Mike opted to record the album on WEA records rather than Charisma and his decision to sing himself was driven by a desire to "get it out of his system" as he explains...

"I look at it as something that you have to do once in your career. Looking back at the album, bits weren't great but probably what made me realise after that album became a struggle was that as a songwriter, if you want the best voice in the world to sing you can get someone to do it. So I thought.. I probably got it out of my system and I did it once and it made me decide I'd never do it again... I can't really sing that well and with someone who can't sing it was a bit frustrating..."

The album also spawned Mike's first solo promotional video for the song Halfway There which included Mike in a dream whilst on an aeroplane and featured amongst other props a gigantic saxophone, bar of chocolate and ten pence piece whose significance is still best known to either Mike or the video director! With his return to recording commitments with Genesis fans were once again deprived of the chance of seeing Mike in a solo context although that particular problem was addressed on his next solo project.

Having decided that the traditional solo album was not the direction to take, Mike opted to submerge his identity within a group format and 1985's project bore the moniker Mike + The Mechanics . Mike's credentials had always been established in the song writing department, it was what he was good at, and to that end he decided to build a song writing co-operative around himself - shades of the formative Genesis again and he enlisted the help of B A Robertson and Chris Neil which was a fortunate pairing, Robertson's ear for a tune and Neil's ability with production enabled Mike to enhance his own creativity and Mike recalls the process...

"Looking back on it, it was a bit like Genesis. I wanted to be a songwriter, so I got together with Chris Neil and B A and we tried to get other people to do our songs.. I always believed in that but it didn't really happen. I suppose making a version of Silent Running didn't seem a good song to cover so once again history was repeating itself.."

History was definitely repeating itself in the choice of the other personnel within the band with Paul Carrack returning to the fold having initially been in the frame as the singer on Mike's first album; Smallcreep's Day although Mike's way of auditioning people does not match your general expectations as Paul explained…

"I didn't actually audition for that no…I bumped into B A Robertson who asked me to sing on a demo for him; he tracked me down. And I did that and he mentioned that he was writing with Mike for a solo album he was doing and would I be interested in coming down? So, B A drove me down there one day and I went in and on Silent Running they didn't even have any lyrics and I just sort of la la'd and made it up and I guess that was an audition…"

The album was eventually put together and released after the initial single had achieved some chart success in the USA and subsequently achieved a healthy chart position in the UK upon its re-release. A further single from the album; the highly catchy All I Need Is A Miracle serve notice that Mike + The Mechanics were no flash in the pan and once again one of Mike's famous "bits" found a place here on the track A Call To Arms which Mike recalls…

"It was a Genesis bit. The main sequence had been discarded from the Genesis album before (Genesis) and I always liked it, so I tried to do it and it didn't come out right. I had a couple of people play on it from a band I'd produced…"

The rest of the personnel for the band were selected including veteran singer Paul Young from the sadly defunct Sad Café who together with Paul Carrack was to form the vocal heart of the new band. Young's introduction to the band was equally as accidental as Carrack's as he recalls…

"I got a 'phone call from Chris Neil and he said; 'I'm doing a solo album for Mike Rutherford, do you want to come down and sing?' So I went down and the first track I tried was All I need is a miracle and they seemed pretty pleased with it and said it was cool for me to do a couple more and so I did and I got a nice cheque and then thought that was the end of it! (laughter). Then I got a call about three months' later saying that Silent Running and Miracle had been top and five respectively in America and we had another one on the boil and did I want to go over there and tour with them.. and we went over there and became Mike + The Mechanics the touring band almost by default really…"

Mike had finally found his song writing collective and the first album's success and the US only tour of June/July 1986 just prior to Genesis' massive tour for their Invisible Touch album enabled Mike to finally establish his bona fides as a songwriter with a wider range of styles than ever displayed within Genesis itself and fans of the band and new ones who were blissfully unaware of Mike's pedigree took to the album making it one of great success stories of 1986 which was a great year all round for Genesis and their various solo off-shoots.

The activities in the Genesis camp surrounding the above mentioned album, Invisible Touch precluded Mike's follow-up on the success of the initial Mike + The Mechanics album for some two years. However, during the spring and summer of 1988, Mike and the band returned to the studio to work on their follow-up which was, upon its release to prove that the success of the first album had certainly not been a fluke. The initial single from the album; Nobody's Perfect was released in November 1988, and charted in the UK top ten. It's rockier nature certainly established Mike's talents as a rock guitarist but it was to be the second single released early in 1989 which was once and for all, to establish Mike + The Mechanics as a force to be reckoned with on the UK music scene. The single; The Living Years which was a personal exorcism of Mike's grief at the recent loss of his father, took the UK charts by storm reaching the number two slot and similar positions elsewhere around the world. The success of the single took even Mike by surprise…

"I don't think that we thought it was going to be a big hit. At the time of doing it, which at the time I was working with Brian by which time we'd both lost our fathers, so it was a very emotional time. That song was so emotional that we thought it might not work and B A and I said we'll try it and if it comes out sugary and sickly, we'll forget it…"

The album displayed a wider range of material than its predecessor including several out and out rock tracks which, when combined with the more traditionally melodic songs on it, made it an album that gained Mike and the band a huge audience across the UK and Europe and the resulting "Living Years" tour of 1989 took in most of the major theatre venues in Europe as well as the band's first handful of gigs in the UK to rapturous welcomes from the crowds. A further single was released from the album later in 1989 to round off the year nicely for the band.

Strangely enough, Mike did not fully capitalise on the increasingly long gaps between Genesis records to produce a further album and work on the next Mike + The Mechanics album did not begin until late 1990. This album was certainly to prove a difficult one for the band especially for Mike and the producer Russ Titelman who was not the right man for the job as Mike remembers…

"I decided to make a change in the choice of producer. Russ was originally producing it and I like his work very much but it just didn't seem to work and on the second day I said to everyone in the band 'I don't think this is going to work' and they all said; 'oh, give it a try…'. Sometimes things would go great but after about two and a half months, I wasn't enjoying it and found myself driving to work slowly! (laughter).."

The resultant album; *Word Of Mouth* was a much more lacklustre affair than its predecessor and although there were certain sparks of magic on it, it is on the whole an album which falls between two stools as Mike himself admits….

"Then Chris Neil came back and we weeded out some songs and by then the whole thing had become a bit of a problem. I'd lost interest and it was laboured. I'm sure that was reflected on the album but having said that; some stuff was very good. Get Up I like very much and Word of mouth as well…There's a bit more drive to it and the Mechanics are more about moods and atmospheres and somehow I think that was missing from this album…"

In all, there were some three singles from the album although none of them emulated the success of the previous record and with no tour for the album due in large part to Mike's return to Genesis for what was to prove to be a pivotal album in the band's development, Word Of Mouth was to be very much an undervalued album.

Late 1991 and 1992 saw Mike fully occupied with writing and touring commitments with Genesis for their hugely successful album; We Can't Dance which proved to be Phil Collins' swan song with the band. Mike finally returned to his own recording studio to begin work on the next Mechanics album in early 1994 and expectations were high for this project and, as it proved, those expectations were to be proven correct.

First indications of what the new album was to be like appeared upon the release of the first single in the shape of the infectiously catchy Over My Shoulder which stormed up the UK charts upon its release in February 1995. The album Beggar On A Beach Of Gold was in hot pursuit and soon reached the top five in the UK charts and if the previous album was a strain the problems attached to this one were much more palatable as Mike recalls…

"I'm very pleased with this album. To me the Mechanics are more about moods and atmospheres and this album is more like that. I had great difficulty selecting the tracks for this one; there were six that I thought were definite and seven that could be there and I could chop and choose…"

Without doubt this album was the band's "coming of age" there was not a duff track on it and the writing team was now expanded to included both Paul Young and Paul Carrack, something which brought an even wider range of styles into the pot and made for a much more satisfying album both for the guys in the band and the growing horde of fans in the UK which was graced by a massive tour of provincial theatres in June/July 1995. In all, three singles were released from the album with each one achieving a respectable position in the charts. The band were also invited to play a handful of shows in South Africa which happened to coincide with the Rugby Union World Cup which for a band as sport mad as the Mechanics was an added bonus as Paul Young recalls…

"I was very pleased to be there while the rugby was on… they just booed us forever when we wore the rugby shirts… we all got into rugby last year and went to all the matches and sat surrounded by thousands of green shirts and there was one thin line of white shirts, it was great…"

To consolidate upon this hard won success, the Mechanics released a compilation album of their greatest hits in March of 1996 accompanying it by another massive UK tour and the promotional blurb on the album I think sums up the attitude of the band and their fans…

"For a part -time band, the Mechanics have enjoyed huge success around the globe. It's not just the wrinklies who like a good tune ya know…"

Mike brought The Mechanics back together again in late 1998 to record that difficult "sixth" studio album which with a touch of irony, the band titled M6 which could either be interpreted as a reference to its status as the band's sixth album or possibly as a reference to an English motorway system! Either way, the album was another great success reaching the top five in the UK helped no doubt by the initial success of the first single from it; Now That You've Gone which was produced by the team responsible for Cher's massive hit Believe. The band also undertook a highly successful tour of the UK with a scattering of shows in Europe thrown in for good measure. The successful formula that brought the band deserved success was shattered however, with the sudden death on 15th July 2000 of singer Paul Young just prior to the band's scheduled appearances at several European festival gigs.

The band took a considerable period away before deciding to reconvene in 2002 to begin recording on what has recently become the band's seventh studio album: Rewired which was released on 7th June 2004. The previous formula for the Mechanics has been stripped away on this project with the emphasis on experimentation. The resulting album has not been too well received by the fans with the album only achieving a chart position in the lower reaches of the top100 a considerable drop for the band after the successes of their previous outings.

The album can obviously be seen as very much a transitional affair as the gap left by Young's death must have been a difficult one to fill as Mike himself acknowledges..

"Paul and I wrote some songs because we like writing together and not necessarily with a plan for a Mechanics album and then as time ticked by the loss of Paul Young became a little less painful and the songs started to sound very different to what Paul does on his own and I pushed them a bit that way anyway; and then we decided; it must have been the beginning of last year that we would put an album out. And so it was probably very different and probably a transitional album in many ways. Some of the good bits were good and I am not saying that it was all great."

The recent shows in support of Phil Collins have demonstrated that the band still can cut it as a live unit although the reluctance of the band to undertake a tour in support of the album in their own right and especially in the UK where the band's fan base is strongest; has been interpreted by many as an indication that the band do not have the confidence in their latest effort to promote it fully. This may be the case or it may not be, either way the Mechanics are still a viable unit and one whose future although uncertain, has not ended yet.

Mike Rutherford/Mike + The Mechanics UK Discography.

7" and 12" Vinyl Singles

A - Side	B - Side	Catalogue Number/Release Date		
Working in line	**Compression**	CB353	(7")	?.1.80
At the end of the day	Overnight job	CB364	(7" PS)	?.7.80
Halfway there	A day to remember	K79331	(7" PS)	19.8.82
Acting very strange	**Couldn't get arrested (NIX MIX)**	RUTH1	(7" PS)	?.10.82
Acting very strange (Extended) Couldn't get arrested (Extended NIX MIX)		RUTH1T	(12" PS)	?.10..82
Hideaway	**Calypso**	U9967	(7")	?.2.83
Silent running	I get the feeling	U8908	(7" PS)	9.10.85
Silent running	I get the feeling/**Too far gone**	U8908T	(12" PS)	9.10.85
Silent running	I get the feeling	U8908P	(7" PD)	9.10.85
All I need is a miracle	You are the one	U8765	(7" PS)	?.5.86
All I need is a miracle(Remix) You are the one/A call to arms		U8765T	(12" PS)	?.5.86
All I need is a miracle (Remix) You are the one/A call to arms		U8765P	(12" PD)	?.5.86
Nobody's perfect	Nobody knows	U7789	(7" PS)	19.10.88
Nobody's perfect	Nobody knows/All I need is a miracle	U7789T	(12" PS)	19.10.88
The living years	**Too many friends**	U7717	(7" PS)	27.1.89
The living years	**Too many friends/I get the feeling (live)**	U7717T	(12" PS)	27.1.89
Nobody knows	Why me?	U7602	(7" PS)	?.4.89
Nobody knows	Why me?/Nobody's perfect	U7602	(12" PS)	?.4.89
Word of mouth	Let's pretend it didn't happen	VS1345	(7" PS)	4.3.91
Word of mouth	Let's pretend it didn't happen	VST1345	(12" PS)	4.3.91
A time and place	Yesterday, today, tomorrow	VS1351	(7" PS)	27.5.91
A time and place **(East West Mix)**	Yesterday, today, tomorrow/**Word of mouth**	VST1351	(12" PS)	27.5.91
Get Up	**I think I've got the message**	VS1359	(7" PS)+	?.5.91

Stop baby	Get up	VS1376	(7" PS)	30.9.91
Everybody gets a second chance	**The way you look at me**	VS1396	(7" PS)	27.1.92
Over my shoulder	Something to believe in	VS1526	(7" PS) #	13.2.95

Tracks in **Bold** are non album tracks.
+ This single was withdrawn from the stores and its b-side used on the cd of "Stop baby".
# This single was a limited edition numbered edition.

Compact Disc Singles

The living years/**Too many friends/I get the feeling (Live)**	U7717 CD (PS)	27.1.89
Nobody's Perfect/**Nobody's perfect(extended)**/Nobody knows	U7789 CD (PS)	19.10.88
Nobody knows/Why me/Nobody knows	U7602 CD (PS)	?.4.89
Word of mouth/Let's pretend it didn't happen	VSCD1345 (PS)	4.3.91
Word of mouth/**Taken in(live)**/Let's pretend it didn't happen sleeve)	VSCDX1345 (Limited edition numbered	
A time and place/Yesterday, today, tomorrow/**Word of mouth (East West Mix)**	VSCD1351 (PS) 27.5.91	
A time and place/Yesterday, today, tomorrow/**Word of mouth (East West Mix)**	VSCDX 1351	3.6.91
Get up/**I think I've got the message**/Before the next heartache falls	VSCDG1359 (PS) ?.8.91	
(Withdrawn from stores)		
Stop baby/get up/Before the next heartache falls	VSCDG1376 (PS) 30.9.91	
Stop baby/**I think I've got the message/My crime of passion (Acoustic version)**	VSCDT1376 (PS) 7.10.91	
Everybody gets a second chance/**The way you look at me**/At the end of the day	VSCD 1396 (PS) 27.1.92	
Everybody gets a second chance/**The way you look at me**/At the end of the day	VSCDX1396 (PS) 27.1.92	
Over my shoulder/Something to believe in/**Always the last to know**	VSCDG1526 (PS)13.2.95	
Over my shoulder/Something to believe in/Word of mouth/**Over my Shoulder (Live)**	VSCDX1526 (PS) 20.2.95	
Beggar on a beach of gold(Edit)/Help me/Nobody told me	VSCDT1535 (PS) 6.7.95	
Beggar on a beach of gold/**Boys at the front/Little boy/Beggar On a beach of gold (Acoustic version)**	VSCDX1535 (PS) 6.7.95	
Another cup of coffee/**You never change/You don't know what Love is**	VSCDG1554 (PS) 21.8.95	
Another cup of coffee/**The living years/Everyday hurts/How long?**	VSCDX1554 (PS) 21.8.95	
(Limited edition in embossed box with set of postcards tracks 2-4 are from the Simon Mayo Radio Session)		
All I need is a miracle '96/The way you look at me/Don't	VSCDT1576 (PS) ?.2.96	
All I need is a miracle '96/**Get up(live)/Over my shoulder(live)/ All I need is a miracle'96 (Radio edit)**	VSCDG576 (PS) ?.2.96	
Silent running/Stop baby/Plain & Simple	VSCDT 1585 (PS) ?.4.96	
Now that you've gone (Radio edit)/A beggar on a beach of gold (live)/ Silent running (live)	VSCDT1732 (PS) 24.5.99	
Now that you've gone/**I believe (when I fall in love it will be forever) (live)/ Word of mouth (live)**	VSCDX1732 (PS) 24.5.99	
Whenever I stop/**Now that you've gone (live)/Whenever I stop (Unplugged)**	VSCDT1743 (PS) ?.7.99	
Whenever I stop/**Ordinary girl (Unplugged)/My little island (Live)**	VSCDX1743 (PS) ?.7.99	
Perfect Child/Underscore	Internet release no catalogue number.	

Tracks in **Bold** are non album tracks.
PS denotes a picture sleeve edition.

Vinyl and Compact Disc albums

Smallcreep's Day	Charisma Records	CAS1149/CASCD1149 (CD)	?.10.80
Acting Very Strange	WEA Records	WEA K 99249/80015-2 (CD)	?.9.82
Mike + The Mechanics	WEA Records	252 496-1/252496-2 (CD)	?.10.85
Living years	WEA Records	WX 203 256004-1/256 004-2 (CD)	?.10.89
Word of mouth	Virgin Records	V2662/CDV2662 (CD)	25.3.91
Beggar on a beach of gold	Virgin Records	CDV2772 (CD)	13.2.95
Hits	Virgin Records	CDV2797 (CD)	4.3.96
Mike & The Mechanics	Virgin Records	CDV2885 (CD)/(MD)	31.5.99
Rewired	Virgin Records	CDV2984 (CD)	7.6.04

Soundtracks

Against All Odds (Making a big mistake) Virgin Records   1984

Appendix F: "Putting together the parts and pieces"

Anthony Phillips - Portrait of a solo artist.

Immediately after leaving the band Anthony went on to study music influenced by several classical pieces he heard during his studies...

"I suddenly had this feeling that I must be able to control an orchestra i.e. orchestrate and learn. Therefore it was a question of learning to write music down.."

He spent the years after his departure gaining a licentiate degree from the Royal College of Music in London and he initially drew his income from teaching music which is something which he may still return to in later life.His first foray into the world of music after his departure from the band was to be the much vaunted but sadly unreleased composition 'Silver Song' which he had written in 1969 as a tribute to the original Genesis drummer: John Silver. This putative single featured Anthony along with Mike Rutherford and Phil Collins and was to have been released under Phil's name but was shelved by Charisma and has yet to see the light of day.

Even in those early post Genesis days, Anthony was not afraid to experiment and one project which has only recently come to light illustrates this more than most. Anthony had been involved with a friend of Richard MacPhail's in a student film project called Substitute which sadly no longer exists; but a further film project based on the French character Fantomas; the amoral "hero" of some 32 pre 1914 stories.

Anthony worked with Richard's friend Philip Black and Anthony was primarily involved with the music; some extracts of which have finally seen the light of day as part of the second Archive Collection album released in 2004. There is even a Genesis connection here too as Anthony recalls...

"I remember that for the opening music Philip wanted something a bit humorous. A lot of the music in the film is quite serious, quite dark and moody. The idea for the opening music was almost a piece that used bass, drums and piano - invoking a feel of black humour is the thing that springs to mind.... There as no budget for this - in fact I don't think I got paid for it and just did it for experience. So John Silver had to do it for experience as well! I had to find somebody I knew well who wouldn't mind doing it for free and I think that John had come back from Cornell university in the holidays. The only other drummer I knew at this time was Phil Collins, who obviously was impossible to get at that time and I had lost contact with Chris Stewart so I got John to come down and do it...."

This project and many others have been revealed by the diligent researches of Jonathan Dann in Anthony's tape archives and it is fortunate that much of this music is now not only being preserved for posterity but finding its way to Anthony's fans as well.

Many other pieces of music and songs were co-written by Anthony and Mike during the early seventies and a couple of these have recently seen the light of day on the re-issues of Anthony's albums. The collaboration also produced the hymn 'Take This Heart' which was released on a Charisma album of religious songs in 1975 and which is now one of the most collectable items in Anthony's catalogue...

"I just asked the music master at Charterhouse if he'd entertain the idea and he said yes. I took down a rough score as I didn't know how to write down the vocal parts...Brian Roberts did the live recording in the Chapel at Charterhouse...I loved it, to us it was very thrilling, it reminded us of our school days in a way..it was very much co-written lyrically...

Creative collaboration with Mike was eventually to lead to the first proper solo album by Anthony in 1977. The Geese and the Ghost began life in the mid seventies as a collaboration between Mike and Anthony, however, trends and tour schedules were to conspire against it as Anthony explained...

"It began as a co thing between Mike and myself. It was when Genesis did 'The Lamb,,' and that became a double album and Mike lost the time and it just became impractical really and he felt more comfortable making it and calling it my solo album, which was probably fair enough..."

With no interest from any record companies to speak of, the album was recorded under quite primitive conditions on board Tom Newman's floating studio in Little Venice and the process was not entirely without incident as Anthony remembers..

"It had to be done on the cheap (laughter) and Tom's barge was going through teething problems and so was the studio on it and we kept having breakdowns all the time...and the barge also kept on being rammed by other barges.."

Despite the problems, the album was finally released in March 1977 on Charisma's subsidiary Hit & Run Records, in fact it was their first release. The album also appeared on Passport Records in the USA the first of a long standing record deal with that company that served Anthony well until the late 1980's. As a first effort the album was a great surprise to fans and drew upon all of Anthony's musical influences to create a many layered soundscape that was totally unique. Perhaps from a fans' perspective, the most interesting thing about this album is the history of some of the pieces...

"I think one can divide the material on it mainly between two eras; there's one or two extras but basically..some of it represents bits and pieces from what I used to call the 1969 era of writing with Mike Rutherford which was stuff we used to do on twelve strings...Collections was from that period, from '69 on piano and a lot of the stuff from The Geese and the Ghost itself also dates from that period, but not all of it...The next bulk of material was from just after I left the band because in the last four or five months nobody seemed to be writing anything or if they were it was in secret...so after I left, after having done very little creative work, there was a great outpouring of material...all of the stuff like God if I saw her now, Which way the wind blows, most of Henry.. all came steaming out..."

However, the delay in releasing the album meant that when it finally emerged it was into the new dawn of the Punk era and as such it was crucified by the press eager to jump on the new bandwagon that labelled any recording artist of Anthony's ilk as being redundant at best and pretentious at worst, an accusation which cannot be levelled at Anthony's music by anyone who has really listened to it. To many of Anthony's fans the album still represents one of his finest moments although at the time Anthony had his reservations about recording more material...

"after putting all that effort into The Geese & The Ghost there didn't seem to be much point... I found that if I stopped I couldn't face the fact that I'd put all this effort into the album and nothing had happened so I just had to keep working to not think about it..."

Musically, The Geese & The Ghost firmly nailed Anthony's musical colours to the mast and indeed this album can be seen as the blueprint for his subsequent work. Within the album's sixteen tracks there is to be found everything which makes Anthony's music special: a microcosmic depiction of Tudor England in the delightful suite: Henry: Portraits From Tudor Times which magnificently evokes the ethos of that vanished era.

The Geese & The Ghost itself, works through soundscapes and imaginative instrumentation to create an eerie and yet strangely comforting mood whilst the album's three songs: Which Way The Wind Blows, God If I Saw Her Now and Collections demonstrated his abilities as a lyricist; especially the glorious elegy to lost love God If I Saw her Now which features one of Phil Collins' finest vocal performances and Anthony's own unique vocal style is premiered on Collections.

The connection with Philip Black also carried over into this album. Philip as a member of the famous (or should that be "infamous"?) Barge Rabbble as he recalls…

"I don't remember too many details as I remember having far too much to drink! Somebody put on a very nice lunch and drinks on the canal and I seem to remember going up and down the canal. I'm not sure whether that was before or after the recording session; it should have been before as we were quite jolly by then…. Barge Rabble describes exactly what it was; it was an odd collection of friends who just made up an impromptu choir. I do remember Richard being rather impressed by my voice as he didn't think I could sing…"

During this period music was written that would eventually see the light of day on other projects..

"during the first part of 1976 I recorded things like Tregenna Afternoons, I did all the Macbeth project which ended up as Reaper and parts of the Scottish Suite, loads and loads of things, we did all the first demos of Tarka..."
It was also during that year that another surprising twist in Anthony's career appeared. Peter Gabriel had finally walked out of the Genesis "machinery" the previous autumn and he had worked on some unreleased demo material with Peter and Mike Rutherford and lyricist Martin Hall, as reported in the press at that time.

Peter called upon Ant's services again in the spring of 1976 for a further series of recordings which included early versions of Flotsam & Jetsam, Slowburn, here Comes The Flood and three as yet unreleased tracks. Sadly none of these recordings were ever used officially although Anthony recalls the sessions at Trident Studios…

This was in a way a really big surprise as by then I had studied piano a fair bit and was much more a pianist than I had been while I was with Genesis when it was very much still as a songwriter. I wasn't by any means an accomplished pianist but Pete clearly felt that he couldn't handle some of the keyboard stuff at a slightly higher level and I think he wanted a slightly different approach than Tony Banks might have had. Maybe having Tony along with Mike and Phil would have been too much Genesis so what we had were the Genesis rhythm section; John Goodsall who was playing with Phil in Brand X and myself, so it was an odd collection of people..." The proliferation of material available to Anthony from this period was to serve him well over the next few years. His US record company; Passport Records who had the initial faith to release his first album continued albeit they required a more commercial album than The Geese & the Ghost...

"Anyway, it was songs and I was able to draw upon quite a lot of songs..like Birdsong which was from just after I left Genesis, certainly the verse..that sequence was very much after leaving. Regrets was from a couple of years before. Squirrel was from straight after Genesis...Paperchase was written before..in '76 but the songs I wrote..the new stuff were; We're all as we lie, Moonshooter, Pulling faces was another new one...Wise after the event that guitar riff was very much a new thing in that was the Rickenbacker big sound new funny sort of pedals and things. Now what (are they doing to my little friends?) was inspired by an awful tv programme about blokes culling seals and so the album was a mix of old, middling and new.."

The new album, titled "Wise After The Event" certainly drew upon a wider range of material than its more pastorally tinged predecessor even spawning Anthony's first UK single; We're All As We Lie which was coupled with two non album tracks; Squirrel and Sitars & Nebulous which were omitted due to lack of space making the single another major collector's item. The album also included an impressive array of talents to augment Anthony's own including Mike Giles (ex of King Crimson), John Perry and orchestrator Jeremy Gilbert. Production was by Rupert Hine already making a name for himself in the world of record production and no mean musician in his own right and he remembers the album fondly...

"I was always interested in pushing Anthony to do the singing himself and some days he'd feel good about that, some days he'd feel that other people could be doing it better. There were pressures from the record company and management side but on this album we tried very much to pursue the course of Anthony's character being his voice as much as his guitar...

John Perry also remembers Wise after the event...

"Well, basically it hurt! I must admit it took me a little while, probably half a day to understand where Anthony was coming from...When somebody like Anthony comes along it's not like painting by numbers,it's not something that falls into a pattern. Anthony has a very personalised style and you're trying to contribute to that, it's a case of stopping and putting your thinking cap on..."

Certainly the fans had to put their thinking caps on even from looking at the album sleeve which, once again, bore a staggeringly original piece of artwork by Anthony's friend Peter Cross including an amazing array of zany characters over its gatefold sleeve. However, by now the fierce detractors in the British music press had little time for the progressive music that they themselves had lauded so fiercely only three years previously and reviews tended to vary from totally antagonistic to deprecating at best.

Taking the courageous decision to sing on the album himself rather than use a guest vocalist; Anthony delivered a delightful album full of marvellous moments. The witty; We're All As We Lie and Wise after the Event itself. There is also the heartrending Regrets another wonderful love song and the brilliantly observed Now What (Are They Doing To My Little Friends?) which is a superb examination of the stupidity of hunting and man's cruelty to animals perfectly illustrated by the accompanying illustrations on the album's cover, To his fans, however, Wise After The Event was a fine follow up to his opening salvo but with commercial success still eluding him in an increasingly hostile marketplace, the question remained "What do I do next..?

1979 was to prove a memorable year for the British public in many ways; Margaret Thatcher became our first woman Prime Minister, a winter of discontent blew through the country and musically the UK was still very much in the grip of the "New Wave".

Into this atmosphere of aggression and frustration Anthony gave his fans what were to prove to be two of his finest albums; Sides, and the first of what is now a series of albums all bearing the generic title; Private Parts & Pieces. Far from being an inhabitant of some remote ivory tower, Anthony too, was clearly affected by the ongoing mood of frustration and anger current in the UK at this time and this shines through on several of the tracks on the Sides album especially the opening track 'Um And Aargh' a clear reference to record company pressures and the hypocrisy of the music press...

"nevertheless coming back into the scene and trying to make my name being at the mercy of the press was pretty tough actually...you heard these stories about A & R men who really didn't have a clue - they were very posey..."

The album includes several of Anthony's finest tracks including the lyrically gorgeous 'I Want Your Love' and 'Bleak House' but even this was not enough to save the album from the surgery of the record company..

"There were two completely instrumental pieces; one twelve string which could have been a Geese and the Ghost thing, and another synth based piece which would have preceded Slow Dance by about ten years...Rupert Hine was very keen to go with those being an instrumental composer himself ..he was getting his instructions from the record company..."

Rupert confirms this view himself ...

"I don't think Sides gained a lot more by the attempts at more commercial songwriting; outside singers and so on...with Sides you can hear these attempts to make the music more widely appealling for better or worse..."

Other problems beset the recording of the album including pressure to complete the recording process which had the knock on effect of squeezing the amount of time available for rehearsal and preparation...

"The thing that was iffy about the album was the fact that my overdubbing time got really squeezed. We started off in style if you like, and ended in style mixing at Trident but the middle part was dodgy. We did the overdubs at this place called Matrix which was dreadful! I wanted to spend more time on nightmare on the overdubs, but it all had to be done extremely quickly - it was almost a case of getting all the overdubs done in a day.."

With the added help of such excellent musicians as Mike Giles and John Perry, however, the album managed to rise above these problems and presented a truer picture of Anthony's talents both as a songwriter and instrumentalist and certainly one capable of writing material of more worth than the pop culture into which the album was born. Nightmare and Sisters Of Remindum certainly demonstrated that Anthony's rock sensibilities were still as keen as ever. His lyrical sensibilities were thrown into sharp contrast with Lucy Will and its acid commentary on fame and how it changes people and the truly wonderful tribute to Dickens in Bleak House. It is no wonder that many fans mark this album down as their favourite from Antony's catalogue.

At the same time as this album, another appeared which was to display the rich legacy of Anthony's instrumental talents; Private Parts and Pieces was to serve as the template for a whole series of albums encompassing all the facets of music which Anthony has explored. Initially released in the USA, the album was subsequently issued in the UK as a limited edition free with the first five thousand copies of the Sides album, a genuinely nice gesture towards his fans, the album includes archival material from the mid '70's mainly acoustic guitar and piano pieces ...

"Home recording studios didn't really stretch to doing anything with much scope or a great number of tracks on it. So, I just used to record acoustic guitar and piano pieces..."

The mixture of elements on the album served as a useful indicator of the influences which have guided Anthony's music and a couple of the tracks have a lengthy pedigree...

"Field Of Eternity was an early long instrumental piece which I took the guitar piece out.."

Anthony freely admits that he was lucky in having an abundance of music from which he could select a "best of" so to speak. The exigencies of the music business did not make for plain sailing with the album, however;

"When I took the tapes to Trident studios to master it, Ray Staff had to do a lot of work on it as there were so many problems with it..."

Anthony had done most of the recording in his home studio which was not as well equipped as a commercial studio..

"There's all sorts of weird and wonderful things going on if you listen to the album closely.." In fact, some of the instruments themselves are quite surprising on an album by a supposed "rock" artist; including as they did; a harmonium, and a "pin" piano which in fact was an ordinary piano with drawing pins under the hammers to create a harpsichord effect!"

Altogether the album was certainly a welcome addition to the growing canon of Anthony's works and even gained him some plaudits both at the time of release and subsequently upon its re-issue on cd. However, the album was never intended to break into the mass commercial market and by now the situation for "serious" musicians was practically untenable in the UK unless you were already an established name.

Into this atmosphere was born the second of the Private Parts & Pieces albums, subtitled; "Back To The Pavilion". Indicative of Anthony's increasing frustration with the music scene in the UK was the dedication on the back cover: *"This album is dedicated to all those who still champion the 'Old Fashioned' ideals of beauty lyricism and grandeur in art against the tide of cynical intellectualism and dissonance.."* Anthony was not prepared to meekly collaborate with the ongoing butchery of the music that had been his mainspring and inspiration which was currently going on in Britain and particularly the cynical attitude of the music press against whom he had already fired a salvo on Sides. His attitude had become even harder since then.

"that was really cynical with the turncoats that one day had been praising the bands and the next day when the new thing was in, started rubbishing them..."

The album was the first in a whole batch of albums by Anthony which only appeared in the USA because of the contractual situation (or lack of it) in the UK:

"After the two so-called commercial albums; Wise after the event and Sides hadn't done anything and after Sides hadn't been the great commercial top ten hit that they thought it would be; that contract went. This was before the contract with RCA but I had an existing contract with Passport and so the only outlet for this album was Passport.."

Once again, Anthony found himself having to draw on existing material for the album...

"There were no advances coming from them so the music that could be used had to be available, hence the use of guitar and piano pieces and material that was available.."

Included in this list was the "Scottish Suite" ostensibly written for an ambitious project based around Shakespeare's play MacBeth which was to set the dialogue to music composed by rock musicians. Sponsored initially by Genesis's publishers Fuse Music, the project never really got off the ground. The ambitious nature of some of this music was finally demonstrated with the release in 2004 of the Scottish Suite II on the second Archive Collection album where a variety of much more experimental music from this project was finally released.

However, the album itself was another intriguing mixture of music including several further pieces dating back to the early Seventies including I Saw You Today, and Back To The Pavilion. Finally the missing "links" from Wise After The Event were also included and the eventual cd re-issue of the album also included another delightful classic; Lucy An Illusion. The album heralded Anthony's survival into the new decade, and his next project was to surprise both his fans and critics alike....

Late 1980 saw Anthony without a record deal in the UK and with the wind set fair against his style of music, his only avenue was his existing deal with American record company Passport Records who were to remain his champions throughout the Eighties until their eventual demise in 1988. With the relative lack of success attaching to both of Ant's previous attempts at song oriented records, the question was very much "What do I do now?" as Anthony himself recalls...

"It was a question of trying to look for a different angle which didn't require a lot of money but which wasn't an acoustic album..."

Anthony had been contacted earlier in the year to write the theme and incidental music for a tv series called "Rule Britannia" and having been given far greater leeway on the composition he decided to use his recently acquired synthesisers on that project and with a certain amount of cross referencing the music began to take on an extra element...

"During the summer of 1980 I did actually record what became the Prelude separately to the whole plan and that was done just out of the blue; I just had an idea and I recorded it very quickly in about three or four hours. The Anthem was done in a similar way..."

At last Anthony was being paid to be inventive in the studio and the resulting music was startlingly original in both its style and use in the six programmes in the series. It was also during this period that Anthony began to pick up tv and jingle work which are very much a composer's stock in trade and it is this area of endeavours which has increasingly featured in Anthony's work schedule. Having started this project Anthony was intending to use a Polymoog piece which he had left over from Sides and this encouraged him to explore further in this area aided by his friend Richard Scott who worked with him on the album...

"I started working on this extra keyboard piece, which I wanted to be a more modern, short five-minute piece - and that ended up as the whole album..."

Recording the album was no easy process, with Anthony only having access to 8 track facilities and all the percussion tracks having to be individually recorded and then the whole thing transferred on to 16 track which involved a multitude of sub-edits...

"It was a complete nightmare for the engineer, Chris David because it was all in sections as there were a lot of cuts and changes. I'd put some edits into pieces to lay the guide synth parts down and then he had to take the edits apart again and then put them together again at the sixteen track stage.."

Nor was composing the music for the tv series a piece of cake either, as Anthony recalls...

"I was handed a list of words like; 'Greed' and 'Irony'...I had to sit and write ideas to 'Greed'!...The Rule Britannia team were quite exceptional - they were all very interested not just to listen to the title music but to listen to all the music I'd done...I think I was lucky, I think television work isn't normally like that..."

Intriguingly enough at the same time, Anthony also wrote a symphony and the Rule Britannia theme was one of the major themes from it. Sadly the symphony itself has yet to see the light of day. RCA Records signed Anthony up on the strength of the album and even went as far to release a single coupling Prelude '84 with Anthem 1984 which was awarded "Single of the week" status by Record Mirror of all things in July 1981. The album itself also garnered a complimentary press in the main although an instrumental album was never going to give Anthony his big break unless attached to a major film or tv series, some things never change! Nevertheless, the album was a refreshing change both for Anthony and his fans and the idea of longer conceptual pieces of music linked by a common theme or story was to be further investigated as both Anthony and Richard Scott continued their partnership and embarked upon a foray into the world of musicals so often fraught with pitfalls.

As if the prospect of being involved full-time in a musical wasn't enough for Anthony, he also found time during late 1981/82 to compile another of the generic Private Parts & Pieces albums; "Antiques" was to be the third in the series to date. Unlike its predecessors however, this album was more of a collaborative effort between Ant and his Argentinian friend Henrique Berro Garcia...

"I got together with Quique and played some music informally...I took round some of my duets which I'd actually scored such as 'Old Wives Tale' and some parts of the 'Hurlingham Suite'..it was a great time that summer (1981). I remember about the time that '1984' came out I did the 'Masquerade' stuff with Richard at Send, I also did a lot of stuff with Dennis Quinn; I helped him record his first lot of demos about that time as well.."

Musically the album was purely driven by the informal 'jams' that the two musicians performed often in the evening after dinner, and the relaxed atmosphere of these shines through in the music. With one or two exceptions, the music also broke with the tradition of the series by using new music rather than archival material..

"It was all pretty much new stuff. We started off saying that we should keep it simple and then we got one or two ideas for slight variations like at the end of 'Old Wives Tale' where all those extra guitars come in and we started dubbing up a bit..."

The entire process of recording took a little over a month although listening to the music gives no indication of the brevity of the project and it is to the enduring credit of both musicians that this is the case. Unusually for an album in this series, "Antiques" was also released in the UK as well as the USA although this was more down to good luck than planning..

"RCA still had me on board, although '1984' didn't do what they wanted it to do. This wasn't the next proper album as far as they were concerned and they weren't interested in it. Tony Smith managed to persuade them to put it out over here. He had to insist that they put it out for an advance of £1! The pressure was already building up for what eventually became 'Invisible Men'. The usual thing happened with Passport; it just drifted out in the States without any great fanfare.."

The album's relaxed aura gives no indication of the trials and tribulations that lay in wait for Anthony over the next two or so years which mainly concerned a young lady by the name of "Alice"..

Rock musicians and musicals have had a somewhat chequered history from Pete Townshend's opus "Tommy" in the mid 1960's very few if any musicians have made the transition successfully. So what exactly motivated Anthony to try his hand at something so radically different to the fields in which he had been working? The "Alice" project evolved out of another musical effort a putative attempt to transfer Kit Williams's book "Masquerade" onto the musical stage. Anthony's involvement stemmed from his association with producer Rupert Hine and his manager Tony Smith and Anthony's involvement was supposed to be very much on the sidelines. However, Rupert's work with many of the then "in" musicians of the current New Wave of the English music scene meant that Anthony gradually became more involved..

"I wrote lots and lots of stuff...we eventually got three or four demos out which were ok but it never felt cohesive at all..."

Rumours abounded that Kate Bush and other alumni of the music industry were to take part but sadly none of these high flown ideas ever developed and Anthony was left with a plethora of material which he was determined to develop further and in order to further that goal he turned to his friend Richard Scott with whom he developed several pieces..

" with encouragement from Tony Smith we demoed four or five songs which worked out pretty well..the funny thing is that not much in Alice came through from Masquerade but some pieces were influenced and inspired by it..."

A suggestion was made that the pair contact Leeds Playhouse an innovative theatre company on the look out for something more adventurous. As Anthony recalls..

"There was an idea of this new dream team of Richard's ideas coupled with Nicholas Hytner's theatrical experience and know-how would manage to carve a brilliant product.."

Nicholas Hytner has since gone on to achieve major musical success with "Miss Saigon" and also the recent Oscar nominated film "The Madness of King George" and so, it was an enthralling prospect.
Not quite so enthralling was the prospect of spending a wintry March in Leeds especially with a Germanic landlady who, if Anthony is to be believed was like one of Wagner's Valkyries! Anthony and Richard spent most of 1983 working on full demos for the musical after Leeds commissioned them and by the end of that year there were about eight songs shaped up. The discipline of a musical however, does not rely solely on the music, drama is the most important aspect and if the music doesn't fit the music MUST be changed as Anthony recalls...

"the great discipline I learned was that in most of the songs the action has to flow through them you can't have frozen moments where you are talking about an emotion except for the odd ballad.."

If nothing else Anthony gained a wider experience of musical styles having to write pieces from quadrilles to boogie woogie for the project...

"There were a couple of set pieces with three sort of washerwomen type characters doing a silly sort of dance and I had to learn boogie woogie for one track called 'Duck and Dive'. It was a million miles away from working with Genesis and that was quite good actually but I'd be sitting in this rehearsal room and having to learn how to do it - so much for the great composer! "

The musical had a budget of £80,000 which sounds an enormous amount of money but compared to the £2000, 000 spent on "Starlight Express" at the same time it is amazing to think that the musical was ever completed at all. Budgetary constraints were not the only problems rehearsals were conducted in a fragmentary way and Anthony was prevailed upon to write the arrangements for the show with only a few weeks to go....

"I have never worked as hard in my life...I would have three hours' sleep a night and I'd wake up in a state of complete panic and start work again..."

The entire project was finally completed and ran for six weeks in March - April 1984 and was deemed a success playing to packed houses every night and it was certainly worthwhile experience for any musician. Sadly the musical has not been staged since it's debut in 1984 and the music, in the main, remains unheard although a couple of pieces have been released elsewhere. The lovely song "Walls And Bridges" was given the instrumental treatment on Anthony's fourth Private Parts & Pieces album under the title of "Lights On The Hill".

Useful experience or no, the musical left Anthony with some serious decisions to make. During this period he had finally moved up to London into his first house, an arduous process for anyone but to a musician faced with limited earnings from royalties and deprived of the opportunity of earning money from sessions due to commitment to the musical..

"I actually lost money over those six months and it was a ludicrous thing to do at the time because I'd just moved into a new house and had a mortgage and a house full of lodgers...I was really back against the wall when it came down to it..."

Faced with the prospect of no big advance from a record company and the need to recoup some lost momentum (and money) Anthony and Richard decided to develop some of the music they had been writing over the past year or so and record an album of more blatantly commercial songs, an album that was certainly to surprise most long standing fans.

At the same time as the "Alice" project was getting under way Anthony and Richard Scott also began work on what was, almost a year later to emerge as Anthony's next album. The exigencies of the time have to be borne in mind when considering this project; Ant had not long moved in to his first house in London and the lupine pest of household bills and other nasties made frequent and unwelcome appearances. To try and alleviate the situation Ant considered a variety of options...

"As far as the direction was concerned; I'd done Private Parts & Pieces albums, I'd done all sorts of things which were all ticking over and making bits of money but nothing was pulling in a lot so, therefore the attitude from Tony Smith and the Genesis office was; 'this is the demands of the time; this is the era Post Punk, New Romantic whatever you want to call it, this is what you need to do..."

The very idea of Anthony being cast in the same mould as the likes of Duran Duran and Spandau Ballet may seem very far fetched now but there was the clear understanding that in order to gain a wider acceptance in a marketplace that was becoming increasingly polarised; a mainstream album was what was required. Always a fan of rock, Anthony set about the task with a vengeance and also taking on board the fact that his Genesis cohorts; Mike and Tony were currently recording albums on which they had decided to sing, Anthony took the plunge himself and had some singing lessons..

"What was happening at the time; Mike Rutherford and Tony Banks were both doing solo albums (Acting Very Strange and The Fugitive respectively) and they were doing their own vocals and I think there was a feeling that in the absence of knowing anybody particularly well; I'll have a crack at it myself.."

Listening to the album now it is difficult to imagine the problems that beset both Richard and Anthony as the work progressed. From a promising beginning with four or five songs it became increasingly difficult to sustain interest in a project which, after all, had been dictated more at the behest of the record company than by any genuine desire of Ant's to become a "pop" star...

"early in 1983 there was all this stuff about 'looking the part' and there was all this stuff about trying to make an image out of it and the Anthony Phillips Band and all that stuff.. "

Musically however, despite the problems the album did contain many fine moments; the emotion of "Women Were Watching" and "Exocet" which caught the frustration of the time with the political situation in the UK over the Falklands War and I am sure if they had been promoted better either track could have been a success. As it was sensibilities prevailed and "Exocet" was dropped from the UK version of the album and fans had to wait almost ten years to hear it again on the Virgin CD re-issue of the album in 1991.

Going For Broke could well be seen as an accurate statement of Anthony's current position with regard to where his musical future lay.

Elsewhere within the album there were several tracks which could have brought the "band" chart success. The delightfully tongue-in-cheek Golden Bodies was a definite contender for an imaginative promotional video with plenty of opportunities for humour. This was also the case with the equally as humorous Love In A Hot Air Balloon which would have worked equally well with a visual accompaniment. My Time Has Come darkly echoed the story of Close Encounters whilst Sally once again demonstrated that Anthony had a fine eye for social realism with a story of the frustrated attempts of a young man "pursuing the unattainable".
As an exercise in compromise however, the album perhaps took Anthony as far as anyone could reasonably expect him to go although even the American record label were not completely happy rejecting several cuts from the album...

"We took the rough mixes to RCA who had been quite keen on 1984 and the guy was quite complimentary but said 'there's no single here'.."

Eventually the album surfaced in the UK on small independent label: Street Tunes who actually picked up on the album while Ant was occupied with the "Alice" musical in Leeds. Writing and recording were no problem however and over thirty tracks were recorded many in quick fire order..

"We used to work incredibly fast and we didn't even work evenings. Richard would arrive at about 10.30 am and we'd have a backing track done by lunch time! I remember I wrote "Bouncer" one morning before he arrived, literally that was it; pick up a twelve string 'right, he's not here yet, let's record this..' "

Many of the tracks were tried in different permutations both by Richard and Anthony and a few found a place on other projects most notable being the compilation album "Harvest Of The Heart" release by Street Tunes in 1985 as well as a couple of others which surfaced on the cd re-issue. Of the remainder, they still exist and who knows, some may find their way on to a future compilation?

Having flirted with the risk-laden world of the charts and musicals; Anthony returned to what he considers himself to be best at; a new instrumental album, the fourth in the Private Parts and Pieces series, subtitled "A Catch At The Tables". In fact, the years 1984 - 87 were to be dominated by volumes in this series with no less than four appearing in that time. Of these, "A Catch At The Tables" is perhaps the most rounded of the series representing as it does, most of the facets of Anthony's music from beautiful acoustic pieces and keyboard works as well as a new song; "Sistine". The next albums to be released by Anthony were also in the Private Parts & Pieces series although both Private Parts & Pieces V and VI were quite radically different from previous offerings in the series. Private Parts & Pieces V, which was subtitled 'Twelve' was an album of Spartan elegance utilising solely acoustic guitars to develop themes based around the twelve months of the year, if you like this album can almost be seen as Anthony's "Four Seasons".

The music is tightly developed but it lacks the usual warmth associated with Anthony's work but nonetheless demonstrated admirably his command of form and style.1986's "Ivory Moon" the sixth album in the series demonstrated a similar notion only this time the instrument used was piano, piano NOT synthesiser. The result was another elegant charming but somewhat characterless album although there were brief snatches of the old Phillips humour among some of the titles. Interestingly enough, this album also included a couple of the pieces from the abortive Masquerade project for which Anthony had written much material as he recalls..

"I wrote stacks for it and it sort of petered out...So I had some experience of writing things in that sort of declamatory style when you have to project songs...So there were two things on Ivory Moon which were, if you like, my attempts at songs for Masquerade..."

These pieces served to give his fans a brief look at what might have been.

The eighteen months or so that followed the release of the sixth Private Parts & Pieces album saw radical changes in Anthony's career. 1987 started well enough with the release once again in the USA only, of the seventh of the Private Parts & Pieces albums subtitled "Slow Waves Soft Stars" a return to the mixed format of album which characterised most of its predecessors and was in a way a reaction of Anthony's against the rather purist feel of the previous two albums in the series...

"Private Parts & Pieces V and VI had to be done...it was great to do albums like that but I felt I couldn't do another album of...purity is fine but too much purity becomes Spartan you know and I think it is quite taxing to listen to an album of one sound...

Certainly Anthony's fans could not accuse him of too much purity with this offering, which had all the usual trademarks on it; delightfully whimsical acoustic guitar pieces and some intriguing synthesiser pieces which had many fans wondering whether Ant had succumbed to the current "New Age" trends?

"...When I came to do Private Parts & Pieces VII this New Age thing.. the upturn hadn't really happened. I had a few synth pieces from library albums that I'd done which were sort of too dreamy because a lot of the things they want for library albums have to have some kind of pulse to them and were almost too kind of dreamy, too ethereal.."

At the time of the album's release, Anthony did a spot of promotional work as guest vj on the VH1 programme "New Visions" in the USA and he referred to the album as "a collection of subversive synthesiser pieces..." however, nothing could be further from the truth. Sure, the synth pieces were an interesting novelty but the meat of the album still resided in the acoustic tracks which were sandwiched between them.

This album is still one of the hardest to find outside of the US a situation aggravated by the fact that at the time of its release the record company were in the midst of financial problems which were to lead to their bankruptcy in late 1988. Irritatingly enough, the company has apparently since been reconstituted but with no legal obligations to any of their previous artists... Hey ho, that's show business, folks! So, by the beginning of 1988 Anthony was faced with the dual problem of having to earn a living as a recording musician without an outlet for his recordings. Library and tv work had become the staff of life for many musicians and Anthony was lucky in having that outlet for some of his work. However, as an album artist it is sadly necessary to have a record company prepared to support you unless you are sufficiently wealthy to do it on your own and so, what was Anthony to do? Ironically, it was to be a work which had been shelved in the mid 1970's during the New Wave backlash against so-called Progressive Rock which was to provide Anthony with a much need breather.

Anthony had worked with Harry Williamson (later of Gong fame) in the late '60's and early '70's on a variety of projects including an instrumental work based around Harry's father's book "Tarka The Otter"...

"Then around 1973-74 we started doing more serious two acoustic guitar things and he told me about his father's book and we became terribly inspired by that...originally we hoped to get the score to the film that they were doing of Tarka The Otter in 1977-78 and we thought it was a good nepotistic line.. Harry being Henry's son but it was a bit far-fetched

I think...Hit & Run put up some money to finish the orchestral score and it sounded pretty good actually..."

Hit & Run who were still Anthony's management at the time were not ultimately responsible for the completion of the project which is run by Simon MacCorkindale and Susan George and they heard it and loved it and wanted to use it in one of their films and even based a script re-write around it. Sadly the film; "The Dragon Under The Hill" has yet to see the light of day, but the album "Tarka" finally emerged into the daylight on 31st October 1988.

In many ways this album was a watershed for Anthony's music. First of all, it was the first of his albums to be issued on compact disc in this country, and it was the largest scale composition that Anthony had attempted up to this point one which was well received in most quarters at the time of its release. Certainly this is a field of endeavours to which Anthony is well suited and indeed, well qualified. Unfortunately, Anthony was to be dogged by bad luck on this project, and within a few months of the album's release in October 1988, the record company had gone bankrupt (no doubt Anthony had a certain feeling of déjà vu at this point).

As a stop gap measure, Anthony issued the first of what has since become a growing series of albums under the generic title of "Missing Links" initially on his own label; "Occasional Records" as a cassette-only edition which was also used to finance the creation of his own fan club; "The Pavilion" which was established in 1991. The album contained a selection of his library music which previously had been unheard by the public and which formed a nice contrast to the other strand of archival music covered by the Private Parts & Pieces albums.

Anthony's career took a turn for the better in 1990 when Virgin Records signed him up for a five album deal which began auspiciously enough with 1990's Slow Dance album although this had already been composed and recorded before the deal was signed. This album proved that Anthony's talents were not just confined to small scale work but could expand to the broader palette require for film work. This album with its soaring instrumentation and lush use of orchestral and rock colour is to my mind one of his finest works and one of which Anthony is justifiably proud although sadly not used in a film as yet, it remains a score "in waiting " for some far sighted film executive to take up and put to good use.

Anthony's connections with Virgin continued and at last the record company had the good sense to release Anthony's back catalogue on compact disc over a period of several months between November 1990 and October of 1991. Most of these albums had never appeared on compact disc before and to these were added bonus tracks including thankfully the long lamented single B-sides to Anthony's relatively few and very hard to find singles. There were also several interesting other additions including several demos and out-takes all of which greatly enhanced the desirability of the discs and ensured that the "Great Re-Issue Rip Off" tag levelled at so many artists could not be aimed at these releases!

The first proper album recorded under their auspices was to be 1992's Private Parts & Pieces VIII: New England which continued the tradition so nobly maintained by the previous albums in this series by integrating both keyboard and guitar work into a broader picture illuminating further Anthony's talents as a composer and musician. Once again Anthony was able to continue a series which has become a trademark to his fans although not quite as simple as that as he explains....

"At the time that Virgin were releasing the back catalogue on CD, the last group of albums we released were Private Parts & Pieces V-VII and it seemed a good idea to coincide with that the release of the new material in a similar genre. I was always keen if possible, to keep the Private Parts & Pieces series going ,because that was the forum if you like for simple acoustic pieces; the kind of material you wouldn't consider putting on another kind of album... I think the essential difference is that it is almost chamber pieces really; very intimate, very direct pieces where you can get away with just playing one instrument..."

The album does contain a mix of music and one of Anthony's rare songs: Unheard Cry which is a heart-rending description of a baby AIDS victim. Anthony's vocals deliver a rare poignancy here and the song is emotionally charged and certainly dispels any myths that Anthony cannot write songs that actually SAY something!
Sadly however, the Virgin deal was to be curtailed in 1993 when Richard Branson sold Virgin to commercial giant EMI who took an axe to Virgin's roster of artists and sadly Anthony was one of those out in the cold again.
His work as a composer has always been Anthony's mainstay and it was fortunate for him that his services were in demand and he could maintain his career through this work whilst seeking an alternative outlet for his recorded work. Finding such an outlet proved quite difficult and it was not until 1994. However, the deal that was arranged has since then proven to be an infinitely more workable one which gives Anthony greater artistic freedom than he has had for many years.

The deal was with Voiceprint Records, an independent record label established at the tail end of the 1980's by Rob Ayling and whose advertising slogan sums up their attitude to music quite nicely: "The best music you never heard". Determined to bring the music of composers either maligned or ignored by the mainstream to a greater audience, Voiceprint and its subsidiary Blueprint have enabled Anthony's work to reach a wider audience beginning in 1994 with the second of the Missing Links albums subtitled, "The Sky Road" which continued the trend set by its predecessor by including further pieces from his television work as well as new compositions and a couple of gems from the very early days of his career as Anthony explains…

"What I am doing with the Missing Links albums is choosing the best of the commissioned music in simple terms of music where I have been told what to do…. It still concerns me slightly when people wonder 'well why isn't this just called Private Parts & Pieces IX?' There must be a definite distinction between albums I think which includes chunks of stuff that are written to order. Then it is not Private Parts & Pieces material because it is what the public ordered such as with Lifeboat which is OK but there were moments when I was trying to sound like Vaughan Williams…"

Between writing new material for various projects; Anthony also managed to revisit a couple of projects which had been shelved a LONG time ago. His next two albums were works of great contrast. First out of the traps was the soundtrack to the 1992/93 Whitbread Round The World Yacht Race which appeared in 1994 under the title Sail The World.

This was a major commission for Anthony and the race itself was televised in the UK and spanned some 36 weeks in all which was excellent coverage for Anthony's music! Once again, this was very much programme music and as such had to emphasise everything from dramatic race sequences to encounters with whales, penguins and other aquatic fauna and the more mundane happenings such as being becalmed. The final selection of music on the CD certainly managed to paint the broadest possible picture and served once again to emphasise Anthony's talents as a composer.

Following this release was an album with a VERY long pedigree. Gypsy Suite began life in the early 1970's as a collaborative effort with Harry Williamson whom Anthony also worked with on the Tarka project mentioned earlier, not long after Anthony's departure from Genesis. The rustic nature of the music can in part be attributed to the experience Anthony had when he visited Harry's father ….

He was quite eccentric by that stage and it was a quite primitive living style, although the house was quite nice it was never really properly furnished and it had log fires which is quite nice. However, although I am very sort of game for the striding over headlands sort of thing but when I come back I quite like the mod cons actually. I love looking at fires but I have never been particularly good at making them whereas Harry was into a basic rough way of life…"

There is a rustic and basic campfire quality to the music; an essential earthiness which is quite charming. The opportunity to work with Harry came at just the right time for Anthony, who by his own admission was finding life outside Genesis quite daunting…

I got very depressed at that point trying to read music and I was also trying to start a lot more guitar writing but it was all very insular stuff. It was my first co-writing after leaving Genesis you see, after about a year of locking myself away during which time I had learned how to play the piano. So it was actually very exciting and refreshing …and there were no boundaries; no barriers really…."

This album was followed by the first compilation of Anthony's material since 1985's Harvest Of The Heart. The Anthology album was a fine introduction to Anthony's back catalogue followed by a "Live In Studio" album; "The Living Room Concert" initially recorded for an American Public Service Radio series called "Echoes"; there was sufficient interest from the fan base to justify this release as an album. Initially accompanied by a booklet with transcripts to the lyrics to nearly all of the songs from Anthony's albums; this was certainly an eye opener for Anthony's fans who have long cherished the hope that their hero might consider concert performance at some point.

Another outing for the Private Parts & Pieces series followed, the ninth in the series: Dragonfly Dreams which once again, mixed old and new material including a couple of pieces from his earlier collaborations with Henrique Berro Garcia. This was in turn followed by another collaborative effort this time with Guillermo Cazenave and titled: The Meadows of Englewood which once again, contained several interesting compositions.
The third volume of the Missing Links series: Time And Tide and a compilation from Anglia TV of many of the best pieces of music from their "Survival" wildlife series titled: Survival: The Music Of Nature thoroughly documented Anthony's work as a TV composer of some stature.

A further trip back into the archives was next on the agenda with the release in 1998 of the first Archive Collection album. This coincided with the release of the first Genesis Box set, a happy but unintentional coincidence which gave Anthony's fans even more archival material to get their teeth into including the legendary F#1 demo, more commonly known to Genesis fans as The Musical Box, here in its embryonic stages.

The album was not intended to "cash in" on the interest in Genesis but also to satisfy the desires of Anthony's own fans to hear some of the material which had been shelved for one reason or another. The efforts expended on ensuring that the material used was both representative but also of suitable quality was to ensure that Anthony's fans were to declare themselves highly satisfied with the end result.

A further edition of the Private Parts & Pieces series emerged in 1999. Titled Soiree it is the second edition to be totally piano-based. The first piano album; Ivory Moon was a somewhat Spartan affair and Anthony had his own reservations about another single instrument album…

"The Whole thing came about I suppose because a number of people had said to me; 'please will you do another album of piano pieces?' I wasn't sure because you know already my reservations about single instrument CDs possibly being a little unchanging in timbre and therefore possibly not giving people the variation…it was nice this time to mainly write new music…"

Despite the use of one instrument, there is definitely more of a flow and variation to this project and as usual there is a certain wry humour in some of the titles! The album serves to reinforce the fact that Anthony is equally at home on the keyboard as he is on the guitar.

The period since the release of Soiree has been one of both looking backward and forward for Anthony. Thanks again to Jonathan Dann's continued researches into Anthony's tape archives and the preservation of much of that musical legacy, Anthony has not only been able to provide his fans with a further delving into that archive in the shape of 2004's second Archive Collection release, a double CD which captured many previously unsuspected tracks from Anthony's lengthy career. A further couple of library albums: English Pastoral and Ancient Civilisations have also occupied a fair amount of Anthony's time in the studio.

The delving has also unearthed much material which will prove useful for the remaining albums from the Virgin contract which have yet to be properly re-mastered in to CD. These include the original master recordings for The Geese & The Ghost as well as a substantial body of demo and rehearsal recordings for that album and for the others awaiting re-issue: Wise after the Event and 1984. It is hoped that when Voiceprint finally acquire the reversionary rights to these albums in 2005, a complete repackaging of these three essential albums can finally be done.

So much for the looking backwards The forward looking projects include another major library album for Atmosphere on which Anthony was currently working at the time this was written and also new music for his first fill-scale album since 1999. Titled Field Day, a double album of acoustic guitar music released by Voiceprint on 10th October 2005.

No matter what else happens, one thing is for sure, Anthony Phillips will be creating new music for many more years yet.

ANTHONY PHILLIPS SOLO RELEASES

7" VINYL SINGLES

A- Side	B-Side	Record Company/Catalogue Number	Release Date
We're all as we lie	Sitars & Nebulous/Squirrel	ARIST 192 (UK)	?.06.78
We're all as we lie	Sitars & Nebulous/Squirrel	PS 7914 (USA)	?.06.78
Um & Aargh	Souvenir	ARIST 252 (UK) (PS)	?.03.79
Prelude '84	Anthem 1984	RCA 102 (UK) (PS)	?.07.81
The Anthem from Tarka	The Rising Spring	PYS 18 (UK) (PS)	10.11.88

12" VINYL SINGLES

Sally	Women were watching/Exocet	JJ 102-12 (UK) (PS)	?.02.84

COMPACT DISC SINGLES

The Anthem from Tarka (Single mix)/The Rising Spring/Excerpt from Tarka (Mvt1)/Excerpt from Tarka (Mvt3)/The Anthem from Tarka (Single mix extended version)   PYD 18   (UK) (PS)   ?.11.88

VINYL ALBUMS

ALBUM TITLE	RECORD COMPANY/ CATALOGUE NUMBER	RELEASE DATE
Beyond an empty dream	Charisma CAS1101	1975 (UK)

(Compilation album featuring 'Take this heart' hymn co-written by Anthony and Mike Rutherford) Intergalactic Touring Band 1977 (UK)

ALBUM TITLE	RECORD COMPANY/ CATALOGUE NUMBER	RELEASE DATE
The Geese & The Ghost	Passport PVC8905	?.03.77 (US)
The Geese & The Ghost	Hit & Run HIT001	?.04.77 (UK)
Wise after the event	Arista SPART1063	?.05.78 (UK)
Wise after the event	Passport PB9828	?.05.78 (US)
Wise after the event (Picture disc album)	Passport PB9828	?.05.78 (US)
Sides	Arista SPART1085	?.06.79 (US)
Sides	Passport PB9834	?.06.79 (US)
Private Parts & Pieces	Arista AFLP1	?.06.79 (UK)

(Limited edition with 1st 5000 copies of 'Sides)

ALBUM TITLE	RECORD COMPANY/ CATALOGUE NUMBER	RELEASE DATE
Private Parts & Pieces	Passport PVC 7909	?.06.79 (US)
Private Parts & Pieces II: Back to the Pavilion	Passport PVC 7913	?.03.80 (US)
1984	RCA RCA LP 5036	?.06.81 (UK)

(Initial copies contained a black and white poster of Anthony in the studio)

ALBUM TITLE	RECORD COMPANY/ CATALOGUE NUMBER	RELEASE DATE
Private Parts & Pieces III: Antiques	RCA INTS 5228	?.05.82 (UK)
Private Parts & Pieces III: Antiques	Passport PVC 7985	?.?.82 (US)
Invisible Men	Passport PB 6023	?.08.83 (US)
Private Parts & Pieces IV: A catch at the tables	Passport PVC 8919	?.07.84 (US)
Invisible Men (1 track different to US)	Street Tunes STLP0013	?.06.84 (UK)
Private Parts & Pieces V: Twelve	Passport PVC 8926	?.09.84 (US)
Harvest of the heart (Compilation)	Cherry Red BRED 66	?.?.85 (UK)
Private Parts & Pieces VI: Ivory Moon	Passport PVC 8946	?.?.85 (US)
Private Parts & Pieces VII: Slow waves soft stars	Audion SYN 308	?.?.87 (US)
Tarka	PRT PYL 18	31.10.88 (UK)
Slow dance	Virgin V2638	24.09.90 (UK)

Slow dance was to be Anthony's last commercial album to be available on the vinyl format although his various library albums continue to be issued on vinyl although these are not available to the general public.

CASSETTE ALBUMS

The Geese & The Ghost	Passport PVCC8905	?.03.77 (US)
The Geese & The Ghost	Hit & Run HIT C001	?.04.77 (UK)
Wise after the event	Arista TCART1063	?.05.78 (UK)
Wise after the event	Passport PBCC8928	?.05.78 (US)
Sides	Arista TCART1085	?.06.79 (UK)
Sides	Passport PBC 9834	?.06.79 (US)
Private Parts & Pieces	Passport PBC 9837	?.06.79 (US)
Private Parts & Pieces II	Passport PBC 7913	?.03.80 (US)
1984	RCA 102	?.06.81 (UK)
1984	Passport PBC 7946	?.06.81 (US)
Private Parts & Pieces III	RCA INTS 5228	?.05.82 (UK)
Private Parts & Pieces III	Passport PBC 8909	?.05.82 (US)
Invisible Men	Passport PBC 6023	?.08.83 (US)
Private Parts & Pieces IV	Passport PBC 8919	?.06.84 (US)
Invisible Men	Street Tunes STC0013	?.06.84 (UK)
Private Parts & Pieces V	Passport PBC 8926	?.11.84 (US)
Private Parts & Pieces VI	Passport PBC 8946	?.05.85 (US)

COMPACT DISC ALBUMS

The Geese & The Ghost	Passport PVCD 8905	?.?.85 (US)
The Geese & The Ghost	Virgin CDOVD 315	?.03.90 (UK)
Wise after the event	Virgin CDOVD 322	?/?.90 (UK)
Sides	Virgin CDOVD 316	?.03.90 (UK)
Sides (Picture disc)	Blueprint BP205CD	?.?.95 (UK)
Private Parts & Pieces	Virgin CDOVD 317	?.02.91 (UK)

Private Parts & Pieces (picture disc)	Blueprint BP202CD	?.?.95 (UK)
1984	Virgin CDOVD 321	?.02.91 (UK)
Private Parts & Pieces II	Virgin CDOVD 318	?.02.91 (UK)
Private Parts & Pieces II (Picture disc)	Blueprint BP203CD	?.?.95 (UK)
Private Parts & Pieces III	Virgin CDOVD 319	?.02.91 (UK)
Private Parts & Pieces III (Picture disc)	Blueprint BP204CD	?.?.95 (UK)
Private Parts & Pieces IV	Virgin CDOVD 320	?.02.91 (UK)
Private Parts & Pieces IV (Picture disc)	Blueprint BP205CD	?.?.95 (UK)
Invisible Men	Virgin CDOVD 323	?.04.91 (UK)
Invisible Men (picture disc)	Blueprint BP211CD	?.?.95 (UK)
Private Parts & Pieces V	Virgin CDOVD 324	?.04.91 (UK)
Private Parts & Pieces V (Picture disc)	Blueprint BP206CD	?.?.95 (UK)
Private Parts & Pieces VI	Virgin CDOVD 325	?.04.91 (UK)
Private Parts & Pieces VI (Picture disc)	Blueprint BP207CD	?.?.95 (UK)
Private Parts & Pieces VII	Audion SYNCD 308	?.?.87 (US)
Private Parts & Pieces VII	VirginCDOVD326	?.04.91 (UK)
Private Parts & Pieces VII (Picture disc)	Blueprint BP208CD	?.?.95 (UK)
Tarka	PRT PYC 18	31.10.88 (UK)
Tarka	Baillemont BPE104	31.10.88 (France)
Tarka (picture disc)	Blueprint BP219CD	31.07.96 (UK)
Slowdance	Virgin CDV2638	24.09.90 (UK)
Slowdance (picture disc)	Blueprint BP213CD	?.?.95 (UK)
Missing Links Vol 1: Finger Painting	Brainworks BWKD208	?.05.92 (UK)
Missing Links Vol 1: Finger Painting (picture disc)	Blueprint BP209CD	?.05.92 (UK)
Private Parts & Pieces VIII	Virgin CDVE319	24.08.92 (UK)
Private Parts & Pieces VIII (Picture disc)	Blueprint BP212CD	?.?.95 (UK)
Sail the world	Resurgence RES102CD	?.05.94 (UK)
Missing Links Vol 2: The Sky Road	Brainworks BWKD212	15.06.94 (UK)
The Gypsy Suite	Voiceprint VP189CD	?.?.95 (UK)
Echoes (free cd with lyric book)	Voiceprint VP184CD	15.05.95 (UK)
Anthology (Compilation cd)	Blueprint BP201CD	16.10.95 (UK)
The Living Room Concert (Re-issue of Echoes cd without booklet) Blueprint BP218CD		?.?.96 (UK)
Private Parts & Pieces IX: Dragonfly Dreams Blueprint BP229CD		04.11.96 (UK)
The Meadows of Englewood	Astral 999CD	1996 (Spain)
The Giants Dance (album by R Runn & D Thomas long time friends of AP who plays on several tracks)		
	Blueprint BP223CD	21.10.96 (UK)
Survival - The Music of nature (Compilation) Virgin VTCD148		02.08.97 (UK)
Missing Links III: Time & Tide	Blueprint BP272CD	13.10.97 (UK)
Live Radio Sessions (Compilation)	Discmedi Blau DM15 02	?.?.97 (Spain)
The Archive Collection Volume One	Blueprint BP279CD	31.03.98 (UK)
(This collection was also issued free to all current members of Anthony's fan club; "The Pavilion" first 1000 copies came with additional 5 track cd ep)		
The Archive Collection Volume One	Blueprint BP279CD	31.3.98 (UK)
(Standard edition of above without bonus cd ep)		
Private Parts & Pieces X: Soiree	Blueprint BP319CD	8.11.99 (UK)
Radio Clyde Session	Blueprint BP354CD	?.06.03 (UK)
Intergalactic Touring Band	Voiceprint VP251CD	?.06.03 (UK)
Battle Of The Birds	Blueprint BP359CD	?.?.03 (UK)
Archive Collection Volume 2	Blueprint BP360CD	?.5.04 (UK)
Field Day (Double album)	Blueprint BP362CD	10.10.05 (UK)

COMPILATION AND LIBRARY ALBUMS

Double Exposure (Double album featuring the unreleased track 'Promenade') No Man's Land Records 1986 (UK)
The best of both worlds (Audio sampler including 'Through the black hole' and 'Pluto Garden by Anthony)
 Audion SYN 108 1987 (US)

Terra X (German tv series soundtrack double cd including 'Drama' and 'Aurora' from Anthony's library music)
CBS 467595 2   1990 (Germany)

All Our Lives (Double CD re-packaged version of The Meadows Of Englewood and Live Radio Sessions albums).
Astral Records Astral CD 1725 (2 CD set).
Soft Vivace Astral Records Astral CD 1728.

VINYL LIBRARY ALBUMS

Ahead of the field	Rouge RMS/LP159
Electronic Music	Atmosphere ATMOS 001
Landscape	Atmosphere ATMOS 005
Modern Christmas Music	Atmosphere ATMOS 009
Deeper Mysteries	Atmosphere ATMOS 011
Around the world	Atmosphere ATMOS 018
Classical Spirit	Atmosphere ATMOS 022

COMPACT DISC LIBRARY ALBUMS

Shortcuts	Atmosphere ATMOS- CD3
Classical Spirit	Atmosphere ATMOS-CD4
Science - Mystery	Atmosphere ATMOS-CD7
Christmas, Kids & Comedy	Atmosphere ATMOS-CD15
Travelogues 1	Atmosphere ATMOS-CD23
Horror, Tension, Suspense	Atmosphere ATMOS-CD28
Short Cuts	Atmosphere ATMOS-CD30
Travelogues 2	Atmosphere ATMOS-CD41
Travelogues 3	Atmosphere ATMOS-CD42
Travelogues 4 - Drama	Atmosphere ATMOS-CD44
Horror, Tension, Suspense 2	Atmosphere ATMOS-CD55
Travelogues 5	Atmosphere ATMOS-CD58
Drama, Action, Suspense	Atmosphere ATMOs-CD61
Short Cuts 4	Atmosphere ATMOS-CD62
Art House	Atmosphere ATMOS-CD63
Soundscapes	Atmosphere ATMOS-CD80
Virtual Corporation	Atmosphere ATMOS-CD92
Loops & Grooves	Atmosphere ATMOS-CD94
Hard Drama	Atmosphere ATMOS-CD96
Weird	Atmosphere ATMOS-CD102
Space & Science	Atmosphere ATMOS-CD104
Hard Drama 2	Atmosphere ATMOS-CD106
Catastrophe	Atmosphere ATMOS-CD115
English Pastoral	Atmosphere ATMOS-CD 117
Millennium	Atmosphere ATMOS-CD 120
Total Movie	Atmosphere ATMOS-CD125
Sport & Leisure	Themes International TIM25

(This is the album which contains the theme co-written by Anthony and Mike Rutherford for TV South's show jumping series for which Mike's wife Angie also did the commentating).

The Natural World	Themes International TIM31
Mystery & Documentary	Atmosphere ATMOS-CD 134
Russia	Atmosphere ATMOS-CD 138
Ethereal Journeys 4	Atmosphere ATMOS-CD 154
True Stories	Atmosphere ATMOS-CD 156
Drones	Atmosphere ATMOS-CD 169
Ancient Civilisations	Atmosphere ATMOS-CD175
Ethereal Journeys 5	Atmosphere ATMOS-CD186
Eccentrics	Atmosphere ATMOS-CD 191
The Rhythm Guide	Atmosphere ATMOS-CD 199
Soundscapes 2	Atmosphere ATMOS-CD204
Acoustic Guitar Solos	FTV Media 01(*)
Piano Solos	FTV Media 02 (*)

(*) Essentially these two albums are compilations of material from the various Private Parts & Pieces albums as samplers for potential TV use.

Library albums are comprised of music written specifically for television and film and give producers of such programmes literally a "library" of music to choose from for their respective programmes. These discs are not available commercially to the public, and in the case of the discs mentioned above, many of these are not solely comprised of material by Anthony but by other composers as well.

Touch Sampler II (Includes unreleased track 'Dansa Cucaracha)   Touch T02 1996 (UK)
Survival - The Music of Nature (Compilation of music from Anglia TV "Survival" wildlife series 13 tracks by AP an
Joji Hirota)   Virgin VTDCD184 1997 (UK)
Legend: Una Antologia Inedita Del Ex-Genesis   Melopea CDMPV1112   1997   (Argentina)
The Sky Goes All The Way Home (Double CD set including unreleased track: Sky Dawn)
                                           Voiceprint no catalogue number 1999 (UK)
Legend: Una Antologia Inedita Del Ex-Genesis (1976/1999) Astral CD39   1999   (Spain)
Soundscapes - An Anthology   Snapper Music SMCD458   ?.4.03 (UK)

RAY WILSON: The Actor Revealed.

Ray's part on the Genesis story may well have been short but for some of us it was certainly sweet! Ray was born in 1968; the year in which Genesis finally unleashed their first recordings upon an unsuspecting public.

His musical experience began with school bands several of which he saw from the spectator's viewpoint as he watched his older brother Steve perform at school concerts and other events as his brother Steve recalls..

"Tay and I have been in bands since I was thirteen basically. I used to be a singer (laughter) loosely termed anyway! Ray actually watched me in a school band; I used to play in school bands. We had quite a vibrant musical scene at school and he watched me singing and about three months later we had another school concert thing and he ended up taking over the singing and I stuck to the guitar and we have been in bands together ever since. " (1)

The experience stood him in good stead and history indeed seems to have repeated itself with the earliest recorded efforts seeing the light of day as a self-produced CD under the band name: Guaranteed Pure. This CD; Swing Your Bag was recorded under similar financial strictures as the formative Genesis had experienced. Eventually Ray was successful with an audition to join the Grunge- Rock influenced band Stiltskin who in 1993/94 topped the charts with the Seattle Rock influenced single: Inside aided by its use as the music for a Levi Jeans advert. The album: The Mind's Eye was a qualified success and the band enjoyed live success both in the UK and Europe although relationships within the band were not exactly cordial at times. In fact, the title track of the first album by Ray's next band; Cut, was a dig at the behaviour of the founder of Stiltskin as Ray himself recalled…

"Millionairhead was really about Peter's treatment of the band ; Peter Lawlor; the guitarist in Stiltskin who treated us like complete bastards really, and used to intimidate us with his wealth because he was a very wealthy guy and there were times when he said to me; he owed me quite a lot of money and it was in a suspense account because there was a legal dispute between one of the band members and all the rest of it and I said to him 'I could do with this money' and this was before Genesis…" (2)

The band did not last long and a second Stiltskin album was never recorded although several songs from that period were carried over into Ray's next band: Cut which reconvened around the core of Ray, Steve and keyboard player Paul Holmes, whom the guys had met in a piano bar in Edinburgh in 1990. The resulting album: Millionairhead was already recorded before Ray got his call-up to join Genesis although it did not see the light of day until 1999.

Still heavily influenced by the grunge and heavy rock side of things, the album certainly demonstrated Ray's abilities as a song -writer although it has to be said that the album is not a joyous affair by any means even a healthy nod to David Bowie's influence in the form of a cover version of Space Oddity. One track in particular: Ghost, summed up the difficult situation that Ray found himself in after the relative failure of the Genesis "experiment" as his brother Steve recalls…

"It was the only song written AFTER Ray went to Genesis and it is really about his feelings when the American tour was cancelled, you know.. it was the reaction to the press murdering him about ..you know 'Genesis Singer Flops' you know and he got a bit of it up here too and I think it was really written about how he felt about it you know the fact that he was giving 150% and it was actually going fine but try and convince a press reporter of that…" (3)

Ray's decision to join Genesis was ultimately to prove costly to him when the band decided not to extend the option on a second album in the wake of the comparative failure of Calling All Stations. Ray had invested heavily in a new house and other trappings of rock stardom and found himself financially embarrassed again, a situation which was not made any easier by the position of Ray as an ex-member of the highly unfashionable Genesis as his brother reflected on the situation of trying to get a UK release for the Millionairhead project…

It hasn't helped in some respects Ray being in Genesis, because he does get that tag especially here in the UK - he's made it bloody impossible for us in the UK to be honest, hence we have no record deal here… we are on sale in fifteen territories in Europe alone and I think we are suffering from the Genesis credibility problem here…" (4)

The one thing that the album did prove more than anything else was that Ray had been sadly undervalued as a songwriter. Many of the songs are wry observations on life and its vicissitudes: Jigsaw for instance being about someone trying to piece their broken life together; Ghost about the situation with the cancellation of the American tour although not as some suspected, as a dig against Genesis fans themselves as Ray explained…

"When I wrote Ghost I hadn't even played a gig with Genesis yet, I actually remember writing that song in November or December 1997 when I read an article in the Daily Record (a Scottish newspaper) and it was just not very nice. Because the American tour had been cancelled … it all happened at once I was giving everything I had and it just

wasn't enough and it was breaking me into pieces. When we started to tour my feelings changed. When you get in front of an audience and you see the audience accept you very quickly that changed everything. That made me feel that I was part of it. By the time we got to the end of the tour and the festivals in Germany I really did feel part of the band and it had nothing to do with Mike and Tony as they always tried to make me feel part of the band but you have to try and develop and it takes time ;live work and gigs and I think I owe a great deal to Genesis fans because they gave me a great deal of support ..." (5)

With his Genesis days firmly behind him, 1999 saw Ray reconvene and regroup with the support of his brother Steve and another Genesis refugee: Nir Zidkyahu and the rest of the guys in Cut to establish their bona fides in Europe with a series of gigs mainly in Germany where their fan base was quickly established.   A highly successful series of concerts at the was captured for posterity in the enormously enjoyable Unplugged album which was eventually released in 2001. This album showcased not only Ray's time with Genesis bit also many tracks from Cut and Stiltskin and his first album as well as several covers of classics by some of Ray's favourite musicians. In all, this was an ideal way to demonstrate that Ray was not merely a one-trick pony and that the criticism he had received in the press and by the "fans" in some quarters was totally unjustified. He was sufficiently impressive to be asked to tour as opening act for The Scorpions which enhanced his profile enormously and no doubt gave him the confidence boost that must have been sorely needed after the Genesis fiasco.

However, logistical problems ensured that Ray's next album was to be a solo effort. Several of the guys in Cut were not resident in the UK (Paul lives in Norway and Nir in New York) which made rehearsing and playing together difficult and so Ray opted for the logical choice which was to record his stuff himself . The resultant album: Change continued the development of Ray as a singer and songwriter in fine style with a wide variety of musical styles… rock, folk all stripped down to a nucleus of Ray, his brother Steve and vocalist Amanda Lyon it is very much music without "props" as Ray himself explained…

"I did enjoy going back to basics with my music and not having the big production sound whether that was with Stiltskin or Genesis. I had to rediscover my love for music and basically I did that by going back to the beginning and picking up a guitar and writing three or four minute songs…"

Basic or not, the album continued the almost organic development of Ray's musical and vocal talents although not all of the songs are as simple as you might think! Beach for instance, which is a lovely song is actually about two children being murdered on a beach and based on actual events … there is a darker and more complex side to Ray and his music which should never be underestimated.

The album was released again in Germany and extensive tours of that country and other parts of Europe continued to occupy Ray throughout most of 2002 nd 2003 with another highly successful series of gigs at the Edinburgh Festival where Ray seems to have become almost a permanent feature.

Ray's latest album: The Next Best Thing was released in 2005, consolidating his position as a songwriter of note even further and I am sure that he will continue to grow and develop into another fine songwriter whose music will delight his fans for many years to come. His recent tours however, have placed the emphasis firmly on Genesis and in fact his most recent outing was titled "The World Of Genesis" in which he performed not only material from the Genesis catalogue but also dipped into the band's solo catalogues too with performances of material by Phil, Peter and Mike & The Mechanics to varying degrees of success. He has left himself wide open to charges of exploiting his associations with the band by doing so, and has even been accused of being the ultimate Genesis "tribute" band but whether people like it or not, Ray WAS a member of Genesis and he has ever right to perform material from that canon.   His tenure in Genesis may not have been a long one but it was a vibrant and vital one and one of which he and the band can be proud.

RAY WILSON SOLO ALBUMS/SINGLES

…. As "Guaranteed Pure"

Swing Your Bag	Guaranteed Pure GPCD1	1992.
"Outpatients '93"	Dick Brothers D Dick 1 CD	1994.

(This was a compilation album of tracks from artists who had recorded at the Funny Farm recording Studios for former Marillion front man - Fish's record company. Guaranteed Pure's contribution to the album was the track; "Swing your bag").

<h2 style="text-align:center">….As "Stiltskin"</h2>

The Mind's Eye	White Water Records/Virgin 7243 8399522-6-PM527 (CD) (UK)	1994.
The Mind's Eye	Eastwest Records 61785-2 (CD) (US)	1994.

(Both versions of this album contained a different running order and differing tracks)

Inside/America/Inside (Extended version)	White Water Records CD Single LEV1CD	1994 (PS)
Footsteps/Sunshine & Butterflies(Live)/Footsteps (Extended Version)		
	White Water Records CD Single WWR D2	1994 (PS)
Rest In Peace/The Poltroon/Inside (Acoustic Version)		
	White Water Records CD Single WWR D3	1995 (PS)

All of the above singles were also released as vinyl and cassette editions.

<h2 style="text-align:center">….As "CUT"</h2>

Another Day/I Hear You Calling/Adolescent Breakdown (Monitor Mix)		
	Virgin Germany CD Single 8 95634 2	8/2/99 (PS)
Millionairehead	Virgin Germany (CD) 8 47060	8/3/99

<h2 style="text-align:center">…. As "Ray Wilson"</h2>

Ray Wilson - Unplugged	Sandport (CD) WilsonCD1	?/12/01
Goodbye Baby Blue	Inside Out 6 93723 60423 7	2003
Change	SPV (CD) 055-65523	2003
The Next Big Thing	Inside Out 6 93723 60782	28.6.04
These Are The Changes (Benztown Mixdown)/These Are The Changes (Live)/Gouranga (Live)		
	Inside Out 6 93723 60883 3	2004
Ray Wilson - Live	Sandport (CD) (No catalogue number)	2005

<h2 style="text-align:center">ASSOCIATED ARTISTS AND TRIBUTE ALBUMS</h2>

Over the years there have been a few recordings issued by musicians associated with the band especially the longstanding "live band" members, Daryl Stuermer and Chester Thompson as well as a couple of others as well as an increasing number of "Tribute" albums to the band and their work. The following are details of the most easily available albums in both category.

<h3 style="text-align:center">DALE NEWMAN SOLO ALBUMS</h3>

Dale has been in the service of the band since he was enlisted as Mike's guitar technician way back in 1973. Since then he has not only continued in that position but is now responsible for the day to day administration of the group's recording studio: The Farm. Dale's first recorded work was as one of the vocalists on Anthony Phillips' "Sides" album in 1978 and he has only recently decided to "go solo" himself initially with a CD EP of songs.

The Eyes Have it	Decision Products DP1306206-2	1998
The Little Things That Matter		1999
Cubed		2003

DARYL STUERMER SOLO ALBUMS

Daryl is no stranger to Genesis fans being the guy who bravely stepped into Steve Hackett's shoes in 1977 and continued as the band's live guitarist until 1992. In addition of course, he has also been in all of Phil Collins' live bands since Phil went solo in 1982. Initially Daryl released a series of albums with his brother in the mid Seventies under the generic title of : "Sweetbottom" the only album for which details are readily available is as follows:

Sweetbottom	Elektra Records K52110	1978
Sweetbottom Live		2003

Daryl has more recently released two albums of his own music although these are not commercially available here in the UK, they are nonetheless, well worth trying to track down.

Steppin' Out	GRP Records A-9573 (LP)	1988
Steppin' Out	GRP Records D-9573 (CD)	1988
Live and Learn	Urban Island Music (no catalogue number)	1998
Another Side Of Genesis	Urban Island Music 56437 19612	2000
Waiting In The Wings	Urban Island Music #19622	2001
Retrofit		2004

CHESTER THOMPSON SOLO ALBUMS.

Chester has long been regarded as the "backbone" of Genesis' live sound and fans have often wondered what a solo album by this genius of the percussion would sound like. In 1991 they finally got their wish when Chester finally released his first and so far only solo album: *A Joyful Noise* initially only available in the USA it was released in the UK and Europe in May of this year by Steve Hackett's record company: Camino Records.

A Joyful Noise	Moo Records RZ 79341 (CD)	1991
A Joyful Noise	Camino Records CAMCD16	24.5.99

GENESIS "TRIBUTE" ALBUMS

Over the past few years the growth of the "Tribute" band has inspired a cottage industry of bands recreating the music of their heroes live on stage and Genesis and their solo members have been well served by their own tributes both at home and further a field and this is a list of the available CDs by these bands/artists….

Various Artists	The River of Constant Change(Double CD)	Mellow Records MMP270	1995
Various Artists	Supper's Ready	Magna Carta Records MA 9004-2	1995
ReGenesis	ReGenesis Live	Mystic Records MYSCD112	1997
Various Artists	The Fox Lies Down	Eagle Records EAGCD057	1998
The Musical Box	Live (promo only CD)		1999
ReGenesis	Here it comes again	Mystic Records MYSCD126	1999
Domino	Under Construction	No Tape Productions	2000
Face Value	Face Value	Face Value FVG1	2000
G2enesis	Live Seconds		2001
Sledgehammer	Sledgehammer		2001
Sledgehammer	Sledgehammer/Steam (2 track demo)		2001
ReGenesis	Lamb For Supper	Mystic Records MYS CD 149	2001
Acoustic Moods	Total Genesis		2000
Acoustic Moods	Conventional Wisdom		2001
Guddal/Matte	Genesis For Two Grand Pianos	Camino Records CAMCD28	2002
ReGenesis	2002 Tour Official Bootleg	Mystic Records MYSCD177	2004
David Myers:	David Myers Plays Genesis	Experience Records EXP2 207	2005

There are even some tribute band "bootlegs" believe it or not! Here is a selection …

The Musical Box	Royal Centre Nottingham	31.5.02 (Selling England By The Pound Show)
The Musical Box	Royal Albert Hall London	1.6.02 (Selling England By The Pound show with Steve Hackett)
The Musical Box	Guildhall Southampton	30.10.03 (Foxtrot show)
The Musical Box	Union County Arts Center Rahway NJ	17.10.04 (The Lamb Lies Down on Broadway show)
The Musical Box	Grand Casino Geneva	23.2.05 (The Lamb… show with Phil Collins)

G2enesis	Kings Head London	3.12.02
G2enesis	Limelight Club Crewe	15.2.04

Face Value	Limelight Club Crewe	6.4.02
Face Value	Seconds In	2003
Face Value	One Side Live	2001

Seconds Out   Tralf Concert Club Buffalo NY   2.1.02

And even some TV and private film footage too…

Carpet Crawlers The Mersey Clipper Tranmere   22.9.05   (Private film)

Face Value

The Astoria London	27.5.06	(Private film)
Thwaites Empire Theatre Blackburn	24.6.06	(Private film)

ReGenesis

The Orange London	12.8.96	(Private film)
Cine Bar London	1997	(Private film)
West One Four London	15.5.99	(Private film)

Strictly Banks Orchard Theatre Dartford   6.9.98   (Private film)

The Musical Box

Montreal Canada	17.7.93	(Private film)
Promotional film	1998	(Official VHS)
Une Soir	4.11.93	(Canadian TV)
CTV Pulse News	5.11.93	(Canadian TV)
City Beat	27.1.94	(Canadian TV)
Montreal Sports Arena	14.11.98	(Private film)
Milan Palatrussardi	22.4.04	(Private film)
Turin Teatro Colsosseo	10.6.04	(Private film)
From Genesis To Recreation	2004	(Official DVD) +

+ Withdrawn due to technical problems

GENESIS GIG GUIDE 1968-

VENUE NAME	CITY/TOWN	COUNTRY	DATE	WITH/AS SUPPORT

From Genesis To Revelation 1968/9

VENUE NAME	CITY/TOWN	COUNTRY	DATE	WITH/AS SUPPORT
BBC Technical College	Evesham	England	1968	

(This was a training session for Brian Roberts at the BBC's training college the band performed In Hiding while Brian filmed them. Sadly, this film is now lost).

| Rehearsals Send Barns | Surrey | England | 9-22.9.69 | |

(During this period parts of what later emerged as The Musical Box were written, rehearsed and recorded at Anthony Phillips' parents' home along with material that was to surface on his first solo album: The Geese & The Ghost in 1977)

| Balmes's dance | Chobham | England | 23.9.69 | |
| Brunel University | Acton | England | 4.11.69 | **Caravan** |

(This was the band's first gig in front of a paying crowd rather than gigs for friends and family)

Twickenham Technical College	London	England	15.11.69	
Kingston Hotel	London	England	23.11.69	
Warley Social Club	Birmingham	England	14.12.69	
Cheadle Hulme Social Club	Manchester	England	16.12.69	
Brunel University	Acton	England	?.12.69	**Fairport Convention**
Twickenham Technical College	London	England	?.12.69	
Kingston Hotel	London	England	?.12.69	**Piblokto**
Rolleston Youth Club	Rolleston	England	?.12.69	
Eel Pie Island	Twickenham	England	?.12.69	

1968/69 saw the band embark on the first of an increasingly gruelling series of tours to, in the first instance, gain an audience for their music and later, to extend that audience. Live sets at this time are hard to document but it is highly likely that the band performed some or all of the following tracks… In The Beginning/The Serpent/**Pacid**y/**Key To Love**/Visions Of Angels/**Going Out To Get You**/Stagnation/**Little Leaf** /The Knife.

Trespass Tour 1970/71.

VENUE NAME	CITY/TOWN	COUNTRY	DATE	WITH/AS SUPPORT
BBC Studios	London	England	2.1.70	

(Training film organised by Brian Roberts who was working for the BBC at the time. Film has never been shown and is now, sadly believed lost)

| Country Club | Havesrtock Hill | England | 4.1.70 | |
| BBC Studios | Shepherds Bush London | England | 9.1.70 | |

(Recording session for BBC production which was never released now referred to as the "Jackson Tapes")

Technical College	Watford	England	17.1.70	**Spirit Of John Morgan**
Technical College	Ewell	England	24.1.70	**Atomic Rooster/Nick Drake**
Kingston Technical College	London	England	28.1.70	
Technical College	Leicester	England	29.1.70	
Locarno Ballroom	Sunderland	England	30.1.70	
Queen Mary College (2 shows)	London	England	4.2.70	
Brunel University	Uxbridge	England	12.2.70	
Technical College	Uxbridge	England	13.2.70	**John Dummer Band**
Leicester University Students Union	Leicester	England	14.2.70	**Nick Drake**
Kingston Hotel	London	England	15.2.70	
The Dome	Brighton	England	18.2.70	**T Rex**
Hurlingham Tennis Club	Fulham	England	20.2.70	
BBC Studios	Maida ValeLondon	England	22.2.70	

(BBC"Night Ride" Session Comprising performances of: Pacidy/Shepherd/Let Us NowMake Love/Stagnation/Dusk)

| Revolution Club | London | England | 25.2.70 | |
| Blaises Club | London | England | 26.2.70 | |

(This is the gig that Mike made famous by bowing up a woman's skirt with his cello bow)

Brunel University	Uxbridge	England	27.2.70	
Essex University	Colchester	England	28.2.70	
Farx Club	Southall	England	1.3.70	**Mott The Hoople**
Mistrale Club	Beckenham	England	2.3.70	
Ronnie Scott's Club	London	England	3.3.70	
Ronnie Scott's Club	London	England	10.3.70	
Roundhouse Club	London	England	11.3.70	David Bowie

(This performance was for the Atomic Sunrise Festival and was captured on both film and 8 track sound recording both of which reputedly still exist along with a privately recorded film source)

College of Technology	Watford	England	14.3.70	**Atomic Rooster**
Ronnie Scott's Club	London	England	17.3.70	
Farx Club	Southall	England	22.3.70	
Ronnie Scott's Club	London	England	24.3.70	
Ronnie Scott's Club	London	England	31.3.70	

Ronnie Scott's Club	London	England	7.4.70	
Cooksferry Inn	Edmonton	England	9.4.70	
Eel Pie Island	London	England	10.4.70	
Central Hall	Chatham	England	11.4.70	**Deep Purple**
Friars Club (2 shows)	Aylesbury	England	13.4.70	
Ronnie Scott's Club	London	England	14.4.70	
The Temple	London	England	17.4.70	
Farx Club	Potter's Bar	England	18.4.70	
One Oak Inn	Camberley	England	19.4.70	
Imperial College	London	England	25.4.70	**P C Kent**
Ronnie Scott's Club	London	England	5.5.70 *	
Eliot College	Canterbury	England	8.5.70	**The Who(?) ***
Ronnie Scott's Club	London	England	9.5.70 *	
Great Hall Surrey University	Guildford	England	16.5.70 *	
Angel Inn	Godalming	England (Rehearsals)	17-23.5.70 *	
Marquee Club	London	England	24.5.70 *	
Angel Inn	Godalming	England (Rehearsals)	25-31.5.70 *	
Technical College	Fanrborough	England	27.5.70	**Nimbo ***

* All gigs/rehearsals in May were cancelled due to Anthony Phillips' illness he was recuperating in Cornwall
for three weeks with his parents

Lyceum Theatre	London	England	6.6.70	
Parish Hall	Dudley	England	8.6.70	
Marquee Club	London	England	14.6.70	**Junco Partners**
Borough Assembly Room (Friars)	Aylesbury	England	15.6.70	
Ronnie Scotts	London	England	16.6.70	
Carshalton College	Surrey	England	20.6.70	
Ronnie Scott's Club	London	England	23.6.70	
Surrey Free Festival	Guildford University	England	27.6.70	

(This is the gig that John Mayhew refers to with the band tuning up on the football/cricket pitch)

Technical College (evening show)	Hackney	England	27.6.70	
Farx Club	Southall	England	28.6.70	
Ronnie Scott's Club	London	England	30.6.70	
College for Distributive Trades	London	England	3.7.70	
Polytechnic	Kingston	England	9.7.70	
St Joan's	Rickmansworth	England	11.7.70	
Star Hotel	Croydon	England	17.7.70	
	Haywards Heath	England	18.7.70	

(This was Anthony Phillips and John Mayhew's last gig with Genesis, after which, they played gigs as a four piece)

(Phil Collins officially joins Genesis on 4th August 1970).

Gaumont Cinema	Doncaster	England	6.8.70	
Parish Hall	Dudley	England	8.8.70	
Central Methodist Hall	Coventry	England	13.8.70	
Maltings	Farnham	England (Rehearsals)	24-26.8.70	
Transport House	Bristol	England	27.8.70	
New Imperial Hotel	Birmingham	England	28.8.70	
Metropole Hotel	Colwyn Bay	Wales	29.8.70	
Marquee Club	London	England	30.8.70	
Maltings	Farnham	England (Rehearsals)	1-5.9.70	
Assembly Rooms	Rotherham	England	3.9.70	
Maltings	Farnham	England (Rehearsals)	7-12.9.70	
Polytechnic	Huddersfield	England	10.9.70	
Maltings	Farnham	England (Rehearsals)	14-19.9.70	
	Wakefield	England	17.9.70	

(The above gigs were cancelled whilst Phil carried out final contractual obligations with Flaming Youth and
rehearsals with Genesis)

Medway Technical College	Chatham	England	2.10.70	**Blonde On Blonde**

(This was Phil's first actual gig with Genesis)

Technical College	Farnborough	England	3.10.70	**Bram Stoker**
Marquee Club	London	England	4.10.70	**Stackridge**
British Legion Hall	Princes Risborough	England	6.10.70	**Chameleon**

(This gig featured Ronnie Caryl on guitar)

Birdcage Club	Harlow	England	7.10.70	
A B C Theatre	Blackpool	England	8.10.70	
Tomorrow Club (Capital Ballroom)	Wallasey	England	9.10.70	
Corn Exchange	Colchester	England	10.10.70	**Tiny Clanger**
Maltings	Farnham	England (Rehearsals)	12.10.70	
Fishmonger's Arms	Wood Green London	England	13.10.70	**Trapeze**

Rex Cinema	Cambridge	England	16.10.70	**Matthews Southern Comfort**
Maltings	Farnham	England (Rehearsals)	19-22.10.70	
Friars Club Addison Centre	Bedford	England	23.10.70	**Medicine Head**
Maltings	Farnham	England (Rehearsals)	26-29.10.70	
?	West Hampstead London	England (Rehearsals)	30-10-1.11.70	
Resurrection Club	Barnet	England	3.11.70	**Trapeze**

(This was Mick Barnard's first gig with the band)

?	West Hampstead London	England (Rehearsals)	4.11.70	
University	Salford	England	6.11.70	**Curved Air/Greasy Bear**
Brunel University	Uxbridge	England	7.11.70	**Argent**
Victoria Hall	Chelmsford	England	8.11.70	
?	West Hampstead	England (Rehearsals)	10.11.70	
Marquee Club	London	England	10.11.70	**Jackson Heights**
?	West Hampstead	England (Rehearsals)	11-12.11.70	
Kent University Rutherford College Canterbury		England	13.11.70	**Fairport Convention**
Technical College (afternoon)	Watford	England	14.11.70	**Steamhammer/Farm**
BBC Studios	London	England "Disco Two"	14.11.70	

(Genesis's first television appearance and their only recorded appearance with Mick Barnard; Anthony Phillips's replacement in the band. This video performance of The Knife is now sadly believed lost. Other performers on this now legendary lost performance included: Duncan Brown/Dream Police and Zoo)

Herriott Watt College	Edinburgh	Scotland	20.11.70	
Lido Ballroom	Ballock	Scotland	21.11.70	
Kinema Ballroom	Dunfermline	Scotland	22.11.70	
Hermitage Ballroom	Hitchin	England	25.11.70	**National Head Band**
Dead End	Blackpool	England	26.11.70	
Neville's Cross College	Durham	England	27.11.70	
Imperial College	London	England	28.11.70	**Van der Graaf Generator**
Northcote Arms (Farx Club)	Southall	England	29.11.70	
Youth Club	Letchworth	England	30.11.70	
Maltings	Farnham	England	2-3.12.70	
College of Education	Worcester	England	4.12.70	
Mother's Club	Birmingham	England	6.12.70	**Rare Bird**
Marquee Club (Charisma Christmas Party)	London	England	9.12.70	
Café Royal	London	England	11.12.70	**East Of Eden**
Grammar School	Aylesbury	England	16.12.70	
Civic College	Ipswich	England	17.12.70	
Hatton Centre	High Wycombe	England	18.12.70	**Farm**

(Mick Barnard's last gig with Genesis)

Humberstone Foundation School	Cleethorpes	England	19.12.70	
Angel Hotel	Godalming	England	20.12.70	
Lyceum Theatre	London	England	28-29.12.70	

(The last of these two shows was where Steve Hackett saw the band for the first time)

1970 had many important developments for Genesis. Increasingly their music was drawing an audience from the university and college circuit eager for their adventurous and imaginative music. The summer months also saw the band having to cope with the departure of two key personnel from the line-up; guitarist Anthony Phillips, and drummer John Mayhew. Phillips's replacement for several weeks in the winter of 1970 was Aylesbury guitarist Mick Barnard who was with them on their first television appearance; BBC's forerunner to The Old Grey Whistle Test; Disco Two where, in November 1970 they played The Knife. John Mayhew's replacement who joined in the Autumn of 1970 was to have a more lasting impact on Genesis. He was of course; Phil Collins. Continuing to expand their repertoire under the tutelage of Charisma Records they increased the length and scope of their music although many of these experiments remain sadly unheard, a further selection of tracks from these halcyon days finally appeared on the first Genesis "Boxed set" which was released on 15th June 1998 giving fans another glimpse into what might have been. The band began to pick up a live following in a big way due to their incessant touring and sets from this period would have included most of the following…**Grandma/Let Us Now Make Love/Little Leaf/** Dusk/Stagnation/White MountainTwilight Alehouse/Visions Of Angels/**Key To Love/I've Been Travelling All Night Long/ Going Out To Get You/Shepherd/**Looking For Someone/**Jamaican Longboat/Pacidy/**The Knife

Nursery Cryme Tour 1971/72.

University Arts Laboratory	Manchester	England	3.1.71	**Hawkwind**
Slough College	Bedford	England	8.1.71	
Technical College	Ewell	England	9.1.71	**Kevin Ayers/Queen**
Farx Club	Southall	England	10.1.71	

(These gigs were played as a four piece with Tony Banks doubling on guitar on certain songs).

University College	London	England	14.1.71	**Steve Hackett's first gig**
Technical College	High Wycombe	England	15.1.71	
Tower Theatre	Blackpool	England	17.1.71	

Assembly Rooms	Derby	England	19.1.71	
City University	London	England	22.1.71	**Steamhammer**
Lyceum Theatre	London	England	24.1.71	**Van Der Graaf Generator/ Lindisfarne**
Town Hall	Birmingham	England	25.1.71	"　　　"　　　"
Colston Hall (Afternoon)	Bristol	England	26.1.71	"　　　"
Town Hall (Evening)	Watford	England	26.1.71	**Johnny Winter**
City Hall	Sheffield	England	27.1.71	**VanDer Graaf Generator/ Lindisfarne**
St George's Hall	Bradford	England	28.1.71	"　　　"　　　"
Free Trade Hall	Manchester	England	30.1.71	"　　　"　　　"
City Hall	Newcastle	England	31.1.71	"　　　"　　　"
?	Hatton	England	5.2.71	"　　　"　　　"
Friars Club	Aylesbury	England	6.2.71	
Rainbow Theatre	London	England	9..271	
The Dome	Brighton	England	11.2.71	"　　　"　　　"
Winter Gardens	Bournemouth	England	13.2.71	"　　　"　　　"
City Hall	Hull	England	19.2.71	
University	Southampton	England	20.2.71	
Colston Hall	Bristol	England	22.2.71	
Blaises Club	London	England	23.2.71	**Paladin**
Mountford Hall	Liverpool	England	25.2.71	
University	Durham	England	28.2.71	
Tower Theatre	Blackpool	England	4.3.71	
University Great Hall	York	England	5.3.71	
Lyceum Theatre	Birmingham	England	6.3.71	**Steamhammer**
La Ferme	Woluwe St Lambert	Belgium	7.3.71	**(Genesis's first overseas gig)**
Belgian tv studios	Brussels	Belgium (TV)	8-9.3.71	

(Session performances for Pop Shop - Genesis' first overseas TV appearance and one which sadly appears to have been erased from the TV company's archives)

University Great Hall	Essex	England	13.3.71	**Curved Air**
East Street Hall	London	England	?.3.71	
Sophia Gardens	Cardiff	Wales	?.3.71	
Dacorum College	Hemel Hempstead	England	2.4.71	
Technical College	Farnborough	England	3.4.71	
Angel Hotel	Godalming	England	?.4.71	
Lyceum Theatre	London	England	9.4.71	
Fairfield Hall	Croydon	England	11.4.71	**Van DerGraaf Generator/ Lindisfarne**
Guildhall	Portsmouth	England	13.4.71	"　　　"　　　"
Civic Hall	Guildford	England	15.4.71	"　　　"　　　"
Floral Hall	Southport	England	22.4.71	"　　　"　　　"
Green's Playhouse	Glasgow	Scotland	23.4.71	"　　　"　　　"
Caird Hall	Dundee	Scotland	24.4.71	"　　　"　　　"
Caley Cinema	Edinburgh	Scotland	25.4.71	"　　　"　　　"
Free Trade Hall	Manchester	England	26.4.71	"　　　"　　　"
Arts College	Kingston	England	30.4.71	
Resurrection Club	Hitchin	England	1.5.71	
Guildhall	Portsmouth	England	4.5.71	
Marquee Club	London	England	6.5.71	
University of East Anglia	Norwich	England	7.5.71	
Clarence's	Halifax	England	8.5.71	
BBC Studios	Shepherds Bush London	England	10.5.71	

("Sounds of The Seventies" session tracks perfomed: The Musical Box/Stagnation)

Youth Centre	Bletchley	England	21.5.71	**Capability Brown**
Kingston Hall	Watford	England	22.5.71	
TV Studios	Brussels	Belgium	4-6.6.71	

(Possible session for Pop Shop TV Show . Exact details of the broadcast are not currently available)

Lyceum Theatre	London	England	8.6.71	
Queen Margaret College	Edinburgh	Scotland	12.6.71	
Cheltenham Girls College	Cheltenham	England	18.6.71	
Friars Club	Aylesbury	England	19.6.71	
Reading Festival	Reading	England	26.6.71	
Friars ClubAddison Centre	Bedford	England	2.7.71	
Farx Club	Southall	England	3.7.71	
Marquee Club	London	England	9.7.71	
Lyceum Theatre	London	England	14.7.71	
Jemelle	Brussels	Belgium	7-8.8.71	
Weeley Festival	Clacton	England	28.8.71	**Van der Graaf Generator / King Crimson**

Pavilion	Hemel Hempstead	England	5.9.71	**Lindisfarne**
Civic Centre	Gravesend	England	16.9.71	**Daniel's Band**
The Temple	London	England	18.9.71	**Good Habit/Albert Monk**
Surrey Rooms	Kennington	England	22.9.71	
Town Hall	Kensington	England	23.9.71	
Sevens The Leas	Letchworth	England	25.9.71	
Kingham Hall	Watford	England	9.10.71	
William Street Club	Windsor	England	12.10.71	
Lyceum Theatre	London	England	14.10.71	**Van der Graaf Generator**
Guildhall	Preston	England	16.10.71	**" " "**
The Halls	Dorking	England	19.10.71	**" " "**
Town Hall	Oxford	England	21.10.71	**" " "**
University Great Hall	Exeter	England	22.10.71	
University	Essex	England	23.10.71	
Guildhall	Southampton	England	26.10.71	**Van der Graaf Generator**
Town Hall	Birmingham	England	27.10.71	**" " "**
City Hall	Newcastle	England	28.10.71	**Audience**
Lake Hall	Birmingham	England	29.10.71	
Guildhall	Plymouth	England	31.10.71	**Lindisfarne**
The Dome	Brighton	England	1.11.71	**Lindisfarne**
Starlight Club	Crawley	England	2.11.71	
Kings Hall	Derby	England	3.11.71	**Van der Graaf Generator**
Tower Theatre	Blackpool	England	4.11.71	
College of Technology	Slough	England	6.11.71	**Redwing**
City Hall	Salisbury	England	7.11.71	**Van der Graaf Generator**
Community Centre	Slough	England	19.11.71	
Sevens The Leas	Letchworth	England	20.11.71	
Surrey Rooms	Kennington	England	22.11.71	
Lyceum Theatre	London	England	24.11.71	**Lindisfarne**
Corn Exchange	Cambridge	England	25.11.71	
Eton College	Windsor	England	26.11.71	
City Hall	Newcastle	England	28.11.71	
City Hall	Sheffield	England	30.11.71	
Lyceum Theatre London	London	England	2.12.71	**Lindisfarne**
Red Lion	Leytonstone	England	3.12.71	
Lawkins Centre	Cottingham	England	4.12.71	
Hobbit's Garden	Wimbledon	England	7.12.71	**Gravy Train/Roxy Music**
Technical College	Kings Lynn	England	8.12.71	
Teeside Polytechnic	Middlesborough	England	9.12.71	
Culham College	Abingdon	England	10.12.71	
Cranbrook School	High Wycombe	England	11.12.71	
Windrush Twilight Club	High Wycombe	England	12.12.71	
Big Brother Club	Greenford	England	15.12.71	
Grammar School	Weymouth	England	16.12.71	
South Parade Pier	Portsmouth	England	21.12.71	
Kingham Hall	Watford	England	23.12.71	

During 1971 Genesis drafted guitarist Steve Hackett into the band and with his arrival, what many fans consider to be the "Classic" Genesis line-up was finally complete. The band's career was taking off with a vengeance and they appeared in two Charisma package tours titled the "Six Bob Tours" because the ticket price was pegged at 6Shillings (six "bob") these tours took place in April and October of that year and they shared the billing on each tour with fellow Charisma artists; Van Der Graaf Generator and Lindisfarne although Genesis were the opening act on these tours they regularly outshone the other artists. The band's third album; "Nursery Cryme also appeared during the year and garnered several plaudits from the music press. 1971 also saw the band's first appearances outside of the UK and their first television appearances outside the UK. The band's live shows gradually increased in length as they headlined more and more of their own shows instead of supporting other artists and as a result, their live set increased in length too and comprised the following songs… Happy The Man/ Fountain Of Salmacis/Seven Stones/Twilight Alehouse/**The Light**/White Mountain/ The Musical Box/Harlequin/The Knife/**Going Out To Get You/** The Return Of The Giant Hogweed.

The Roundhouse	Dagenham	England	1.1.72	
Maltings	Farnham (Rehearsals)	England	4-6.1.72	
Technical College	Bradford	England	7.1.72	
Baths Hall	Epsom	England	8.1.72	
BBC Studios	Shepherds Bush London	England	9.1.72	

(Recordings made for both Sounds Of The Seventies and Top Gear programmes tracks performed: Harold TheBarrel Harlequin/The Fountain Of Salmacis/The Return of The Giant Hogweed.)

Maltings	Farnham (Rehearsals)	England	11-13.1.72
?	Brussels (Rehearsal)	Belgium	14.1.72
Salle Petite	Arlon	Belgium	15.1.72
Festival	Charleroi	Belgium	16.1.72

| Maltings | Farnham (Rehearsal) | England | 17.1.72 | |
| Island | Ilford (Rehearsal) | England | 18.1.72 | |

(The band also recorded another Top Gear performance for the BBC on this date)

College of Education	Coventry	England	19.1.72	
St Johns College	Manchester	England	20.1.72	
L'Atheneee Royal Du Woluwe St Pierre				
	Brussels	Belgium	22.1.72	

(Possibly a performance for either "Pop Shop" or "Rock of the Seventies" exact details are unknown and the footage appears to have been erased from the TV company's archives)

| Palais des Beaux Arts | Charleroi | Belgium | 23.1.72 | |
| TV Studios | Brussels | Belgium | 24.1.72 | |

(Possibly a performance for either "Pop Shop" or "Rock Of The Seventies" exact details are unknown at present and the films have not been seen on tv since 1972/3 and it is suspected that they have been wiped)

Trocadero	Liege	Belgium	24.1.72	
Toby Jug	Tolworth	England	27.1.72	
Town Hall	High Wycombe	England	28.1.72	
University of Surrey	Guildford	England	29.1.72	
Black Prince	Bexley Heath	England	30.1.72	
Maltings	Farnham (Rehearsals)	England	1-3.2.72	
Queen Elizabeth Halls	London	England	4.2.72	**Lindisfarne**
College of Technology	Luton	England	5.2.72	
Lancing College	Sussex	England	6.2.72	
Maltings	Farnham (Rehearsals)	England	8.2.72	
Rainbow Theatre	London	England	9.2.72	
The Dome	Brighton	England	10.2.72	
Winter Gardens	Penzance	England	11.2.72	
Van Dyke Club	Plymouth	England	12.2.72	
University College of Wales	Aberystwyth	Wales	14.2.72	
Green's Playhouse	Glasgow	Scotland	16.2.72	
City Hall	Sheffield	England	17.2.72	
Medway Technology College	Maidstone	England	18.2.72	

(This gig was cancelled apparently due to a power cut in the locality)

Alex Disco	Salisbury	England	19.2.72	
The Greyhound	Croydon	England	20.2.72	
Winter Gardens	Cleethorpes	England	21.2.72	
City Hall	Newcastle	England	22.2.72	
Polytechnic	Leicester	England	23.2.72	
Town Hall	High Wycombe	England	24.2.72	
Locarno Ballrooms	Sunderland	England	25.2.72	
Sports Centre	Bracknell	England	26.2.72	
Civic Centre	Chelmsford	England	28.2.72	

(This gig was cancelled and the band undertook a day's rehearsals instead)

?	West Hampstead (Rehearsals)	England	29.2.72	
Civic Centre	Chelmsford	England	1.3.72	
BBC Paris Studios	London	England	2.3.72	

("In Concert" Live radio session including: The Fountain of Salmacis/The Musical Box/The Return Of The Giant Hogweed)

Island Studios	London (Recording session)	England	3.3.72	
Technical College	Watford	England	4.3.72	
?	West Hampstead (Rehearsals)	England	7-9.3.72	
South Parade Pier	Portsmouth	England	10.3.72	
Friars Club	Aylesbury	England	11.3.72	
The Tram Shed	Woolwich (Rehearsals)	England	13-15.3.72	
Princes Theatre	Hull	England	16.3.72	
Aston University	Birmingham	England	17.3.72	
Fete Saint Gratien	Troyes	France	18-19.3.72	
TV Studios	Brussels	Belgium	20-21.3.72	

(Earliest surviving visual document of the band featuring: Fountain Of Salmacis/Musical Box/Twilight Alehouse and The Return Of The Giant Hogweed performed for the Pop Shop TV programme)

Essex University Chelmsford	Essex	England	24.3.72	
Carshalton College	Essex	England	25.3.72	
The Manor	Essex (Recording session)	England	26.3.72	
?	Blackheath (Rehearsals)	England	29-31.3.72	
Trident Studios	London (Mixing session)	England	4.4.72	
Heathrow Airport	London	England	5.4.72	

(Band sets off for first Italian tour)

Palasport	Beluno	Italy	6.4.72	
Apollo 2000	Godega di S Urbano Treviso	Italy	7.4.72	
Dancing Paradiso	Trieste	Italy	8.4.72	

(This show was cancelled by the police and Peter dedicates the following night's show to the people of Trieste)

Lem (2 shows)	Verona	Italy	9.4.72
Palasport	Pesaro	Italy	11.4.72
Palasport	Reggio Emillia	Italy	12.4.72
Le Rotonde	Cuorgne Turin	Italy	13.4.72
Palasport (2 shows)	Pavia	Italy	14.4.72
Hit Parade (2 shows)	Lugo di Romagna Ravenna	Italy	15.4.72
Supertivoli	Travagliato Brescia	Italy	16.4.72
Palasport	Siena	Italy	17.4.72
Piper Club (2 shows)	Rome	Italy (Italian tv/radio)	18.4.72

(Extracts from this gig have been rebroadcast and also featured as part of The Genesis Story documentary)

Teatro Mediterraneo	Naples	Italy	19.4.72
Cambridge Technical College	Arlon	Belgium	22.4.72
Zoom Club	Frankfurt	Germany	23.4.72

Foxtrot Tour 1972/73

The Greyhound	Croydon	England	25.4.72
Van Dyke Club	Plymouth	England	26.2.72
Branton (?)	Essex (Rehearsal)	England	27.4.72
Polytechnic	Kingston	England	28.4.72
Polytechnic	Isleworth	England	29.4.72
Civic Hall	Guildford	England	30.4.72
Red Lion	Leytonstone	England	5.5.72
University College	Bangor	Wales	6.5.72
University of Essex	High Wycombe	England	8.5.72
Town Hall	Oxford	England	9.5.72
Cleopatra's	Derby	England	11.5.72
Mecca Ballrooms	Newcastle	England	19.5.72
City Hall	StAlban's	England	20.5.72
Youth Centre	Bletchley	England	21.5.72
Winter Gardens	Penzance	England	25.5.72
Van Dyke Club	Plymouth	England	26.5.72
Technical College	Farnborough	England	27.5.72
Great Western Festival	Lincoln	England	28.5.72

(Joe Cocker/Status Quo/Monty Python/The BeachBoys/Van Der Graaf Generator)

The Pier	Hastings	England	2.6.72
Technical College	Luton	England	3.6.72
Lyceum Theatre	London	England	4.6.72
Olympia Theatre	Paris	France	5.6.72
The Rock Club	Wellingborough	England	6.6.72
Polytechnic	Leeds	England	9.6.72
Argus	Peterlee	England	11.6.72
Corn Exchange	Cambridge	England	12.6.72
?	Blackheath (Rehearsals)	England	13-15.6.72
Friars Corn Exchange	Bedford	England	16.6.72
The Rock	Wellingborough	England	17.6.72
Top Rank	Swansea	Wales	19.6.72
?	Blackheath (Rehearsals)	England	20-22.6.72
Castle	Durham	England	23.6.72
Pier Pavilion	Felixstowe	England	24.6.72
Town Hall	Watford	England	25.6.72
Olympia Theatre	Paris	France	26.6.72

(Show with Van derGraaf Generator and Lindisfarne)

Town Hall	Watford	England	28.6.72	
Town Hall	Shoreditch	England	29.6.72	**Fusion Orchestra /Shamelady**
Community Centre	Slough	England	30.6.72	
The Greyhound	Croydon	England	2.7.72	
?	Blackheath (Rehearsals)	England	3-5.7.72	
Marquee Club	London	England	7.7.72	
Carre Hotel	Amsterdam	Holland	8.7.72	
Island Studios	London (Recording sessions)	England	10-12.7.72	
Uppingham School	Uppingham	England	13.7.72	

(This was a rehearsal for the band's gig at The Lyceum London the following night)

Lyceum Theatre	London	England	14.7.72
Coatham Hotel	Redcar	England	16.7.72
?	Blackheath (Rehearsals)	England	17-20.7.72
Red Lion	Leytonstone	England	21.7.72
Alex Disco	Salisbury	England	22.7.72
The Wake Arms	Epping	England	23.7.72
Civic Hall	Solihull	England	25.7.72

Winter Gardens	Cleethorpes	England	27.7.72	
Archer Hall	Billericay	England	28.7.72	
?	Blackheath (Rehearsals)	England	31.7.72	
?	Blackheath (Rehearsals)	England	4.8.72	
Island Studios	London (Recording session)	England	6.8.72	
Carre Hotel	Amsterdam	Holland	7.8.72	
Festival	Bilsen	Belgium	8.8.72	
Island Studios	London (Recording sessions)	England	9-10.8.72	
Reading Festival	Reading	England	11.8.72	
Island Studios	London (Recording session)	England	11.8.72	
Palasport	Reggio Emilia	Italy	15.8.72 ?	
Corte Malatestana	Fano	Italy	16.8.72	**Jumbo/Osanna**
Dancing Lago delle Rose	Monselice	Italy	18.8.72	" "
Jolly Club (2 shows)	Ravenna	Italy	19.8.72	" "
Piper 2000 Club (2 shows)	Viareggio	Italy	20. 8.72	" "
Palasport	Albegna	Italy	21.8.72	" "
Teatro Alcione	Genoa	Italy	22.8.72	" "
La Locanda del Lupo (2 shows)	Rimini	Italy	23.8.72	" "
Island Studios	London (Mixing sessions)	England	25-27.8.72	
Civic Hall	Merton	England	1.9.72	**Fruup**
Friars Club	Aylesbury	England	2.9.72	
Chelsea Village	Bournemouth	England	3.9.72	
Seloncourt Festival Halle Polyvalente Montbeliard		France	9.9.72	
Big Brother Club	Greenford	England	13-15.9.72	
Sports Centre	Bracknell	England	16.9.72	
The Greyhound	Croydon	England	17.9.72	
Marquee Club	London	England	19.9.72	
Friars Club	Aylesbury	England	22.9.72	
Tait Hall	Kelso	Scotland	23.9.72	
BBC Studios	London	England	25.9.72	

("Sounds Of The Seventies" session. Tracks performed: Watcher of The Skies/Twilight Alehouse/Get 'Em Out By Friday)

National Stadium	Dublin	Eire	28.9.72	**Lindisfarne**
Friars Club	Aylesbury	England	29.9.72	
Kennington Oval	London	England	30.9.72	

(ELP/Wishbone Ash/Argent/Focus/Fudd "Melody Maker" Poll Winner's Party)

City Hall	Newcastle	England	1.10.72	**Lindisfarne**
City Hall	Sheffield	England	3.10.72	**Lindisfarne/Rab Noakes**
Music Hall	Aberdeen	Scotland	4.10.72	" "
Green's Playhouse	Glasgow	Scotland	6.10.72	" "
Empire Theatre	Edinburgh	Scotland	7.10.72	" "
Free Trade Hall	Manchester	England	10.10.72	" "
St George's Hall	Bradford	England	11.10.72	" "
De Montfort Hall	Leicester	England	12.10.72	" "
Winter Gardens	Bournemouth	England	13.10.72	" "
Polytechnic	Kingston	England	14.10.72	**Rab Noakes**
Coliseum	London	England	15.10.72	**Lindisfarne/Rab Noakes**
Top Rank	Liverpool	England	16.10.72	" "
City Hall	Hull	England	17.10.72	
Top Rank	Watford	England	18.10.72	" "
Trentham Gardens	Stoke on Trent	England	19.10.72	" "
Top Rank	Bristol	England	20.10.72	" "
New Theatre	Oxford	England	21.10.72	" "
Guildhall	Preston	England	22.10.72	" "
Guildhall	Portsmouth	England	24.10.72	" "
Odeon Theatre	Birmingham	England	25.10.72	" "
Top Rank	Cardiff	Wales	26.10.72	" "
Top Rank	Brighton	England	27.10..72	" "
Odeon Theatre	Lewisham	England	29.10.72	" "
Cooksferry Inn	Edmonton	England	30.10.72	
Hard Rock Concert Theatre	Stretford	England	2.11.72	
Civic College	Ipswich	England	3.11.72	
University	Leeds	England	4.11.72	
The Wake Arms	Epping	England	5.11.72	
WinterGardens	Cleethorpes	England	6.11.72	
Sundown Club (Rehearsals)	Mile End Brixton London	England	8-9.11.72	
Brunel University	Uxbridge	England	10.11.72	

(This gig featured the first public performance of Suppers Ready)

Marquee Club	London	England	11.11.72	
Alex Disco	Salisbury	England	11.11.72	

Fairfield Hall	Croydon	England	12.11.72	**Capability Brown**
Lyceum Theatre	London (Rehearsals)	England	13-14.11.72	
Polytechnic	Kingston	England	15-16.11.72	
Essex University	Chelmsford	England	17.11.72	**Capability Brown**
Imperial college	London	England	18.11.72	**String Driven Thing**
Town Hall	Cheltenham	England	19.11.72	
Corn Exchange	Kings Lynn	England	24.11.72	
The Belfry Hotel	Sutton Coldfield	England	25.11.72	
Lords Club Civic Hall	Gravesend	England	26.11.72	**Jumping Jack's Experiment**
Sundown Club	Mile End	England	6.12.72	**Capability Brown**
University	Southampton	England	7.12.72	
Guildhall	Plymouth	England	8.12.72	
Brandeis University	Boston	USA	16.12.72	
Carnegie Hall	New York NY	USA	17.12.72	
Salle D'Expositions	Mulhouse	France	19.12.72	
Salle Penfield	Strasbourg	France	20.12.72	

(There is still some doubt about these two gigs taking place advertising documentation does exist although like so many gigs in this period, they may have been cancelled and have included them here for the sake of completeness).

1972 saw the band continuing to expand playing their first gigs in France, Germany, Italy and the USA and also an increasing number of television and radio appearances both at home and abroad and their appearance in their first tour programmes and with the appearance in October of their fourth studio album; "Foxtrot" the band finally had arrived on the UK music circuit and continued to build their reputation as one of the UK's most innovative acts. The early part of 1972 saw a continuation of the set from 1971 with additions from the forthcoming new album which increased the length of theband's set to include… Watcher Of The Skies/Fountain Of Salmacis/Musical Box/Get 'Em Out By Friday/Can-Utility & The Coastliners/Supper's Ready/Twilight Alehouse/The Knife/**Going Out To Get You**/ The Return Of The Giant Hogweed.

The Greyhound	Croydon	England	7.1.73	
Place D'Hiver	Marseilles	France	9.1.73	
Bataclan Club	Paris	France	10.1.73	

(Performed and recorded for the TV show "Pop Deux" and recently re-broadcast on French TV including footage of The Return Of The Giant Hogweed/Supper's Ready/The Musical Box and The Knife and includes only known footage of Peter wearing the red dress and fox head)

Congresshalle	Hamburg	Germany	13.1.73	
Stadthalle	Heidelburg	Germany	15.1.73	
Stadthalle	Offenbach	Germany	16.1.73	
Jahrhunderthalle	Frankfurt	Germany	17.1.73	

(This show was also filmed and broadcast as part of the "Best of British" Festival which had taken place in Frankfurt, strangely enough! The footage still exists and the band played: Watcher of The Skies/Musical Box and Supper's Ready)

Palasport	Rome	Italy	19.1.73	

(Genesis performed with Lindisfarne/Capability Brown/Balletto Di Bronzo)

Palasport	Reggio Emilia	Italy	20.1.73	

(Genesis performed with Lindisfarne/Capabiluty Brown/Balletto Di Bronzo)

Palasport	Rome	Italy	21-22.1.73	

(Genesis performed with Lindisfarne/Capability Brown/Balletto Di Bronzo)

Sundown Club	Mile End London (Rehearsals)	England	30.1.73 - 1.2.73	
Arts Festival	Lanchester	England	2.2.73	
Hippodrome	Bristol	England	4.2.73	**String Driven Thing**
Rainbow Theatre	London (Rehearsal)	Rngland	8.2.73	
Rainbow Theatre	London	England	9.2.73	" " "
The Dome	Brighton	England	10.2.73	" " "
Guildhall	Plymouth	England	12.2.73	" " "
University Great Hall	Exeter	England	14.2.73	" " "
Green's Playhouse	Glasgow	Scotland	16.2.73	" " "
City Hall	Sheffield	England	17.2.73	" " "
Town Hall	Biringham	England	18.2.73	" " "
New Theatre	Oxford	England	19.2.73	" " "
University Great Hall	York	England	21.2.73	" " "
City Hall	Newcastle	England	22.2.73	" " "
University Great Hall	Lancaster	England	23.2.73	" " "
Free Trade Hall	Manchester	England	24.2.73	" " "
De Montfort Hall	Leicester	England	25.2.73	" " "
Civic Hall	Dunstable	England	26.2.73	" " "
US Radio "Bob Harris Show"	New York NY	USA	1.3.73	
Carnegie Hall	New York NY	USA	2.3.73	
Grand Theatre	Quebec City	Canada	3.3.73	
Montreal Forum	Montreal	Canada	4.3.73	
Gusman Hall	Miami FL	USA	5.3.73	
Carnegie Hall	New York NY	USA	8.3.73	
Tower Theatre	Upper Darby PA	USA	10.3.73	

Alpine Arena	Pittsburgh PA	USA	13.3.73	**Lou Reed**
Alexander Hall	Princeton NJ	USA	28.3.73	
Student Centre Seton Hall University	East OrangeNJ	USA	31.3.73	
Philharmonic Hall	New York NY	USA	2-3.4.73	
Grand Theatre	Quebec	Canada	6.4.73	
Maple Leaf Gardens	Toronto	Canada	7.4.73	
Community Centre	Sherbrooke	Canada	8.4.73	
Maple Leaf Gardens	Toronto	Canada	9.4.73	
Sargent Gymnasium Boston University	Boston MA	USA	10.4.73 (Cancelled)	
War Memorial Auditorium	Rochester NY	USA	11.4.73	
Case Western University	Cleveland OH	USA	15.4.73	
Henry Levitt Arena	Wichita KS	USA	17.4.73	
Aragon Ballroom	Chicago IL	USA	20.4.73	
University	Princeton NJ	USA	22.4.73	
Brandeis University	Watltham MA	USA	23.4.73	
Music Hall	Boston MA	USA	24.4.73	
Olympia Theatre	Paris	France	7.5.73	

(Recorded for French "Musicorama" radio show)

Ancienne Belgique	Brussels	Belgium	8.5.73	
ORTF TV Sessions	Paris	France	6.7.73	
Olympia Theatre	Paris	France	7.7.73	**Peter Hammill**
Reading Festival	Reading	England	26.8.73	
Olympia Theatre	Paris	France	19.9.73	
Munsterhalle	Munster	Germany	25.9.73	
Congresshalle	Hamburg	Germany	26.9.73	
?	Darmsdorff	Germany	27.9.73	
Palais de Beaulieu	Lausanne	Switzerland	29.9.73	
Festhalle	Frankfurt	Germany	30.9.73	

Selling England By The Pound Tour 1973/74

Apollo Theatre	Glasgow	Scotland	5.10.73	**Ron Geesin**

(Gig cancelled due to electrical problems and rescheduled for 9th October)

Opera House	Manchester	England	6.10.73
New Theatre	Oxford	England	7.10.73
Apollo Theatre	Glasgow	Scotland	9.10.73
Gaumont Theatre	Southampton	England	11.10.73
Winter Gardens	Bournemouth	England	12.10.73
The Dome	Brighton	England	15.10.73
Colston Hall	Bristol	England	16.10.73
De Montfort Hall	Leicester	England	18.10.73
Rainbow Theatre	London	England	19-20.10.73
Empire Theatre	Liverpool	England	23.10.73

(Interestingly enough;this show featured the inclusion of The Return Of The Giant Hogweed due to technical problems with Mike's guitar lead)

City Hall	Sheffield	England	25.10.73
City Hall	Newcastle	England	26.10.73
Trident studios	London	England	27.10.73

(Recording sessions for Silver Song/Only Your Love putative Phil Collins solo single which has sadly never been released)

Hippodrome	Birmingham	England	28.10.73
Shepperton Film Studios	Borehamwood	England	30-31.10.73

(Filming for the "Tony Stratton-Smith Presents : Genesis In Concert" film from which a live promo clip for I Know What I Like was selected but subsequently rejected).

Capitole Theatre	Quebec QC	Canada	7.11.73
Massey Hall	Toronto ONT	Canada	8.11.73
Queens University Bartlett Gym	Kingston ONT	Canada	9.11.73
University Sports Arena	Montreal QC	Canada	10.11.73
State University Auditorium	Buffalo NY	USA	11.11.73
Kosh Auditorium	Lawrence NY	USA	13.11.73
Tower Theatre	Upper Darby PA	USA	15.11.73
Tufts University Cohen Auditorium	Medford MA	USA	17.11.73
Bergen Community College	Paramus NJ	USA	18.11.73
Felt Forum	New York NY	USA	22.11.73
McCarter Theatre Princeton University	Princeton NJ	USA	24.11.73
Gusman Hall	Miami FL	USA	26.11.73
Institute of Technology	Rochester NY	USA	27.11.73
The Agora	Columbus OH	USA	29.11.73

Allen Theatre	Cleveland OH	USA	30.11.73
State University New Gym	Buffalo NY	USA	1.12.73
North Western University Cahn Auditorum Chicago IL		USA	3.12.73
Perdue Regional Ballroom	Fort Wayne IN	USA	7.12.73
Peace Auditorium	Ypsilpanti MI	USA	8.12.73
Hara Theatre	Toledo OH	USA	9.12.73
Ford Auditorium (?)	Detroit MI	USA	?.12.73
Roxy Theatre (2 shows)	Hollywood CA	USA	17.12.73
Roxy Theatre (2 shows)	Hollywood CA	USA	18.12.73
Roxy Theatre (2 shows)	Hollywood CA	USA	19.12.73
NBC Studios "Midnight Special "	Burbank CA	USA	20.12.73

(Recorded tracks were: WatcherOf The Skies and The Musical Box both of which were slightly different to their album counterparts).

1973 and the band's stature continues to grow with their first headlining tour of the UK's larger auditoriums and an extensive tour of the East coast of the USA. The shows recorded at Manchester's Free trade Hall and Leicester's De Montfort Hall are recorded by US radio show The King Biscuit Flower Hour and parts of these are subsequently issued in August as the band's first live album; "Genesis Live" . October sees the band record a live film at the Shepperton Film Studios part of which was used for the putative promotional video for "I know what I like" the single from the band's new studio album; "Selling England by the Pound" which pierces the lower reaches of the UK charts in October 1973 but sadly the remainder of the film has never seen the light of day officially. The band round off the year with six sell-out shows at Los Angeles's prestigious Roxy Theatre. By the time the band emerged with the follow up to 1972's *Foxtrot* album, their status as headliners meant that their show was now approaching two hours in length and comprised the following tracks with occasional "additions"…Watcher Of The Skies/Dancing With The Moonlit Knight/Cinema Show/I Know What I Like/Firth Of Fifth/Musical Box/More Fool Me/The Battle Of Epping Forest/Horizons/Supper's Ready/ **Harold The Barrel.**

Hippodrome Theatre	Bristol	England	13.1.74
Drury Lane Theatre Royal	London	England	15-16.1.74
Drury Lane Theatre Royal	London	England	18-20.1.74
Vorst Nationale	Brussels	Belgium	26.1.74
Congresshalle	Hamburg	Germany	27.1.74
Eulach Halle	Winterthur	Switzerland	28.1.74
Victoria Koncertshalle	Geneva	Switzerland	29.1.74
Philipshalle	Dusseldorf	Germany	30.1.74
Stadthalle	Offenbach	Germany	31.1.74
Palasport	Turin	Italy	3.2.74
Palasport	Reggio Emilia	Italy	4.2.74
Palasport	Rome	Italy	5.2.74
Teatro Mediteranneo	Naples	Italy	6.2.74
Salle Vaubier	Winterthur	Switzerland	8.2.74
Palais des Sports	Marseilles	France	9.2.74
Palais d'Hiver	Lyon	France	10.2.74
ORTF TV Studios	Paris "Melody" Programme	France	12.2.74

(Features a VERY strange performance of I Know What I Like and Supper's Ready)

Capitol Theatre	Passaic NJ	USA	1.3.74
Tower Theatre	Upper Darby PA	USA	2-3.3.74
East Wind Ballroom	Baltimore MD	USA	4.3.74
T P Warner Theatre	Washington DC	USA	5.3.74
Sports Arena	Fort Wayne IN	USA	7.3.74
Fox Theatre	Atlanta GA	USA	8.3.74
Gusman Philharmonic Hall	Miami FL	USA	9.3.74
Muthers	Nashville TN	USA	12.3.74
North Hall	Memphis TN	USA	13.3.74
Armadillo World Headquarters	Austin TX	USA	17.3.74
Civic Plaza Assembly Hall	Phoenix AZ	USA	20.3.74
Civic Reunion Centre	Santa Monica CA	USA	21-22.3.74
Winterland Arena	San Francisco CA	USA	24.3.74
Arena	Seattle WA	USA	26.3.74
Garden Auditorium	Vancouver	Canada	27.3.74
Philharmonic Hall	New York NY	USA	2.4.74
Orpheum Theatre	Davenport IO	USA	3.4.74
Embassy Theatre	Fort Wayne IN	USA	5.4.74
Student Union Auditorium	Toledo OH	USA	6.4.74
The Agora	Columbus OH	USA	7.4.74
Centre Culturel Grande Salle	Sherbrooke QC	Canada	8.4.74
Guthrie Theatre (Cancelled)	Minneapolis MN	USA	9.4.74
Spectrum	Philadelphia PA	USA	10.4.74
Auditorium Theatre	Chicago IL	USA	11.4.74
Convention Centre	Indianapolis IN	USA	12.4.74
Kiel Theatre	St Louis MO	USA	13.4.74

Memorial Hall	Kansas City MO	USA	14.4.74
Ford Auditorium	Detroit OH	USA	16.4.74
McGaw Hall	Evanston IL	USA	17.4.74
Centre de Congres	Quebec QC	Canada	18.4.74
Civic Centre	Ottawa ON	Canada	19.4.74
University Sports Arena	Montreal QC	Canada	20-21.4.74 **Peter Hammill**
Auditorium Theatre	Rochester NY	USA	22.4.74
Music Hall	Boston MA	USA	24.4.74
A G Hall	Allentown PA	USA	25.4.74
Century Theatre	Buffalo NY	USA	27.4.74
Allen Theatre	Cleveland OH	USA	28-29.4.74
Massey Hall (2 shows)	Toronto ON	Canada	2.5.74
Syria Mosque	Pittsburgh PA	USA	3.5.74
Academy of Music	New York NY	USA	4 &6.5.74

The Lamb Lies Down On Broadway Tour 1974/75

City Hall (fan club show?)	Newcastle	England	29.10.74	(*)
City Hall	Newcastle	England	30.10.74	(*)
Palace Theatre	Manchester	England	1-2.11.74	(*)
Empire Pool	Wembley London	England	4.11.74	(*)
Usher Hall	Edinburgh	Scotland	6-7.11.74	(*)
Hippodrome	Bristol	England	8-9.11.74	(*)
Hippodrome	Birmingham	England	11-12.11.74	(*)

(*) Original dates for UK shows cancelled as a result of Steve Hackett's hand injury

Auditorium Theatre	Chicago IL	USA	20-21.11.74
Indiana Convention Center	Indianapolis IN	USA	22.11.74
Ambassador Theatre	St Louis MO	USA	23.11.74
Music Hall	Cleveland OH	USA	25-26.11.74
Veterans Memorial Coliseum	Columbus OH	USA	27.11.74
Masonic Temple	Detroit MI	USA	28.11.74
National Guard Armory	Fort Wayne IN	USA	29.1174
Syria Mosque	Pittsburgh PA	USA	30.11.74
Lyric Theatre	Baltimore MD	USA	1.12.74
Warner Theater	Washington DC	USA	2 (or) 3.12.74
(originally 2-3 November are days off from the tour schedule)			
Mosque	Richmond VA	USA	4.12.74
Philadelphia Civic Center	Philadelphia PA	USA	5.12.74
Academy of Music	New York NY	USA	6-7.12.74
Palace Theatre	Providence RI	USA	8.12.74
Music Hall	Boston MA	USA	9.12.74
Palace Theatre	Albany NY	USA	11.12.74
Palace Theatre	Waterbury CT	USA	12.12.74
Capitol Theatre	Passaic NJ	USA	13.12.74
Market Square Arena	Indianapolis IN	USA	14.12.74
(This date is not on original tour schedule)			
Forum	Montreal QC	Canada	15.12.74
Maple LeafGardens	Toronto ONT	Canada	16.12.74
The Dome	Rochester NY	USA	17.12.74
Century Theatre	Buffalo NY	USA	18.12.74
Gusman Auditorium University Of Miami Miami FL		USA	9-10.1.75
Lakeland Civic Center Concert Hall Lakeland FL		USA	11.1.75
Fox Theatre	Atlanta GA	USA	12.1.75
Music Hall	New Orleans LA	USA	15.1.75
Houston Music Hall	Houston TX	USA	17.1.75
McFarland Auditorium (Cancelled) Dallas TX		USA	18.1.75
Civic Centre Music Hall	Oklahoma City OK	USA	19.1.75
Civic Centre	Phoenix AZ	USA	20.1.75
(This date was originally not on the tour schedule)			
Macky Auditorium University of			
Colorado at Boulder	Boulder CO	USA	21.1.75
Berkeley Community Theatre	Berkeley CA	USA	22.1.75
Old Waldorf Astoria	San Francisco CA	USA	23.1.75
(22 and 23 January not included on original tour schedule)			
Shrine Auditorium	Los Angeles CA	USA	24.1.75

(Excerpts of In The Cage, Colony Of Slippermen and Musical Box are film recorded for a WDR German TV profile of Billy Graham the promoter of the Shrine gig. It is unknown if the entire gig was filmed and these clips remain the only acknowledged official footage from The Lamb,… tour).

Golden Hall	San Diego CA	USA	25.1.75
Berkeley Community Theatre	Berkeley CA	USA	26.1.75
Civic Centre	Phoenix AZ	USA	28.1.75
Queen Elizabeth Theatre	Vancouver BC	Canada	2.2.75
Kansas Memorial Hall	Kansas City MO	USA	1.2.75
Grand Valley State College	Grand Rapids MI	USA	2.2.75
Allen County Memorial Coliseum	Fort Wayne IN	USA	3.2.75
Arie Crown Theater McCormick Place Chicago IL		USA	4.2.75

(last five US dates not included on original tour itineraries)

Ekeberghallen	Oslo	Norway	19.2.75
Falkoner Theatrit	Copenhagen	Denmark	21.2.75
Niedersachsenhalle	Hannover	Germany	22.2.75
Eishalle (Deutschlandhalle)	Berlin	Germany	23.2.75
Theatre Carre	Amsterdam	Holland	24-25.2.75
Palais des Grottes	Cambrai	France	26.2.75
Parc D'Expositions	Colmar	France	28.2.75
Parc D'Expositions	Dijon	France	1.3.75
Palais des Sports	St Etienne	France	2.3.75
Palais des Sports	Paris	France	3.3.75
Pavilhao dos Desportos	Cascais nr Lisbon	Portugal	6-7.3.75
Nuevo Pabellon Club Juventud	Badalona	Spain	9-10.3.75
Pabellon Real Madrid	Madrid	Spain	11.3.75

(Italian Tour supposed to take place between 13th March and 27th March cancelled due to political unrest)

Porte de Versailles	Paris	France	17.3.75
Salle D'Expositions	Annecy	France	22.3.75
Palasport Parco Rufino	Turin	Italy	24.3.75
Messezentrum Halle A	Nuremberg	Germany	27.3.75
Festhalle	Bern	Switzerland	29.3.75
Saarlandhalle	Saarbrucken	Germany	30.3.75
Friedrich Ebert Halle	Ludwigshafen	Germany	1.4.75
Killesberghalle 14	Stuttgart	Germany	2.4.75
Jahrhunderthalle	Frankfurt	Germany	3.4.75
Zirkus Krone	Munich	Germany	4.4.75
Stadthalle	Heidelberg	Germany	5.4.75
Philipshalle	Dusseldorf	Germany	6.4.75
Westfalenhalle 3	Dortmund	Germany	7.4.75
Congress Centrum	Hamburg	Germany	8.4.75
Martinihal-Centrum	Groningen	Holland	10.4.75
Ahoy Sportpaleis	Rotterdam	Holland	11.4.75
Vorst Nationale	Brussels	Belgium	12.4.75
Empire Pool	London	England	14-15.4.75
Gaumont Theatre	Southampton	England	16.4.75
Empire Theatre	Liverpool	England	17-19.4.75
Usher Hall	Edinburgh	Scotland	22-23.4.75
City Hall	Newcastle	England	24-25.4.75
Palace Theatre	Manchester	England	27-28.4.75
Colston Hall	Bristol	England	29-30.4.75
Hippodrome	Birmingham	England	1-2.5.75
Ostseehalle	Kiel	Germany	10.5.75
Grugahalle	Essen	Germany	11.5.75
Rhein am Main Halle	Wiesbaden	Germany	12.5.75
Stadthalle	Bremen	Germany	13.5.75
Patinoire	Rheims	France	15-16.5.75
Velodromo Anoeta	San Sebastian	Spain	18.5.75
Porte de Versailles	Paris	France	20.5.75
Palais des Grottes	Cambrai	France	21.5.75
Parc D'Expositions	Colmar	France	23.5.75
Palais des Sports	Dijon	France	25.5.75
Palais des Sports	Besancon	France	27.5.75

1974/75 sees the band on an upward curve playing bigger and better shows and with two successful albums under their belts; "Selling England by the Pound" and their most controversial album ; "The lamb lies down on Broadway" which they play in its entirety on their biggest tour to date through late 1974 and early 1975 although it was originally to have been even bigger but the enforced cancellation of several shows due to poor ticket sales and in the case of an sixteen date tour of Italy, cancelled due to political unrest in the country at the time made it a slightly shorter affair but still their largest tour to-date. However, fans are taken by surprise by Peter Gabriel's announcement in August 1975 that he is quitting the band. A live recording of the band's show at the shrine Auditorium in Los Angeles is made part of which features as a b-side to one of the band's singles the rest of this recording finally surfaces on the first Genesis "Boxed Set" released on 15th June 1998. The band's show continued as outlined above for 1973 until the beginning of *The Lamb Lies Down On*

Broadway tour. From that moment an entirely new set was played which comrpised the ENTIRE Lamb... album with encores which comprised one or two of the following tracks...Watcher Of The Skies/Musical Box/The Knife. There is still some debate over the exact number of shows played on this tour, several were cancelled and others were added, especially to the second European leg to compensate for the cancellation of the Italian tour. Official sources state that 102 dates were performed on this tour; as you can see from this list; more were added, and maybe more are still to be documented!

Author's Note: The tour itinerary referred to in this section of the Gig Guide is that which was provided to working members of the road crew. My thanks to David Lawrence chief projectionist on both legs of the US and first leg of the European Lamb... tours for providing this information.

Genesis Gig Guide

Part Two: "The Phil Collins Years"

VENUE NAME	CITY	COUNTRY	DATE

A Trick Of The Tail Tour 1976.

VENUE NAME	CITY	COUNTRY	DATE
Reunion Centre (Rehearsals)	Las Colinas TX	USA	18-24.3.76
Civic Centre	London Ontario ONT	Canada	25.3.76
Auditorium	Kitchener ONT	Canada	27.3.76
Century Theatre	Buffalo NY	USA	28.3.76
Hamilton Place Great Hall	Hamilton ONT	Canada	29.3.76
Maple Leaf Gardens	Toronto ONT	Canada	31.3.76
Forum	Montreal QC	Canada	2.4.76
Ottawa Civic Centre	Ottawa ONT	Canada	3.4.76
Colisee de Jeunesse	Quebec QC	Canada	4.4.76
Tower Theatre (2 shows)	Upper Darby PA	USA	7.4.76
Beacon Theatre	New York NY	USA	8.4.76
Beacon Theatre (2 shows)	New York NY	USA	9.4.76
Orpheum Theatre	Boston MA	USA	10.4.76
Lyric Theatre	Baltimore MD	USA	12.4.76
Syria Mosque	Pittsburgh PA	USA	13.4.76
Music Hall	Cleveland OH	USA	14.4.76
Ohio Theatre (Cancelled)	Columbus OH	USA	15.4.76
Music Hall	Cleveland OH	USA	15.4.76
(Replacing postponed show at Columbus)			
Auditorium Theatre	Chicago IL	USA	16-17.4.76
Ohio Theatre	Columbus OH	USA	19.4.76
(Rescheduled show from 15th)			
Ford Auditorium	Detroit MI	USA	20.4.76
Riverside Theatre	Milwaukee WI	USA	21.4.76
Civic Centre	Grand Rapids MI	USA	22.4.76
Ambassador Theatre	St Louis MO	USA	23.4.76
Memorial Hall	Kansas City MO	USA	25.4.76
Community Centre	Berkeley CA	USA	29.4.76
Warner Theatre	Fresno CA	USA	30.4.76
Starlight Bowl	Burbank CA	USA	1.5.76
Sports Arena	San Diego CA	USA	3.5.76
Memorial Auditorium	Austin TX	USA	5.5.76
Music Hall	Houston TX	USA	6.5.76
Will Rogers Auditorium	Fort Worth TX	USA	7.5.76
Hammersmith Odeon	London	England	9-14.6.76
New Bingley Hall	Stafford	England	15.6.76
Ahoy Sportpaleis	Rotterdam	Holland	16.6.76
Philipshalle	Dortmund	Germany	18.6.76
Deutshlandhalle	Berlin	Germany	19.6.76
Vorst Nationale	Brussels	Belgium	22.6.76
Pavilion de Paris	Paris	France	23.6.76
Palais des Sports	Lyon	France	24.6.76
Festhalle	Berne	Switzerland	26.6.76
Olympiahalle	Munich	Germany	27.6.76
Festhalle	Berne	Switzerland	28.6.76
Congresshalle	Hamburg	Germany	29..6.76
Scandinavium	Gothenburg	Sweden	30.6.76

Philipshalle	Dusseldorf	Germany	2.7.76
Loreley Freiluftbuhne	St Goarshausen	Germany	3.7.76

(Show interrupted when a drug den at the side of the stage was raided by the police and subseqently set on fire. This show is documented by the "We're Hot On Your Tail" bootleg. This was the very first Loreley Festival).

Rhein Neckar Halle	Heidelberg	Germany	4.7.76
Apollo Theatre	Glasgow	Scotland	8-9.7.76
New Bingley Hall	Stafford	England	10.7.76
Sports Centre	Luton	England	11.7.76 (*)

(*) Gig cancelled, the band actually played an additional night at Stafford in place of this show.

1976 saw Genesis enter a new phase in their development. Peter's departure and Phil's entry into the vocalist's role gave the band a more accessible feel to their music as evidenced by their new album : "A Trick of the tail". Steve's solo success the previous year with his first solo album; "Voyage of the acolyte" had proven that their was still interest in the band and their new tour was stunning. Taking over the drum seat live performances was Yes and King Crimson stalwart Bill Bruford. The band took another stab at a live concert film by recording their shows Glasgow and Stafford for a film which was premiered the following summer under the title of "Genesis in concert" the premiere of which was attended by Princess Anne! From this point onwards, Genesis's live sets increasingly tended toward being the same every night with a typical set running as follows… Dance On A Volcano/The Lamb Lies Down On Broadway-Broadway Melody Of '74-Fly On A Windshield-Carpet C (medley sometimes introduced as "Lamb Stew" or "Lamb Casserole")/Cinema Show/Robbery Assault & Battery/WhiteMountain/Firth Of Fifth/Entangled/Supper's Ready/Squonk/I Know What I Like/Los Endos/It-Watcher Of The Skies (instrumental),with the exception of the first three shows of the tour at which Supper's Rady was omitted because Phil was uncertain about performing it. Two soundboard recordings of th shows at Kichener and Buffalo have recently emerged documenting these unusual shows.

Wind & Wuthering Tour 1977.

Farmyard Studios (Rehearsals)	Little Chalfont	England	17 -30.12.76
Rainbow Theatre	London	England	31.12.76

(Full dress rehearsal gig for the commencement of the 1977 tour)

Rainbow Theatre	London	England	1-3.1.77

(Footage from one of these three shows was filmed for Japanese TV)

Odeon Theatre	Birmingham	England	7-8.1.77
Empire Theatre (2 shows)	Liverpool	England	9.1.77
Free Trade Hall	Manchester	England	10-11.1.77
Playhouse Theatre (2 shows)	Edinburgh	Scotland	14.1.77
Caird Hall	Dundee	Scotland	15.1.77
City Hall	Newcastle	England	16-17.1.77
Gaumont Theatre	Southampton	England	19-20.1.77
De Montfort Hall (2 shows)	Leicester	England	21.1.77
De Montfort Hall	Leicester	England	22.1.77
Hippodrome (2 shows)	Bristol	England	23.1.77

(These gigs were the last time that All In A Mouse's Night was performed as part of the live set)

Mackey Auditorium	Boulder CO	USA	2.2.77
Municipal Theatre	Tulsa OK	USA	4.2.77
Municipal Auditorium	Kansas City MO	USA	5.2.77
Kiel Auditorium	St Louis MO	USA	6.2.77
Orpheum Theatre	Minneapolis MN	USA	8.2.77
Dane County Memorial Coliseum	Madison WI	USA	9.2.77
Auditorium	Milwaukee WI	USA	10.2.77
Ballrooms	Nashville TN	USA	11.2.77
Masonic Auditorium	Detroit OH	USA	12.2.77
Wings Stadium	Kalamazoo MI	USA	13.2.77
Auditorium Theatre	Chicago IL	USA	15-17.2.77
Winnipeg Auditorium	Winnipeg MN	Canada	19.2.77
Memorial Auditorium	Kitchener ONT	Canada	21.2.77
Madison Square Garden	New York NY	USA	23.2.77
Bushnell Auditorium	Hartford CT	USA	25.2.77
Onondaga County War Memorial	Syracuse NY	USA	26.2.77
Richfield Coliseum	Cleveland OH	USA	27.2.77
Buffalo Memorial Auditorium	Buffalo NY	USA	28.2.77
Forum	Montreal QC	Canada	2.3.77
Colisee de Quebec	Quebec QC	Canada	3.3.77
Maple Leaf Gardens	Toronto ONT	Canada	4.3.77
Ottawa Civic Centre	Ottawa ONT	Canada	5.3.77
Maple Leaf Gardens	Toronto ONT	Canada	6.3.77
The Spectrum	Philadelphia PA	USA	8.3.77
Civic Centre	Baltimore MD	USA	9.3.77
Civic Arena	Pittsburgh PA	USA	10.3.77
Vanderbilt University	Nashville TN	USA	12.3.77
Fox Theatre	Atlanta GA	USA	13-14.3.77

Municipal Auditorium	New Orleans LA	USA	16.3.77
Sam Houston Coliseum	Houston TX	USA	17.3.77
Texas Hall	Arlington TX (Cancelled)	USA	18.3.77
Moody Coliseum	Dallas TX	USA	19.3.77

(A 25 minute segment of film from this gig was filmed as a promotional item for the subsequent Seconds Out live album featuring Dance On A Volcano/Los Endos/The Lamb…/Musical Box).

Municipal Auditorium	Austin TX	USA	21.3.77
Forum	Los Angeles CA	USA	24.3.77
Winterland Arena	San Francisco CA	USA	25-26.3.77
Sports Centre	San Diego CA	USA	27.3.77
Civic Centre	Phoenix AZ	USA	29.3.77
Paramount Theatre	Portland OR	USA	1.4.77
Coliseum	Vancouver BC	Canada	2.4.77
Paramount Northwest	Seattle WA	USA	3.4.77
Starlight Bowl	Burbank CA	USA	1.5.77
Gigantinho Stadium	Porto Allegre	Brazil	10-11.5.77
Maracananzinho Stadium (2 shows)	Rio de Janeiro	Brazil	14.5.77
Maracananzinho Stadium (2 shows)	Rio de Janeiro	Brazil	15.5.77
Anhembi Stadium	Sao Paolo	Brazil	18-19.5.77
Ibirapuera Stadium (2 shows)	Sao Paolo	Brazil	21.5.77
Ibirapuera Stadium (2 shows)	Sao Paolo	Brazil	22.5.77

(Apparently these shows were filmed by Brazilian TV and the footage is still in existence in the TV archives).

Olympiapark Olympialle	Munich	Germany	2.6.77
Isstadion	Stockholm	Sweden	4.6.77
EisSporthalle	Berlin	Germany	6.6.77
Isstadion	Stockhom	Sweden	7.6.77
Palais des Sports (2 shows)	Paris	France	11.6.77
Palais des Sports (2 shows)	Paris	France	12.6.77
Palais des Sports	Paris	France	13-14.6.77

(There is reputed to be a complete concert film from one of the Paris gigs but this is unsubstantiated and the footage is not in the band's film archive)

| Muengersdorfer Sportstadion | Cologne | Germany | 17.6.77 |
| Stadion Bieberer Berg | Offenbach | Germany | 19.6.77 |

(Open air festival with Manfred Mann's Earth Band/Lake/Gentle Giant also on the bill)

| Earls Court Arena | London | England | 23-25.6.77 |

(Special guest at these shows was Woodstock veteran Richie Havens)

Vorst Nationale (2 shows)	Brussels	Belgium	28.6.77
Ahoy Sportpaleis	Rotterdam	Holland	29.6.77
Parc Des Expositions	Colmar	France	1.7.77
Hallenstadion	Zurich	Switzerland	2.7.77
Olympiahalle	Munich	Germany	3.7.77

(This show was Steve Hackett's last performances with the band)

1977 and Genesis are riding high on a wave of public adulation that sees them go from five nights at the 3000 seater Hammersmith Odeon to three nights at London's 18000 seater Earls Court Arena and with their first ever number one album ; "Wind & Wuthering" under their belts,the band defy the critics who pan their brand of music so vehemently and continue to attract ever more fans. The year also see the band's first shows in South America and numerous awards for their work. For live performances, the band recruit American drummer Chester Thompson who soon becomes an integral part of the Genesis live sound.

Outside of the band, Phil helps to form free-form jazz outfit Brand X and Mike is reunited with former guitarist Anthony Phillips on his first solo album; "The Geese & the Ghost". The band record their five nights at the Palais des Sports in Paris for a long overdue second live album. It is during the mixing of this album that Steve announces his decision to quit the band to pursue solo projects. The band, with typical British sense of humour title the live album; "Second's out" . The band's massive tour to promote *Wind & Wuthering* resulted in a couple of alternative tracks in the set which usually ran as follows… Eleventh Earl Of Mar/Carpet Crawl/**All In A Mouse's nNight**/ Firth Of Fifth/Your Own Special Way/Robbery Assault & Battery/Unquiet Slumbers For The Sleepers/In That Quiet Earth/Afterglow/**Lilywhite Lilith/Wot Gorilla?**/One For The Vine/Supper's Ready/Squonk/Dance On A Volcano/Los Endos/The Lamb Lies Down On Broadway/Musical Box (end section). For the band's inaugural visit to Brazil **Inside & Out** replaced Your Own Special Way which also appeared in the set for their shows at Earls Court in June which wasalso where **The Knife** made a welcome appearance as additional encore.

And Then There Were Three Tour 1978.

Las Colinas (Showco rehearsals)	Dallas TX	USA	21-25.3.78
Broome County Arena	Binghamton NY	USA	28.3.78
Buffalo Memorial Auditorium	Buffalo NY	USA	29..3.78
Rochester Community War Memorial	Rochester NY	USA	30.3.78
The Spectrum	Philadelphia PA	USA	31.3.78
Rockland Fieldhouse Rockland Community College			
	Suffern NY	USA	1.4.78
Penn State University Scranton	Pennsylvania PA	USA	2.4.78
Met Centre	Bloomington OH	USA	3.4.78
Wings Auditorium	Kalamazooo MI	USA	4,4,78
Horton Fieldhouse	Normal IL	USA	5.4.78
Stadium	Chicago IL	USA	6.4.78
Richfield Coliseum	Cleveland OH	USA	7.4.78
Hara Arena	Dayton Ohio OH	USA	8.4.78
Assembly Hall Indiana University	Bloomington IN	USA	9.4.78
Kiel Opera House	St Louis MO	USA	10.4.78
Coliseum	Oakland CA	USA	14.4.78
Sports Arena	San Diego CA	USA	15.4.78
Forum	Inglewood Los Angeles CA	USA	17.4.78
Forum	Montreal QC	Canada	22.4.78
Sportshalle	Cologne	Germany	14.5.78
Festhalle	Frankfurt	Germany	15.5.78
Olympiahalle	Munich	Germany	16.5.78
Eistadion	Mannheim	Germany	17.5.78

(Parts of this show were filmed for inclusion in the BBC TV documentary "Three Dates With Genesis)

Sporthalle	Cologne	Germany	18.5.78
Groenoordhal	Leiden	Holland	20.5.78

(Parts of this show were filmed for inclusion in the BBC TV documentary "Three Dates With Genesis")

Vorst Nationale	Brussels	Belgium	21-22.5.78
Jaap Edenhal	Amsterdam	Holland	24.5.78
Palais des Sports	Paris	France	26-29.5.78
Palais des Sports	Poitiers	France	30.5.78
Palais des Sports	Lyon	France	1.6.78
Palais de Congres	St Etienne	France	2.6.78
Palais des Sports	Dijon	France	3.6.78
Hallenstadion	Zurich	Switzerland	4.6.78
Ishallen	Malmo	Sweden	6.6.78
Scandinavium	Gothenburg	Sweden	7.6.78
Ekeberghallen	Oslo	Norway	8.6.78
Ishallen	Helsinki	Finland	9.6.78
Deutschlandhalle	Berlin	Germany	11.6.78
Stadthalle	Bremen	Germany	12.6.78
Ernst Merckt Halle	Hamburg	Germany	13.6.78
Westfalenhalle	Dortmund	Germany	14.6.78
Knebworth Park	Stevenage	England	24.6.78

(Festival line-up included; Roy Harper/Atlanta Rhythm Section/Tom Petty & The Heartbreakers/Devo/Brand X/Jefferson Starship. The band's soundcheck and mimed performance of The Lady Lies also f eatured in the BBCTV documentary "Three Dates With Genesis")

Maple Leaf Gardens	Toronto ON	Canada	3.7.78
CNE Exhibition Stadium	Toronto ON	Canada	10.7.78
Forum	Montreal QC	Canada	12-13.7.78
Pine Knob Performing Arts Centre	Clarkston MO	USA	14.7.78
Cobo Hall	Detroit MI	USA	15-16.7.78
Summerfield Gardens	Milwaukee WI	USA	17-19.7.78
Richfield Coliseum	Cleveland OH	USA	21.7.78
Civic Arena	Pittsburgh PA	USA	22.7.78
Onondaga County War Memorial	Syracuse NY	USA	23.7.78
Merriweather Post Pavilion	Columbia PA	USA	25-26.7.78
The Scope	Norfolk VA	USA	27.7.78
Coliseum	Hampton Roads VA	USA	28.7.78
Madison Square Garden	New York NY	USA	29.7.78
Waterbury Theatre	Providence RI	USA	30.7.78
Saratoga Performing Arts Centre	Saratoga Springs NY	USA	31.7.78

Stadthalle	Vienna	Austria	20..8.78	
Friedrichsau-Festplatz	Ulm	Germany	26.8.78	**John McLaughlin/Alvin Lee/Ten Years Later/Joan Baez**
Stadthalle	Vienna	Austria	28.8.78	
Messegelande Halle 20	Hannover	Germany	30.8.78	
Radreunbahn	Cologne	Germany	1.9.78	
Ludwigsparkstadion	Saarbrucken	Germany	3.9.78	**John McLaughlin/Alvin Lee/Ten Years Later/Joan Baez**
Eurohal	Maastricht	Holland	4.9.78	
Rijnhal	Arnhem	Holland	5.9.78	
Ahoy Sportpaleis	Rotterdam	Holland	6.9.78	
Fete De L'Humanite	La Courneuve Paris	France	9.9.78	

- (Festival line-up included: Joan Baez/John McLaughlin/Alvin Lee/ Ten Years Later/The Scorpions/Brand X)

Sportatorium	Hollywood CA	USA	29.9.78
Civic Centre	Lakeland CA	USA	30.9.78
The Omni Centre	Atlanta GA	USA	4.10.78
Boutwell Auditorium (Cancelled)	Birmingham AL	USA	5.10.78
Riverside Centroplex	Baton Rouge LA	USA	6.10.78
Nashville Municipal Auditorium	Nashville TN	USA	8.10.78
St Johns Centre	Columbus OH	USA	10.10.78
MSU Jenison Fieldhouse	Lansing MI	USA	11.10.78
Aseembly Hall	Champaign IL	USA	12.10.78
Uptown Theatre	Chicago IL	USA	13.10.78
Civic Arena	Evansville KY	USA	14.10.78
Coliseum	Springfield OH	USA	16.10.78
Kemper Arena	Kansas City MO	USA	17.10.78
Edwin Nutter Centre	Norman IL	USA	18.10.78
Municipal Auditorium	Austin TX	USA	20.10.78
Reunion Centre	Dallas TX	USA	21.10.78
Hofheinz Pavilion University Of Houston	Houston TX	USA	22.10.78
Sun Plaza Hall	Tokio	Japan	27.11.78
Kosei Nenkin Hall	Tokio	Japan	28.11.78
Sun Plaza Hall	Tokio	Japan	29.11.78
Castle Hall	Osaka	Japan	30.11.78
(A privately shot film of thisgig exists)			
Kosei Nenkin Hall	Tokio	Japan	2.12.78
Sun Plaza Hall	Tokio	Japan	3.12.78

(Several songs from this gig were filmed by Japanese TV and subsequently broadcast including: 11th Earl Of Mar/Dance On A Volcano and I Know What I Like. It is also alleged that a complete film of this gig was made by Japanese TV)

1978 and Genesis finally achieve the impossible : a hit single! "Follow You Follow Me" the first release from their new album; "And Then There Were Three" achieves a top ten spot in the UK and elsewhere. A massive tour is undertaken in support of the album which includes three separate tours of the USA and Canada and the band's first shows in Japan. For live duties the band recruit another American; Daryl Stuermer. The tour lasts eight months and features one of the largest lighting rigs seen including six computerised mirrors and numerous laser effects and Boeing 747 landing lights _ all in all the stage production costs a staggering £150,000 PER DAY to run! The 1978 tours saw the band vary their live set depending on which territory they were in beginning with the April US tour which was as follows… Eleventh Earl Of Mar/In The Cage/Burning Rope/Ripples/Deep In The Motherlode/Fountain Of Salmacis/Down & Out/One For The Vine/Say It's Alright, Joe/Squonk/The Lady Lies/Cinema Show/Follow You Follow Me/Dance On A Volcano/Los Endos/I Know What I Like. The tour in Europe had a couple of alterations including rare performances of **Ballad Of Big.** The band's Autumn US tour also saw a set change with the inclusion of **Dancing With The Moonlit Knight** at several shows December saw the band's inaugural visit to japan for which a revised set was played…. Eleventh Earl Of Mar/In The Cage/Burning Rope/Ripples/Deep In The Motherlode/One For The Vine/Squonk/Say It's Alright, Joe/The Lady Lies/Cinema Show/In That Quiet Earth/Afterglow/Follow You Follow Me/Dance On A Volcano/Los Endos/I Know What I Like.

Duke UK/US Tour 1980

Shepperton Film Studios (Rehearsals)Borehamwood		England	17-25.3.80
Winter Gardens	Bournemouth	England	26.3.80 (*)
Hammersmith Odeon	London	England	27-29.3.80 (*)
New Theatre	Oxford	England	31.3.80 (*)
Gaumont Theatre	Ipswich	England	1.4.80 (*)
ABC Theatre	Great Yarmouth	England	2.4.80 (*)
ABC Theatre	Peterborough	England	3.4.80 (*)
Odeon Theatre	Birmingham	England	4-5.4.80 (*)
ABC Theatre	Blackpool	England	6.4.80 (*)
Trentham Gardens	Stoke-On-Trent	England	8.4.80 (*)
Sophia Gardens	Cardiff	Wales	9.4.80 (*)
Gaumont Theatre	Southampton	England	11.4.80 (*)
Conference Centre	Brighton	England	12.4.80 (*)
Theatre	Coventry	England	13.4.80 (*)
De Montfort Hall	Leicester	England	15.4.80 (*)
Assembly Rooms	Derby	England	16.4.80 (*)
City Hall	Sheffield	England	17.4.80 (*)
Apollo Theatre	Manchester	England	18-19.4.80 (*)
St George's Hall	Bradford	England	21.4.80 (*)
Odeon Theatre	Edinburgh	Scotland	23.4.80 (*)
Caird Hall	Dundee	Scotland	24.4.80 (*)
Capitol Theatre	Aberdeen	Scotland	25.4.80 (*)
Apollo Theatre	Glasgow	Scotland	27-28.4.80 (*)
City Hall	Newcastle	England	29-30.4.80 (*)
Market Hall	Carlisle	England	1.5.80 (*)
Empire Theatre	Liverpool	England	2-3.5.80 (*)

(*) Original UK tour dates some of which were re-scheduled due to Phil's illness with laryngitis. As can be seen, other gigs were added to the itinerary and some planned gigs were dropped from the final itinerary.

Festival Hall	Paignton	England	17-18.3.80
University	Exeter	England	19-20.3.80
Friars	Aylesbury	England	22.3.80
Hexagon	Reading	England	23.3.80
Civic Hall	Guildford	England	24.3.80
Hammersmith Odeon	London	England	27-29.3.80
New Theatre	Oxford	England	31.3.80
Gaumont Theatre	Ipswich	England	1.4.80
ABC Theatre	Great Yarmouth	England	2.4.80
ABC Theatre	Peterborough	England	3.4.80
Odeon Theatre	Birmingham	England	4-5.4.80
ABC Theatre	Blackpool	England	6.4.80
Trentham Gardens	Stoke on Trent	England	8.4.80
Sophia Gardens	Cardiff	Wales	9.4.80
Gaumont Theatre	Southampton	England	10.4.80
Conference Centre	Brighton	England	12.4.80
ABC Theatre	Coventry	England	13.4.80
De Montfort Hall	Leicester	England	15.4.80
Assembly Rooms	Derby	England	16.4.80
City Hall	Sheffield	England	17.4.80
Apollo Theatre	Manchester	England	18-19.4.80
St George's Hall	Bradford	England	21.4.80
Odeon Theatre	Edinburgh	Scotland	23.4.80
Capitol Theatre	Aberdeen	Scotland	24.4.80
Caird Hall	Dundee	Scotland	25.4.80
Apollo Theatre	Glasgow	Scotland	27-28.4.80
City Hall	Newcastle	England	29-30.4.80
Market Hall	Carlisle	England	1.5.80
Empire Theatre	Liverpool	England	2-3.5.80

(ITV documentary filmed at the first of these two shows and broadcast the following night)

Theatre Royal Drury Lane	London	England	4.5.80

(Recorded for BBC transmission which has never been released)

Lyceum Ballrooms	London	England	6-7.5.80

(Both shows recorded for BBC Radio and TV the second show was eventually broadcast and edited
highlights of the film of that show were also broadcast two years later on the BBC's Whistle Test programme)

Guildhall	Portsmouth	England	9.5.80
Northland Coliseum Bowl	Edmonton AL	Canada	17.5.80

Max Bell Memorial Auditorium	Calgary AL	Canada	18.5.80
PNE Coliseum	Vancouver BC	Canada	20.5.80
Coliseum	Oakland	USA	23.5.80
Arena	Long Beach CA	USA	24.5.80
The Roxy	Hollywood CA	USA	25.5.80
Sports Arena	San Diego CA	USA	26.5.80
Greek Theatre	Los Angeles CA	USA	27.5.80
The Summit	Houston TX	USA	30,5,80
Sanger Theatre	New Orleans LA	USA	31.5.80
Fox Theatre	Atlanta GA	USA	1.6.80
Park West	Chicago IL	USA	3.6.80
Kemper Arena	Kansas City MO	USA	4.6.80
Kiel Open House	St Louis MO	USA	5.6.80
Rosemont Horizon	Chicago IL	USA	6.6.80
Mecca Arena	Milwaukee WI	USA	7.6.80
Pine Knob	Clarkston WI	USA	9-10.6.80

(The second of these two gigs was played without Daryl Stuermer who was ill)

Richfield Coliseum	Cleveland OH	USA	11.6.80
Music Hall	Cincinatti OH	USA	12.6.80
Stanley Theatre	Pittsburgh OH	USA	13.6.80
Merriweather Post Pavilion	Columbia OH	USA	14.6.80
The Spectrum	Philadelphia PA	USA	16-17.6.80
Orpheum Theatre	Boston MA	USA	18.6.80
Forum	Montreal QC	Canada	19-20.6.80
Ottawa Civic Centre	Ottawa ONT	Canada	22.6.80
Maple Leaf Gardens	Toronto ONT	Canada	23-24.6.80
Rochester Community War Memorial	Rochester NY	USA	25.6.80
Buffalo Memorial Auditorium	Buffalo NY	USA	26.6.80
Capitol Theatre	Passaic NJ	USA	28.6.80
Madison Square Garden	New York NY	USA	29.6.80
Saratoga Performing Arts Centre	Saratoga Springs NY	USA	30.6.80

1980 and for fans who complained that the UK was being ignored at the expense of Europe and the USA there was a treat in store as the band embarked on their largest tour of the UK since the mid '70's and in THEATRES to boot! The new album; "Duke" spawned several hit singles both here and in the USA where the band went from strength to strength.
For once even the UK television got in on the act with this "happening" band with both ITV and BBC covering shows in the UK.

During the lull in activities between the end of the 1978 tour and the start of the "Duke" sessions Tony and Mike take advantage of Phil's time away dealing with his family problems to finally record and release their first solo projects; Tony's "A Curious Feeling" appears first in 1979 followed by Mike's "Smallcreep's Day" early in 1980. The return to theatres also brought a revised set list which comprised the following tracks **Back in NYC**/Deep in the Motherlode/Dancing with the moonlit knight/CarpetCrawl/Squonk/One for the vine/Behind thelines/Duchess/Turn it on again/Duke's Travels/Dukes' end/**Say it's alright, Joe**/The lady lies/In the cage/Raven-Cinema show medley/Afterglow/Follow you follow me/Dance on a volcano/Los Endos/I know what I like/**The knife**

Abacab European/US Tour 1981.

Shepperton Film Studios (Rehearsals) Borehamwood		England	7-21.9.81
Plaza de Toros Monumental	Barcelona	Spain	25.9.81

(This show also saw the inclusion of Me & Virgil in the set subsequently dropped).

Velodromo Anoeta	San Sebastian	Spain	27.9.81
Amphitheatre	Frejus	France	29.9.81
Parc des Expositions	Avignon	France	30.9.81
Palais des Sports	Lyon	France	1.10.81
Halle Rhenus	Strasbourg	France	2.10.81
Groenoordhal	Leiden	Holland	3-4.10.81
Stadthalle	Bremen	Germany	5.10.81
Grugahalle	Essen	Germany	6.10.81
Olympiahalle	Munich	Germany	8.10.81
Messehalle	Nuernburg	Germany	9.10.81
Karl Diehm Halle	Wuerzburg	Germany	10.10.81
EisSporthalle	Kassel	Germany	11.10.81
Eilenriedhalle	Hanover	Germany	13.10.81
Ostseehalle	Kiel	Germany	14.10.81
Congresshalle	Hamburg	Germany	15.10.81
Sportshalle	Cologne	Germany	16-17.10.81
L'Hippodrome Pantin	Paris	France	19-21.10.81
Vorst Nationale	Brussels	Belgium	22.10.81
Parc des Expositions	Metz	France	23.10.81

Hallenstadion	Zurich	Switzerland	24-25.10.81
Westfalenhalle	Dortmund	Germany	27.10.81
Freidrich Eberthalle	Ludwigshafen	Germany	28.10.81
Sporthalle	Stuttgart	Germany	29.10.81
Festhalle	Frankfurt	Germany	30-31.10.81
Deutschlandhalle	Berlin	Germany	2.11.81
Dane County Memorial Coliseum	Madison WI	USA	12.11.81
Rosemont Horizon	Chicago IL	USA	13-15.11.81
Civic Arena	Milwaukee WI	USA	16.11.81
Notre Dame University	South Bend IN	USA	17.11.81
Joe Louis Arena	Detroit MI	USA	18.11.81
Civic Arena	Pittsburgh PA	USA	19.11.81
Riverfront Coliseum	Cincinatti OH	USA	21.11.81
Richfield Coliseum	Cleveland OH	USA	22-23.11.81
The Spectrum	Philadelphia PA	USA	25-27.11.81
Savoy Theatre	New York NY	USA	28.11.81
Nassau Coliseum	Long Island NY	USA	29.11.81

(Show recorded for the Three Sides Live video/album)

Capital Centre	Largo NY	USA	30.11.81

(This show featured a rare performance of Like It Or Not)

Hartford Civic Centre	Hartford CT	USA	2.12.81
Forum	Montreal QC	Canada	3-4.12.81
Ottawa Civic Centre	Ottawa ONT	Canada	5.12.81
Maple Leaf Gardens	Toronto ONT	Canada	6-7.12.81
Buffalo Memorial Auditorium	Buffalo NY	USA	8.12.81
Brendan Byrne Arena	East Rutherford NJ	USA	10.12.81
Madison Square Garden	New York NY	USA	11.12.81
Wembley Arena	London	England	17-19.12.81
National Exhibition Centre	Birmingham	England	20-23.12.81

(Last night also recorded for the Three Sides Live album/video)

1981 the inexhaustible Genesis return with "Abacab" an album that takes fans by surprise once again with its stripped down sound and the inclusion of the Earth Wind & Fire horn section on one track! The tour also saw the introduction of what is now a standard lighting effect; the vari-lite which Genesis helped create and which gave their stage show even more clout. An unusual experience awaited the band at their show in Leiden Holland where they were booed! The band always ones for a challenge returned for a second night there and took the audience by storm. 1981 also saw the emergence of Phil Collins as a solo artist with the release of his first solo album; "Face Value".
In keeping with the radical new album the band's set underwent a similar reorganisation with the following tracks as part of their live show...
Behind thelines/Duchess/The lamb lies down on Broadway/Dodo/Lurker/Abacab/CarpetCrawl/Me & Sarah Jane/Misunderstanding/No reply a all/Firthof fifth/Man on the corner/Who-dunnit/In the cage/Cinema show-Raven medley/Afterglow/Turn it on again/Dance on a volcano/Los endos/I know what I like. In addition to these, at the band's shows in Spain a new song; **Me & Virgil** was included in the show and at their shows in Philadelphia and Largo **Like it or not** was performed and the band also trotted out **The knife** again as an encore at their final show in Birmigham.

Three Sides Live US/European Tour 1982.

Civic Centre	Peoria IL	USA	1.8.82
Poplar Creek Hoffman Estates	Chicago IL	USA	2-3.8.82
Greek Theatre	Berkley CA	USA	6-7.8.82
Forum	Los Angeles CA	USA	9-10.8.82
Memorial Auditorium	Phoenix AZ	USA	11.8.82
Reunion Arena	Dallas TX	USA	13.8.82
The Summit	Houston TX	USA	14.8.82
Myriad Convention Centre	Oklahoma City OK	USA	15.8.82
Checkerdome	St Louis MO	USA	16.8.82
Pine Knob Music Centre	Detroit MI	USA	18.8.82
Merriweather Post Pavilion	Columbia MD	USA	19.8.82
John F Kennedy Stadium	Philadelphia PA	USA	21.8.82
Forest Hills	New York NY	USA	22-23.8.82

(These gigs also included guest appearances on stage by the Phoenix Horns who performed No Reply At All and Paperlate with the band)

Coliseum	New Haven CT	USA	25.8.82
Saratoga Performing Arts Centre	Saratoga Springs NY	USA	26.8.82
Rochester Community War Memorial	Rochester NY	USA	27.8.82
CNE Grandstand	Toronto ONT	Canada	28.8.82
Jarry Park	Montreal QC	Canada	29.8.82

(This gig included a rare performance of Like It Or Not as part of the set)

Stade de Charmilles	Geneva	Switzerland	3.9.82

Amphitheatre	Frejus	France	4.9.82	
Tirennia Film Studios	Pisa	Italy	6.9.82	
Palasport	Rome	Italy	7-8.9.82	
Wilhelm Koch Stadion	Hamburg	Germany	10.9.82	**King Crimson**
Johanneshovs Isstadion	Stockholm	Sweden	12.9.82	
Broendbyhallen	Copenhagen	Denmark	13.9.82	
Scandinavium	Gothenburg	Sweden	14.9.82	
Vorst Nationale	Brussels	Belgium	16.9.82	
Coliseum	St Austell	England	18.9.82	
Showering Pavilion	Shepton Mallet	England	19.9.82	
National Exhibition Centre	Birmingham	England	20-21.9.82	
Leisure Centre	Deeside	England	22.9.82	
Queens Hall	Leeds	England	24.9.82	
Inglistone Hall	Edinburgh	Scotland	25-26.9.82	
Marquee Club	London	England	27.9.82	
Hammersmith Odeon	London	England	28-30.9.82	
Concert Bowl	Milton Keynes	England	2.10.82	

(Line-up included a re-formed Genesis with Peter Gabriel AND Steve Hackett/Talk Talk/The Blues Band/John Martyn. Despite rumours to the contrary, this gig WAS filmed for at least one band member's archives).

1982 and Genesis continue to captivate audiences with a tour to support their third live album; "Three Sides Live" which is also the title of their first commercial concert video, and an ep of songs from the "Abacab" sessions achieves a healthy position in the charts. Both Phil and Mike release their second solo albums. Highlight of 1982 however, is the long dreamed about reunion between Genesis and their ex frontman Peter Gabriel and Steve Hackett for a charity gig at an extremely wet Milton Keynes Bowl on 2nd October. The band's live show for this tour is perhaps one of their most balanced with just about every era represented by at least one song in the set which was as follows... Dance On A Volcano/Behind The Lines/Follow You Follow Me/Dodo/Lurker/Abacab/Supper's Ready/Misunderstanding/**Man On The Corner**/Who-Dunnit/In The Cage/Cinema Show-Raven-Afterglow medley/Turn It On Again/Los Endos/TheLamb Lies Down On Broadway/Watcher Of The Skies/ **I Know What I Like**. At several of the band's US shows, The Phoenix Horns joined them onstage to perform **Paperlate.** 1982 also saw the reunion with Peter Gabriel for which a special set was rehearsed... Back In NYC/Dancing With The Moonlit Knight/CarpetCrawl/Firth Of Fifth/Musical Box/Solsbury Hill/Turn It On Again/The Lamb Lies Down On Broadway/Fly On A Windshield/Broadway Melody Of '74/In The Cage/Supper's Ready/I Know What I Like/The Knife.

Genesis "Mama" US/UK Tour 1983/84

Las Colinas (Rehearsals)	Dallas TX	USA	22.10 - 3.11.83	
Horton Fieldhouse	Normal IL	USA	6.11.83	(Cancelled)
Horton Fieldhouse	Normal IL	USA	7.11.83	
Iowa state University	Ames IA	USA	8.11.83	
Civic Centre	St Paul MN	USA	9.11.83	
Civic Centre	Milwaukee WI	USA	10.11.83	
Rosemont Horizon	Chicago IL	USA	11-13.11.83	
Joe Louis Arena	Detroit MI	USA	14.11.83	
Capital Centre	Landover MD	USA	16.11.83	
Madison Square Garden	New York NY	USA	17-18.11.83	
Forum	Montreal QC	Canada	20-21.11.83	
Maple Leaf Gardens	Toronto ONT	Canada	23-24.11.83	
Spectrum	Philadelphia NY	USA	25-27.11.83	
Worcester Centrum Cetnre	Worcester MA	USA	28-30.11.83	
Hartford Civic Centre	Hartford CT	USA	1.12.83	
Carrier Dome	Syracuse NY	USA	2.12.83	
Buffalo Memorial Auditorium	Buffalo NY	USA	3.12.83	
Richfield Coliseum	Cleveland OH	USA	4-5.12.83	
Civic Centre	Pittsburgh PA	USA	7.12.83	
Riverfront Coliseum	Cincinnatti OH	USA	8.12.83	
The Scope	Norfolk VA	USA	10.12.83	
Coliseum	Greensborough NC	USA	11.12.83	
Municipal Coliseum	Nashville TN	USA	12.12.83	
The Omni Centre	Atlanta GA	USA	13.12.83	
Veterans Memorial Coliseum	Jacksonville FL	USA	15.12.83	
Lakeland Civic Centre	Lakeland FL	USA	16.12.83	
Hollywood Sportatorium	Miami FL	USA	17.12.83	
Cow Palace	San Francisco CA	USA	6.1.84	
PNE Coliseum	Vancouver BC	Canada	9.1.84	
Tacoma Dome	Seattle WA	USA	10.1.84	
Forum	Los Angeles CA	USA	12-14.1.84	
ASU Activity Centre	Tempe AZ	USA	15.1.84	
McNichols Sports Arena	Denver CO	USA	17.1.84	
Lloyd Nobel Centre	Norman CO	USA	19.1.84	

Assembly Centre	Tulsa OK	USA	20.1.84
Reunion Arena	Dallas TX	USA	21.1.84

(A TV Special entitled "Five Songs Live" was recorded in Dallas and subsequently broadcast in mainland Europe and Home By the Sea/Second Home By The Sea from this performance were used as the promotional video for the single release in several overseas territories)

The Summit	Houston TX	USA	22.1.84 (Cancelled)
The Summit	Houston TX	USA	23.1.84
Frank Erwin Centre	Austin TX	USA	24.1.84
Lakefront Arena	New Orleans LA	USA	25.1.84
Mid South Coliseum	Memphis TN	USA	26.1.84
MIS Arena	St Louis MO	USA	28.1.84
Kemper Arena	Kansas City MO	USA	29.1.84

(This show featured a set interrupted by a power failure - almost like old times!)

Rupp Arena	Lexington KY	USA	31.1.84
Market Square Arena	Indianapolis IN	USA	1.2.84
Civic Auditorium Arena	Omaha NB	USA	3.2.84
Civic Centre	Peoria IA	USA	4.2.84
Dane County Memorial Coliseum	Madison Wisconsin WI	USA	5.2.84
Civic Centre	St Paul MN	USA	7.2.84
The Arena	Winnipeg MA	Canada	9.2.84
Olympic Saddledome	Calgary AL	Canada	11.2.84
Northlands Coliseum	Edmonton AL	Canada	12.2.84
The Pavilion Boise State University	Boise ID	USA	14.2.84
Lawlor Events Centre	Reno NV	USA	16.2.84
Thomas & Mack Centre	Las Vegas NV	USA	17.2.84
Coliseum	Oakland CA	USA	19-20.2.84

(A complete audience shot of this gig exists)

National Exhibition Centre	Birmingham	England	25-29.2.84

(These gigs were filmed for the "MamaTour Live" video released in1985)

1983/84 and Genesis embark on their biggest tour of the USA and Canada; a massive seventy dates between November 1983 and February 198 with heir most adventurous light show to date. The five shows in the UK at the end of the tour are recorded for a video of the tour; "The Mama Tour". The group's eponymous album; "Genesis" spawns three hit singles including the classic "Mama". Phil finds time during the tour to pen yet another hit single; "Against all odds" and Tony manages to put out two solo albums; "The Wicked lady" and "The Fugitive". The band continued to expand their set which was now almost two and a half hours long and which for this tour usually comprised the following songs at their first show… Dodo/Carpet Crawl/That's All/Mama/Illegal Alien/Eleventh Earl Of Mar-Ripples-Squonk-Firth Of Fifth medley/Man On The Corner/Who-Dunnit?/Home ByThe Sea/Second Home ByThe Sea/Keep It Dark/It's Gonna Get Better/Follow You Follow Me/In The Cage-Cinema Show-Unquiet Slumbers For The Sleepers-Afterglow/Abacab/Misunderstanding/Turn It On Again. After this show th set generally ran as follows…Dodo/Abacab/That's All/Mama/Eleventh Earl of Mar-The lamb lies down on Broadway-Musical Box-Firth of fift medley/illegal Alien/home by the sea/Second home by the sea/Keep it dark/It's gonna get better/Folow you follow me/In the cage/Cinema show raven-In that quiet earth medley/Afterglow/Los Endos/Misunderstanding/ Turn it on again (with Sixties medley)

Invisible Touch World Tour 1986/87

Joe Louis Arena	Detroit MI	USA	18-20..9.86
CNE Grandstand	Toronto ONT	Canada	22.9.86
The Spectrum	Philadelphia PA	USA	24-27.9.86
Madison Square ardens	New York NY	USA	29.9-3.10.86
Rosemont Horizon	Chicago IL	USA	5-8.10.86
Rosemont Horizon	Chicago IL	USA	10.10.86
Forum	Los Angeles CA	USA	13-17.10.86
Oakland Coliseum	Oakland CA	USA	19-24.10.86
Weston Springs	Auckland	New Zealand	23.11.86
Entertainment Centre	Sydney	Australia	25-27.11.86
Boondall Centre	Brisbane	Australia	29-30.11.86
Westlakes Oval	Adelaide	Australia	2.12.86
Entertainment Centre	Perth	Australia	5.12.86
Subiaco Oval	Perth	Australia	6.12.86
National Tennis Centre	Melbourne	Australia	9-11.12.86
Olympic Park	Melbourne	Australia	13.12.86
Entertainment Centre	Sydney	Australia	15-20.12.86

(All of the Australian shows featured a string section on stage with the band due to local Musicians' Union rules. They played with the band on Your Own Special Way and In Too Deep)

The Summit	Houston TX	USA	15-16.1.87

Venue	City	Country	Date	Support
Reunion Arena	Dallas TX	USA	18-19.1.87	
Kemper Arena	Kansas City MO	USA	21-22.1.87	
Dean Smith Centre	Chapel Hill NC	USA	23.1.87	
Hoosier Dome	Indianoplis IN	USA	24.1.87	
Richfield Coliseum	Cleveland OH	USA	25-27.1.87	
Capital Centre	Landover MD	USA	29.1.87	
Dean Smith Arena	Chapel Hills NC	USA	31.1.87	
Rupp Arena	Lexington KN	USA	1.2.87	
Hartford Civic Centre	Hartford CT	USA	15.2.87	
Worcester Centrum Centre	Worcester MA	USA	16-18.2.87	
Coliseum	Hampton Roads VA	USA	20-21.2.87	
Dean Smith Centre	Chapel Hill KS	USA	22.2.87	
Greensboro Coliseum	Greensboro GA	USA	23.2.87	
The Omni Centre	Atlanta GA	USA	25-26.2.87	
Citrus Bowl	Orlando FL	USA	28.2.87	
Orange Bowl	Miami FL	USA	1.3.87	
Nippon Budokan Hall	Tokio	Japan	13-16.3.87	
Castle Hall	Osaka	Japan	18-19.3.87	
Football Stadium	Malaga	Spain	10.5.87	**Paul Young**
Vicente Calderon Stadium	Madid	Spain	13.5.87	" "
Stade Sept Deniers	Toulouse	France	15.5.87	" "
Casino	Montreux	Switzerland	16.5.87	" "
Flaminio Stadium	Rome	Italy	17.5.87	" "
San Siro Stadium	Milan	Italy	19.5.87	
Dodger Stadium	Los Angeles CA	USA	22.5.87	
Three Rivers Stadium	Pittsburgh PA	USA	24.5.87	
Robert F Kennedy Memorial Stadium	Washington DC	USA	26.5.87	
Veterans Stadium	Philadelphia NY	USA	28-29.5.87	
Giants Stadium	East Rutherford NJ	USA	30-31.5.87	
Palais Omnisports de Bercy	Paris	France	2.6.87	**(Indoor show)**
L'Hippodrome de Vincennes	Paris	France	3.6.87	**Paul Young**
Gentofte Stadium	Copenhagen	Denmark	5.6.87	" "
Niedersachsenstadion	Hanover	Germany	7.6..87	" "
Reichstagsgelande	Berlin	Germany	8.6.87	" "
Westfalenhalle	Dortmund	Germany	10.6.87	**(Indoor show)**
Feyernoord Stadium	Rotterdam	Holland	11.6.87	**Paul Young**
St Jakob Football Stadium	Basle	Switzerland	13.6.87	" "
Marcel Picot Stadium	Nancy	France	14.6.87	" "
Wiener Prater Stadium	Vienna	Austria	16.6.87	" "
Nepstadion	Budapest	Hungary	18.6.87	" "
Maimarktgelande	Mannheim	Germany	20.6.87	" "
Olympic Stadium	Munich	Germany	21.6.87	" "
Stade de la Beaujoire	Lyon	France	23.6.87	" "
L'Hippodrome de Vincennes	Paris	France	24.6.87	" "
Hampden Park Stadium	Glasgow	Scotland	26.6.87	" "
Roundhay Park	Leeds	England	28.6.87	" "
Wembley Stadium	London	England	1-4.7.87	" "

1986/87 Well, where do you begin? Genesis decided to break all the rules and record books with their 1986 album "Invisble Touch".
First of all the album spawned an incredible FIVE hit singles and the tour they undertook saw them playing stadium gigs all over the world including their first in New Zealand and Australia where the local regulations about employing local musicians meant that fans were treated to a string section sharing the stage with the band for versions of In too deep and Your own special way. The triumphant tour atmosphere was dampened somewhat in early1987 with the sad news of the death of Charisma Records founder and long time supporter of the band; Tony Stratton-Smith. 1985/86 also saw Phil Collins consolidate his solo status with another sell-out tour in support of his latest solo album; "No jacket required" and Mike finally got the success he deserves with the first single from his new Mike & The Mechanics project; "Silent Running" and a successful US tour with this new band before the Genesis tour. This tour, the band's biggest to date was to see several different live sets performed over its ten month course,beginning with the USA..mama/Abacab/Land of confusion/That's all/Domino/in too deep/ The Brazilian/Follow you follow me/Home by the sea/Second homeby the sea/Throwing it all away/in the cage-
Unquiet slumbers for the sleepers-in that quiet earth-**Apocalypse in 9/8** medley/Invisible Touch/Los Endos/
turn it onagain (with Sixties medley).

This was followed by the band's inaugural shows in Australia and new Zealand for which another set was performed…Mama/Abacab/Domino/**Your own special way**/In too deep (or) Follow you follow me/TheBrazilian/That's all/Home by the sea/Second home by the sea/Throwing it all away/In the cage-Unquiet slumbers for the sleepers-in that quiet earth-**Apocalypse in 9/8** medley/Invisible touch/Los endos/Turn it on again (with Sixties medley).
The band's US, Japanese and European shows of 1987 were fundamentally the same show in each territory comprising the following tracks…
Mama/Abacab/Domino/That's all/The Brazilian/In the cage/Unquiet slumbers for the sleepers-In that quiet earth-In the cage medley/Afterglow/land of confusion/Tonight tonight tonight/Throwingit all away/Home by the sea/Second home by the sea/Invisible touch/Los Endos/Turn it on again (with Sixties medley)

Madison Square Garden	New York NY	USA	15.5.88	

(Band performed special medley as part of the "Atlantic At Forty" Birthday celebrations for Atlantic Records)

Knebworth Park	Stevenage	England	30.6.90	

(Both Genesis and Phil performed sets aspart of the Silver Clef Concert)

The gaps between Genesis projects grew to epic proportions with only two appearances by the band between 1987 and 1992 the Atlantic Records fortieth birthday concert in 1988 at which both Phil AND Genesis played and the Silver clef concert in 1990 in aid of the Nordoff Robbins music charity at which once again, both Genesis AND Phil played separate sets. Solo success continued for both Mike and Phil with further solo outings for both musicians during the intervening years between "Invisible Touch" and the next Genesis project and Tony kept his hand in with two further solo albums of his own.

We Can't Dance US/European Tour 1992.

Texas Stadium (Rehearsals)	Irving TX	USA	4-7.5.92	
Texas Stadium	Irving TX	USA	8.5.92	
Astrodome	Houston TX	USA	9.5.92	
Joe Robbie Stadium	Miami FL	USA	16.5.92	
Tampa Stadium	Tampa FL	USA	17.5.92	**(Cancelled after 2 songs)**
R F K Memorial Stadium	Washington DC	USA	19.5.92	
Hoosier Dome	Indianapolis IN	USA	21.5.92	
Ohio State University Stadium	Columbus OH	USA	22.5.92	
Pontiac Silverdome	Pontiac Michigan MI	USA	24.5.92	
Municipal Stadium	Cleveland OH	USA	25.5.92	
Three Rivers Stadium	Pittsburgh PA	USA	26.5.92	
Foxboro Stadium	Foxboro MA	USA	28.5.92	
Stade Du Parc Olympique	Montreal QC	Canada	29.5.92	
Veterans Stadium	Philadelphia PA	USA	31.5-1.6.92	
Giants Stadium	East Rutherford NJ	USA	2-3.6.92	
Carrier Dome Syracuse University	Syracuse PA	USA	5.6.92	
Skydome	Toronto ONT	Canada	6.7.92	
Carrier Dome Syracuse University	Syracue PA	USA	7.6.92	
Camp Randall Stadium UW	Madison WI	USA	9.6.92	
Hubert H Humphrey Metrodome	Minneapolis MN	USA	10.6.92	
Commonwealth Stadium	Edmonton AL	Canada	12.6.92	
British Columbia Place Stadium	Vancouver BC	Canada	14.6.92	
Tacoma Dome	Tacoma WA	USA	15.6.92	
Dodger Stadium	Los Angeles CA	USA	18.6.92	
Hornet Field CSU at Sacramento	Sacramento CA	USA	19.6.92	
Oakland Coliseum Stadium	Oakland CA	USA	20.6.92	
Cyclone Stadium	Ames IA	USA	23.6.92	
World Music Theatre	Tinley Park IL	USA	24-25.6.92	
Festival Showground	Werchter	Belgium	28.6.92	
L'Espace Tony Garnier	Lyon	France	30.6.92	
Stade Gerland	Lyon	France	1.7.92	**(Cancelled)**
L'Hippodrome de Vincennes	Paris	France	2.7.92	
Parkstadion	Gelsenkirchen	Germany	3.7.92	
HockenheimRing	Hockenheim	Germany	4.7.92	
Olympic Stadium	Munich	Germany	5.7.92	
Ullevi Stadium	Gothenburg	Sweden	7.7.92	
Gentofte Stadium	Copenhagen	Denmark	8.7.92	
Niedersachsenstadion	Hanover	Germany	10-11.7.92	
Maifeld Stadium	Berlin	Germany	12.7.92	
Niedersachsenstadiom	Hanover	Germany	13.7.92	
Maimarktgelande	Mannheim	Germany	15.7.92	
Wiener Pater Stadion	Vienna	Austria	16.7.92	
San Siro Stadium	Milan	Italy	17.7.92	
Stadio del Alpi	Turin	Italy	18.7.92	**(Cancelled)**
Stade de L'Ouest	Nice	France	19.7.92	
L'Espace Grammont	Montpellier	France	20.7.92	
Estadio Alvalade	Lisbon	Portugal	22.7.92	
Estadio Vicente Calderon	Madrid	Spain	24.7.92	**(Cancelled)**
St Jakob Football Stadium	Basle	Switzerland	26.7.92	
Muengersdorfer Sportstadion	Cologne	Germany	27.7.92	
Feyernord Stadium	Rotterdam	Holland	28.7.92	
Nordmark Sportfeld	Kiel	Germany	29.7.92	
Roundhay Park	Leeds	England	31.7.92	

Knebworth Park	Stevenage	England	1.8.92 **(Cancelled)**
Knebworth Park	Stevenage	England	2.8.92

We Can't Dance UK Tour 1992.

Working Mens' Club (Rehearsals)	Chiddingfold	England	15-22.10.92
Mayflower Theatre	Southampton	England	23.10.92
City Hall	Newcastle	England	28.10.92
Playhouse	Edinburgh	Scotland	29.10.92
Apollo Theatre	Manchester	England	30.10.92
Earls Court Arena	London	England	2-4.11.92
Earls Court Arena	London	England	6-8.11.92
Centre	Torquay	England	10.11.92
Civic Centre	Newport	Wales	11.11.92
Theatre Royal	Nottingham	England	13.11.92
Centre	Brighton	England	15.11.92
Royal Albert Hall	London	England	16.11.92
Civic Hall	Wolverhampton	England	17.11.92
Cowdray Ruins	Sussex	England	18.9.93

1992/93 saw Genesis return to the fold after their longest lay off yet. In the meantime all of the band had put out a further range of solo projects to varying degrees of success. The 1992 tour also featured another innovation the first three Sony "Jumbotron" video screens which enabled the band to play to even bigger audiences and in the open air . The "We can't dance" album continued the successful trend set by its predecessor with a whole series of hit singles and several appearances by the band on Top of the Pops! In the autumn the band undertook a short tour of theatres in the UK as a gesture to their UK fans and another video was filmed at their shows in London's Earls Court Arena. The 1993 Cowdray Ruins charity gig also turned out to be Phil's last appearance with the band.

The band's shows for their 1992 tour were their biggest to date with a set which comprised the following songs... Land of confusion/ No son of mine/Driving the last spike/Dance on a volcano-The lamb lies down on Broadway-Musical Box-Firth of fifth-I know what I like-That's all-illegal alien-Stagnation-Follow you follow me medley/Throwing it all away/Fading lights/Jesus he knows me/Home by the sea/ Second home by the sea/Hold on my heart/Domino/Drum duet/I can't dance/Tonight tonight tonight/Invisible touch/Turn it on again. For the band's UK indoor shows later in the year the set also included **Dreaming while you sleep** and at the first of the provincial theatre shows the band also threw in the golden oldie **Carpet crawlers**.

Genesis Gig Guide

Part Three: "Life after Phil Collins..."

Calling All Stations European Tour 1998.

Working men's club (Rehearsals)	Chiddingfold	England	?.8.97- 5.10.97
BT Tower (album launch gig)	Berlin	Germany	26.8.97
Kennedy Space Centre	Cape Canaveral FL	USA	28.8.97
RTL Studios	Paris	France	17.11.97
Danish Radio Studios	Copenhagen	Denmark	15.12.97
Pepsi Arena	Albany NY	USA	5.11.97*
Civic Arena	Pittsburgh PA	USA	7.11.97*
Marine Midland Arena	Buffalo NY	USA	8.11.97*
Bryce Jordan Centre	Pennsylvania PA	USA	9.11.97*
Edwin Nutter Centre	Dayton OH	USA	11.11.97*
Van Andel Arena	Grand Rapids MI	USA	12.11.97*
Palace of Auburn Hills	Detroit MI	USA	14.11.97*
Gund Arena	Cleveland OH	USA	15.11.97*
Dance County Memorial Coliseum	Madison Wisconsin WI	USA	18.11.97*
Bradley Centre	Milwaukee WI	USA	19.11.97*
Kiel Centre	St Louis MO	USA	21.11.97*
Rosemont Horizon	Chicago IL	USA	22.11.97*
Corel Arena	Ottawa ONT	Canada	25.11.97*
Maple Leaf Gardens	Toronto ONT	Canada	27.11.97*
Molson Centre	Montreal QC	Canada	28.11.97*
Colisee Arena	Quebec QC	Canada	30.11.97*
Madison Square Garden	New York NY	USA	4.12.97*
Corestate Centre	Philadelphia PA	USA	5-6.12.97*
Fleet Centre	Boston MA	USA	9.12.97*

Civic Centre	Hartford CT	USA	11.12.97*
Nassau Coliseum	Uniondale LI	USA	12.12.97*
USAir Arena	Landover MD	USA	13.12.97*
Arena	Miami FL	USA	18.12.97*
Arena	Orlando FL	USA	19.12.97*
Ice Palace	Tampa FL	USA	21.12.97*

(*) "Calling All Stations" US Arena tour cancelled dates.

Riverside Theatre	Milwaukee WI	USA	5.11.97+
Braden Auditorium	Normal IL	USA	8.11.97+
Rosemont Theatre	Chicago IL	USA	9.11.97+
Fox Theatre	St Louis MO	USA	12.11.97+
Palace of Auburn Hills	Auburn Hills MI	USA	14.11.97+
Veterans Memorial Auditorium	Columbus OH	USA	15.11.97+
Hummingbird	Toronto ONT	Canada	17-18.11.97+
Civic Centre theatre	Ottawa ONT	Canada	21.11.97+
Beacon Theatre	New York NY	USA	23-24.11.97+
Molson Centre Theatre	Montreal QC	Canada	28.11.97+
Quebec Colisee	Quebec City QC	Canada	29.11.97+
Orpheum Theatre	Boston MA	USA	4.12.97+
Meadows Music Theatre	Hartford CT	USA	6.12.97+
Tower Theatre	Upper Darby PA	USA	10-11.12.97+
MCI Centre	Washington DC	USA	14.12.97+
A J Palumbo Centre	Pittsburgh PA	USA	15.12.97+
Van Andel Arena	Grand Rapids MI	USA	18.12.97+
Music Hall	Cleveland OH	USA	19-20.12.97+

(+) "Calling All Stations" US Theatre tour cancelled dates.

Telecom Tower (TV Show)	Berlin	Germany	22.8.97
Kennedy Space Centre (TV Show)	Cape Canaveral FL	USA	26.8.97
Hotel Richmond (Radio show)	Copenhagen	Denmark	15.11.97
RTL Studios (Radio Show)	Paris	France	13.12.97
Bray Film Studios (Production rehearsals) Windsor		England	5.1.98-25.1.98
Bray Film Studios (Pre-tour warm-up gig) Windsor		England	23.1.98
Sportshall (Warm-up gig)	Budapest	Hungary	28.1.98
Sportshall	Budapest	Hungary	29.1.98
Spodek	Katowice	Poland	31.1.98
Sportovinhala	Prague	Czech Republic	2.2.98
Maimarktgelande	Mannheim	Germany	4.2.98
Messehalle 7	Leipzig	Germany	5.2.98
Velodrom	Berlin	Germany	6.2.98
(original venue for above show was the Max Schmelling Halle)			
La Galaxie	Metz	France	8.2.98
Westfalenhalle	Dortmund	Germany	10.2.98
Schleyerhalle	Stuttgart	Germany	12.2.98
Hallenstadion	Zurich	Switzerland	13.2.98
Stadthalle	Vienna	Austria	15.2.98
Palasport Casalecchio	Bologna	Italy	17.2.98
Palasport	Rome	Italy	18.2.98
Filaforum	Milan	Italy	19.2.98
Halle Tony Garnier	Lyon	France	20.2.98
Palais Omnisports de Bercy	Paris	France	23.2.98
National Exhibition Centre	Birmingham	England	25-26.2.98
Earls Court Arena	London	England	27.2.98
Scottish Exhibition & Conference Centre Glasgow		Scotland	1.3.98
Telewest Arena	Newcastle	England	2.3.98
International Arena	Cardiff	Wales	4-5.3.98
NYNEX Arena	Manchester	England	6.3.98
The Point Theatre	Dublin	Eire	8.3.98
Vorst Nationale	Brussels	Belgium	10.3.98
Ahoy Sportpaleis	Rotterdam	Holland	11.3.98
Zenith	Lille	France	13.3.98
Amphitheatre 4000	Angers	France	15.3.98
Patinoire de Malley	Bordeaux	France	16.3.98
Zenith	Pau	France	18.3.98
Pabellon dos Desportos	Madrid	Spain	19.3.98
Palau St Jordi	Barcelona	Spain	20.3.98
Le Dome	Marseilles	France	22.3.98

Maison des Sports	Clermont Ferrand	France	23.3.98
Zenith	Caen	France	24.3.98
Halle Rhenus	Strasbourg	France	26.3.98
Olympiahalle	Munich	Germany	27.3.98
Messehale	Erfurt	Germany	28.3.98
Sporthalle	Hamburg	Germany	30.3.98
Seidenstickerhalle	Bielefeld	Germany	31.3.98
(Show subsequently cancelled)			
Forum	Copenhagen	Denmark	1.4.98
(Show subsequently cancelled)			
Erikhallen	Oslo	Norway	2.4.98
Globe	Stockholm	Sweden	3.4.98
Hartwall Arena	Helsinki	Finland	5.4.98
Rock in Ring Festival	Nurburgring	Germany	30.5.98
Rock im Park Festival			
Frankenstadion	Nurnberg	Germany	31.5.98
Dorchester Hotel	London	England	21.9.00

(Managerial awards dinner for Tony Smith for which Tony and Mike were briefly reunited with former frontman Phil Collins for a short acoustic set)

1996/98 has seen perhaps the biggest upheaval in Genesis's fortunes since the departure of Peter Gabriel. Both Mike and Phil continued to enjoy massive solo successes in the intervening years and Tony also turned in his most convincing solo album in ages with 1995's underrated "Strictly Inc" project. The announcement on 6th June 1997 that Phil Collins had quit the band stunned fans of the band and had many writing the obituaries that had been proven to be so premature all those years ago. Holding high the spirit of Genesis, Tony and Mike decided to continue with the band and enlisted the talents of former frontman for grunge rock group Stiltslkin; Ray Wilson as their new singer and drafting in talented session musicians Nir Tsidkyahu on drums and Anthony Drennan on guitars. The resultant album; "Calling all stations" the band's fifteenth studio album was released on 2nd September 1997 and was a welcome return to the darker and more melodramatic sound of vintage Genesis. The album entered the UK charts at the number two slot and gained respectable positions elsewhere with the notable exception of the USA where its poor showing in the charts led to a hasty re-arrangement and eventual cancellation of the band's proposed US tour .

The band undeterred by events in the USA toured mainland Europe and the UK during January/April 1998 and turned in convincing shows proving that for Genesis there is life after Phil Collins. For their new shows billed as *"Genesis through the ages"* the band drew more extensively on their back catalogue for a show thatincluded the f ollowing songs… No son of mine/Land of confusion/The lamb lies down on Broadway/Calling all stations/Carpet crawlers/**There must be some other way/Alien afternoon**/Domino/Firth of fifth (instrumental end section only)/Congo/Home by the sea/Second home by the sea/Dancing with the moonlit knight/Follow you follow me/Lover's leap/**Not about us**/Mama/The dividing line/Invisible touch/Turn it on again/Throwing it all away/I can't dance. At the band's dress rehearsal gig on 23rd January 1998 both **Hold on my heart** and **That's all** were included in the set after Calling al lstations but subsequently dropped from the set.

TURN IT ON AGAIN – THE TOUR 2007

Olympic Stadium	Helsinki	Finland	11.6.07
Messecenter	Herning	Denmark	14.6.07
AOL Arena	Hamburg	Germany	15.6.07
Stade De Suisse	Berne	Switzerland	17.6.07
Gugglesstadium	Linz	Austria	18.6.07
Puskas Ferenc Stadium	Budapest	Hungary	20.6.07
Slaski Stadium	Katowice	Poland	21.6.07
AWD Arena	Hannover	Germany	23.6.07
LTU Arena	Dusseldorf	Germany	26.6.07
LTU Arena	Dusseldorf	Germany	27.6.07
Gottlieb-Daimler Stadium	Stuttgart	Germany	29.6.07
Parc Des Princes	Paris	France	30.6.07
Holland Arena	Amsterdam	Holland	1.7.07
Olympiastdion	Berlin	Germany	3.7.07
Zentralstadion	Leipzig	Germany	4.7.07
Commerzbankarena	Frankfurt	Germany	5.7.07
Old Trafford Football Stadium	Manchester	England	7.7.07
Twickenham Stadium	London	England	8.7.07
Olympiastadion	Munich	Germany	10.7.07
Louis II Stadium	Monaco	Monaco	12.7.07
Telecomcerto at Colosseo	Rome	Italy	14.7.07

Just when we thought the band had effectively folded, they took everyone by surprise by announcing a series of shows under the title of "Turn It On Again – The Tour" for major European venues in the summer of 2007. At time of printing details of the intended set list for these gigs was not available.

Tracks in **Bold** type are either unreleased or alternative tracks not played at every show on a tour.

This gig guide has been compiled over the last ten or so years from a variety of sources. The original idea for a listing of Genesis gigs came from Peter Morton at "The Waiting Room" and has been expanded upon by the following people: Alan Hewitt (The Waiting Room), Carol Willis (Hit & Run Music/Tony Smith Personal Management Services Ltd), Annie Callingham (Philip Collins Ltd) Mario Giammetti (Dusk Magazine), Helmut Janisch (It Magazine), Mal Lord, Mel Huang, Jack M Beermann,Tom Oastler, George German III, Mike Jackson , Thomas Holter, Vernon Parker, Bill McCormick, Margaret Banks; Richard MacPhail; PeterVickers; David Lawrence and numerous others whose work and contributions are gratefully acknowledged. Copyright: A Hewitt 2006.

PHIL COLLINS SOLO GIG GUIDE

VENUE NAME	CITY	COUNTRY	DATE

Phil's Gigs Pre- 1970

Even in his youth, Phil was always gigging,although as yet exact details ofmore than a handful of his gigs with the bands he was in prior to joining Genesis,are hard to come by. Here are such details as have come to light so far.

Marine Theatre	Lyme Regis	England	4.5.68	**(Freehold)**
Planetarium	London	England	2.10.69	**(Ark Two album launch)**
BBC Studios	London	England	27.10.69	
(Dave Lee Travis Show Session broadcast on 2.11.69)				
BBC Studios	London	England	8.11.69	
(Howard & Blakely appear on "Tony Brandon Meets The Saturday People" Show BBCRadio 1)				
?	Hilversum	Holland	10.11.69	
(TV/Radio Session exact details are still unknown)				
Lyceum Ballroom	London	England	14.11.69	
BBC Studios	London	England	23.12.69	
("Night Ride Session broadcast on 21.1.70)				
New Joints Club	Wimbledon	England	4.2.70	
BBC Studios	London	England	5.3.70	
(Radio One Club Session broadcast)				
Roundhouse	Chalk Farm London	England	12.4.70	
The Temple	Wardour St London	England	20.6.70	
Roundhouse	Chalk Farm London	England	28.6.70	
Van Dyke Club	Plymouth	England	15.8.70	
?	Penzance	England	16.8.70	

(My thanks to Jonathan Dann at the BBC for the information on the above gigs and sessions)

Phil's Gigs with Brand X

London School of Economics	London	England	?.12.75
Friars New Addison Centre	Bedford	England	20.12.75
Marquee Club	London	England	30.7.76
BBC Studios (John Peel session)	London	England	2.8.76
Reading Festival	Reading	England	26.8.76
Ronnie Scott's Club	London	England	1.9.76
Hammersmith Odeon	London	England	12.11.76
Free Trade Hall	Manchester	England	15.11.76
New Vic Theatre **(with Marscape)**	London	England	20.11.76
Marquee Club	London	England	1.4.77
Fete de L'Humanite La Courneuve	Paris	France	10.9.77
Glass Onion	Rochester NY	USA	28.9.77
Beginnings Club	Shambourg Chicago IL	USA	16.11.77
Old Waldorf Theatre	San Francisco CA	USA	28.11.77
Mountford Hall Students Union	Liverpool	UK	1.9.79
The Venue Club	London	UK	16.9.79
Old Waldorf Theatre **(2 shows)**	San Francisco CA	USA	20.9.79
The Roxy **(2 shows)**	Hollywood CA	USA	21-23.9.79
Park West **(2 shows)**	Chicago IL	USA	25.9.79
Bottom Line Club NYC	Ne w York NY	USA	26.9.79

Tower Theatre	Upper Darby PA	USA	30.9.79
Long Island Coliseum	Long Island NY	USA	28.10.79
Theatre Royal	London	UK	9-10 &12.9.81
(Secret Policeman's Other Ball Charity gigs)			

See Peter Gabriel Gig Guide section for details of gigs Phil performed with Peter in 1979-80.

"Hello, I Must Be Going" World Tour 1982 - 1983"

Concertgebouow	Den Haag	Holland	21.11.82
Olympia Theatre	Paris	France	22.11.82
Jahrhunderthalle	Frankfurt	Germany	23.11.82
Congresshalle	Hamburg	Germany	25.11.82
Vorst Nationale	Brussesls	Belgium	26.11.82
Hammersmith Odeon **(2 shows)**	London	England	28.11.82
Hammersmith Odeon	London	England	29.11.82
Hammersmith Odeon	London	England	30.11.82
Hammersmith Odeon	London	England	1.12.82
Maple leaf Gardens	TorontoONT	Canada	6.12.82
Ritz Theatre	New York NY	USA	7.12.82
Palladium Theatre	New York NY	USA	8.12.82
Tower Theatre	Upper Darby PA	USA	9-10.12.82
Holiday Star Theatre	Merriville IL	USA	12.12.82
Auditorium Theatre	Chicago IL	USA	13.12.82
Berkeley Community Theatre	San Francisco CA	USA	16.12.82
Universal Amphitheatre	Los Angeles CA	USA	17-18.12.82
The Roxy	Hollywood CA	USA	19.12.82
Music Hall	Houston TX	USA	21-22.1.83
Perkins Palace	Pasadena CA	USA	23.1.83
Tarrant County centre	Fort Worth TX	USA	24.1.83
Brady Theatre	Tulsa TX	USA	25.1.83
Memorial Auditorium	Kansas City KS	USA	26.1.83
University of Illinois	Normal IL	USA	28.1.83
University of Indiana	Bloomington IL	USA	29.1.83
Cincinnatti Gardens	Cincinnatti MO	USA	30.1.83
Veterans Auditorum	Columbus OH	USA	31.1.83
University of Minnesota	Minneapolis MO	USA	2.2.83
Milwaukee Auditorium	Milwaukee WI	USA	3.2.83
Wings Stadium	Kalamazoo WI	USA	4.2.83
University of Michigan	Ann Arbor MI	USA	5.2.83
Richfield Coliseum	Cleveland PA	USA	7.2.83
Civic Arena	Pittsburgh PA	USA	8.2.83
Rochester Community War Memorial	Rochester NY	USA	9-10.2.83
War Memorial	Syracuse NY	USA	12.2.83
University Park	Penn State University PA	USA	13.2.83
Stabler Arena	Allentown PA	USA	14.2.83
Forum	Montreal QC	Canada	15-16.2.83
University of Massachussetts	Amherst MA	USA	17.2.83
Orpheum Theatre	Boston MA	USA	18.2.83
Warner Theatre	Washington DC	USA	20.2.83

"The Principle Of Moments Tour" with Robert Plant

Civic Centre	Peoria IL	USA	26.8.83
Wings Auditorium	Kalamazoo MI	USA	27.8.83
Rosemont Horizon	Chicago IL	USA	29.8.83
Kiel Auditorium	St Louis MO	USA	30.8.83
Civic Arena	Milwaukee WI	USA	31.8.83
Joe Louis Arena	Detroit IL	USA	3.9.83
Richfield Coliseum	Cleveland OH	USA	4.9.83
Reunion Arena	Dallas TX	USA	5.9.83
Worcester Centrum Centrum	Worcester MD	USA	6.9.83
Forum	Montreal QC	Canada	8.9.83
Buffalo Memorial Auditorium	Buffalo NY	USA	9.9.83
Maple Leaf Gardens	Toronto ONT	Canada	10.9.83
Madison Square Garden	New York NY	USA	12.9.83
HartfordCivic Centre	Hartford CT	USA	13.9.83
The Spectrum	Philadelphia NY	USA	14.9.83
Mid-South Coliseum	Memphis TN	USA	16.9.83
Louisiana State University	Baton Rouge TN	USA	18.9.83
The Summit	Houston TX	USA	20.9.83
Frank Erwin Centre	Austin TX	USA	21.9.83
Reunion Arena	Dallas TX	USA	22.9.83
McNichols Sports Arena	Denver CO	USA	24.9.83
Sports Arena	San Diego CA	USA	26.9.83
Forum	Los Angeles CA	USA	27.9.83

Coliseum	Oakland CA	USA	28.9.83
Coliseum	Seattle WA	USA	30.9.83
PNE Coliseum	Vancouver BC	Canada	1.10.83

1982/83 and Phil Collins solo artist bursts upon the concert scene. Consolidating his highly successful first solo album; "Face Value" released the previous year, Phil soon takes the world by storm with his second solo album; "Hello; I must be going" released in 1982 and which included his first number one hit; the hilarious take off of The Supremes's classic; You can't hurry love, in which he played ALL of the Supremes! Phil's first live gig was at the Concertgebouuw in Holland and a tour of Europe and the USA followed including a show at Perkins Palace in Pasadena which was filmed for his first solo live video release; "Live from Perkins Palace". Phil's first solo tour proved beyond doubt that he was capable of performing outside of Genesis proving it by playing a set which drew upon material from his forst two albums as well as a few classics… I don't care anymore/Thunder & Lightning/I cannot believe it's true/This must belove/Thrue these walls/I missed again/Behind the lines/You know what I mean/The roof is leaking/Don't let him steal your heart away/The west Side/If leaving me is easy/In the air tonight/ Like China/You can't hurry love/It don't matter to me/Hand in hand/And so to F../Why can't it wait til morning/ People get ready.

As if all of that wasn't enough, Phil also found the time to take part in Robert Plant's tour in the summer of 1983 as his drummer having guested on the album itself - where did he get the energy from?!

"The No Jacket Required World Tour" 1985

Royal Theatre	Nottingham	England	11.2.85
Apollo Theatre	Manchester	England	12.2.85
Apollo Theatre	Glasgow	Scotland	13.2.85
City Hall	Newcastle	England	14.2.85
City Hall	Sheffield	England	16.2.85
Royal Albert Hall	London	England	17-22.2.85
National Exhibition Centre	Birmingham	England	23.2.85
Philipshalle	Dusseldorf	Germany	25.2.85
Vorst Nationale	Brussels	Germany	26.2.85
Ahoy Sportpaleis	Rotterdam	Holland	27.2.85
Scandinavium	Gothenburg	Sweden	1.3.85
Isstadion	Stockholm	Sweden	2.3.85
Valbyhallen	Copenhagen	Denmark	3..385
Stadthalle	Bremen	Germany	4.3.85
Palais Omnisports de Bercy	Paris	France	6.3.85
Festhalle	Frankfurt	Germany	7.3.85
Olympiahalle	Munich	Germany	8.3.85
Hallenstadion	Zurich	Switzerland	10.3.85
Boeblingen	Stuttgart	Germany	11.3.85
Patinoire de Malley	Nantes	France	13.3.85
Salle D'Expositions	Bordeaux	France	14.3.85
Masion des Sports	Toulouse	France	15.3.85
L'Espace Tony Garnier	Lyon	France	16.3.85
Halle des Fetes Beaujoire	Lausanne	Switzerland	17.3.85
National Exhibition Halls	Sydney	Australia	3-4.4.85
National Exhibition Halls	Sydney	Australia	6-7.4.85
National Exhibition Halls	Sydney	Australia	10-11.4.85
National Tennis Centre	Melbourne	Austraila	13-14.4.85
Westlakes Oval	Adelaide	Australia	17.4.85
Entertainment Centre	Perth	Australia	20.4.85
The Big Egg	Tokio	Japan	23.4.85
The Dome	Fukuoka	Japan	25.4.85
Castle Hall	Osaka	Japan	26.4.85
Rainbow Hall	Nagoya	Japan	27.4.85
Worcester Centrum Centre	Worcester MD	USA	12.5.85
Forum	Montreal QC	Canada	13.5.85
Madison Square Garden	New York NY	USA	15-17.5.85
The Spectrum	Philadelphia NY	USA	20.5.85
Virginia Coliseum	Hampton VA	USA	21.5.85
Coliseum	Greensboro NC	USA	22.5.85
The Omni Centre	Atlanta GA	USA	23.5.85
Mid South Coliseum	Memphis TN	USA	25.5.85
Lakefront Arena	New Orleans LA	USA	26.5.85
Sam Houston Centre	Houston TX	USA	28.5.85
Reunion Arena	Dallas TX	USA	29.5.85
Frank Erwin Centre	Austin TX	USA	30.5.85
Veterans Memorial Coliseum	Phoenix AZ	USA	1.6.85
Irvine Meadows	Laguna Hills CA	USA	2-3.6.85
Forum	Los Angeles CA	USA	4-6.6.85
Forum	San Francisco CA	USA	7-8.6.85
Memorial Auditorium	Sacramento CA	USA	11.6.85
McNichols Sports Centre	Denver CO	USA	13.6.85
Kemper Arena	Kansas City KS	USA	15.6.85
Rosemont Horizon	Chicago IL	USA	17.6.85
Riverfront Coliseum	Cincinnatti OH	USA	19.6.85
Merriweather Post Pavilion	Columbia MD	USA	21.6.85
Hartford Civic Centre	Hartford CT	USA	22.6.85
Saratoga Performing Arts Centre	Saratoga Springs NY	USA	23.6.85

Maple Leaf Gardens	Toronto ONT	Canada	25.6.85
Joe Louis Arena	Detroit OH	USA	27.6.85
Blossom Music Center	Cuyahoga Falls NY	USA	28.6.85
Madison Square Garden	New York NY	USA	1.7.85

"Behind the Sun Tour" 1986/87 with Eric Clapton

Kalvoyre Festival (Isle of Calves)	Oslo	Norway	3.7.86
Roskilde Festival	Roskilde	Denmark	4.7.86
Grand Casino (Jazz Festival)	Montreux	Switzerland	10.7.86
Juan Les Pins Festival	Antibes	France	12.7.86
National Exhibition Centre	Birmingham	England	14-15.7.86
Royal Albert Hall	London	England	11-12.1.87
Coliseum	Oakland CA	USA	11.4.87
Pacific Amphitheatre	Costa Mesa CA	USA	13.4.87
Forum	Los Angeles CA	USA	14.4.87
Ebony Showcase Theatre	Los Angeles CA	USA	15.4.87 **(with BB King)** McNichols Sports
Arena	Denver CO	USA	16.4.87
Civic Centre	St Paul MO	USA	18.4.87
Rosemont Horizon	Chicago IL	USA	19.4.87
Limelight Club	Chicago IL	USA	19.4.87 **(with BB King)**
Market Square Arena	Indianapolis IN	USA	21.4.87
Joe Louis Arena	Detroit MI	USA	22.4.87
Richfield Coliseum	Cleveland OH	USA	23.4.87
Capital Centre	Landover MD	USA	25.4.87
Civic Centre	Providence RI	USA	26.4.87
Madison Square Garden	New York NY	USA	27.4.87
Wembley Arena	London	England	6.6.87

1985 Phil's rise to super stardom is assured by the release of his third solo album; "No jacket required" in February of that year coming as it did after two years' hard graft with Genesis and the success of the film "Against all odds" which included hi song of the same name. Phil's tour in support of the album took him further afield than ever including his first visit to Australia and another visit to Japan. Phil had dispelled any doubts about his solo abilities with his first tour in 1982 and he continued to build on that success with a tour which included the following in the live set…I don't care anymore/Only you & I know/I cannot believe its true/This must be love/Against all odds/inside out/Who said I would?/If leaving me is easy/Sussudio/Behind thelines/Don't lose my number/The West Side/One more night/In the air tonight/Like China/ You can't hurry love/it don't matter to me/Hand in hand/Take me home/ People get ready/And so to F…
Phil's constant desire to be working led him in 1986/87 to work with his long time friend Eric Clapton on his "Behind the sun" album and inevitably,Phil could not resist the desire to be part of the band and he travelled as part of Eric's band for several shows (other commitments permitting) during the latter's several tours in support of the album as well as turning in several charity shows on behalf of the "Prince's Trust".

Civic Hall	Guildford	England	7.2.88 **(With Eric Clapton)**
Wintershall	Guildford?	England	2.7.88 **(With Eric Clapton)**
City Hall	Sheffield	England	16.1.89 **(With Eric Clapton)**
City Hall	Newcastle	England	17.1.89 **(With Eric Clapton)**
Playhouse Theatre	Edinburgh	Scotland	18.1.89 **(With Eric Clapton)**
Royal Albert Hall	London	England	20-26.1.89 **(With Eric Clapton)**

"But Seriously World Tour" 1990

Seto-Shi Bunka Centre **(Rehearsal)**	Nagoya	Japan	23.2.90
Seto-Shi Bunka Centre **(Rehearsal)**	Nagoya	Japan	26.2.90
Castle Hall	Osaka	Japan	27-28.2.90
Sun Plaza hall	Hiroshima	Japan	3.3.90
Yokohama Arena	Yokohama	Japan	5.3.90
Yoyogi Olympic Pool	Tokio	Japan	6-9.3.90
Entertainment centre	Sydney	Australia	13-15.3.90
Entertainment Centre	Brisbane	Australia	17-18.3.90
National Tennis Centre	Melbourne	Australia	21.3.90
National Tennis Centre	Melbourne	Australia	23-25.3.90
Entertainment Centre	Sydney	Australia	27-29.3.90
Memorial Drive	Adelaide	Australia	31.3.90
Entertainment Centre	Perth	Australia	4-5.4.90
Vorst Nationale	Brussels	Belgium	16.4.90
Palais Omnisports de Bercy	Paris	France	17-20.4.90*
(*) gig on 18th cancelled.			
Royal Albert Hall	London	England	22.4.90
Deutschlandhalle	Berlin	Germany	24.4.90
Wembley Arena	London	England	28.4.-2.5.90
Ahoy Sportpaleis	Rotterdam	Holland	4.5.90
Congresshalle	Hamburg	Germany	5.5.90
Scandinavium	Gothenburg	Sweden	6.5.90
Globe	Stockholm	Sweden	8.5.90
Festhalle	Frankfurt	Germany	10.5.90
Olympiahalle	Munich	Germany	12.5.90

Hallenstadion	Zurich	Switzerland	15.5.90
Palatrussardi	Milan	Italy	16.5.90
Palaeur	Rome	Italy	17.5.90
L'Espace Tony Garnier	Lyon	France	19.5.90
Amphitheatre	Nimes	France	20.5.90
Nuevo Pabellon	Barcelona	Spain	21.5.90
Palais Omnisports de Bercy	Paris	France	23.5.90+

(+) Replacing gig cancelled on 18th April

Nassau Coliseum	Long Island LI	USA	3.6.90
Rosemont Horizon	Chicago IL	USA	14-17.6.90
Greatwestern Forum	Los Angeles CA	USA	20-21.6.90
Great western Forum	Los Angeles CA	USA	23-25.6.90
Knebworth Park "Silver Clef" Festival	Stevenage	England	30.6.90
Inglistone Centre	Edinburgh	Scotland	1.7.90
The Point Theatre	Dublin	Eire	5-6.7.90
National Exhibition Centre	Birmingham	England	7-10.7.90
Philipshalle	Dortmund	Germany	12-13.7.90
Waldebuehne	Berlin	Germany	14-15.7.90
Meadowlands Arena	New York NY	USA	10-11.8.90
Forum	Montreal QC	Canada	13-14.8.90
Palace of Auburn Hills	Auburn Hills NY	USA	16-17.8.90
Richfield Coliseum	Cleveland OH	USA	19-20.8.90
The Spectrum	Philadelphia NY	USA	22-25.8.90
Capital Centre	Landover MD	USA	27-28.8.90
Starlake Amphitheatre	Pittsburgh PA	USA	29-30.8.90
Dean E Smith Centre	Chapel Hill PA	USA	1.9.90
Lakewood Amphitheatre	Atlanta GA	USA	2.9.90
Civic Centre Coliseum	Birmingham GA	USA	3.9.90
Starwood Amphitheatre	Nashville TN	USA	4.9.90
"MTV Awards"	Los Angeles CA	USA	6.9.90
Summit Arena	Houston TX	USA	7.9.90
Starplex Amphitheatre	Dallas TX	USA	8-9.9.90
McNichols Sports Arena	Denver CO	USA	11.9.90
PNE Coliseum	Vancouver BC	Canada	13.9.90
The Dome	Tacoma WA	USA	14-15.9.90
Shoreline Amphitheatre	San Francisco CA	USA	17-19.9.90
ARCO Arena	Sacramento CA	USA	20.9.90
Irvine Meadows Amphitheatre	Los Angeles CA	USA	22-23.9.90
Wiltern Theatre	Los Angeles CA	USA	24.9.90
Beacon Theatre	New York NY	USA	27.9.90
Madison Square Garden	New York NY	USA	28-29.9.90
Madison Square Garden	New York NY	USA	1-3.10.90

1989/90 and Phil's star is firmly in the ascendant! His fourth solo album; "But seriously" hits the top of the charts worldwide and the debut single; Another day in paradise becomes a multi million selling hit and it is even used by the UN commission on homelessness as part of heir campaign on this issue. Phil's tour takes him even further around the globe than ever before and his success is assured with his most convincing shows to date. The 1990 tour was Phil's largest to date and the live set increased in length accordingly with a show now almost THREE HOURS long comprising the following tracks...Hand in hand/Hang in long enough/Behind thelines/Against all odds/Doesn't anybody stay together anymore?/All of my life/Don't lose my number/Do you remember?/Something happened on the way to heaven/Another day in paradise/Separate lives/I wish it would rain down/Saturday night, Sunday morning/The West Side/That's just the wayit is/Heat on the street/One more night/Colours/In the air tonight/You can't hurry love/Two hearts/Find a way to my heart/Sussudio/A groovy kind of love/Easy lover/Always/Take me home. On occasions there were changes including performances of Inside out and The roof is leaking in place of Behind thelines or Something happened on the way to heaven.

Royal Albert Hall	London	England	5-7.2.91 **(With Eric Clapton)**

"Both Sides Of The Story" World Tour 1994

Prins van Oranje Hal **(Load in and set up)**	Utrecht	Holland	30.3.94
Prins van Oranje Hal **(Rehearsal)**	Utrecht	Holland	31.3.94
Prins van Oranje Hal	Utrecht	Holland	1-2.4.94
The Globe	Stockholm	Sweden	4.4.94
Spectrum	Oslo	Norway	6-7.4.94
Prinz van Oranje Hal	Utrecht	Holland	9-10.4.94
Flanders Expo	Ghent	Belgium	12-13.4.94
Westfalenhalle	Dortmund	Germany	15-18.4.94
La Galaxie	Metz	France	21.4.94
Hallenstadion	Zurich	Switzerland	22-23.4.94
Forum Assago	Milan	Italy	25.4.94
Patinoire de Malley	Lausanne	Switzerland	26.4.94
L'Espace Tony Garnier	Lyon	France	28.4.94
Palais Omnisports de Bercy	Paris	France	29.4.94
Palais Omnisports de Bercy	Paris	France	1.5.94
Palais des Sports	Toulouse	France	2.5.94
Palau St Jordi	Barcelona	Spain	4.5.94
Plaza de Toros de las Ventas	Madrid	Spain	5.5.94

Estadio Alvalade	Lisbon	Portugal	7.5.94
Sports Palace **(Load in and set up)**	Mexico City	Mexico	16.5.94
Sports Palace	Mexico City	Mexico	17-18.5.94
Sports Palace	Mexico City	Mexico	20-21.5.94
Teatro Funidora Amphitheatre	Monterrey	Mexico	23.5.94
Cynthia Woods-Mitchell Pavilion	The Woodlands	USA	25.5.94
The Summit Arena	Houston TX	USA	26.5.94
Reunion Arena	Dallas TX	USA	27.5.94
Florida Thunderdome	St Petersburg FL	USA	29.5.94
Miami Arena	Miami FL	USA	30-31.5.94
Orlando Arena	Orlando FL	USA	2.6.94
Lakewood Amphitheatre	Atlanta GA	USA	4.6.94
Blockbuster Pavilion	Charlotte VA	USA	5.6.94
Walnut Creek Amphitheatre	Raleigh NC	USA	7.6.94
Great Woods	Mansfield OH	USA	9-10.6.94
Saratoga Performing Arts Centre	Saratoga Springs NY	USA	11.6.94
The Forum	Montreal QC	Canada	13-14.6.94
Skydome	Toronto ONT	Canada	16-17.6.94
The Spectrum	Philadelphia PA	USA	19-20.6.94
The Spectrum	Philadelphia PA	USA	22.6.94
USAir Arena	Landover MD	USA	23.6.94
Meadowlands Arena	East Rutherford NJ	USA	25-26.6.94
Palace of Auburn Hills	Auburn Hills NY	USA	28-29.6.94
Star Lake Amphitheatre	Burgettstown NY	USA	30.6.94
Jones Beach Amphitheatre	Wantagh NY	USA	2-3.7.94
Hartford Civic Centre	Hartford CT	USA	5.7.94
Madison Square Garden	New York NY	USA	6-7.7.94
Hershey Park Stadium	Hershey PA	USA	9.7.94
Richfield Coliseum	Cleveland OH	USA	11-12.7.94
Polaris Amphitheatre	Columbus OH	USA	14.7.94
Deer Creek Amphitheatre	Indianapolis IN	USA	15.7.94
Marcus Amphitheatre	Milwaukee WI	USA	16.7.94
Riverbend Music Centre	Cincinatti WI	USA	18.7.94
Rosemont Horizon	Chicago IL	USA	20-21.7.94
The Park	Moline IL	USA	22.7.94
Riverport Amphitheatre	Maryland Heights MD	USA	24.7.94
Sandstone Amphitheatre	Kansas City KS	USA	25.7.94
Fiddler's Green Amphitheatre	Englewood CA	USA	27.7.94
Delta Centre	Salt Lake City UT	USA	28.7.94
MGM Grand Garden	Las Vegas NV	USA	30.7.94
Blockbuster Desert Sky Pavilion	Phoenix AZ	USA	31.7.94
ARCO Arena	Sacramento CA	USA	4.8.94
Shoreline Amphitheatre	Mountain View CA	USA	5-6.8.94
Greatwestern Forum	Englewood CA	USA	8-9.8.94
Wembley **(MTV Unplugged)**	London	England	30.8.94
Maifeld **(Load in and set up)**	Berlin	Germany	31.8.94
Maifeld	Berlin	Germany	1.9.94
Niedersachsenstadion	Hanover	Germany	3-4.9.94
Niedersachsenstadion	Hanover	Germany	6-7.9.94
Palais Omnisports de Bercy	Paris	France	9-10.9.94
Palais Omnisports de Bercy	Paris	France	12-13.9.94
Schleyerhalle	Stuttgart	Germany	15-16.9.94
Schleyerhalle	Stuttgart	Germany	18-19.9.94
Olympiahalle	Munich	Germany	21-22.9.94
Olympiahalle	Munich	Germany	24.9.94
Festhalle	Frankfurt	Germany	26-28.9.94
Le Galaxie	Metz	France	30.9.94
Le Galaxie	Metz	France	1.10.94
National Exhibition Centre	Birmingham	England	3-4.10.94
King's Hall	Belfast	Northern Ireland	7-8.10.94
The Point Theatre	Dublin	Eire	9-10.10.94
The Point Theatre	Dublin	Eire	12.10.94
Arena	Sheffield	England	23-24.11.94
Royal Albert Hall	London	England	26.11.94
G-Mex Centre	Manchester	England	28-29.11.94
Scottish Exhibition & Conference Centre	Glasgow	Scotland	1-2.12.94
National Exhibition Centre	Birmingham	England	4-5.12.94
Wembley Arena	London	England	7-8.12.94
Wembley Arena	London	England	10-11.12.94
Wembley Arena	London	England	13-14.12.94

"The Far Side World Tour" 1995"

Ellis Park Rugby Stadium	Johannesburg	South Africa	17.3.95
Kingsmead Cricket Ground	Durban	South Africa	19.3.95
Indoor stadium	Singapore	Singapore	22-23.3.95
Impian Jaya Anool	Jakarta	Indonesia	25.3.95
Thai Army Stadium	Bangkok	Thailand	27.3.95
Thai Army Stadium	Bangkok	Thailand	28.3.95*
(*)Show cancelled			
Entertainment Centre	Perth	Australia	30.3.95
Memorial Drive	Adelaide	Australia	1.4.95
National Tennis Centre	Melbourne	Australia	2-3.4.95
National Tennis Centre	Melbourne	Australia	5-6.4.95
Entertainment Centre	Brisbane	Australia	8-9.4.95
Entertainment Centre	Sydney	Australia	11-12.4.95
Entertainment Centre	Sydney	Australia	14-15.4.95
Estadio Carlos de Apoquindo	Santiago	Chile	18-19.4.95
Estadio Monumental	Buenos Aires	Argentina	22-23.4.95
MuelaUno	Lima	Peru	25.4.95
Esatdio de Pacaembu **(Cancelled)**	Sao Paolo	Brazil	27.4.95
Conplejo Cultural DeTeresa Careno	Caracas	Venezuela	27.4.95
(Show replacing planned Sao Paolo show)			
Praca da Apoteose **(Cancelled)**	Rio de Janeiro	Brazil	29.4.95
Hiram Bithorn Stadium	San Juan	Puerto Rico	28.4.95
(Show replacing planned Rio de Janeiro show)			
Coliseum	Hong Kong	Hong Kong	3-4.5.95
Fukuoka Dome	Fukuoka	Japan	6-7.5.95
(This gig was televised via satellite link to the city of Kobe wich had recently been devastated by an earthquake Phil dedicated the gig to the inhabitants of Kobe)			
Yoyogi Gymnasium	Tokio	Japan	9-10.5.95
Yokohama Arena	Yokohama	Japan	11.5.95
Chung Shan Football Stadium	Taipei	Taiwan	13.5.95
Ultra Football Stadium	Manila	Philippines	15-16.5.95

1994/95 sees Phil reach the peak of his popularity so far with another highly successful album; "Both Sides" although the press opted to cover the breaking story of his marriage difficulties. The album again reached number one both in the UK and worldwide and the tour that he undertook to promote it was his biggest yet, being a truly "World Tour" even being divided into two halves; the "Both Sides" tour of Europe and the USA which ran from April to December 1994 and the "Far Side" tour which ran from February to May 1995 and which, as its title suggests was a tour of exotic locations including Phil's first solo gigs in South Africa, South America and even gigs in Hong Kong! Also here was a special satellite linked concert made from Fukuoka in Japan to the earthquake ravaged city of Kobe which was to have been on Phil's original tour schedule.

Phil's tours just keep getting bigger and the 1994/95 tour was ENORMOUS and the live set was equally so comprising the following tracks...Drum solo intro/I don't careanymore/Don'tlose my number/Everyday/Survivors/Another day in paradise/I can't find my way/I wish it would rain down/One more night/Agroovy kind of love/We wait and we wonder/I've forgotten everything/Both sides of the story/ In the air tonight/Hang inlong enough/Find a way tomyheart/It don't matter to me/I missed again/Behind thelines/Easy lover/Only you & I know/Something happened on the way to heaven/You can't hurry love/Two hearts/Sussudio/ Helpless heart/Knockin' on heaven's door/ My girl/Against all odds/Take me home. Other interesting variations included Phil playing the didgeridoo in Autsralia and knocking out a surprisingly good version of Amazing Grace on the bagpipes during the later UK shows. His first show in Utrecht also saw rare performances of Burn Down The Misson and Always

Big Band Jazz Tour 1996

Grand Casino	Geneva	Switzerland	26.1.96
Grand Casino (Rehearsals)	Montreux	Switzerland	1-9.7.96
Royal Albert Hall	London	England	11.7.96
Monaco Sporting Club	Monte Carlo	Monaco	12-13.7.96
Giardini del Frontone	Perugia	Italy	15.7.96
La Pinede	Antibes	France	16.7.96
Stavinski Auditorium	Montreux	Switzerland	17.7.96
Polediportivo de Mendizorroza	Vittoria	Spain	20.7.96
Jardine de los viveros	Valencia	Spain	21.7.96
Radio City Music Hall	New York NY	USA	28.10.96

1996 and Phil takes everyone by surprise with a tour as part of a Big Band style jazz combo playing a handful of shows at prestigious jazz festivals in Europe. The show at the Royal Albert Hall is given in the presence of both HRH the Queen but also the newly elected president of South Africa; Nelson Mandela. The tour is filmed for a BBC documentary which is screened on 29thDecember 1996 and a recording is also made for future release as a live album and video. Before year's end, Phil has also released his sixth solo album; "Dance into the light" The set for the jazz tour included a selection of Phil's solo material and Genesis tracks along with several jazz standards and a typical set included the following...Two hearts/That's all/The west Side/Agains all odds/Hand in hand/Tony Bennett solo set/Drum-percussion duet/Los Endos/Don't do nothin' til you hear from me/Sussudio.

Phils set for the Dance in to the light tour of 1997 was changed between the US and European legs with the two sets running as folows... (USA) Hand in hand/Hang in long enough/Don't lose my number/River so wide/Take me down/Find a way to my heart/Another day in Paradise/Against all odds/Just another story/Lorenzo/Separate lives/The times they are a-changin'/You know what I mean/One more night/In the air tonight/Timbantiocha/Loco in Acapulco/Dance into thelight/Easy lover/Wear myhat/You can't hurry love/Two hearts/Something happened on the way to heaven/Sussudio/The same moon/Take me home. (Europe/UK) Hand in hand/Hang in long enough/Don't lose my number/River so wide/Take me down/Find a way to my heart/Another day in paradise/Just another story/Againstall odds/Lorenzo/Separate lives/Both sides of the story/Do you remember?/Long long way to go/One more night/In the air tonight/Timbantiocha/Easy lover/Dance into thelight/Wear my hat/You can't hurry love/Two hearts/Somethinghappened on the way to heaven./Sussudio/take me home.

"The Dance Into The Light World Tour" 1997

The Arena **(Rehearsals)**	Lakeland FL	USA	1-25.2.97
Ice Palace **(load-in only)**	Tampa FL	USA	27.2.97
Ice Palace	Tampa FL	USA	28.2.97
Orlando Arena	Orlando FL	USA	1.3.97
Miami Arena	Miami FL	USA	3.3.97
USAir Arena	Landover MD	USA	5.3.97
Civic Arena	Pittsburgh PA	USA	7.3.97
Marine Midland Arena	Buffalo NY	USA	8.3.97
Palace of Auburn Hills	Detroit MI	USA	10.3.97
Edwin Nutter Centre	Dayton OH	USA	11.3.97
Madison Square Garden	New York NY	USA	13.3.97
(A show scheduled for the 14th at the above venue was cancelled due to illness)			
Colisee Arena	Quebec City QC	Canada	16.3.97
Molson Centre	Montreal QC	Canada	17-18.3.97
Skydome	Toronto ONT	Canada	20.3.97
Corel Centre	Ottawa ONT	Canada	21-22.3.97
Fleet Centre	Boston MA	USA	24.3.97
Pepsi (Knickerbocker) Arena	Albany NY	USA	25.3.97
Hartford Civic Centre	Hartford CT	USA	27.3.97
Corestate Centre	Philadelphia NY	USA	29.3.97
Bryce Jordan Arena	Penn State PA	USA	30.3.97
Van Andel Arena	Grand Rapids MI	USA	3.4.97
Gund Arena	Cleveland OH	USA	4.4.97
Rosemont Horizon	Chicago IL	USA	6.4.97
Market Square Arena	Champaign IL	USA	8.4.97
Bradley Centre	Milwaukee WI	USA	10.4.97
Kiel Centre	St Louis MO	USA	11.4.97
Kemper Arena	Kansas City KS	USA	12.4.97
San Jose Arena	San Jose CA	USA	15.4.97
ARCO Arena	Sacramento CA	USA	16.4.97
America West Arena	Phoenix AZ	USA	`18.4.97
MGM Grand Garden	Las Vegas AZ	USA	19.4.97
Arrowhead Pond	Los AngelesCA	USA	21.4.97
Palau St Jordi **(Rehearsal)**	Barcelona	Spain	6.10.97
Palau St Jordi	Barcelona	Spain	7.10.97
Filaforum	Milan	Italy	9.10.97
Halle Tony Garnier	Lyon	France	11.10.97
Arena	Geneva	Switzerland	12-13.10.97
Hallenstadion	Zurich	Switzerland	15-16.10.97
Deutschlandhalle	Berlin	Germany	18-19.10.97
Festhalle	Frankfurt	Germany	21-23.10.97
Globe Arena	Stockholm	Sweden	25.10.97
Spektrum	Oslo	Norway	26.10.97
Ahoy Sportpaleis	Rotterdam	Holland	28-29.10.97
Messehalle 2	Hanover	Germany	31.10.97
Messehalle 2	Hanover	Germany	1.11.97
Flanders Expo	Ghent	Belgium	3-4.11.97
National Exhibition Centre	Birmingham	England	6-7.11.97
Arena	Newcastle	England	9-10.11.97
NYNEX Arena	Manchester	England	18-19.11.97
Westfalenhalle	Dortmund	Germany	21-23.11.97
Schleyerhalle	Stuttgart	Germany	25-26.11.97
Olympiahalle	Munich	Germany	28-29.11.97
Stadthalle	Vienna	Austria	1.12.97
Sportovinhala	Prague	Czech Republic	2.12.97
Messehalle 7	Leipzig	Germany	4-6.12.97
Palais Omnisports de Bercy	Paris	France	8-9.12.97
Westfalenhalle	Dortmund	Germany	11.12.97
Earls Court Arena	London	England	13-14.12.97
Earls Court Arena	London	England	16-17.12.97

Big Band Jazz Tour 1998.

Historic Mountain Winery	Saratoga NY	USA	12-13.6.98
County Bowl	Santa Barbara CA	USA	14.6.98
Greek Theatre	Los Angeles CA	USA	15.6.98
Woodlands Pavilion	Houston TX	USA	18.6.98
City Stages	Birmingham AL	USA	19.6.98

Chastain Park Amphitheatre	Atlanta GA	USA	20.6.98
I C Light Amphitheatre	Pittsburgh PA	USA	21.6.98
Nautica Stage	Cleveland OH	USA	22.6.98
Meadow Brook	Detroit MI	USA	23.6.98
Taste of Chicago	Chicago IL	USA	25.6.98
Summerfest	Milwaukee WI	USA	26.6.98
Boston Globe Jazz Festival	Harborlights MA	USA	28.6.98
Carnegie Hall	New York NY	USA	29.6.98
Tivoli Gardens Jazz Festival	Copenhagen	Denmark	7.7.98
Waldebuehne	Berlin	Germany	8.7.98
North Sea Jazz Festival	The Hague	Holland	10.7.98
Nice Jazz Festival	Nice	France	13.7.98
Montreux Jazz Festival	Montreux	Switzerland	14.7.98
Pori Fest	Helsinki	Finland	17.7.98
Villa Erba Cernobbio	Milan	Italy	19.7.98
Fourviere	Lyon	France	20.7.98
Grand Rex	Paris	France	21.7.98
Royal Festival Hall	London	England	23.7.98
Symphony Hall	Birmingham	England	24.7.98

1998 and Phil takes out his Big Band combo for a proper tour of the USA and Europe with a set which drew from the best of his own material and that of Genesis as well as several jazzstandards again for an almost three hour musical extrvaganza comprising the following tracks... Two hearts/That's all/I don't care anymore/Against all odds/The west Side/hand in hand/Rad Dudeski/Hold on my heart/In the air tonight/Chips & Salsa/Georgia on my mind/Don't lose my number/Milestones/Los Endos/Do nothin' til you hear from me/The way you look tonight/Always/Sussudio.

Tarzan Showcase	New Orelans LO	USA	20.2.99
Tarzan Showcase	Las Vegas NA	USA	10-11.3.99
El Capitan Theater	Los Angeles CA	USA	11-12.6.99
RadioCity Music Hall	New York NY	USA	14.6.99
"Tonight Show With Jay Leno" US TV	New York NY	USA	16.6.99
Tarzan Showcase	Munich	Germany	30.10.99
Madison Square Garden	New York NY	USA	1.11.99
?	Berlin	Germany	13.11.99
Ruud de Wild Dutch TV?	Amsterdam	Holland	19.11.99
Academy Awards Ceremony	West Hollywood CA	USA	26.3.00
Theatre des Champs Elysees	Paris	France	4.7.01
Grand Casino	Geneva	Switzerland	19.2.02
Buckingham Palace	London	England	3.6.02
RTL Studios	Paris	France	30.10.02
The Scala	London	England	6.11.02
On Line Arena	Hamburg	Germany	8.11.02
Cipriani	New York NY	USA	13.11.02
Star Academy Chateau Des Vives	Paris	France	29-30.11.02

The New York show in 1999 was to promote the Tarzan movie and Phil's short set comprised: Against All Odds/You'll be In My Heart/Separate Lives/Take Me Home/In the AirTonight (Solo piano version)

Phil's recent viral infection and the problems that has created, coupled with his new found family commitments led to his scaling down touring commitments to a handful of promotional shows in support of the Testify album. His shows drew on material from all of his albums and could almost be classed as a "Greatest Hits" show with a set including the following songs:

In TheAir Tonight/Something Happened On The Way To Heaven/AnotherDay In Paradise/Can't StopLoving You/Driving Me Crazy/I Missed Again/You'll Be In My Heart/One More Night/Separate Lives/Easy Lover/Two Hearts/Sussudio/Take Me Home/My Girl/GetReady.

Grand Casino	Geneva	Switzerland	12.8.03

This was a further charitable performance in aid of the "Little Dreams Foundation" and Phil wasjoined on stage by his old Genesis cohort Mike Rutherford for this performance which included... You Can't Hurry Love/Easy Lover/Follow You Follow Me/I Can't Dance/Throwing It All Away.

"FIRST FINAL FAREWELL TOUR 2004 - 06"

Venue	City	Country	Date	
Filaforum	Milan	Italy	1.6.04	
Ernst Happel Stadion	Vienna	Austria	3.6.04	
Letzigrund Stadium	Zurich	Switzerland	5.6.04 +	
Olympic Stadium	Munich	Germany	6.6.04 +	
Festhalle	Frankfurt	Germany	7.6.04	
The Globe	Stockholm	Sweden	9.6.04	
Waldebuehne	Berlin	Germany	11.6.04 +	
Rhein Energie Stadion	Cologne	Germany	12.6.04 +	
Hannover Arena	Hannover	Germany	13.6.04	
Palais Omisports de Bercy	Paris	France	15-16.6.04	
Palais Omnisports de Bercy	Paris	France	17.6.04	
Amsterdam Arena	Amsterdam	Holland	19.6.04 +	Werchter Classic
Rock Festival	Werchter	Belgium	20.6.04 +	
Leipzig Arena	Leizpig	Germany	21.6.04 +	
Schleyerhalle	Stuttgart	Germany	23.6.04	
Halle Tony Ganier	Lyon	France	24.6.04	
Zenith Amphitheatre	Nancy	France	25.6.04 +	
Wembley Arena	London	England	27.6.04	
M E N Arena	Manchester	England	28.6.04	
Palau St Jordi	Barcelona	Spain	1.7.04 +	
	Alicante	Spain	2.7.04 +	
Restelo Stadium	Lisbon	Portugal	3.7.04 +	
Zenith	Toulouse	France	5.7.04	
Arena	Geneva	Switzerland	6.7.04	
Stravinsky Auditorium	Montreux	Switzerland	7.7.04	
Arrowhead Pond	Anaheim CA	USA	26.8.04	
MGM Grand	Las Vegas NV	USA	28.8.04	
Arena	San Jose NV	USA	30.8.04	
America West Arens	Phoenix AZ	USA	1.9.04	
Ford Center	Oklahoma City OK	USA	3.9.04	
American Airlines Center	Dallas TX	USA	4.9.04	
Toyota Center	Houston TX	USA	5.9.04	
Bradley Center	Milwaukee WI	USA	7.9.04	
United Center	Chicago IL	USA	8.9.04	
The Palace	Detroit MI	USA	10.9.04	
Gund Arena	ClevelandOH	USA	11.9.04	
HSBC Arena	Buffalo NY	USA	12.9.04	
Bell Centre	Montreal QE	Canada	14.9.04	
Fleet Center	Boston MA	USA	15.9.04	
Madison Square Garden	New York NY	USA	17.9.04	
Air CanadaCentre	Toronto ONT	Canada	20.9.04	
Mohegan Sun Casino Arena	Uncasville	USA	21.9.04	
Wachonia Center	Philadelphia NY	USA	22.904	
Van Andel	Grand Rapids MI	USA	24.9.04	
Schottenstein Center	ColumbusOH	USA	25.9.04	
Mellon Arena	Pittsburgh PA	USA	26.9.04	
TD Waterhouse Center	Orlando FL	USA	28.9.04	
St Petersburg Times Forum	Tampa FL	USA	29.9.04	
Office Depot Center	Fort Lauderdale FL	USA	30.9.04	

+ = Gigs performed with Mike & The Mechanics

For this tour, Phil once again present what is fundamentally a "Greatest Hits" package comprising the following tracks; Drum Trio (Inc: Los Endos/Timbantiocha)/Something Happened On The Way To Heaven/Against All Odds/A Groovy Kind Of Love/One More Night/Don't LoseMy Number/You'll Be In My Heart/Can't Stop Loving You/No Way Out/Another Day In Paradise/Separate Lives/In The Air Tonight/Easy Lover/You Can't Hurry Love/Two Hearts/Dance Into The Light/Wear My Hat/Sussudio/Always/Take Me Home/ I Missed Again.

The US tour saw Phil and the band play aslightly diferent set which usually ran as follows... Drum Trio (Inc: Los Enndos/Timbantiocha)/Something Happened On The Way To Heaven/AgainstAll Odds/Don't Lose My Number/You'll Be In My Heart/One More Night/Can't Stop Loving You/Hang In Long Enough/True Colours/Come With Me/A Groovy Kind Of Love/I Missed Again/AnotherDay In Paradise/Misunderstanding/No Way Out/In The Air Tonight/Dance Into The Light/You Can't Hurry Love/Two Hearts/Wear My Hat/Easy Lover/Sussudio/It's Not Too Late/Drum Thing/Take Me Home.

Venue	City	Country	Date
Saku Suurhall	Tallinn	Estonia	13.10.05
Hartwall Arena	Heksinki	Finland	14-15.10.05
Saku Suurhall	Tallin	Estonia	16.10.05
New Ice Arena	St Petesburg	Russia	18.10.05
Olympic Arena	Moscow	Russia	20.10.05
Siemens Arena	Vilnius	Lithuania	22.10.05
Sazka Arena	Prague	Czech Republic	24-25.10.05(*)
Budapest Arena	Budapest	Hungary	26.10.05
Dom Sportova	Zagreb	Croatia	27.10.05

Belgrade Arena	Belgrade	Serbia	28.10.05
Romaero (Baneasa)	Bucharest	Romania	30.10.05
Love And Peace Stadium	Athens	Greece	1.11.05
Adbi Ipekci Stadium	Istanbul	Turkey	3.11.05
B I E L	Beirut	Lebanon	5.11.05
Bloomfield Stadium	Tel Aviv	Israel	7.11.05
Dubai Autodrome	Dubai	United Arab Enirates	10.11.05
LTU Arena	Dusseldorf	Germany	12-13.11.05
The Point	Dublin	Republic Of Ireland	15.11.05
Odyssey Arena	Belfast	Northern Ireland	17.11.05
Scottish Exhibition And Conference Centre	Glasgow	Scotland	19-20.11.05
Sazka Arena	Prague	Czech Republic	23-24.11.05

(*) = Re-scheduled gigs

PETER GABRIEL SOLO GIG GUIDE

VENUE NAME	CITY	COUNTRY	DATE

Peter Gabriel 1 Tour 1977

Capitol Theatre	Passaic NJ	USA	5.3.77
Civic Auditorium	Rochester NY	USA	6.3.77
Orpheum Theatre	Davenport NY	USA	9.3.77
Uptown Theatre	ChicagoIL	USA	11.3.77
Masonic Auditorium	Detroit OH	USA	13.3.77
Music Hall	Cleveland OH	USA	15.3.77
Century Hall	Buffalo NY	USA	16.3.77
Tower Theatre	Upper Darby PA	USA	17-18.3.77
Palladium Theatre	New York NY	USA	19.3.77
Massey Hall	Toronto ONT	Canada	22.3.77
City Hall	Quebec QC	Canada	23.3.77
Stanley Theatre	Pittsburgh PA	USA	26-28.3.77
Music Hall	Cleveland OH	USA	29.3.77
Kiel Open House	St Louis MO	USA	30.3.77
Uptown Theatre	Kansas City KS	USA	1,4,77
Convention Centre	Dallas TX	USA	2.4.77
Music Hall	Houston TX	USA	3.4.77
Winterland Arena	San Francisco CA	USA	7.4.77
The Roxy	Hollywood CA	USA	9-10.4.77
Polytechnic	Hatfield	England	23.4.77
Hammersmith Odeon	London	England	24-26.4.77
Empire Theatre	Liverpool	England	28.4.77
Apollo Theatre	Manchester	England	29.4.77
New Vic Theatre	London(2 shows)	England	30.4.77
Ockenden Theatre (Warm Up)	Haslemere	England	30.8.77
Pavilion Des Sports	Courtrai	Belgium	2.9.77
Maison Des Sports	Antwerp	Belgium	3.9.77
Rijnhal	Arnhem	Holland	4.9.77
Doelen Halle	Rotterdam	Holland	7.9.77
VorstNationale	Brussels	Belgium	8.9.77
Fete de l'Humanite	La Corueuve Paris	France	10.9.77
City Hall	Newcastle	England	13-14.9.77
Apollo Theatre	Glasgow	Scotland	15.9.77
City Hall	Sheffield	England	17.9.77
Trentham Gardens	Stoke on Trent	England	18.9.77
The Dome	Brighton	England	19.9.77
De Montfort Hall	Leicester	England	21.9.77
St George's Hall	Bradford	England	22.9.77
Empire Theatre	Liverpool	England	23.9.77
Odeon Theatre (2 shows)	Birmingham	England	25.9.77
Apollo Theatre	Manchester	England	27-28.9.77
Free Trade Hall	Manchester	England	29.9.77
Gaumont Theatre	Southampton	England	30.9.77
Capitol Theatre	Cardiff	Wales	1.10.77
Hippodrome	Bristol(2 shows)	England	2.10.77
Olympia Theatre	Paris	France	4.10.77
Halle des Fetes	Lyon	France	5.10.77
Salle D'Expositions	Colmar	France	6.10.77
Congresshalle	Hamburg	Germany	8.10.77
Tivolis Conzertsal	Copenhagen	Denmark	9.10.77
Konserthuset	Stockholm	Sweden	10-11.10.77
Munsterlandhalle	Munster	Germany	13.10.77
Rhein-Main-Halle	Wiesbanden	Germany	14.10.77
Festhalle	Berne	Switzerland	15.10.77

Chapiteau	Strasbourg	France	16.10.77
Sporthalle	Cologne	Germany	18.10.77
Stadthalle	Offenbach	Germany	19.10.77
Philipshalle	Dusseldorf	Germany	20.10.77
Deutschlandhalle	Berlin	Germany	21.10.77
Zirkus Krone	Munich	Germany	22.10.77
Palais des Sports	Dijon	France	24.10.77
Porte des Expositions	Nantes	France	25.10.77
Palais de Congres	Lille	France	26.10.77
Arena	Poitiers	France	27.10.77
Patinoire de Malley	Bordeaux	France	28.10.77
Palais des Sports	Toulouse	France	29.10.77
Nouvel Hippodrome	Paris	France	30.10.77
Sports & Leisure Centre	Bath	England	1.11.77

Peter could not long resist returning to the recording and performing fray and his first solo album was well received by fans and critics alike; as were his live shows which drew on the new album as well as at least one reference to Genesis and a tacit acknowledgement to Peter's Motwon roots in a set which ran as follows....

Here Comes The Flood/On The Air./Moribund The Burgermeister/Waiting For The Big One/Why Don't We?/Excuse Me/Humdrum/Solsbury Hill/Ain't That Peculiar/Indigo/All Day, And All Of The Night/Here Comes The Flood/Slowburn/ Modenr Love/Down The Dolce Vita/Back in NYC.
During the course of this first tour; two other new songs were also included occasionally: On The Air and Indigo under their respective working titles of "Song Without Words" and "Mickey Mouse".

The second leg of the '77 tour saw some changes in the typical set with the revised European set running as follows...
Here Comes The Flood/Slowburn/Moribund The Burgermeister/Modern Love/Indigo/Humdrum/White Shadow/I Heard It Thru The Grapevine/Excuse me/Waiting For The Big One/Solsbury Hill/Down The Dolce Vita/On The Air/All Day And All Of The Night/HereComes The Flood/Back in NYC. Ocasionally another new song; Animal Magic was added as an extra encore.

Peter's opening act on this tour was Nona Hendryx.

Peter Gabriel 2 Tour 1978

New Theatre	Oxford	England	23.8.78
Assembly Rooms	Derby	England	24..8.78
University Great Hall	Lancaster	England	25.8.78
Chateau Neuf	Oslo	Norway	31.8.78
Grona Lund	Stockholm	Sweden	1.9.78
Concerthal	Gothenburg	Sweden	2.9.78
Tivoli	Copenhagen	Denmark	3.9.78
Stadthalle	Bremen	Germany	4.9.78
CongressCentrum	Hamburg	Germany	6.9.78
Deutschlandhalle	Berlin	Germany	7.9.78
Knebworth Park Festival	Stevenage	England	9.9.78
Congressgebouow	Den Haag	Holland	10.9.78
Vorst Nationale	Brussels	Belgium	12-13.9.78
Battersea Park Festival	Battersea Park London	England	15.9.78
Grugahalle	Essen	Germany	17.9.78
The Roxy	Hollywood CA	USA	30.9.-1.10.78
Bottom Line Club (2 shows)	New York NY	USA	4.10.78
Civic Auditorium	Rochester NY	USA	5.10.78
USACollege	Oswego NY	USA	6.10.78
Music Hall	Geneseo NY	USA	7.10.78
King Concert Hall	Fredonia NY	USA	8.10.78
Wilkins Theatre	Unionville PA	USA	9.10.78
Colisee de Quebec	Quebec City QC	Canada	13.10.78
University	Montreal QC	Canada	15.10.78
Maple Leaf Gardens	Toronto ONT	Canada	16.10.78
Cleinhams Music Hall	Buffalo NY	USA	17.10.78
Uptown Theater	Chicago ILL	USA	19.10.78
Masonic Auditorium	Detroit ILL	USA	20.10.78
State University	Kent OH	USA	21.10.78
Stanley Theatre	Pittsburgh PA	USA	22.10.78
Hudson Civic Center	Poughkeepsie NY	USA	25.10.78
Lyric Theater	BaltimoreML	USA	26.10.78
University	Stoneybrook NJ	USA	28.10.78
Capitol Theatre	Passaic NJ	USA	29.10.78
Paradise Theater	Boston MA	USA	30-31.10.78
Palladium Theatre	New York NY	USA	4.11.78
Crawford Hall	Irvine NY	USA	18.11.78
Union Hall UCLA	Ackerman CA	USA	21.11.78
Terrace Theatre	Long Beach CA	USA	22.11.78
J Eden Hal	Amsterdam	Holland	30.11.78
Parc De La Beaujoire	Nantes	France	2.12.78
Palais Des Sports	Rheims	France	3.12.78
Pavilion Des Sports	Besancon	France	4.12.78

Palais des Sports	Lyon	France	5.12.78
Fredrich EbertHalle	Ludwigshafen	Germany	6.12.78
Ahoy Sportpaleis	Rotterdam	Holland	7.12.78
Pavilion Baltard	Nogent Marne	France	9-10.12.78
RTL French tv studios	Paris	France	10.12.78
Philipshalle	Dusseldorf	Germany	12.12.78
Festhalle	Frankfurt	Germany	13.12.78
Deutshces Museum	Munich	Germany	14.12.78
Mozartsaal	Mannheim	Germany	15.12.78
Congreshalle	Basle	Switzerland	16.12.78
Patinoire	Geneva	Switzerland	17.12.78
The Venue Club	London	England	20.12.78
Hammersmith Odeon	London	England	20-24.12.78

1978 and Peter's second album, a much darker one than its predecessor is released. Also titled "Peter Gabriel" it includes work by King crimson stalwart Robert Fripp who also produced the album and guested with Peter's band under the moniker of "Dusty Road". During the tour which coincided with that of Peter's former band; Genesis, Peter was briefly reunited with them during their performance of "The Lamb lies down on Broadway" at New York. The show at the Grugahalle Essen was also filmed for tv and captures the excitement of one of these shows including Peter's resurrection of his alter-ego "Rael" for a marvellous version of "The lamb.." as an encore. Peter rounds off the year with four sell-out gigs at London's prestigious Hammersmith Odeon in the company of Tom Robinson. The set for this tour usually ran as follows...

Me & My Teddy Bear/On The Air/Moribund The Burgermeister/Animal Magic/Flotsam & Jetsam/White Shadow/Have A Wonderful Day(In AOneWay World)/Humdrum/I Don't Remember/Home SweetHome/DIY/A Whiter Shade Of Pale/HereComes The Flood/ Slowburn/Modern Love/Perspective/The Lamb Lies Down On Broadway/Down The Dolce Vita.

It was during this tour that Peter also began to experiment with other language versions of his songs including "Moi Et Mon Teddy Bear" and "Ich Und Mein Teddy Bear" .

The special Christmas show also featured a special set comprising songs by Peter, Tom Robinson and their other special guests which ran as follows...

Ding Dong/DIY/Don't Take No For An Answer/Humdrum/Red Cortina/HereComes The Flood/Truce/Hold Out/Solsbury Hill/ I Don't Remember/Bully For You/Do-Wa-Diddy/Jumping Jack Flash/You Gotta Go/Saturday Night's Alright (For Fighting) 2; 4; 6; 8;Motorway.

Brilling Arts Centre	Bath	England	5.5.79
Hammersmith Odeon	London	England	12.5.79
Glastonbury Fayre	Glastonbury	England	23.6.79
Friars Club	Aylesbury	England	24.8.79
Reading Festival	Reading	England	26.8.79

1979 and only a handful of shows from Peter at which he took the opportunity of premiering several tracks from his forthcoming third solo album which is still almost a year away. These gigs featured Phil Collins on drums. . The Reading and Glastonbuy sets ran as follows...

Biko/On The Air/DIY/Humdrum/And Through The Wire/White Shadow./MotherOf Violence/Animal Magic/I Don't Remember/ Modern Love/Moribund The Burgermeister/Perspective/Solsbury Hill/HereComes The Flood/The Lamb Lies Down On Broadway.

Peter Gabriel Three Tour 1980

University	Exeter	England	20.2.80
Odeon Theatre	Taunton	England	21.2.80
Odeon Theatre	Birmingham	England	23.2.80
De Montfort Hall	Leicester	England	24.2.80
City Hall	Sheffield	England	25.2.80
Caird Hall	Dundee	Scotland	27.2.80
Capitol Theatre	Aberdeen	Scotland	28.2.80
Apollo Theatre	Glasgow	Scotland	29.2.80
Odeon Theatre	Edinburgh	Scotland	1.3.80
City Hall	Newcastle	England	3.3.80
Empire Theatre	Liverpool	England	4.3.80
Apollo Theatre	Manchester	England	5.3.80
Sophia Gardens	Cardiff	Wales	7.3.80
Gaumont Theatre	Southampton	England	8.3.80
Hammersmith Odeon	London	England	11-13.3.80
Conference Centre	Brighton	England	15.3.80
University	Bath	England	16.3.80
Clubhouse	Santa Ana TX	USA	17.6.80
Arlington Theatre	Santa Barbara CA	USA	18.6.80
Greek Theatre Griffith Park	Los Angeles CA	USA	19.6.80
Civic Theatre	San Jose CA	USA	21.6.80
Fox Warfield Theatre	San Francsisco CA	USA	22-23.6.80
Uptown Theatre	Chicago IL	USA	26.6.80
Music Hall	Cleveland OH	USA	27.6.80

Auditorium	Rochester NY	USA	28.6.80
Kleinhans Music Hall	Buffalo NY	USA	29.6.80
Ottowa Civic Centre	Ottowa ONT	Canada	2.7.80
Maple Leafe Gardens	Toronto ONT	Canada	3.7.80
Forum Concert Bowl	Montreal QC	Canada	4.7.80
Parc de Jeunesse	Quebec QC	Canada	5.7.80
Central Park	New York NY	USA	7.7.80
Orpheum Theatre	Boston MA	USA	8.7.80
Convention Hall	Asbury Park MA	USA	9.7.80
Tower Theatre	Upper Darby PA	USA	10.7.80
Diplomat Hotel	New York NY	USA	12.7.80
Nuevo Pabellon	Barcelona	Spain	3.8.80
Erikhallen	Stockholm	Sweden	30.8.80
Scandinavium	Gothenburg	Sweden	31.8.80
Audimax	Hamburg	Germany	1.9.80
Kuppelsaal	Hanover	Germany	2.9.80
Eisporthalle	Berlin	Germany	4.9.80
Philipshalle	Dortmund	Germany	5.9.80
NeumusikCentrum	Utrecht	Holland	6.9.80
Olympia Theatre	Paris	France	10-13.9.80
Palais de Congres	Nantes	France	14.9.80
Stadthalle	Offenbach	Germany	15.9.80
Alexpo	Grenoble	France	20.9.80
Pavilion Des Sports	Geneva	Switzerland	21.9.80
Patinoire De Malley	Bordeaux	France	24.9.80
Palais Des Sports	Toulouse	France	25-26.9.80
Parco Cascine	Florence	Italy	28.9.80
Palasport	Genoa	Italy	29.9.80
Hallenstadion	Zurich	Switzerland	30.9.80
Parc des Expositions	Avignon	France	1.10.80
Palais Des Sports	Lyon	France	2.10.80
Pabellon De Los Deportes	Barcelona	Spain	3.10.80
Pavilhao Dos Desportos	Cascais	Portugal	6-7.10.78
Pavilhao Dos Desportos	Porto	Portugal	8.10.80

1980 and Peter's success continues this time with the brilliant "Games without frontiers" single and third solo album. For reasons which still remain uncertain, Peter titled his tour "The Tour of China 1984" maybe a veiled reference to all the artists scrambling to play behind the Iron Curtain as a status symbol who knows, who cares? The tour itself is another great success. A typical 1980 set usually ran as follows….

Intruder/The Start/I Don't Remember/Solsbury Hill/Family Snapshot/Milgrams' 37/Modern Love/Not One Of Us/Lead A Normal/ Life/Moribund The Burgermeister/MotherOf Violence/White Shadow/Bully For You/Games Withot Frontiers/And Through The Wire/I Go Swimming/Biko/On The Air/HereComes The Flood..

Once again, several songs were tried out in the language of the respective country in which the band were playing, resulting in such Favourites being rendered as "Giocchi Senza Frontiere", "Jeux Sans Frontieres" ; "Ein Normales Leben", Und Durch Den Draht" and "Jetzt Kommt Die Flut.

Opening act on this tour: Random Hold who include a promising guitarist by the name of David Rhodes.

Peter Gabriel Four Tour 1982/83

Showering Pavilion	Sheptom Mallet	England	16.7.82
Showering Pavilion	Shepton Mallet	England	18.7.82
Orpheum Theatre	Boston MA	USA	28.10.82
Stoneybrook University	Long Island LI	USA	29.10.82
Rutgers University	Livingstone NJ	USA	31.10.82
Mid Hudson Civic Centre	Poughkeepsie NY	USA	1.11.82
Stanley Theater	Utica NJ	USA	2.11.82
Horton Fieldhouse	Normal IL	USA	3.11.82
Colisee de Quebec	Quebec City QC	Canada	4.11.82
Forum	Montreal QC	Canada	5.11.82
Ottawa Civic Centre	Ottawa ONT	Canada	6.11.82
Maple Leaf Gardens	Toronto ONT	Canada	8.11.82
Shea's Theatre	Buffalo NY	USA	9.11.82
Rochester Community War Memorial	Rochester NY	USA	11.11.82
Orpheum Theatre	Boston MA	USA	12.11.82
Capitol Theatre	Passaic NJ	USA	13.11.82
Warner Theatre	Washington DC	USA	14.11.82
Spectrum	Philadelphia PA	USA	16.11.82
Hara Arena	Dayton OH	USA	18.11.82
Michigan Theatre	Ann Arbor MI	USA	20.11.82
University of Indiana	Bloomington MI	USA	21.11.82
Wings Auditorium	Kalamazoo MI	USA	22.11.82

Richfield Coliseum	Cleveland OH	USA	24.11.82
Ritz Theatre	New York NY	USA	25-26.11.82
Dane County MemorialColiseum	Madison WI	USA	28.11.82
Performing Arts Centre	Milwaukee WI	USA	1.12.82
Pavilion	Chicago IL	USA	2.12.82
Horton Fieldhouse	Normal IL	USA	3.12.82
Memorial Auditorium	Kansas City KS	USA	4.12.82
North Illinois University	De KalbIL	USA	6.12.82
Southern Illinois University	Carbondale IL	USA	7.12.82
Agora	Dallas TX	USA	9.12.82
Music Hall	Houston TX	USA	10.12.82
Coliseum	Austin TX	USA	11.12.82
Sports Arena	San Diego CA	USA	14.12.82
Universal Amphitheatre	Los Angeles CA	USA	15-16.12.82
Civic Centre	San Francisco CA	USA	18.12.82
Civic Center	San Jose CA	USA	19.12.82
Parc des Expositions	Rouen	France	30.6.83
Palais des Sports **(2 shows)**	Paris	France	1.7.83
Tourhout Festival	Tourhout	Belgium	2.7.83
Werchter Festival	Werchter	Belgium	3.7.83
Stadio Communale	Ferrara	Italy	5.7.83
Stadio Communale	Prato	Italy	7.7.83
Selhurst Park Football Ground	London	England	9.7.83

(Other artists on the bill include The Thompson Twins)

Agora Ballroom	Hartford CT	USA	14.7.83
Lehigh University	Bethlehem PA	USA	15.7.83
Agora Ballroom	Lancaster PA	USA	16.7.83
Landsdowne Park	OttawaONT	Canada	17.7.83
CNE Bandshell	Toronto ONT	Canada	18.7.83
Palace Des Nations	Montreal ONT	Canada	20.7.83
Civic Center	Ottawa ONT	Canada	21.7.83
Arts Centre	Holmdel PA	USA	22.7.83
Mann Music Centre	Philadelphia PA	USA	23.7.83
Performing Arts Centre	Saratoga Springs NY	USA	24.7.83
E M Lowe Theatre	Worcester MD	USA	27.7.83
Tennis Centre	Forest Hills NY	USA	29.7.83
Meriweather Post Pavilion	Columbia MD	USA	30.7.83
Poplar Creek Centre	Pine Knob MI	USA	31.7.83
Poplar Creek Centre	Chicago IL	USA	2.8.83
Hampton Roads	Vancouver BC	Canada	3.8.83
Commonwealth Stadium	Edmonton BC	Canada	7.8.83 **Supporting David Bowie**
British Columbia Place	Vancouver BC	Canada	8.8.83 **Supporting David Bowie**
Paramount Theatre	Seattle WA	USA	10.8.83
Civic Theatre	Berkeley CA	USA	12-13.8.83
Golden Hall	San Diego CA	USA	15.8.83
Greek Theatre	Los Angeles CA	USA	16-17.8.83
Coliseum	St Austell	England	4.9.83
Gaumont Theatre	Southampton	England	5.9.83
Hammersmith Odeon	London	England	7-9.9.83
National Exhibition Centre	Birmingham	England	10.9.83
Apollo Theatre	Glasgow	Scotland	12.9.83
Playhouse	Edinburgh	Scotland	14.9.83
City Hall	Newcastle	England	15.9.83
Apollo Theatre	Manchester	England	17.9.83
Empire Theatre	Liverpool	England	18.9.83
Vorst Nationale	Brussels	Belgium	26.9.83
Concertgebouow	Den Haag (2 shows)	Holland	27.9.83
Ekeberghallen	Oslo	Norway	29.9.83
Johanneshovs Istadion	Stockholm	Sweden	30.9.83
Falkoner Theatrit	Copenhagen	Denmark	1.10.83
Congresshalle	Hamburg	Germany	2.10.83
Philipshalle	Dusseldorf	Germany	4.10.83
Alte Oper	Frankfurt	Germany	5.10.83
Zirkus Krone	Munich	Germany	6.10.83
Stadthalle	Vienna	Austria	8.10.83
Niedersachsenhalle	Hanover	Germany	10.10.83
Eisporthalle	Berlin	Germany	11.10.83
Boeblingen Sporthalle	Stuttgart	Germany	12.10.83
Halle 7	Lausanne	Switzerland	14.10.83
Maison des Sports	Clermont Ferrand	France	15.10.83
Palais des Sports	Toulouse	France	16.10.83
Patinoire	Bordeaux	France	17.10.83
Parc Exposition Chateau Blanc	Avignon	France	18.10.83
Alexpo	Grenoble	France	20.10.83
Chapiteau	Dijon	France	21.10.83
Chapiteau	Strasbourg	France	22.10.83
Foire de Lille Halle B	Lille	France	24.10.83
Espace Baktard	Paris	France	25.10.83
Palais de Beaujoire	Nantes	France	27.10.83

| La Petite Salle Penfield | Brest | France | 28.10.83 |

1982/83 sees Peter's fourth album released to a critically mixed reception. Its mixture of rhythms and over all darker texture make it a trying proposition but the shows in support of the album blow away any doubts as Peter and his band turn in superb performances which are impressive enough to persuade rock alumnus David Bowie to invite Peter on to the bill at several of his US/Canadian shows on the "Serious Moonlight" tour during the summer of 1983.

The opening show of this tour saw Peter premiering more material from his unheard four th album with a set which ran as follows…

San Jacinto/The Family & The Fishing Net/I Have The Touch/Lay Your Hands On Me/Shock The Monkey/I Go Swimmimg/ The Rhythm of The Heat/Shosholosa/Kiss Of Life/Biko.

His second night at Shepton Mallet saw a much more improvised set comprising mainly instrumental pieces…

A Ritual Mask/Dog One/Dog Two/Dog Three/Indian Melody/Across The River/Across The River (reprise)..

The tour proper featured a set drawing on all of Peter's albumns and the US 1982 set ran as follows….

Rhythm Of The Heat/I Have TheTouch/Not One Of Us/The Family & The Fishing Net/Shock The Monkey/Family Snapshot/ Intruder/I Go Swimming/Lay Your Hands On Me/Solsbury Hill/I Don't Remember/San Jacinto/On The Air/Kiss Of Life/Biko.

At a hanf dful of shows on this tour, another new song; "John Has A Headache" was included in the set. This elusive track remains Unreleased.

The European and second US tour in 1983 contained several changes to the previous set and included….

Across TheRiver/I Have TheTouch/Not One Of Us/TheFamily & The Fishing Net/Shock The Monkey/Family Snapshot/Intruder/ Games Without Frontiers/Lay Your Hands On Me/Solsbury Hill/I Don't Remember/San Jacinto/On The Air/Biko/HereComes The Flood.
Several other tracks were also played eitherin place of some of the above or in addition to them including; Humndrum; Rhythm Of The Heat; KissOf Life; Milgrams 37; and DIY as well as No Self Control and Wallflower. Peter's language experiments continued, with "Schock Den Affen" (Shock The Monkey); "Kontakt" (I Have The Touch); as well as old favourites such as "Spiele Ohne Grenzen" (Games Without Frontiers) an d "Jetzt KommtDie Flut" (HereComes The Flood) all of which were also sung in Italian or French versions in those territories.

Comspiracy Of Hope "Amnesty International Tour 1986

Cow Palace	San Francisco CA	USA	4.6.86
Sports Arena	Los Angeles CA	USA	6.6.86
Coliseum	Denver CO	USA	9.6.86
The Omni Centre	Atlanta GA	USA	11.6.86
Rosemont Horizon	Chicago IL	USA	13.6.86
Giants Stadium	East Rutherford NJ	USA	15.6.86
Clapham Common	London	England	28.6.86

("Freedom Beat" Concert filmed and subsequently released. Peter's contribution was a performance of Biko)

| United Nations Building | New York NY | USA | 15.9.86 |

1986 sees Peter embark on his most ambitious schedule yet including two separate tours. First of all is his active participation in the "Conspiracy of Hope" tour of the US in the company of Bryan Adams, The Police, U2 and various major acts in support of the Amnesty International charity including an impromptu gig outside the UN building in New York on 15th September 1986 the 38th anniversary of the signing of the "Declaration of Human Rights".

The set for this short tour was a greatest hitspackage comprising the following tracks: Red Rain/Games Without Fromtiers/In Your Eyes/Shock The Monkey/Sledgehammer/Biko.

Peter then embarks on his lengthiest tour to-date in support of his new album; "So" which sees his success reach new heights including an Unheard of THREE hit singles both in the UK and elsewhere. Peter is joined at the last night of his stint at London's Earls Court Arena By Kate Bush for an emotional rendition of Don't Give Up. The US set usually featured the following songs:

Floating Dogs(intro)/San Jacinto/Red Rain/Shock The Monkey/Family Snapshot/No Self Control/Mercy Street/This Is The Picture/ The Family & The Fishing Net/Don't Give Up/Big Time/Lay Your Hands On Me/Sledgehammer/HereComes The Flood/In Your Eyes/ Biko.
Ata couple of early shows on this leg of the tour; ThatVoice Again was played instead of The Family & TheFishing Net.

Peter's sets for the two "Japan Aid" gigs ran as follows:

2Oth December1986: HereComes The Flood/Red Rain/Shock The Monkey/San Jacinto/Sledgehammer/Biko/In Your Eyes.

21st December 1986: Red Rain/Shock The Monkey/No Self Control/Sledgehammer/In Your Eyes/Biko.

For the second tour in 1987; Peter's set included the following tracks:

Floating Dogs (intro)/Red Rain/Shock The Monkey/Family Snapshot/The Faily & TheFishing Net/F Games Without Frontiers/ No Self Control/Mercy Street/This Is The Picture/Big Time/Don't Give Up/Solsbury Hill/Lay Your Hands On Me/Sledgehammer/

HereComes The Flood/In Your Eyes/Biko.

Peter Gabriel Five "So" Tour 1987/87

Civic Center **(Warm-up gig)**	Poughkeepsie NY	USA	2.11.86
Rochester Community War Memorial	Rochester NY	USA	7.11.86
Civic Arena	Pittsburgh PA	USA	8.11.86
Civic Arena	Syracuse NY	USA	9.11.86
Civic Arena	New Haven CT	USA	11.1.186
Capital Theatre	Landover MD	USA	12.11.86
The Gardens	Cincinnatti IL	USA	14.11.86
Assembly Halls	Champaign IL	USA	15.11.86
Joe Louis Arena	Detroit MI	USA	17.11.86
Richfield Coliseum	Cleveland OH	USA	18.11.86
Municipal Auditorium	Buffalo NY	USA	19.11.86
Worcester Centrum Centre	Worcester MD	USA	21-22.11.86
Ottawa Civic Centre	Ottawa ONT	Canada	24.11.86
Forum	Montreal QC	Canada	25.11.86
Maple Leaf Gardens	Toronto ONT	Canada	26-27.11.86
The Spectrum	Philadelphia PA	USA	29-30.11.86
Madison Square Garden	New York NY	USA	1-2.12.86
Rosemont Horizon	Chicago IL	USA	4-5.12.86
The Summit	Houston TX	USA	7.12.86
Reunion Arena	Dallas TX	USA	8.12.86
Oakland Coliseum	San Francisco CA	USA	12-13.12.86
Forum	Los Angeles CA	USA	15-16.12.86
Jingu Stadium	Tokio	Japan	20-21.12.86
Palladium Theatre	London	England	28-29.3.87
Maison des Sports	Clermont Ferrand	France	1.6.87
Patinoire Meriadec	Bordeaux	France	2.6.87
Salle de Beaujoire	Nantes	France	3.6.87
Palais Omnisports de Bercy	Paris	France	5-7.6.87
Palatrussardi	Milan	Italy	10.6.87
Palasport	Bologna	Italy	12.6.87
Palasport	Rome	Italy	13.6.87
Olympiahalle	Munich	Germany	15.6.87
Schleyerhalle	Stuttgart	Germany	16.6.87
Frankenhalle	Nurnburg	Germany	17.6.87
Sporthalle	Cologne	Germany	19.6.87
Alster Dorfer Sporthalle	Hamburg	Germany	20.6.87
Stadthalle	Bremen	Germany	21-22.6.87
Scottish Exhibition & Conference Centre	Glasgow	Scotland	23.6.87
Earls Court Arena	London	England	25-28.6.87
National Exhibition Centre	Birmingham	England	29.6.-1.7.87
Tourhout Festival	Tourhout	Belgium	2.7.87
Werchter Festival	Werchter	Belgium	3.7.87
Landsdowne Park	OttawaONT	Canada	10.7.87
CNE Fairgrounds	Toronto ONT	Canada	11.7.87
Forum	Montreal QC	Canada	12-13.7.87
Great Woods Centre	Boston MA	USA	15-16.7.87
Meadowlands Stadium	East Rutherford NJ	USA	17-18.7.87
The Spectrum	Philadelphia PA	USA	20-21.7.87
Pine Knob Music Centre	Detroit OH	USA	22.7.87
Performing Arts Centre	Poplar Creek OH	USA	24.7.87
Marcus Amphitheatre	Milwaukee WI	USA	25.7.87
Blossom Music Centre	Cleveland OH	USA	27.7.87
Merriweather Postgate Pavilion	Columbia MD	USA	28.7.87
Hvidovre Stadium	Copenhagen	Denmark	28.8.87
Kalvoyre Festival	Isle of Calves	Norway	30.8.87
Ishallen	Helsinki	Finland	1.9.87
Johanneshovs Isstadion	Stockholm	Sweden	3.9.87
Scandinavium	Gothenburg	Sweden	6.9.87
Ahoy Sportpaleis	Rotterdam	Holland	8-9.9.87
Waldebuehne	Berlin	Germany	11.9.87
Ruhrstadion	Bochum	Germany	12.9.87
Offenbachstadion	Offenbach	Germany	13.9.87
MTK Stadium	Budapest	Hungary	15.9.87
Stadthalle	Vienna	Austria	16.9.87
Piazza Bra' Amphitheatre	Verona	Italy	18.9.87
Piazza Grande	Locarno	Switzerland	19.9.87
St Jakob Football Stadium	Basle	Switzerland	21.9.87
Patinoire de Malley	Lausanne	Switzerland	22.9.87
Chapiteau	Strasbourg	France	23.9.87
Palais des Sports	Lyon	France	24.9.87
Palais des Sports	Toulouse	France	26.9.87

Velodromo Anoeta	San Sebastian	Spain	27.9.87
Palacio de los Desportos	Barcelona	Spain	29-30.9.87
Lykabettus Hill Theatre	Athens	Greece	5-9.10.87

Special guest on the second leg of the 1987 tour are: Youssou N'Dour and Les SuperEtoiles deDakar.

Royal Albert Hall	London	England	5-6.6.88
Wembley Stadium	London	England	11.6.88
Coliseum	St Austell	England	28.8.88

The Wembley Stadium set ran as follows: Across The River/African Shuffle/Red Rain/Don't Give Up/No Self Control/Islamic Offbeat/Sledgehammer/In Your Eyes/Biko.

"Human Rights, Now!" Amnesty International Tour 1988.

Wembley Stadium	London	England	2.9.88
Palais Omnisports de Bercy	Paris	France	4-5.9.88
Nepstadion	Budapest	Hungary	6.9.88
Stadio Communale	Turin	Italy	8.9.88
Nou camp Stadium	Barcelona	Spain	10.9.88
Estadio Nacional	San Jose	Costa Rica	13.9.88
Maple Leaf gardens	TorontoONT	Canada	15.9.88
Stade Olympique	Montreal QC	Canada	17.9.88
John F Kennedy Stadium	Philadelphia PA	USA	19.9.88
Memorial coliseum	Los Angeles CA	USA	21.9.88
Oakland Coliseum	Oakland CA	USA	23.9.88
The Big Egg	Tokio	Japan	27.9.88
Jawaharlal Nehru Stadium	Delhi	India	30.9.88
Olympiako Stadium	Athens	Greece	3.10.88
New Stadium	Harare	Zimbabwe	7.10.88
Stade Houpouet Boigny	Abidjan	Ivory Coast	9.10.88
Estadio Palmeiras	Sao Paolo	Brazil	12.10.88
Estadio Mundialista	Mendoza	Argentina	14.10.88
Estadio Rio Plata	Buenos Aires	Argentina	15.10.88

1988 and Peter, already well known for his activities on behalf of human rights undertakes his most ambitious tour as part of the "Human Rights Now!" tour package along with Sting, Bruce Springsteen, Youssou N'Dour and TracyChapman for a jaunt around the world spreading Amnesty International's message on human rights culminating with a gig in Buenos Aires on the 40th anniversray of the signing of the "Declaration of Human Rights".

The usual set for these gigs was as follows: Of These Hope/Games WithoutFrontiers/Family Snapshot/Shock The Monkey/Don't Give Up/Sledgehmmer/Biko.

Glastonbury Fayre	Glastonbury	England	18.6.89
National Exhibition Centre	Birmingham	England	23.9.89
(Special guest appearance at Simple Minds gig, performing Biko)			
Wembley Stadium	London	England	16.4.90
("Mandela Day" Concert)			
Estadio Nacional	Santiago	Chile	13.10.90
("Abrazo de Esperanza" Concert)			
Stade De L'Amite	Dakar	Senegal	3.4.91
(Guest appearance at gig by Youssou N'Dour)			
Statenhal	Den Haag	Holland	9.5.91
("Simple Truth" concert)			
Real World Studios Marquee	Bath	England	18.8.91
Glastonbury Fayre	Glastonbury	England	24.6.92
Rivermead Leisure Centre	Bath	England	18.7.92
Royal Victoria Park	Bath	England	16.8.92
Royal Victoria Park	Bath	England	17.8.92
Royal Victoria Park	Bath	England	23.8.92

"Secret World" Tour 1993/94.

Botanic Park **(Womadelaide)**	Adelaide	Australia	19-20.2.93
Grand Slam Club **(Rehearsals)**	Los Angeles CA	USA	6-7.3.93
Academy of Music **(Warm-up gig)**	New York NY	USA	13.3.93

The Globe	Stockholm	Sweden	13.4.93
Spektrum	Oslo	Norway	14.4.93
Sporthalle	Hamburg	Germany	15.4.93
Deutschlandhalle	Berlin	Germany	17.4.93
Hallenstadion	Zurich	Switzerland	19.4.93
Festhalle	Frankfurt	Germany	20.4.93
Schleyerhalle	Stuttgart	Germany	21.4.93
Galaxie	Amneville	France	23.4.93
Le Zenith	Paris	France	24-25.4.93
Ahoy Sportpaleis	Rotterdam	Holland	27-28.4.93
Flanders Expo	Ghent	Belgium	30.4.93
Stade Couvert Reg	Lieven	Belgium	1.5.93
Halle Expo	Caen	France	2.5.93
Patinoire Meriadec	Bordeaux	France	4.5.93
WOMAD Festival	Madrid	Spain	6.5.93
WOMAD Festival	Caceres	Spain	7.5.93
Velodromo	Valencia	Spain	9.5.93
Palau St Jordi	Barcelona	Spain	10.5.93
Palais des Sports	Toulouse	France	11.5.93
Les Arenes	Nimes	France	13.5.93
Halle Tony Garnier	Lyon	France	14.5.93
Patinoire de Malley	Lausanne	Switzerland	15.5.93
Forum	Mailand	Italy	17.5.93
Palaghiaccio Marino	Rome	Italy	18.5.93
Olympiahalle	Munjch	Germany	20.5.93
Frankenhalle	Nurnburg	Germany	21.5.93
Westfalenhalle	Dortmund	Germany	22.5.93
Arena	Sheffield	England	24.5.93
National Exhibition Centre	Birmingham	England	25.5.93
Scottish Exhibtion & Conference Centre Glasgow		Scotland	26.5.93
The Point Theatre	Dublin	Eire	27.5.93
Festival Showground "Peace Together Festival" Belfast		Northern Ireland	29.5.93 *
(*) Festival cancelled.			
Earls Court Arena	London	England	31.5.93
Earls Court Arena	London	England	1.6.93
Rochester Community War Memorial Rochester NY		USA	18.6.93
Worcester Centrum Centre	Worcester MD	USA	19-20.6.93
Capital Centre	Landover MD	USA	22.6.93
Giants Stadium	East Rutherford NJ	USA	23.6.93
Madison Square Garden	New York NY	USA	24.6.93
Skydome	TorontoONT	Canada	26.6.93
Colisee de Quebec	Quebec City QC	Canada	28.6.93
Forum	Montreal QC	Canada	29-30.6.93
Palace of Auburn Hills	Detroit IL	USA	2.7.93
Richfield Coliseum	Cleveland OH	USA	3.7.93
The Spectrum	Philadephia PA	USA	6-8.7.93
Rosemont Horizon	Chicago IL	USA	10-11.7.93
Saddledome	Calgary BC	Canada	14.7.93
PNE Coliseum	Vancouver BC	Canada	16.7.93
Tacoma Dome	Seattle WA	USA	17.7.93
Coliseum	Oakland CA	USA	19-20.7.93
Great Western Forum	Los Angeles CA	USA	22.7.93
Sports Arena	San Diego CA	USA^	23.7.93
America West Arena	Phoenix AZ	USA^	24.7.93
McNichols Sports Arena	Denver CO	USA^	27.7.93
Reunion Arena	Dallas TX	USA^	29.7.93
Summit Arena	Houston TX	USA^	30.7.93
The Omni Centre	Atlanta GA	USA^	1.8.93
Orlando Arena	Orlando FL	USA^	3.8.93
Miami Arena	Miami FLA	USA^	4.8.93
Royal Victoria Park (WOMAD)	Bath	England	8.8.93
Cesmes (WOMAD)	Cesmes	Turkey	28.8.93
Estadio Alvalade (WOMAD)	Lisbon	Portugal^	29.8.93
Coliseum (WOMAD)	St Austell	England	30.8.93
Maple Leaf Gardens	Toronto ONT	Canada^	4.9.93
Forum (WOMAD)	Montreal QC	Canada^	5.9.93
SaratogaPerforming Arts Centre (WOMAD) Saratoga Springs NY		USA^	6.9.93
Starlake Amphitheatre (WOMAD)	Pittsburgh PA	USA^	8.9.93
Buckeye Lake (WOMAD)	Columbus OH	USA^	10.9.93
World Music Theatre (WOMAD)	Chicago IL	USA^	11.9.93
Marcus Amphitheatre (WOMAD)	Milwaukee WC	USA^	12.9.93
Deer Creek (WOMAD)	Indianapolis IN	USA^	13.9.93
Fiddler's Green (WOMAD)	Denver CO	USA^	16.9.93
Velodrome (WOMAD)	Los Angeles CA	USA^	18.9.93
Golden Gate Park (WOMAD)	San Francisco CA	USA^	19.9.93
ARCO Arena	Sacramento CA	USA^	21.9.93
Oakland Coliseum	Oakland CA	USA^	22.9.93
Sports Palace	Mexico City	Mexico	24-26.9.93

Pista Atletica	Santiago	Chile	29.9.93
Chateau Carreras Stadium	Cordoba	Argentina	1.10.93
Velez Sarfeld	Buenos Aires	Argentina	2.10.93
Rosario stadium	Rosarui	Argentina	4.10.93
Ibirapuera	Sao Paolo	Brazil	6.10.93
Imperator	Rio de Janeiro	Argentina	7.10.93
Poliedro Parking Lot	Caracas	Venezuela	9.10.93
Maimarktgelande	Mannheim	Germany^	4.11.93
Deutschlandhalle	Berlin	Germany^	6.11.93
Congresshalle	Hamburg	Germany^	7-8.11.93
Philipshalle	Dortmund	Germany^	10.11.93
Hallenstadion	Zurich	Switzerland^	12.11.93
Le Summum	Grenoble	France^	13.11.93
Zenithe Omega	Toulon	France^	14.11.93
Palasport	Modena	Italy^ <<	16-17.11.93
Palaghiaccio Marino	Rome	Italy^	19.11.93
Palasport	Florence	Italy^	20.11.93
Forum Assago	Milan	Italy^	22.11.93
Palais Omnisports de Bercy	Paris	France^	24.11.93
Le Zenith	Paris	France^	25.11.93
Indira Gandhi Stadium	Delhi	India	11.2.94
Palace Grounds	Bangalore	India	14.2.94
Brabourne Stadium	Bombay	India	17.2.94
Entertainment Centre	Perth	Australia	21.2.94
Entertainment Centre	Adelaide	Australia	23.2.94
National Tennis Centre	Melbourne	Australia	24-25.2.94
Entertainment Centre	Brisbane	Australia	27.2.94
Entertainment Centre	Sydney	Australia	1-2.3.94
Supertop	Auckland	New Zealand	4.3.94
Budokan Hall	Tokio	Japan	7-8.3.94
Castle Hall	Osaka	Japan	10.3.94
Stadium	Hong Kong	Hong Kong	14.3.94
Messehalle	Nurnburg	Germany	19.5.94
"Rock in Reim" Festival	Munich	Germany	21.5.94
"Rock am Ring" Festival	Nuremburg	Germany	22.5.94
Nelson's Beach (WOMAD)	Taba	Egypt	18.6.94
Hayarkon Park (WOMAD)	Tel Aviv	Israel	19.6.94
Le Zenith	Paris	France	21.6.94
"Rock Productions"	Bratislava	Czech Republic	23.6.94
"Schulschuss" Festival	Wels	Austria	24.6.94
"Glastonbury Fayre"	Glastonbury	England	26.6.94
"Kalvoyre Festival"	Isle of Calves	Norway	29.6.94
"Roskilde Festival"	Roskilde	Denmark	1.7.94
Tourhout Festival	Tourhout	Belgium	2.7.94
Werchter Festival	Werchter	Belgium	3.7.94
North Sea Jazz Festival	Den Haag	Holland	6.7.94
"Out in the Green" Festival	Winterthur	Switzerland	8.7.94
Forum	Mailand	Switzerland	9.7.94
Parco Acquatico	Milan	Italy	10.7.94
Lakewood Amphitheatre	Atlanta GA	USA	12.7.94
Polaris Amphitheatre	Columbus OH	USA	14.7.94
Merriweather Postgate Pavilion (WOMAD) Columbia MD		USA	15.7.94
Jones Beach (WOMAD)	New York NY	USA	16.7.94
Saratoga Performing Arts Centre	Saratoga Springs NY	USA	17.7.94
Great Woods Amphitheatre	Boston MA	USA	19.7.94
Stabler Arena	Allentown NY	USA	10.8.94
Beacon Theatre	New York NY	USA	11.8.94
Tower Theatre	Upper Darby PA	USA	12.8.94
Saugerties "Woodstock 25th Anniversary" New York State NY		USA	14.8.94

This massive tour saw several changesto the set and a typical set ran as follows…..

Come Talk To Me/Steam/Games Without Frontiers/Across the River/Zaar/Shaking The Tree/Blood Of Eden/San Jacinto/
Love Town/Kiss That Frog/Washing Of The Water/Solsbury Hill/Digging In TheDirt/Sledgehammer/SecretWorld/In Your Eyes/
Biko/HereComes The Flood.

Palais Omnisports de Bercy	Paris	France	10.12.98

Amnesty '98 set: Red Rain/Signal To Noise/In Your Eyes.

WOMADFestival Marymoor Park	Seattle BC	Canada	29.7.01

Seattle 01 set: HereComes the Flood/Red Rain/Digging In The Dirt/Family Snapshot/Come Talk To Me/Mercy Street/Solsbury
Hill/Signal To Noise/In Your Eyes/FatherTo Son/When You're Falling (With Afro Celts)

Munchner Konigsplatz	Munich	Germany (*)	31.8.02
Piazza Centrale	Aezachena	Italy (*)	7.9.02
Alcataz	Milan	Italy (*)	16.9.02

Alcataz	Milan	Italy (*)	18.9.02
Theatre De la Mutualite	Paris	France (*)	21.09.02

(*) These shows were promotional warm-up shows for which varying sets were played as follows…

Munich: Darkness/Red Rain/Growing Up/Solsbury Hill/Mercy Street/The Barry Williams Show/More Than This/Digging In The Dirt/ Family Snapshot/Jetzt Kommt Die Flut.

Arzachena: Solsbury Hill/Red Rain/Growing Up/No Way Out/Mercy Strete/The Barry Williams Show/Downside Up/More Than This/ Digging In The Dirt/Sledgehammer/In Your Eyes.

Milan (16th) : Darkness/Red Rain/Growing Up/No Way Out/Mercy Street/My Head Sounds Like That/The Barry Williams Show/More Than This/Digging In The Dirt/Animal Nation/Sledgehammer/In Your Eyes/FatherTo Son.

Milan (18th) : Darkenss/Red Rain/Growing Up/No Way Out/Mercy Street/Downside Up/The Barry Williams Show/Solsbury Hill/More Than This/Digging In The Dirt/The TowerThat Ate People/Sledgehammer/In Your Eyes/Here Comes The Flood.

Paris: Darkness/Red Rain/Growing Up/Downside Up/No Way Out/Mercy Street/My Head Sounds Like That/The Barry Williams Show/More Than This/Diggir The Dirt/Animal Nation/Sledgehammer/In Your Eyes/FatherTo Son.

"Growing Up" US Tour 2002.

Supper Club	New York NY	USA	24.9.02
Azteca Stadium	Mexico City	Mexico	3-4.11.02
Philips Arena	Atlanta GA	USA	5.11.02
(This show was cancelled)			
Quebec City Arena	Quebec City QC	Canada	8.11.02 (Rehearsals)
United Center	Chicago IL	USA	12.11.02
United Center	Chicago IL	USA	14.11.02
TargetCenter	Minneapolis MN	USA	15.11.02
Continental Airlines Arena	EastRutherford NJ	USA	17.11.02
First Union Center	Philadelphia PA	USA	18.11.02
Gund Arena	Cleveland OH	USA	19.11.02
Madison Square Garden	New York NY	USA	21.11.02
MCI Center	Washington DC	USA	24.11.02
Fleet Center	Boston MA	USA	25.11.02
Mohegan Sun Casino	Uncasville CT	USA	26.11.02
Bell Centre	Montreal QC	Canada	28.11.02
Bell Centre	Montreal QC	Canada	29.11.02
Quebec City Arena	Quebec QC	Canada	30.11.02
Air Canada Centre	Toronto ON	Canada	2.12.02
Palace of Auburn Hills	Auburn Hills MI	USA	3.12.02
Pepsi Center	DenverCO	USA	5.12.02
San Diego Sports Arena	San Diego CA	USA	8.12.02
Convention Center	Anaheim CA	USA	10.12.02
Staples Center	Los Angeles CA	USA	11.12.02
America West Arena	Phoenix AZ	USA	12.12.02
Oakland Arena	Oakland CA	USA	14.12.02
HP Pavilion At San Jose	San Jose CA	USA	15.12.02
Marymoor Park	Seattle BC	USA	17.12.02

The years following the end of the 1993/94 Secret World tour had been relatively quiet ones performance wise for Peter, but now with the release of his first priper solo album in ten years; the recently released UP, things have picked up for Peter and his North American tour in support of this album , which preceded by a few European warm-up shows, has just begun featuring a set list mainly drawn from his ast couple of albums which runs as follows… Darkness/R Rain/SecretWorld/My Head Sounds Like ThatAnimal Nation/Sky Blue/More Than This/Mercy Strete/Growing Up/Downside Up/No Way Out/Solsbury Hill/Th TowerThatAte People/The BarryWilliams Show/Signal To Noise/Sledgehammer/Digging In The Dirt/HereComes The Flood

Growing Up European/US Tour 2003.

The Globe	Stockholm	Sweden	24.4.03
Colorline Arena	Hamburg	Germany	26.4.03
Velodrom	Berlin	Germany	27.4.03
Arena	Leipzig	Germany	29.4.03
Konig Pilsner Arena	Oberhausen	Germany	30.4.03
Ahoy Hal	Rotterdam	Holland	2.5.03
Vorst Nationale	Brussels	Belgium	3.5.03
Olympiahalle	Munich	Germany	5.5.03
Palamalaguli	Bologna	Italy	6.5.03
Filaforum	Milan	Italy	8-9.5.03
Palarassini	Ancona	Italy	11.5.03
Palasport	Florence	Italy	12.5.03
Palais Omnisports De Bercy	Paris	France	14.5.03

Hallenstadion	Zurich	Switzerland	15.5.03
Manchester Evening News Arena	Manchester	England	18.5.03
National Exhibition Centre	Birmingham	England	19.5.03
Wembley Arena	London	England	21-22.5.03
Schleyerhalle	Stuttgart	Germany	24.5.03
Arena	Cologne	Germany	25.5.03
Halle Tony Garnier	Lyon	France	27.5.03
Palais Nikaia	Nice	France	28.5.03
Stadion Lech	Posnan	Poland	30.5.03
Palau St Jordi	Barcelona	Spain	1.6.03
Shoreline Amphitheater	San Francisco CA	USA	7.6.03
Verizon Amphitheater	Los Angeles CA	USA	8.6.03
Sminall	Dallas TX	USA	11.6.03
Woodlands	Houston TX	USA	12.6.03
Coral Sky Amphitheater	West Palm Beach FL	USA	14.6.03
Chastain Park	Atlanta GA	USA	16.6.03
Tweeter Center	Boston Ma	USA	18.6.03
PNC Bank Arts Pavilion	Holmdel	USA	20.6.03
TweeterCenter	Philadelphia PA	USA	21.6.03
DC Nissan Pavilion	Washington DC	USA	22.6.03
JonesBeach	Wantaugh	USA	24.6.03
Marcus Amphitheater	Milwaukee WI	USA	26.6.03
TweeterCenter	Chicago IL	USA	28.6.03
DTE Music Pavilion	Detroit IL	USA	29.6.03
Germain Amphitheater	Columbus OH	USA	1.7.03
Verizon Wireless MusicCenter	Noblesville IN	USA	2.7.03
Molson Amphiteatre	Toronto ONT	Canada	4.7.03
Labatt Center	London ONT	Canada	5.7.03
Bell Center	Montreal QE	Canada	6.7.03
?	Merthyr Tydfil	Wales	22.11.03
Conference Centre	Brighton	England	25.11.03
Greenpoint Stadium	Cape Town	South Africa	29.11.03

As usual, Peter continued to mix and match his sets with no two nights' performances being exactly the same. Here are a couple of examples of the set list from the 2003 tour...

Poznan 30th May 2003: Here Comes The Flood/Darkness/Red Rain/Secret World/Sky Blue/Downside-Up/The Barry Williams Show/ More Than This/Mercy Street/Digging In The Dirt/Growing Up/Animal Nation/Solsbury Hill/Sledgehammer/SignalTo Noise/in Your Eyes/ Biko.

Camden New Jersey 21st June 2003: Red Rain/More Than This/Secret World/Games Without Frontiers/Mercy Street/Darkness/Digging In The Dirt/Don't Give Up/No Way Out/The Tower That Ate People/Growing Up/Shock The Monkey/Solsbury Hill/Sledgehammer/Signal To Noise/In Your Eyes/Come Talk To Me/Father To Son.

Still Growing Up European Tour 2004.

?	Ischgl	Austria	1.5.04
Westfalemnhalle	Dortmund	Germany	5.5.04
Ahoy Hal	Rotterdam	Holland	6.5.04
Velodrom	Berlin	Germany	8.5.04
Festhalle	Frankfurt	Germany	9.5.04
Filaforum	Milan	Italy	11.5.04
Arena	Pesaro	Italy	12.5.04
Stadthalle	Vienna	Austria	14.5.04
Arena	Budapest	Hungary	15.5.04
Sportovinhala	Prague	Czech Republic	17.5.04
Arena	Nurnburg	Germany	18.5.04
Preussag Arena	Hannover	Germany	20.5.04
Colorline Arena	Hamburg	Germany	21.5.04
Galaxie	Amneville	France	23.5.04
Hallenstadion	Zurich	Switzerland	24.5.04
Vorst Nationale	Brussels	Belgium	26.5.04
Palais Omnisports De Bercy	Paris	France	27.5.04
Zenith	Lille	France	28.5.04
Bela Vista Park	Lisbon	Portugal	29.5.04

(This was broadcast live by Portuguese TV as part of the annual the "Rock In Rio" Festival which last year was hosted in Portugal instead of Brazil just to confuse people!)

National Indoor Arena	Birmingham	England	1.6.04
Hallam FM Arena	Sheffield	England	2.6.04
Arena	Newcastle	England	4.6.04
Scottish Exhibition And Conference Centre	Glasgow	Scotland	5.6.04
Wembley Arena	London	England	7-8.6.04

Seebuhne	Bregenz	Austria	12.6.04
Anfiteatro	Cagliari	Italy	14.6.04
Piazza del Mare Fiera	Genoa	Italy	16.6.04
Rockwave Festival	Athens	Greece	18.6.04
One Love Festival	Istanbul	Turkey	20.6.04
Palace Of Culture	Sofia	Bulgaria	21.6.04
Sala Palatului	Bucharest	Romania	22.6.04
Kings Dock Arena	Liverpool	England	30.6.04
Festival Nuisilac	Aix Les Bains	France	2.7.04
Teatro Antico	Taormina	Italy	4.7.04
Area Magna Grecia	Catanzaro	Italy	5.7.04
Neapolis Festival Arena Flegrea	Naples	Italy	7.7.04
IppodromoLe Campannelle	Rome	Italy	8.7.04
Moon And Stars Festival Piazza Grande	Locarno	Switzerland	9.7.04
	Carminha	Portugal	16.7.04
?	Santiago de Compostella	Spain	17.7.04
Piazza Napoleone	lucca	Italy	19.7.04
Paleo Festival	Nyon	Switzerland	21.7.04
Jazz Festival	Nice	France	22.7.04
Amphitheatre	Nimes	France	23.7.04
Stifplatz	Kaiserslautern	Germany	25..7.04

Special Guest at the UK shows was Real World artist: Sizer Barker.

Once again, expect the unexpected was the order of the day with Peter altering the set at the majority of these gigs, here are a couple of examples…

Ischgl 1 st May 2004: Red Rain/Burn You Up, Burn You Down/Secret World/Games Without Frontiers/|Downside-Up/The Tower That Ate People/More Than This/Mercy Street/Digging In The Dirt/Growing Up/Solsbury Hill/Sledgehammer/Signal ToNoise/In Your Eyes/Jetzt Kommt Die Flut.

Filaforum Milan 11 th May 2004: Here Comes The Flood/Darkness/Red Rain/SecretWorld/White Ashes/Games Without Frontiers/Burn You Up, Burn you Down/Downside-Up/The TowerThat Ate People/More Than This/San Jacinto/Digging In The Dirt/Growing Up/Solsbury Hill/ Sledgehammer/Signal T Noise/In Your Eyes/Come Talk To Me/Father To Son.

This gig guide has been compiled by Alan Hewitt with the help of Mary Lane at "Real World" Mario Giametti and Vernon Parker whose help has been of inestimable value.

Steve Hackett Gig Guide 1978-

| VENUE | CITY | COUNTRY | DATE |

"Please Don't Touch" Tour 1978.

Chateau Neuf	Oslo	Norway	4.10.78
Gota Lejon	Stockholm	Sweden	5.10.78
Konserthuset	Gothenburg	Sweden	14.10.78
Olympia Theatre	Paris	France	16.1.078
Palais Des Fleurs	Aix-Les-Bains	France	17.10.78
BeatClub	Bremen	Germany	18.10.78

(This gig was filmed for television and subsequently broadcast both in Germany and the UK and recently released as a DVD by ARD)

Congresshal	Den Haag	Holland	19.10.78
University	Cardiff	Wales	23.10.78
Apollo Theatre	Manchester	England	24.10.78
Apollo Theatre	Glasgow	Scotland	26.10.78
Friars (Maxwell Hall)	Aylesbury	England	28.10.78
Odeon Theatre	Birmingham	England	29.10.78
Hammersmith Odeon	London	England	30.10.78

1978 and Steve's first solo outing which follows on the back of his second highly successful solo album; "Please don't touch". This tour finally gives Steve the opportunity to prove exactly what Genesis were missing from his contribution to the band's sound and indeed 1978 was a rich year for Genesis fans with tours by Genesis, Steve AND Peter Gabriel. Steve's live set for this tour incorporated material from the first two solo albums as well as tryng out some tracks from the as yet unrecorded third album; and a set usuallly ran as follows… Please Don't Touch/Racing In A/Carry On Up The Vicarage/Ace Of Wamds/Hands Of The Priestess(pt1)/Icarus Ascending/Narnia/ Guitar solo-Horizons/Kim/A Tower Struck Down/Spectral Mornings/StarOf Sirius/Shadow Of The Hierophant/Clocks- The Angel Of Mons/I Know What I Like.

"Spectral Mornings" Summer Tour 1979.

Concerthaus	Gothenburg	Sweden	25.5.79
Chateau Neuf	Oslo	Sweden	29.5.79
Liederhalle	Stuttgart	Germany	2.6.79
Hosschulekuenste	Berlin	Germany	3.6.79
Alte Oper	Frankfurt	Germany	4.6.79
Zirkus Krone	Munich	Germany	5.6.79
Hugenottenhalle	Neu Isenburg	Germany	6.6.79
Sartory Saal	Cologne	Germany	8.6.79
Audimax	Hamburg	Germany	9.6.79
Ancienne Belgique	Brussels	Belgium	10.6.79
Pavilion de Paris	Paris	France	11.6.79
Theatre Sebastapol	Lille	France	12.6.79
La Bourse du Travail	Lyon	France	14.6.79
Theatre de Verdune	Nice	France	15.6.79
Musik Centrum	Utrecht	Holland	17.6.79
Odeon Theatre	Edinburgh	Scotland	21.6.79
City Hall	Sheffield	England	22.6.79
University	Leicester	England	23.6.79
Empire Theatre	Liverpool	England	24.6.79
The Dome	Brighton	England	25.6.79
Pavilion	Hemel Hempstead	England	27.6.79
Civic Hall	Wolverhampton	England	28.6.79
Gaumont Theatre	Southampton	England	29.6.79
Hammersmith Odeon	London	England	30.6.79
New Theatre	Oxford	England	1.7.79
Reading Festival	Reading	England	26.8.79

"Spectral Mornings" Autumn Tour 1979

Capitol Theatre	Aberdeen	Scotland	22.10.79
Apollo Theatre	Glasgow	Scotland	23.10.79
Apollo Theatre	Manchester	England	24.10.79
Royal Court Theatre	Liverpool	England	25.10.79
Victoria Halls	Hanley	England	26.10.79
City Hall	Newcastle	England	27.10.79
Town Hall	Middlesborough	England	28.10.79
Maxwell Hall	**Aylesbury**	**England**	**28.10.79**
(This date and venue appeared in advertising for the tour, the Middlesbrough gig appears in the 1979 Tour itinerary)			
St George's Hall	Bradford	England	29.10.79
Odeon Theatre	Birmingham	England	31.10.79
Colston Hall	Bristol	England	1.11.79
Odeon Theatre	Chelmsford	England	3.11.79
Gaumont Theatre	Ipswich	England	4.11.79
Assembly Rooms	Derby	England	5.11.79
West Runton Pavilion	Cromer	England	6.11.79
Polytechnic	Plymouth	England	8.11.79
Brunel University	Uxbridge	England	9.11.79
Theatre Royal Drury Lane	London	England	11.11.79
Arts Centre	Poole	England	12.11.79

1979 and Steve releases the album by which all his future releases will be measured; "Spectral Mornings" a glorious album accompanied by a highly successful tour , two tours in fact, of the UK and Europe with Steve continuing to consolidate his growing success including a stunning performance at the Reading Rock Festival. Performing two tours during the year; Steve also varied the set for both of them with a set for the summer tour running as follows….

Please Don't Touch/Tigermoth/Everyday/Narnai/The Red Flower Of Taichi Blooms Everywhere/Ace Of Wands/Carry On Up The Vicarage/ Acoustic Set/Horizons/The Optigan/A Tower Struck Down/Spectral Mornings/StarOf Sirius/Shadow Of The Hierophant/Racing In A/Ace Of Wands/I Know What I Like.

The set for the second tour usually ran as follows; including even mor e previously unreleased material…..

Please Don't Touch/Tigermoth/Everyday/Ace of Wands/The Virgin & The Gypsy/The Steppes/Narnai/Sentimental Institution/The Red Flower Of Tai Chi Blooms Everywhere/Star Of Sirius/Spectral Mornings/A Tower Struck Down/Clocks/Acoustic set/Horizons/The Ballad Of The Decomposing Man/Hercules Unchained/Racing In A.

"Defector Tour" 1980

Assembly Rooms	Derby	England	11.6.80
Playhouse	Edinburgh	Scotland	13.6.80
Apollo Theatre	Glasgow	Scotland	14.6.80
City Hall	Newcastle	England	15.6.80
Apollo Theatre	Manchester	England	16.6.80
City Hall	Sheffield	England	17.6.80
City Hall	Hull	England	19.6.80
Guildhall	Preston	England	20.6.80

Odeon Theatre	Birmingham	England	21.6.80
New Theatre	Oxford	England	22.6.80
De Montfort Hall	Leicester	England	23.6.80
Davenport Arts Centre	Coventry	England	24.6.80
Civic Centre	Guildford	England	26.6.80
Gaumont Theatre	Southampton	England	27.6.80
Arts Centre	Poole	England	28.6.80
Top Rank	Cardiff	Wales	29.6.80
Royal Court Theatre	Liverpool	England	1.7.80
Odeon Theatre	Hammersmith	England	4-5.7.80
Odeon Theatre	Canterbury	England	6-7.7.80
Grand Casino	Montreux	Switzerland	13.7.80

(Steve's performance was filmed for broadcast by Japanese television and has recently surfaced again after an absence of almost twenty one years!)

Palais Montcalm	Quebec QC	Canada	19.9.80
O'Keefe Centre	Toronto ONT	Canada	21.9.80
Club Montreal Theatre	Montreal QC	Canada	22.9.80
Paradise Theatre	Boston MA	USA	24.9.80
Toad's Place	Newhaven CT	USA	25.9.80
Uncle Sam's	Syracuse NY	USA	26.9.80
Auditorium Theatre	Rochester NY	USA	27.9.80
Uncle Sam's	Buffalo NY	USA	28.9.80
Bottom Line Club	New York NY	USA	29-30.9.80
Hillwood Hall	Long Island LI	USA	1.10.80
Bergen Community College	New Jersey NJ	USA	3.10.80
Tower Theatre	Philadelphia PA	USA	4.10.80
Bayou Club	Washington DC	USA	5.10.80
The Agora	Cleveland OH	USA	7.10.80
Harpo's	Detroit OH	USA	9.10.80
The Parkwest	Chicago IL	USA	10.10.80
Uptown Theatre	Milwaukee WI	USA	11.10.80
Dooley's	Phoenix AZ	USA	14.10.80
The Roxy	Hollywood CA	USA	15-16.10.80
Old Waldorf Theatre	San Francisco CA	USA	17-18.10.80
Civic	San Jose CA	USA	19.10.80
Paramount Theatre	Seattle WA	USA	22.10.80
Commodore	Vancouver	USA	23.10.80
Chateau Neuf	Oslo	Norway	11.11.80
Gota Lejon	Stockholm	Denmark	12.11.80
Rijnhal	Arnhem	Holland	14.11.80
Musik Centrum	Utrecht	Holland	15.11.80
Palasport	Turin	Italy	24.11.80
Palasport	Bologna	Italy	25.11.80
Palasport	Rome	Italy	26.11.80
Palasport	Turin	Italy	27.11.80
Palasport Cavergnaghi	Mestre-Venice	Italy	28.11.80
Palasport Pianella	Cantu	Italy	29.11.80
Palasport E I B	Brescia	Italy	30.11.80
Palasport	Genoa	Italy	1.12.80

1980 sees Steve continuing to attract audiences to his own brand of rock with a new album "Defector". The year also sees him put in an appearance at the prestigious Montreux Jazz festival and also perform his first solo shows in the USA. The set for the 1980 tour usually comprised these tracks....
Slogans/Everyday/TheRed Flower Of Tai Chi Blooms Everywhere/Tigermoth/Kim/Time To GetOut/The Steppes/Acoustic set/Horizons/ Sentimental Institution/Jacuzzi/Spectral Mornings/A TowerStruck Down/Clocks/Please Don't Touch/The Show/It's Now or Never/Hercules Unchained.

"Cured Tour" 1981

Leas Cliff Pavilion	Folkestone	England	22.8.81
Arts Centre	Poole	England	23.8.81
Coliseum	St Austell	England	24.8.81
Gaumont Theatre	Ipswich	England	26.8.81
Rock City	Nottingham	England	27.8.81
Reading Festival	Reading	England	28.8.81
Carre Theatre	Amsterdam	Holland	31.8.81
Vorst Nationale	Brussels	Belgium	1.9.81
Hallenstadion	Zurich	Switzerland	3.9.81
Palasport	Milan	Italy	5.9.81
Festival	San Remo	Italy	6.9.81
Palasport	Trento	Italy	7.9.81
Rolling Stone Theatre	Milan	Italy	8-9.9.81
Palasport	Reggio Emilia	Italy	10.9.81
Palasport	Viareggio	Italy	11.9.81
Castel Sant' Angelo	Vatican City	Italy	13.9.81
Parco Virgiliano	Naples	Italy	14.9.81
Zirkus Krone	Munich	Germany	17.9.81

Festhalle	Mannheim	Germany	18.9.81
SalleD'Expositions	Colmar	France	19.9.81
Congreshalle	Hamburg	Germany	20.9.81
Ostseehalle	Kiel	Germany	21.9.81
Waldebuehne	Berlin	Germany	22.9.81
Grugahalle	Essen	Germany	23.9.81
Festhalle	Frankfurt	Germany	24.9.81
Concerthal	Den Haag	Holland	25.9.81
Casino (2 shows)	Hertogenbosch	Holland	26.9.81
L' Hippodrome Pantin	Paris	France	27.9.81
Guildhall	Portsmouth	England	29.9.81
Colston Hall	Bristol	England	30.9.81
Leisure Centre	Gloucester	England	1.10.81
Victoria Hall	Hanley	England	2.10.81
Empire Theatre	Liverpool	England	3.10.81
City Hall	Newcastle	England	4.10.81
Playhouse	Edinburgh	Scotland	5.10.81
City Hall	Sheffield	England	6.10.81
Odeon Theatre	Birmingham	England	7.10.81
Apollo Theatre	Manchester	England	8.10.81
University Great Hall	York	England	9.10.81
Hammersmith Odeon	London	England	11-12.10.81
The Agora	Cleveland OH	USA	26.10.81
Park West	Chicago IL	USA	27.10.81
Toad's Place	Newhaven CT	USA	29.10.81
Triangle Theatre	Rochester NY	USA	30.10.81

(A complete concert film of this gig still exists although it has never been broadcast outside of the USA)

Uncle Sam's	Buffalo NY	USA	1.11.81
Massey Hall	Toronto ON	Canada	2.11.81
Pavillion de la Jeunesse	Quebec QC	Canada	4.11.81
Le Club	Montreal QC	Canada	5-7.11.81
State University New York	Oswego NY	USA	8.11.81
Savoy Theatre	New York City NY	USA	10-11.11.81
Paradise Theatre	Boston MA	USA	12.11.81
Tower Theatre	Philadelphia PA	USA	13.11.81
North Stage Theatre	Glencove LI	USA	15.11.81
The Bayou	Washington DC	USA	16.11.81
The Agora	Atlana GA	USA	18.11.81
McAllister Auditorium	New Orleans MO	USA	19.11.81
Agora	Dallas TX	USA	22.11.81
Dooley's	Phoenix AZ	USA	24.11.81
Bachanale	San Diego CA	USA	25.11.81
The Roxy	Hollywood CA	USA	26-28.11.81
Perkins Palace	Pasadena WI	USA	29.11.81
The Old Waldorf	San Francisco CA	USA	2-3.12.81
Civic	San Jose CA	USA	4.12.81
University of Washington	Seattle WA	USA	6.12.81
Commodore	Vancouver BC	Canada	7.12.81
Royal Theatre	Victoria BC	Canada	8.12.81

1981 saw Steve out again with another album ; "Cured" which saw his first attempts at singing vocals himself. Generally well received, the tour saw Steve continue to broaden the spectrum of his audiences by playing the first gigs by any member of Genesis behind the Iron Curtain in Yugoslavia as well as further dates in the USA. The 1981 set usually ran as follows….
The Air-Conditioned Nightmare/Jacuzzi/FunnyFeeling/Ace Of Wands/Picture Postcard/The Steppes/Everyday/The Red Flower Of Tai Chi Blooms Everywhere/Tigermoth/Horizons/Kim/Overnight Sleeper/Hope I Don't Wake/Slogans/A TowerStruck Down/Spectral Mornings/ Please Don't Touch/TheShow/Clocks.

Elixii Festival	Brest	France	15.7.82
Venue Club	London	England	18.12.82

1982 and 1983 saw Steve hard at work with no less than two albums appearing in 1983; the electric "Highly Strung" was first out in March 1983 with another highly successful UK tour and a HIT single in the shape of "Cell 151". The autumn of 1983 saw Steve's second release the acoustic "Bay of kings" album for which Steve embarked upon a tour of the University and college circuit in the UK and played in places which hadn't seen an artist of his calibre since the early days of Genesis. The gig at Guildford in January 1983 also saw Steve reunited again with Peter Gabriel and Mike Rutherford for a charity show in aid of Tadworth Children's Hospital. The sets for the Venue Club and Guildford Civic Hall shows ran as follows….

The Venue: The Steppes/Funny Feeling/Can't Let Go/HackettTo Pieces/A TowerStruck Down/Spectral Mornings/Acoustic Set/Horizons/ Overnight Sleeper/Slogans/Please Don't Touch/The Show/Clocks/The Air-Conditioned Nightmare/Hackett's Boogie.

Guildford Civic Hall: The Steppes/FunnyFeeling/Jacuzzi/HackettTo Pieces/Everyday/A Tower Struck Down/Horizons/Kim/Overnight Sleeper/Slogans/The Show/Clocks/HereComes The Flood/Solsbury Hill/Reach Out (I'll Be There)/I Know What I Like.

Once again, Steve went into overdive with not one but TWO tours in 1983. The first in the spring in support of his new rock album "Highly Strung" for which Seve and the band played the following set….

The Steppes/Camino Royale/Funny Feeling/Weightless/Always Somewhere Else/HackettTo Pieces/Slogans/Give ItAway/Spectral Mornings/Acoustic Set/Kim/Overnight Sleeper/Cell 151/Please Don't Touch/Everyday/Walking Through Walls/The Show/Clocls/ Hackett's Boogie.

"Highly Strung" UK Tour 1983

Civic Centre	Guildford	England	29.1.83
Pavilion	Worthing	England	19.4.83
Odeon Theatre	Birmingham	England	20.4.83
City Hall	Newcastle	England	21.4.83
Apollo Theatre	Manchester	England	22.4.83
Playhouse	Edinburgh	Scotland	23.4.83
Leisure Centre (Coatham Bowl)	Redcar	England	24.4.83

(A complete private film recording ofthis gig is reputed to exist)

University	Bradford	England	25.4.83
Empire Theatre	Liverpool	England	26.4.83
Colston Hall	Bristol	England	27.4.83
Queensway Hall	Dunstable	England	28.4.83

(A complete private film recordingof this gig is reputed to exist)

Gaumont Theatre	Southampton	England	29.4.83
Hammersmith Odeon	London	England	30.4.-1.5.83
Apollo Theatre	Oxford	England	2.5.83

(This gig is in press advertisements for the tour but not in the tour programme)

Cliffs Pavilion	Southend	England	3.5.83

(This date appears in press advertisements for the tour but not in the tour programme)

Derngate Centre	Northampton	England	4.5.83
City Hall	Sheffield	England	5.5.83
Royal Centre	Nottingham	England	6.5.83
Winter Gardens	Margate	England	7.5.83
Arts Centre	Poole	England	8.5.83
University of East Anglia	Norwich	England	9.5.83

The autumn tour in support of the acoustic "Bay Of Kings" album featured the following tracks in its set ; inlcuding many Rock tracks in an acoustic setting for the first time…..

Horizons/Time Lapse At Milton Keynes/Bay of Kings/Calmaria/Hands Of The Priestess/Jacuzzi/Overnight Sleeper/The Barren Land/Blood On The Rooftops/Tales Of The Riverbank/Second Chance/Chinese Improvisation/Petropolis/Kim/Butterfly (also known as: The Water Wheel)/Jazz On A Summer's Night/ The Journey/Ace Of Wands/Cradle Of Swans/Munich/Horizons.

"Bay Of Kings" UK Tour 1983

University	Warwick	England	26.10.83
Mountford Hall	Liverpool	England	27.10.83
University	Leeds	England	28.10.83
University	Loughnborough	England	29.10.83
Ashton Metro	Ashton-Under-Lyme	England	30.10.83 (Cancelled)
Polytechnic	Plymouth	England	1.11.83
University	Keele	England	2.11.83
University	Newcastle	England	3.11.83
Heriot Watt University	Edinburgh	Scotland	4.11.83
University	Dundee	Scotland	5.11.83
Civic Centre	Corby	England	6.11.83
Barbican Centre	London	England	7.11.83
Festival Hall	Corby	England	8.11.83
Leas Cliff Hall	Folkestone	England	9.11.83
Polytechnic	Oxford	England	11.11.83
Surrey University	Guildford	England	12.11.83
Leisure Centre	Mansfield	England	13.11.83
Vanbrugh Dining Rooms (University)	York	England	14.11.83
Town Hall	Birmingham	England	15.11.83
St Davids Hall	Cardiff	Wales	16.11.83
Taliesin Theatre	Swansea	Wales	17.11.83

There was to be a two year gap between these tours and Steve's next outing and when he next appeared it was as part of the AOR supergroup GTR With Steve Howe! Steve had released another album in 1984; the sadly underrated (and un toured) "Til we have faces". Steve's involvement with GTR led to a highly successful album and another hit single; When the heart rules the mind and a high profile tour of the USA and Europe. Steve succumbed to supergroup fever for this project, and the set drew on both Steves' material for twin acoustic sets before the band took the stage for The main show and a set for the GTR tour would have included the following tracks….

Hackett acoustic set (including Horizons/Blood On The Rooftops)/Howe acooustic set (including Clap/Mood For A Day)/From A Place Where Time Runs Slow/Jekyll & Hyde/Here I Wait/Prize Fighters/Imagining/HackettTo Pieces/Hackett-Genesis medley/Toe The Line/Sketches In TheSun/Pennants/Roundabout/The Hunter/You Can Still GetThrough/Reach Out (NeverSay No)/When The HeartRules The Mind.

Hammersmith Odeon	London	England	6.2.86

G T R US/UK/European Tour 1986

Lyric Theatre	Baltimore MD	USA	20.6.86
Stanley Theatre	Utica NY	USA	21.6.86
Ulster Performing Arts Centre	New York NY	USA	22.6.86
Orpheum Theatre	Boston MA	USA	23.6.86
Beacon Theatre	New York NY	USA	25.6.86
Palace Theatre	Newhaven CT	USA	27.6.86
Tower Theatre	Upper Darby PA	USA	28.6.86
Constitution Hall	Washington DC	USA	29.6.86
Convention Centre	Quebec QC	Canada	2.7.86
Congress Centre	Ottawa ON	Canada	3.7.86
Verdune	Montreal QC	Canada	4.7.86
Massey Hall	Toronto ON	Canada	5.7.86
Music Hall	Cleveland OH	USA	6.7.86
Syria Mosque	Pittsburgh PA	USA	8.7.86
State Theatre	Detroit OH	USA	9.7.86
Riviera Theatre	Chicago IL	USA	10.7.86
Performing Arts Centre	Milwaukee WI	USA	11.7.86
The Orpheum	Minneapolis IN	USA	12.7.86
Music Hall	Omaha NB	USA	13.7.86
Mc Nichols Centre	Denver CO	USA	15.7.86
Warfield Theatre	San Francisco CA	USA	18.7.86
Wilton Theatre	Los Angeles CA	USA	19.7.86
California Theatre	San Diego CA	USA	21.7.86
Arizona State University	Mesa CA	USA	22.7.86
Coliseum	Austin TX	USA	24.7.86
Bronco Bowl	Dallas TX	USA	25.7.86
Music Hall	Houston TX	USA	26.7.86
Sam Gore Theatre	New Orleans LA	USA	27.7.86
Bayfront Theatre	St Petersburg FL	USA	30.7.86
Arena	Miami FL	USA	31.7.86
Apollo Theatre	Manchester	England	8.9.86
Odeon Theatre	Birmingham	England	10.9.86
Hammersmith Odeon	London	England	12.9.86
Apollo Theatre	Glasgow	Scotland	14.9.86
Alabamahalle	Munich	Germany	22.9.86
Hammersmith Odeon	London	England	29.9.86

"Momentum" UK/EuropeanTour 1988

Rehearsals	London	England	23.4.88	
Town Hall	Cheltenham	England	25.4.88	
Leas Cliff Pavilion	Folkestone	England	26.4.88	
University	Warwick	England	27.4.88	
University of East Anglia	Norwich	England	28.4.88	
The Dome	Brighton	England	29.4.88	
Essex University	Colchester	England	30.4.88	
Opera House	Manchester	England	1.5.88	
Derngate Arena	Northampton	England	2.5.88	
Colston Hall	Bristol	England	3.5.88	
Polytechnic	Leicester	England	4.5.88	
Wessex Hall	Poole	England	5.5.88	
The Forum	Hatfield	England	6.5.88	
Saddlers Wells Opera House	London	England	7.5.88	The Panic Brothers
Cliffs Pavilion	Southend	England	8.5.88	
Corn Exchange	Cambridge	England	10.5.88	
Civic Hall	Guildford	England	11.5.88	
St Davids Hall	Cardiff	Wales	12.5.88	
Concert Hall	Lewisham	England	13.5.88	
Royal Centre	Nottingham	England	14.5.88	
Alexandra Theatre	Birmingham	England	15.5.88	
The Orchard Theatre	Dartford	England	16.5.88	
Hexagon Theatre	Reading	England	17.5.88	
Teatro Colosseo	Turin	Italy	19.5.88	
(An edited private film of this gig exists)				
Teatro Orfeo	Milan	Italy	20.5.88	
Teatro Verdi	Genoa	Italy	21.5.88	
Teatro Tenda a Strisce	Rome	Italy	22.5.88	
Osterpoort	Groningen	Holland	24.5.88	
Music Centrum	Utrecht	Holland	25.5.88	
Paradiso Theatre	Amsterdam	Holland	26.5.88	
De Doelen	Rotterdam	Holland	27.5.88	
Het Noorderlight	Tilburg	Holland	28.5.88	
(A private filmof this gig exists)				

Ancienne Belgique	Brussels	Belgium	29.5.88
Craigtoun Park	St Andrews	Scotland	24.7.88
"Rock Glasnost" Festival	Tallinn	Estonia	26.8.88
Central Tejo	Lisbon	Portugal	3.9.88
Teatro Rivoli	Opporto	Portugal	4.9.88
Festa della Unita	Modena	Italy	5.9.88
Sardines	Oslo	Norway	8.9.88
Gota Lejon	Stockholm	Sweden	9.9.88
Saga Theatre	Copenhagen	Denmark	11.9.88
Quartier Latin	Berlin	Germany	12.9.88
Markthalle	Hamburg	Germany	15.9.88
Zeche	Bochum	Germany	16.9.88
(A private film of this gig exists)			
Scala	Ludwigsburg	Germany	17.9.88
New Morning	Paris	France	19.9.88

Special Guest on this tour: Mae McKenna and The Panic Brothers (Sadlers Wells gig only)

Fans were amazed by Steve's acoustic tour in support of the "Momentum" album an album which achieved top ten status in the classical charts and which drew favourable comments from music virtuoso Yehudi Menuhin. Steve also fulfilled an ambition to play Vivaldi's Guitar Concerto as guest of the London Chamber Orchestra proving once again that there was more to Steve Hackett than meets the eye! The set for these acoustic shows drewon Steve's full repertoire of material and a set usually ran as follows. ..

Horizons/Bay Of Kings/A Bed, Achair & A Guitar/Time Lapse At Milton Keynes/Tales Of The Riverbank/Ace Of Wands/Hands Of The Priestess/ Overnight Sleeper/Cavalcanti/Second Chance/Portrait Of A Brazilian Lady/Still Life/Jazz On A Summer's Night (previously known as Butterfly)/ Munich/Notre Dame Des Fleurs/GuitarSynth Improvisation (including Katchachurian's "Sabre Dance" or Sibelius' "Finlandia")/Kim/Untitled Piece (The Vigil)/TheCarrot That Killed My Sister.

Fans then had to wait four years before Steve returned to the live circuit again in the meantime, he continued to work on building his own studio and the only releases to appear were a long overdue live album ironically titled "Timlapse" and a compilation album byVirgin Records titled "The Unauthorised Biography".In 1992 Steve took to the road again to roadtest material for his first rock album in almost tenyears; the as yet unreleased "Guitar Noir" and alive set for these shows usually comprised the following tracks….

Myopia Medley/A Vampyre With A Healthy Appetite/Flight Of The Condor(SierraQuemada)/Take These Pearls/Always Somewhere Else/In The Heart Of The City/Walking Away From Rainbows/There Are Many Sides To The Night/In That QuietEarth/Dark As The Grave/Etruscan Serenade/Depth Charge/Everyday/Cuckoo Coccoon/Blood On The Rooftops/Horizons/The Stumble.

"Tour Noir" US Tour 1992.

Le Spectrum	Montreal QE	Canada	14.8.92
El Mocambo	Toronto ONT	Canada	15.8.92
D'Auteuil	Quebec QE	Canada	16.8.92
Bottom Line Club	New York NY	USA	18.8.92
Birchmere Auditorium	Alexandria NY	USA	19.8.92
The Penguin	Ottawa ONT	Canada	22.8.92
Impaxx Concert Theatre	Buffalo NY	USA	23.8.92
Shank Hall	Milwaukee WI	USA	25.8.92
The Agora	Cleveland OH	USA	27.8.92
The Marquee	Detroit MI	USA	28.8.92
City Limits	Dallas TX	USA	2.9.92
Concert Theatre	Ventura AZ	USA	5.9.92
The Cave	Las Vegas NV	USA	7.9.92
The Strand	Redondo Beach CA	USA	8.9.92
Coach House	San Juan Capistrano CA	USA	9.9.92
Mason Jar	Tempe CA	USA	10.9.92
Cabaret	San Jose CA	USA	12.9.92
Club Soda	Montreal QE	Canada	19.9.92
Bottom Line Club	New York NY	USA	20.9.92
Max's on Broadway	Baltimore MD	USA	23.9.92
23 East Cabaret	Philadelphia PA	USA	24.9.92
Club Bene	South Amboy NJ	USA	27.9.92

"Guitar Noir" Tour 1993

Grand Rex Theatre	Buenos Aires	Brazil	16-17.4.93
Canecao	Rio de Janeiro	Brazil	20.4.93
Palace Theatre	Sao Paolo	Brazil	22.4.93
Town Hall (Rehearsals)	Whitchurch	England	20.5.93
Neptune Theatre	Liverpool	England	21.5.93
Renfrew Ferry	Glasgow	Scotland	22.5.93
Coatham Bowl	Redcar	England	23.5.93
Spring Street Theatre	Hull	England	24.5.93
Hop & Grape	Manchester	England	25..5.93
The Old Bourbon (Cancelled)	Harrogate	England	26.5.93
Wulfrun Hall	Wolverhampton	England	27.5.93

De Montfort Hall	Leicester	England	28.5.93
University of East Anglia	Norwich	England	29.5.93
Lead Mill	Sheffield	England	31.5.93
Assembly Halls	Worthing	England	1.6.93
Princess Hall	Aldershot	England	2.6.93
Leas Cliff Pavilion	Folkestone	England	3.6.93
Polygon	Southampton	England	4.6.93
Wedgewood Rooms	Portsmouth	England	5.6.93
The Swan Theatre	High Wycombe	England	6.6.93
Bierkeller	Bristol	England	7.6.93
The Grand Theatre	Clapham Junction London	England	8,6,93
Arts Centre	Kendal	England	11.6.93
Woughton Centre	Milton Keynes	England	12.6.93
St George's Hall (Cancelled)	Bradford	England	13.6.93
Villa Torlonia	Frascati	Italy	5.7.93
Centro Sportivo	Selvazzano nr Padua	Italy	6.7.93
(A private film of this gig exists)			
Castello	Brescia	Italy	7.7.93
Stadio del Pini	Sassari	Italy	9.7.93
Stadietto San Gaviro	Ozieri	Italy	10.7.93
Teatro Tenda	Cagliari	Italy	11.7.93
Irving Plaza	New York NY	USA	26.10.93
Charity's	Clifton Park NY	USA	28.10.93
The Icon	Buffalo NY	USA	29.10.93
El Mocambo	Toronto ONT	Canada	30.10.93
Café du Palais	Sherbrooke ONT	Canada	1.11.93
D'Auteuil (2 shows per night)	Quebec QE	Canada	2-3.11.93
Club Soda	Montreal QE	Canada	4-5.11.93
The Penguin	Ottawa ONT	Canada	6.11.93
The Town Pump	Vancouver BC	Canada	8.11.93
Chillers	San Diego CA	USA	10.11.93
The Coach House	San Juan Capistrano CA	USA	11.11.93
Cabaret	San Jose CA	USA	12.11.93
(A private film of this gig exists)			
The Strand	Redondo Beach CA	USA	13.11.93
Ventura Theatre	Ventura CA	USA	14.11.93

Steve's touring schedule increased dramatically during 1992/93 with a lengthy tour of the USA and UK as well as several shows in Brazil (Steve's first in that country since the 1977 Genesis tour). Another new album; "Guitar Noir" was well received by fans and Critics alike and Steve's profile remained high throughout theperiod. Steve toured in South America, the UK and Italy and the US again During the spring and summer of 1993 an dthe live set fopr these shows ran as follows....

Myopia medley/Camino Royale/A Vampyre With A Healthy Appetite/Sierra Quemada/Take These Pearls/In The Heart Of The City/ Walking Away From Rainbows/ThereAre Many Sides To The Night/Dark As TheGrave/Depth Charge/In That QuietEarth/Bass-drum Duet/ Always SomewhereElse/LostIn Your Eyes/Every Day/Blood On The Rooftops/Horizons/Cinema Paradiso/SpectralMornings/Firth Of Fifth/Clocks- The Angel Of Mons.

"There Are Many Sides To The Night" Tour 1994

Vorst Nationale	Brussels	Belgium	3.5.94*
Teatro Teresa Carrenas	Caracas	Venezuela	7-8.5.94*
Planet Pul Festival	Uden	Holland	4.6.94
Stadthalle	Vienna	Austria	8.6.94*
Tanzbrunnen	Cologne	Germany	12.6.94*
Rock Summer Festival	Tallinn	Estonia	17.6.94
Golden Stag TV Festival	Brasov	Romania	7.9.94
Standard	Barcelona	Spain	12.11.94
Sonny Boy	Treviso	Italy	24.11.94
(A private film of this gig exists)			
Teatro C T M	Brescia	Italy	25.11.94
Teatro Aurora	Como	Italy	26.11.94
Teatro Michetti	Pescara	Italy	28.11.94
Teatro Palladium	Rome	Italy	29.11.94
Teatro Metropolitan	Palermo	Italy	1.12.94
Teatro Nuovo	Catania	Italy	2.12.94

(*) shows as part of David Palmer's Orchestral presentation of the music of Pink Floyd, Genesis and Jethro Tull

1994 saw Steve continue to perform including shows as part of the David Palmer presentation of music by Pink Floyd, Genesis, and Jethro Tull. Steve also indulged his love of The Blues with an album of blues standards and new tracks written in the blues style titled; "Blues with a feeling" although no tour was undertaken to promote this album. + Later in the year Steve's acoustic tour in Italy was recorded and released as a live acoustic album under the title "There are many sides To the night".

The concert set for the Palmer shows was as follows...Turn ItOn Again/WholeLottaLove/Money/LosJigos/LivingIn The Past/Drum Solo/BlackLight/ BloodOn The Rooftops/CuckooCocoon-Chinese Improvisation-Unquiet Slumbers For The Sleepers/Horizons/Cavalcanti/Tales Of The Riverbank/ Classical Piece/The Journey/Notre Dame Des Fleurs/Silence/Run Like Hell/Owner Of A Lonely Heart/Roundabout.

The live set for the Italian acoustic tour comprised further acoustic renditions o fmany of Steve's classic tracks, and a set usually included these tracks….

Horizons/Black Light/TheSkye BoatSong/Time Lapse At Milton Keynes/Beja Flor/Kim/Second Chance/Oh How I Love You/The Journey/ Baroque/Walking Away From Rainbows/Cavalcanti/Andante In C/Concerto In D (Largo)/A Blue Part of Town/ThereAre Many Sides To The Night/Ace of Wands/Cinema Paradiso/Blues Coda/Jazz On A Summer's Night/End of Day.

"Genesis Revisited" Japanese Tour 1996

Sun Plaza Hall	Tokio	Japan	16-17.12.96
Castle Hall	Osaka	Japan	19.12.96
Rainbow Hall	Nagoya	Japan	20.12.96

1995/98 saw Steve increasingly prolific; a re-issue of the king Biscuit Flower Hour's recording of the 1986 GTR set revived interest in that band and Steve followed that with an orchestral interpretation of Shakespeare's "A Midsummer Night's Dream" for the Classics division of EMI Records. Steve also found time to indulge in a little nostalgia by putting together an album of re-worked Genesis classics and several new pieces And a couple of previously unheard tracks under the title of "Genesis revisited" initially released in Japan in 1996 and subsequently elsewhere in1997. Steve put together a band to perform a handful of shows in Japan in December 1996 and the resulting recording titled "The Tokio Tapes" is his third live album documenting the live set for these shows which ran as follows….

Watcher Of TheSkies/Riding The Colossus/Firth Of Fifth/Battle Lines/Camino Royale/In TheCourt of The Crimson King/Horizons/Walking Away From Rainbows/Heat Of The Moment/In ThatQuiet Earth/A Vampyre With A Healthy Appetite/I Talk To The Wind/Shadow Of The Hierophant/Los Endos/Black Light/TheSteppes/I Know WhatI Like.

Italian Tour 2000

Ritz Studios (Rehearsals)	Putney	England	1-6.7.00
Festival	Vivegano	Italy	9.7.00
(Private footage of this gig exists)			
Castello Malatestiana	Cesena	Italy	11.7.00
(Private footage of this gig exists)			
Teatro de la Ciminiera	Catania	Italy	13.7.00
Piazza Duomo Vecchio	Molfetta	Italy	14.7.00
Arena Stella Maris	Pescara	Italy	15.7.00 (Cancelled)

The last couple of years have seen Steve expand his repertoire even further with the recent release of a "covers" album with a difference. "Sketches Of Satie" Steve's most recent release is, as its title suggests; an album of renditions of pieces by the French impressionist composer: Erik Satie, performed by Steve and his brother John. Steve has also embarked upon the creation of a larger studio complex for his work with several projects in the pipeline.

The recent Italian tour also saw Steve take his first proper steps back in to the touring circuit and his current South American tour may be the beginning of a more regular schedule of live appearances. Steve's set for the recent tours has included more as yet unreleased material and The set usually ran as follows… Mechanical Bride/Serpentine/Watcher of The Skies/Hairless Heart/Firth Of Fifth/Riding The Colossus/Pollution/The Steppes/Gnossienne No 1/ Walking Away From Rainbows/Sierra Quemada/Slavegirls/A Vampyre With A Healthy Appetite/A Tower Struck Down/Lucridus/Darktown/Camino Royale/In Memoriam/Horizons/Los Endos/In That QuietEarth.

"Somewhere In South America" Tour 2001

Auditorio La Fundacion	Rosario	Argentina	28.6.01
Teatro Real	Cordoba	Argentina	29.6.01
Bristol Martinez	Buenos Aires	Argentina	30.6.01
Coliseao Gimnasio	Buenos Aires	Argentina	1.7.01
Santa Rosa Las Condes	Santiago	Chile	3.7.01
Canal De La Musica	Curitiba	Brazil	5.7.01
Teatro Carlos Gomez	Blumenau	Brazil	6.7.01
Teatro CIC	Florianopolis	Brazil	7.7.01
Teatro Opiniao	Porto Alegre	Brazil	8.7.01
Cenecao	Rio De Janeiro	Brazil	9.7.01
Funchal	Sao Paolo	Brazil	10.7.01
Casa Hacienda Moreyra	Lima	Peru	12.7.01
Santa Rosa De Lima	Caracas	Venezuela	14-15.7.01
Frogs	Panama	Panama	16.7.01
Melico Salazar	Costa Rica	Costa Rica	18.7.01
Premiere	Mexico City	Mexico	20.7.01
Premiere	Mexico City	Mexico	21.7.01
Premiere	Mexico City	Mexico	22.7.01

The touring bug has continued to bite and Steve undertook an extnsive tour of South America in the summer of 2001 for which his set comprised the following tracks….Mechanical Bride/Hackett To Bits/Serpentine/Watcher of The Skies (instrumental)/Hairless Heart/Firth Of Fifth/Riding The Colossus/ Pollution/The Steppes/Gnossiene No 3/Walking Away From Rainbows/Sierra Quemada/A Vampyre With A Healthy Appetite/A Tower Struck Down/ Lucridus/ Darktown/Camino Royale/In Memoriam/Acoustic Set: Black Light/Horizons/Los Endos/In That QuietEarth.

Odaiba Aqua City	Tokio	Japan	12-14.1.02
Petofi Hall	Budapest	Hungary	26.1.02

Italian /USTour 2002

Teatro Solva	Rosignano Pisa	Italy	23.4.02
Teatro Mediterraneo	Naples	Italy	24.4.02
Auditorio San Domenico	Foligno	Italy	25.4.02
Barfly	Ancona	Italy	27.4.02
Teatro Sociale	Trento	Italy	28.4.02

Steve returned to his acoustic roots for the recent Italian tour for which a typical set ran as follows....

Horizons/Gnossienne 1/Bacchus/Firth of Fifth/Bay Of Kings/Syrinx/Imagining(intro)/Second Chance/Jacuzzi/Overnight Sleeper/The Barren Land/ Kim/Time Lapse At Milton Keynes/Blood On The Rooftops/Improvisation/Concerto In D/Hairless Heart/Mustardseed/Gymnopedie 1/ Jazz On A Summer's Night/Cavalcanti/Walking Away From Rainbows/Tales Of The Riverbank/Concert For Munich/The Journey/ Medley: Skye Boat Song-By Paved Fountain/Hands Of The Priestess/Ace Of Wamds/Three Humoresques: Idylle-Aubade-Meditation/Hairless Heart (reprise)

The Birchmere	Alexandria VA	USA	27.6.02
BB Kings	New York NY	USA	28.6.02
NEARFest Trenton War Memorial	Trenton NJ	USA	30.6.02
Theatre Of Living Arts	Philadelphia PA	USA	1.7.02
L'International	Trois Rivieres QC	Canada	3.7.02
Quebec City Festival	Quebec City QC	Canada	4.7.02

The set for the US shows ran as follows: The Floating Seventh/Mechanical Bride/Myopia Medley - Myopia-Los Endos-Imaging-Ace Of Wands-Hackett To Pieces/Serpentine Song/Watcher Of The Skies/Hairless Heart/Firth of Fifth/Riding The Colossus/Pollution/The Steppes/Gnossienne No 1/Walking Away From Rainbows/in Memoriam/Slave Girls/A Vampyre With A Healthy Appetite/Spectral Mornings/Lucridus/Darktown/ Camino Royale/Everyday/Horizons/Fire Hydrant/Los Endos/Sierra Quemada.

Bridgewater Hall	Manchester	England	19.7.02
Festival Hall	London	England	21.7.02
(Both of these shows are as accompaniment to Evelyn Glennie)			
Piazza Del Popolo	Todi	Italy	25.7.02
Corte Del Castello	Falconara	Italy	26.7.02
Cortile Teresiano	Pavia	Italy	27.7.02
Waterfront Hall	Belfast	N Ireland	22.8.02
(Show with Evelyn Glennie)			
Teatro Sala Tripovich	Trieste	Italy	20.10.02
Manoel Theatre	St Julians	Malta	28-29.10.02
Naima	Forli	Italy	1.11.02
Teatro Toniodei	Lanusei (NU)	Italy	2.11.02

The set for the Italian shows this time ran as follows...

Intro/Horizons/Bay Of Kings/Colony Of Slippermen/Cuckoo Cocoon/Unquiet Slumbers For The Sleepers/Blood On The Rooftops/The Journey/ The Barren Land/Cavalcanti/Black Light/Tales Of TheRiverbank/Time Lapse At Milton Keynes/The Sky Boat Song/By Paved Fountain/End Of Day/Mustardseed.

To Watch The Storms Tour 2003

PR3 Radio Studios	Warsaw	Poland	?.6.03
Guilfest Acoustic Stage	Stone Park Guildford	England	5.7.03
Borders Bookstore	New York NY	USA	5.8.03
Borders Bookstore	White Plains NY	USA	6.8.03
Borders Boostore	Philadelphia PA	USA	8..803
Borders Bookstore	Bryn Mawr PA	USA	8.8.03
Borders Booksktore	Monroeville PA	USA	9.8.03
Borders Booksktore	Columbus OH	USA	10.8.03
Borders Bookstore	Cleveland Heights OH	USA	11.8.03
Borders Booksktore	Chicago IL	USA	12.8.03
Borders Bookstore	Minneapolis MN	USA	13.8.03
Akasaka Blitz	Tokyo	Japan	29.8.03
Nanba Hatch	Osaka	Japan	1.9.03
(These shows were recorded for the "GuitarWars" DVD featuring Steve, Nuno Bettencourt, John Paul Jones and Paul Gilbert)			
Boerderij	Zoetermeer	Holland	28.9.03
Het Noorderlight	Tilburg	Holland	29.9.03
The Stables	Milton Keynes	England	3-4.10.03
Wulfrun Hall	Wolverhampton	England	5.10.03
City Varieties	Leeds	England	6.10.03
Palace Theatre	Newark	England	7.10.03
Huntingdon Hall	Worcester	England	9.10.03
Coal Exchange	Cardiff	Wales	10.10.03
Oakwood Centre	Rotherham	England	11.10.03
Renfrew Ferry	Glasgow	Scotland	12.10.03
Neptune Theatre	Liverpool	England	13.10.03

Whelans	Dublin	Republic Of Ireland	15.10.03
Waterfront Hall	Belfast	Northern Ireland	16.10.03
Opera House	Newcastle	England	18.10.03
Academy 3	Manchester	England	19.10.03
De Montfort Hall	Leicester	England	20.10.03
Town Hall	High Wycombe	England	21.10.03
Astor Theatre	Deal	England	25.10.03
Quen Elizabeth Hall	London	England	28.10.03
Fairfield Hall	Croydon	England	29.10.03
Nalen	Stockholm	Sweden	31.10.03
KB	Malmo	Sweden	2.11.03
Tradgarn	Gothenburg	Denmark	3.11.03
Fabrik	Hamburg	Germany	5.11.03
LiveMusic Hall	Cologne	Germany	6.11.03
(Private film footage of this gig exists)			
Colosaal	Aschaffenburg	Germany	7.11.03
Meier Music Hall	Braunschweig	Germany	8.11.03
Villa Berg	Stuttgart	Germany	9.11.03
Capitol	Mannheim	Germany	10.11.03
Centre De Culture	Limbourg	Belgium	11.11.03
Wisla Hall	Krakow	Poland	14.11.03

To Watch The Storms, Steve's seventeenth studio album also sawhimundertake his first proper European and UK tours forover ten years with a set which drew Heavily on hs back catalogueand even some Genesis classics…

Mechanical Bride/Serpentine Song/Watcher Of The Skies/HairlessHeart/Darktown/CaminoRoyale/The Steppes/Acoustic Set/WalkingAway From Rainbows/Slogans/Everyday/Please Don't Touch/Firth Of Ffth (instrumental)/A Vampyre With A Healthy Appetite/ Clocks/ SpectralMornings / BrandNew/ Myopia/Los Endos/In That Quiet Earth.

The shows at Rotherham Leicester saw special appearances by Steve's brother John on flute for an extra acoustic performance of Jacuzzi and an acoustic performance of Kim at the showin Croydon

The shows at Stuttgart, Mannheim and Krakow also included an extra encore: In Memoriam

To Watch The Storms/Live Archive Tour 2004

Mick Jagger Centre	Dartford	England	4.3.04
Derngate Theatre	Northampton	England	5.3.04
PacificArts Centre	Birkenhead	England	6.3.04
St George's Hall	Blackburn	England	7.3.04
Lead Mill	Sheffield	England	11.3.04 (Cancelled)
Corn Exchange	Cambridge	England	12.3.04
Shepherds Bush Empire	London	England	13.3.04 Circus
Colston Hall	Bristol	England	14.3.04
Alexandra Theatre	Birmingham	England	15.3.04
RockCity	Nottingham	England	16.3.04
Town Hall	Middlesbrough	England	18.3.04
New Theatre	Oxford	England	19.3.04
Guildhall	Southampton	England	20.3.04
Phoenix	Exeter	England	21.3.04
SpiritOf 66	Verviers	Belgium	23.3.04
Kubo	Turin	Italy	25.3.04
(Private film footage of this gig exists)			
Marghera	Venice	Italy	26.3.04
Musictheater Rex	Lorsch	Germany	30.3.04
Gewerkschafthaus	Erfurt	Germany	31.3.04
Dietrich-Keuning-Haus	Dortmund	Germany	1.4.04
Petofi Csarnok	Budapest	Hungary	3.4.04
Laiterie	Strasbourg	France	7.4.04 (Cancelled)

Steve certainl;y took the fans's advice with regard to his set list and for this second tour in support of To Watch The Storms the set list became his most representative todate with tracks from practially every solo album played, and a healthy dose of Genesis material too.
A standard set ran as follows…
Valley Of The Kings/Mechanical Bride/ Circus Of Becoming/Frozen Statues/Slogans/Serpentine Song/AceOf Wands/HammerIn The Sand/
Acoustic Set: Classical Gas-BlackLight-Horizons-Imagining/Second Chance/Blood On The Rooftops/Fly On A Windshield/Please Don't Touch/
Fith Of Fifth/A Dark Night In Toytown/Darktown/Brand NewThe Air-ConditionedNightmare/Clocks/Spectral Mornings/ Every Day/Los Endos.

Stadio Centrale del Tennis Foro Italico	Rome	Italy	26.7.04
Teatro di Verdura	Palermo	Italy	28.7.04
(Private film footage of this gig exists)			
Fort Manoel Manoel Island	Valetta	Malta	1.8.04

The summer shows featured a slightly shorter set which ommitted Valley Of The Kings and A Dark Night In Toytown (If You Can't Find Heaven).

UK/EUROPEAN ACOUSTIC TOUR 2005

Grand Theatre (Spirit Of 66)	Verviers	Belgium	13.3.05
Oakwood Centre	Rotherham	England	26.3.05
Pacific Arts Cenntre	Birkenhead	England	30.3.05
The Lowry Centre	Manchester	England	31.3.05
The Platform	Morecambe	England	1.4.05
Assembly Rooms	Derby	Rngland	2.4.05
Queen Elizabeth Hall	London	England	3.4.05
Komedia	Brighton	England	4.4.05
Huntingdon Hall	Worcester	England	5.4.05
St George's Hall	Bristol	England	7.4.05
Carnglaze Caverns	Liskeard	England	8.4.05
Wulfrun Hall	Wolverhampton	England	10.4.05
Maddermarket Theatre	Norwich	England	11.4.05
Th e Stables	Milton Keynes	England	13.4.05
The Stables	Milton Keynes	England	14.4.05
The Broadway	Barking	England	16.4.05
Ashcroft Theatre	Croydon	England	17.4.05
Luz de Gas	Barcelona	Spain	19.4.05
Clamores	Madrid	Spain	21.4.05
TVE 3 TV Studios (live TV broadcast)	Madrid	Spain	21.4.05
Saschall	Florence	Italy	26.4.05
Teatro Metropolitan	Catania	Italy	27.4.05
Teatro Elena	Sesto San Giovanni (MI)	Italy	28.4.05 (Finisterre)
Teatro Astra	Schio (VI)	Italy	29.4.05
Staatheater	Oldenburg	Germany	13.6.05
Haus der Jugend	Osnarbruck	Germany	14.6.05
St Jakobi Kirche	Braunschweig	Germany	15.6.05
Harmonie	Bonn	Germany	16.6.05
St Maximin	Trier	Germany	17.6.05

"Two Days Of Love & Peace" Festival

Waldbuhne	Wuppertal (Open Air)	Germany	18.6.05

(Festival lineup: Savoy Brown/Litmus/Caravan/Steve Hackett/Pavlov's Dog/Mother's Finest)

"Three Days Of Love & Peace" Festival

St Goarshausen	Loreley (Open Air)	Germany	19.6.05

(Festival lineup: Iron Butterfly/Savoy Brown/Pavlov's Dog/Caravan/Canned Heat/Mother's Finest/Steve Hackett/Jefferson Starship)

Imperial De Quebec	Quebec QC	Canada	28.9.05
Le Medley	Montreal QC	Canada	29.9.05
Markham Theatre For Performing Arts	Toronto ON	Canada	30.9.05
Capital Music Hall	Ottawa ON	Canada	1.10.05
Hamilton Place Theatre - The Studio	Hamilton ON	Canada	2.10.05
IMAC Theater	Huntington NY	USA	7.10.05
Society For Ethnic Culture	New York NY	USA	8.10.05
Summerville Theater	Boston MA	USA	9.10.05
Troy Savings Bank Music Hall	Troy NY	USA	10.10.05
The State Theater	Falls Church VA	USA	12.10.05
Keswick Theater	Glenside Pasadena PA	USA	13.10.05
The Sphere	Buffalo NY	USA	14.10.05
The Kent Stage	Kent OH	USA	15.10.05
Royal Oak Music Theater	Detroit MI	USA	16.10.05
Shank Hall	Milwaukee WI	USA	18.10.05
The Abbey	Chicago IL	USA	19.10.05
Springfield Center For The Arts	Springfield IL	USA	20.10.05
Rosses Blue Star Room	Minneapolis MN	USA	22.10.05
The Triple Door	Seattle	USA	25.10.05
Aladdin Theater	Portland OR	USA	26.10.05
The Swedish American Music Hall	San Francisco CA	USA	27.10.05
Galaxy Concert Theatre	Santa Ana CA	USA	28.10.05
Centro Cultural Ollin Yolizrli	Col Isidro Fabela Del Tlalpan		
	Mexico City	Mexico	30.10.05

Leaving the lasers and smoke machines behind, Steve embarked on a further acoustic tour in 2005 as a trio with his brother and keyboard player; Roger King. Once again, the emphasis was on musical excellence and the set was a healthy mix of old and new with a typical show comprising the following tracks: Intro/Japonica/Andante In C/Tribute To Segovia/Metamorpheus medley/Bay Of Kings/Classical Jazz/Sapphires/Mexico City/BlackLight/Skye Boat Song/Pease Blossom/Horizons/Jacuzzi-Overnight Sleeper/Bacchus/Firth Of Fifth/Whole Tone Jam-The Red Flower Of Taichi Blooms Everywhere-Hands Of The Priestess/After The Ordeal/Hairless Heart/M3/Imagining/Second Chance/Jazz On A Summer's Night/ Next Time Around/Kim/Aubade/Meditation/Idylle/The Journey/Ace Of Wands/Walking Away From Rainbows/Gnossienne #1.

The TVE 3 Studio performance in Madrid lasted half an hour and comprised a performance of the following tracks: Jam/Jacuzzi/Overnight Sleeper/Horizons/ Walking Away From Rainbows/Bacchus-Firth Of Fifth-Bacchus/The Pool Of Memory And The Pool Of Forgetfulness/Bay Of Kings/After The Ordeal/Hairless Heart/Ace Of Wands.

Steve performed an abbreviated set at both the open air festivals which comprised: Horizons/Jacuzzi/Bacchus/Whole Tone Jam-The Red Flower Of Taichi Blooms Everywhere-Hands Of The Priestess/After The Ordeal/Hairless Heart/Imagining/Second Chance/Classical Jazz/Mexico City/ Black Light/Kim/The Journey/

Jazz on A Summer's Night/Walking Away From Rainbows/Ace Of Wands.

At the Loreley gig, Steve also got up and performed an impromptu "jam" with Mother's Finest who were the headlining act on that day.

Soundstage Studios	WestActon London	England	22.4.06
Charterhouse Public School	Godalming	England	1.5.06
Boardwalk Club	Sheffield	England	20.5.06
Astoria	London	England	28.5.06

Steve guested with his brother John and his band at these handful of inaugural gigs for the newly formed John Hackett Band. The set comprised A mix of material from John's own solo album: Checking Out Of London along with several classics from Steve's repertoire and material from both Nick Magnus and Tony Patterson's albums.

Kulturhus	Bodo	Norway	28.9.06
(A gig at the Tivoli in Utrecht Holland was originally scheduled for this date and subsequently cancelled)			
Kulturhuset	Tromso	Norway	29.9.06
Quartier Modo	Berlin	Germany	1.10.06
Peter Paul Kirche	Reichenbach	Germany	2.10.06
Abbaye De Neu Munster	Luxembourg	Luxembourg	4.10.06
Karlstatdt Kulturcafe	Nurnburg	Germany	5.10.06
Christuskirche	Bochum	Germany	6.10.06
Alte Statdthalle	Melle	Germany	7.10.06
Blue Note	Nagoya	Japan	24.11.06
STB 139	Tokyo	Japan	25-26.11.06
Blue Note	Osaka	Japan	27.11.06
Teatro Comunale	Belluno	Italy	21/3/07
Teatro Verdi	Pisa	Italy	22/03/07
Stazione Birra	Roma	Italy	23/03/07
Teatro Chiabrera	Savona	Italy	24/03/07

Steve's latest gigs with the acoustic trio performing predominantly the same set as that of the 2005 tour. With Steve's new rock album; Wild Orchid released on 11th September it won'tbe long before he is out again promoting it in front of enthusiastic crowds

This part of the Gig Guide has been compiled by Alan Hewitt with the assistance of: Billy Budis,Vernon Parker; PhilMorris, NickMagnus and Pam Bay of the "Steve Howe Appreciation Society".

JOHN HACKETT GIG GUIDE

VENUE NAME	CITY	COUNTRY	DATE
Soundstage Studios (Warm-up gig)	Acton (London)	England	23.4.06
Charterhouse School	Godalming	England	1.5.06
The Boardwalk	Sheffield	England	20.5.06
The Borderline	London	England	21..5.06 (Cancelled)
The Astoria	London	England	28.5.06

John Hackett has been a constant presence in his brother Steve's live touring line-up since 1978 and it was something of a surprise when he finally stepped out of his big brother's shadow to gig in his own right after the release of 2005's Checking Out Of London album. With a band comprising another ex-Hackett man; Nick Magnus on keyboards and the services of one the singer and guitarist from one of the UK -based Genesis tribute bands: Re-Genesis, John took the bold step of performing in his own right for the first time with a set which drew on material from both of his own solo albums, material from Nick Magnus's excellent albums and a healthy smattering of material from Hackett senior's back catalogue too.

The set list was as follows... Ace Of Wands/Whispers/Late Trains/Fantasy/Another Life/DNA/Brother Son, Sister Moon/Double Helix/Dream Town/Let It Rain Down/Winter/Jacuzzi/Hands Of The Priestess/A Tower Struck Down/Ego And Id/More.

MIKE + THE MECHANICS GIG GUIDE

VENUE NAME	CITY	COUNTRY	DATE
"The Miracle Tour" US Tour 1986			
Sunrise Theatre	Miami FL	USA	5.6.86
Curtis Hixon Centre	Tampa Bay FL	USA	6.6.86
Southern Star Amphitheatre	Atlanta GA	USA	8.6.86
?	Memphis TN	USA	10.6.86
Kiel Open House	St Louis MO	USA	11.6.86
Midland Theatre	Kansas KS	USA	12.6.86
Holiday Star	Merrivale KS	USA	14.6.86

Timber Wolf	Cincinatti OH	USA	15.6.86
Allen Theatre	Cleveland OH	USA	16.6.86
Kingswood	Toronto ON	Canada	17.6.86
Tower Theatre	Upper Darby PA	USA	19.6.86
Finger lakes Performing Arts Centre	Rochester NY	USA	21.6.86
Syria Mosque	Pittsburgh PA	USA	22.6.86
The Pier	New York NY	USA	23-24.6.86
Six Flags over Texas	Dallas TX	USA	27.6.86
Seven Stars Amphitheatre	Houston TX	USA	30.6.86
Universal Amphitheatre	Los Angeles TX	USA	1.7.86
Pavilion	Concord NH	USA	5.7.86
Paramount Theatre	Seattle WA	USA	8.6.86
Expo Theatre	Vancouver BC	Canada	9.7.86

Mike is the late developer in terms of solo performances. His first outing in 1986 was on the back of his THIRD solo album; the highly successful "Mike & The Mechanics" debut album which appeared in 1985. The tour was a USA/Canada only affair between stints with Genesis and fans in Europe and the UK had to wait a further three years to see Mike's "part-time" band in action.

The set for the inaugural US tour ran as follows:

Hanging By A Thread/Half Way There/Silent Running/Taken In/I Don't Wanna Know/Maxine/Par Avion/Call To Arms/Tempted/
I GetThe Feeling/Take The Reins/All I Need Is A Miracle/Gimme Some Lovin'.

"Living Years"European/US Tour 1989

Volkshaus	Zurich	Switzerland	22.2.89
Palatrussardi	Milan	Italy	23.2.89
Forum	Ludwigsburg	Germany	24.2.89
Niedersachsenhalle	Hanover	Germany	26.2.89
Philipshalle	Dusseldorf	Germany	27.2.89
Broendbyhallen	Copenhagen	Denmark	1.3.89
Gota Lejon	Stockholm	Sweden	2.3.89
Apollo Theatre	Manchester	England	5.3.89
Hammersmith Odeon	London	England	6.3.89
Leas Cliff Pavilion	Folkestone	England	7.3.89
Deutsches Museum	Munich	Germany	9..3.89
Rheingoldhalle	Mainz	Germany	10.3.89
Salle des Fetes Thonex	Geneva	Switzerland	11.3.89
Olympia Theatre	Paris	France	13.3.89
Ancienne Belgique	Brussels	Belgium	14.3.89
Vredenburg	Utrecht	Holland	15.3.89
Playhouse	Edinburgh	Scotland	17.3.89
City Hall	Newcastle	England	18.3.89
Hammersmith Odeon	London	England	19.3.89
?	DaytonFL	USA	23.3.89
?	Miami FL	USA	24.3.89
Straub Park	St Petersburg FL	USA	25.3.89
The Omni Centre	Atlanta GA	USA	26.3.89
?	Raleigh NC	USA	27.3.89
?	Washington DC	USA	28.3.89
Lyric Theatre	Baltimore MD	USA	29.3.89
Tower Theatre	Upper Darby PA	USA	30.3.89
The Scope	Norfolk VA	USA	2.4.89
Orpheum Theatre	Boston MA	USA	7.4.89
Bally's Grand Grandstand	Atlantic City NJ	USA	10.4.89
Coliseum	Springfield OH	USA	12.4.89
?	Courtland State NY	USA	14.4.89
?	Albany NY	USA	15.4.89
Rochester Community War Memorial	Rochester NY	USA	17.4.89
Hamilton Place	Hamilton ON	Canada	21.4.89
Tower Theatre	Philadelphia PA	USA	22.4.89
Allen Theatre	Cleveland OH	USA	24.4.89
?	Ann Arbor MI	USA	25.4.89
Holiday Star	Merriville MI	USA	26.4.89
?	Milwaukee WI	USA	27.4.89
?	Minneapolis WI	USA	28.4.89
?	Warrensburg VA	USA	29.4.89
The Roxy	Hollywood CA	USA	30.4.89
Lake Compounce	Bristol RI	USA	28.7.89
L'Agora	Quebec QC	Canada	29.7.89
La Ronde	Montreal QC	Canada	30.7.89
Ontario Place Forum	Toronto ON	Canada	31.7.-1.8.89
Garden State Arts Centre	Holmdel NY	USA	3.8.89
Jones beach Amphitheatre	WantaughNJ	USA	4.8.89
Bally's Grand Grandstand	Atlantic City NJ	USA	5.8.89
Amphitheatre	Doswell NJ	USA	6.8.89
Merriweather Post Pavilion	Columbia MD	USA	7.8.89

Ohio State Fair Grandstand	Columbus OH	USA	8.8.89
Pine Knob Music Theatre	Clarkston MI	USA	10.8.89
Timberwolf Amphitheatre	King's Island MI	USA	11.8.89
Old Glory Theatre	St Louis MO	USA	12.8.89
Poplar Creek Music Theatre	Hoffman Estates MI	USA	13.8.89
Grandstand Stagefair	Springfield OH	USA	15.8.89
Lakewood Amphitheatre	Atlanta GA	USA	17.8.89
The Summit	Houston TX	USA	19.8.89
Music Mill Amphitheatre	Arlington TX	USA	20.8.89
Ventura County Theatre	Ventura CA	USA	23.8.89
Concord Concord	Concord WA	USA	24.8.89
Greek Theatre	Los Angeles CA	USA	25.8.89
Pacific Amphitheatre	Costa Mesa CA	USA	27.8.89
Entertainment Centre	Sydney	Australia	1.9.89*
Entertainment Centre	Brisbane	Australia	4.9.89*
National Tennis Centre	Melbourne	Australia	6.9.89*
Apollo Entertainment Centre	Adelaide	Australia	8.9.89*
Superdome	Perth	Australia	10.9.89*

(*) Austalian tour dates cancelled.

1988 saw Mike & The Mechanics hit the big time with a world wide number one hit single with the title track to their second album; Living years. Number one everywhere except mysteriously in the UK where it weighed in at number two! With two solid albums under their belts and a settled line-up, the band undertook an extensive tour of Europe where they were supported by progressive rockers IQ. Two US tours followed and a handful of shows were planned for Australia but these were cancelled at the last minute nonetheless, 1989 saw Mike & The Mechanics arrive on the concert stage and play for keeps. The tour drew extensively on the material from the band's two studio albums and the set usually ran as follows...

Nobody's Perfect/Seeing Is Believing/Silent Running/Don't/Nobody Knows/Hanging By A Thread/Why Me?/Taken In/Beautiful Day/Black & Blue/ParAvion/A Call To Arms/The Living Years/I GetTheFeeling/Take The Reins/All I Need Is A Miracle/Poor Boy Down.
The second US tour also occasionally featured the additional encore of the band's coverversion of The Beatles' classic: "Revolution".

Special Guests on the UK leg of the tour: IQ

A third album; "Word of mouth" followed in 1991 although Mike was unable to capitalise on the band's profile fort his one due to other commitments with Gene and it was to be a further four years before the Mechanics hit the road again.

"Beggar On Beach Of Gold" Tour 1995

The Manor Studios (Virgin Records 21st birthday) Oxford		England	24.8.94
Victory Club (album launch gig)	London	England	18.1.95
World Earth Day Festival	Boston MA	USA	22.4.95
Standard Bank Arena	Johannesburg	South Africa	1-2.6.95
Village Green	Durban	South Africa	3.6.95
Sandton Towers	Johannesburg	South Africa	5.6.95
(This gig was captured on film by South African television)			
Saambo Arena	Pretoria	South Africa	6.6.95
Freiluftbuhne	Lorlei	Germany	10.6.95
Capitol Theatre	Hanover	Germany	11.6.95
Offenbach Theatre	Frankfurt	Germany	12.6.95
Guildhall	Portsmouth	England	14.6.95
Royal Concert Hall	Nottingham	England	15.6.95
Wembley Stadium (Supporting R Stewart) London		England	17.6.95
International Centre	Bournemouth	England	18.6.95
Trinity College	Cambridge	England	19.6.95
Apollo Theatre	Oxford	England	20.6.95
Civic Hall	Wolverhampton	England	21.6.95
St David's Hall	Cardiff	Wales	22.6.95
St Gallen Festival	Zurich	Switzerland	24.6.95
Park Pop Festival	?	Holland	25.6.95
Congreshalle	Hamburg	Germany	27.6.95
Tivolis Conzertsal	Copenhagen	Denmark	28.6.95
Metron	Gothenburg	Sweden	29.6.95
Midtfyns Festival	Roskilde	Denmark	1.7.95
Lalauna	Brussels	Belgium	4.7.95
Demain Du Monde (Cancelled)	Paris	France	5.7.95
Culture Tent	Luxembourg	Luxembourg	6.7.95
Festival	Imst	Austria	8.7.95
Prague Festival (Cancelled)	Prague	Czechoslovakia	9.7.95
Colston Hall	Bristol	England	11.7.95
Pavilion	Plymouth	England	12.7.95
The Dome	Brighton	England	13.7.95
Summer Rock Festival	Tallinn	Estonia	15.7.95
The Island	Ilford	England	17.7.95
Shepherds Bush Empire	London	England	18.7.95
Coliseum	Watford	England	19.7.95

Roundhay Park "Heineken Festival"	Leeds	England	21.7.95
City Hall	Newcastle	England	23.7.95
Sands Centre	Carlisle	England	24.7.95
Assembly Rooms	Derby	England	25.7.95
Festival	Langelands	Denmark	27.7.95
Mean Fiddler	Dublin	Eire	29-30.7.95
Festival	Jubeck	Germany	12.8.95
?	?	Belgium	13.8.95

1994/95 saw Mike's "other" band take off in a big way with the hugely successful "Beggar on a beach of gold" album which produced no less than three top ten singles. The band's tour took them to South Africa in time for the Rugby World Cup before touring Europe and the UK on their most successful tour to-date for which the set usually ran as follows:

BeggarOn A Beach Of Gold/Get Up/Silent Running/Over My Shoulder/AnotherCup Of Coffee/Someone Always Hates Someone/
You Really Got A Hold On Me/Web Of Lies/Every Day Hurts/How Long?/I Can't Dance/TheLiving Years/All I Need Is A Miracle/I Believe/Word Of Mouth.

 To capitalise on this success, Mike's record company released the "Hits" album in 1996 and organised the band's biggest tour of the UK; a 31 date tour round the theatres and city halls of the UK to packed audiences. Playing a "Greatest Hits" package of songs in keeping with the album itself. The set included the following….

Silent Running/Seeing is Believing/GetUp/A Beggar On A Beach Of Gold/Someone Always Hates Someone/Don't/Plain & Simple/Another Cup Of Coffee/Eyes Of Blue/Nobody's Perfect/Every Day Hurts/How Long?/I Can't Dance/TheLiving Years/All I Need Is A Miracle/Word Of Mouth/Over My Shoulder.

Special Guests on this tour: The Swans.

 Mike then returned to his "Full time" band; Genesis to begin work on what would become their seventeenth studio album in 1997.

"Hits" UK Tour 1996

Working Men's Club (Rehearsals)	Chiddingfold	England	21-27.2.96
The Island	Ilford	England	28.2.96
Mayfield Leisure Centre	Belfast	Northern Ireland	1.3.96
Stadium	Dublin	Eire	2.3.96
Guildhall	Portsmouth	England	4.3.96
Colston Hall	Bristol	England	5.3.96
Royal Concert Hall	Nottingham	England	7-8.3.96
Apollo Theatre	Manchester	England	9.3.96
City Hall	Sheffield	England	11.3.96
City Hall	Newcastle	England	12.3.96
Sands Centre	Carlisle	England	13.3.96
Usher Hall	Edinburgh	Scotland	14.3.96
Capitol Theatre	Aberdeen	Scotland	16.3.96
Royal Concert Hall	Glasgow	Scotland	18.3.96
St George's Hall	Bradford	England	19.3.96
Civic Hall	Wolverhampton	England	21.3.96
Corn Exchange	Cambridge	England	23-24.3.96
Assembly Rooms	Derby	England	5.4.96
Apollo Theatre	Oxford	England	6.4.96
Hexagon	Reading	England	7.4.96
Centre	Brighton	England	9.4.96
International Centre	Bournemouth	England	10.4.96
De Montfort Hall	Leicester	England	11.4.96
Apollo Theatre	Manchester	England	12.4.96
Empire Theatre	Liverpool	England	14.4.96
St David's Hall	Cardiff	Wales	15.4.96
Fairfield Halls	Croydon	England	16.4.96
Royal Albert Hall	London	England	18-19.4.96
"Rock am Ring Festival"	Hockenheim	Germany	24.5.96
"Rock in Park Festival"	Frankenburg	Germany	25.5.96

Special Guests on the UK tour : Blessid Union Of Souls.

The "Hits" tour proved to be Mike + The Mechanics' biggest success to date with sell-out shows across the UK and with a hit album under their belts the Mechanics were to go their separate ways to concentrate on their various solo projects.

Mike & The Mechanics M6 UK Tour 1999

Hanover Club (Warm-up show)	London	England	10.5.99
Barbican Centre	York	England	13.5.99
Apollo Theatre	Manchester	England	14.5.99
Apollo Theatre	Manchester	England	15.5.99
City Hall	Sheffield	England	17.5.99
City Hall	Sheffield	England	18.5.99
International Conference Centre	Bournemouth	England	20.5.99 (Canvelled)

The Conference Centre	Brighton	England	21.5.99	
Corn Exchange	Cambridge	England	22.5.99 (Cancelled)	
Royal Albert Hall	London	England	24-25.5.99	
The Pavilion	Plymouth	England	26.5.99	
Colston Hall	Bristol	England	28.5.99	
St Davids Hall	Cardiff	Wales	29.5.99	
St David's Hall	Cardiff	Wales	30.5.99	
The Royal Theatre	Hanley	England	31.5.99	
Symphony Hall	Birmingham	England	1.6.99	
Symphony Hall	Birmingham	England	2.6.99	
Fairfield Hall	Croydon	England	3.6.99	
Armadillo Centre	Glasgow	Scotland	5.6.99	
Royal Centre	Nottingham	England	6.6.99	
St George's Hall	Bradford	England	8.6.99	
City Hall	Newcastle	England	9.6.99	
City Hall	Newcastle	England	10.6.99	
Stadtpark Festival	Hamburg	Germany	13.6.99	
Museumsmeile	Bonn	Germany	18.6.99	
Guildhall	Portsmouth	England	20.6.99	
Fairfield Halls	Croydon	England	21.6.99	
Derngate Centre	Northampton	England	22.6.99	
Corn Exchange	Cambridge	England	23.6.99	**(Re-scheduled gig)**
Olympia Theatre	Dublin	Eire	1-2.7.99	
"T in the Park" Hyde Park	London	England	4.7.99	
Don Valley Stadium	Sheffield	England	6.7.99	**(Supporting Celine Dion)**
Wembley Stadium	London	England	10-11.7.99	**(Supporting Celine Dion)**
TV Studios "Ohne Filter"	Baden Baden	Germany	19.9.99	

(This show was to be The Mechanics' last performance before the untimely death of their singer; Paul Young)

| Langelands Festival | ? | Denmark | 28.7.00 | |
| Drobak Festival | Oslo | Norway | 29.7.00 | |

(Both of these gigs were subsequently cancelled due to the death of Paul Young)

After a four year hiatus the band returned with their fifth studio album, confusingly titled "M6" and setabout touring the UK
and selected European venues again, once again thrilling their audiences with a set comprising the following songs…

A Beggar On Abeach Of Gold./GetUp/Ordinary Girl/Now That You've gone/AnotherCup Of Coffee/Whenever I Stop/|My Little
Island/All The Light I Need/Every DayHurts/How Long?/I Can't Dance/The Living Years/All I Need Is A Miracle/Over My
Shoulder/Word of Mouth.

Paul Young's tragic death in late 1999 has led to much speculation about the future of The Mechanics,although most recent indications
are that Mike and Paul Carrack are continuing to write together and with other musicians..
2004 sees the release of the seventh studioalbumby The Mechanics: Rewired and a handful of dates as the opening act for
former Genesis compatriot: PhilCollins. With the prospect of more shows to follow the Mechanics's story is far from over, it seems

Rewired Tour 2004.

Letzigrund	Zurich	Switzerland	5.6.04	**PhilCollins**
Olympic Stadium	Munich	Germany	6.6.04	**Phil Collins**
Waldebuhne	Berlin	Germany	11.6.04	**Phil Collins**
Rhein Energie Stadion	Cologne	Germany	12.6.04	**PhilCollins**
Arena	Amsterdam	Holland	19.6.04	**Phil Collins**
Classic Festival	Werchter	Belgium	20.6.04	**Phil Collins**
Stadium	Leipzig	Germany	21.6.04	**PhilCollins**
Le Zenith	Nancy	France	25.6.04	**PhilCollins**
PalauSt Jordi	Barcelona	Spain	1.7.04	**PhilCollins**
	Alicante	Spain	2.7.04	
Restelo Stadium	Lisbon	Portugal	3.7.04	**PhilCollins**
VIG Festival	Copenhagen	Denmark	10.7.04	
Empire Theatre	Shepherds Bush London	England	7..9.04	

The band's set whilst supporting Phil Collins included the following songs; Falling/Now That You've Gone/Silent Running/If I Were You/One LeftStanding/Livin
Years/Over My Shoulder/Word Of Mouth.

The gig at the Shepherds Bush Empire was a benefit gig for the Nordoff Robbins Music Therapy charity and was filmed for a subesequent live DVD
release which featured the following set list: Falling/Now That You've Gone/Get Up/If I Were You/Another Cup Of Coffee/A Beggar On A Beach Of Gold/Perfe
Child/Whenever I Stop/All The Light I Need/One Left Standing/Silent Running/The Living Years/OverMy Shoulder/Word Of Mouth.

| Highclere Castle | Newbury | England | 20.5.06 | |

(Charity gig in aid of the Countryside Alliance featuring both Mike Rutherford and Paul Carrack with Roger Waters and Gary Brooker)

This gig guide has been compiled by Alan Hewitt with help from Carol Willis at Hit & Run Music/Tony Smith PersonalManagement Services.

Face Value

PHIL COLLINS & GENESIS TRIBUTE BAND

Friday 21st February 2003
Farnworth Vets Club
Farnworth, Bolton
Doors 7.30pm

Tickets £6

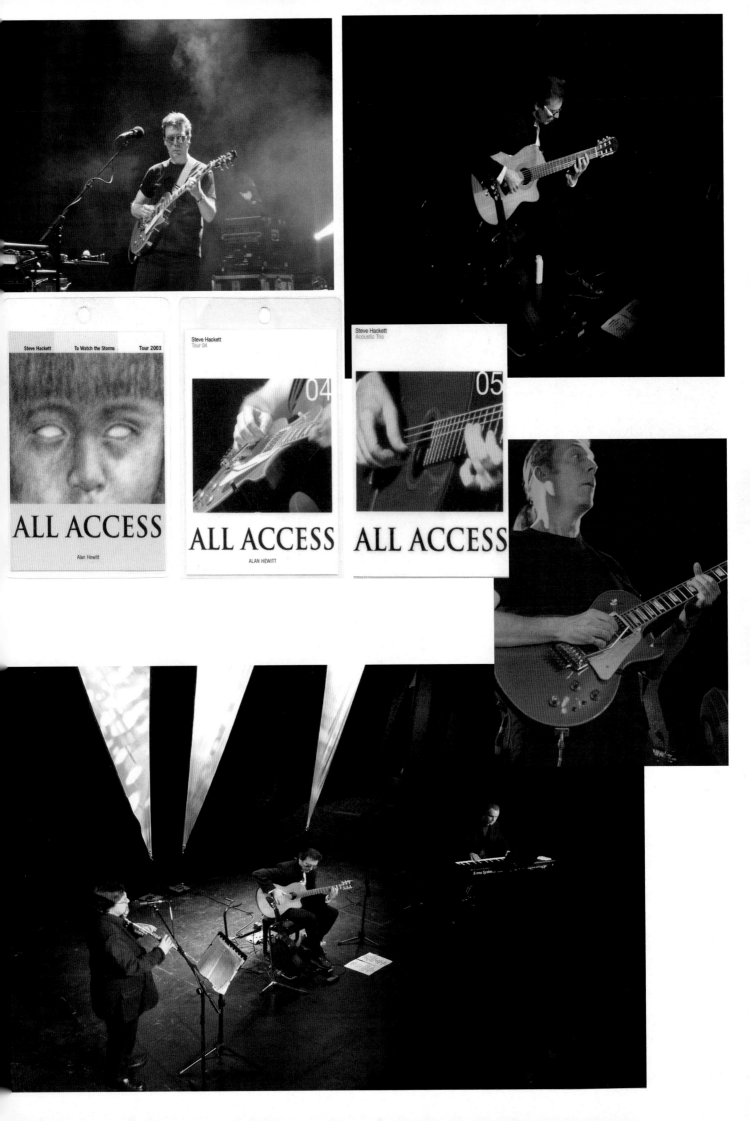

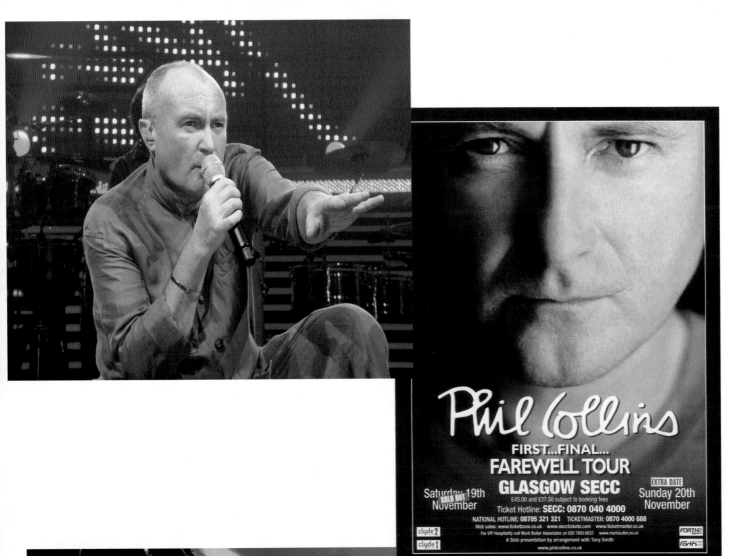

PETERGABRIELSTILLGROWINGUPLIVE2004

John Hackett
Checking Out of London

RAY WILSON GIG GUIDE

CUT GIG GUIDE

VENUE NAME	CITY	COUNTRY	DATE
Room at the Top Night Club	Bathgate	Scotland	27.4.99
Eisstadion	Deggendorf	Germany	30.4.99
Congress Centrum	Stuhl	Germany	1.5.99
Festhalle	Frankfurt	Germany	3.5.99
Schleyerhalle	Stuttgart	Germany	4.5.99
Frankenhalle	Nurnberg	Germany	6.5.99
Olympiahalle	Munich	Germany	8.5.99
Messehalle	Leipzig	Germany	10.5.99
Boerdelandhalle	Magdeburg	Germany	11.5.99
Sporthalle	Hamburg	Germany	12.5.99
Gerry-Weber-Stadion	Halle	Germany	14.5.99
Koln Arena	Cologne	Germany	15.5.99
Berlin Arena	Berlin	Germany	17.5.99
Oberhausen Arena	Oberhausen	Germany	18.5.99
Eissporthalle	Memmingen	Germany	20.5.99
Niedersachsenstadion	Hanover	Germany	22-23.5.99
Parkstadion	Gelsenkirchen	Germany	26.5.99
Weserstadion	Bremen	Germany	29.5.99
Olympiastadion	Munich	Germany	2.6.99
Rheinstadion	Dusseldorf	Germany	5-6.6.99
Waidstadion	Frankfurt	Germany	11-12.6.99
Colossaal	Aschaffenburg	Germany	13.6.99
Olympiastadion	Berlin	Germany	16.6.99
Trabrennbahn	Hamburg	Germany	19.6.99

RAY WILSON BAND GIG GUIDE

Alexanders Club	Chester Cheshire	England	4.4.02
The Limelight Club	Crewe Cheshire	England	5.4.02
(The Crewe gig was as the opening night of the three day "Genesis Weekend" held at The Limelight Club)			
Herringthorpe Leisure Centre	Rotherham S Yorkshire	England	6.4.02
Mill Race Lane Rock Café 2000	StourbridgeW Midlands	England	7.4.02
The Musician	Leicester Leicestershire	England	9.4.02
Park Cult Tour Open Air Festival	Duisburg	Germany	15.6.02
Kaue	Gelsenkirchen	Germany	16.6.02
David McTaggart Foundation	Munich	Germany	23.6.02
Audimax	Foyer	Germany	16.10.02
Kirche	Hohennau nr Rathenow	Germany	12.11.02
Rex	Wuppertal	Germany	14.11.02
Parkhaus	Duisburg	Germany	15.11.02
Musicfabrik	Celle	Germany	16.11.02
Bluesgarage	Hannover	Germany	17.11.02
Hearbeat	Zwonittz	Germany	19.11.02
Haus der Jugend	Ingolstadt	Germany	21.11.02
Alte Weberei	Cottbus	Germany	22.11.02
Musikkneipe Pur	Plaue/Brandenburg	Germany	23.11.02
The Limelight Club	Crewe Cheshire	England	24.11.02
Alexanders Club	Chester Cheshire	England	25.11.02
Spectrum	Augsburg	Germany	23-24.2.03
Spirit of 66	Verviers	Belgium	26.2.03
De Boerdrij	Zoeterme	Holland	27.2.03
De Kade	Zaandam	Holland	28.2.03
Podium	Harbende	Holland	1.3.03
Spirit Of 66	Verviers	Belgium	2.3.03
Trabendo	Paris	France	3.3.03
Centre Culture	Plomeurs	France	4.3.03
Podium	Harbende	Holland	5.3.03
Robin Hood Club	Brierley Hill W Midlands	England	6.3.03
Mean Fiddler	London	England	7.3.03
Oakwood Centre	Rotherham S Yorkshire	England	8.3.03
Garage	Saarbrucken	Germany	11.3.03
Theatrehaus	Stuttgart	Germany	12.3.03
E-Werk	Cologne	Germany	13.3.03
Stadthalle	Cloppenburg	Germany	14.3.03

Halle 101	Speyer	Germany	15.3.03
Roxy	Ulm	Germany	16.3.03
Stadthalle	Lichtenfe	Germany	18.3.03
Lowensaal	Nurnburg	Germany	19.3.03
Z-7	Pratteln	Switzerland	20.3.03
Hafen	Innsbruck	Austria	21.3.03
Posthof	Linz	Austria	22.3.03
Hugenottenhal	Neu Isenburg	Germany	24.3.03
Turbinehalle	Oberhausen	Germany	25.3.03
GF 36	Hamburg	Germany	26.3.03
Jolly Joker	Brauschweig	Germany	27.3.03
Halle 39	Hildesheim	Germany	28.3.03
PC 69	Bielefeld	Germany	30.3.03
Museumsmeile	Bonn	Germany	11.7.03 **(Supporting Joe Jackson)**
Blues Festival	Pistoia	Italy	13.7.03
Freilichtbuhne	Zwickau	Germany	19.7.03
Rock Café	Prague	Czech Republic	20.7.03
Riders Café	Lubeck	Germany	22.7.03
Burg Satzvey	Mechernich	Germany	23.7.03
Colos-saal	Aschaffenburg	Germany	24.7.03
?	Krefeld	Germany	25.7.03
Capitol	Hannover	Germany	26.7.03 **(Supporting Joe Jackson)**
World Nature Festival	Munich/Eichenried	Germany	16.8.03
IFA	Berlin	Germany	28.8.03 **(Rehearsal)**
ImmerWiderSonntags	Rust	Germany	31.8.03
Landhaus Walter	Hamburg	Germany	12.9.03
Music Hall	Worpswede	Germany	13.9.03
Bluesgarage	Hannver	Germany	14.9.03
Elfenbein	Bielefeld	Germany	17.9.03
Kaue	Gelsenkirchen	Germany	18.9.03
Festival	Wolnzach	Germany	19.9.03
Lindenbrauerei	Unna	Gemany	20.9.03
De Boerderij	Zoetermeer	Holland	21.9.03
Colos-saal	Aschaffenburg	Germany	23.9.03
Spectrum	Augsburg	Germany	24.9.03
Jazz Club Minden	Minden	Germany	26.9.03
Underground	Cologne	Germany	29.9.03
(WDR TV concert performance for "Live Im Rockpapast" series)			
Hobbit Hohle	Kaltenkirchen	Germany	30.9.03
Marktlocke	Hamburg	Germany	1.10.03
Alte Brauerei	Stralsund	Germany	2.10.03
Otto-Flick Halle	Kreutzal	Germany	3.10.03
Burg Satzvey	Mechernich	Gemany	4.10.03
The Claddagh Ring	Monchengladbach	Germany	28.5.04
Welkers	Fulda	Germany	29-30.5.04
Musikcafe Heartbeat	Zwonitz	Germany	31.5-1.6.04
MusikforumKatharinenekirche	Stendal	Germany	3.6.04
Kulturscheune	Thyrow	Germany	4.6.04
Kulturzentrum	Rathenow	Germany	5.6.04
Isernhagen Bluesgarage	Hannover	Germany	6.6.04
Bergkeller	Reichenbach/Vogtland	Germany	24.6.04
Plaue	Kneipe	?	25.6.04
Schenna Gompm	Alm	Italy	27.6.04
Radionave	Porto Sant'Elpidio	Italy	22.7.04
?	Molinara	Italy	23.7.04
Rosse Blues Festival	Tortoli Sardinia	Italy	24.7.04
Severino Blues Festival	Tolentino	Italy	25.7.04
The Lighthouse	Edinburgh	Scotland	10-12.8.04
The Lighthouse	Edinburgh	Scotland	14.8.04
The Lighthouse	Edinburgh	Scotland	17-19.8.04
The Lighthouse	Edinburgh	Scotland	21.8.04
The Lighthouse	Edinburgh	Scotland	24-26.8.04
The Lighthouse	Edinburgh	Scotland	28.8.04

(The Edinburgh shows are as part of the annual Edinburgh Festival)
(All of the above are acoustic performances)

The Next Best Thing Tour 2004.

Downtown Bluesclub	Hamburg	Germany	1.10.04
Prime Club	Cologne	Germany	3.1.0.04
Batschkapp	Frankfurt	Germany	4.10.04
Planet Music	Vienna	Austria	7.10.04
Spectrum	Augsburg	Germany	14.10.04
Kitchen Club	Nabburg	Germany	15.10.04

Zur Linde	Affalter	Germany	16.10.04
Otto-Flick-Halle	Kreutzal	Germany	23.10.04
Spirit 0f 66	Verviers	Belgium	24.10.04
Oakwood Centre	Rotherham	England	30.10.04 (Cancelled)
The Olympiad Leisure Centre	Chippenham	England	31.10.04 (Cancelled)
Paget Rooms	Cardiff	Wales	1.11.04 (Cancelled)
Malzhaus	Plauen	Germany	6.11.04
Riders Café	Lubeck	Germany	11.11.04
Musichall	Worpswede	Germany	13.11.04
Twish Heimathaus	Twist	Germany	14.11.04
Burg Satzvey	Mechernich	Germany	19.11.04
Zeche	Bochum	Germany	22.11.04
Little John	Rheine	Germany	23.11.04
Lindenbrauerei	Unna	Germany	26.11.04
Rock It	Aalen	Germany	12.2.05
Eifel	Mechernich	Germany	13.2.05
KKC Uni Club	Essen	Germany	14.2.05
Musikforum Katherinkirche	Stendal	Germany	16.2.05
Kulturscheune	Thyrow	Germany	17.2.05
Bluesgarage	Hannover	Germany	18.2.05
Kneipe PUR	Plaue	Germany	19.2.05
Musikcafe Heartbeat	Zwonitz	Germany	22.2.05
Q24	Pirna	Germany	23.2.05
KIK	Wernigerod	Germany	24.2.05
Kulturwekrkstatt	Melle-Buer	Germany	25.2.05
Gasthaus am Schmolderpark	Monchengladbach	Germany	26.2.05
Harmonie	Bonn	Germany	8.3.05
Lindenkeller	Friesing	Germany	10.3.05
Klosterkirche	Remscheid	Germany	18.3.05
Od Zmierzchv	Wroclav	Poland	19.3.05
Teatro Del Liberator San Martin	Cordoba	Argentina	5.4.05
Cine Plaza	Montevideo	Uruguay	6.4.05
Teatro Gran rex	Buenos Aires	Argentina	9.4.05
Canecao	Rio de Janeiro	Brazil	13.4.05
Via Funchal	Sao Paolo	Brazil	15.4.05
Sala Garbo	San Jose	Costa Rica	17.4.05
Next Disco	Panama City	Panama	20.4.05
Room At The Top	Bathgate	Scotland	27.5.05 (Full Band)
Alte Gasometer	Zwickau	Germany	30.6.05 (Acoustic Trio)
Tanzschule	Kassel	Germany	2.7.05 (Acoustic Trio)
Stadtfest	Celle	Germany	13.8.05
Open Flair Festival	Eschwege	Germany	14.8.05
The Lighthouse On The Shore	Edinburgh	Scotland	24-25.8.05 (Acoustic Trio)
The Fleece & Firkin	Bristol	England	21.9.05
The Point	Cardiff	Wales	22.9.05
Sheune Semlin	Rathenau	Germany	30.9.05
Stadthalle	Torgelow	Germany	1.10.05
Dieselstrasse	Esslingen	Germany	20.10.05 (Full Band)
Musica Hall	Worpspwede	Germany	21.10.05 (Full Band)
Bluesgarage	Hannover	Germany	22.10.05 (Full Band)
UNI Club KKC	Essen	Germany	24.10.05
Spectrum	Augsburg	Germany	26.10.05
KKB Q24	Pirna	Germany	27.10.05 (Full Band)
Od Zmierzchu Do Switu	Wroclav	Poland	28.10.05 (Full Band)
Zur Linde	Affalter	Germany	29.10.05 (Full Band)
Brauhaus Radigk	Finsterwalde	Germany	30.10.05
Kukturschmiede	Stralsund	Germany	18.11.05
Klosterkirche	Remscheid	Germany	2.12.05
Downtown Bluesclub	Hamburg	Germany	6.12.05
Kniepe PUR	Plaue	Germany	18.12.05

The World Of Genesis Tour 2006.

Pavilion Theatre	Rhyl	Wales	4.5.06
Civic Hall	Grays	England	5.5.06
The Stables	Milton Keynes	England	6.5.06
Carnegie Hall	Dunfermline	Scotland	23.5.06
Gaiety Theatre	Ayr	Scotland	24.5.06
Forum 28	Barrow-In-Furness	England	26.5.06
Music Hall	Shrewsbury	England	27.5.06
Mechanics	Burnley	England	28.5.06
Alban Arena	St Albans	England	30.5.06
Cutstom House	South Shields	England	2.6.06
Playhouse	Whitley Bay	England	3.6.06
Orchard Theatre	Dartford	England	7.6.06
The Playhouse	Harlow	England	8.6.06
Corn Exchange	Kings Lynn	England	9.6.06
Central Theatre	Chatham	England	10.6.06

Embassy Theatre	Skegness	England	11.6.06
Civic Theatre	Motherwell	Scotland	13.6.06
Benbridge	Isle Of Wight	England	17.6.06
Concert Hall	Perth	Scotland	19.6.06
Theatre	Camberley	England	22.6.06
Royal Spa Theatre	Leamington Spa	England	23.6.06
Assembly Hall	Worthing	England	24.6.06
Millfield Theatre	Edmonton	England	25.6.06
Broadway Theatre	Catford	England	28.6.06
St Davids Hall	Cardiff	Wales	29.6.06
Playhouse	Weston Super Mare	England	30.6.06
Marina Theatre	Lowestoft	England	2.7.06
Rheinkutlur Festival	Bonn	Germany	7.7.06
Park-Kult-Tour Festival Im Parkhaus	Duisburg	Germany	8.7.06
Radio 21 Stage	Melle	Germany	14.7.06
Sachsenring	Hochenstein Ernstahl	Germany	15.7.06
Bergkeller Art Rock Festival	Reichenbach	Germany	16.7.06
Stadtfest 800 Jahre Dresden	Dresden	Germany	17.7.06
Der Club	Heiligenhaus	Germany	19.7.06
Burg Lissingen Sommerscheune	Gerolstein	Germany	20.7.06
Bluesgarage	Hannover	Germany	21.7.06
Harry's Ranch	Eichenried	Germany	4.8.06
Reha Westphalz	Landsbuhl	Germany	5.8.06
L'Attache At Rutland	Edinburgh	Scotland	9-12.8.06
L'Attache At Rutland	Edinburgh	Scotland	16-19.8.06
L'Attache At Rutland	Edinburgh	Scotland	23-26.8.06
Dachsbergfest	Premnitz	Germany	27.8.06
Landhaus Walter	Hamburg	Germany	14.10.06 (Stiltskin)
Kulturbahnof	Uslar	Germany	3.11.06
Kiliankirche	Mullhausen	Germany	4.11.06
Hot Jazz Club	Munster	Germany	5.11.06
Backstage	Munich	Germany	6.11.06
Spectrum	Augsburg	Germany	7.11.06
Fritz Club im Postbahnhof	Berlin	Germany	9.11.06
Music Hall	Worpswede	Germany	10.11.06

"Who said it?" Index of sources of quotations.

The text of this book contains references to works other than my own and also to works contained within other publications. The following is a list of those sources and their relevant authors.

"The Secret history of Anon" published in #11 of The Pavilion Magazine interview with Anthony Phillips by Jonathan Dann.

"How I came to be involved in underwater archery" published in #7 of The Waiting Room Magazine Anthony Phillips interview with Alan Hewitt.

"The A to Z of Genesis" (Pt1) interview with Tony Banks as published in #27 of The Waiting Room Magazine. Interview by: Alan Hewitt/Peter Morton/Jonathan Dann.

"One From The Fans" Interview in #15 of The Pavilion. Interview by: Mike Costa.

"Lest We Trespass" Published in #61 of The Waiting Room Online. John Mayhew interview with Alan Hewitt.

Interview with Paul Whitehead published in #38 of The Waiting Room Magazine. Interview by Alan Hewitt/Thomas Holter.

"In Conversation" Interview with Mike Rutherford and Tony Banks published in #53 of The Waiting Room Online. Interview with Alan Hewitt, Stuart Barnes and Richard Nagy.

"Another trip down Memory Lane" interview with Mike Rutherford published in #34 of The Waiting Room Magazine interview with Alan Hewitt.

"Genesis: The Evolution of a rock band" Armando Gallo (Sidgwick & Jackson) 1978.

"Looking For Someone" Interview with Kim Shaheen and Mick Barnard published in #38 of Dusk Magazine. Interview by: Mario Giammetti.   "Genesis Revelations" interview with Steve Hackett published in #33 of The Waiting Room Magazine interview by Alan Hewitt.

"Memories of a tour promoter" Interview with Andrew Kilderry published in #39 of The Waiting Room Magazine interview by Tony Emmerson.

"Melody Maker" 28/1/71.

"Waiting for the Big One" interview with Armando Gallo published on The Waiting Room Magazine's web site November 1998. Interview by: Alan Hewitt/Thomas Holter.

"First supper" Andy Wilkinson feature published in #39 of The Waiting Room Magazine.

"Melody maker" 1972

BBC Transcription disc.

"The eyes have it" interview with Dale Newman published in #12 of The Pavilion Magazine interview by Alan Hewitt/Simon Pound/Ian Jones.

"Just for the record" Interview with Steve Hackett published in #36 of The Waiting Room Magazine interview by Alan Hewitt.

Andy Wilkinson feature on Genesis 1974 Lyceum concert published in #39 of The Waiting Room Magazine.

BBC Radio One interview.

"The Insane Ramblings of an old Genesis roadie" Interview with David Lawrence published in #43 of The Waiting Room Magazine".

"Portrait of an artist" interview with Kim Poor published in #38 of The Waiting Room Magazine interview by Alan Hewitt.

"Lamb Memories" feature by Andy Wilkinson published in #39 of The Waiting Room Magazine.

"Genesis: A History" video Virgin Vision 1991.

"The Genesis of a guitarist" interview with Steve Hackett published in #37 of The Waiting Room Magazine interview by Alan Hewitt.

"John Peel Show" BBC Radio February 1976.

"Have Drum Will Travel" Bill Bruford feature in "Sounds" 10th April 1976.

"Melody Maker" concert review by Chris Welch January 1977.

Capitol Radio transcript.

Genesis Information Magazine.

Phil's introduction quoted from a live audio recording of Hamburg concert 10/9/82.

Hit & Run Music Publishing (lyrics).

NME June 1986.

"We can't dance" press release Virgin Records.

"I can't dance but I can play a mean bass guitar" Interview with Mike Rutherford published in #37 of The Waiting Room Magazine interview by Alan Hewitt.

Knebworth Park concert 2.8.92 television broadcast.

Virgin Records Press release "The way we walk Volume One: The Shorts".

"An alien afternoon" interview with Tony Banks published in #35 of The Waiting Room Magazine interview by Alan Hewitt/Simon Pound/Ian Jones.

"Another Chiddingfold afternoon" interview with Ray Wilson published in #36 of The Waiting Room Magazine interview by Alan Hewitt/Simon Pound/Ian Jones.
Tony Smith interview with Alan Hewitt Lyon 20th February 1998 (unpublished).
Interview with Chris "Privet" Hedges and Dave Hill at Birmingham NEC 26th February 1998 previously unpublished.
"Archivally Speaking" Interview with Tony Banks published in #51 of The Waiting Room Online. Interview by: Alan Hewitt and Mark Hughes.
Interview with Ray Wilson in #35 of Dusk Magazine interview by: Mario Giammetti.
Interview with Nick Davis published in #50 of The Waiting Room Online. Interview by: Stuart Barnes.
Interview with Phil Collins published in #51 of The Waiting Room Online. Interview by: Alan Hewitt and John Wilkinson.
Interview with Tony Banks and Mike Rutherford published in #53 of The Waiting Room Online. Interview by: Alan Hewitt, Stuart Barnes and Richard Nagy.
Unpublished interview by the author with Kim Poor 29th May 2006.

OTHER SOURCES .....

The Silent Sun single review Melody Maker February 1968.
"Genesis Build" A Winter's Tale single review Melody Maker May 1969.
"Stagnation" review Melody Maker 7th November 1970.
"The Babes From The Nursery Onto The Stage" Sounds March 4th 1972.
Tony Tyler interview Melody Maker September 1972.
"The Book Of Genesis" Chris Welch Melody Maker interview 1972.
"The Band Who Want to Be Booed" Melody Maker September 23rd 1972
"What Genesis Did On Their Holidays" Melody Maker July 28th 1973.
"Flying High!" Melody Maker September 28th 1974.
"Mickey Mouse Lies Down On Broadway" Sounds interview with Barbara Charone October 26th 1974.
"Public School Boy Reprimands Critics" New Musical Express 2nd November 1974.
"Here Beginneth The Second Chapter Of Genesis" Melody Maker September 27th 1975.
"Genesis: Chapter II" Interview with Barbara Charone Sounds February 1976
"Have Drum Will Travel" Sounds interview with Bill Bruford 10th April 1976.
"It Helps You Make It On The Night" New Musical Express 2nd July 1977
"Genesis Track By Track" Hugh Fielder interview with Mike Rutherford Sounds 1st April 1978.
"Genesis Hit Back" Melody Maker 19th August 1978.
"The Return Of Getting It Together In The Country" Hugh Fielder feature in Sounds 27th October 1979.
"Duke No Hazard" Sounds 10th May 1980.
"The Great Escape" Sounds interview with Hugh Fielder 26th September 1981.
"Mothercare" Sounds 17th September 1983
Record Mirror feature June 1986.
"Brum Punch" Kerrang Magazine January 1984.
"We Can't Dance" Vox Magazine feature December 1991.
"Genesis Cut Loose" Vox Magazine feature December 1992.
"In The Beginning" Dartford Saturday Observer 3rd June 2006.

Appendix A: "The Fugitive from fame" A biography of Tony Banks.

"Portrait of an artist" Interview with Tony Banks published in #27-28 of The Waiting Room Magazine   interview by Alan Hewitt
"Strictly in conversation" Interview with Tony Banks published in #30 of The Waiting Room Magazine interview by Alan Hewitt/Richard Nagy/Andrew Nagy.
Magnificent Seven" Interview with Tony Banks published in #50 of The Waiting Room Online. Interview by: Alan Hewitt/Mark Hughes.

Appendix B: "No drumkit required" A biography of Phil Collins.

"Genesis A History" Video Virgin Video 1991.
BBC Radio One interview 1974.
Phil Collins News Magazine #1.
Phil Collins News Magazine #2.
Phil Collins News Magazine #3.

Genesis Information Magazine.
"In Conversation" The Waiting Room #52 Online interview 28th June 2004.
Electronic Press Kit for Testify album 2002.

OTHER SOURCES…..

"Facing Up To New Values" Melody Maker February 7th 1981.
"The Sound Of The Basker-Phils" Sounds December 25th 1982.
"The Hit That Nearly Wasn't"   Daily Star 1985.
"Phil Collins…. Profiled!" Atlantic Records interview disc 1989.
"Phil Collins - The Story (The Interview Disc) Atlantic Records 1993.
"Phil Collins - Shaped" interview disc 1996
"Dance Into The Light" interview disc.   Face Value Records 1996.

Appendix C: "From the cocoon to the secret world" A biography of Peter Gabriel.

New Musical Express review of Battersea Park concert 1978.
"Peter Gabriel: An authorized biography" Spencer Bright (Sidgwick & Jackson) 1988.
"The South Bank Show" ITV 31.10.82.
Sounds June 1982.
Genesis Information Magazine.
"The South Bank Show" ITV 31.10.82.
Various press reports on "So" album.

OTHER SOURCES…

"The Lamb Stands Up - The Real Peter Gabriel" Sounds 16th April 1977
"Hi, I'm Peter Gabriel, Remember Me?" Sounds April 1977.
"An Angel At Work" Record Mirror 7th May 1977.
"Gabriel: The Image Gets A Tweak" New Musical express 10th June 1978.
"Fame Without Frontiers" Smash Hits Magazine 1980.
"The Ever-Changing Face Of Peter Gabriel" Melody Maker 14th February 1981.
"Don't Touch Me There" Sounds 2nd October 1982.
"Peter Gabriel Hits Out" Record Mirror May 1986.
"From Brideshead To Shrunken Heads" Musician Magazine July 1986.
"My Brilliant Career" Sounds December 1986
"So What About Us" Vox Magazine October 1992.
"Scene And Heard"   Evening Standard 19th September 2002.
"Dome Head" Sunday Times Magazine 2003.

Appendix D: "The Acolyte's Voyage to a blue part of town" A Biography of Steve Hackett.

"The Defector Speaks Out" Interview with Steve Hackett published in #26 of The Waiting Room Magazine interview by Alan Hewitt
"Sounds" Hugh Fielder interview published 16.6.80.
"From the Camino Royale to the Bay of Kings" interview with Steve Hackett published in #28 of The Waiting Room Magazine interview by Alan Hewitt.
"The unauthorised biography of a guitar noir" interview with Steve Hackett published in #29 of The Waiting Room Magazine interview by Alan Hewitt.
"Interview with Steve Hackett published in #30 of The Waiting Room Magazine interview by Alan Hewitt.
"I owe it all to the Richmond Hill tuna sandwiches!" Interview published in #31 of The Waiting Room Magazine interview by Alan Hewitt/Richard Nagy/Andrew Nagy.
"Widening the landscape" Interview with Steve Hackett published in #33 of The Waiting Room Magazine interview by Alan Hewitt/Richard Nagy/Andrew Nagy.
"Between the tape deck and the teacup" Interview with Steve Hackett published in #35 of The Waiting Room Magazine interview by Alan Hewitt.
Camino Records Press release for the "Darktown" album 1999.
"Sketches of Hackett" Interview with Steve Hackett published in #41 of The Waiting Room Magazine. Interview by: Alan Hewitt.

"Talking about Feedback" interview with Steve Hackett published in #42 of The Waiting Room Magazine. Interview by Alan Hewitt.

"To mix or re-mix" Steve Hackett interview published in #39 of The Waiting Room Magazine. Interview by Alan Hewitt.

"A Tale Of Thirteen Bungalows" Steve Hackett interview published in # 49 of The Waiting Room Online. Interview by Alan Hewitt.

"In Conversation" Steve Hackett interview published in #54 of The Waiting Room Online. Interview by Alan Hewitt.

"Memoirs Of An Inveterate Dreamer" Steve Hackett interview published in #59 of The Waiting Room Online. Interview by Alan Hewitt.

"Let's Get Technical" Steve Hackett and Roger King interview published in #59 of The Waiting Room Online. Interview by Stuart Barnes.

Interview with Kim Poor Crown Studios 29th May 2006.

OTHER SOURCES...

"Painter Of Sound Pictures" Melody Maker 18th October 1975.
"Steve Hackett - A Solo Voyage" Beat Instrumental June 1978.
"Steve Hackett Solos In Style" Circus Magazine 1978.
"When In Rome" Melody Maker September 26th 1981.
"Steve Hackett - His Five Year Exodus From Genesis" Guitar Player April 1982.
"Steve's Dreams (Are Made Of This)" Kerrang April 1983.
"Walking Through Walls" Sounds May 14th 1983.
Music Week 4th June 1988
"Rebel Steve's Kind Of Music" Dartford Advertiser (?) April 1988.

Appendix: E "The Genesis of a Mechanic" A biography of Mike Rutherford.

In the beginning there was Smallcreep" Interview with Mike Rutherford published in #31 of The Waiting Room Magazine interview by Alan Hewitt/Richard Nagy/Andrew Nagy.

"Trouser Press" June 1982.

"Whistling while you work" interview with Mike & The Mechanics published in #32 of The Waiting Room Magazine interview by Alan Hewitt/Matthew Skelland/Jonathan Guntrip.

"From the factory floor to chief mechanic" Interview with Mike Rutherford published in #30 of The Waiting Room Magazine interview by Alan Hewitt/Richard Nagy/AndrewNagy.

"Life's a beach then you write an album about one" Interview with Mike Rutherford published in #29 of The Waiting Room Magazine interview by Alan Hewitt/Richard Nagy/Andrew Nagy.

Virgin Records Press release for "Hits" album.

Appendix F "Putting together the parts & pieces" A biography of Anthony Phillips.

"The Geese & The Glenfiddich" interview with Anthony Phillips published in #3 of The Pavilion Magazine interview by Alan Hewitt/Jonathan Dann.

"The Humbert Ruse interview" interview with Rupert Hine published in #6 of The Pavilion Magazine interview by Jonathan Dann.

"I want to go home...I want to go home now!" interview with John G Perry published in #5 of The Pavilion Magazine interview by Jonathan Dann.

"Talking Sides" interview with Anthony Phillips published in #5 of The Pavilion Magazine interview by Alan Hewitt/Jonathan Dann.

"The Humbert Ruse interview" (as above).

"Private Parts & Pieces" interview with Anthony Phillips published in #6 of The Pavilion Magazine interview by Alan Hewitt/Jonathan Dann.

"1984: An Antique Year" interview with Anthony Phillips published in #7 of The Pavilion Magazine interview by Alan Hewitt/Jonathan Dann.

"A Masquerade for Alice" Anthony Phillips interview published in #9 of The Pavilion Magazine interview by Alan Hewitt.

"Making the invisible visible" Anthony Phillips interview published in #10 of The Pavilion Magazine interview by Alan Hewitt.

"How I became involved in underwater archery" Anthony Phillips interview published in #8 of The Waiting Room Magazine interview by Alan Hewitt.

Appendix G "The Actor Revealed" Ray Wilson.

Interview with Cut published in #39 of The Waiting Room Magazine interview by: Alan Hewitt and Martin Dean. E-mail interview with Ray Wilson unpublished.

Photo Index

Section One Genesis (black and white)

1) Letter Confirming receipt of the band's contract appointing there first manager (Courtesy of Anthony Phillips)
2) Various press cuttings and group publicity photo 1968 – 70
3) Phil, Mike and Tony "The 70's Look" 1972 – 73
4) Peter experiencing various identity crises 1973
5) "Memories of the Lamb….." 1974
6) "A Trick of the Triumph" The Band defy the critics and survive Peter's Departure 1976 – 77
7) "Memories of the Giant Knebworth" 1978
8) "Phil sinks to new depths in the Fashion stakes" Duke Tour 1980
9) "The Streamlined Genesis 1981 Model"
10) "Encore tour Memories" Leeds and Hamburg 1982
11) " Reunion ? What Reunion ? ! " The Band wowing Sixty Thousand Bedraggled fans at Milton Keynes 2nd October 1982
12) Tony and Daryl 1983
13) Mike and Phil both displaying lousy dress sense on the Invisible Touch Tour, Europe 1987
14) The Band proving that they can't dance on Peter's Pop Show and in Lyon on the 1992 European Tour
15) Calling All Stations Memorabillia
16) "Congo" Video shoot and Captured in concert during the 1998 European Tour

(Memorabillia from the Collections of The Author and E Sayers)

Section Two Solo (black and white)

1) Tony Banks Tickling the Ivories and pondering the pros and cons of an Album of Tuned Percussion
2) "For Perverts Only" Phil fogest to get dressed for his Hammersmith Gigs, Publicity Shots (Fully Clothed of Course)
3) "Serious tour, Serious Travel" Phil and Hhis Expanding Band caught live in Melbourne, Zurich and Lyon on the 1990 Tour
4) "From the trash can to Jazz" Memories of 1994, 1997 and the 1998 Tours
5) "Farewell, Adieu" Phil's First Final Farewell Tour
6) "Expect the Unexpected" Peter Gabriel in Various guises during the 1977, 1978, 79 and 80 Tours
7) "Behind The Mask" Peter in Concert at Shepton Mallet and Liverpool 1982/93 and at the Giants Stadium during The 1986 "Conspiracy of Hope" Tour
8) "The Man is Back" Memories of the 1993/1994 'US' tour
9) "Careful with that Zimmer Frame ! " Wembley 2004 & Publicity Photo (Courtesy of Real World Records)
10) "The Acolyte Steps Out" (Photos Courtesy of Cchrysalis Records)
11) "So How Does This One Go?" Steve and Gandalf 1992, Richmond Hill Hotel 1993 and with Brother John 2000
12) "The Changing face of Anthony Phillips" (Photos Courtesy of Passport, PRT and Virgin Venture Records
13) "Now about this Album for Charango and Tuned Warthog….." Dale Newman and Henrique Berro Garcia Ponder working with Anthony again while Anthony himself tries to tame the offending Charango
14) "The Mechanics ROAR out of the Garage" Manchester 1989
15) "A Grand Day Out" The Mechanics at the Hanover Grand 1999
16) "The Actor Revealed" The Various guises of Ray Wilson

(Memorabillia from the Collections of the Author, E Sayers and M Kenyon)

Photo Index

Page

Memorabilla from the collections of The Author, T Sayers and M Kenyon

Front Cover photograph provided by Stephanie Stratton, taken at Earls Court November 1992
Back Cover photograph provided by S Barnes taken at Fisher Lane Farm Decemeber 2004

Photographry Credits

The photographs contained in this volume are the work of the following individuals (you should all know what your own work looks like, folks!). The photographic content is based on on the same chronological output as the text – which should make figuring out where each photo fits in the grand scheme of things relatively easy and saves me a great amount of time writing photo captions!

David Scheinmann   www.davidscheinmann.com
Alan Perry   www.concertphotos.uk.com

Mark Kenyon, Richard Nagy, Stuart Barnes, Alan Hewitt, Mike Ainscoe, Jon Guntrip www.twronline.net
Stephanie Stratton
David Beaven
Guido Truffer
Ted Sayers
David Birtwell
Albert Gouder
Frederic Martin
Anthony Hobkinson
Kurt Arrigo
David Lawrence
Jack Beermann
Carol Willis
Helmut Janisch
Ulrich Klemt
Sakura

If we have forgotten anyone, please let us know.